Silent Activism

Barbara Holub

Stiller Aktivismus

Edition Angewandte
Book series of the University of Applied Arts Vienna
Edited by Gerald Bast, Rector

Edition Angewandte
Buchreihe der Universität für angewandte Kunst Wien
Herausgegeben von Gerald Bast, Rektor

edition:'ʌngewʌndtə
Universität für angewandte Kunst Wien
University of Applied Arts Vienna

Barbara Holub –
Stiller Aktivismus / Silent Activism

Başak Şenova (Hrsg./Ed.)

DE GRUYTER

IV. Systems, Secrecy, Voices

V. Missing Things—Noisy Activism

IV. Systeme, Geheimnis, Stimmen

V. Dinge, die fehlen – geräuschvoller Aktivismus

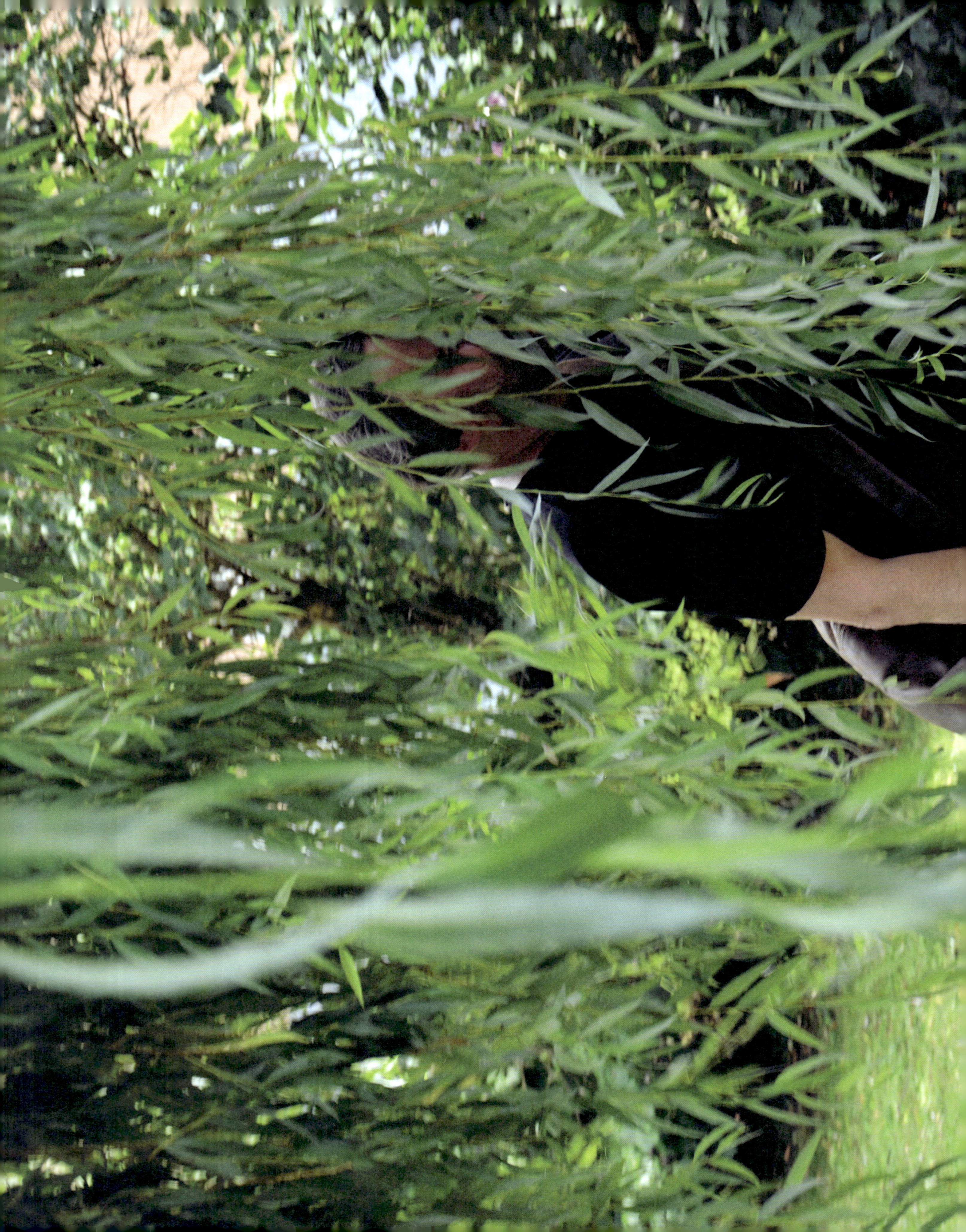

(refusing tabloid messages)

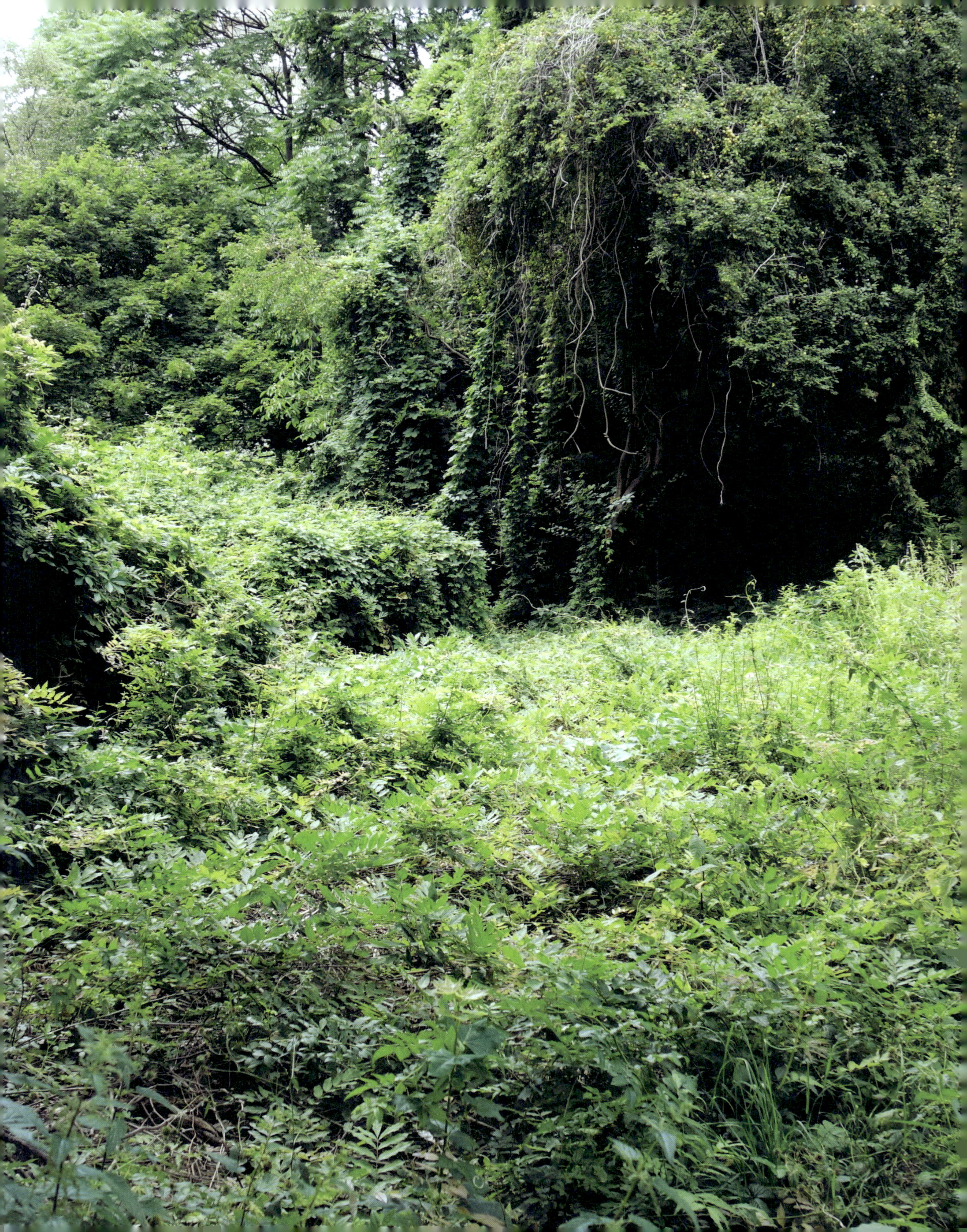

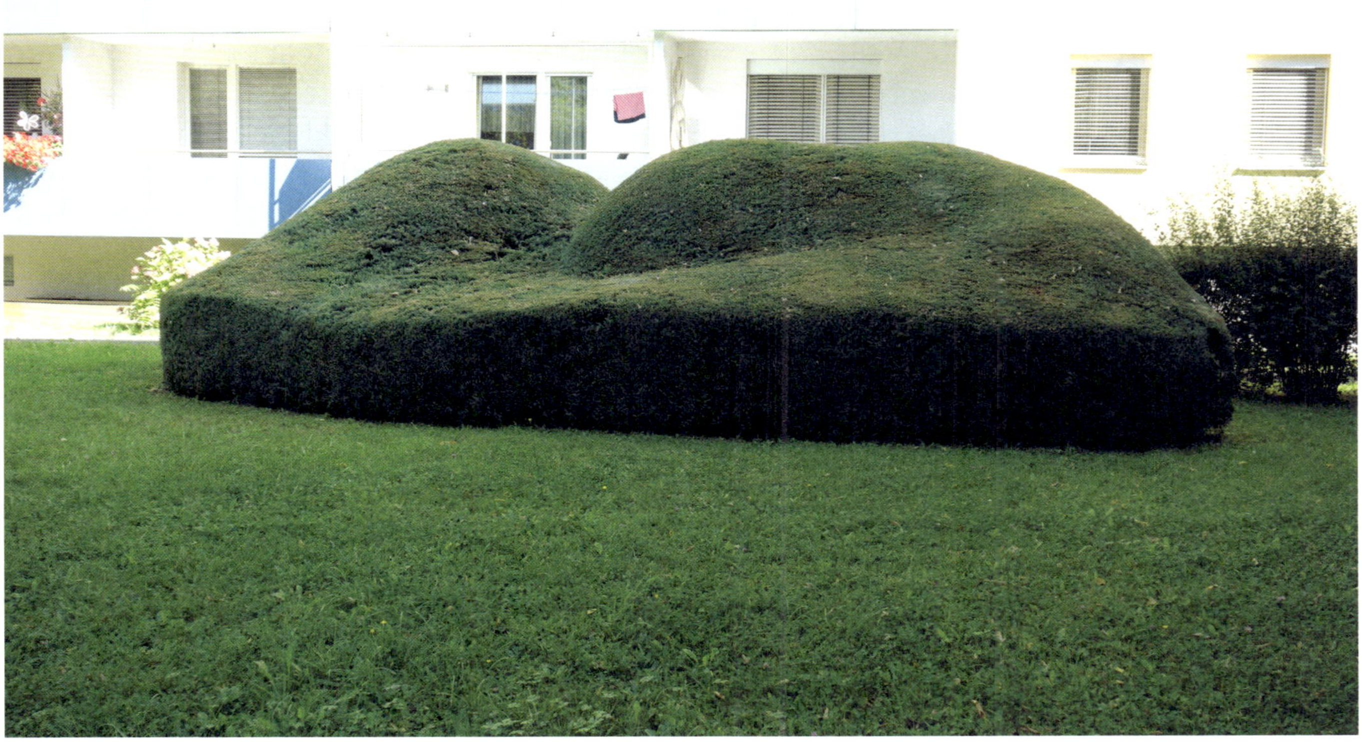

SILENT ACTIVISM
Preface by Başak Şenova

This monograph spans Barbara Holub's three decades of work by tracing her Œuvre, which largely consists of socially and politically engaged works and actions, at times discrete or even clandestine, at times more direct, an ambivalence significant for her silent activism. Holub has a special focus on what constitutes the awareness and criticality of the public through current urban and societal issues. Hence, she often also expands her artistic practice with excursions into other fields, while emphasizing that her action comes from her position as an artist, employing artistic strategies and thought in order to intervene in various systems of society.

In a politically informed and cautious way, Holub recognizes and acts upon the urgencies of specific contexts. Her work communicates an embodied research across the imperatives of socio-political justice and corresponding artistic counteractions and reflections. Despite the participatory nature of many of her projects, these often filter through a very distinctive artistic language and standpoint that intervenes in structural and social transformation. Holub has been deliberately creating an ever-growing distributive network of projects, situations and settings—with a performative and interactive focus—that complement each other through different links, knots, and intersections over time.

Through "silent activism," a term she coined around 2015, Holub has developed a discourse based on thinking, (re)producing, sharing, and questioning current conditions and systems. To be silently active is to persistently insist on engaging the public/audience not as the public in general, but as active individuals capable of taking the initiative and realizing a vision, while avoiding the trap of direct engagement with "tabloid activism." This engagement can be traced already in her earlier works from

STILLER AKTIVISMUS
Vorwort von Başak Şenova

Die vorliegende Monografie beschreibt Barbara Holubs seit über drei Jahrzehnten andauerndes künstlerisches Schaffen, ein Œuvre, das in erster Linie aus sozial und politisch engagierten Arbeiten und Aktionen besteht, die zum Teil diskret, um nicht zu sagen klandestin, zum Teil direkter und unmittelbarer angelegt sind – eine Ambivalenz, die charakteristisch für ihren stillen Aktivismus ist. Holubs besonderes Augenmerk in ihrer Auseinandersetzung mit aktuellen urbanen und gesellschaftlichen Problemen gilt der Wahrnehmung und dem kritischen Bewusstsein in Bezug auf das Öffentliche. Aus diesem Grund erweitert Holub ihre künstlerische Tätigkeit oftmals durch Exkurse in andere Bereiche, wobei sie stets als Künstlerin agiert, sich künstlerischer Strategien und Denkansätze bedient, um in unterschiedlichen gesellschaftlichen Kontexten Interventionen zu setzen.

Holubs politisch informiertes, von genauer Beobachtung geprägtes Schaffen richtet sich nach der wahrgenommenen Dringlichkeit der jeweiligen Situationen. Ihre Arbeiten bestehen aus den Rechercheprozessen selbst, die sich vom Aufruf gesellschaftspolitischer Veränderung bis hin zu entsprechenden künstlerischen „Gegen-Aktionen" und Reflexionen spannen. Trotz des partizipatorischen Charakters vieler ihrer Projekte lassen diese meist eine unverkennbare künstlerische Sprache und die Absicht erkennen, strukturelle und gesellschaftliche Veränderungen herbeizuführen. Holub hat bewusst ein beständig wachsendes Netzwerk aus performativen und interaktiven Projekten, Situationen und Kontexten geschaffen, die sich im Lauf der Zeit gegenseitig ergänzen, miteinander verbinden und überlagern.

Unter dem Begriff „stiller Aktivismus", den Holub etwa 2015 prägte, hat sie einen künstlerischen Ansatz entwickelt, der gegenwärtige

the 1990s, where she critically engaged with various corporate systems.

Holub's artistic inquiries have drawn a line between the urgency for structural revision in society and the need to continually question the role art plays in society. This monograph shows her rhizomatic thinking—connecting projects, topics, and sites over time—by presenting a non-linear selection of her projects that demonstrate multiple strategies and approaches. Some of these projects have been realized by transparadiso, a collaborative and transdisciplinary practice involving art, artistic urban intervention, architecture, and urbanism, which she founded with architect/urbanist Paul Rajakovics in 1999. By intertwining her artistic practice with the transdisciplinary fields that transparadiso addresses, her silent activism becomes even more fluid and ambiguous as it incorporates both "silence" and "directness"—as in "direct urbanism," a term transparadiso coined for how art and artistic strategies can engage in urban development on a durational level—when addressing today's challenges of urban planning, reacting to unforeseen changing parameters, and furthering a socially engaged urban development.

Andreas Spiegl opens the book by discussing Holub's consistent artistic approach of taking local politics and social dynamics into consideration, starting with "stuttering" or "laughing" as a notion of helplessness. He continues addressing the "silence" in Holub's activism by turning to another angle of silent activism: silence as a means of expression for people who are silent, since they are in the position of not being heard. Then the artist, in conversation with the editor, discusses her consistent working patterns and accumulative knowledge production, rotating between poetics and pragmatics, opening up space for the in-between. This discussion is followed by texts by Enrico Lunghi, Jonatan Habib Engqvist, and Paul O'Neill that discuss the politics, social conditions, urgencies, artistic strategies and acts that orbit around Holub's and transparadisos works. Lunghi covers the current political climate in general while giving

Bedingungen und Systeme reflektiert, diese (re)produziert, teilt und hinterfragt. Stiller Aktivismus heißt aber auch, beharrlich darauf zu bestehen, die Öffentlichkeit/das Publikum nicht als Allgemeinheit zu begreifen, sondern als einzelne handelnde Individuen, die Initiativen ergreifen und Visionen verwirklichen, ohne dabei in die Falle des bloßen Mitmachens eines „Boulevard-Aktionismus" zu tappen. Diese Form der Partizipation ist bereits in ihren früheren Arbeiten aus den 1990ern zu finden, in denen Holub sich kritisch mit verschiedenen Unternehmensstrukturen auseinandersetzte.

Holubs künstlerische Recherche verbindet die Notwendigkeit struktureller Veränderungen in der Gesellschaft mit der Notwendigkeit, die Rolle, die Kunst in der Gesellschaft einnimmt, ständig zu hinterfragen. Die vorliegende Monografie spiegelt Holubs rhizomatische Denkweise – das Verbinden von Projekten, Themen, Schauplätzen im Lauf der Zeit – wider, indem sie eine nicht linear angeordnete Auswahl ihrer Projekte zeigt, die durch vielfältige Strategien und Ansätze gekennzeichnet sind. Einige dieser Projekte wurden von transparadiso realisiert, ein von Holub 1999 mit dem Architekten/ Urbanisten Paul Rajakovics gegründetes transdisziplinäres Kollektiv, das Kunst, künstlerische Interventionen im urbanen Raum, Architektur und Urbanismus miteinander verbindet. Wenn Holub ihre künstlerische Herangehensweise mit dem transdisziplinären Feld, das transparadiso bespielt, verflicht, wird ihr stiller Aktivismus noch vieldeutiger und engmaschiger, weil dadurch die Eigenschaften „still" und „direkt" aufeinandertreffen. Letztere ist dem Begriff des direkten Urbanismus entnommen, der von transparadiso für die Art und Weise, wie Kunst und künstlerische Strategien langfristig in urbane Stadtentwicklungsprozesse eingreifen können, geprägt wurde. Dieser stille Aktivismus ist Holubs künstlerischer Ansatz, um aktuelle Themen der Stadtplanung aufzugreifen, auf unvorhergesehene Paradigmenwechsel zu reagieren und eine sozial engagierte Stadtentwicklung weiter voranzutreiben.

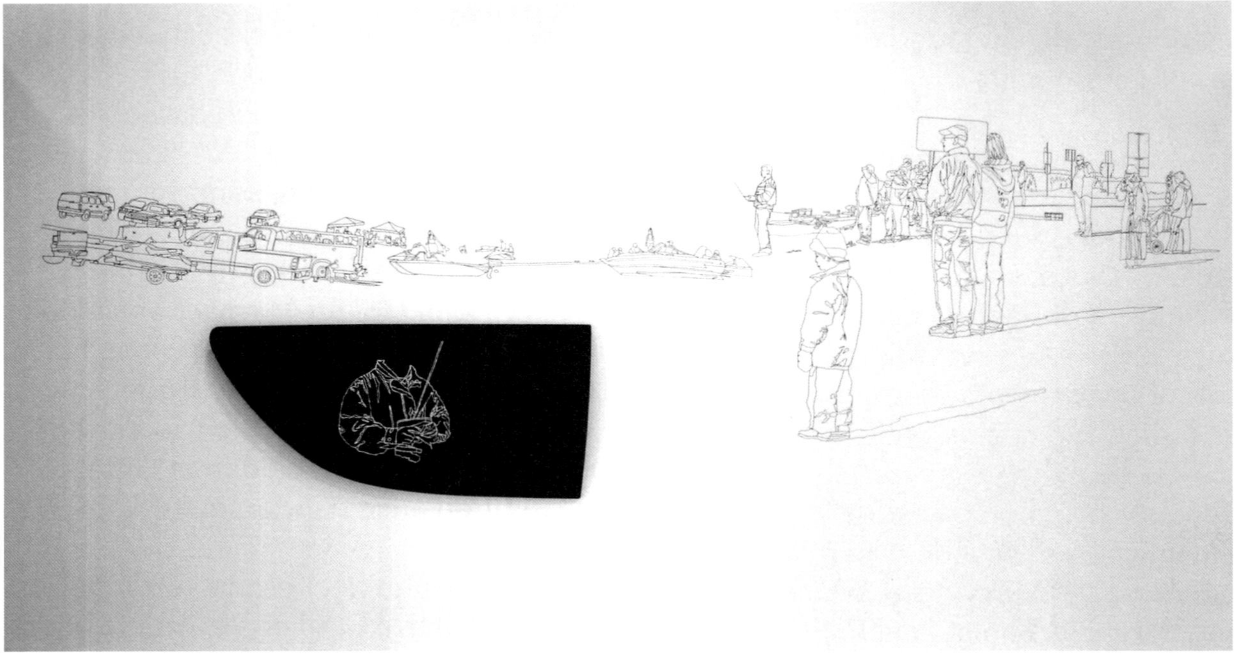

LEISURE ENERGY, OMV, Vienna, 2006
In this installation, various recreational activities overlap: In the man-made Castaic Lake (north of Los Angeles), motorboats turn in circles as if in an oversized model boat pond due to overuse, while remote-controlled model boats in Greifenstein near Vienna seem to steer SUVs with their boat trailers in Castaic Lake. LEISURE ENERGY thus questions our (leisure) consumption behavior and energy resources, and who is in control.

LEISURE ENERGY, OMV, Wien, 2006
In dieser Installation überlagern sich verschiedene Freizeitaktivitäten: Im künstlich angelegten Castaic Lake (nördlich von Los Angeles) drehen sich die Motorboote aufgrund der Übernutzung im Kreis wie in einem überdimensionalen Modellboot-Teich, während die ferngesteuerten Modellboote in Greifenstein bei Wien die SUVs mit ihren Bootsanhängern im Castaic Lake zu steuern scheinen. LEISURE ENERGY hinterfragt damit unser (Freizeit-) Konsumverhalten und Energieressourcen, und wer in Kontrolle ist.

broad reflections on the term "silent activism," emphasizing what art can do in the seemingly helpless state of neoliberal society. Engqvist tackles the question of normalcy, a recurrent theme in Holub's work, and the increasing quest for the "return to normal," suggesting that social emancipation has become self-emancipation. He indicates that it is from this form of existence—which has generated a longing for inclusive contexts where we can appreciate what we are and not just what we achieve—that Holub's works often take their point of departure. O'Neill presents a close reading of Holub and transparadiso's works by focusing on layers of social and civic action, exemplified especially in NORMAL and the WORLD CONGRESSES OF THE MISSING THINGS. He then explores how Holub's silent activism contributes to the core of collaborative practice discourses.

Each chapter takes elements of silent activism into consideration: political engagement, participatory strategies, macro-utopian visions and speculative fictions, different forms of dialog,

Andreas Spiegl leitet in die Publikation mit einer Diskussion der konsequenten Berücksichtigung von lokaler Politik und sozialen Dynamiken in Holubs künstlerischem Werk ein, wobei er „Stottern" und „Lachen" als Ausdruck der Hilflosigkeit zum Ausgangspunkt seiner Betrachtungen nimmt. In der Folge arbeitet er einen weiteren Aspekt der Stille von Holubs Aktivismus heraus, nämlich den des „Schweigens als Ausdrucksmittel für jene, die nicht gehört werden, wenn sie die Stimme erheben". Anschließend erörtert Holub im Dialog mit der Herausgeberin wiederkehrende Merkmale ihres Arbeitsprozesses und die damit verbundene Wissensproduktion, die zwischen Poetik und Pragmatik zirkuliert und Raum für das Dazwischen öffnet. Es folgen Beiträge von Enrico Lunghi, Jonatan Habib Engqvist und Paul O'Neill, die sich mit politischen Themen, sozialen Rahmenbedingungen, drängenden Fragen sowie künstlerischen Strategien und Handlungen rund um Holubs und transparadisos Arbeiten auseinandersetzen. Lunghi geht in seiner ausführlichen Reflexion über den Begriff „stiller Aktivismus"

performative situations, the politics of borders, the production of knowledge, often informed by unpronounced pedagogical layers. The introductory texts create a framework for exemplifying Barbara Holub's artistic methodology and structural approach by presenting the selected projects in a non-linear and non-chronological order, an open structure of cross-references and overlapping issues, a rhizomatic exploration. Consequently, Jane Rendell's "Index"—which counteracts the conventional form of an index—closes the book by providing an exceptional cross-reading of the artist's work by underlining its non-linear, non-hierarchical, multidisciplinary and open-ended aspects.

im Allgemeinen auf das aktuelle politische Klima ein und im Besondern auf die Frage, was Kunst angesichts der scheinbaren Hilflosigkeit unserer neoliberalen Gesellschaft tun kann. Engqvist beschäftigt sich mit dem Thema Normalität, das sich als kontinuierliche Fragestellung durch Holubs Arbeiten zieht, dem zunehmenden Streben nach einer „Rückkehr zum Normalität" sowie der These, dass sich soziale Emanzipation zu einer „Selbst-Emanzipation" gewandelt habe. Er verortet in dieser Existenzform – die eine Sehnsucht nach inklusiven Kontexten geweckt hat, in denen wir sein können, wer wir sind, und nicht nur nach unserem Erfolg gemessen werden – den Ausgangspunkt für viele von Holubs Projekten. O'Neill unternimmt ein Close Reading der Arbeiten Holubs und transparadisos mit Fokus auf die einzelnen Ebenen der sozialen und zivilgesellschaftlichen Interventionen, insbesondere das Projekt NORMAL und der WORLD CONGRESSES OF THE MISSING THINGS. Nicht zuletzt untersucht O'Neill den Beitrag, den Holubs stiller Aktivismus zum Diskurs kollaborativer Praktiken leistet.

In jedem Kapitel werden unterschiedliche Elemente von stillem Aktivismus reflektiert: politisches Engagement, partizipatorische Strategien, makroutopische Visionen und spekulative Fiktionen, verschiedene Dialogformen, performative Situationen, Grenzpolitik, Wissensproduktion, die oft auf einer nicht expliziten pädagogischen Ebene vermittelt werden. Die einleitenden Texte legen Holubs künstlerische Herangehensweisen innerhalb der nicht linearen und nicht chronologischen Anordnung ausgewählter Projekte dar: eine offene Struktur aus Querverweisen und einander überlappenden Themen, eine rhizomatische Erkundung. Entsprechend beschließt Jane Rendells „Index", der die eigentliche Form eines Index konterkariert, das Buch mit einer außergewöhnlichen Art des Querlesens von Holubs Œuvre, das sich ebenso durch nicht lineare, nicht hierarchische, multidisziplinäre Aspekte und eine offene Betrachtungsweise auszeichnet.

I. Silent Activism and Political Commitment

Stiller Aktivismus und politisches Engagement

THEATER OF THE PUBLIC

Andreas Spiegl

Stuttering[1] or laughing[2] when at a loss for words, even out of despair, unable to continue speaking anymore because words are insufficient or the language is no longer understood by anybody because it is dying out—like the minorities[3] who still use it and regard it as a part of their cultural heritage, as part of a diversity that is being marginalized and denied relevance in the cultural hegemony; a display of speechlessness[4], screaming soundlessly when all demands and arguments remain unheard. The last possibility being to remain silent, the last way to say something, an unheard silence that interrupts the supposed "order of things."[5] This silence, which also features in Silent Activism and is used in the title of this catalog, alludes to something more than just pausing for reflection—it is a means of expression for those who are not heard when they raise their voices, the people nobody listens to when they try to articulate their wishes or suggestions. It is what remains, a last resort, the flipside of language contrasted against eloquence, a representational silence manifested in silenced speech, a loud, even shrill silence that can only be heard with the eyes, an unheard "loud transcription" that addresses the eyes as it falls upon deaf ears, a silence that bears witness to speechlessness and wants to be witnessed—nobody wants to listen, while everybody sees the speechlessness.

"Can the Subaltern Speak?"[6] is a question that asks whether, how, and under what conditions people can speak who are excluded from hegemonic cultures or pushed to the various margins of society. This not only provides the title for Gayatri Spivak's essay, but is also the point of departure for Barbara Holub's art projects. In this sense, LISTEN TO THE QUIET VOICE[7] also presents itself not only as an imperative, and the title of one of her works, but as the paradigm behind her entire practice. Over the decades her work has pursued listening, a listening to, and hearing of, the concerns and demands of those "quiet voices" who were not born mute, while they have been silenced—for fear of persecution, for fear of being marginalized even further, or for the experience of merely becoming acquainted with hopelessness. With this listening to other voices—however quiet, wounded or silenced they may be—as the basis of her approach, Holub has turned away from a concept of art that seeks to associate or identify the "artwork" with the person of the artist.

Far from engaging with autonomous artistic production, Holub is committed to heteronomy as a precondi-

DAS THEATER DER ÖFFENTLICHKEIT

Andreas Spiegl

Stottern[1], wenn es einem die Sprache verschlägt, Lachen[2], auch aus Verzweiflung, wenn man nichts mehr sagen kann, weil die Sprache nicht hinreicht oder von niemandem mehr verstanden wird, weil sie ausstirbt, wie die Minderheiten[3], die sie noch sprechen und als Teil ihrer Kultur verstehen, als Teil einer Diversität, die von der hegemonialen Kultur verdrängt und negiert wird; die Sprachlosigkeit zur Schau stellen[4], wenn alle Forderungen und Argumente ungehört bleiben, das Schweigen hinausschreien, ein Verstummen als letzte Möglichkeit, das Wort zu erheben, eine unerhörte Stille, die die vermeintliche „Ordnung der Dinge"[5] unterbricht. Diese Stille, die auch im stillen Aktivismus und Titel dieser Publikation zur Sprache kommt, meint etwas anderes als ein bloßes Innehalten – sie ist Ausdrucksmittel für jene, die nicht gehört werden, wenn sie die Stimme erheben, denen niemand zuhört, wenn sie ihre Wünsche oder Vorschläge zu kommunizieren suchen, sie ist das, was übrigbleibt, ein letztes Mittel, die Kehrseite von Sprache, die der Beredsamkeit entgegen gehalten wird, eine gegenständliche Stille, die sich verdinglicht und das Sprechen als Schweigen materialisiert, eine laute, ja schrille Stille, die nur mit den Augen gehört werden kann, eine unerhörte „Laut-Schrift", die sich an die Augen wendet, wenn die Ohren nicht zuhören wollen, ein Schweigen, das von der Sprachlosigkeit Zeugnis ablegt und bezeugt werden will – keine/r wollte sie hören, aber ihre Sprachlosigkeit haben alle gesehen.

„Can the Subaltern Speak?"[6] Diese Frage, ob und wie und unter welchen Bedingungen Menschen sprechen können, die von hegemonialen Kulturen ausgeschlossen oder an die verschiedenen Ränder einer Gesellschaft gedrängt werden, liefert nicht nur den Titel für den gleichnamigen Text von Gayatri Spivak, sondern zugleich den Ausgangspunkt für die künstlerischen Projekte von Barbara Holub. In diesem Sinne erscheint auch das LISTEN TO THE QUIET VOICE[7] nicht nur als Imperativ und Titel einer ihrer Arbeiten, sondern paradigmatisch für ihre gesamte Praxis. Seit Jahrzehnten folgt ihre Arbeit einem Zuhören, einem Hinhören und Vernehmen der Anliegen und Forderungen jener „Quiet Voices", die nicht stumm geboren wurden und dennoch zum Verstummen gebracht wurden – aus Angst vor Verfolgung, aus Angst, noch weiter marginalisiert zu werden oder aus der Erfahrung, sich nur mehr mit der Hoffnungslosigkeit anfreunden zu können. Mit diesem Vernehmen anderer Stimmen – so leise, verletzt oder verstummt diese sein mögen – als Ausgangspunkt ihrer künstlerischen Praxis hat sich Holub von einem Kunstbegriff abgewandt, der das „Kunstwerk" mit der Person der Künstlerin assoziieren oder identifizieren will.

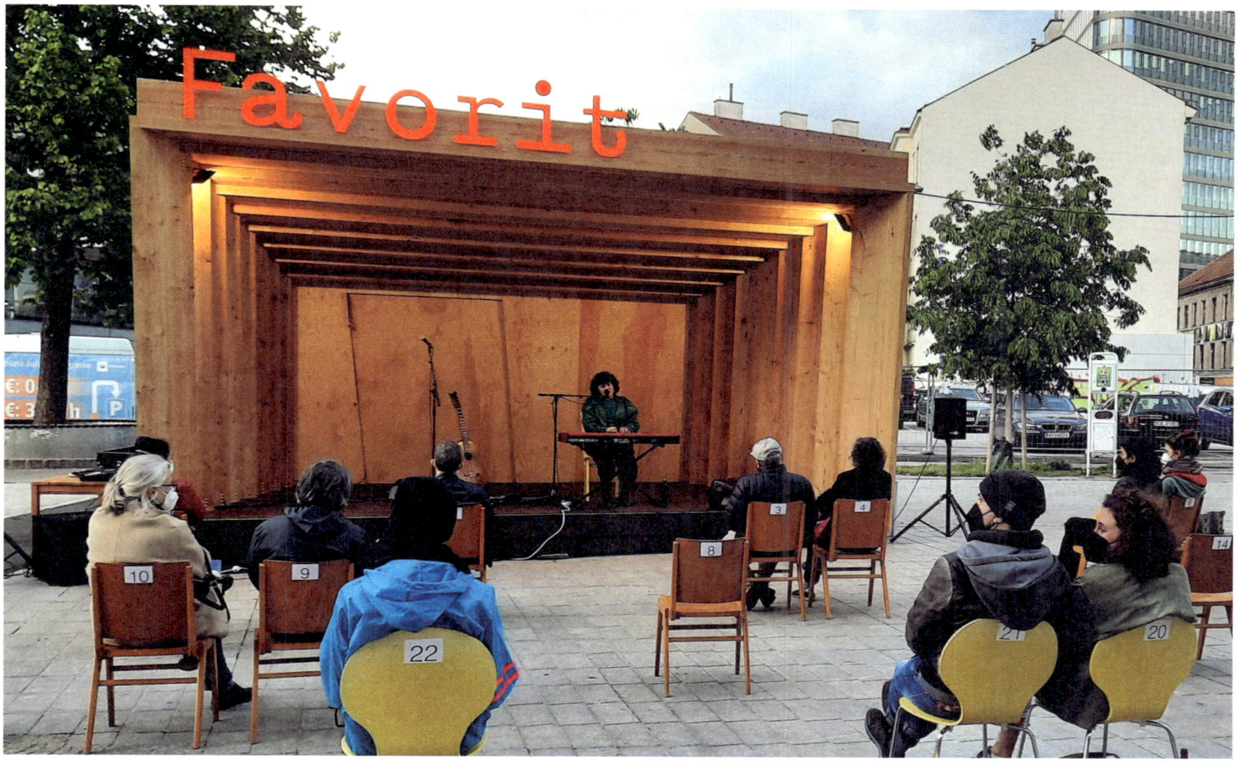

FAVORIT (transparadiso), Sonnwendplatz, Vienna, 2021
This square–transformer–performer is an informal pavilion stage bridging "high culture" and "popular culture," between the everyday and staged performances, at the entrance of Favoriten, Vienna's 10th district, which is undergoing a massive process of transformation. FAVORIT offers its stage to the original inhabitants as a platform to present their various cultures.

FAVORIT (transparadiso), Sonnwendplatz, Wien, 2021
Dieser Platz-Transformer-Performer ist eine informelle Pavillon-Bühne zwischen „Hochkultur" und „Volkskultur", zwischen Alltagsnutzung und Performances am Eingang zu Favoriten, dem 10. Bezirk in Wien, der sich in einem massiven Transformationsprozess befindet. Der FAVORIT stellt diese Bühne den ursprünglich hier „Beheimateten" als Plattform zur Verfügung um ihre verschiedenen Kulturen in der Öffentlichkeit zu präsentieren.

tion for a politicized approach that deliberately makes her (inter)dependent on those whose independence or autonomy is continually—and structurally—endangered, whose independence or autonomy is threatened or being undermined; these are men and women for whom inequality and their treatment as unequal essentially defines their everyday lives. Hence the diverse and globally dispersed set of people she collaborates with in her projects—covering a spectrum of contexts ranging from migration experiences[8], minority and refugee politics[9] to suburban peripheries[10] and social and economic marginalization. In such collaborations, artistic practice essentially transitions into an artistic investigation of perception and reception in the broadest sense. The classical division of roles that used to assign separate tasks to artists and recipients—people who were supposed to produce works of art, and the people who were supposed to view them—is dissolved here. In hearing the concerns of others, the artistic approach starts off from the reception and subsequently transforms it into an act of participation, of sharing and attempting to proactively communicate this sharing to others "activistically."

By refusing to orientate her artistic practice toward an audience that is solely assigned the passive role of

Weit davon entfernt einer Autonomie des künstlerischen Schaffens das Wort zu reden, verpflichtet sich Holub der Heteronomie als Voraussetzung für ihre Praxis, die sich wissentlich und politisch (gegenseitig) abhängig macht von jenen, deren Unabhängigkeit oder Eigenständigkeit unentwegt und strukturell gefährdet, bedroht oder negiert wird, für die die Ungleichheit und ihre Behandlung als Ungleiche wesentlich den Alltag definieren. Daraus folgt auch die diverse und weltweit verstreute Menge derer, mit denen sie in ihren Projekten zusammenarbeitet – ein Spektrum, das von Migrationserfahrung[8], Minoritäts- und Flüchtlingspolitik[9] über suburbane Peripherien[10] bis hin zur sozialen und ökonomischen Marginalisierung reicht. In dieser Zusammenarbeit geht die künstlerische Praxis wesentlich in ein künstlerisches Vernehmen über, in ein Wahrnehmen und Rezipieren im weitesten Sinne. Die klassische Rollenaufteilung, die KünstlerInnen und RezipientInnen je getrennte Aufgaben zugeteilt hat – auf der einen Seite die, die Kunstwerke hervorbringen sollte und auf der anderen Seite jene, die diese betrachten sollten –, wird hier aufgelöst. Im Vernehmen der Anliegen anderer nimmt die künstlerische Praxis ihren Ausgangspunkt in der Rezeption und verwandelt diese im Anschluss daran selbst in einen Akt der Teilhabe, des Anteilhabens und des Versuchs, dieses Teilen auch aktiv(istisch) wieder anderen mitzuteilen.

reception, for years Holub has been pursuing a path that Jacques Rancière outlined—in parallel to the production of her works—with the concept of *the* "emancipated spectator": "What is required is a theatre without spectators, where those in attendance learn from as opposed to being seduced by images; where they become active participants as opposed to passive voyeurs."[11] In this sense, Holub works on an art without spectators—not to keep her art hidden nor to keep it secret, but to reject the "uncanny"[12] division of roles between the artist and audience. What is then presented as an artwork corresponds more to an installative setting of tools for use in making one's own voice (publicly) heard and thus for generating a public. The image of a giant megaphone with which people could shout out their concerns or demands across a river to the other bank as part of her work CALL AGAINST THE BORDER[13] (2019) is not merely documentation, it shows the operative paradigm. The same applies to FAVORIT[14] (2021), a wooden pavilion with an integrated stage installed on a public square in Vienna, primarily to provide a tool to empower what had been an audience to now step onto the stage themselves, to participate proactively and voice their own concerns.

The art begins with hearing and the awareness of the need to be heard—to join others in engaging with a shared concern. The emancipatory act consists of hearing silence, the not-being-heard, the experience of being left alone with a problem or having been forgotten—while seeing possibilities in sharing and communicating this experience, speaking in a language that does not have to be either translated into the "governing" hegemonic jargon or to assimilate itself in order to be heard. In this sense, Holub does not adopt a position of advocating and promoting the concerns of "others" because this would merely be rehashing a personal experience of being unable to speak, to speak for oneself. Instead of representing others, a moment of solidarity is expressed here, without necessarily negating or neutralizing the inequality and difference between the positions from which somebody is speaking or remaining silent. It is a moment that expresses an essential suspension or abrogation of any pre-structured boundaries of competence or concern.

For the role as an artist, this also means questioning their role for themselves, exercising doubts about their own expressive power or expressiveness, about their own capacity, about the difference that separates their own talent from the others' reception. What emerges here is also an act of renunciation, an action that consists of withdrawing, of experiencing, of not finding better words or stories for people who might not have them at hand, so to speak, of not replacing or compensating for their silence and stillness with the artist's own eloquence. Instead, the implicit challenge, what wants to be heard in silent activism, is aimed at a practice that would have, in Macharey's words, "the task of measuring silence,

Mit der Weigerung, die künstlerische Praxis auf ein Publikum hin auszurichten, dem allein die passive Rolle der Rezeption zugedacht wird, verfolgt Holub seit Jahren einen Weg, den Jacques Rancière, zur gleichen Zeit wie die der Entstehung ihrer Arbeiten, mit dem Begriff des „emanzipierten Zuschauers" skizziert hat: „Man braucht ein Theater ohne Zuschauer, wo die Anwesenden lernen, anstatt von Bildern verführt zu werden, wo sie aktive Teilnehmende werden, anstatt passive Voyeurs zu sein."[11] In diesem Sinne arbeitet Holub an einer Kunst ohne ZuschauerInnen – nicht um ihre Kunst im Verborgenen und geheim zu halten, sondern um die „unheimliche"[12] Aufteilung der Rollenzuteilungen zwischen Publikum und KünstlerInnen zurückzuweisen. Was dann als „Arbeit" vorgestellt wird, entspricht eher einem installativen Setting von Instrumenten, die in Anspruch genommen werden können, um der je eigenen Stimme (öffentlich) Gehör zu verschaffen und damit selbst eine Öffentlichkeit zu generieren. Das Bild von einem riesenhaften Megaphon, mit dem Menschen im Rahmen ihrer Arbeit RUF GEGEN DIE GRENZE[13] (2019) ihre Anliegen oder Forderungen über einen Fluss hinweg bis ans andere Ufer hinausschreien konnten, ist hier weniger dokumentarischer als paradigmatischer Natur. Gleiches gilt für den FAVORIT[14], einen Holzpavillon mit integrierter Bühne, die sie 2021 auf einem öffentlichen Platz in Wien installiert hat, um primär ein Instrument zur Verfügung zu stellen, das es dem einstigen Publikum ermöglichte, nun selbst die Bühne zu betreten, aktiv(istisch) teilzuhaben und die Stimme zu erheben.

Die künstlerische Arbeit beginnt mit einem Vernehmen, einem Wahrnehmen des Bedarfs danach (an)gehört zu werden und Angehörige/r eines Anliegens zu werden. Der emanzipatorische Akt besteht darin, das Schweigen, das Nicht-gehört-Werden, die Erfahrung, mit einem Problem allein gelassen oder vergessen zu werden zu vernehmen, die Möglichkeit zu sehen, diese Erfahrung teilen und mitteilen zu können, sprechen zu können in einer Sprache, die nicht übersetzt werden muss in den „vor/herrschenden" hegemonialen Jargon oder sich assimilieren muss, um gehört zu werden. In diesem Sinne übernimmt Holub auch nicht die Position einer Fürsprecherin, einer Repräsentantin der Anliegen „anderer", denn dies würde die Erfahrung, nicht selbst und nicht für sich selbst sprechen zu können, nur unter anderen Vorzeichen wiederholen. Anstelle der Vertretung äußert sich hier ein Moment des Solidarisierens, das nicht bedeutet, die Ungleichheit und Differenz der Positionen, aus denen heraus man spricht oder schweigt, zu negieren oder zu neutralisieren, sondern das ein wesentliches Außer-Kraft-Setzen der vorab strukturierten Zuständigkeits- oder Betroffenheitsgrenzen zum Ausdruck bringt.

Dies bedeutet für die künstlerische Rolle, diese auch selbst zu hinterfragen, Zweifel zu üben an der eigenen Ausdruckskraft oder Ausdrucksstärke, am eigenen Vermögen, an der Differenz, die die eigene Begabung von der Rezeption durch andere trennt. Was sich hier abzeichnet, ist auch ein Akt des Verzichtens, eines Handelns, das darin besteht, sich zurückzunehmen, zu

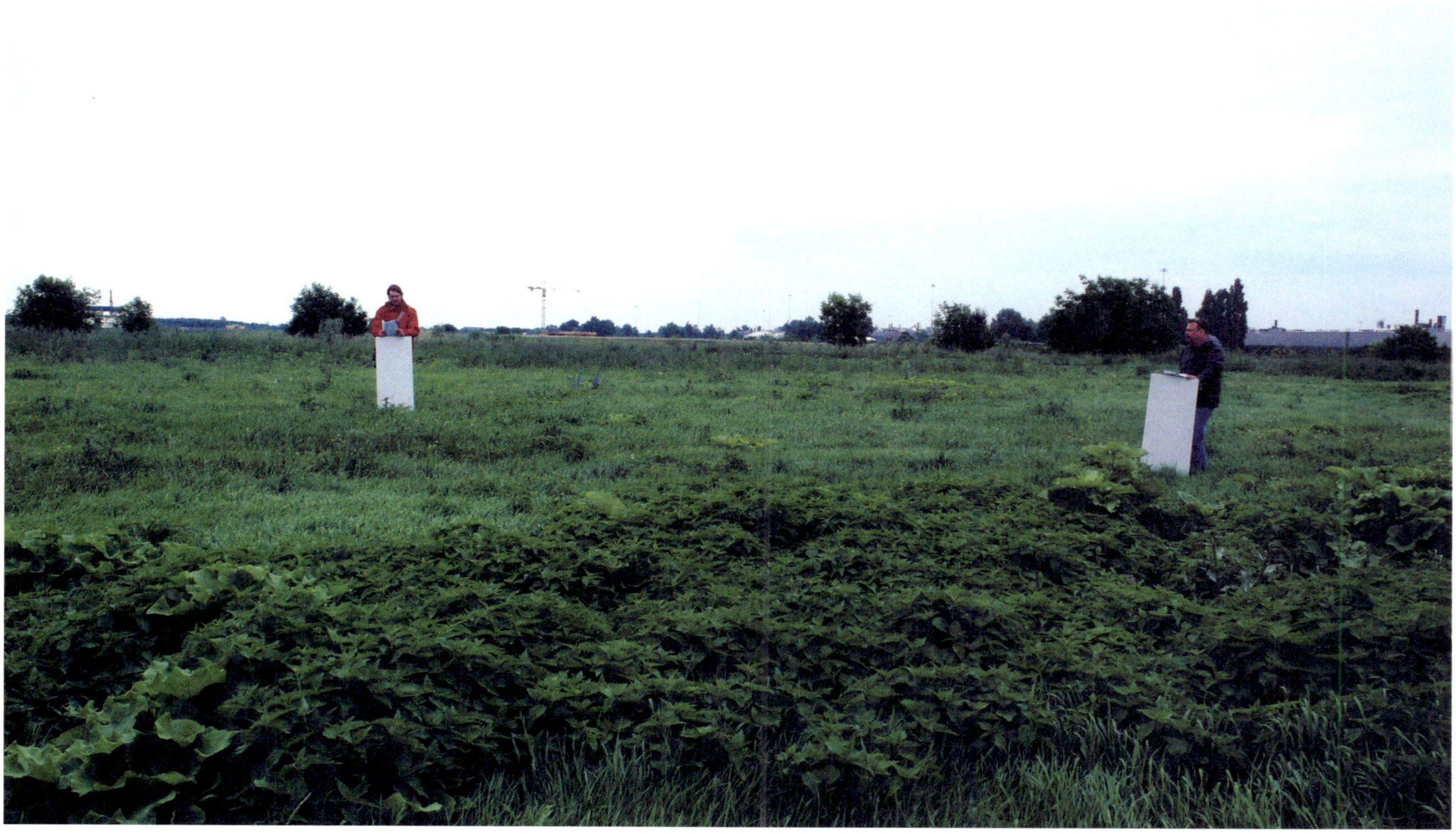

2nd WALK AT THE URBAN PERIPHERY, June 20, 2010, with "Voices From a Future International City"; performers: Dirk Nocker, Sönke Schnitzer Text: Barbara Holub

2. STADTRANDSPAZIERGANG, 20. Juni 2010, mit „Stimmen aus einer internationalen Stadt der Zukunft"; Performer: Dirk Nocker, Sönke Schnitzer Text: Barbara Holub

whether acknowledged or unacknowledged."[15] While, he continues, "what work cannot say is important, because there the elaboration of the utterance is acted out in a sort of journey to silence."[16] What is invoked here as silence is not being silent or secretive, but rather a mode of articulation—an expression of the encounter with discriminatory structures that do not provide a right to, nor a place for, rebuttal and reply unless adhering to the difference of Us and You, One and the Other, not equating a notion of the public arena and democracy with the notion of the majority. If "public" places should by definition be open to diverse, contradictory and inhomogeneous group affiliations—i.e. for a society that is aware of its intrinsic differences—then hegemonic and normative notions of the public arena fall short of precisely this openness. They present themselves as places of exclusion and marginalization. If talk of integration implies that it is about fitting in somewhere, adapting to the conditions of this "inside" and assimilating, then every deviance from this normative inside, it is inferred, is an "outside" and the concept of the public arena is to a certain extent "internalized" and de-differentiated. Only what belongs is heard and what is not supposed to belong remains unheard. What then remains is a public arena that is not open to differences and conveys the experience of only being heard when remaining silent—and sometimes not even that: then silence turns into a form of non-existence, into

erfahren, nicht die besseren Worte oder Geschichten für jene zu finden, die diese nicht zur Verfügung hätten, deren Schweigen und Stille nicht durch die eigene Beredsamkeit zu ersetzen oder zu kompensieren. Anstelle dessen zielt das Vernehmen, das im „Stillen Aktivismus" gehört werden will, auf eine Praxis, die „die Aufgabe hätte, das Schweigen zu vermessen, ob dieses Schweigen eingestanden oder uneingestanden ist."[15] Macherey: „Wichtig ist […] vielmehr das, was das Werk nicht sagen kann, denn hier, in einer Art Reise des Schweigens, spielt sich die Ausformung der Rede ab […]."[16] Was hier als Schweigen aufgerufen wird, ist kein Verschweigen und keine Verschwiegenheit, sondern ein Modus der Artikulation – Ausdruck für die Begegnung mit diskriminierenden Strukturen, die kein Recht und keinen Platz für Entgegnungen und Widerreden vorsehen, die nicht der Differenz von Uns und Euch, den einen und den anderen Folge leisten, die einen Begriff von Öffentlichkeit und Demokratie nicht mit der Vorstellung von Mehrheit gleichsetzen. Sollten „öffentliche" Plätze per Definition offen sein für diverse, widersprüchliche und inhomogene Gruppenzugehörigkeiten – mithin für eine Gesellschaft, die um ihre immanenten Differenzen weiß, dann verfehlen hegemoniale und normative Vorstellungen von Öffentlichkeit genau diese Offenheit, dann vermitteln sie sich als Orte des Ausschlusses und der Ausgrenzung. Wenn die Rede von Integration schon skizziert, dass es darum geht, sich irgendwo einzufügen, sich an die Bedingungen dieses

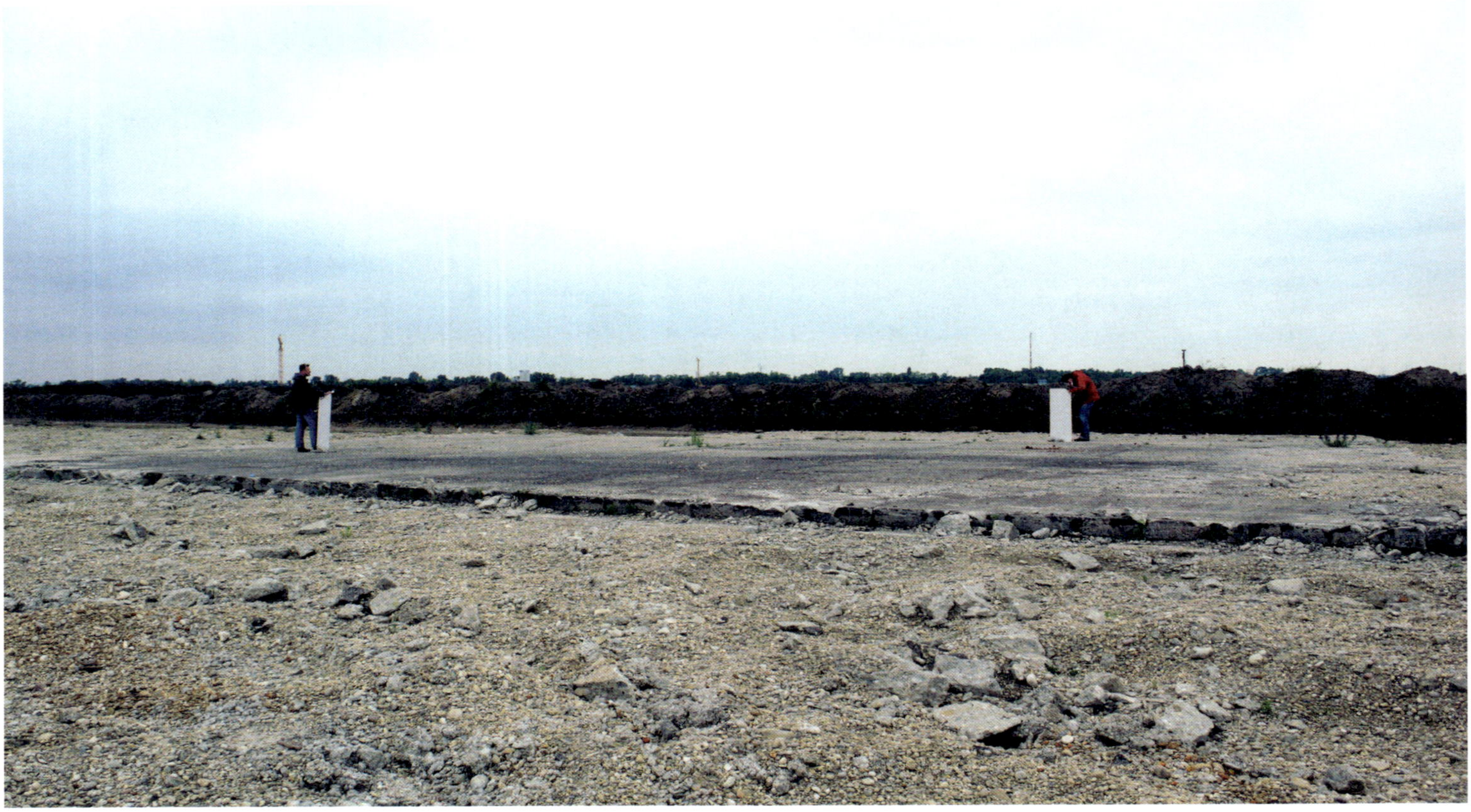

2nd WALK AT THE URBAN PERIPHERY, June 20, 2010, with "Voices From a Future International City"; performers: Dirk Nocker, Sönke Schnitzer Text: Barbara Holub

2. STADTRANDSPAZIERGANG, 20. Juni 2010, mit „Stimmen aus einer internationalen Stadt der Zukunft"; Performer: Dirk Nocker, Sönke Schnitzer Text: Barbara Holub

the experience of understanding one's own presence as synonymous with absence.

Holub locates most of her projects in "public" spaces in order to restore the claim to inclusion in this public arena for precisely those who are already there and are only tolerated as absentees. This means showing solidarity with them as part of the (democratic) public, hearing their silence as a mode of speaking, and confronting the emptied concept of the "public." It is not a matter of bringing "art" to public locations, nor of realizing "art in public space" beyond institutional structures, but rather of making this lost meaning of the public arena itself audible again—in other words, of realizing that a concept of the public arena based on exclusion does not mean a public arena and conceals the significance of being public. Paradoxically, the exclusion-based public arena thus becomes a silenced community—a community that pretends to be the public in order to conceal the diversity and contradictions inherent in the concept.

The silence of those who are not heard only reveals itself as an echo of the secrecy of this illusory public arena. To demonstrate solidarity does not mean becoming part of a community, but to stand up for concerns and demands beyond the boundaries of the respective communities that are denied the claim to

„Innen" anzupassen und zu assimilieren, dann wird implizit jede Devianz von diesem normativen Innen als „Außen" interpretiert und der Begriff von Öffentlichkeit gewissermaßen „verinnerlicht" und entdifferenziert. Gehört wird nur, was dazu gehört, und unerhört bleibt, was nicht dazu gehören soll. Was dann bleibt, ist eine Öffentlichkeit, die nicht offen ist für Differenzen, und die Erfahrung vermittelt, nur schweigend Gehör zu finden – und manchmal nicht einmal das: Dann verwandelt sich das Schweigen in eine Form der Inexistenz, in die Erfahrung, die eigene Anwesenheit als Synonym für Abwesenheit zu verstehen.

Holub lokalisiert die meisten ihrer Projekte in „öffentlichen" Räumen, um gerade denen, die schon da sind und nur als Abwesende geduldet werden, den Anspruch, Teil dieser Öffentlichkeit zu sein, wieder zuzuerkennen. Dies bedeutet, sich mit diesen als Teil der (demokratischen) Öffentlichkeit zu solidarisieren, ihr Schweigen als Modus des Sprechens zu vernehmen und dem entleerten Begriff des Öffentlichen gegenüberzutreten. Es geht nicht darum, „Kunst" an öffentliche Plätze zu bringen oder außerhalb vom institutionellen Gefüge „Kunst im öffentlichen Raum" zu realisieren, sondern diese verloren gegangene Bedeutung von Öffentlichkeit selbst wieder vernehmbar zu machen – mithin zu vergegenwärtigen, dass ein Begriff von Öffentlichkeit, der auf Ausschluss basiert, keine Öffentlichkeit meint und die Bedeutung des Öffentlichen verschweigt. Paradoxerweise wird damit die auf Ausschluss basierende

public relevance. In this sense, solidarity can only be shown with a community to which one does not belong, still supporting it within the horizon of a notion of the public sphere in order to defend the significance of the public arena itself. In short, the public arena must remain open—open to the diversity inherent in the concept of society and open to its inherent indeterminacy. From this perspective, Holub's projects aim equally at a politics and culture of solidarity and a critique of the massive cutbacks that are limiting and restricting the concept of the public arena. If we consider that Holub's projects have been accompanied by a resurgence of nationalist, xenophobic, racist and discriminatory developments on a political level in Austria and Europe over the last twenty years,[17] with anything and everything tried to introduce exclusion and promote mechanisms of exclusion, then her interventions in "public" space imply a political agenda—a critique of emptied concepts of the public arena promoting an opening of public space.

In this context, the concept of art that accompanies it also shifts emphasis. Art in public space does not mean confronting a public with art or familiarizing it with art outside of an institutional framework, rather regarding art itself as a public agenda. Rancière's thesis mentioned above—calling for "a theatre without spectators"[18]—is pursued further in Holub's work in the sense that it calls to mind theater without a theater. In the knowledge of the indeterminacy and differences that are inscribed in a concept of the public arena, the public arena is by its very constitution of a contested and performative nature—and thus of a theatrical nature. The public sphere simply does not exist. It only exists in the form in which it articulates itself and as what it articulates. When Antonin Artaud speaks of a "theatre of cruelty,"[19] this could also be applied to the concept of being public: the public arena as a theater of cruelty. What is cruel about the public arena, however, is not only the battles that are fought in it but, above all, the current policies that do not even allow everybody to participate in these disputes, nor to play or find their own "roles" within them. The theater of the public arena takes place, while under current conditions it only takes place with the exclusion of an open public. The public arena generates itself as a theater where not everybody is supposed to find a seat—as a spectacle to the exclusion of a broad public. Laughter, silence or stuttering are reserved for those who are not allowed in, those excluded from any opening up of what is public. When Holub shows solidarity with various excluded or marginalized groups in her projects, when the artistic act essentially expresses an interrogation and solidarity, then it is in the sense of this opening and restoration of the public arena. It works not only in the public sphere, but above all with the public arena. The theater of the public is the material from which Holub develops her works, and at the same time their location and their destination. What she succeeds in doing is to understand the public arena not only as a theater of cruelty, but also as a theater of

Öffentlichkeit zu einer verschwiegenen Gemeinschaft – zu einer Gemeinschaft, die sich als Öffentlichkeit ausgibt, um die Diversität und Widersprüche, die dem Begriff inhärent sind, zu verschweigen.

Das Schweigen jener, die nicht gehört werden, gibt sich nur als Echo der Verschwiegenheit dieser Scheinöffentlichkeit zu erkennen. Sich zu solidarisieren bedeutet nicht, Teil einer Gemeinschaft zu werden, sondern sich über die Grenzen der jeweiligen Gemeinschaften hinweg für Anliegen und Forderungen einzusetzen, denen der Anspruch auf öffentliche Relevanz vorenthalten wird. In diesem Sinne kann man sich nur mit einer Gemeinschaft solidarisieren, der man nicht angehört, und sie dennoch im Horizont eines Begriffs von Öffentlichem unterstützen, um die Bedeutung von Öffentlichkeit selbst zu verteidigen. Kurz gesagt: Öffentlichkeit muss offenbleiben – offen für die Diversität, die dem Gesellschaftsbegriff inhärent ist, und offen auch für die Unbestimmbarkeit, die diesem innewohnt. Aus dieser Perspektive zielen die Projekte von Holub gleichermaßen auf eine Politik und Kultur des Solidarisierens wie auf eine Kritik an den massiven Einschnitten, die den Öffentlichkeitsbegriff limitieren und einschränken woll(t)en. Wenn man sich vergegenwärtigt, dass die Projekte von Holub in den letzten 20 Jahren auf politischer Ebene in Österreich und Europa durch ein Wiedererstarken nationalistischer, xenophober, rassistischer und diskriminierender Entwicklungen,[17] die mit allen Mitteln versucht haben, Ausgrenzungs- und Ausschlussmechanismen einzuführen, begleitet wurden, dann weisen ihre Interventionen im „öffentlichen" Raum auf eine politische Agenda hin – auf eine Kritik an entleerten Öffentlichkeitsbegriffen und auf ein „Öffnen öffentlicher Räume".

In diesem Horizont verschiebt sich auch der Kunstbegriff, der damit einhergeht. Kunst im öffentlichen Raum heißt dann nicht, eine Öffentlichkeit mit Kunst zu konfrontieren oder mit dieser außerhalb der institutionellen Rahmen vertraut zu machen, sondern Kunst selbst als öffentliche Agenda zu betrachten. Die eingangs erwähnte These von Rancière, ein „Theater ohne Zuschauer"[18] zu fordern, wird durch die Arbeiten von Holub in dem Sinne erweitert, dass man darüber hinaus auch an ein Theater ohne Theater denken kann. Im Wissen um die Unbestimmtheit und Differenzen, die einem Öffentlichkeitsbegriff eingeschrieben sind, ist Öffentlichkeit konstitutiv von umstrittener und performativer Natur – mithin von theatralischer Natur. Öffentlichkeit existiert nicht einfach so, es gibt sie nur in der Form, wie sie sich und als was sie sich artikuliert. Wenn Antonin Artaud von einem „Theater der Grausamkeit"[19] spricht, dann könnte man dies auch auf den Öffentlichkeitsbegriff übertragen – auf Öffentlichkeit als Theater der Grausamkeit. Das Grausame am Öffentlichen sind aber nicht nur die Kämpfe, die darin ausgetragen werden, sondern vor allem die aktuellen Politiken, die es nicht einmal allen zugestehen, an diesen Auseinandersetzungen teilzuhaben und ihre „Rolle" darin zu spielen oder zu finden. Das Theater des Öffentlichen findet statt, aber es findet unter den gegenwärtigen Bedingungen nur unter Ausschluss einer offenen Öffentlichkeit statt.

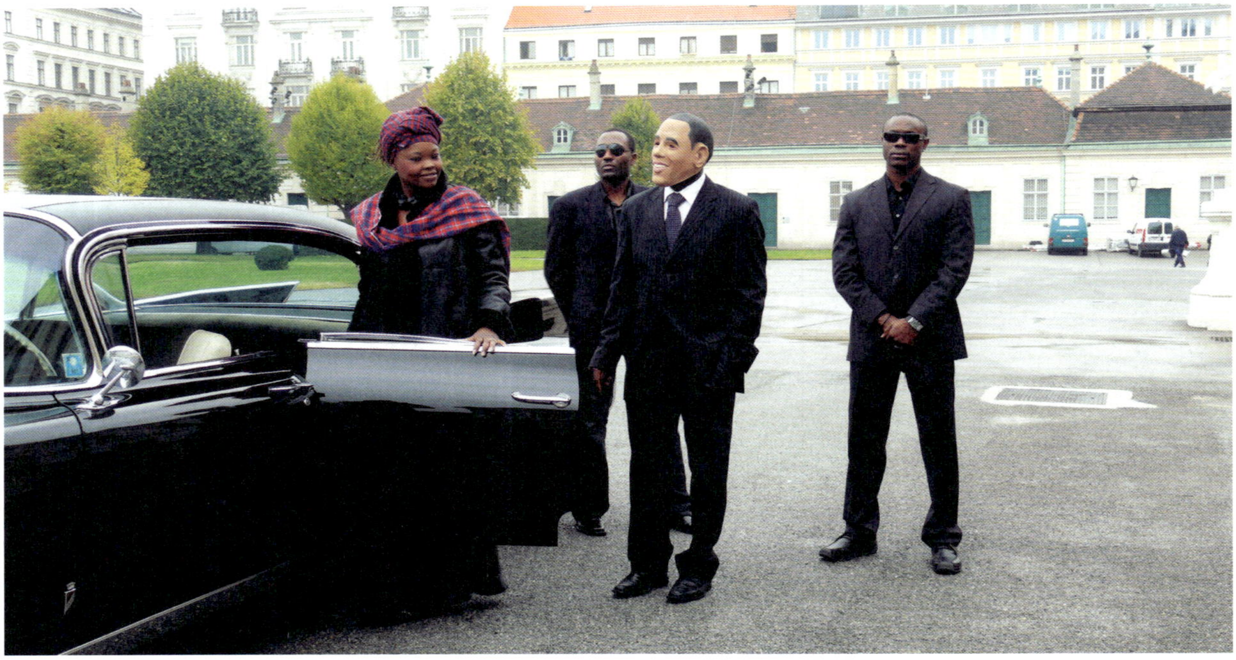

ISH BIN EIN...(transparadiso/Bernd Vlay), in: *Waypoints Like Sharon's Stone*, curated by Andrea Börner and Bärbel Müller, Kunsthalle Exnergasse, Vienna, 2007
For the exhibition, which examined "African spaces in Vienna," transparadiso staged a state visit by Barack Obama and his wife Michelle as an anticipatory fiction—which became reality through his election as president of the USA in 2009.

ISH BIN EIN... (transparadiso/Bernd Vlay), in: *Waypoints Like Sharon's Stone*, kuratiert von Andrea Börner und Bärbel Müller, Kunsthalle Exnergasse, Wien, 2007
Für die Ausstellung, in der „afrikanische Räume in Wien" untersucht werden sollten, inszenierte transparadiso einen Staatsbesuch von Barack Obama und seiner Frau Michelle als antizipatorische Fiktion – die durch seine Wahl zum Präsidenten der USA 2009 Realität wurde.

solidarity that can only articulate itself in public—as a horizon of commonality despite the diversity, contradictions and differences that are also allowed to be tested, played out and performed in line with a concept of the public arena: theater freed of the theatrical.

1 Cf. the performance BREAKING QUIET (2001) by Barbara Holub in collaboration with Christine Hohenbüchler at the BONE Performance Art Festival in Berne (CH): www.barbaraholub.com/breaking-quiet.html.

2 Cf. THE LAUGHTER THAT GETS CAUGHT IN YOUR THROAT, a performance by Barbara Holub and transparadiso at the Vienna Biennale 2015, in cooperation with the Integrationshaus, SOS-Mitmensch and the Vinzi-Rast in Vienna: www.barbaraholub.com/the-laughter-that-gets-caught-in-your-throat.html.

3 Cf. A STATE VISIT TO THE BLUE FROG SOCIETY BY MINORITY NATIONALITIES, developed by Barbara Holub for the *CrossSections* project (curated by Başak Şenova, 2018): www.barbaraholub.com/the-blue-frog-society.html.

4 Cf. MORE OPPORTUNITIES (Plymouth, 2007) by Barbara Holub. Demonstrators rallied through the streets holding blank banners: www.barbaraholub.com/more-opportunities.html.

5 Cf. Michel Foucault, The Order of Things (London/New York: Routledge, 1970). In Foucault's original essay "Les mots et les choses" (published in 1966 by Edition Gallimard), he describes the interrelationship between words and things, their formal expressions and how they merge and stand for one another, how they might be interchangeable. The thing can only be "read" as a word when the word is treated as a thing.

6 Cf. the book of the same title by Gayatri Chakravorty Spivak, Can the Subaltern Speak? Reflections on the History of an Idea (New York, Columbia University Press, 2010).

7 Barbara Holub's LISTEN TO THE QUIET VOICE (2008) was screened at the Regionale in Feldbach (AT): www.barbaraholub.com/listen-to-the-quiet-voice. html.

Öffentlichkeit generiert sich so als Theater, in dem nicht alle Platz finden sollen – als Schauspiel unter Ausschluss der Öffentlichkeit. Das Lachen, das Schweigen oder Stottern ist jenen vorbehalten, die nicht reindürfen, ausgeschlossen werden vom Offenen des Öffentlichen. Wenn sich Holub in ihren Projekten mit verschiedenen ausgeschlossenen oder marginalisierten Gruppen solidarisiert, wenn der künstlerische Akt wesentlich ein Vernehmen und Solidarisieren zum Ausdruck bringt, dann im Sinne dieses Öffnens und Wiederherstellens des Öffentlichen. Sie arbeitet nicht nur in der Öffentlichkeit, sondern vor allem mit dem Öffentlichen. Das Theater der Öffentlichkeit ist das Material, aus dem Holub ihre Arbeiten entwickelt, und zugleich deren Ort und Destination. Was ihr dabei gelingt, besteht darin, die Öffentlichkeit nicht nur als Theater der Grausamkeit zu verstehen, sondern auch als ein Theater der Solidarität, das sich nur öffentlich artikulieren kann – als ein Horizont von Gemeinsamkeit trotz der Diversität, Widersprüche und Differenzen, die im Sinne eines Öffentlichkeitsbegriffs auch erprobt, gespielt und vorgetragen werden dürfen. Ein Theater ohne Theater.

1 Vgl. dazu die Performance BREAKING QUIET, die Barbara Holub gemeinsam mit Christine Hohenbüchler beim BONE Performance Art Festival in Bern 2001 gezeigt hat: https://www.barbaraholub.com/breaking-quiet.html (Zugriff: 25.2.2022).

2 Vgl. dazu THE LAUGHTER THAT GETS CAUGHT IN YOUR THROAT, eine Performance, die Barbara Holub mit transparadiso bei der Vienna Biennale 2015 in Kooperation mit dem Integrationshaus, SOS-Mitmensch und der Vinzi-Rast in Wien gezeigt hat: https://www.barbaraholub.com/the-laughter-that-gets-caught-in-your-throat.html (Zugriff: 25.2.2022).

8 Cf. Je suis arabe (2015) by Barbara Holub, realized with the performer Akram al Halabi in Salzburg, where a Tunisian poem was transmitted in the original Arabic and in German: www.barbaraholub.com/je-suis-arabe.html.

9 Cf. TIMES OF DILEMMA and the "Ghana dialogs" (2018) by Barbara Holub: www.barbaraholub.com/times-of-dilemma.html.

10 Cf. AT THE URBAN PERIPHERY (2010) in Vienna or INITIATIVE ISLAND (2008) in Birmingham, both of which short-circuit peripheral territory with social marginalization: www.barbaraholub.com/at-the-urban-periphery.html www.barbaraholub.com/initiative-island1.html.

11 Jacques Rancière, The Emancipated Spectator (London/New York: Verso, 2009), p. 4.

12 The term "uncanny" is used here in Sigmund Freud's interpretation: "the uncanny [the 'unhomely'] is what was once familiar ['homely', 'homey']. The negative prefix un- is the indicator of repression." Here, quoted from Sigmund Freud, The Uncanny, translated by David McLintock (London: Penguin, 2013), p. 260.

13 Cf. www.barbaraholub.com/call-against-the-border.html.

14 Cf. the work of the same title with transparadiso: www.barbaraholub.com/favorit.html.

15 Pierre Macherey, A Theory of Literary Production, translated from the French by Geoffrey Wall (London/New York: Routledge, 1978), p. 97.

16 Ibid., pp. 97f.

17 Here, reference to the involvement in the Austrian government of a radical right-wing, xenophobic political party like the FPÖ suffices to show the local context for these developments. The European dimension of this policy of exclusion is clearly expressed in the sealing off of Europe and the strengthening of the Schengen borders against the admission of people seeking asylum. The equally restrictive policies in place stretching from the USA to Australia indicate the global dimension of the same developments. In the foreword to the German translation of Gayatri Spivak, Can the Subaltern Speak? Hito Steyerl writes, "It is solidarity as such that has become subaltern today, as there is no language in which it can be audibly articulated." (Columbia University Press, 2010; Can the Subaltern Speak? Postkolonialität und subalterne Artikulation; translated by Alexander Joskowicz and Stefan Nowotny, Vienna: Verlag Turia + Kant, 2008, p. 15).

18 Rancière, The Emancipated Spectator, p. 4.

19 Cf. Antonin Artaud, "The Theater of Cruelty," The Theater and its Double, translated by Mary Caroline Richards (New York: Grove Press, 1958), pp. 84ff.

3 Vgl. dazu die Arbeit A STATE VISIT TO THE BLUE FROG SOCIETY BY MINORITY NATIONALITIES, die Barbara Holub für das *CrossSections*-Projekt (kuratiert von Başak Şenova) 2018 entwickelt hat: https://www.barbaraholub.com/the-blue-frog-society.html (Zugriff: 25.2.2022).

4 Vgl. dazu die Arbeit MORE OPPORTUNITIES, die Barbara Holub 2007 in Plymouth gezeigt hat, bei der DemonstrantInnen mit unbeschriebenen Bannern durch die Straßen gezogen sind: https://www.barbaraholub.com/more-opportunities.html (Zugriff: 25.2.2022).

5 Vgl. dazu Michel Foucault, Die Ordnung der Dinge, Frankfurt am Main, 1974 (Orig.: Les mots et les choses, Edition Gallimard, 1966; übersetzt von Ulrich Köppen). Foucault beschreibt in diesem Buch „die Wörter und Dinge", wie der originale Titel seines Texts heißt, das Verhältnis zwischen den beiden, die Formen, wie sie ineinander übergehen, für einander einstehen oder einander ersetzen sollen, das Wort wie ein Ding behandelt und das Ding nur mehr als Wort „gelesen" werden kann.

6 Vgl. dazu das gleichnamige Buch von Gayatri Chakravorty Spivak, Can the Subaltern Speak? Postkolonialität und subalterne Artikulation, übersetzt von Alexander Joskowicz und Stefan Nowotny, Wien 2008 (1985).

7 Vgl. dazu die Arbeit LISTEN TO THE QUIET VOICE von Barbara Holub, die sie im Rahmen der regionale 2008 in Feldbach in Österreich gezeigt hat: https://www.barbaraholub.com/listen-to-the-quiet-voice.html (Zugriff: 25.2.2022)

8 Vgl. dazu die Arbeit Je suis arabe, die Barbara Holub gemeinsam mit dem Performer Akram al Halabi 2015 in Salzburg realisiert hat. Dabei wurde das Gedicht eines tunesischen Dichters auf Arabisch und Deutsch gewissermaßen „verlautbart": https://www.barbaraholub.com/je-suis-arabe.html (Zugriff: 25.2.2022).

9 Vgl. dazu Barbara Holubs Arbeit TIMES OF DILEMMA und die so genannten „Ghana dialogs" (2018): https://www.barbaraholub.com/times-of-dilemma.html (Zugriff: 25.2.2022).

10 Vgl. dazu die Arbeiten AT THE URBAN PERIPHERY (2010) in Wien oder INITIATIVE ISLAND in Birmingham (2008), die gleichermaßen die territoriale Peripherie mit einer sozialen Marginalisierung kurzschließen: https://www.barbaraholub.com/at-the-urban-periphery.html und https://www.barbaraholub.com/initiative-island1.html (Zugriff: 25.2.2022).

11 Jacques Rancière, Der emanzipierte Zuschauer, übersetzt von Richard Steurer, Wien 2009, S. 14 (Orig.: Le spectateur émancipé, 2008).

12 Der Begriff des „Unheimlichen" folgt hier der Interpretation von Sigmund Freud: „Das Unheimliche ist also [...] das ehemals Heimische, Altvertraute. Die Vorsilbe ‚un' an diesem Worte ist aber die Marke der Verdrängung." Sigmund Freud, „Das Unheimliche" (1919), in: ders., Psychologische Schriften, Studienausgabe, Frankfurt am Main 1970, S. 267.

13 Siehe https://www.barbaraholub.com/call-against-the-border.html (Zugriff: 25.2.2022).

14 Vgl. dazu die gleichnamige Arbeit mit transparadiso: https://www.barbaraholub.com/favorit.html (Zugriff: 25.2.2022)

15 Pierre Macherey, Zur Theorie der literarischen Produktion, (1966) 1974; zitiert nach Spivak, a. a. O., S. 54.

16 Ebd., S. 54–55.

17 Hier sei der Hinweis auf die Einbindung einer rechtsradikalen und fremdenfeindlichen Partei wie der FPÖ in die österreichische Regierung genug, um den lokalen Kontext dieser Entwicklungen zu erwähnen. Die Abschottung Europas und die Stärkung der Schengen-Grenzen gegen die Aufnahme hilfesuchender Menschen unterstreicht die europäische Dimension dieser Ausgrenzungspolitik. Die gleichfalls restriktive Politik, die von den USA bis Australien reicht, markiert die globale Dimension dieser Entwicklungen. Hito Steyerl: „Es ist die Solidarität als solche, die heute subaltern geworden ist, da es keine Sprache gibt, in der sie vernehmbar artikuliert werden kann." Hito Steyerl, „Die Gegenwart der Subalternen", in: Gayatri Spivak, Can the Subaltern Speak, a. a. O., S. 15.

18 Siehe Fußnote 11.

19 Vgl. dazu Antonin Artaud, „Das Theater der Grausamkeit", in: ders., Das Theater und sein Double, übersetzt von Gerd Henninger, Berlin 2012.

I. *This is the Gallery, and the Gallery is Many Things*, curated by Gavin Wade, Eastside Projects, Birmingham (UK), 2008, permanent installation 2008–2018

This is the Gallery, and the Gallery is Many Things, kuratiert von Gavin Wade, Eastside Projects, Birmingham (UK), 2008, permanente Installation 2008–2018

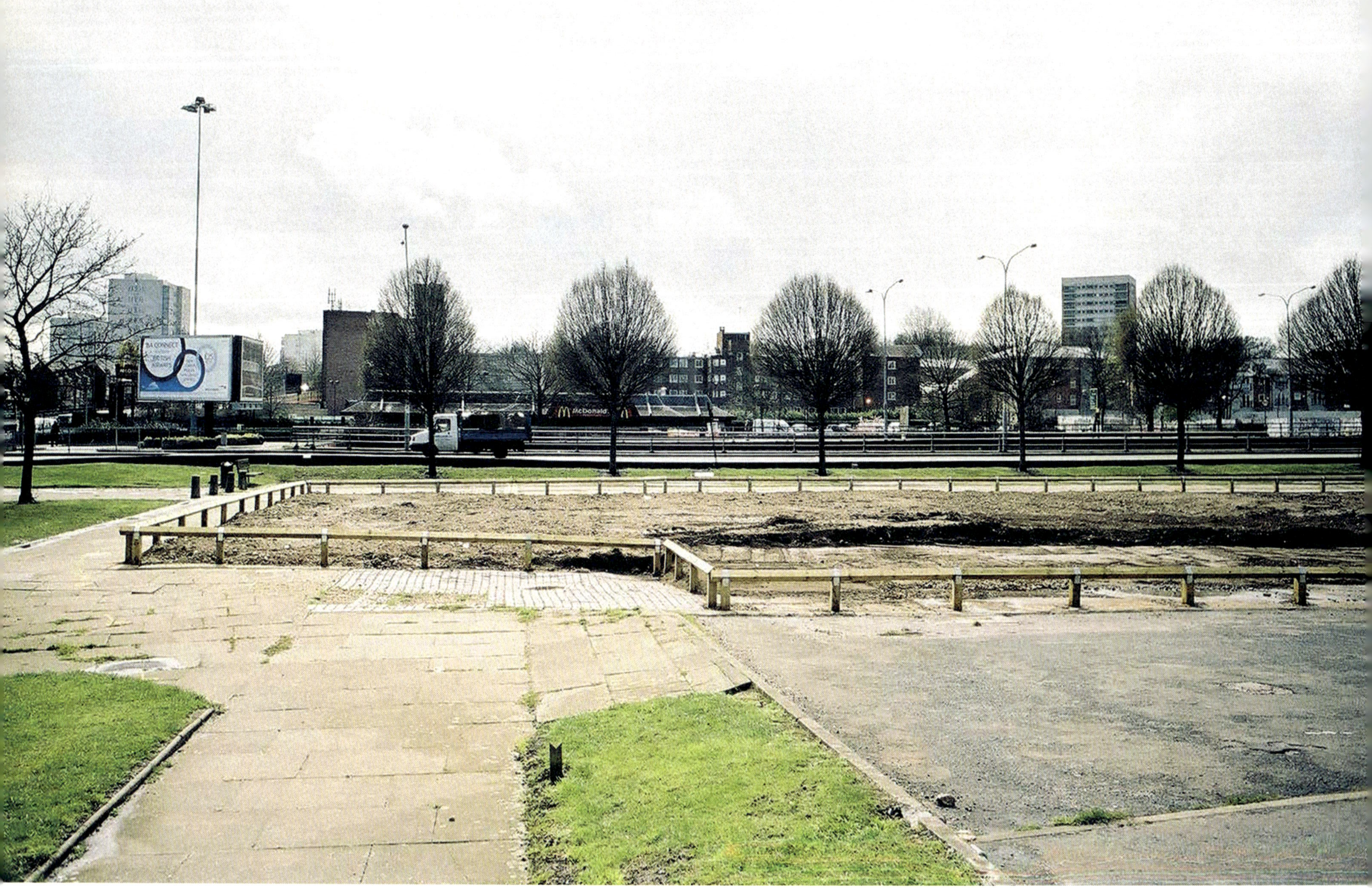

Haddon Tower, Birmingham, 2008. This 20-storey tower block (1967), was demolished in 2006 to give way for Park Central, the largest urban renewal project in the UK outside London.

Haddon Tower, Birmingham, 2008. Dieses 20-geschoßige Wohnhochaus (1967) wurde 2006 abgerissen, um Platz zu machen für Park Central, das größte Stadterneuerungsprojekt im UK außerhalb Londons.

INITIATIVE ISLAND

The starting point of the project was to look at urban transformation focusing on social housing and the demolition of tower blocks. In the UK, the typology of architecture is often blamed for social problems, in lieu of understanding that a lack of maintenance and infrastructure causes a (social) decline. As a consequence, tower blocks were demolished in Birmingham, to be replaced by two-story buildings, again with no urban design concept of public space and infrastructure. By anchoring this transformation in the new exhibition venue Eastside Projects—a change-over from a factory building in the former industrial area of Digbeth in Birmingham into a contemporary art space—INITIATIVE ISLAND explored the phases/faces of urban developments.

The large-scale curtain installed in the exhibition space took the cartographic surface in a social direction. Dated 2008, the map pointed out the segregation among the demolished buildings, buildings destined to be demolished, and buildings that remain. Holub conceived a map showing the current state of social housing projects in Birmingham, conveyed like a "galactic map." It manifested itself as an outcome of Holub's extensive research on the tower blocks/social housing of Birmingham. Through this map, the project made visible the tension between advocating a progressive urban renewal and its destructive side effects. Moreover, the map was embroidered on black stage molleton by asylum seekers located temporally at the House of Integration in Vienna. Since this fabric is mostly used for theater backdrops, the story behind the production of this installation embraced the audience with further symbolic connotations.

The curtain addresses the ambivalence of being a backdrop for other exhibitions (also shown by the "cheap"/non-representative material of molleton) and its role as a representation (entering the exhibition space through the back of the curtain); the cartography already becoming historic evidence of the change of the city throughout the years.

In addition, this inaugural exhibition of Eastside Projects, "This is the Gallery, and the Gallery is Many Things," presented two billboards with the headline "Choose your second life in real life—bid on your future" both exhibited inside and on the façade of the building.
The curtain was permanently installed as a backdrop for shows from 2008–2018 at Eastside Projects.[BS]

INITIATIVE ISLAND

Ausgangspunkt des Projekts war eine Untersuchung urbaner Transformationsprozesse, insbesondere im Bereich des sozialen Wohnbaus.
Im Vereinigten Königreich wird für gesellschaftliche Probleme oft die Typologie der Architektur verantwortlich gemacht und nicht gesehen, dass (sozialer) Verfall mitunter durch deren ungenügende Wartung und fehlende Infrastruktur verursacht wird. Infolgedessen wurden in Birmingham Wohnhochhäuser abgerissen, um sie durch zweistöckige Gebäude zu ersetzen – wieder einmal ohne jegliches städtebauliche Konzept in Bezug auf öffentlichen Raum und Infrastruktur. INITIATIVE ISLAND transportierte diese Aspekte der Stadtentwicklung in den neu gegründeten Ausstellungsort Eastside Projects, der durch die Adaptierung eines ehemaligen Fabrikgebäudes im ehemaligen Industriebezirk Digbeth entstand.

Die umfangreichen Recherchen zum sozialen Wohnbau/zu den Wohnhochhäusern in Birmingham wurden auf einem mit einer großflächigen kartografischen Darstellung bestickten Vorhang repräsentiert, der entlang der Wände des Ausstellungsraums installiert wurde. Als eine Art „galaktisches Netzwerk" angelegt, spiegelte die Karte den Stand des sozialen Wohnbaus in Birmingham von 2008 wider, unterteilt in Wohnblocks, die entweder bereits abgerissen oder zum Abriss bestimmt waren, und solchen, die weiterhin bestehen sollten. Auf diese Weise machte die Karte das Spannungsverhältnis zwischen der fortschreitenden Stadterneuerung und deren destruktiven Auswirkungen sichtbar. Der damit oft einhergehende Verdrängungsprozess wurde dadurch betont, dass die Karte von Asylsuchenden des Wiener Integrationshauses auf schwarzen Molton gestickt wurde, ein „armes" Material, das vorzugsweise im Theater Verwendung findet. Diese Herstellungsgeschichte verleiht dem Vorhang eine zusätzliche soziale Dimension und fügt dem Objekt weitere Bedeutungen hinzu.

Die Installation des Vorhangs thematisiert seine ambivalente Doppelrolle als Hintergrund für nachfolgende Ausstellungen und hinterfragt die Repräsentation von Kunst im Ausstellungskontext, zumal der Ausstellungsraum von der Rückseite des Vorhangs betreten werden musste.
Die Kartografie ist mittlerweile zur historischen Zeugin der gesellschaftlichen wie architektonischen Veränderung geworden.

In der Eröffnungsausstellung waren außerdem zwei Plakatwände zu sehen, mit der Aufschrift „Choose your second life in real life – bid on your future" an der Außenfassade, und der Aufschrift INITIATIVE ISLAND im Hauptraum. Der Vorhang war in Eastside Projects von 2008 bis 2018 als permanenter Hintergrund für die Ausstellungen installiert.[BS]

"Her billboard on the outside of the Eastside Projects building depicts several chains of black pearls, quoting the rotary airer/ chandelier produced for Plymouth Arts Centre. The billboard inside the gallery is entitled 'Initiative Island,' this reference to a—presumably—real estate property indicates that something is to become reality within an unknown future. "Initiative Island invites the many people who are not heard in a regeneration program to speak up; it refers to a utopian space." To the billboard on the façade a slogan is added: 'Choose your second life in real life, bid on your future—here and now!'"

Marjolein Schaap

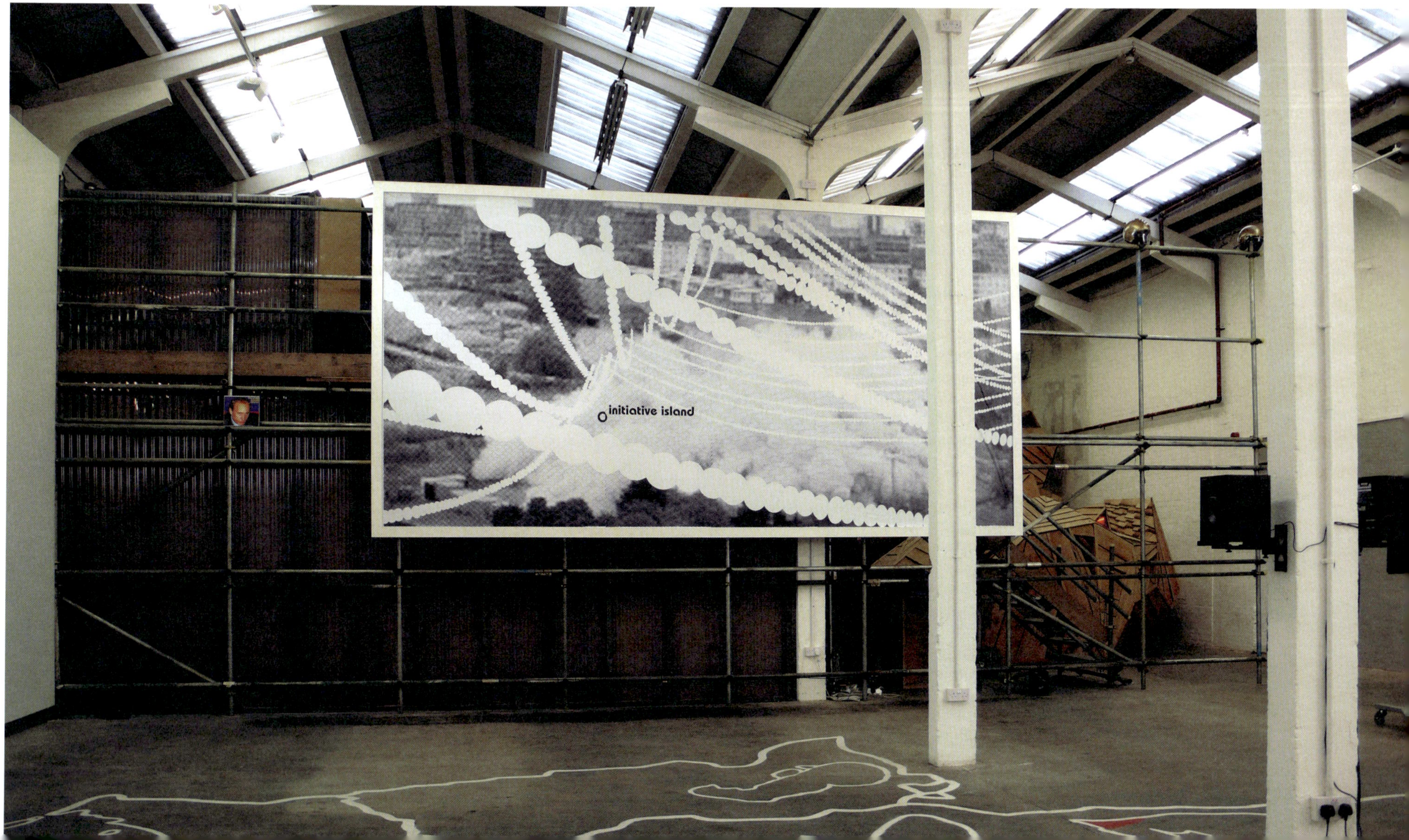

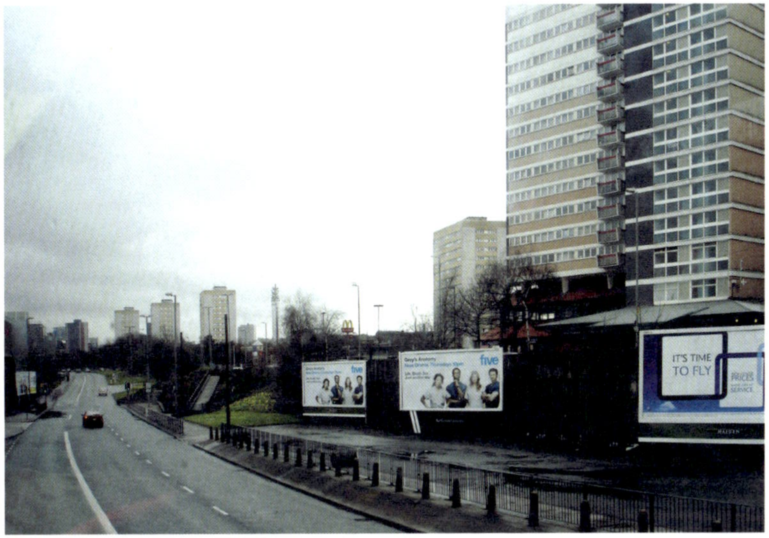

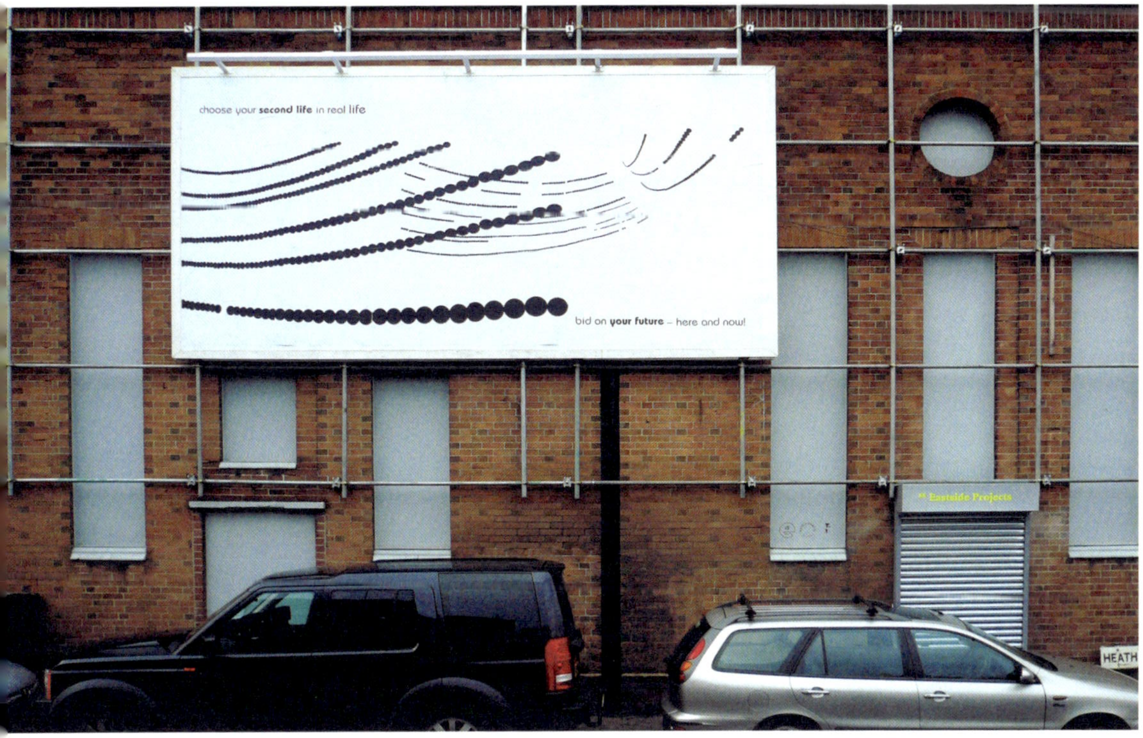

~~Abingdon Tower~~
Adelaide Tower
Albany House
~~Albert Shaw House~~
~~Andover House~~
~~Argosy House~~
Arlington House
~~Auster House~~
Avery House
Avon House*
~~Avro House~~
Bakeman House
Baldwin House
Banbury House
~~Barford House~~
Barn House
Barratts House
Barry Jackson Tower
~~Bartley House~~
~~Bayley Tower~~
Beale House
Bellfield House
Birchfield Tower
~~Blakemere House~~
Boundary House
~~Bovingdon Tower~~
~~Bower House~~
Bradbeer House
Brecon Tower
Bridge Meadow House
~~Bridgnorth House~~
Bridport House
Brinklow Tower
~~Brisbane House~~
Broadheath House*
~~Broadmeadow House~~
~~Brook House~~
~~Brooks Tower~~
Brookpiece House
Browning Tower*
Brunswick House
Buckland House
Burcombe Tower
Calder Tower
California House
Cambridge Tower
Camrose Tower
~~Canberra House~~
Canterbury Tower
Cantlow House
~~Carbrooke House~~
~~Castle House~~
~~Cedar House~~
~~Centre 8~~
Century Tower
Chadwick House
Chamberlain House
~~Charlecote Tower~~
~~Chatsworth Tower~~
~~Chestnut House~~
~~Chillinghome Tower~~
Chiswick House
Chivenor House*
Claverdon House
~~Clayton House~~
Cleeve House*
Cleveland Tower*
~~Clyde Tower~~
Clydesdale Tower*
Collings House
~~Comet House~~
~~Compton House~~
Copeshill Court
Coldfield
~~Concorde Tower~~
Coppice House
Cornwall Tower
~~Cosford Tower~~
Crabtree House
~~Cranwell Tower~~
Crescent Tower*
Danesmoor House*
~~Donnington House~~
~~Dorset Tower~~
Dovey Tower
Drews House
~~Dunchurch House~~
Durham Tower
~~Earlswood House~~
Elizabeth and Margaret Court
~~Elm Tree Tower~~
~~Ensign House~~
Essington House
Fairbourne Tower*
Fallows House
Faraday House
~~Farclose House~~
~~Firs House~~
~~Flint Tower~~
~~Freemantle House~~
Frogmoor House*
Galton Tower*
Geach Tower
Giles Close House
Gosmoor House*
~~Haddon Tower~~
~~Hampden House~~
~~Harlech Tower~~
~~Hawker House~~
Heath House
~~Hercules House~~
~~Hermes House~~
Heron Court*
High Tower
Hillcroft House
Hillside House
Hodgson Tower
Hogarth House*
Holbrook Tower
Hollowmeadow House
Hollypiece House
Home Meadow House
Home Tower
Humber Tower
Inkerman House
James House
~~Javelin House~~
Jordan House
~~Juniper House~~
~~Kemble Tower~~
Kempsey House
~~Kenchester House~~
Kendal Tower
Kenilworth House
Kenrick House
Kentmere Tower*
~~Kents House~~
~~Kesterton Tower~~
Kestrel House
Kineton House
Kingspiece House
Kingswood House
Lakehouse Court
Lansdown House*
~~Lappath House~~
~~Lapworth House~~
~~Larch House~~
Lea House
~~Lebanon House~~
Ledbury House
Leominster House
Lincoln Tower
Lloyd House
~~Longleat Tower~~
Ludlow House
~~Lyncham Tower~~
~~Lysander House~~
~~Maitland House~~
Manton House
Martineau Tower
Medway Tower
~~Melbourne House~~
~~Meteor House~~
Middlefield House
Mill House
Monmouth House
~~Moundsley House~~
Moor House
Muntz House
Nash House*
~~Near Oak House~~
Norfolk Tower
~~Normansell Tower~~
Normanton Tower*
~~Northolt Tower~~
Norton Tower*
~~Oakington House~~
Oast House
Osbourne Tower
~~Oscott Court~~
Ottawa House*
~~Packwood House~~
Park Court*
Parker House
Pennycroft House
~~Pine House~~
~~Pioneer House~~
Pitmeadow House
Pleck House
Primrose Tower
~~Princethorpe Tower~~
Pritchett Tower
Quarry House
~~Quebec Tower~~
Queens Tower
Radcliffe Tower
Rea Tower
Redditch House
~~Rednal House~~
Redway Court
Reynolds House
Rushmore House
Sadler House
Salisbury Tower
Sapphire Tower
Saxelby House
~~Sayer House~~
Scholefield Tower
Severn Tower
~~Shawbury Tower~~
Shelley Tower*
~~Sorrel House~~
~~Souters House~~
South Tower
Southam House
Stafford House
~~Stephenson Tower~~
~~Stoneycroft Tower~~
Studley Tower
Sycamore House
~~Sydney House~~
~~Tenbury House~~
~~Ternhill House~~
Teviot Tower
Thames Tower
The Sentinels: Clydesdale and Cleveland Tower*
Thistle House
Thornton House
Topcliffe House*
Topfield House
Trent Tower
~~Trident House~~
Truro Tower
Tweed Tower
~~Valiant House~~
~~Vanguard House~~
Vaughton House
Victor Tower
~~Viscount House~~
~~Vulcan House~~
Ward End House
Warstone Tower
~~Wellesbourne Tower~~
Wells Tower
Wendover House
Weston House
Wheeldon House
Whitbourne House
~~White House~~
Wickets Tower
~~Wiggin Tower~~
Wilmcote Tower
Woburn House
Woodstock House
Wyrley House

August 2008:
http://ukhousing.wikia.com
+ aerial views

existing tower blocks
refurbished or planned to be refurbished*
~~demolished or planned to be demolished~~

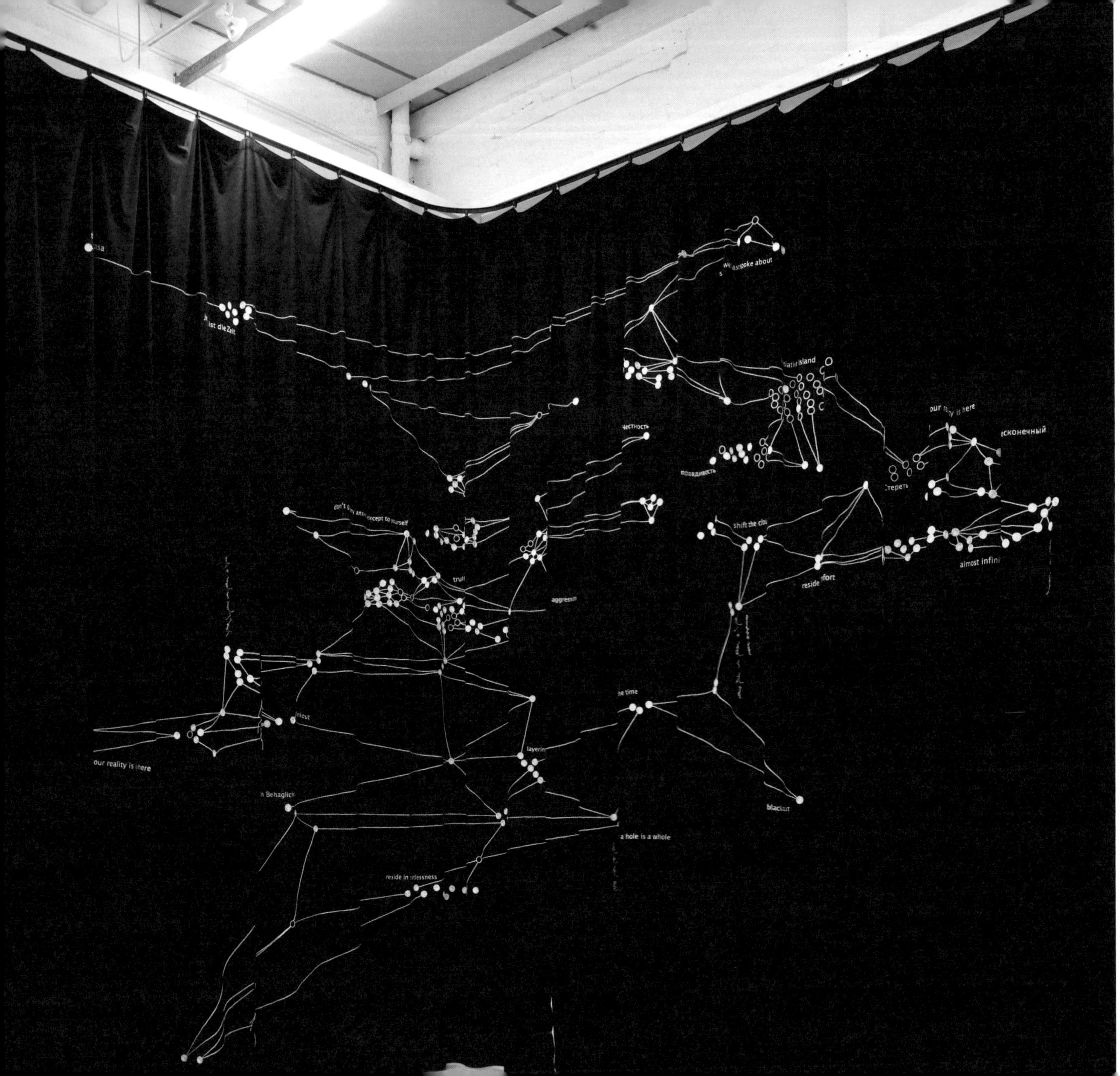
ist dieZeit
честность
reside
almost infini
a hole is a whole
our reality is here

Installation view, Eastside Projects, Birmingham, 2008

Installationsansicht, Eastside Projects, Birmingham, 2008

"Strangers in Vienna are giving an evidence of visibility to the ethnic diversities in Birmingham as is marked by their 'autographs.' The English text lines on the curtain are translated into Mongolian and Russian—the languages of thc embroiderers."

Marjolcin Schaap

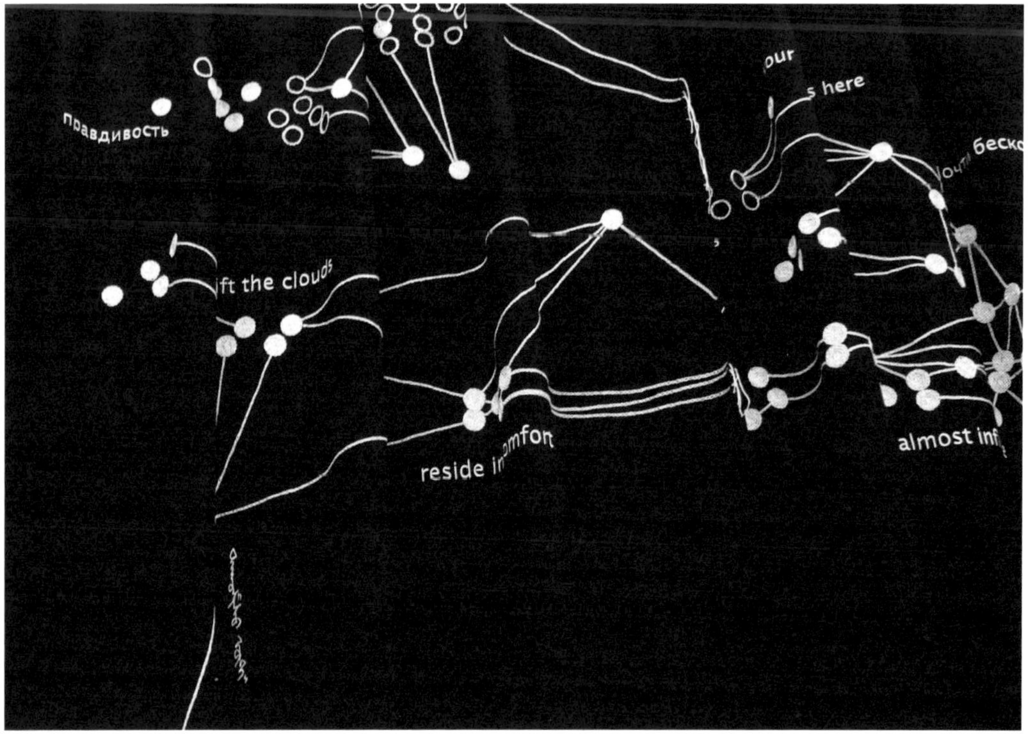

to the right of INITIATIVE ISLAND: Peter Fend & Jenny Holzer, *Political Economies After Oil*, 1980, in: *This is the Gallery and the Gallery is Many Things*, 2008

rechts von INITIATIVE ISLAND: Peter Fend & Jenny Holzer, *Political Economies After Oil*, 1980, in: *This is the Gallery and the Gallery is Many Things*, 2008

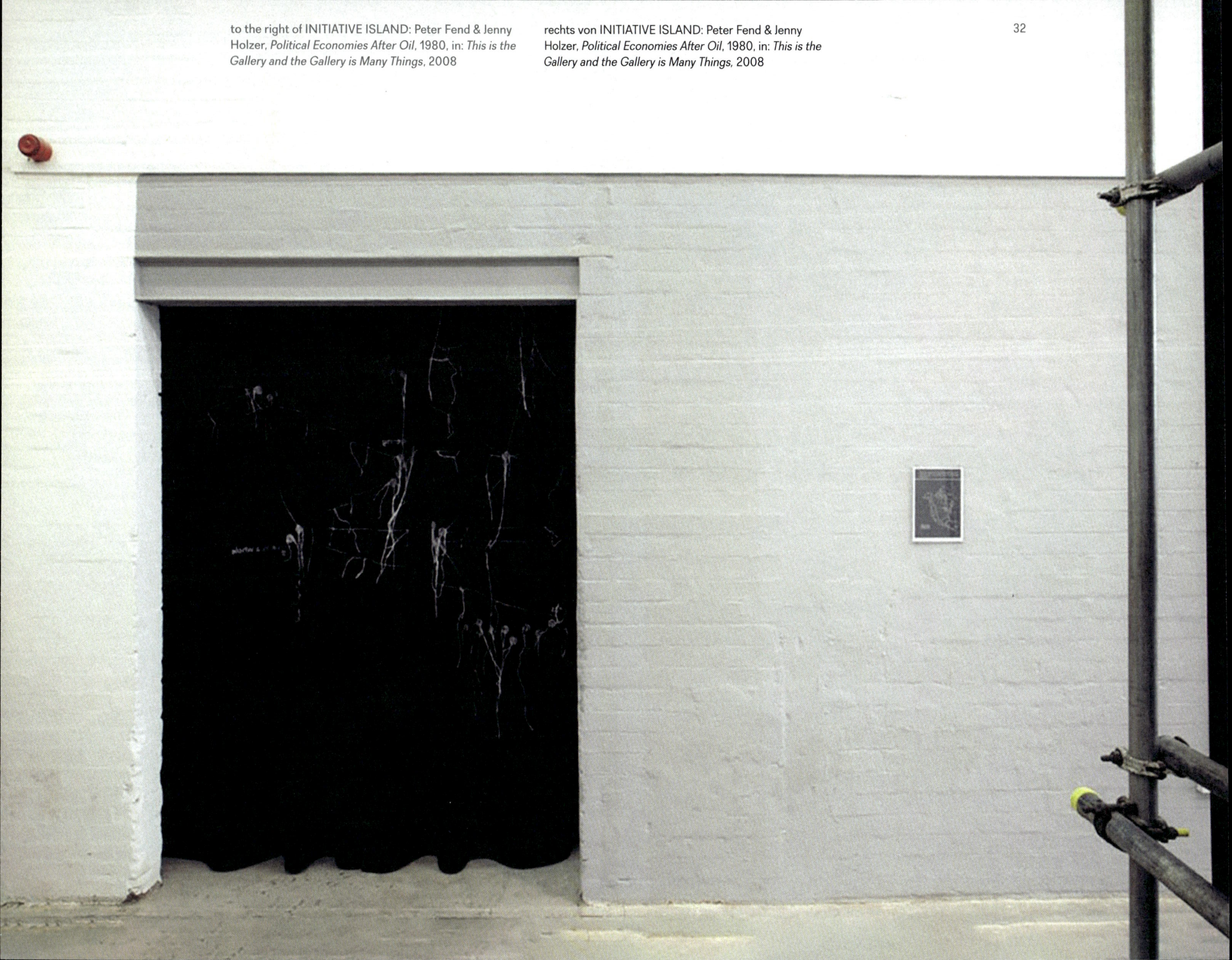

Installation views
with INITIATIVE ISLAND

Installationsansichten
mit INITIATIVE ISLAND

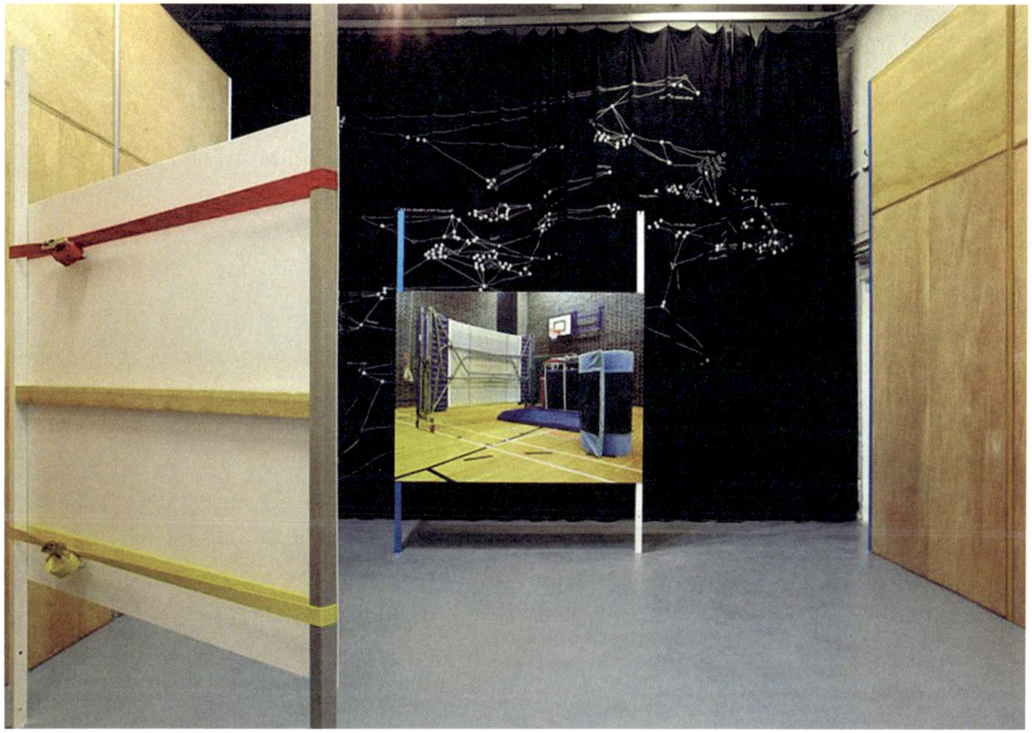

Jim Howieson,
Sports Hall Sessions, 2013

Jim Howieson,
Sports Hall Sessions, 2013

Roger Coward,
You and Me Here We Are, 2015

Roger Coward,
You and Me Here We Are, 2015

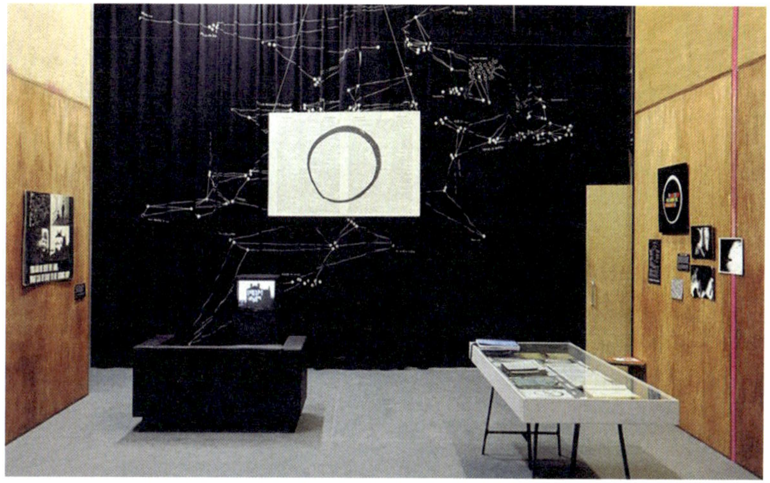

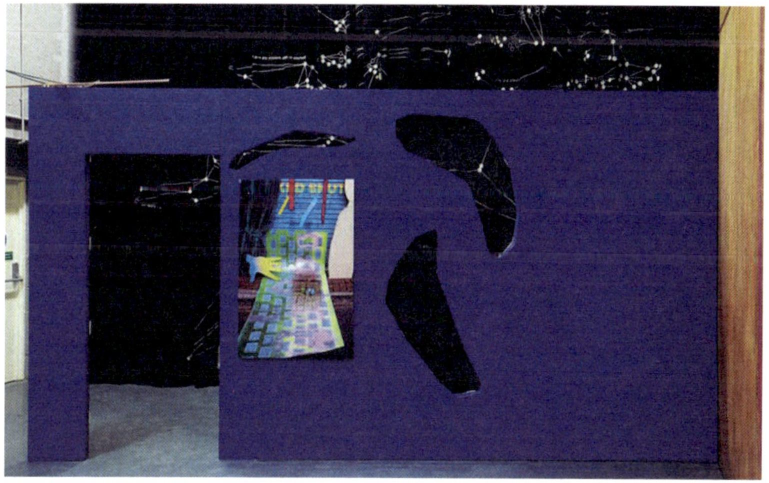

Flore Nové-Josserand,
City Growth Blues, 2015

Flore Nové-Josserand,
City Growth Blues, 2015

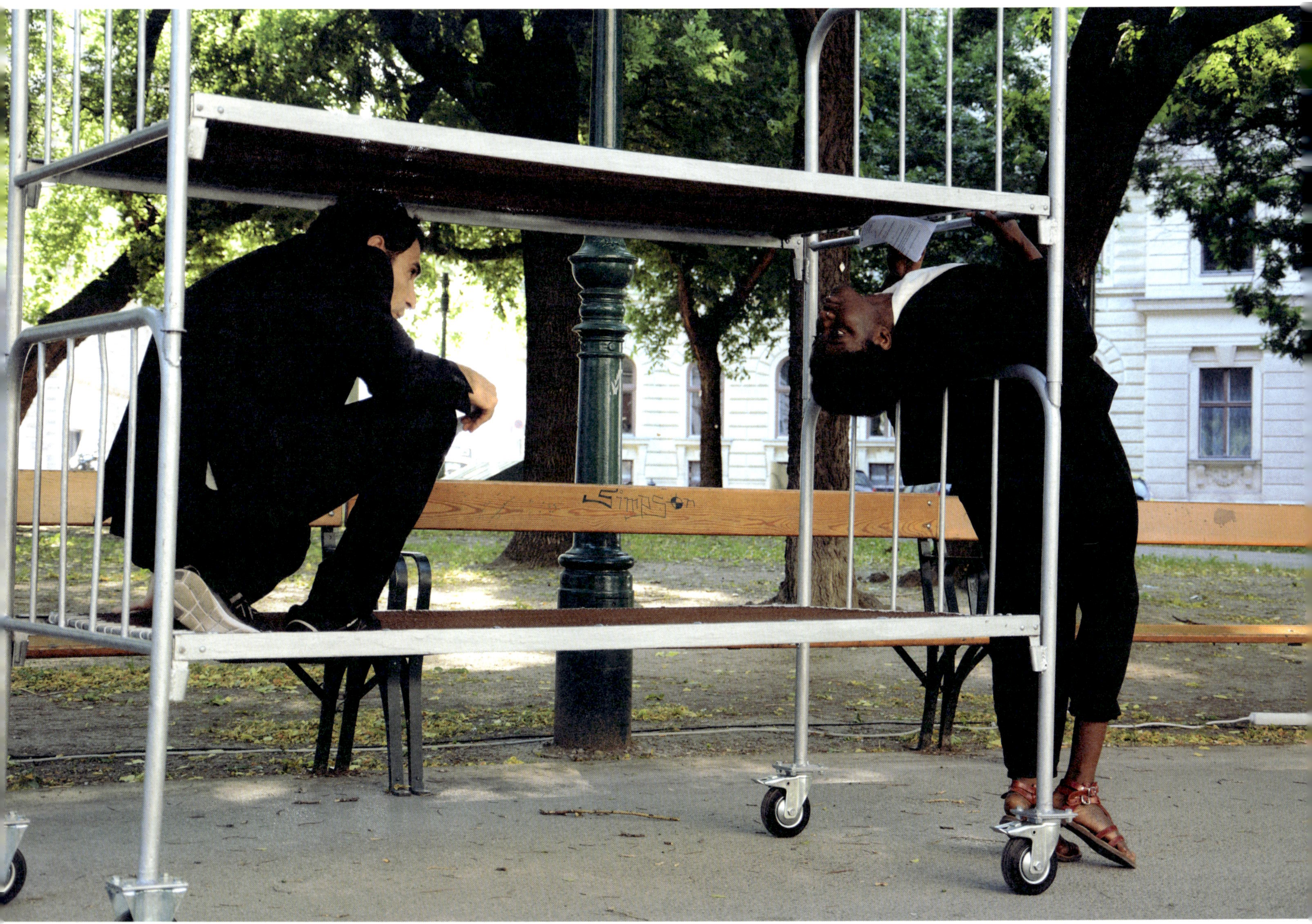

THE LAUGHTER THAT GETS CAUGHT IN YOUR THROAT

THE LAUGHTER THAT GETS CAUGHT IN YOUR THROAT was an urban intervention held at the 2015 Vienna Biennale. Using scripts based on texts by Herbert Marcuse, Joseph Beuys, Henri Bergson and others, this "laughter performance" involved five people reading to each other and a small crowd gathered by the path in Sigmund-Freud-Park. Hidden among this audience were members of the refugee choir Hor 29. Novembar, who at a given signal (bird noise), would laugh sarcastically. Choreographed by composer Tamara Friebel, the performers moved up and down in a procession and interacted with two metal bed frames that functioned as a moveable prop, wheeled in front of the Votive Church, where seventy asylum seekers had sought refuge in 2012 as a protest against conditions in their refugee camp in Traiskirchen. THE LAUGHTER THAT GETS CAUGHT IN YOUR THROAT revived this moment of protest, reminding us of the draconian policy of Austria's Minister of Interior Affairs, Johanna Mikl-Leitner, who sent many asylum seekers back to their home countries, including Syrians displaced by war.

Political demonstrations usually happen in response to an issue in the present. But that issue often gets buried by other events, which collectively compete for media coverage. THE LAUGHTER THAT GETS CAUGHT IN YOUR THROAT (The Laughter) reminds us that the consequences of present-day issues continue to play out after their media coverage stops. As a kind of "commemorative" protest, this intervention renews the political narratives that shaped the event, giving it new life by staging something that feels ontologically fresh, blurring the boundary between art and life, performer and audience, and audience and lingering passersby unsure of what they were witnessing but laughing along with the "laughing choir" anyway. Laughter can be genuine, and laughter can be mirthless, a nervous response to things we don't understand.[SA]

A project by transparadiso

The performance was based on stage directions by composer Tamara Friebel: the performers were each assigned a page of the script, from which they were to perform passages of text freely. At certain moments, Tamara Friebel intoned a bird's twitter—as a signal for the deployment of the laughter choir.

Script for *The Laughter That Gets Caught in Your Throat* by Barbara Holub,
The script includes quotes from the following texts: Vilém Flusser, *Von der Freiheit des Migranten*, 1994; Interview with Johanna Mikl-Leitner, ZIB 2, 20.4.2015; Herbert Marcuse, *Repressive Toleranz*, 1966. *Das Lachen und das Komische*, Zeitschrift für Literatur- und Theatersoziologie, März 2012; Henri Bergson, *Das Lachen*, 1900, Joseph Beuys, *Aufruf zur Alternative*, 1978

Performers: Christiane Beinl, Xenia Gala, Akram al Halabi, Nancy Mensah-Offei, Johanna Orsini-Rosenberg; composition: Tamara Friebel, together with the Vienna refugee choir Hor 29. Novembar; in cooperation with SOS Mitmensch, Integrationshaus, and Vinzi-Rast, Vienna.

DAS LACHEN, DAS EINEM IM HALSE STECKEN BLEIBT

Bei dieser „Lach-Performance" im Sigmund-Freud-Park trugen fünf Personen eine von der Künstlerin verfasste Textcollage mit Zitatenvon Herbert Marcuse, Joseph Beuys, Henri Bergson u. a. vor. Unter das Publikum hatten sich Mitglieder des MigrantInnenchors Hor 29. Novembar gemischt, die auf ein vereinbartes Zeichen (Vogelgeschrei) sarkastisch zu lachen begannen. Choreografiert von der Komponistin Tamara Friebel bewegten sich die PerformerInnen mit zwei fahrbaren Metallbetten auf einem Parkweg vor der Votivkirche auf und ab. In dieser hatten 2012 siebzig Asylsuchende aus Protest gegen die Bedingungen im Flüchtlingslager Traiskirchen Zuflucht gesucht. DAS LACHEN, DAS EINEM IM HALSE STECKEN BLEIBT ließ diesen Moment des Protests wiederaufleben und kritisierte die drakonischen Maßnahmen der damaligen österreichischen Innenministerin, die viele Asylsuchende, einschließlich syrischer Kriegsvertriebener, in ihre Heimatländer abschob.

Politische Demonstrationen finden gewöhnlich als Reaktion auf ein aktuelles Problem statt. Aber das eine Problem wird schnell vom nächsten überlagert, das nun wiederum die Aufmerksamkeit der Medien auf sich zieht. DAS LACHEN, DAS EINEM IM HALSE STECKEN BLEIBT erinnert daran, dass die Probleme fortbestehen, auch wenn tagesaktuell nicht mehr darüber berichtet wird. Als eine Art „Gedenk"-Protest ruft diese Intervention die politischen Narrative, die das Ereignis prägten, in Erinnerung, haucht ihnen durch eine Inszenierung, die sich ontologisch frisch anfühlt, neues Leben ein. Das verwischt die Grenze zwischen Kunst und Leben, PerformerInnen und Publikum, aber auch Publikum und PassantInnen, von denen viele stehen blieben, ohne recht zu wissen, was da vor sich ging, aber dennoch mit dem „Lach-Chor" mitlachten. Lachen kann aus vollem Herzen kommen, kann aber auch gänzlich trostlos sein: eine nervöse Reaktion auf etwas, das man nicht versteht.[SA]

Ein Projekt von transparadiso

Die Performance basierte auf Regieanweisungen der Komponistin Tamara Friebel: Den PerformerInnen wurde jeweils eine Seite des Skripts zugeteilt, aus der sie Textpassagen frei aufführen sollten. In bestimmten Momenten stimmte Tamara Friebel ein Vogelgezwitscher an – als Zeichen für den Einsatz des Lachchors.

Barbara Holub, Skript für *Das Lachen, das einem im Halse stecken bleibt*
Das Skript inkludiert Zitate von folgenden Textquellen: Vilém Flusser, *Von der Freiheit des Migranten*, 1994; Interview mit Johanna Mikl-Leitner, ZIB 2, 20.4.2015; Herbert Marcuse, *Repressive Toleranz*, 1966; *Das Lachen und das Komische*, Zeitschrift für Literatur- und Theatersoziologie, März 2012; Henri Bergson, *Das Lachen*, 1900; Joseph Beuys, *Aufruf zur Alternative*, 1978

Performerinnen: Christiane Beinl, Xenia Gala, Akram al Halabi, Nancy Mensah-Offei, Johanna Orsini-Rosenberg; Komposition: Tamara Friebel unter Mitwirkung des MigrantInnenchors Hor 29. Novembar; in Kooperation mit SOS Mitmensch, Integrationshaus und Vinzi-Rast, Wien.

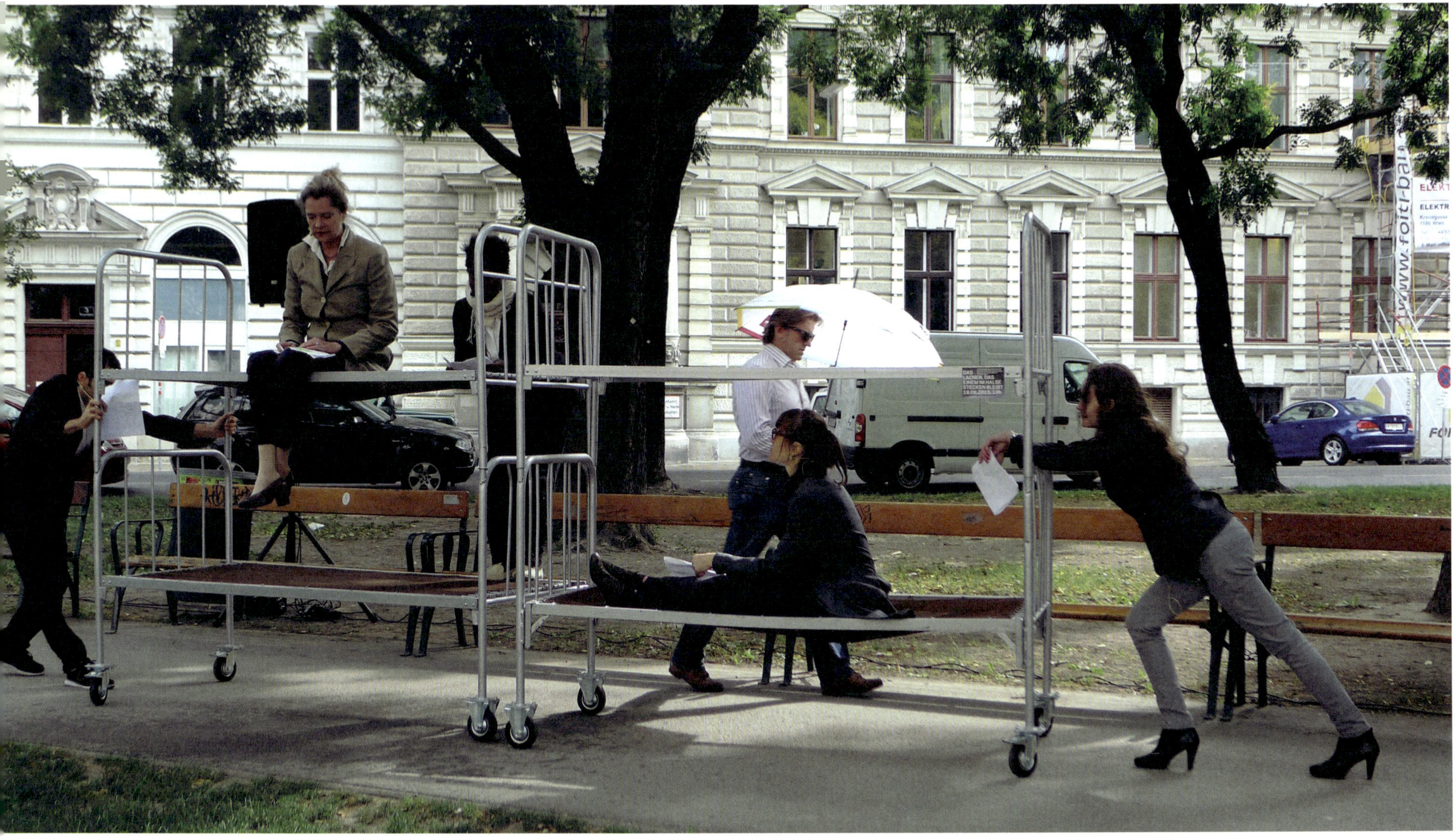

Seite 1 – Johanna

JO (VF Vilém Flusser „Von der Freiheit des Migranten“, S. 20) Die Soziologen scheinen uns zu belehren, dass die geheimen Codes der Heimat von Fremden erlernt werden können, da ja die Beheimateten selbst sie zu lernen hatten. [...] Daher könnte ein Heimatloser von Heimat zu Heimat wandern und in jede von ihnen einwandern, wenn er nur an seinem Schlüsselbund alle notwendigen Schlüssel zu diesen Heimaten mit sich trägt.

Bei der Einwanderung entsteht zwischen den schönen Beheimateten und den hässlichen Heimatlosen ein polemischer Dialog:

Seite 2 – Nancy

NM (ML) Auch ich bin ungeduldig, mir wäre lieber, unser Projekt „Leben Retten“ wäre schon umgesetzt, wir haben einen wichtigen Schritt erzielt.

XG (R) keine Betonung, natürlich sprechen

NM (ML) Wir müssen ...

XG (R) Wir müssen ...

Alle Wir müssen ...

Schönen
Guten

JO (Off) Henri Bergson ist nicht erschienen.

NM (ML) „Eine Katastrophe, eine menschliche Tragödie die uns zum Handeln zwingt und zwar zum raschen Handeln."

XG (R) Eine Katastrophe. Und das bedeutet ...
bedeutet Bedeutung,

JO (Off) Man muss es nur oft genug wiederholen, dann hat es keine Bedeutung mehr, dann hört man nur noch das Wort.

XG (R) „Rasches Handeln"??? rrrrraschschhhhh

NM (ML) Ja eine unfassbare Tragödie.

JO (Off) Worte des Bedauerns ... werden ausge
drückt und verharren in Belanglosigkeit.

NM (ML) Hier sind heute einige konkrete
Vorschläge gemacht worden.

CB (HM) Es ist Aufgabe und Pflicht des Intellektuellen, an geschichtliche Möglichkeiten, die zu utopischen geworden zu sein scheinen, zu erinnern.

AH (J) ... und es ist nichts passiert.

NM (ML) Es ist ganz wichtig und dringend erforderlich, dass wir Anlaufstellen von UNHCR direkt in den Nordafrikanischen Ländern schaffen. Es braucht einen Paradigmenwechsel im Mittelmeer. wir müssen ... einschreiten ...

CB (HM) Der Verfasser ist sich dessen voll bewusst, dass gegenwärtig keine Macht, Autorität oder Regierung vorhanden ist, die eine befreiende Toleranz in die Praxis übersetzen würde.

NM (ML) Das heißt einen Paradigmenwechsel, um hier den Schleppertaten ein Ende zu setzten. Dass wir eben die geretteten Menschen nicht direkt nach Europa bringen, sondern direkt zurück in die nordafrikanischen Ländern in die UNHCR Anlaufstellen, wo die Erstprüfung stattfinden soll.

AH (J) Ist das nicht zynisch?

NM (ML) Wir, Europa, können doch die Last nicht alleine tragen

JO (Off) Worte des Fragens greifen um sich:
Welche Last? Ist nicht die Ungleichheit die Last, die auf uns allen lastet?

——— *LC 1* ———

JO (off) Wir brauchen einen Paradigmenwechsel einer anderen Art

CB (HM) Die Idee der Toleranz erscheint, mit anderen Worten, heute wieder als dasjenige, was sie an ihren Ursprüngen war, zu Beginn der Neuzeit – als ein unparteiliches Ziel, ein subversiver, befreiender Begriff und als ebensolche Praxis.

NM (ML) Lassen Sie mich.... Lassen Sie mich noch ganz kurz ausreden.

Seite 3 – Christiane

CB (HM) Toleranz ist ein Selbstzweck.

NM (ML) .... Lassen sie mich, das ist die einzige Chance.
.... Die Lösung ist nicht einfach, aber wir müssen Stück für Stück damit beginnen, mit der Umsetzung.

JO (off) Und das Publikum ist sich nicht sicher,
wie es sich verhalten soll
halten soll
halt

——— *LC 2* ———

JO (off) Sicherheit, wir wollen ihnen doch Sicherheit garantieren

CB (HM) Es ist Aufgabe und Pflicht des Intellektuellen, an geschichtliche Möglichkeiten, die zu utopischen geworden zu sein scheinen, zu erinnern.

JO (off) das Publikum, das Öffentliche,
im öffentlichen Interesse
ist gewohnt
ist sich nicht sicher
das öffentliche Interesse
ist leise

——— *LC 3* ———
(kurz)

NM (JB, modifiziert) Ich frage euch: Was können wir tun? Und ich frage euch davor:
Wie müssen wir denken? Damit der phrasenhafte Umgang mit den höchsten Idealen der Menschheit, die alle Parteiprogramme heute verkünden, nicht weiterhin als Ausdruck des krassen Gegensatzes zur Lebenspraxis unserer wirtschaftlichen, politischen und kulturellen Wirklichkeit sich fortpflanzt.

JO Die Gewohnheit des Rauschens,
des Blattrauschens,
des Verkehrsrauschens,
des Aufmerksamkeitrauschens,
des Publikumsrauschens, ...
... dieses vielfältige Rauschen drängt an uns vorbei.

CB (HM) Diese Art von Toleranz stärkt die Tyrannei der Mehrheit, gegen welche die wirklichen Liberalen aufbegehren. ... Toleranz wird von einem aktiven in einen passiven Zustand übergeführt, von der Praxis in eine Nicht-Praxis.

Seite 4 – Xenia

XG (LK) Warum lachen wir in einigen Fällen frei heraus, während wir uns das Lachen in anderen verkneifen?

AH Das Gewöhnliche ... verdrängt unsere leisen Stimmen ...

Alle ... verdrängt unsere lllleiiisen (laut gesprochen) Stimmen.

CB (HM) Toleranz gegenüber dem radikal Bösen erscheint jetzt als gut, weil sie dem Zusammenhalt des Ganzen dient auf dem Wege zum Überfluss oder zu größerem Überfluss.

JO (off)_ wir entledigen uns des Gewöhnlichen. Ein Beigeschmack des Verdrängten.

——— *LC 4* ———
(kurz, aber länger als vorher)

NM (ML) Ja eine unfassbare Tragödie, wo natürlich die Worte des Bedauerns zu wenig sind
... und da braucht es doch die Unterstützung der nordafrikanischen Länder.

AH (J) ... Wie wollen sie denn das eigentlich ... erklären, dass

NM (ML) Wir brauchen hier die Unterstützung ... deswegen ist es wichtig und ich habe heute betont bei der Sitzung ...

JO (off) Und sie wiederholten Fragen und Antworten, die die Verantwortung ansprachen. Und SIE wiederholte, dass doch auch die Anderen Verantwortung übernehmen müssten. Das reiche Europa alleine könne das nicht bewältigen ...

CB (HM) In der gegenwärtigen Periode wird das demokratische Argument zunehmend dadurch hinfällig, dass der demokratische Prozess selbst hinfällig wird.

XG Unser Lachen passt zum Krieg. Wir brechen unversehens in hysterisches Gelächter aus, doch plötzlich fängt einer an zu weinen.

CB Wir widmen uns dem Lachen. Ob der Zustände können wir nur lachen.

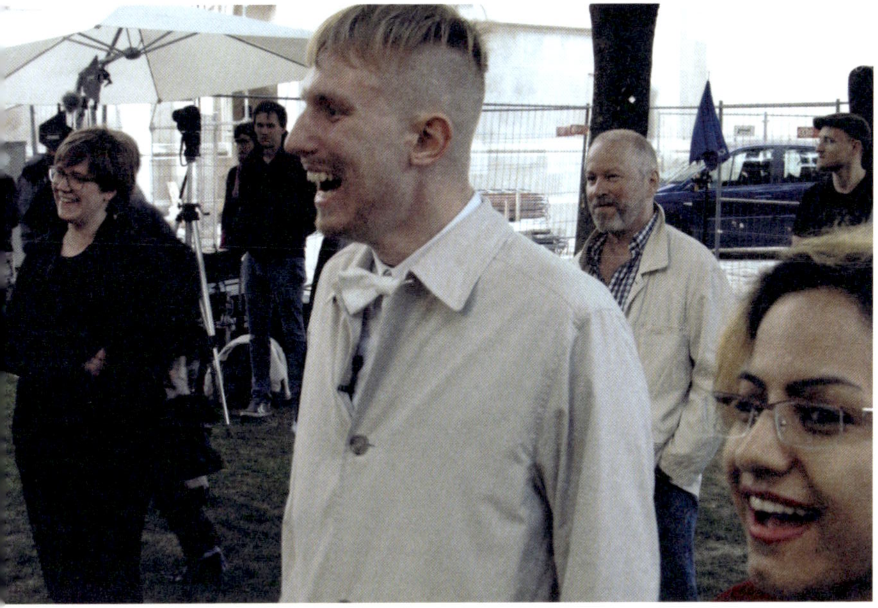

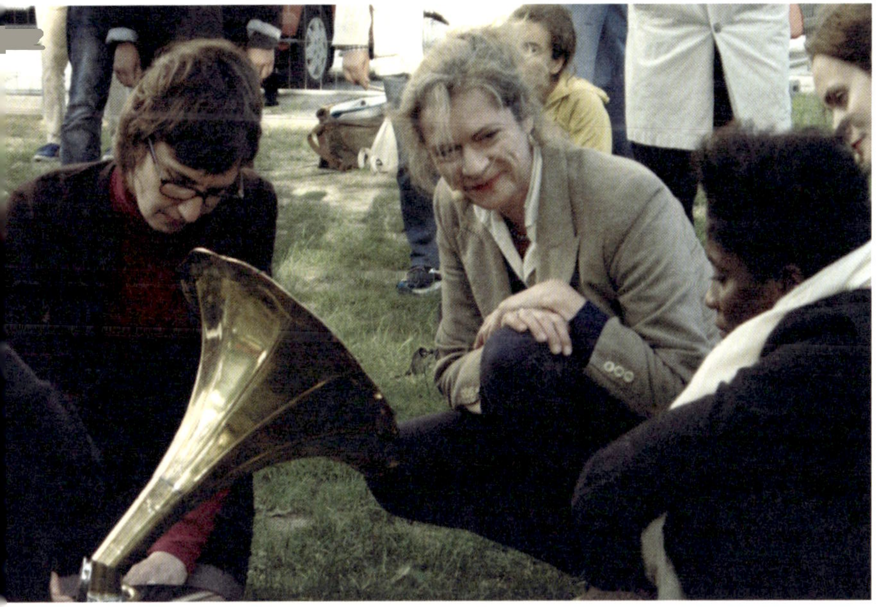

Alle	Können wir nur lachen.
JO (off) (LK (S. 88)	Ein Narr lacht überlaut, ein Weiser lächelt ein wenig. Ein vernünftiger Mensch solle sich also auch beim Lachen mäßigen.
Alle	Da können wir nur umso lauter lachen.

LC 5

JO (off)	Ratlosigkeit überfällt die Performer und das Publikum, aber
Alle (SZ)	Humor könne ein Mittel sein, mit dieser Ratlosigkeit umzugehen. Die Syrer seien immer schon ein humorvolles Volk gewesen.
XG (HB)	Man steigert die Ironie, wenn man sich durch die Idee des Guten, das sein sollte, immer höher tragen lässt.
Alle	Wir wollen doch alle das Gute!

LC 6

(Kürzer, gequält)

NM (VF)	Die Wirklichkeit ist anders. Die geheimen Codes der Heimaten sind nicht aus bewussten Regeln, sondern größtenteils aus unbewussten Gewohnheiten gesponnen Um in eine Heimat einwandern zu können, muss der Heimatlose zuerst die Geheimcodes bewusst erlernen und dann wieder vergessen. Der Einwanderer ist für den Beheimateten noch befremdender, unheimlicher als der Wanderer dort draußen, weil er das dem Beheimateten Heilige als Banales bloßlegt
JO (off)(LK (S. 89)	Im gemeinsamen Lachen verschwinden soziale Unterschiede.
Alle	Das braucht Übung. Viel Übung. Üben wir also.

LC 7

(nach langem Lach-Chor / Ende > zu Grammophon gehen)

Operation Goldhaube, curated by Eva Jandl-Jörg and Ernestine Hutter, Folklore Museum/Monatsschlössl Hellbrunn, Salzburg Museum, Salzburg, 2015

JE SUIS ARABE— A RIGHT TO POETRY

In this performance, transparadiso interpret the golden bonnet in terms of its semantic ambivalence between Austrian cultural heritage and the Austrian air defense system named after it since 1975. While the latter was installed for military purposes, the traditional golden bonnet is an item of head-dress dating back to the 13th century that remains a part of women's traditional costume in Salzburg and Upper Austria today.

Wearing special golden bonnets of gilded satellite dishes, made especially for the occasion and connected with each other by CB radio, Barbara Holub and Akram al Halabi alternately recited *La volonté de vivre* (*The Will to Live*, 1933) in German and Arabic, a poem by the Tunisian poet Aboul-Qacem Echebbi that has since become part of Arab cultural heritage. Between the Hellbrunner Park and the Monatsschlössl (Folklore Museum) and outside and inside the Schwarzenberg Barracks, where the air defense system was first tested—both locations are, in different ways, equally committed to the concept of homeland—the protagonists enter into a dialog that quotes the poetic "Hymn of the Arab Spring."

JE SUIS ARABE—A RIGHT TO POETRY thus not only critically scrutinizes emotions such as "love of the homeland" and "fear of foreigners," often abused for political purposes, but also juxtaposes the "defense of the Fortress Europe" with a central work of Arab cultural heritage that is largely unknown in Europe—not least with the aim of grasping migration as a "creative situation" in the sense implied by Vilém Flusser ("The Freedom of the Migrant," 1994).[BR]

A project by transparadiso

Operation Goldhaube, kuratiert von Eva Jandl-Jörg und Ernestine Hutter, Volkskundemuseum/Monatsschlössl Hellbrunn, Salzburg Museum, Salzburg, 2015

JE SUIS ARABE – EIN RECHT AUF POESIE

transparadiso interpretiert die Goldhaube in ihrer semantischen Ambivalenz zwischen österreichischem Kulturgut und dem danach benannten Luftraumüberwachungssystem Österreichs. Während Letzteres in der zweiten Hälfte des 20. Jahrhunderts zu militärischen Zwecken installiert wurde, ist die traditionelle Goldhaube ein Kopfschmuck, der, bis in das 13. Jahrhundert zurück nachweisbar, noch heute Bestandteil heimischer Frauentracht ist.

Mit eigens angefertigten Spezialgoldhauben aus vergoldeten Satellitenschüsseln, die über CB-Funk miteinander verbunden sind, trugen Barbara Holub und Akram al Halabi das zum arabischen Kulturgut avancierte Gedicht *La volonté de vivre* (*Der Wille zum Leben*, 1933) des tunesischen Schriftstellers Abou el Kazem Chebbi abwechselnd in deutscher und arabischer Sprache vor. Zwischen Hellbrunner Park und Monatsschlössl (Volkskundemuseum) sowie vor und in der Schwarzenbergkaserne, jenem Ort, wo das Luftraumüberwachungssystem erstmals getestet wurde – und beides Orte, die sich auf unterschiedliche Weise gleichermaßen dem Heimatbegriff verpflichtet fühlen – treten die ProtagonistInnen in einen Dialog, der die poetische „Hymne des Arabischen Frühlings" zitiert.

JE SUIS ARABE – EIN RECHT AUF POESIE nimmt daher nicht nur auf vielfach politisch missbrauchte Emotionen wie „Heimatliebe" und „Fremdenangst" kritisch Bezug, sondern stellt auch der „Verteidigung der Festung Europa" ein zentrales Werk arabischen Kulturguts gegenüber, das im europäischen Raum weitgehend unbekannt ist – nicht zuletzt, um im Sinne Vilém Flussers („Von der Freiheit des Migranten", 1994) „Migration als eine kreative Situation" zu begreifen.[BR]

Ein Projekt von transparadiso

Performance of "Will to Live" (by Aboul-Qacem Echebbi) as an Arab-German dialog between Monatsschlössl and Hellbrunn Park

Aufführung von „Wille zum Leben" (von Abou el Kazem Chebbi) als arabisch-deutscher Dialog zwischen Monatsschlössl und Park Hellbrunn

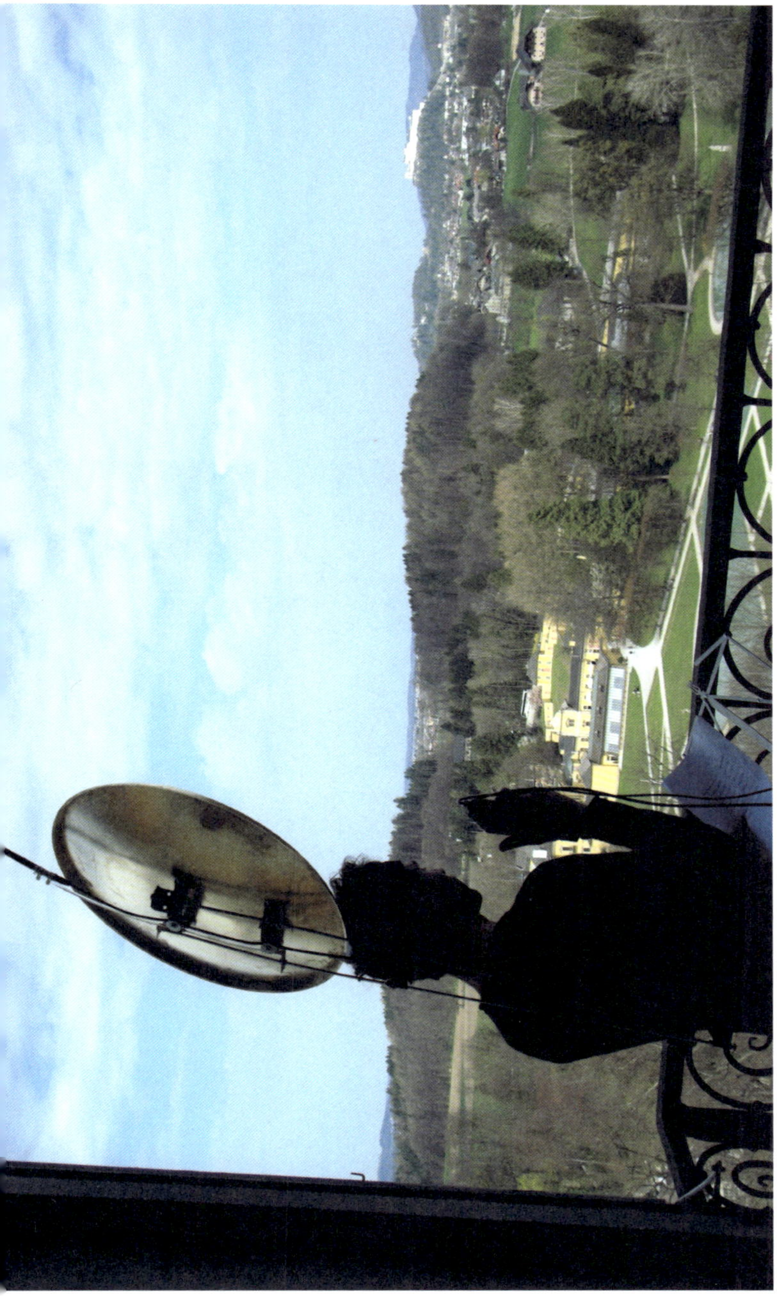

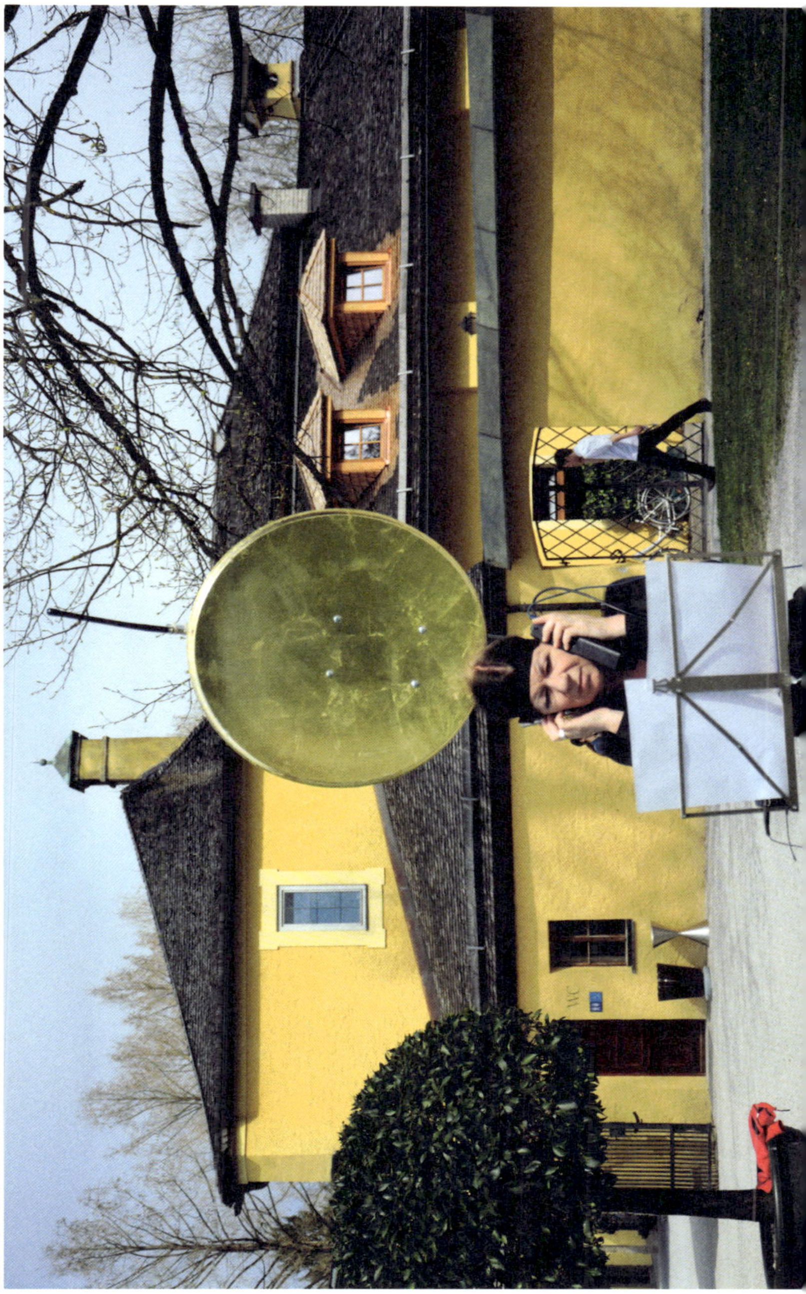

Der Wille zum Leben

Wenn das Volk eines Tages das Leben einfordert, dann muss das Schicksal das gewähren. Die Nacht muss weichen, die Ketten müssen gesprengt werden.

Und wen die Sehnsucht nach Leben nicht erfasst, der verdunstet in seiner Atmosphäre und verschwindet. Wehe dem, den das Leben nicht mit Sehnsucht erfüllt, vor dem Schlag des triumphierenden Nichts. So sprachen die Lebewesen zu mir. Dies verriet mir ihr verborgener Geist.

Der Wind raunte in den Schluchten, auf den Bergen und unter den Bäumen. Wenn ich nach einem Ziel strebe, reite ich den Wunsch und vergesse die Vorsicht, befürchte weder die Beschwerlichkeit des Weges noch die lodernden Feuerkugeln. Denn wem es nicht liegt, Berge zu erklimmen, der muss sein Dasein im Abgrund verbringen.

إرادة الحياة

إذا الشعبُ يوماً أرادَ الحَيَاةَ / فلا بدّ أن يستجيبَ القدرْ

ولا بدّ لليلِ أنْ ينجلي / ولا بدّ للقيدِ أنْ ينكسرْ

ومَنْ لمْ يعانقْهُ شوقُ الحَيَاةِ / تبخّرَ في جوّها واندثرْ

فويلٌ لمَنْ لمْ تشُقْهُ الحياةُ / من صفعةِ العدمِ المنتصرْ

كذلكَ قالتْ ليَ الكائناتُ / وحدّثني روحُها المستترْ

ودمدمتِ الريحُ بينَ الفجاجِ / وفوقَ الجبالِ وتحتَ الشجرْ

إذا ما طمحْتُ إلى غايةٍ / ركبْتُ المُنى ونسيتُ الحذرْ

ولمْ أتجنّبْ وعورَ الشعابِ / ولا كبّةَ اللهبِ المستعرْ

ومَنْ لا يحبُّ صعودَ الجبالِ / يعشْ أبدَ الدهرِ بينَ الحفرْ

Akram al Halabi in front of the Schwarzenberg Barracks

Akram al Halabi am Eingang der Schwarzenbergkaserne

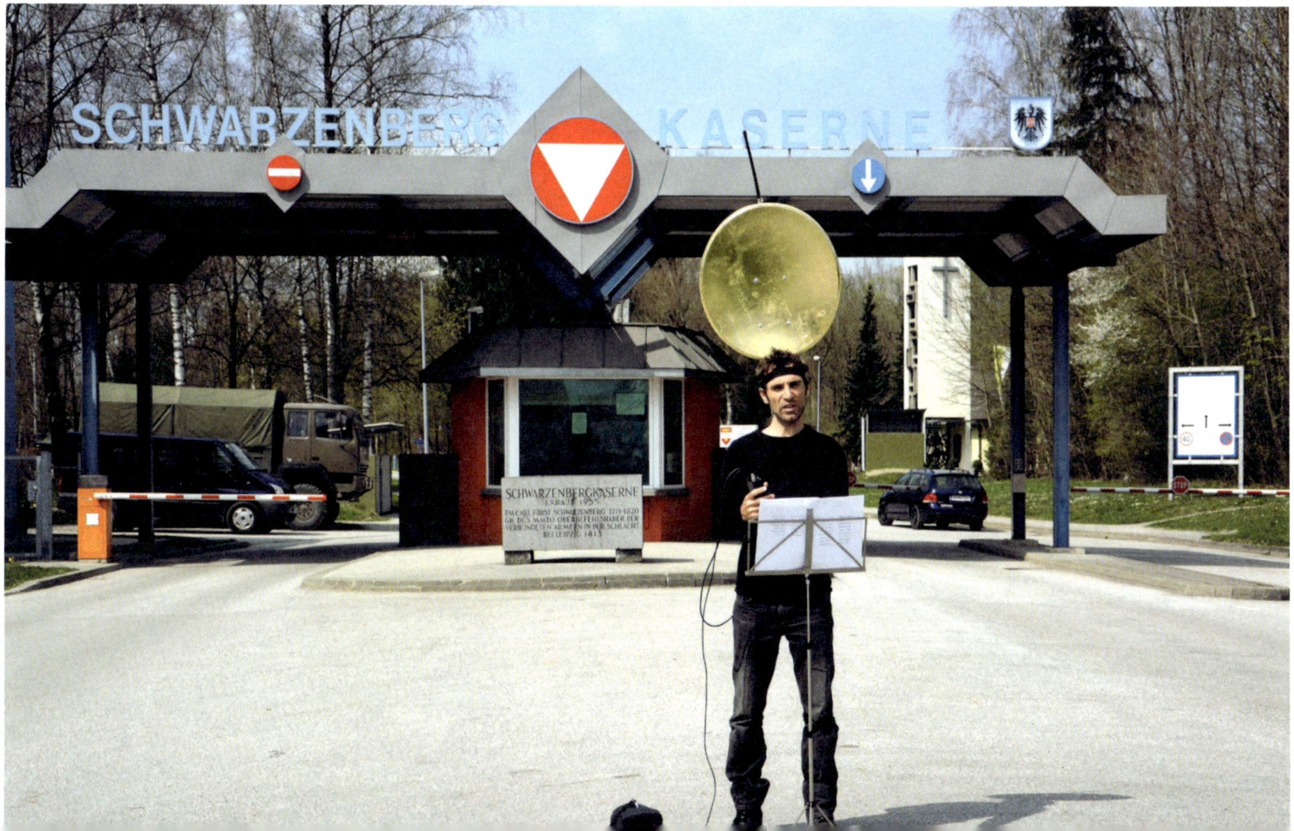

Das Licht wird euch segnen, empfängt die Fruchtbarkeit des Lebens. Wer in seinen Träumen dem Licht huldigt, den segnet das Licht auf seinem Weg. In nur einem Moment, nicht länger als ein Flügelschlag, erstarkte ihr Wunsch und triumphierte.

Sie durchbrachen den Boden, der auf ihnen lastete Und eine reiche Vegetation trat hervor, um die Schönheit der Schöpfung zu sehen. Das Licht ist in meinem Herzen und in meiner Seele, Warum sollte ich mich fürchten, in der Dunkelheit zu gehen? Lieber hätte ich die Welt niemals betreten und niemals unter den Sternen gebadet. Lieber hätte die Morgenstund' niemals meine Träume geküsst und das Licht nicht meine Augen liebkost. Lieber hätte ich niemals aufgehört zu sein, was ich war, Ein freies Licht verstreut über das gesamte Leben.

“؟رَشَبَلا نَيِهَرْكَتَ لْهَ مُأ اَيَأ /: تُلْأَس اَمَل - ضُرْأَلا ىل تْلَاقَو
رَطَخلا بوُكُر ذِلَتْسَي نْمَو /حوُمُطلا لْهَأ سِانلا ىف كِرابُأ„
رَجَحلا شِيْعَ شْيَعِ لَاب عُنَقْيَو /نَاحَزلا ىشامُي ال نْمَ نُعَلْأَو
رُبَك اَمَهَم تَيَمْلا رُقَتْحَيَو /ةايَحلا بِحُي ،ىَحُ نْوَكلا وُه
رهَزلا تَيَم مُثْلَي لْحَنلا الَو /روُيُطلا تَيَم نُضْحَي قُفُأَلا الَف
رَفُحلا كَلْت تَيَمْلا تَمَض اَمَل / موُؤرلا ىبْلَق ةَموُمُأ الْوَلَو
رِصَتْنُمْلا مَدَعلا ةَنْعَل نْم /ةايَحلا هُقْشَت مَل نَمِل لٌيَوَف

Barbara Holub next to the site at the Schwarzenberg barracks where the airspace surveillance *Goldhaube* was tested in the 1980s.

Barbara Holub unweit jenes Ortes in der Schwarzenbergkaserne, an dem das Luftraum-überwachungssystem Goldhaube in den 1980er-Jahren getestet wurde.

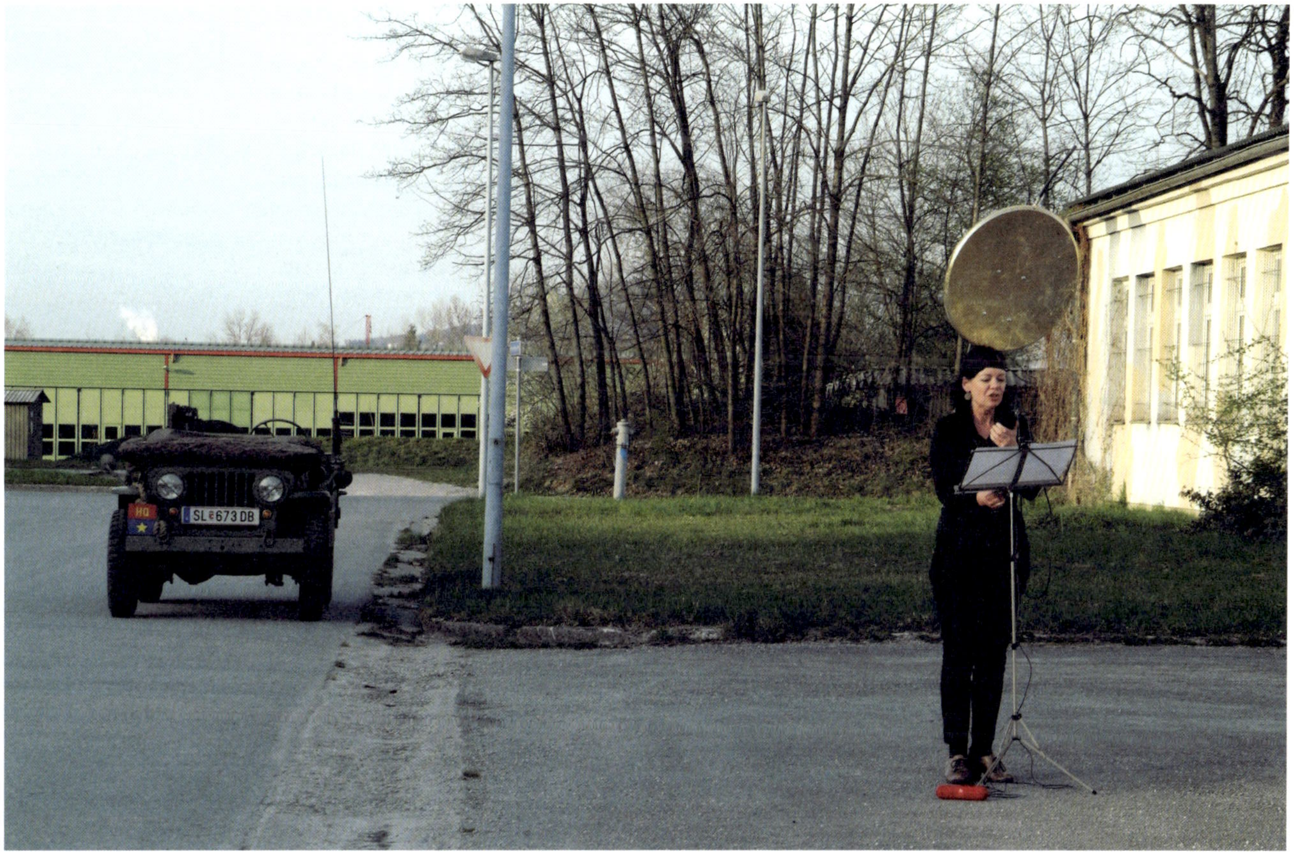

DU BAKCHICH POUR LAMPEDUSA

The UN Convention against Corruption—dated December 2005 and supporting an active stance against corruption as a global movement—anchored the starting point of "Bye, Bye, Bakchich Système," a public art project curated by Tunisian artist Faten Rouissi and funded by the UN Development Program. In the coverage of this project, Du bakchich pour Lampedusa looked at the issue of corruption from a European point of view by addressing the relationship between corruption and social inequality. Corruption not only weakens economic growth and stability, it also distorts the moral values of a society.

A garbage container was transformed into an oversized savings box as a monumental sculpture placed right in front of the Big Mosque in the Medina in Sousse. It was surrounded by screens granting an intimacy similar to an election setting. The residents of Sousse were called to donate ten percent of their irregular income from the last three years—an equivalent percentage was spent on bribery—to the savings box. In an official closing ceremony, the donations were handed over to the humanitarian aid organization African Intelligence, founded and directed by Father Jonathan in Sfax, who has been taking care of refugees sent back from Lampedusa.

As a modest gesture, the project challenged the silence that the issue of corruption is facing in Tunisia, which results in a loss of economic means for providing a solid social substance and perspective for Tunisians. In this way, the project also drew a parallel line between the EU's inhuman migrant policies that have been applied to refugees—risking their lives to enter Europe to provide their children a better future—and the silence that jeopardizes a better future for Tunisia.[BS]

A project by transparadiso

DU BAKCHICH POUR LAMPEDUSA

Die 2005 in Kraft getretene UN-Konvention gegen Korruption bildete den Ausgangspunkt für das von der tunesischen Künstlerin Faten Rouissi kuratierte und vom Entwicklungsprogramm der Vereinten Nationen (UNDP) gesponserte Projekt für Kunst im öffentlichen Raum „Bye, bye, bakchich système". Mit DU BAKCHICH POUR LAMPEDUSA griff transparadiso das Thema aus europäischer Perspektive auf, indem sich die KünstlerInnen mit der Beziehung von Korruption zu sozialer Ungleichheit beschäftigten. Korruption schwächt nicht nur die wirtschaftliche Entwicklung und Stabilität einer Gesellschaft, sondern verzerrt auch ihre moralischen Werte.

Ein Müllcontainer wurde in eine überdimensionale Sparbüchse umfunktioniert, eine monumentale Skulptur wurde direkt vor der Großen Moschee in der Medina von Sousse aufgestellt – verborgen hinter Paravents, wie sie auch bei Wahlen zur Wahrung der Diskretion eingesetzt werden. Die BürgerInnen von Sousse wurden aufgefordert, zehn Prozent ihres illegalen Einkommens aus den letzten drei Jahren zu spenden – ein Prozentsatz, der dem Aufwand für Bestechung entspricht. In einer offiziellen Abschlusszeremonie wurden dann die Spenden dem katholischen Pater Jonathan für seine humanitäre Hilfsorganisation African Intelligence in Sfax überreicht, die sich der abgewiesenen Geflüchteten von Lampedusa annimmt.

Die partizipative Installation forderte das Publikum dazu auf, dem diskreten Schweigen zur Korruption mit einer bescheidenen Geste öffentlich entgegenzutreten, um so eine langfristige soziale Basis für eine Zukunftsperspektive in Tunesien zu schaffen. Dabei zieht die Arbeit auch eine Parallele zwischen der inhumanen Politik der EU gegenüber flüchtenden Menschen, die ihr Leben riskieren, um ihren Kindern eine bessere Zukunft in Europa zu ermöglichen, und dem Schweigen, das eine bessere Zukunft in Tunesien gefährdet.[BS]

Ein Projekt von transparadiso

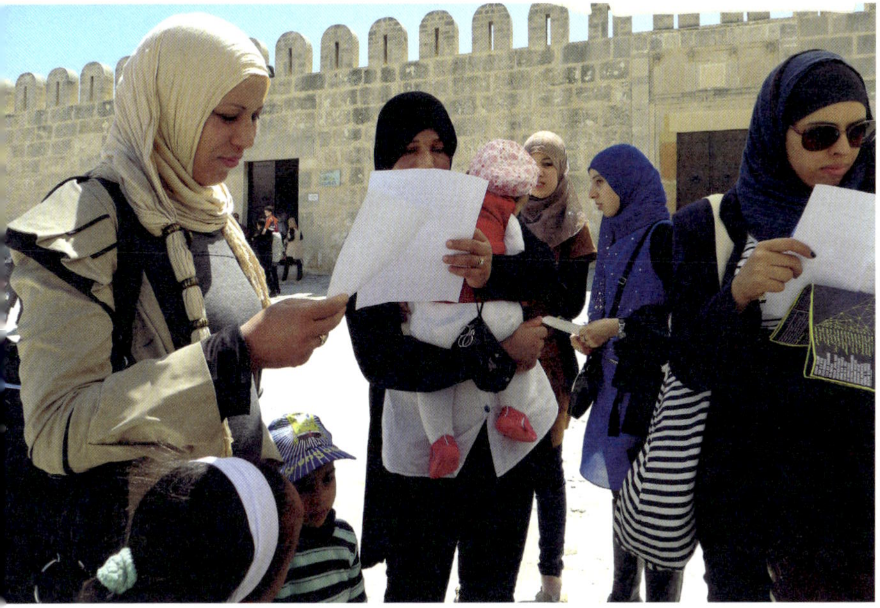

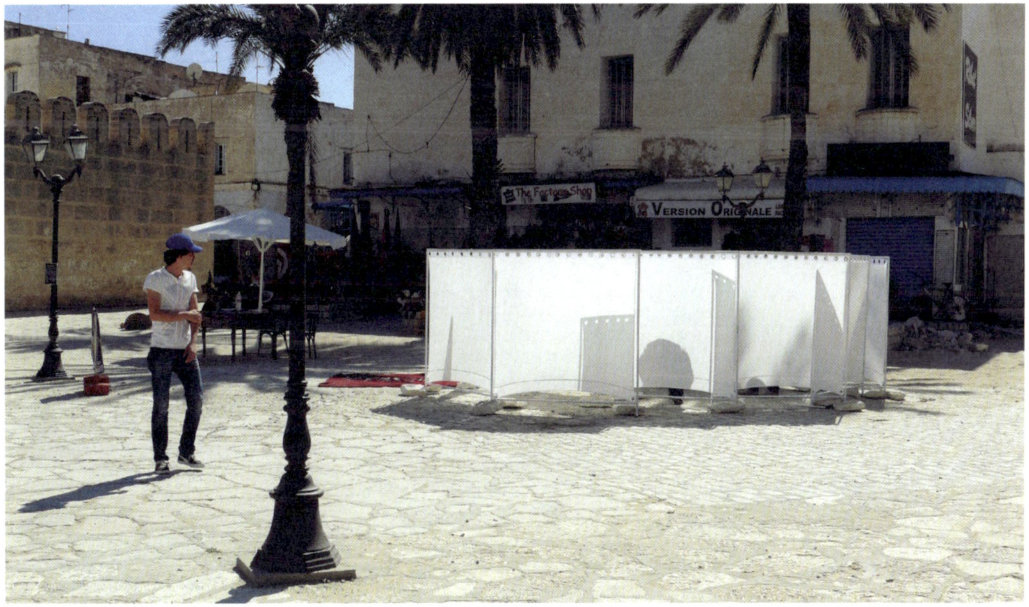

Installation in front of the Great Mosque of Sousse, and appeal to the residents of Sousse to donate 10 % of their irregular income of the last three years.

Installation vor der Großen Moschee in Sousse, sowie Aufruf an die BewohnerInnen von Sousse, 10 % ihres irregulären Einkommens der letzten drei Jahre zu spenden.

transparadiso zt kg
Barbara Holub/ Paul Rajakovics
Gr.Mohreng.34/3
A-1020 Vienne
Autriche
T +43 1 946 07 34
M +43 699 102 79 217
www.transparadiso.com

اَلْبَقْشِيشْ لِلَّمْبَدُوزَة
Du bakchich pour Lampedusa

Vienne, 080414

Madame, Monsieur,

Nous nous permettons de nous adresser à vous en tant que personnalité éminente de Sousse. Nous sommes deux artistes d'Autriche et d'Allemagne qui prenons part à un projet artistique qui aura lieu à Sousse les 19 et 20 avril 2014, « Bye Bye Bakchich Système ». Ce projet fait partie d'une action artistique[1] qui vient en soutien à un projet important en Tunisie « Appui à l'Etablissement d'un système national d'intégrité » qui est promu par le Programme des Nations Unies pour le Développement (PNUD).

Ce projet se veut très marquant pour l'avenir – non seulement pour votre pays – mais aussi dans le cadre de discussions plus approfondies avec l'Europe et plus particulièrement avec l'Autriche et l'Allemagne d'où nous sommes originaires. En participant à ce projet, nous avons le sentiment de créer et travailler pour un futur plus juste, basé sur les Droits de l'Homme, - pas seulement ceux définis par l'ONU - mais élargis aux valeurs sociales et éthiques.

En participant à ce projet politique et artistique, nous voulons marquer notre désaccord avec la politique des frontières européennes, et œuvrer par un acte concret au dialogue sur les valeurs universelles de cohabitation harmonieuse dans le monde.

Nous vous invitons à venir voir les œuvres qui seront exposées près des remparts de la Medina de Sousse les 19 et 20 avril 2014. A cette occasion, notre installation ludique « Du Bakchich pour Lampedusa » (sur la place devant la grande Mosquée) comprendra une grande tirelire destinée à recueillir votre contribution pour venir en aide à vos compatriotes réfugiés à Lampedusa. *Nous espérons récolter 10% de l'argent que chacun aurait reçu en tant que ressources non déclarées dans les trois dernières années, en d'autre terme l'argent de la corruption.* Les fonds ainsi récoltés seront donnés à une organisation qui s'occupe des réfugiés à Lampedusa. Ce geste de générosité constituerait un important signe pour le public – pas seulement tunisien, mais aussi international, en démontrant que la défense des valeurs du bien-être commun domine le seul profit personnel.

Nous sommes confiants que vous voudrez profiter de cette occasion pour apporter votre contribution à la tirelire « Du Bakchich pour Lampedusa ». Si vous le souhaitez, votre geste sera anonyme. Alternativement, vous pourrez profiter de votre geste pour vous présenter en tant que personnalité publique. Vous êtes d'ailleurs invité (e) à participer à l'acte final festif du projet « Du Bakchich pour Lampedusa » pendant lequel nous annoncerons le montant récolté dans la tirelire.

Pour plus d'information sur cet évènement, vous trouverez en annexe, le communiqué de presse. N'hésitez pas à nous contacter si vous souhaitez recevoir plus de détails.

Barbara Holub et Paul Rajakovics

[1] Le projet „Bye Bye Bakchich Système" a été conçu par l'artiste tunisienne et pluridisciplinaire Faten Rouissi, Présidente de l'Association 24 Heures Pour l'Art Contemporain – 24HPAC.

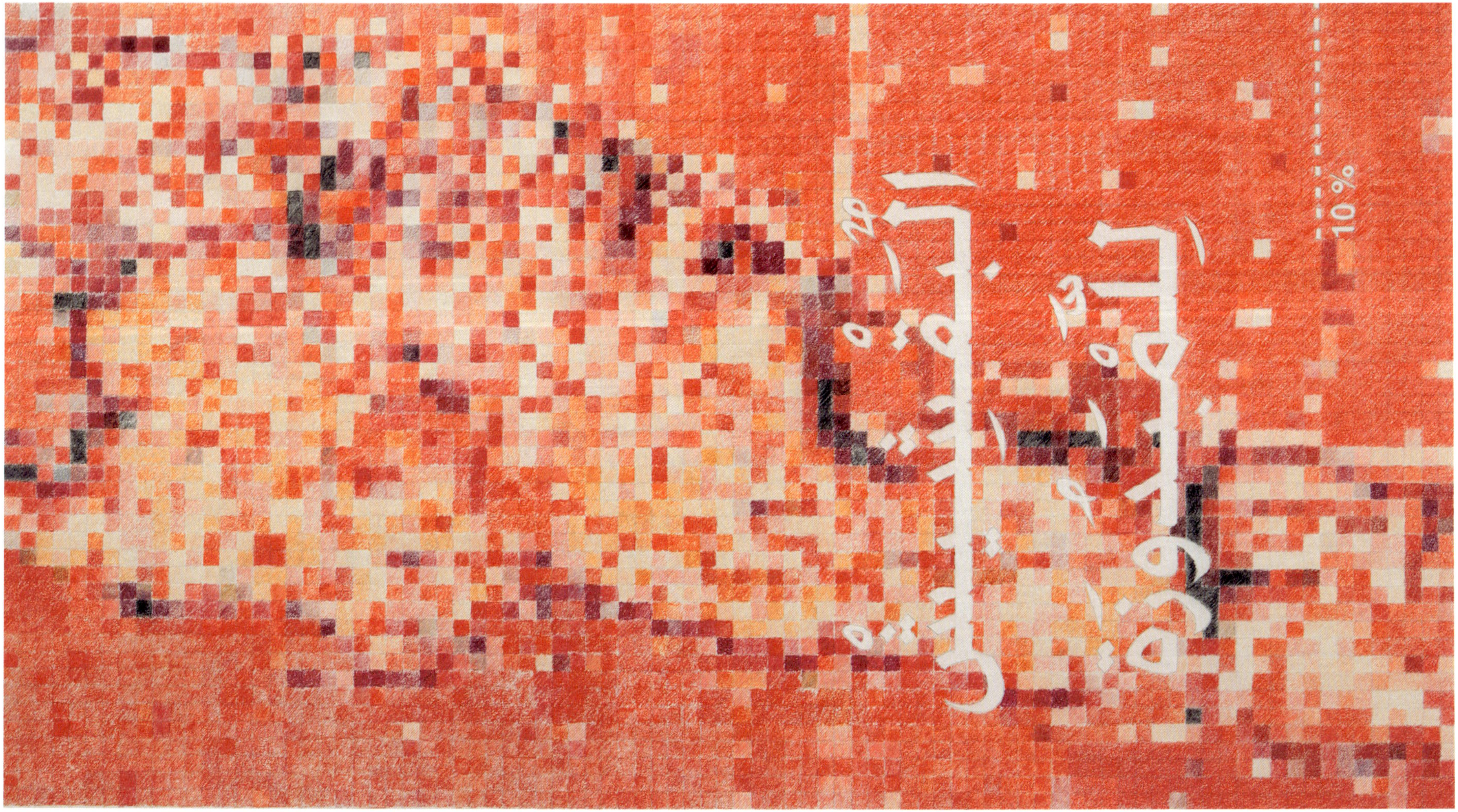

Design for a carpet based on the map of Lampedusa, 2014
transparadiso commissioned a local carpet dealer to produce this carpet for the entrance of the installation. Yet the commission was never executed in this way. A "temporary" carpet was provided for the installation in Sousse, and as the final result of the commission, transparadiso received a monochrome red carpet.

Teppichentwurf, basierend auf der Landkarte von Lampedusa, 2014
Für den Eingang zur Installation gab transparadiso bei einem lokalen Teppichhändler diesen Teppich in Auftrag. Der Auftrag wurde jedoch nie in dieser Form ausgeführt. Für die Installation in Sousse wurde ein „temporärer" Teppich zur Verfügung gestellt, und als Endergebnis des Auftrags erhielt transparadiso einen monochromen roten Teppich.

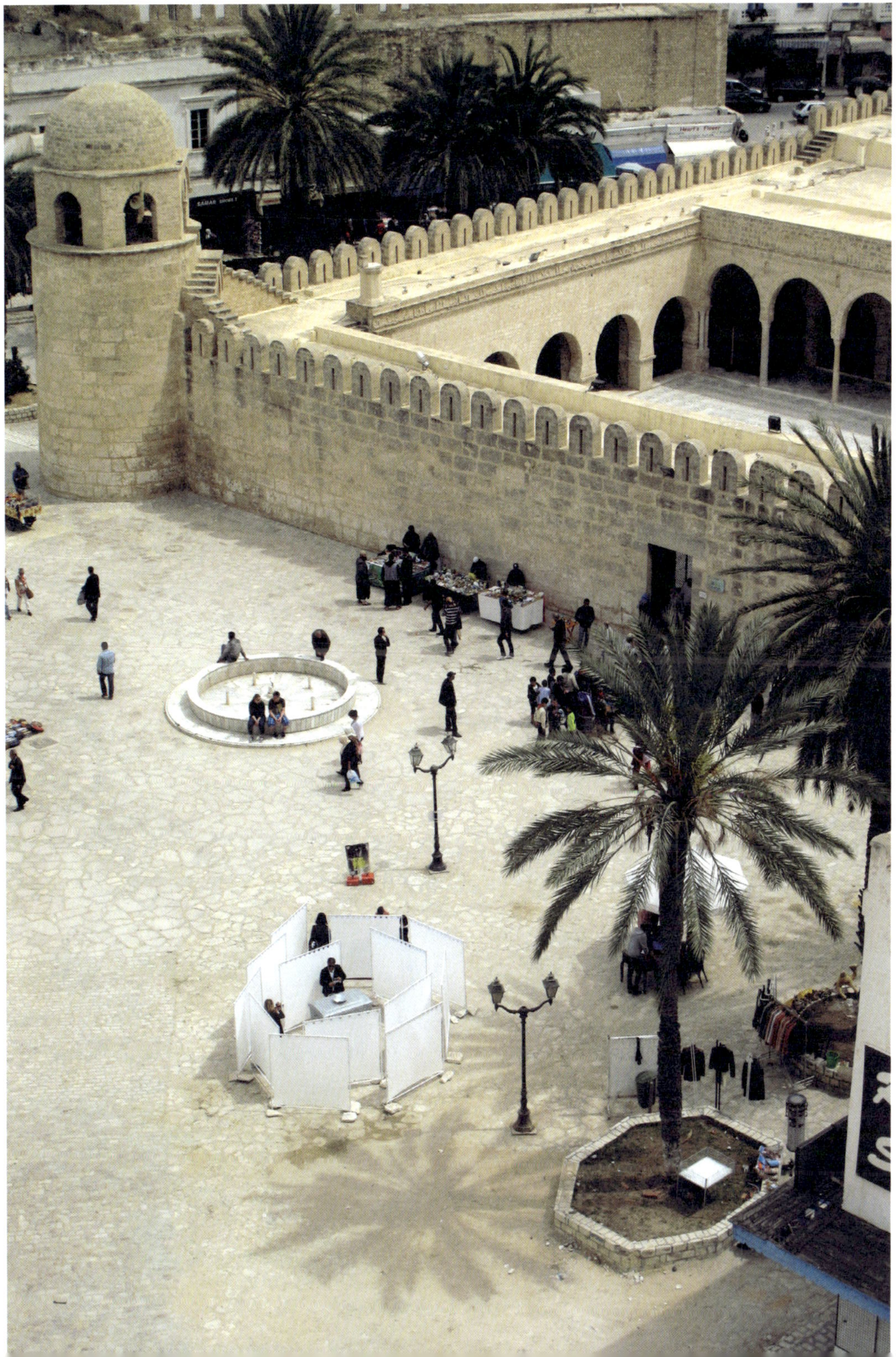

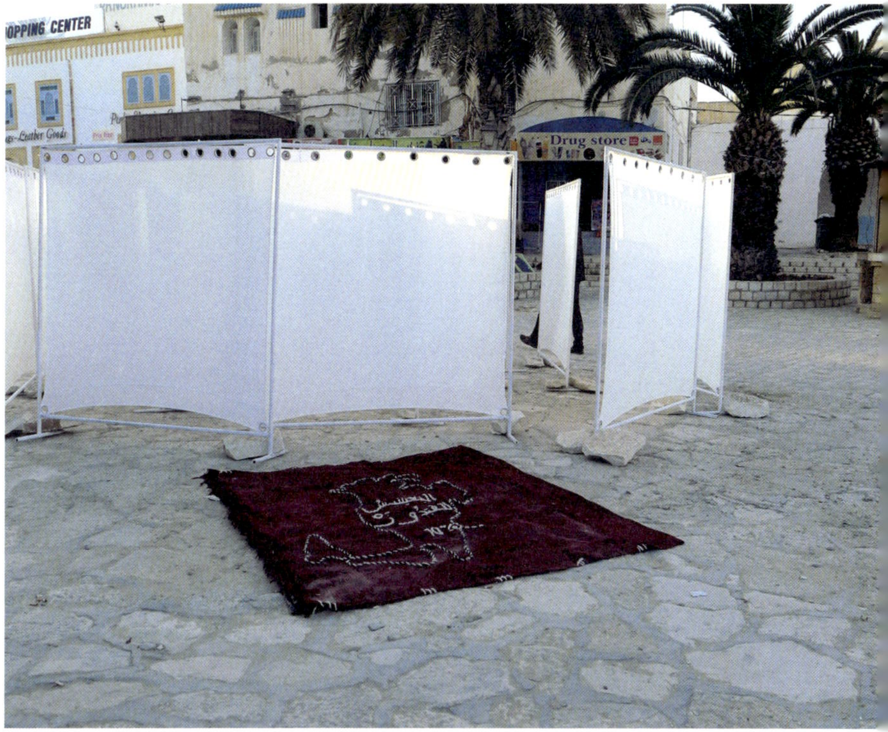
SHOPPING CENTER
Drug store

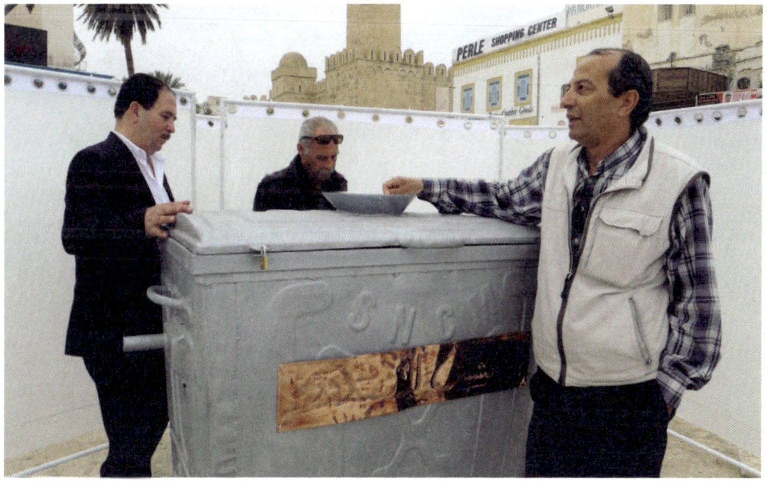
PERLE SHOPPING CENTER

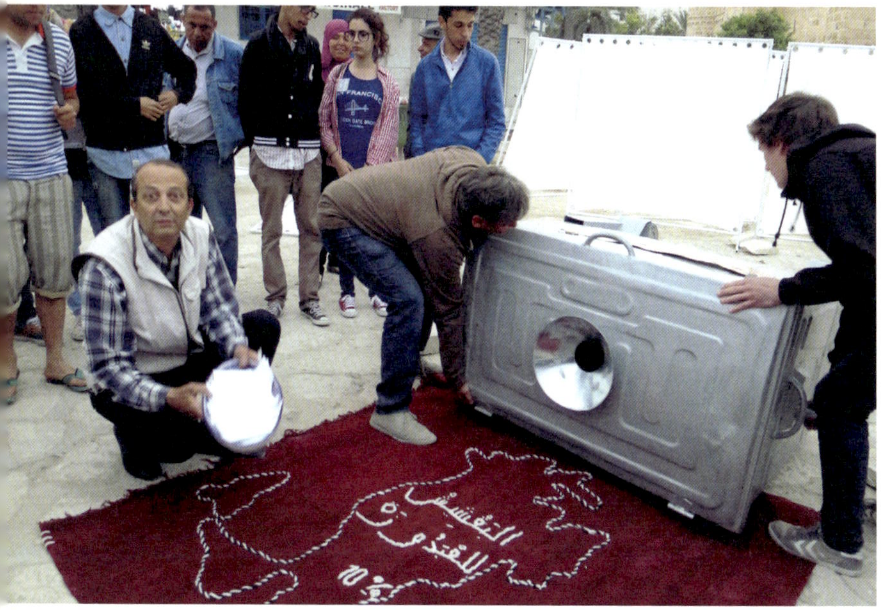

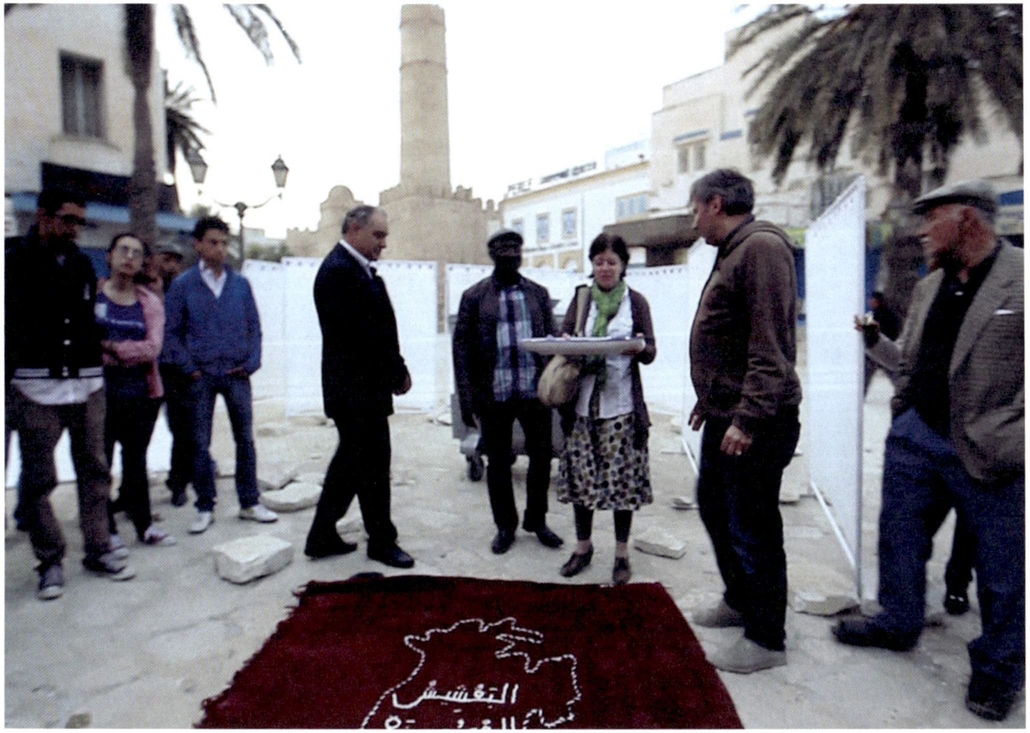

Great Mosque, Rue Othmane Osmane, Sousse
Closing ceremony and handover of donations to Father Jonathan, director of the aid organization African Intelligence in Sfax.

Große Moschee, Rue Othmane Osmane, Sousse
Schlusszeremonie mit Überreichung der Spenden an Père Jonathan, Direktor der Hilfsorganisation African Intelligence in Sfax.

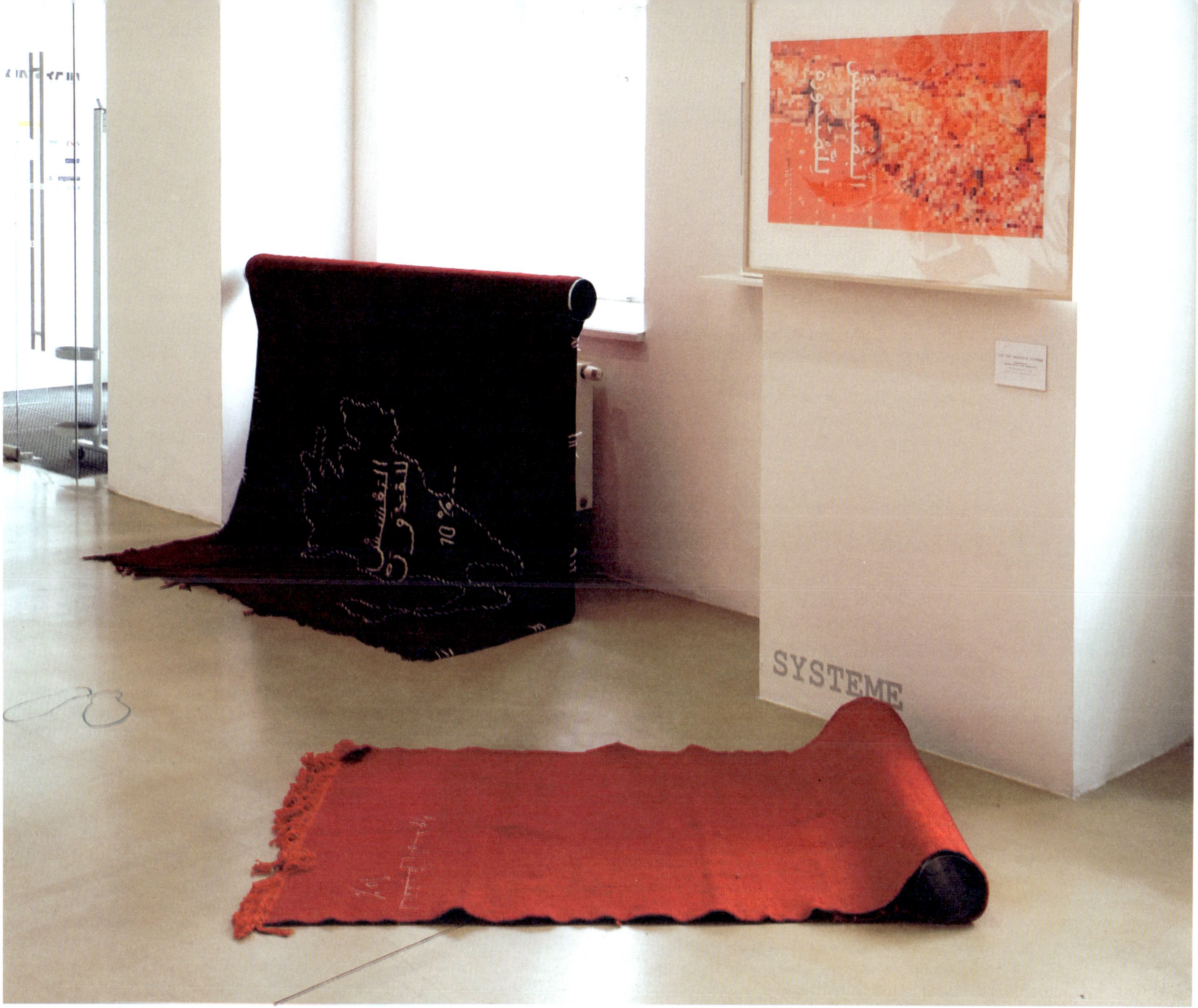

Installation view, *The Turn*, Kunstraum Niederösterreich, Vienna, 2016

Ausstellungsansicht, *The Turn*, Kunstraum Niederösterreich, Wien, 2016

WE PARAPOM!

What sounds like a proclamation of protest is in fact the title of an art project that can also be interpreted as a protest. Conceived for the program of the European Capital of Culture Chemnitz 2025, the project involves planting as many as 2,000 trees of different European apple varieties along an axis that runs right through the city, across districts and property boundaries. Beyond traditional "educational programs" or "events on democratic duties," the residents are invited to become sponsors for tending these trees so as to "produce" collective urban space.[1]

WE PARAPOM! (Eng. parade, apple = pomme, Fr.) thus not only brings together different characteristic social and historical features by focusing on current political topics such as migration, working conditions, ecology, soil sealing, and power systems. It also casts a critical spotlight on the growing apparent necessity of standards: dedicated to apples, whose existence is defined by EU standards, leading to a visible decrease in the range of varieties, WE PARAPOM! also creates space for "strangelings" that/who deviate from the norm.

WE PARAPOM! calls on the public to engage with art projects and artistic strategies so as to test and live out new ways of participating in our democratic self-image and engagement. How can art activate new qualities, and qualities believed lost, under the pressures of an everyday life driven by efficiency and, at the same time, play an active part in social processes?

Until 2025, successive temporary and permanent art projects and artistic urban interventions in various parts of Chemnitz will accompany the tree planting. In 2025, an exhibition in a newly adapted factory building will connect the whole process to parallel interventions from the partner cities including Ustí nad Labem (CZ), presenting further contemporary artworks as well as reflections on the cultural history of the apple and on the parade as representation of power.[BH/BR]

1 Henri Lefebvre's *The Production of Space* (1991) outlines that space is not a container, but produced through the use of its inhabitants, by appropriation.

WE PARAPOM!

Was wie eine Protestansage klingt, ist Titel eines Kunstprojekts und kann auch als Protest verstanden werden. Für das Programm der Kulturhauptstadt Chemnitz 2025 konzipiert, werden in einer Achse quer durch die Stadt, über einzelne Stadtteile und Grundstücksgrenzen hinweg, bis zu 2.000 Bäume unterschiedlicher europäischer Apfelsorten gepflanzt. In weiterer Folge und abseits von klassischen Vermittlungsprogrammen oder „Veranstaltungen zu demokratischen Pflichten" werden die BewohnerInnen dazu eingeladen, PatInnenschaft für deren Pflege zu übernehmen und auf diese Weise kollektiven urbanen Raum zu „produzieren".[1]

Die von Holub kuratierte *Parade der Apfelbäume* (die Parade, der Apfel = pomme, frz.) verbindet auf diese Weise nicht nur unterschiedliche soziale und historische Prägungen entlang aktueller politischer Themen wie Migration, Arbeitsbedingungen, Ökologie, Bodenversiegelung und Machtsysteme. Sie rückt auch die zunehmende, scheinbare Notwendigkeit von Normen ins Scheinwerferlicht: Dem Apfel, dessen Existenz über EU-Normen definiert und dessen Sortenvielfalt dadurch zusehends reduziert wird, widmet sich WE PARAPOM! und schafft zugleich Raum für „Wunderlinge", die aus der Norm fallen.

WE PARAPOM! ruft dazu auf, über Kunstprojekte und künstlerische Strategien eine neue Teilhabe am demokratischen Selbstverständnis und Engagement zu erproben und zu realisieren: Wie kann Kunst neue und verloren gegangene Qualitäten unter dem Druck eines von Effizienz geprägtem Alltagsleben aktivieren und gleichzeitig in gesellschaftlichen Prozessen wirksam werden?

Bis 2025 werden sukzessive temporäre und permanente Kunstprojekte in verschiedenen Vierteln von Chemnitz anlässlich der Pflanzungen realisiert. Eine Ausstellung, die 2025 in einer neu adaptierten Fabrikhalle stattfinden wird, führt den gesamten Prozess mit parallelen Interventionen aus den Partnerinnenstädten wie Ustí nad Labem (CZ) zusammen und ergänzt diese um weitere zeitgenössische Kunstwerke und kulturgeschichtliche Betrachtungen des Apfels sowie die Parade als Mittel zur Repräsentation von Macht.[BH/BR]

1 In *The Production of Space* (1991) beschreibt Henri Lefebvre, dass Raum kein Behältnis ist, sondern dass Raum durch die Benutzung seiner BewohnerInnen, durch Aneignung entsteht.

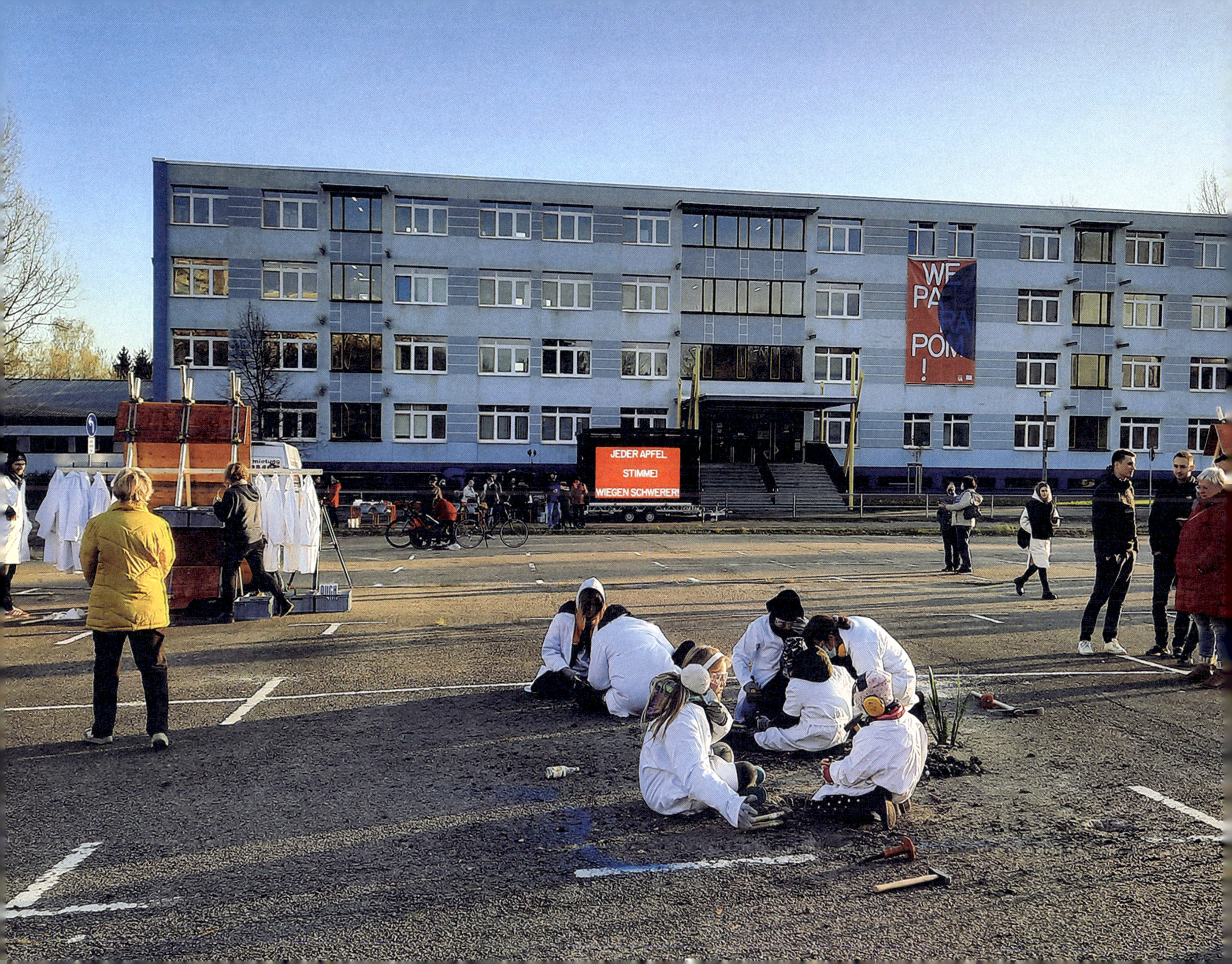
JEDER APFEL
STIMME!
WIEGEN SCHWERER!

Folke Köbberling, "Test Phase #4," Albert-Einstein Primary School/parking lot, Fritz Heckert quarter, Chemnitz, 2021. At the end of the "first public appearance" of WE PARAPOM! a performance took place which addressed different aspects of WE PARAPOM!

Folke Köbberling, „Testphase #4", Albert-Einstein-Grundschule/Parkplatz, Fritz-Heckert-Gebiet, Chemnitz, 2021. Zum Abschluss des „ersten öffentlichen Auftritts" von WE PARAPOM! fand eine Performance statt, die die verschiedenen Aspekte von WE PARAPOM! ansprach.

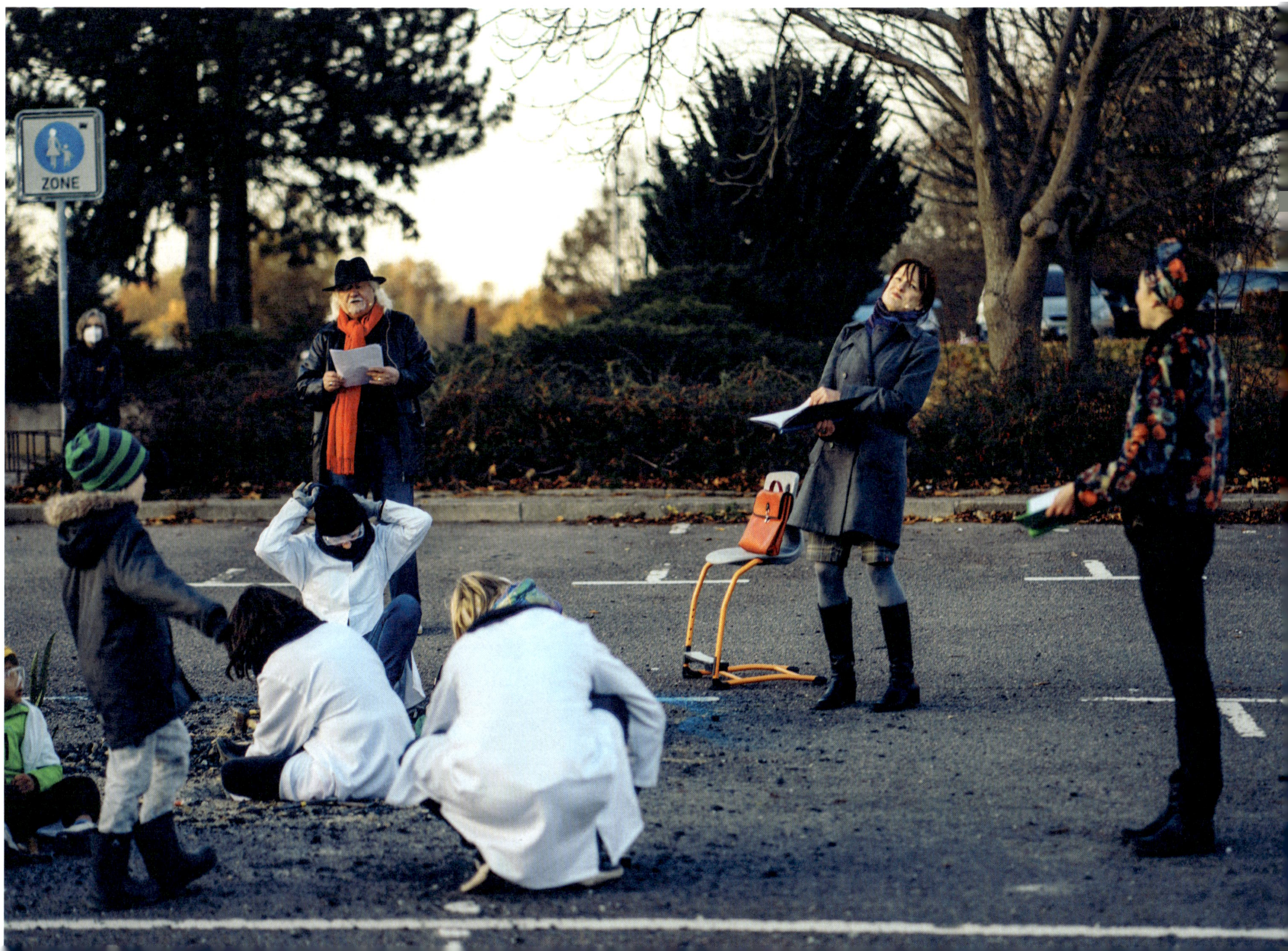

WE wir
Para (*griechisch*) bei neben
Para wie Parade
Pom Pom Pom Pommes (*französisch*)
wie Äpfel
! Rufzeichen wir rufen wir
rufen auf
zur Parade
der Apfelbäume

der vielen
(*sehr schnell sprechen*) die kommen, die
gewünscht wurden,
die nicht mehr entbehrlich sein wollen, die
gepflegt werden wollen,
die Grundlage sein wollen

Nährboden für Gedeihliches
für ein Miteinander

für die
Nachbarschaft
für Partnerschaft

Nicht mehr allein sein
zumindest ein Paar,
zumindest zu zweit,
aber besser ... zu vielen
...

Samen für Patenschaft

für ein kollektives Kunstwerk

für viele künstlerische Interventionen

für Widerspruch!!!

für anregende Debatten

ein Apfel
ein Zankapfel
ein Paradiesapfel

ein Ermöglicher (*Chor, laut*)

dafür werden viele – Ermöglicher – gesucht

in der Stadt
in der Stadtverwaltung
in der
Stadtgesellschaft
in der Kultur
in den Organisationen
in den Vereinen

in den Kunstinstitutionen
in den Museen

im öffentlichen Raum
im
privaten Raum

Das erproben wir (*Chor, sehr laut*)

HEUTE (*Chor, sehr laut*)

Lehnen wir uns hinaus
Weit hinaus, über das übliche

WE PARAPOM! (*Chor, laut*)

(*das folgende mit verteilten Orten: Stimmen, quer über den Platz,*
sehr laut)
Über Grenzen hinweg
Über kulturelle Grenzen hinweg
Über Grundstücksgrenzen hinweg
Über geografische Grenzen hinweg
Über Grenzen von Engstirnigkeit hinweg
Über Grenzen von Einsamkeit hinweg
Über Grenzen von Langeweile hinweg

WE PARAPOM! (*laut > im folgenden leiser werdend*):
POM! POM! POM!

HEUTE
(*Chor, leise*):
Marschieren wir nicht im Gleichschritt
Marschieren wir nicht auf den Boulevards
Marschieren wir nicht als Repräsentation von Macht

HEUTE
marschieren wir
bescheiden
poetisch
recken
wir unsere Blüten empor
für das Erwachen
des Frühlings
für das Versprechen
Früchte zu tragen
für die Hoffnung
auf Früchte

(*PAUSE: eine Geste > zu entwickeln; Klänge eines Instruments ...,*
klopfen auf das Geländer: nacheinander)

Kann ein Apfel verführen?
Zu Genuss?
Erlauben wir uns Momente von Genuss? (*Chor, laut*)
Erlauben wir uns Momente von Genuss! (*Chor, laut)*

Frönen wir der Genusssucht

oder ist das verwerflich

das Genießen

wenn wir einen Apfel betrachten

anschneiden oder hineinbeißen
den Geschmack testen
testen wir den Geschmack der Verführung
den Genuss im Alltag
unentdeckte Momente des
Genusses

entdecken wir sie in Chemnitz in
CHEMNITZ! *(Chor, laut)*
schaffen wir sie in Chemnitz in
CHEMNITZ! *(Chor, laut)*

(Lautes klopfen auf das Geländer; + Instrument? Triangel?)

In this first artistic intervention in the frame of WE PARAPOM! Folke Köbberling manually broke up the asphalt in order to prepare the ground for the planting of apple trees.

In dieser ersten künstlerischen Intervention im Rahmen von WE PARAPOM! brach Folke Köbberling händisch den Asphalt auf, um den Boden für die Pflanzung von Apfelbäumen freizumachen.

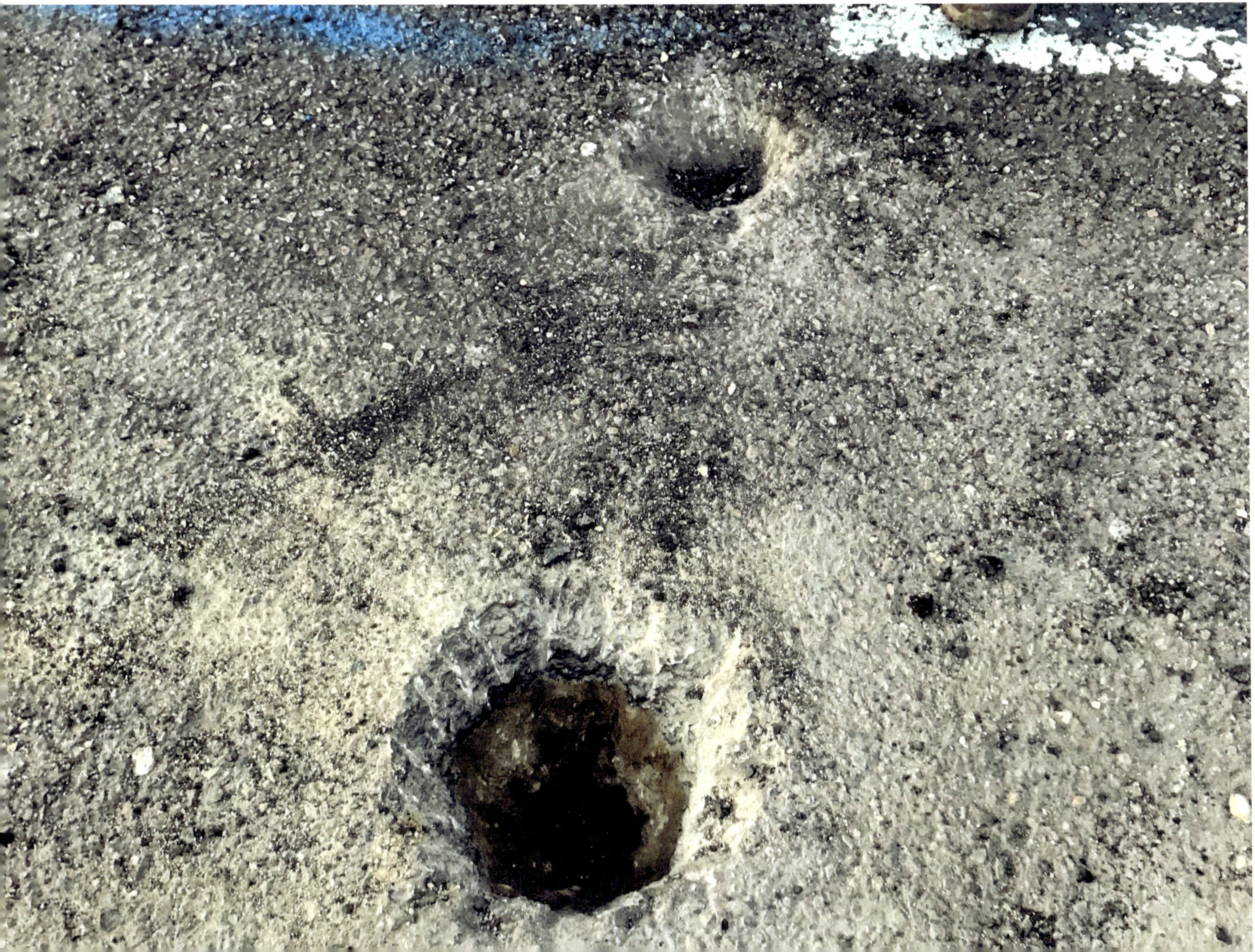

Glossary WE PARAPOM! WE PARAPOM! Glossar

Falling out of the norm Aus der Norm fallen
Not conforming to the norm Nicht der Norm entsprechen
Refusing to conform to the norm Sich der Norm verweigern
Defying efficiency Entgegen der Effizienz
Resisting the demand for efficiency Sich der Forderung nach Effizienz widersetzen
Running wild Wildwuchs
Exposing oneself to difficulties Sich Schwierigkeiten aussetzen
(picking fruits that can only be reached with difficulty) (Pflücken von Früchten, die nur unter Mühsal erreichbar sind)
Sites for secrets (on the apple tree) Orte für Geheimnisse (auf dem Apfelbaum)
Sites for wishes Orte für Wünsche
Sites for visions Orte für Visionen
The (seemingly) unfeasible Das (scheinbar) Nicht-Machbare
Listening (as a quality to be rediscovered) Zuhören (als wieder zu entdeckende Qualität)
Slowness (as a quality to be rediscovered) Langsamkeit (als wieder zu entdeckende Qualität)
Slowness of harvesting fruit Langsamkeit des Früchteerntens
Slowness of learning Langsamkeit des Lernens
Peace (among neighbours) Friede (unter Nachbarn)
The slowness of learning to make peace Die Langsamkeit des Lernens, Frieden zu schließen
New community of godparents Neue Gemeinschaft der PatInnen
(of apple trees–not to be confused with the mafia) (der Apfelbäume – nicht mit der Mafia zu verwechseln)
Overcoming (property) boundaries Überwindung von (Grundstücks-)Grenzen
Parade of underestimated qualities Parade der unterschätzten Qualitäten
Parade of celebration Parade des Feierns
Parade of emancipation Parade der Emanzipation
Parade of standing up for humanistic values Parade des Einstehens für humanistische Werte
Parade against exclusion Parade gegen Ausgrenzung
Parade of crossing borders Parade des Grenzenüberschreitens
Emancipation (of the apple trees) Emanzipation (der Apfelbäume)
Right to work Recht auf Arbeit
Desire for work Lust auf Arbeit
Quality of work Qualität von Arbeit
Migration (of the apples, of the harvesters) Migration (der Äpfel, der ErntearbeiterInnen)
Quality of leisure Qualität von Freizeit
Quality of being involved in the community (in leisure time or professionally) Qualität, sich für die Gemeinschaft zu engagieren (in der Freizeit oder beruflich)
Self-esteem Selbstwertgefühl
Seduction Verführung
The Fall of Man Der Sündenfall
Paradise Paradies
Garden of Paradise Paradiesgarten
The apple of paradise (as a sign of ecology) Der Paradiesapfel (als Zeichen für Ökologie)
The apple of discord Der Zankapfel
New seeds, new community Neue Samen, neue Gemeinschaft
New seeds, swarm intelligence Neue Samen, Schwarmintelligenz
A prime example Ein Paradebeispiel

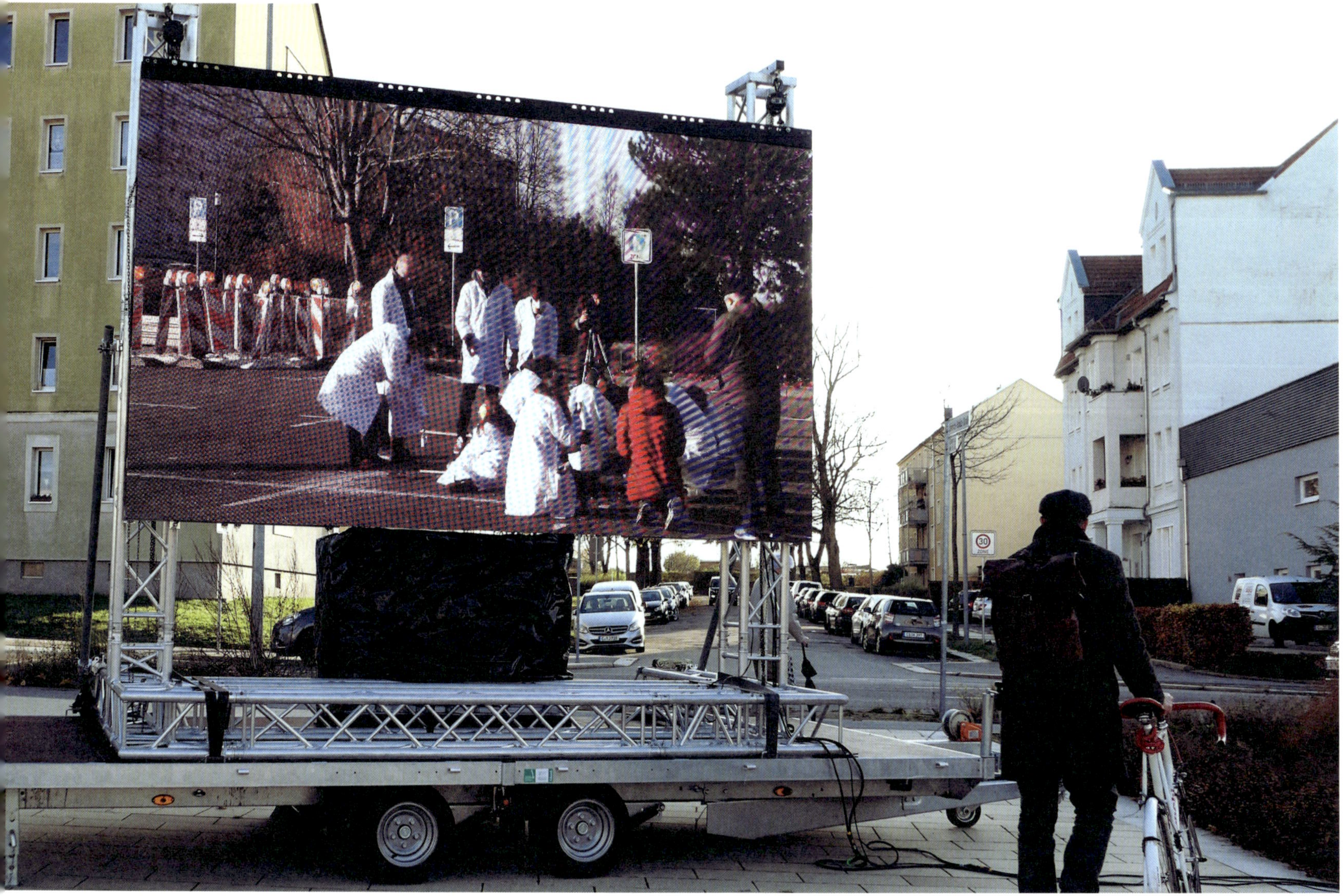

"Test Phase #4" was broadcast live to the site of the first plantings, the Terra Nova Campus.

„Testphase #4“ wurde live an den Ort der ersten Pflanzungen, den Terra Nova Campus, übertragen.

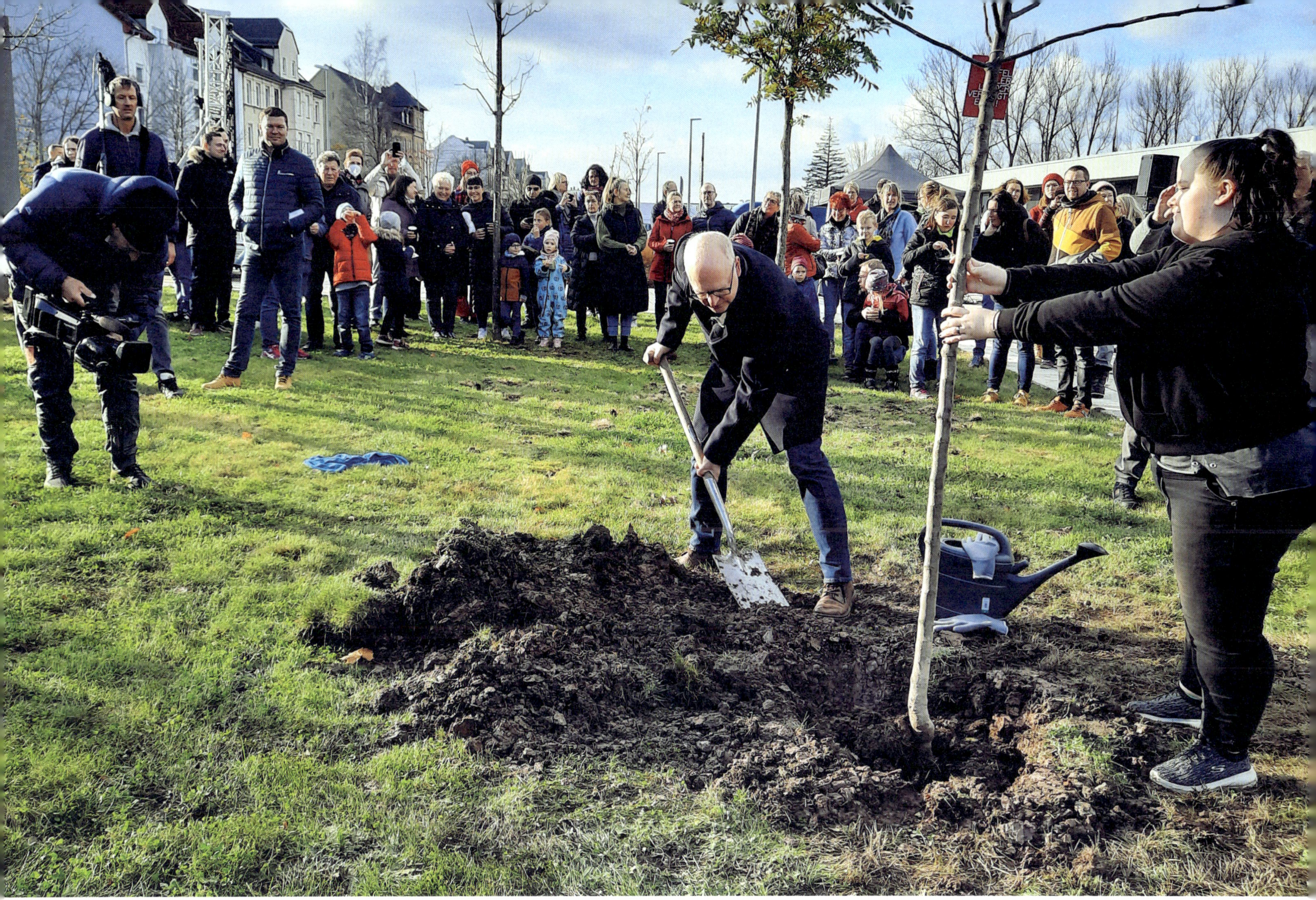

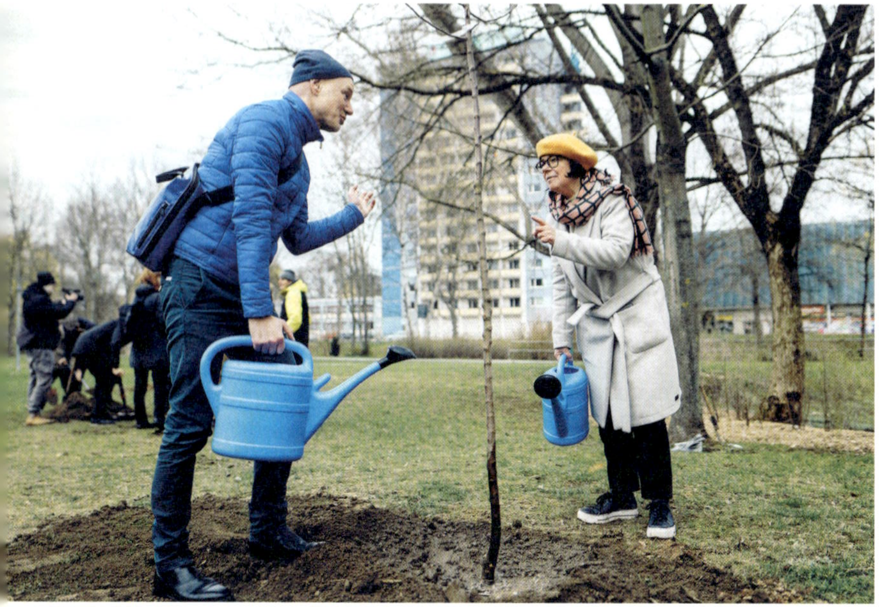

Plantings in the park at Falke Square

Pflanzungen im Park am Falkeplatz

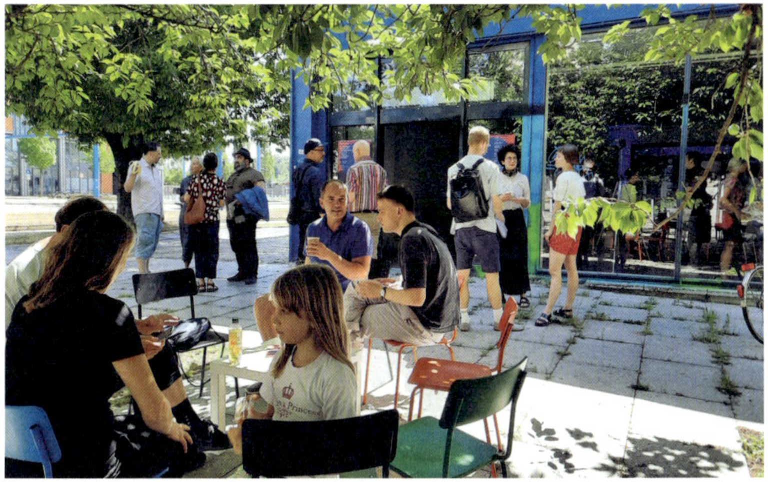

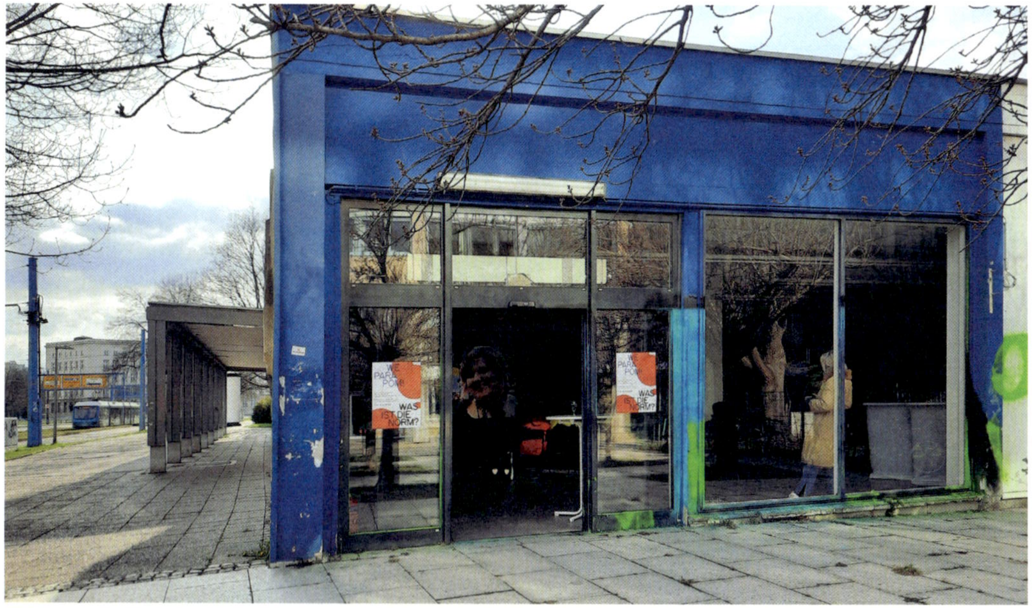

Film screenings in the former EDEKA supermarket/Kaufhalle

Filmscreenings im ehemaligen EDEKA-Markt/Kaufhalle

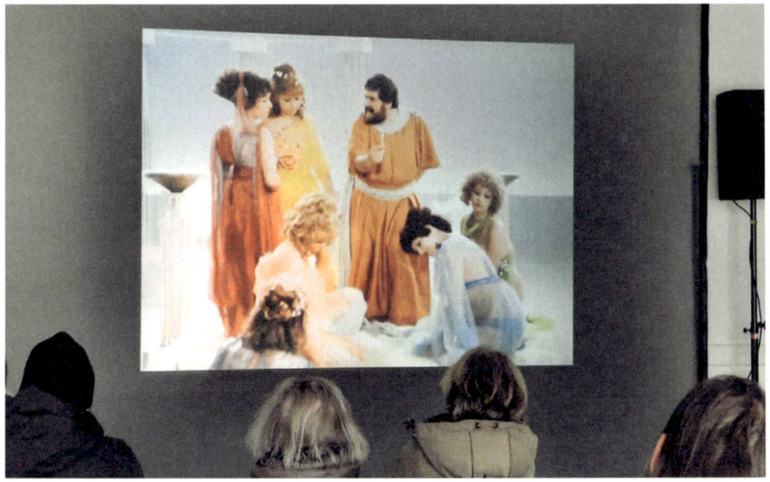

The apple as such (Kurt Barthel, GDR, 1979, 12'32"/ DEFA)

Der Apfel als solcher (Kurt Barthel, DDR, 1979, 12'32"/ DEFA)

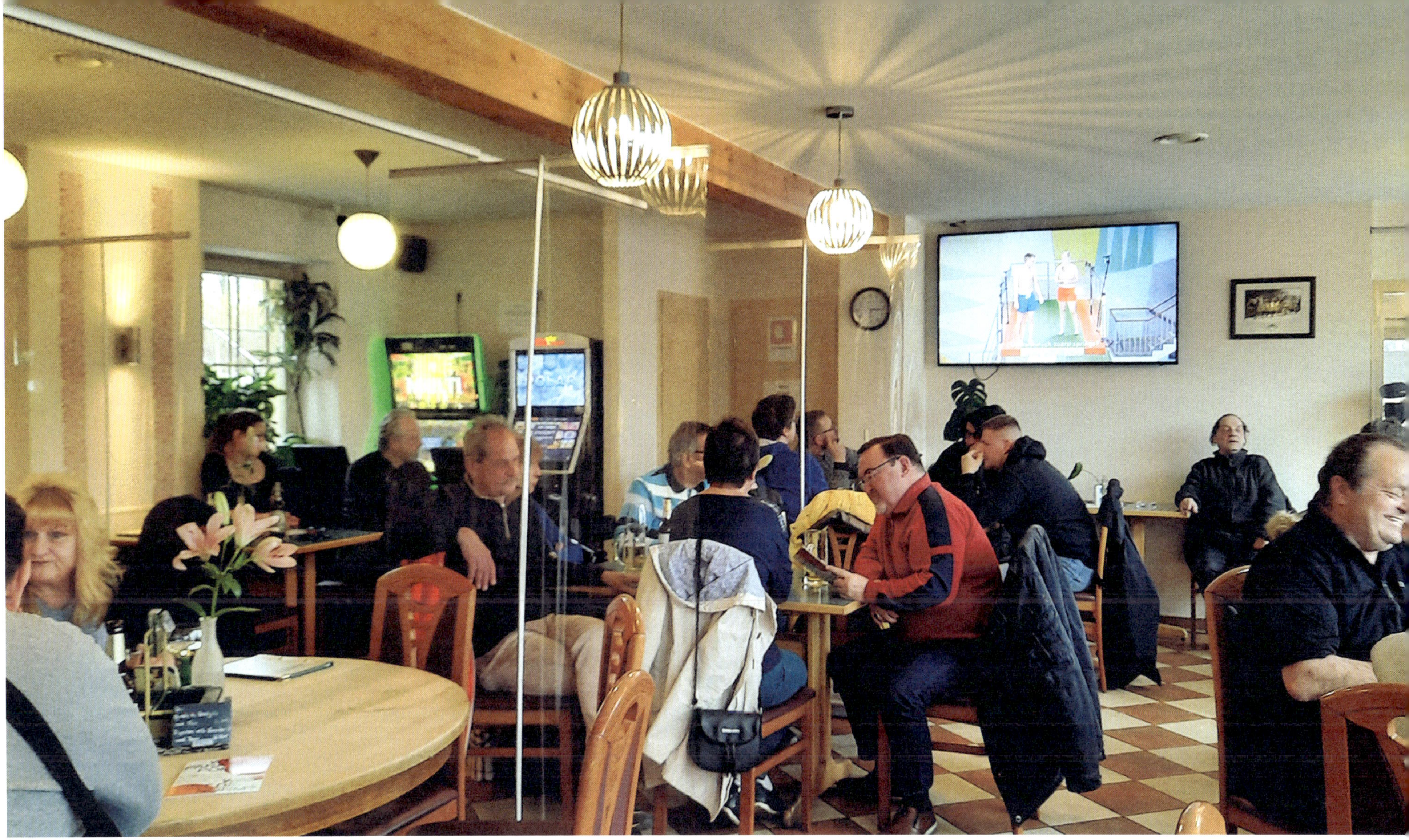

Film screenings at Café Smart

Filmscreenings im Café Smart

The "Second Public Appearance" of WE PARAPOM!, 2022
Public film screenings at various locations in the area of the second planting phase around the Museum Gunzenhauser questioned the concepts of "norm" and "norming" (curated by Beate Kunath).

Der „Zweite öffentliche Auftritt" von WE PARAPOM!, 2022
Öffentliche Filmscreenings an verschiedenen Orten im Bereich der zweiten Pflanzungsphase um das Museum Gunzenhauser hinterfragten „Norm" und „Normierung" (kuratiert von Beate Kunath).

Albert Einstein Grade School/parking lot,
Fritz Heckert quarter, Chemnitz, July 2022
The plantings have developed into green islands and the apple trees are bearing first fruits.

Parkplatz Albert-Einstein-Grundschule,
Fritz-Heckert-Gebiet, Chemnitz, Juli 2022
Die Pflanzungen haben sich zu grünen Inseln entwickelt, und die Apfelbäume tragen erste Früchte.

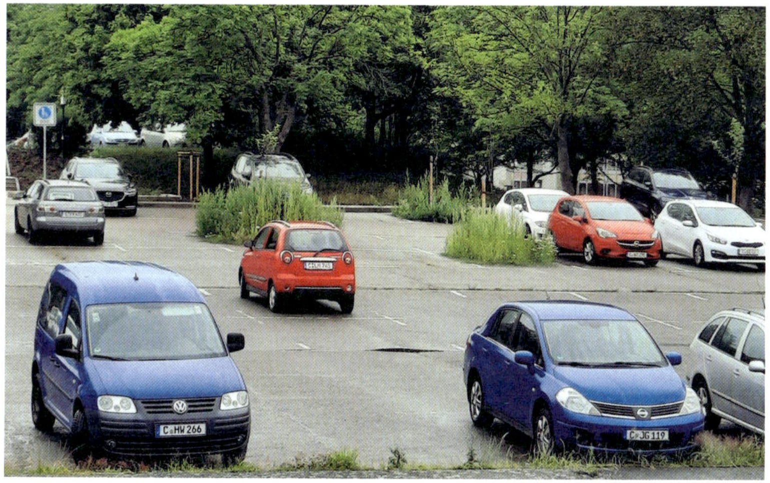

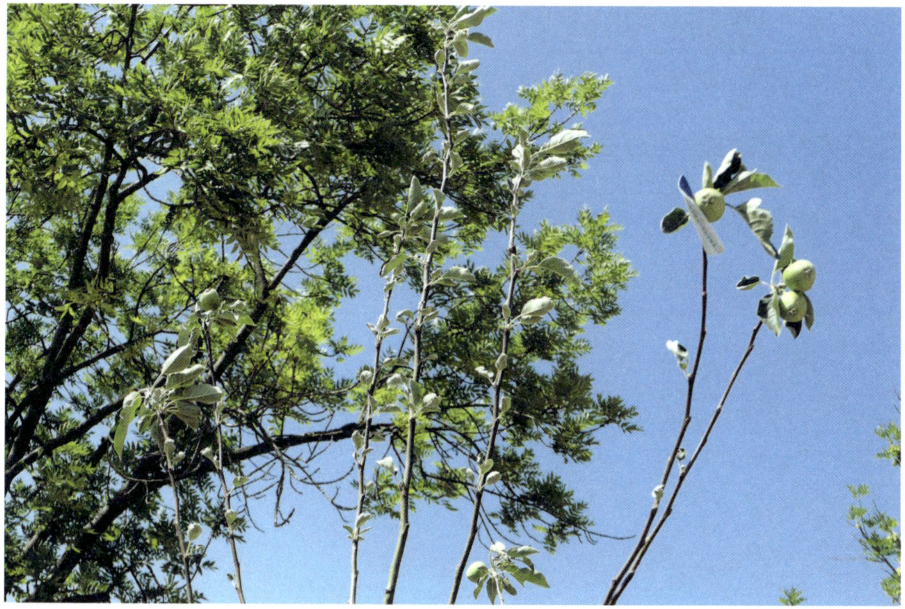

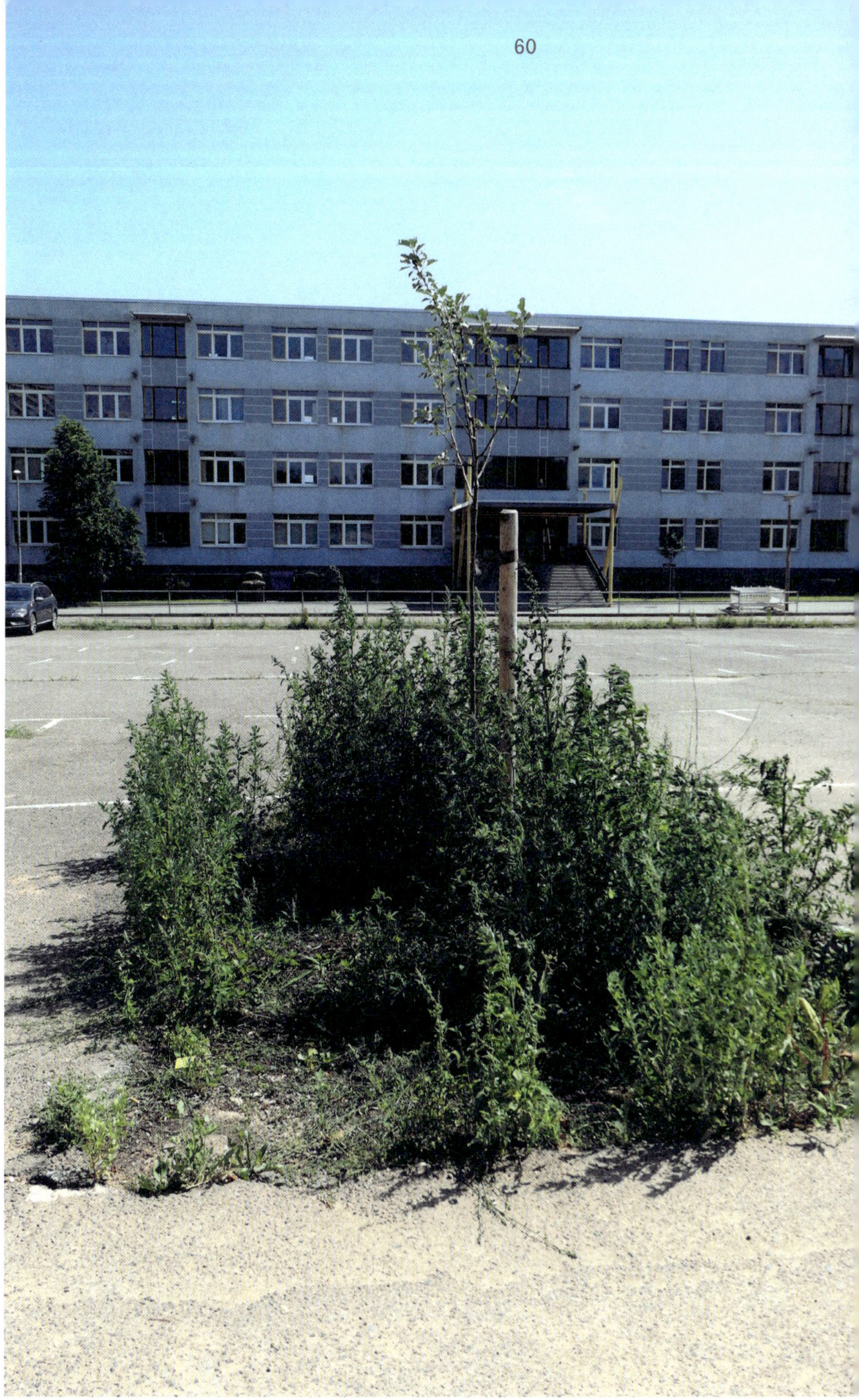

II. Participatory Strategies, Visions, and Speculative Fiction

Partizipative Strategien, Visionen und spekulative Fiktion

SILENT BUT PERSISTENT RESISTANCE

Barbara Holub in conversation with Başak Şenova

BS: Prompted by transdisciplinary research on social and political dynamics, you use various process-based artistic methods and strategies to create situations of social practice and in-situ production through dialog with local communities. As I observe it, your practice is infused with the actions of listening, sharing, empowering, collaborating, reacting, and claiming together, therefore your long-term projects often prompt affective responses to the given problematic social and political conditions. They responsively underline possibilities and strategies for a better future beyond a narrowly construed pragmatic approach addressing and illustrating obstacles. Furthermore, they all follow the same line of inquiry with a subtle move towards questioning and subverting the context. The first time I encountered your work back in 2009, I was struck by the silent but persistent resistance that finds its vocabulary of form through simple actions. How is the notion of "persistence" situated in relation to your artistic practice?

BH: The act of persisting is a quite intensive ongoing interest throughout my projects. Persisting in opening up spaces and situations for the seemingly undoable, in what does not fit, in providing situations for people who seem to not fit the general demands and requests of society. By also taking the experience of one project to the next, this could be considered a golden thread through my practice.

I have always been particularly interested in borders, how to transgress individual, felt or actually existing, geographical or physical borders, how to create situations for addressing these borders. For BETWEEN ROLES (2000) I first installed a garden situation in my new studio space, with a generic Austrian wooden garden fence and basic garden furniture and invited people to have conversations across the fence. A harmless situation, yet quite distinctive for the middle European culture. Garden fences don't exist for example in American (suburban) housing areas, yet when you think of gated communities, the fence already takes on even militant aspects with surveillance cameras, guards etc. For *Enactments of the Self* (Graz, 2002) I expanded this piece at Steirischer Herbst, installing a garden in the exhibition hall—a former factory building—and again inviting specific people to have conversations. This time I asked the director of a prison, the CEO of a company producing prefabricated houses, and an oncologist, among others, to especially address experiences with borders. These were recorded and then shown in the shop window of a furniture store in the city centre. Apart

LEISER, ABER BESTÄNDIGER WIDERSTAND

Barbara Holub im Gespräch mit Başak Şenova

BS: Ausgehend von transdisziplinärer Forschung zu sozialen und politischen Dynamiken stellst du unter Anwendung verschiedener künstlerischer Methoden und prozessorientierter Strategien Situationen einer sozialen Praxis her, die im Dialog mit lokalen Communities vor Ort realisiert werden. Nach meiner Beobachtung ist dein Schaffen geprägt von Situationen des Zuhörens, Teilens, Ermächtigens, Zusammenarbeitens, Reagierens und gemeinsamen Forderns, weshalb deine Langzeitprojekte häufig eine affektive Resonanz auf bestehende soziale und politische Bedingungen hervorrufen. Sie zeigen Möglichkeiten und Strategien für eine bessere Zukunft auf, die über einen eng definierten pragmatischen Ansatz, der nur Hürden anspricht bzw. veranschaulicht, hinausgehen. Überdies folgen sie alle derselben Untersuchungsmethode, die meist mit einer subtilen Hinterfragung und Unterminierung des Kontexts verbunden ist. Bei meiner ersten Begegnung mit deiner Arbeit im Jahr 2009 beeindruckte mich vor allem der stille, aber beharrliche Widerstand, der seine Formensprache aus einfachen Aktionen entwickelt. Wo würdest du den Begriff „Beharrlichkeit" in deiner künstlerischen Praxis verorten?

BH: Der Akt des Beharrens nimmt eine sehr wichtige Rolle in all meinen Projekten ein. Das Beharren auf dem Öffnen von Räumen und Situationen für das scheinbar Unmögliche, das Beharren auf dem Unpassenden, der Herstellung von Situationen für Menschen, die nicht den allgemeinen Erfordernissen der Gesellschaft entsprechen. Aber auch das Beharren auf dem Mitnehmen von Erfahrungen von einem Projekt zum nächsten. Das Beharren könnte demnach als roter Faden durch meine künstlerische Praxis gesehen werden.

Ich habe mich immer besonders für Grenzen interessiert, für die Möglichkeit der Überschreitung gefühlter oder real existierender geografischer oder physischer Grenzen, das Schaffen von Situationen, um sie zu thematisieren. Für ZWISCHENROLLEN (2000) habe ich zuerst in meinem neuen Atelierraum eine Gartensituation installiert, mit einem typisch österreichischen Gartenzaun aus Holz und ein paar elementaren Gartenmöbeln, und dann Leute eingeladen, sich über den Zaun hinweg zu unterhalten. Eine harmlose Situation, aber bezeichnend für die mitteleuropäische Kultur – in amerikanischen Vorstädten zum Beispiel gibt es keine Gartenzäune. Dafür nehmen sie in Gated Communities sogar militärischen Charakter an, mit Überwachungskameras, Wachpersonal und dergleichen Für *Enactments of the Self* (beim Steirischen Herbst in Graz, 2002) erweiterte

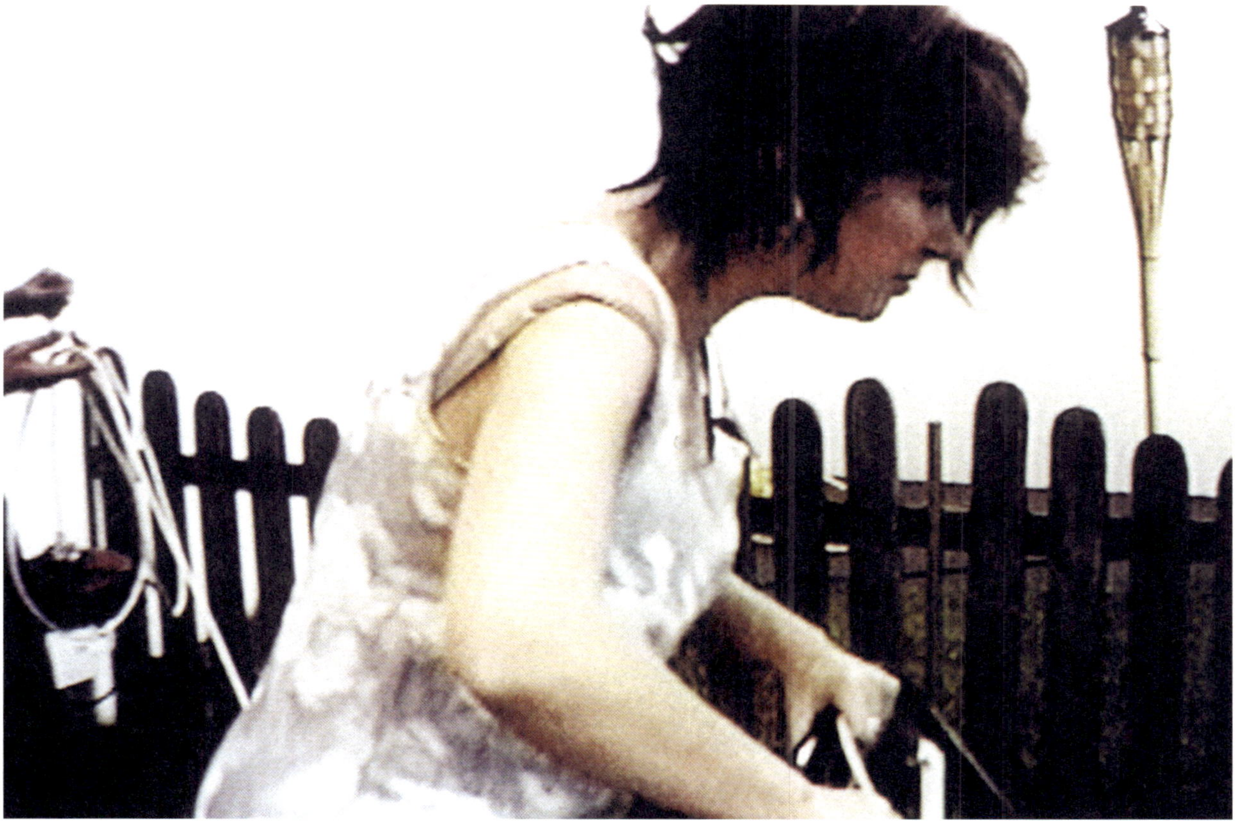

BETWEEN ROLES, Barbara Holub studio, 2000 (see p. 149) ZWISCHENROLLEN, Atelier Barbara Holub, 2000 (siehe S. 149)

from these organized conversations, the garden was open to use by the public. This harmless and ordinary doubling of an outdoor space, and transporting it into an indoor exhibition venue, created an absurd stage—yet familiar enough for the visitors to use.

> In this context, another project, PERSONAL INVESTIGATION (1994), which took place at the Municipal Gallery of Fürstenfeld and tobacco factories located in Linz and Hainburg, also created a space for detecting covert power structures, human conditions, and mechanisms of social order and patterns.

This was actually my first project dealing with a corporation and intervening in their system. I was invited as part of the *Casablanca Gallery*, an art program funded by the Austrian Tobacco Company. During my research, the random generator at the exit of the factory in Hainburg called my special attention. Workers and employees that were selected by the random generator had to undergo a body search for the possible smuggling of cigarettes, the penalty for which had different consequences: if caught, workers would be dismissed immediately whereas employees would (only) receive a warning. This unequal treatment was the starting point to work with the factory staff. I asked them to leave their hand prints on an acrylic plate, which would create an overlay of the many individual traces that couldn't be deciphered, succumbing to the "many." These pieces were then put into context by my electric writing machine tapes, suggesting—to

ich diese Arbeit. Ich installierte einen Garten in der Ausstellungshalle – einem ehemaligen Fabrikgebäude – und lud erneut Leute ein, dort Gespräche zu führen. Diesmal ganz bestimmte Leute, u. a. einen Gefängnisdirektor, den CEO eines Fertighausunternehmens und einen Onkologen, die sich insbesondere über ihre Erfahrungen mit Grenzen austauschen sollten. Die Gespräche wurden aufgezeichnet und im Schaufenster eines Möbelhauses im Stadtzentrum wiedergegeben. Außerhalb dieser organisierten Gesprächsrunden konnte der Garten vom Publikum genutzt werden. Durch diese harmlose und gewöhnliche Verdoppelung eines Außenraums und seine Verlagerung in einen Ausstellungsraum entstand eine absurde Bühne, die aber gleichzeitig doch so vertraut war, dass die BesucherInnen sie benutzten.

> Einen Raum zum Aufspüren verborgener Machtstrukturen, menschlicher Verhältnisse und Mechanismen sozialer Ordnung schuf auch ein anderes Projekt, PERSONAL INVESTIGATION (1994), das in der Stadtgalerie Fürstenfeld und in den Tabakfabriken in Linz und Hainburg stattfand.

Das war mein erstes Projekt, das sich mit einem Unternehmen beschäftigte und in sein System eingriff. Ich war im Rahmen der *Casablanca Gallery*, eines von den Austria Tabakwerken finanzierten Kunstprogramms, eingeladen worden. Im Zuge meiner Recherchen fiel mir der Zufallsgenerator am Ausgang der Tabakfabrik Hainburg besonders in Auge. Die von diesem Zufallsgenerator ausgewählten ArbeiterInnen und Angestellten wurden einer Körper-

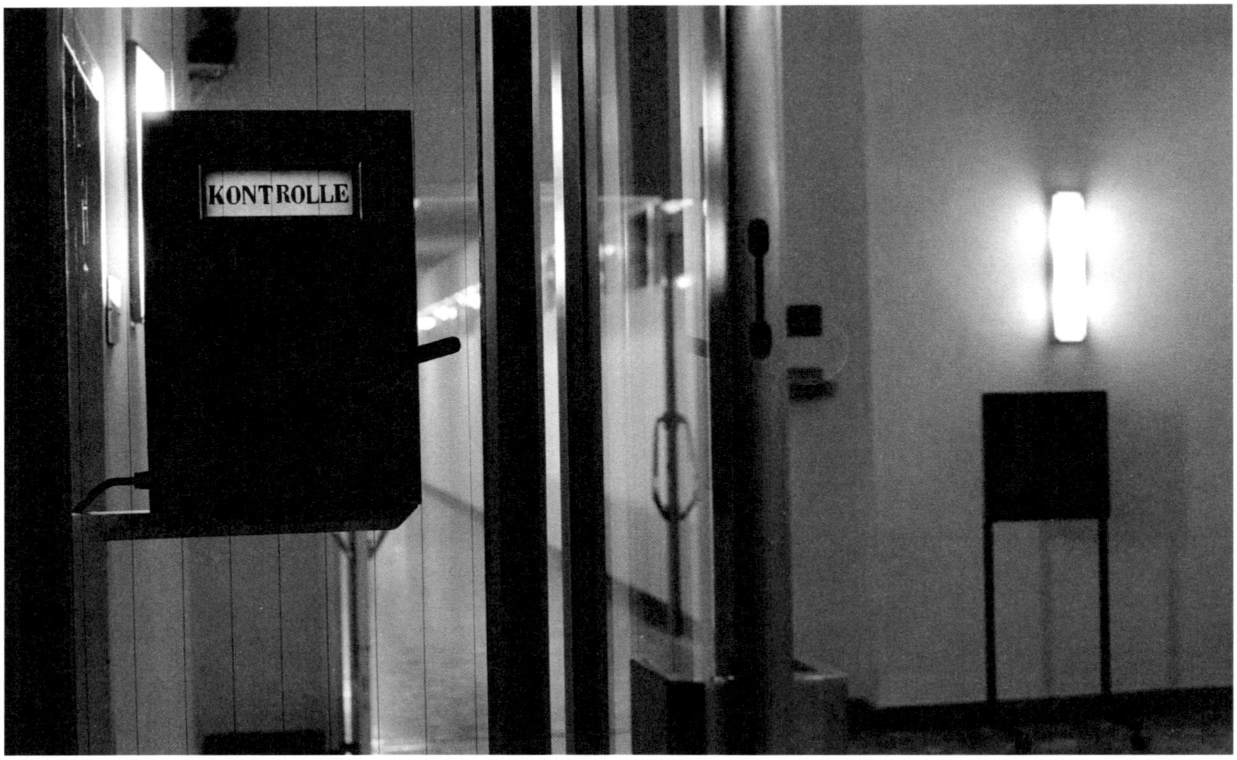

PERSONAL INVESTIGATION, monitoring instrument, tobacco factory in Hainburg, 1994 (see p. 189)

PERSONAL INVESTIGATION, Kontrollapparat in der Tabakfabrik Hainburg, 1994 (siehe S. 189)

the audience of the exhibition at the Municipal Gallery of Fürstenfeld—that one could intrude into my private life. Thus, PERSONAL INVESTIGATION revolves around the work of a private investigator: creating a complex spatial setting by questioning the private and public, personal and communal, and connecting this setting to factory situations. In the presumption that their workers and employees would smuggle, the tobacco company had already put them under suspicion rather than trust.

Have you followed the developments in those factories, and the region, after this particular project?

Due to Austria becoming a member of the EU in 1995, the state monopoly of the Austrian Tobacco Factories (Austria Tabakwerke, 1784–1996) was privatized in 1997 and the art program *Casablanca Gallery* came to an end. The factories were closed one after the other, the last one in Hainburg in 2011. The tobacco factory in Linz is a listed building by architect Peter Behrens, built in 1935. After it closed down, it was first used by Art University Linz and then transformed into an event centre and "creative hotspot."

Then I continued working with the employees of Bene, a high-end office furniture company that had always been engaged in art. This developed into a collaboration over the years. It started with a staged photoshoot with the employees of "what happens under the table," which served as a basis for a permanent installation of light boxes in the façade. A year later I was invited to produce a video on their experiences and then I continued to work

visitation nach geschmuggelten Zigaretten unterzogen. Erwischte man sie beim Schmuggeln, hatte das für ArbeiterInnen und Angestellte unterschiedliche Konsequenzen: Die einen wurden sofort entlassen, wogegen die anderen (lediglich) verwarnt wurden. Diese Ungleichbehandlung war der Ausgangspunkt für die Arbeit mit FabrikarbeiterInnen. Ich bat sie, ihre Handabdrücke auf einer Acrylplatte zu hinterlassen, wodurch eine nicht entzifferbare Überlagerung vieler individueller Spuren zustande kam, eine Unterordnung unter die „Vielen". Diese Platten wurden dann durch die Farbbänder meiner elektrischen Schreibmaschine kontextualisiert, was dem Publikum der Ausstellung in der Stadtgalerie Fürstenfeld nahelegte, man könne in meinem Privatleben herumschnüffeln. PERSONAL INVESTIGATION dreht sich also um die Arbeit einer Privatdetektivin: das Schaffen einer komplexen räumlichen Situation, um Fragen nach dem Privaten und Öffentlichen, dem Persönlichen und Gemeinschaftlichen zu stellen, und diese mit den Arbeitssituationen in den Fabriken zu verknüpfen. Mit der Annahme, dass ihre ArbeiterInnen schmuggeln könnten, hatten die Tabakwerke sie bereits unter Verdacht gestellt.

Hast du die Entwicklung in diesen Fabriken – und ihren Regionen – nach dem Projekt weiter verfolgt?

Als Österreich 1995 EU-Mitglied wurde, fiel das Staatsmonopol auf Tabak. 1997 wurden die Austria Tabakwerke (1784–1996) privatisiert und das Kunstprogramm *Casablanca Gallery* lief aus. Die Fabriken wurden nach und nach geschlossen, als letzte jene in Hainburg 2011. Die von Peter Behrens 1935 erbaute Tabakfabrik in Linz ist ein denkmal-

on installations in their interior spaces, addressing the topic of "game" in relation to work, which connected to my show at the Secession in 1999.

The correlation between your position and critical spatial practice[1] adds another layer to your projects. This red thread also connotes a simultaneity—in parallel with Rosalind Krauss' notion of an "expanded field"[2]—by expanding art production in relation to architecture and its settings.

These projects where I intruded in systems of corporate companies created a parallel layer where I established a relationship of confidence between the workers/employees and myself on an equal level of exchange by using my position as an artist, as someone who is not taken seriously by the commissioning party, referring to what Michel de Certeau describes as *"faire la perruque"*[3]—a clandestine endeavor outside of what would be shown in the exhibition, offering a new experience and presence for people who are probably not familiar with contemporary art and wouldn't visit contemporary art exhibitions. Like a silent contract, whereas, for example, Antje Schiffers created a method of barter, offering a painting (depicting a situation the people whom she wants to talk to can choose) in exchange for conversations.

As I see it, these initial projects started to open up new territories of research in conjunction with the notion of public space.

From engaging in corporations I moved more and more towards public space, while still always interested in addressing diverse audiences, between companies and public space on the one side and the art exhibition context on the other. What you refer to as "sculpture" was for me always the complex spatial setting including the possible engagement of participants. Mary Jane Jacob's seminal project *Culture in Action* (1993) in Chicago created a radical shift in the notion of sculpture, a revolutionary act in reversing the tradition of Sculpture Chicago.[4] This was as relevant for the discourse of how art can engage in societal issues as what Jane Rendell coined "critical spatial practice," coming from an architecture perspective. So, one could maybe say that my work is situated in between. And then, of course, the publication DÜRFEN DIE DAS?[5] put the question to the foreground whether or not and how artists are "allowed" to engage in societal issues without compromising the autonomy of art. Questions I also addressed in PLANNING UNPLANNED (2015).[6]

Such a spatial practice also expands the audience's reach of new associations and context. WITH VEILING HANDS (1999), which was shown in Secession, is a perfect example of how the context is being shifted by channeling a discussion on different roles in relation to its setting.

geschütztes Gebäude. Nach ihrer Schließung wurde sie zunächst von der Kunstuniversität Linz genutzt, dann in ein Event Center und einen „Kreativ-Hotspot" umgewandelt.

Danach arbeitete ich mit Angestellten von Bene weiter, einer High-End-Büromöbelfirma, die sich immer schon im Kunstbereich engagierte hatte. Daraus entspann sich eine jahrelange Zusammenarbeit. Es begann mit inszenierten Fotos mit den Angestellten von dem, „was unter dem Tisch passiert", die als Grundlage für eine permanente Installation von Leuchtkästen an der Außenfassade dienten. Ein Jahr später wurde ich eingeladen, ein Video über ihre Erfahrungen zu drehen, und danach arbeitete ich an Installationen im Inneren der Büroräume zum Thema „Spiel" im Verhältnis zu Arbeit, was mit meiner Ausstellung 1999 in der Secession zusammenhing.

Durch die Nähe deiner Position zur *critical spatial practice*[1] kommt bei deinen Projekten eine weitere Ebene hinzu. Hier besteht auch eine gewisse Parallelität zu Rosalind Krauss' Begriff des „erweiterten Felds"[2] – die Ausweitung der Kunstproduktion hin zur Architektur und ihrem Umfeld.

Diese Projekte, bei denen ich in Systeme von Unternehmen eindrang, ließen eine parallele Ebene entstehen, indem ich ein Vertrauensverhältnis zwischen den ArbeiterInnen/Angestellten und mir herstellte, einen Austausch auf Augenhöhe. Ich nutzte dazu meine Position als Künstlerin, als jemand, der vom Auftraggeber „nicht ganz ernst genommen wird", machte also quasi auf *„la perruque"* – wie Michel de Certeau das nennt[3] – für persönliche Gespräche. Die TeilnehmerInnen entschieden selbst, ob und welche Inhalte davon in die Ausstellung einfließen würden. So bot ich Menschen, die vermutlich nicht mit Gegenwartskunst vertraut sind und auch keine zeitgenössischen Ausstellungen besuchen, eine neue Erfahrung und Präsenz. Es ist eine Art stille Übereinkunft, während zum Beispiel Antje Schiffers ein Tauschverfahren entwickelte, bei dem sie als Gegenleistung für Gespräche ein Gemälde von einer Situation anfertigt, das sich die Person, mit der sie sprechen will, nach ihren Vorstellungen wünschen kann.

Meiner Meinung nach begannen diese frühen Projekte, neue Forschungsfelder in Verbindung mit der Idee des öffentlichen Raums zu erschließen.

Von der Auseinandersetzung mit Unternehmen bewegte ich mich mehr und mehr Richtung öffentlicher Raum, blieb aber weiterhin daran interessiert, unterschiedliche Öffentlichkeiten anzusprechen, zwischen Firmen und öffentlichem Raum auf der einen Seite und dem Kunstkontext auf der anderen. Was andere unter „Skulptur" verstehen, war für mich seit jeher das komplexe räumliche Setting, einschließlich möglicher Teilnahme des Publikums. Mary Jane Jacobs' bahnbrechendes Projekt *Culture in Action* (1993) in Chicago stellte den Skulpturbegriff radikal auf den Kopf, war revolutionär in seiner Umkehrung

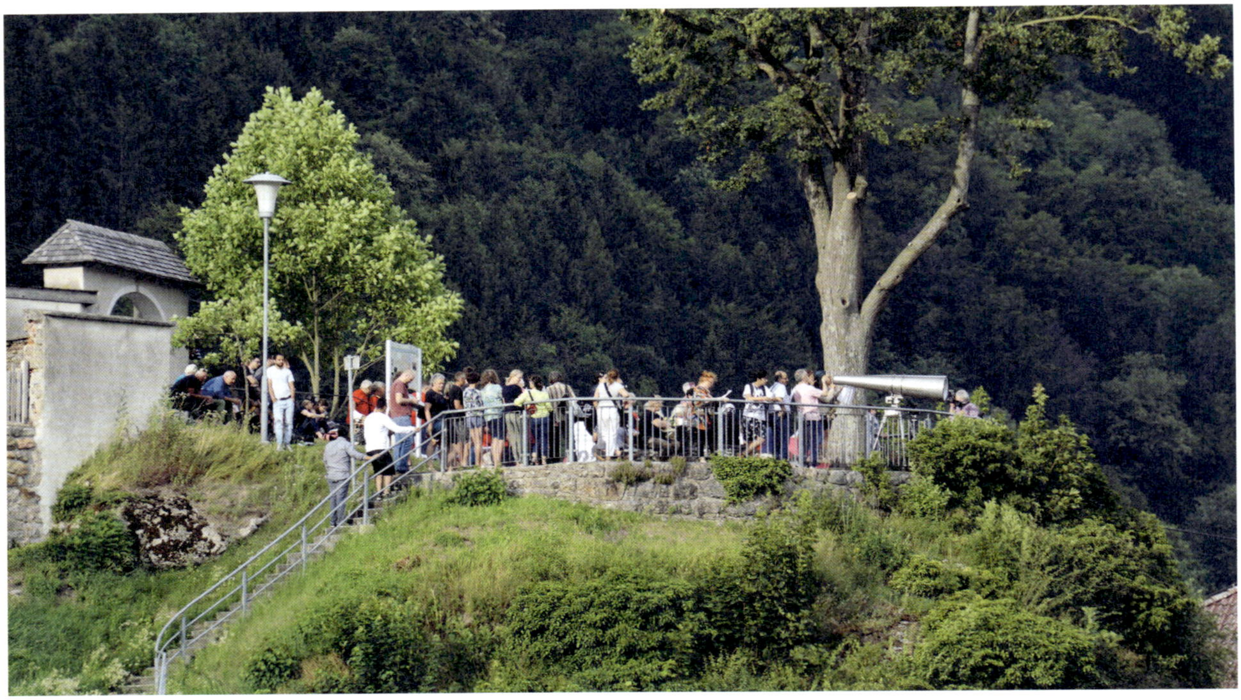

CALL AGAINST THE BORDER
St. Nikola (Upper Austria, AT), 2019 (transparadiso)
For the Festival of Regions, transparadiso addressed the flowing border that runs through the middle of the Danube between Upper Austria and Lower Austria. The megaphone sculptures (based on TIMES OF DILEMMA, see p. 206) transmitted a dialog developed together with residents of Strudengau.

RUF GEGEN DIE GRENZE
St. Nikola (Oberösterreich), 2019 (transparadiso)
Für das Festival der Regionen thematisierte transparadiso die fließende Grenze, die mitten in der Donau zwischen Oberösterreich und Niederösterreich verläuft. Die Megaphon-Skulpturen (basierend auf TIMES OF DILEMMA, siehe S. 206) übertrugen einen Dialog, der gemeinsam mit BewohnerInnen des Strudengaus entwickelt wurde.

WITH VEILING HANDS is a good example of how the experience of a piece I created for the headquarters of Porsche, Porschehof, in Salzburg, was shifted to the exhibition context. Based on interviews with the employees of Porschehof—in parallel to preparing the situation with Carrera race tracks in their lobby, which resulted in a large-scale installation right there—I held interviews with people from my art surroundings questioning the roles of "adultlike" and "childlike" behavior. The spatial setting at the Secession was also particular, since the visitors of the double video projection were seated in an "airport waiting situation," shifted 90° from the projection. So, they actually had to turn their heads to be able to watch the video or engage in conversations with the other "waiting" visitors.

Although WITH VEILING HANDS is a project dated 1999, it immediately gives the early indications of your artistic methodology and process, which undertakes a longer journey of the content and context that is not limited to one shot.

In a recent talk at the Royal College of Art (RCA) in London the question of latency came up. Projects lasting over time, are they ever finished? I re-examine conditions and at certain points they accumulate to having a public moment, a public appearance, an audience, and then they might submit to silence for a period, for being re-awakened in a different context. Withstanding and

der Tradition von Sculpture Chicago[4]. Es war für den Diskurs darüber, wie sich Kunst in gesellschaftliche Fragen einbringen kann, genauso wichtig wie das, was Jane Rendell, von der Architektur kommend, als *critical spatial practice* bezeichnet hat. Man könnte vielleicht sagen, meine Arbeit liegt irgendwo dazwischen. Und dann war da auch noch die Publikation DÜRFEN DIE DAS?[5], die die Frage in den Vordergrund rückte, ob es KünstlerInnen gestattet sei, sich mit gesellschaftlichen Fragen zu befassen, und wenn ja, wie, ohne dadurch die Autonomie von Kunst aufs Spiel zu setzen. Fragen, die ich auch in PLANNING UNPLANNED (2015) thematisiere.[6]

Eine solche Raumpraxis erreicht auch andere Publikumsschichten, über den Kunstkontext hinaus. Die Ausstellung MIT VORGEHALTENER HAND (1999) in der Secession ist ein frühes exemplarisches Projekt für eine Erweiterung des Kontextes, indem verschiedene Rollen in Bezug auf das jeweilige Umfeld diskutiert wurden.

MIT VORGEHALTENER HAND ist ein gutes Beispiel für die Verlagerung einer Arbeit in den Ausstellungskontext, die ich zuvor für das Porsche-hauptquartier, den Porschehof in Salzburg, geschaffen hatt. Ausgehend von Interviews mit Angestellten im Porschehof über die Rolle von „erwachsenem" und "kindlichem" Verhalten, die ich parallel zur Vorbereitung des Spiels mit den Carrera Rennbahnen führte – das schließlich in eine großformatige

counteracting notions of current demands and expectations, trying to engage in a kind of "choreography" that highlights silent or hidden poetic moments, the non-spectacular, whose relevance will only show over time and hopefully contribute to change in the individuals participating, in the audience who might have experienced these moments. John Cage's work altogether, but especially his *lecture on something* and *lecture on nothing* are seminal for me.[7] What is important? What is the material? Especially in the current situation of our world, with ever shorter attention spans, I find it even more important to engage in moments that last beyond the specific moment, that can trigger relevance for the audience and participants over a longer period. And here, chance and play have a significant role. The incalculable, the unexpected, the unplannable. Creating situations with clear parameters, which leave a space open to chance and play.

Speaking of creating situations, who is your audience?

Actually, my whole work has always been questioning the distinction between the author and the public/audience. In terms of reception and discourse, my first audience is the art community, be it the visitor of an exhibition or of a project in the urban public space or project intruding on corporations and systems, where other conditions are at play. Here the passersby are a general audience witnessing the artistic action and, when participants are involved, the border between "audience" and "actor" is blurred.

No matter if I engage in an exhibition context or in public spaces, I want to challenge the viewers to leave their position as "audience," as receivers, and rather trigger moments to actively engage. This means to create an ambivalence where the audience is not quite sure about their role in the situation. This was the case in early pieces like DRIVEN (1997) for the pickup truck gallery (by artist Matthew Girson) in Chicago, where I created an audio play to be experienced by the audience getting on this ride, exposing them to conversations with prostitutes in Vienna, and addressing their expectations as an art audience, asking them to experience the ride with a blindfold not knowing where the ride would take them in Chicago.

In the same vein, TIMES OF DILEMMA (2018) in Malta was quite exceptional as it merged the boundary between collaborator and audience. The collaborative process, through workshops, had already "created" the audience of the project during its preparation.

For TIMES OF DILEMMA we, *transparadiso*, actually achieved a rare collaboration between Għannejja—performers of Għana, a unique Maltese tradition of improvised dialogical singing considered folk, Għannejja mostly coming from a working-class background—and famous Maltese authors, who would usually, maybe, research Għana as scholars. Bridging the boundaries between

Installation in der Lobby des Porschehofs mündete –, interviewte ich Bekannte aus meinem Kunstumfeld zum selben Thema. Das räumliche Setting in der Secession war dann ebenfalls speziell, insofern die BetrachterInnen der Doppel-Videoprojektion in einer Flughafenwartesituation platziert wurden, die in einem 90°-Winkel zur Projektion stand. Sie mussten also den Kopf drehen, um das Video zu betrachten oder mit anderen Wartenden ein Gespräch führen.

Obwohl MIT VORGEHALTENER HAND bereits 1999 entstand, werden darin deine künstlerische Methode und deine Vorgangsweise ersichtlich, die du seither kontinuierlich weiterentwickelt hast.

In einem Vortrag am Royal College of Art (RCA) in London ging es kürzlich um die Frage der Latenz. Sind länger dauernde Projekte jemals abgeschlossen? Ich überprüfe die Rahmenbedingungen zu bestimmten Zeitpunkten, und die Projekte akkumulieren sich dann zu einem bestimmten öffentlichen Moment, in einem bestimmten öffentlichen Erscheinungsbild, für ein bestimmtes Publikum, und fallen dann eine Zeitlang in Stille zurück, um in einem anderen Kontext wiedererweckt zu werden. Es geht darum, sich Vorstellungen von aktuellen Erwartungshaltungen (von KuratorInnen, AuftraggeberInnen) zu widersetzen, sich an einer Art Choreografie zu versuchen, die die stillen, versteckten poetischen Momente betont, das Nicht-Spektakuläre. Dessen Relevanz wird oft erst mit der Zeit sichtbar und kann längerfristig zu einer Veränderung (im Denken und Handeln) bei den beteiligen Personen beitragen, beim Publikum, das diese Momente vielleicht erlebt hat. Das Werk von John Cage insgesamt, vor allem aber sein Vortrag *über nichts* und sein Vortrag *über etwas* sind für mich wesentlich.[7] Was ist wichtig? Was ist das Material? Speziell in unserer heutigen Welt, mit ihren immer kürzeren Aufmerksamkeitsspannen, halte ich es für wichtig, sich mit Momenten zu beschäftigen, die den jeweiligen Augenblick überdauern, die für Publikum und Teilnehmende von längerfristiger Relevanz sind. Und dabei kommen Zufall und Spiel eine entscheidende Rolle zu. Das Unberechenbare, Unerwartete, Unplanbare. Das Kreieren von Situationen mit klaren Parametern, die Raum für Zufall und Spiel lassen.

Apropos Situationen kreieren, wer ist dein Publikum?

Eigentlich ging es bei meiner ganzen Arbeit immer darum, die Unterscheidung zwischen UrheberIn und Öffentlichkeit/Publikum infrage zu stellen. Was Rezeption und Diskurs betrifft, so ist mein primäres Publikum die Kunst-Community, etwa die Besucherin einer Ausstellung, eines Projekts im öffentlichen Raum oder eines Projekts, das in Unternehmen und Systeme eindringt, wobei in Letzterem andere Bedingungen herrschen. In dem Fall bilden PassantInnen ein allgemeines Publikum, das die künstlerische Aktion miterlebt, und, wenn TeilnehmerInnen mit im Spiel sind, sin dem sich die Grenze zwischen Publikum und AkteurIn verwischt.

these very different notions of culture was an intensive process that required an openness from both sides, open also to a nonpreliminary determined result. The Għannejja accepted that, for the first time, Għana dialogs would be scripted and based on issues that had been collected in the workshops. They addressed the current challenges of urban life in Malta, especially the rapid urban transformation due to new construction, the privatization of Manoel island, and its impact on social and community life. Yet a renowned Għanej decided to not participate since he did not agree on writing texts that were not based on his personal interests since the goal of the project was to collectively decide on content. The Maltese authors transformed these issues into literature in the traditional verse of Għana, which means that they agreed on writing in a given format. An eminent role in this process had Rachelle Deguara, a young Għana-rapper, who had already engaged in transforming Għana into a contemporary format. At a certain point we learned that Mikkelina, a renowned older female Għanej, had stepped out. After we heard it was because she was illiterate, we decided that she would have the final voice after each performance, improvising in her way, reflecting on the dialogs and thus reconnecting to the tradition.

Sometimes the singing was carried away by the wind, thus surprising people in various locations in Valletta, on the ferry to Gżira and on Manoel island, a casual and chance audience who did not know where the singing came from, all of a sudden exposed to poetic texts addressing burning societal and political issues. A beautiful moment of silent activism...

Following up on the experience of TIMES OF DILEMMA, one of our big supporters, Chris Micallef (NIDUM, Malta), invited us, in 2019, to start a process for a "production of desires" for Sliema (the area next to Manoel Island also undergoing drastic urban renewal), enhance community engagement for discussing their heritage and existing values of communal life, and employ this method in the Maltese context. This resulted in a contribution to the exhibition *Public Architecture—Future for Europe* at the Shchusev Museum of Architecture in Moscow (2020).

Apart from the amazingly enriching process of TIMES OF DILEMMA, a surprising "reward" came later, in 2021, in the sense that the master plan for Manoel Island had actually been revised due to ongoing protests, drastically reducing luxury housing and instead granting more public space and access to the general public. Maybe TIMES OF DILEMMA did not only have an impact on the personal experience of the people directly involved, but also on a larger scale.

The same approach can also be detected in the iterations of ON THE SLIM PROBABILITY (2014). Even though you shifted the locations and the cities, you had

Ob ich nun im Ausstellungskontext oder im öffentlichen Raum arbeite, ich versuche das Publikum stets herauszufordern, seine Position als Betrachtende, als RezipientInnen aufzugeben und sich aktiv einzubringen. Das heißt, eine Ambivalenz herzustellen, in der sich das Publikum nicht ganz sicher ist, welche Rolle es in der Situation hat. Das war etwa so in frühen Arbeiten wie DRIVEN (1997) für die pickup truck gallery (des Künstlers Matthew Girson) in Chicago der Fall. Dafür produzierte ich ein Hörstück, das die Teilnehmenden während der Autofahrt mit Gesprächen mit Wiener Prostituierten konfrontierte und ihre Erwartungen als Kunstpublikum thematisierte, indem ich sie bat, bei der Fahrt eine Augenbinde zu tragen, sodass sie nicht wussten, wohin in Chicago die Fahrt ging.

In diesem Sinn war auch TIMES OF DILEMMA (2018) auf Malta außergewöhnlich, da die Arbeit die Grenze zwischen Mitwirkenden und Publikum verwischte. Der kollaborative Prozess – in Workshops – hatte bereits in der Vorbereitungsphase das Publikum „geschaffen".

Bei TIMES OF DILEMMA konnten wir, transparadiso, tatsächlich eine ungewöhnliche Zusammenarbeit zwischen Għannejja – meist aus der Arbeiterklasse stammende PerformerInnen des Għana, einer einzigartigen maltesischen Tradition improvisierten dialogischen Singens – und bekannten maltesischen AutorInnen, die Għana sonst eher aus einer wissenschaftlichen Perspektive betrachten würden, herbeiführen. Die Überwindung der Grenze zwischen diesen sehr unterschiedlichen Zugängen zu Kultur war ein intensiver Prozess, der von beiden Seiten Offenheit erforderte, auch in Bezug auf das Ergebnis. Die Għannejja akzeptierten zum ersten Mal, dass Għana-Dialoge geskriptet wurden, basierend auf in den Workshops gesammelten Themen. Sie handelten von den aktuellen Herausforderungen des urbanen Lebens in Malta, vor allem der raschen urbanen Transformation der Städte durch groß angelegte Neubauten, die Privatisierung der Manoel-Insel und deren Auswirkungen auf das soziale Leben und die Gemeinschaft. Ein bekannter Għanej verweigerte die Mitwirkung, weil er nicht mit dem Schreiben von Texten einverstanden war, die nicht auf seinen persönlichen Interessen beruhten, während es das Ziel des Projekts war, sich gemeinsam auf den Inhalt zu einigen. Die maltesischen AutorInnen setzten die Themen dann in Literatur um, verfasst im traditionellen Għana-Vers, akzeptierten also, in einem vorgegebenen Format zu schreiben. Eine wichtige Rolle im gesamten Prozess kam Rachelle Deguara zu, einer jungen Għana-Rapperin, die Għana bereits in ein zeitgenössisches Format transformiert hatte. Irgendwann hörten wir, dass Mikkelina, eine bekannte ältere Għanej, ausgestiegen sei. Als wir erfuhren, dass es daran lag, dass sie Analphabetin war, beschlossen wir, ihr die letzte Stimme in jeder Aufführung zu geben, sie auf ihre übliche Weise improvisieren zu lassen, indem sie mittels Spirtu Pront die Dialoge „kommentierte".

Manchmal wurde der Gesang vom Wind davongetragen und überraschte so Leute an verschiedenen Orten in Valletta,

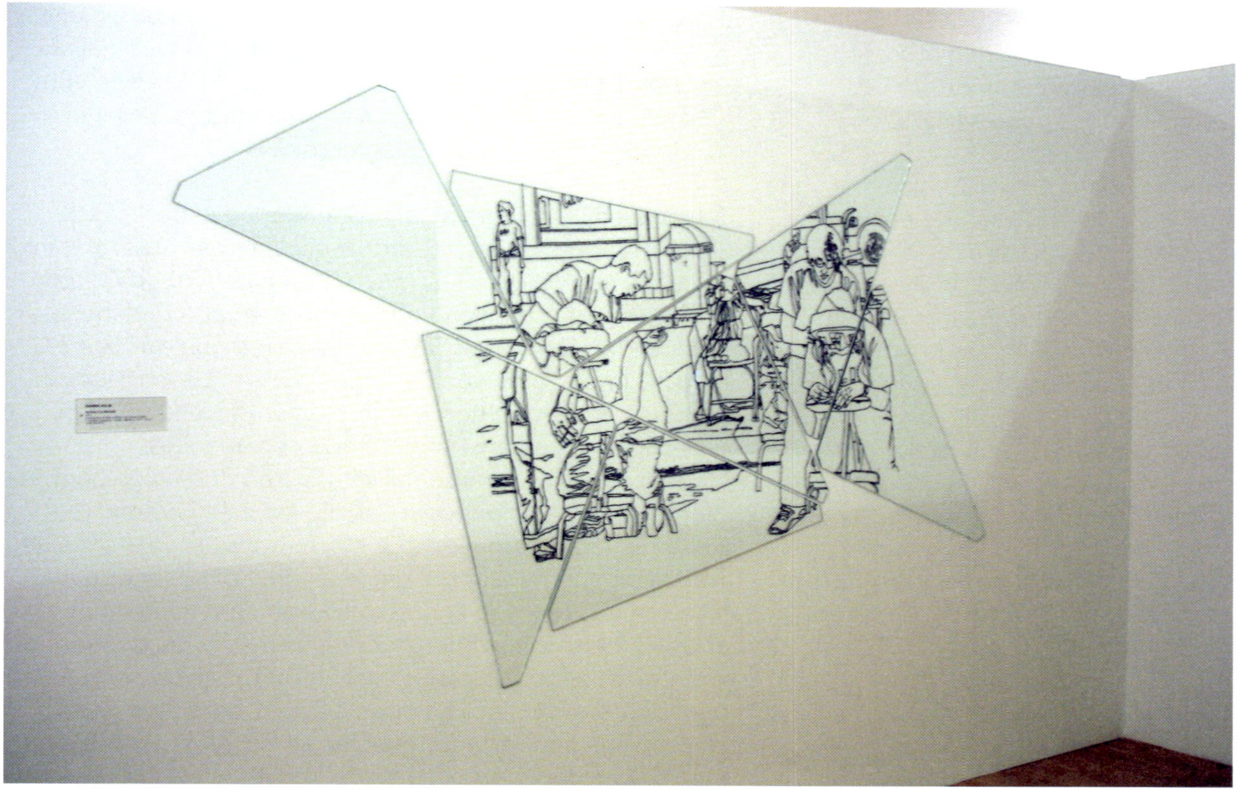

MASSAGE À LA MEXICANA, in: Austria: 1900–2000/Confrontations and Continuities, Essl Collection, Klosterneuburg (AT), 2006

MASSAGE À LA MEXICANA, in: Österreich: 1900–2000/Konfrontationen und Kontinuitäten, Sammlung Essl, Klosterneuburg (AT), 2006

> different audiences that were sharing almost similar situations and living conditions despite the fact that they were subject to different gentrification processes.

Actually, the contexts in the two sites in Berlin and Vienna were quite the opposite. We, as transparadiso, conceived ON THE SLIM PROBABILITY for the horseracing track in Karlshorst, in former East Berlin. Exploring the notion of game and play for *Part of the Game*[8] we decided to concentrate on betting at this horse race track, which had not yet undergone a new "business plan"—as, for example, the horserace track Hoppegarten, also in former East Berlin, which was revitalized as a commercial venue. Karlshorst was a remnant from the GDR, not yet undergoing the gentrification process, still maintaining the quality of sharing an experience without necessarily having to consume (people could bring their own food), offering a meeting place for the community. Therefore, we offered bets dedicated to emphasizing community values rather than mere interests of economical profit. The winning bet was "revaluation contributes to the prosperity of this quarter." The prize for the winning bet was "gilding a gully cover at the corner of Treskower Allee/ Am Carlsgarten." This publicly performed-yet-clandestine action raised awareness about a seemingly insignificant infrastructure, reattributing it a new value, as a real but also symbolic gesture for under-recognized community values. We came back to that gesture in HARBOUR FOR CULTURES (2018), for which we gilded a bollard in the Old Harbor of Trieste, revaluating objects we take

auf der Fähre nach Gżira oder auf der Manoel- Insel. Auf diese Weise wurde ein zufälliges Publikum, das nicht wusste, woher der Gesang kam, plötzlich mit poetischen Texten über drängende gesellschaftliche und politische Probleme konfrontiert. Ein schöner Moment des stillen Aktivismus ...

Aufgrund der Erfahrung mit Times of Dilemma lud uns einer unserer großen Förderer, Chris Micallef (NIDUM, Malta), 2019 ein, eine „Wunschproduktion" für Sliema (ein Nachbarviertel der Manoel-Insel, das ebenfalls einem massiven Stadtumbau ausgesetzt war) zu starten, um das Community-Engagement in Bezug auf das eigene Erbe und die existierenden Werte des Lebens im Viertel anzuregen. Dies führte schließlich zu einem Beitrag für die Ausstellung *Public Architecture–Future for Europe* am Shchusev Museum of Architecture in Moskau (2020).

Ein überraschender Erfolg für TIMES OF DILEMMA, abgesehen vom bereichernden Arbeitsprozess, stellte sich 2021 ein, als der Masterplan für die Manoel-Insel aufgrund der fortgesetzten Proteste dahingehend revidiert wurde, dass das Gebiet für die geplanten Luxuswohnungen reduziert und stattdessen mehr öffentlicher Raum und Zugang für die Allgemeinheit geschaffen wurde. Vielleicht wirkte sich TIMES OF DILEMMA nicht nur auf die persönliche Erfahrung der beteiligten Personen, sondern auch auf einer breiteren Ebene aus.

Derselbe Ansatz findet sich auch im Projekt AUF DIE GERINGE WAHRSCHEINLICHKEIT (2014) wieder.

for granted as a promise to install a HARBOUR FOR CULTURES Centre at Porto Vecchio, which is currently destined to undergo urban development without the notion to consider cultural or communal values.

When we were invited to k48, a project space in Vienna directed by Oliver Hangl, we decided to come back to the horserace track Krieau, at which I had already engaged, for SPIELEN, BEGEHREN, BRAUCHEN (1998) exploring the ambivalence of hidden and obvious desires between gambling, betting, and prostitution (which also contributed to DRIVEN) in various contexts of the Prater in Vienna.

Meanwhile, the horse race track Krieau is the last remnant of this formerly glorious urban public space where people from different social backgrounds mingled, since it was accessible for everybody. Today it is surrounded by "Viertel Zwei," a new luxurious quarter of urban development consisting of office buildings and housing, amputated of its context.

What themes do you pursue in your work?

To undermine and question systems—of belief, of norms—to expand physical and mental borders of thinking and acting, to encourage visions that go beyond the seemingly doable. Unveiling the hidden—hidden potentials—giving space to what seems to be difficult, not accepted by dominant power structures. Altogether (and formulated very generally) throughout my projects I have been interested in questioning the role art can play in society. Revealing existing and positioning new, poetic moments has become increasingly important in my work, together with play and giving space to humor. Connecting diverse audiences while respecting and highlighting their specific backgrounds and modes of reception, but exposing them to something unfamiliar; reading situations from a different perspective. Nothing is too mundane to be considered "material" for my work, drawing attention to the unspectacular, the "normal," where the majority of people's lives play out and what people are busy with. If we believe that art can contribute to societal issues—this is where the attention of the art community and art market, which has increasingly reduced art to a commodity good, is lacking.

At the same time, your approach to collaboration designates a "rhizomatic" structure.

Precisely. In the same line of thinking, Jane Rendell's index does not only connect the different layers of my projects and pieces, but it also shows the rhizomatic structure of my thinking and working, always in progress. What might have been lost in the last project can be reconsidered in the next. Currently I'm facing a wonderful challenge of exemplifying and realizing this rhizomatic structure of my thinking for WE PARAPOM!, a flagship project for the European Capital of Culture in Chemnitz 2025, which dives into the depth of the society in Chemnitz and its

An den Orten der beiden Interventionen in Berlin und Wien waren die TeilnehmerInnen mit unterschiedlichen Lebensbedingungen konfrontiert, die die Stadien von möglicher zukünftiger bzw. bereits stattgefundener Gentrifizierung widerspiegelten.

Tatsächlich waren die beiden Situationen in Berlin und Wien in Bezug auf ihren Kontext sehr gegensätzlich. transparadiso entwickelte AUF DIE GERINGE WAHRSCHEINLICHKEIT ursprünglich für die Trabrennbahn Karlshorst im ehemaligen Ostberlin. Für die Untersuchung des Spielbegriffs im Rahmen von *Part of the Game*[8] beschäftigten wir uns mit Wetten und wählten dafür diese Rennbahn, weil sie noch keinem neuen Businessplan folgte – im Gegensatz etwa zur ebenfalls im Osten Berlins gelegenen Pferderennbahn Hoppegarten, die in einen kommerziellen Veranstaltungsort transformiert worden war. In der Trabrennbahn Karlshorst, die in einem noch nicht gentrifizierten Viertel liegt, konnte man noch gemeinsam etwas erleben, ohne konsumieren zu müssen (die BesucherInnen konnten ihr eigenes Essen mitbringen). Es war ein Treffpunkt für die lokale Community. Daher boten wir dort Wetten an, die Werte für die Gemeinschaft anstatt ökonomische Gewinninteressen fördern sollten. Die SiegerInnenwette lautete „Aufwertung trägt zum Wohlstand dieses Viertels bei" und der Preis bestand in der „Vergoldung eines Gully-Deckels an der Ecke Treskowallee/Am Carlsgarten". Diese öffentlich, aber diskret durchgeführte Aktion förderte das Bewusstsein für ein scheinbar unbedeutendes Stück Infrastruktur. Sie verlieh ihm einen neuen Wert in Form einer realen, aber auch symbolischen Geste gegenüber geringgeschätzten Gemeinschaftsgütern – eine Geste, zu der wir bei HARBOUR FOR CULTURES (2018) zurückkehrten. Dort haben wir einen Poller im alten Hafen von Triest vergoldet, also ein Objekt umgewertet, um damit ein Versprechen für die Realisierung des HARBOUR FOR CULTURES Center zu positionieren – ein transdisziplinäres, zeitgenössisches Kunst- und Kulturzentrum, das insbesondere wichtig wäre, da in den aktuellen Planungen für den Porto Vecchio kulturelle oder gemeinschaftliche Werte kaum berücksichtigt sind.

Als wir vom k48, einem von Oliver Hangl geleiteten Projektraum in Wien, eingeladen wurden, beschlossen wir, wieder an der Trabrennbahn Krieau zu arbeiten, wo ich bereits für SPIELEN, BEGEHREN, BRAUCHEN (1998) die Ambivalenz verborgener und offensichtlicher Wünsche – zwischen Glückspiel, Wetten und Prostitution (was dann auch in DRIVEN einfloss) – in verschiedenen Kontexten des Praters untersuchte.

Mittlerweile ist die Trabrennbahn Krieau der letzte Rest dieses einst gloriosen öffentlichen Stadtraums, in dem sich Leute aus verschiedensten sozialen Milieus mischten, weil er für alle zugänglich war. Heute ist die Trabrennbahn vom „Viertel Zwei" umgeben, einem von diesem Kontext abgekoppelten neuen Luxusquartier aus Büro- und Wohngebäuden.

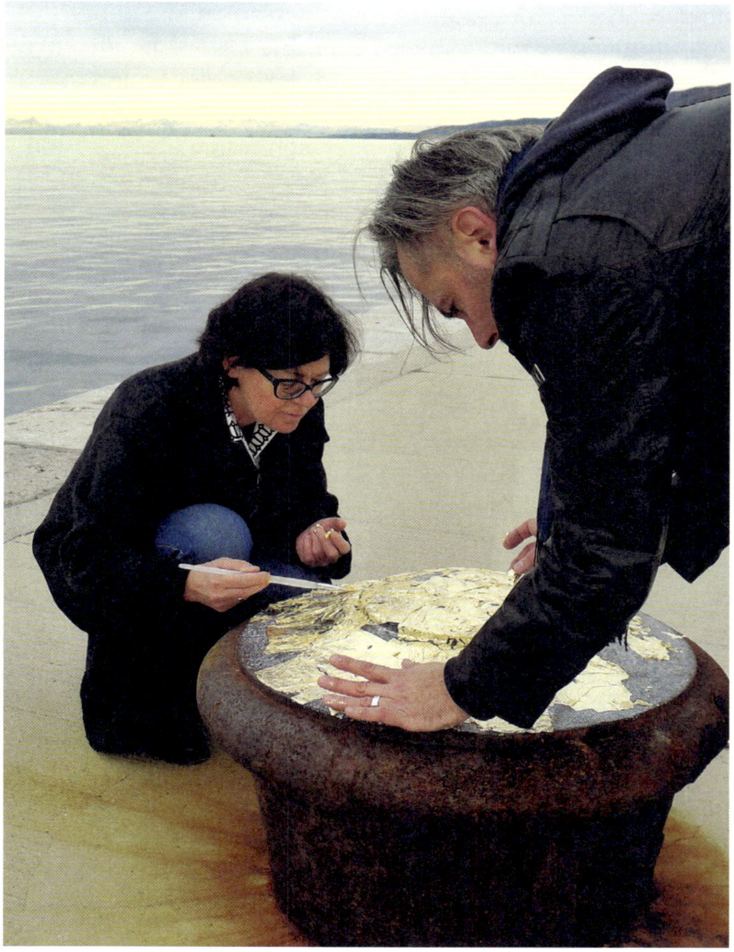

A PROMISE FOR HARBOUR FOR CULTURES, Porto Vecchio, Trieste, Jan. 2, 2018 (transparadiso)
In a clandestine action, transparadiso gilded a bollard as a sign for revaluation—as a vision for the realization of the 100 DESIRES FOR HARBOUR FOR CULTURES (see p. 98).

A PROMISE FOR HARBOUR FOR CULTURES, Porto Vecchio, Triest, 2. Januar 2018 (transparadiso)
In einer klandestinen Aktion vergoldete transparadiso einen Poller als Zeichen für Umwertung – als Vision für die Realisierung der 100 DESIRES FOR HARBOUR FOR CULTURES (siehe S. 98).

urban development, connecting climate and societal issues to participatory engagement and artistic interventions. I could imagine that in 2025 the terms Jane Rendell collected and selected in her index could be re-investigated according to the various projects and complex strands of WE PARAPOM!, as a genuine engagement in non-hierarchical acting, as a promise and vision for a more just society, obviously not only in Chemnitz.

In terms of the societal actions that you would like to trigger with your projects, to what extent do you think there's a discrepancy between acceptance and adaptation?

I have to say that I never really cared about acceptance. I've always been in favor of minority, that also means minority audience, minority acceptance. I'm quite stubborn and undiplomatic, which makes things more complicated, but this is also a method I use to encourage others to withstand or reconsider expectations. I'm quite radical

Welche Absichten verfolgst du mit deiner Arbeit?

Ich möchte mit meinen Arbeiten Systeme, Überzeugungen und Normen hinterfragen und unterlaufen, Denk- und Handlungsräume ausweiten, Visionen fördern, die über das angeblich Machbare hinausgehen; Verborgenes – verborgene Potenziale – zum Vorschein bringen, dem schwierig Erscheinenden, von den herrschenden Machtstrukturen nicht Akzeptierten, Raum geben. Insgesamt war ich in meinen Projekten stets daran interessiert zu ergründen, welche Rolle Kunst in der Gesellschaft spielen kann. Zunehmend wichtig wurde es, in meinen Arbeiten existierende Momente aufzuzeigen und neue poetische Momente zu produzieren, dem Aspekt des Spiels und Humors Raum zu geben; disparate Publikumsgruppen unter Anerkennung und Beleuchtung ihres jeweiligen Hintergrunds und ihrer Rezeptionsweise zu verbinden, und sie dennoch mit etwas Neuem zu konfrontieren; Situationen aus einem anderen Blickwinkel zu betrachten; auf das Unspektakuläre, das Normale hinzuweisen, wo das Leben der Menschen und das, was sie umtreibt, zum größten Teil stattfinden. Nichts ist zu banal, um als „Material" für meine Arbeit in Betracht gezogen zu werden.

Gleichzeitig hat deine Herangehensweise an die Zusammenarbeit etwas Rhizomatisches.

Ganz genau. Auf ähnliche Weise verbindet Jane Rendells Index nicht nur die verschiedenen Ebenen meiner Projekte und Arbeiten, sondern zeigt auch das Rhizomatische meines Denkens und Arbeitens, das ständig in Bewegung ist. Was im letzten Projekt vielleicht versäumt wurde, kann im nächsten neu berücksichtigt werden. Gegenwärtig stehe ich vor der wunderbaren Aufgabe, dieses rhizomatische Denken mit WE PARAPOM! exemplarisch umzusetzen. Dieses ist eines der zentralen Projekte der Europäischen Kulturhauptstadt 2025 in Chemnitz, das tief in die Gesellschaft von Chemnitz und seine Stadtentwicklung eingreift. Es verbindet Klima- und Gesellschaftsfragen mit zivilgesellschaftlichem Engagement und künstlerischen Interventionen. Ich könnte mir vorstellen, dass die Begriffe, die Jane Rendell für ihren Index zusammengetragen hat, nach der Realisierung der verschiedenen Projekte und komplexen Stränge von WE PARAPOM! wieder neu untersucht werden könnten, als genuine Einlassung auf nicht hierarchisches Handeln, als Versprechen und Vision einer gerechteren Gesellschaft, und zwar nicht nur für Chemnitz.

Was das gesellschaftliche Handeln betrifft, das du mit deinen Projekten in Gang setzen willst, inwiefern siehst du da ein Spannungsverhältnis zwischen Akzeptanz und Adaption?

Ich muss sagen, Akzeptanz war nie ein Thema, das mich wesentlich beschäftigt hat. Ich habe mich immer für die Minderheit interessiert und eingesetzt, das heißt auch, für ein Minderheitspublikum, für Minderheitsakzeptanz. Ich bin ziemlich stur und undiplomatisch, was vieles verkompliziert,

in my demands of conditions, yet at the same time very open to input by my conversation partners, as ongoing dialog or polylog, by creating non-hierarchical situations. So here again, overtly emphasizing an ambivalence that counteracts the demand for direct or short "messages" or quick reception. An underestimated space which only art can offer in that way in our society. Of course, while developing projects, negotiations take place between the expectations of the commission parties and my own interests and adaptations are made, but I am very aware of my role as "artist-director." That means that adaptations must not harm the original intention of the project.

How do you define your political stance?

As an attempt, an approach, which I constantly reconsider and question, and as a result reconsidering my artistic means, I can only emphasize that I am engaged in how I, and (socially engaged) art, can contribute to a more just society. To produce pieces and projects that show the complexity of political issues and societal challenges and problems rather than leveling them or trying to find solutions. Actually, I am in favor of re-introducing the word "problems" rather than bowing to the euphemism of "challenges," which disguises the complexity of the issues we are facing. Artists are not problem solvers, but we can raise questions, uncomfortable questions. And "Imagine the Impossible (and work on it)," if I may come back to Issues[3] of the 10 ISSUES OF THE BLUE FROG SOCIETY. Probably, altogether, these state a very good position of my political stance, still valid after all these years.

What is your stance on activism?

As an artist, in my work, I am quite suspicious of activism in a direct sense. I want to offer situations in which others can engage and reflect upon the conditions I create without making them follow my beliefs. Therefore, the situations often have moments of ambivalence, where the audience or participants do not receive a clear message. For instance, in MORE OPPORTUNITIES (2007/2008) the banners for the staged demonstration were devoid of words or slogans, covered with reflective white paint. I realized over the years that this was a golden thread connecting my engagement in different cultural and societal contexts, and that's why I started to use the term "silent activism." Encouraging people to take matters into their own hands, and yes, to get active, but based on their own decisions, according to their own capabilities and capacities. This needs me to build trust and confidence throughout the process of engagement, of developing the project. How does activism relate to activation? I want to activate hidden potentials and qualities in people, poetic moments in specific contexts, moments to question the prevalent pressure to conformity, our lives being submitted to pragmatics and primarily economic interests.

aber auch eine Methode ist, die ich einsetze, um andere zu ermutigen zu widerstehen oder ihre Erwartungen zu überprüfen. Ich bin recht radikal in den Bedingungen, die ich fordere, zugleich aber – durch das Schaffen nicht hierarchischer Situationen – auch sehr offen für Input von GesprächspartnerInnen, in Form eines kontinuierlichen Dialogs oder Polylogs. Ich forciere also auch hier offen eine Ambivalenz, die die Forderung nach direkten oder einfachen Botschaften bzw. leichter Rezipierbarkeit konterkariert. Ein unterschätzter Raum, den in unserer Gesellschaft nur die Kunst bieten kann. Natürlich findet bei der Projektentwicklung ein Abwägen zwischen den Erwartungen der AuftraggeberInnen und meinen eigenen Interessen statt und es werden Dinge adaptiert, aber ich bin mir meiner Rolle als „Künstlerin-Regisseurin" sehr bewusst. Das heißt, dass eventuelle Anpassungen der ursprünglichen Intention des Projekts nicht zuwiderlaufen dürfen.

Wie würdest du deine politische Haltung definieren?

Ich würde meine politische Haltung als einen Versuch, eine Vorgangsweise beschreiben, die ich anhand meiner künstlerischen Mittel ständig überprüfe und infrage stelle, um herauszufinden, wie ich und (sozial engagierte) Kunst zu einer gerechteren Gesellschaft beitragen können. Meine Arbeiten und Projekte wollen die Komplexität der politischen Thematiken und deren gesellschaftliche Herausforderungen und Probleme aufzeigen, anstatt sie zu nivellieren oder Lösungen dafür zu finden. Eigentlich möchte ich Probleme wieder beim Namen nennen, statt den Neologismus „Euphemismus" zu verwenden, der die Komplexität der Sachverhalte, mit denen wir konfrontiert sind, lediglich verschleiert. KünstlerInnen sind nicht für das Lösen von Problemen zuständig, aber wir können Fragen aufwerfen, unangenehme Fragen. Und uns „das Unmögliche vorstellen (und daran arbeiten)", wenn ich Issue[3] der „10 ISSUES OF THE BLUE FROG SOCIETY" zitieren darf. Insgesamt geben diese wahrscheinlich meine politische Haltung sehr gut wieder. Sie sind immer noch gültig nach all den Jahren.

Wie stehst du zu Aktivismus?

Als Künstlerin, und in meinen Arbeiten, ist mir Aktivismus – in einem direkten Sinn – eher suspekt. Ich möchte Situationen schaffen, in denen sich andere engagieren und über die von mir angebotenen Bedingungen nachdenken können, ohne dabei meinen Überzeugungen folgen zu müssen. Darum wohnt den Situationen häufig ein Moment der Ambivalenz inne, insofern, als das Publikum oder die Teilnehmenden keine Instruktionen erhalten, wie sie sich verhalten sollen. Es gibt keine Erwartungshaltung, auch nicht in Bezug auf ein konkretes Ergebnis. So waren zum Beispiel die Banner für die inszenierte Demonstration in MORE OPPORTUNITIES (2007/2008) leer, ohne Slogans, lediglich mit weißer Reflexionsfarbe bestrichen. Mit den Jahren wurde mir klar, dass das eine Art roter Faden ist, ein verbindendes Element meines Engagements in verschiedenen kulturellen und gesellschaftlichen Kontexten, und so begann ich, den Ausdruck stiller

Even though I consider conflict a productive force for negotiating diverse interests, rather than leveling them, my work is based on dialog and collaboration rather than dialectics. Grant Kester coined the term "dialogical aesthetics," which he also elaborated in his talk and text for PLANNING UNPLANNED, an artistic research project I directed at the Vienna University of Technology.

When looking at the terms "direct" (as in "direct urbanism" / transparadiso) and "silent" (as in "silent activism"), they seem to be contradictory, direct versus silent. But they are closely linked. In certain moments the "direct" is more necessary and in the foreground, in others the "silent"—also in the sense of confidential—is more suitable to what I want to achieve. Direct engagement involves people, in a certain context, to produce a piece and sometimes also to (re)frame the setting and engage in producing the situation. At the same time, throughout, I use the process to hold private conversations on a parallel level, establishing a situation of confidence and silently addressing, and possibly activating, the hidden desires and potentials of the participants.

As I see it, the continuity among your projects provides a conceptual scaffold to read your practice as an ongoing undertaking. How does continuity—and sometimes repetition—manifest in your work?

The continuity manifests itself by learning from one project to the next. "Missing Things" as they can be read in the series of WORLD CONGRESSES OF THE MISSING THINGS (2014, ongoing), do not only show the different societal and urban contexts of the locations, but also the evolving changes in society over a longer period of time and therefore a change in what is felt as missing. And then it might turn out that certain missing things are quite similar, no matter what societal or cultural context. Researching new contexts and taking into account, of course, the specific parameters, yet referring to previous experiences. Continuity shows, especially, in returning to sites and re-addressing similar issues in different contexts. Again, THE BLUE FROG SOCIETY as an ongoing project, as a project in real space, and as a vision, together with the 10 Issues, could be considered the framework for continuity, for addressing overarching issues and connecting different contexts. The insistence on continuity and durational processes makes it also difficult at times, since I am suspicious of producing a spectacular visibility or flashy images. But I have to say that I consider repetition an important strategy: repeating as insisting, repeating in variations, of course, sometimes minor, sometimes major, sometimes more overt, sometimes more concealed, repeating what does not want to be heard, to be heard, to insist.

In the same way, each conversation around your work extends beyond its context. Each project compliments the next one and bespeaks fundamental issues

Aktivismus zu verwenden. Leute zu ermutigen, die Dinge selbst in die Hand zu nehmen, und ja, auch aktiv zu werden, aber basierend auf eigenen Entscheidungen und nach eigenen Kräften und Fähigkeiten. Das erfordert von mir, während des ganzen Prozesses der Entwicklung des Projekts Vertrauen aufzubauen. Wie verhält sich Aktivismus zu Aktivierung? Ich möchte verborgene Potenziale und Qualitäten in Menschen sowie poetische Momente in spezifischen Kontexten aktivieren. Momente, die den herrschenden Druck nach Anpassung, nach Ausrichtung unseres Lebens nach Pragmatik, Effizienz und ökonomischen Interessen infrage stellen.

Auch wenn ich Konflikte als eine produktive Kraft für das Verhandeln gegensätzlicher Interessen erachte, finde ich Dialog und Zusammenarbeit wichtiger und produktiver als Dialektik. Ganz im Sinne von Grant Kesters Begriff einer „dialogischen Ästhetik", wie er ihn auch in seinem Text für PLANNING UNPLANNED ausführte.

Hält man sich die Begriffe „direkt" (wie in direkter Urbanismus/transparadiso) und „still" (wie in Stiller Aktivismus) vor Augen, so erscheinen sie als Gegensätze: direkt versus still. Sie hängen aber eng zusammen. In gewissen Momenten ist das Direkte notwendiger und steht im Vordergrund, in anderen ist das Stille – auch im Sinn des Vertraulichen – besser geeignet für das, was ich erreichen will. Direktes Engagement bedeutet Menschen in einen bestimmten Kontext zu involvieren, um eine Arbeit zu produzieren, manchmal auch das Setting (neu) zu formulieren und an der Herstellung einer Situation zu arbeiten. Gleichzeitig und parallel nutze ich den gesamten Prozess für private Gespräche, um Momente des Vertrauens zu schaffen, um im Stillen verborgene Wünsche und Potenziale der Teilnehmenden anzusprechen und vielleicht auch zu aktivieren.

Meines Erachtens bietet die Kontinuität deiner Projekte ein konzeptionelles Gerüst, um deine Praxis als fortlaufendes Unterfangen zu verstehen. Wie manifestiert sich Kontinuität – und manchmal auch Wiederholung – in deinem Werk?

Die Kontinuität manifestiert sich im Lernen von einem Projekt zum anderen. „Missing Things" (fehlende Dinge), wie sie in der Reihe der World Congresses of the Missing Things (seit 2014) sichtbar werden, spiegeln nicht nur die unterschiedlichen gesellschaftlichen und urbanen Kontexte der jeweiligen Situationen, sondern auch die gesellschaftlichen Veränderungen über einen längeren Zeitraum wider. Andererseits können sich gewisse fehlende Dinge auch in sehr unterschiedlichen gesellschaftlichen oder kulturellen Kontexten als ganz ähnlich erweisen. Kontinuität zeigt sich vor allem durch die Rückkehr an frühere Schauplätze und das Aufgreifen ähnlicher Themen in anderen Kontexten. Auch in Bezug auf Kontinuität ließe sich The Blue Frog Society als fortlaufendes Projekt, als Projekt im realen Raum und als Vision, zusammen mit den „10 Issues", als Leitlinie für die Behandlung übergreifender Themen

in such a critical, but also generous, way that they are not only urgent, but also socially and politically binding. By analyzing the accumulation of your projects in time, Andreas Spiegl indicates in his text that you are establishing a sound artistic statement. I read it as a discourse on silent activism that you generate through your artistic methodology.

The shift from my training as an architect to the decision to work as an artist was a decision based on my experience in the architecture field, which is governed by the client. No sidesteps allowed. But that is exactly what I'm interested in, producing sidesteps, being uncomfortable, irritating, raising questions rather than providing "solutions," expanding the context, questioning again, insisting on a process rather than providing final results or "solutions." Today I'm even more convinced that this is what is needed. The more demagogic politicians operate, the more artists are called to action, to counteract and raise questions that address the complexity of our global society. There's no longer simply black and white. We need to create an awareness and sensibility for complexity. It lies in our own hands to change conditions. I want to emphasize that this must not be confused in any way with direct political or social work. I'm always acting from the position of an artist developing specific aesthetics for creating specific situations. The term "silent activism," which I coined some years ago, is still quite appropriate for producing visions of how art can contribute to society and address the political dimension in various and diverse cultural contexts through aesthetics and what I then exemplified as "artistic strategies": exploring missing and hidden agendas, putting the finger in the wound, challenging the expectations of commissioning parties.

In my earlier projects dealing with corporations, it was always important for me to build a situation of mutual trust and respect by sharing personal moments. As I mentioned, I was very aware of my role as an artist, considered "innocent" in a way, without the power to actually intervene in systems of neoliberal economy. But throughout the many projects I experienced, I realized that art actually has a strong and underestimated power because through these personal encounters real visions can be triggered in people. This shows that we must never underestimate the general audience and visitors who may not be accustomed to engaging with art. That's why I'm also suspicious of educational programs. Art must not "educate" in a direct way. For example, *Three Weeks in May* by Suzanne Lacy (1977)[8] is a seminal project, showing how art can intrude on systems (in her project collaborating with the LAPD / Los Angeles Police Department) and create many layers of addressing diverse audiences between the public realm and art exhibition context.

Exhibitions and art projects in public space must consider the participants (be they participants in the direct sense of actor, or viewers/visitors) as equals.

und die Verknüpfung verschiedener Kontexte betrachten. Das Beharren auf Kontinuität und länger andauernden Prozessen ist manchmal auch mit Schwierigkeiten verbunden, denn ich misstraue spektakulärer Sichtbarkeit oder knalligen Bildern. Dabei ist Wiederholung eine wichtige Strategie: Wiederholen als Beharren, natürlich in Variationen, manchmal kleineren, manchmal größeren, manchmal offensichtlicheren, manchmal unauffälligeren. Wiederholen, was nicht gehört werden will. Insistieren.

Ähnlich führt jedes Gespräch über dein Werk über seinen Kontext hinaus. Jedes Projekt weist auf das nächste hin und spricht fundamentale Probleme so kritisch, aber auch großzügig an, dass sie nicht nur als dringend, sondern auch als sozial und politisch unumgänglich erscheinen. In seinem Text, der die im Lauf der Zeit entstandenen Projekte analysiert, deutet Andreas Spiegl dein Werk als klares, fundiertes künstlerisches Statement. Ich verstehe es als Diskurs zum stillen Aktivismus, den du mit deiner künstlerischen Methode entwickelt hast.

Die Entscheidung, als ausgebildete Architektin meine Arbeit als Künstlerin fortzuführen, traf ich aufgrund meiner Erfahrungen in der Architektur, die von AuftraggeberInnen bestimmt ist. Keine Abweichungen erlaubt. Genau das interessiert mich aber, abzuweichen, unbequem und irritierend zu sein, Fragen zu stellen, statt konkrete Ergebnisse oder gar „Lösungen" zu liefern. Heute bin ich mehr denn je überzeugt, dass es genau das braucht. Je demagogischer PolitikerInnen agieren, umso mehr sind KünstlerInnen aufgefordert zu handeln, sich zu widersetzen und Fragen zu stellen, die die Komplexität unserer globalen Gesellschaft kritisch ansprechen. Wir müssen ein Bewusstsein und eine Sensibilität für Komplexität schaffen. Es liegt in der Hand jedes Einzelnen, zur Veränderung von Verhältnissen beizutragen. Ich möchte jedoch ausdrücklich betonen, dass dies in keiner Weise mit direkter politischer oder sozialer Arbeit verwechselt werden darf. Ich handle stets als Künstlerin, die eine bestimmte Ästhetik für die Schaffung bestimmter Situationen entwickelt. Der Begriff „stiller Aktivismus" erscheint mir immer noch adäquat, um zu benennen, wie Kunst Visionen entwickeln, zur Gesellschaft beitragen und die politische Dimension in unterschiedlichsten kulturellen Kontexten mit ästhetischen Mitteln ansprechen kann: Aufdecken fehlender und verborgener Agenden, den Finger in die Wunde legen, Erwartungen der AuftraggeberInnen infrage stellen.

In meinen früheren Projekten mit Unternehmen war es mir immer wichtig, durch das Teilen persönlicher Momente eine Situation gegenseitigen Vertrauens und Respekts herzustellen. Wie gesagt, habe ich mir meine Rolle als Künstlerin, die irgendwie als naiv betrachtet wird, als unfähig, tatsächlich in neoliberale Wirtschaftssysteme einzugreifen, bewusst zunutze gemacht. Im Lauf der vielen Projekte, die ich realisiert habe, habe ich immer mehr die Erfahrung gemacht, welch unterschätzte Macht Kunst besitzt, weil durch persönliche Begegnungen reale Visionen ausgelöst werden können. Das zeigt, dass wir

No matter is too demanding for the artist to communicate and convey their content and ambitions on the highest level. Otherwise, we anticipate and disgrace the participants/audience as "unknowledgeable."

Artists should be called on, as experts, to discuss the burning issues of society (on a parallel level to their art production), as the Artist Placement Group[9] (London) already exemplified in their seminal projects in the 1970s. Yet we have been facing an increasing divide, in recent years, between the art market—where art is handled predominantly as a commodity with speculation no different than stock exchange, whitewashing collectors' neoliberal economic agendas—and artists who engage in societal issues and the public realm. These artists and production fees are not equipped with similar budgets, nor are their works considered valuable collectors' items. So, as you can see, silent activism operates on many parallel levels, always ready to escape, yet present and alert.

1 This term was coined by Jane Rendell; see: www.janerendell.co.uk/chapters/space-place-site-critical-spatial-practice

2 In "Sculpture in the Expanded Field," Rosalind Krauss discusses the possibility of defining sculpture through four distinct categories that define the field as: (i) not-landscape and not-architecture, (ii) not-landscape and landscape, (iii) not-architecture and architecture, and (iv) landscape and architecture. By incorporating these expanded categories, Krauss allows for multiple definitions for an artistic practice that is perceived together with its setting. Rosalind Krauss, "Sculpture in the Expanded Field," October Vol. 8, 1979, p. 34.

3 Michel de Certeau, The Practice of Everyday Life, University of California Press, 1988. Arts de faire, the original in French, was published in 1980.

4 Culture in Action. A public art program of Sculpture Chicago curated by MaryJane Jacob, Seattle: Bay Press. 1995.

5 Eds. Stella Rollig and Eva Sturm, Turia + Kant, 2002.

6 Planning Unplanned. Can Art have a Function? Towards a new Function of Art in Society, eds. Barbara Holub and Christine Hohenbüchler, Nuremberg: Verlag für moderne Kunst Nürnberg, 2015.

7 John Cage, Lecture on Nothing/ Lecture on Something, in: Silence. Lectures and Writings, Marion Boyars London, 1968 (reprinted 2020), pp. 108–145.

8 Cf.: www.suzannelacy.com/three-weeks-in-may (accessed July 21, 2022).

9 Cf.: www.tate.org.uk/artistplacementgroup/(accessed August 30, 2022).

das allgemeine Publikum und BesucherInnen, die nicht mit Kunst vertraut sind, nie unterschätzen dürfen. Darum misstraue ich auch Bildungsprogrammen. Kunst darf nicht auf direkte Art „bilden". So zeigt z. B. die bahnbrechende Arbeit *Three Weeks in May* von Suzanne Lacy (1977)[8], wie Kunst in Systeme (in diesem Fall das Los Angeles Police Department) eindringen und auf vielschichtige Weise unterschiedliche RezipientInnen zwischen öffentlichem Raum und Ausstellungskontext ansprechen kann.

Ausstellungen und Kunstprojekte im öffentlichen Raum müssen die Teilnehmenden (ob nun direkte Mitwirkende oder BetrachterInnen/BesucherInnen) als ebenbürtig behandeln. Kein Inhalt und keine Ambition sind zu anspruchsvoll, um vom Künstler oder der Künstlerin nicht auf höchstem Niveau kommuniziert zu werden. Ansonsten würdigen wir die Teilnehmenden/das Publikum von vorherein als unwissend herab.

KünstlerInnen sollten als ExpertInnen eingeladen werden, zur Diskussion drängender gesellschaftlicher Fragen einen Beitrag zu leisten (auf einer gleichwertigen Ebene zu ihrer Kunstproduktion), so, wie das die Artist Placement Group[9] in London bereits mit ihren wegweisenden Projekten in den 1970ern vorgezeigt hat. Tatsächlich aber sind wir in letzter Zeit mit einer zunehmenden Trennung zwischen Kunstmarkt – wo Kunst oft spekulativ als Ware gehandelt wird und dazu dient, die neoliberalen, ausschließlich ökonomischen Interessen der SammlerInnen „reinzuwaschen" – und KünstlerInnen, die sich für Gesellschaftsfragen und im öffentlichen Raum engagieren, konfrontiert. Dennoch oder gerade deshalb ist Stiller Aktivismus weiterhin auf vielen parallelen Ebenen am Werk, immer auf dem Sprung, präsent und wach.

1 Dieser Begriff wurde geprägt von Jane Rendell; siehe: https://www.janerendell.co.uk/chapters/space-place-site-critical-spatial-practice

2 In „Skulptur im erweiterten Feld" erörtert Rosalind Krauss die Möglichkeit, Skulptur mithilfe von vier Kategorien zu definieren, die das Feld wie folgt bestimmen: (i) als Nicht-Landschaft und Nicht-Architektur, (ii) als Nicht-Landschaft und Landschaft, (iii) als Nicht-Architektur und Architektur und (iv) als Landschaft und Architektur. Durch Einbeziehung dieser erweiterten Kategorien ermöglicht Krauss eine Vielzahl von Definitionen für eine künstlerische Praxis, die zusammen mit ihrer Umgebung wahrgenommen wird. Rosalind Krauss, „Skulptur im erweiterten Feld", in: dies., Die Originalität der Avantgarde und andere Mythen der Moderne, hg. v. Herta Wolf, übers. v. Jörg Heininger, Amsterdam, Dresden: Verlag der Kunst, 2000, S. 331–346.

3 „Eine Perücke aufsetzen": siehe Michel de Certeau, Die Kunst des Handelns, Übers. v. Roland Vouillé, Berlin: Merve 1988. Das franz. Original, Arts de faire, erschien 1980, S. 71.

4 Culture in Action. A public art program of Sculpture Chicago curated by Mary Jane Jacob, Seattle: Bay Press. 1995.

5 Hg. von Stella Rollig und Eva Sturm, Turia + Kant 2002.

6 Barbara Holub und Christine Hohenbüchler (Hg.), Planning Unplanned. Can Art have a Function? Towards a new Function of Art in Society, Nürnberg, Verlag für moderne Kunst Nürnberg, 2015.

7 John Cage, Lecture on Nothing/Lecture on Something, in: Silence. Lectures and Writings, Marion Boyars London, 1968 (reprinted 2020), S. 108–145.

8 Vgl.: https://www.suzannelacy.com/three-weeks-in-may (Zugriff: 21.7.2022).

9 Vgl.: https://www.tate.org.uk/artistplacementgroup/ (Zugriff: 30.8.2022).

Part of the Game, nGbK, Berlin, trotting track Berlin-Karlshorst, 2014; k 48, trotting track Krieau, Vienna, 2014

ON THE SLIM PROBABILITY

Through a search of possible connotations and correlations between the action of betting and the notion of "fortune," transparadiso developed the project ON THE SLIM PROBABILITY. The project first took part in Berlin under the coverage of the exhibition *Part of the Game*, produced by nGbK and curated by Claudia Burbaum, Angus Cameron, Berit Fischer, Folke Köbberling, Pia Lanzinger, and Olivia Plender. Their focus was horserace betting as it draws a picture of where the poor and rich mingle paradoxically for an easy reach for glory in which temptation aligns with hope. At the trotting track of Berlin-Karlshorst (former East Berlin), transparadiso offered urban interventions addressing social qualities in the quarter rather than financial gains—as a promise to break given situations and living conditions. The winning bet was "Revaluation contributes to the prosperity of this quarter" and was realized by an urban intervention of gilding a gully cover on the corner of Treskower Allee and Am Carlsgarten.

The project was extended to a complex area of inner-city transformation in Vienna. On invitation by the k48 project space, the trotting track Krieau was used as a significant venue for another betting performance. As the last remnant of this former lively public space, once a meeting point for people from different social and financial backgrounds, the Krieau is now surrounded by a newly developed and luxurious business and housing quarter. As results of the winning bets, two performances addressed the changing profile of the area by referring its glorious past: Bet no. 3: "Social justice: Golfing for everybody," Bet no. 4; "On the winning side: Prosecco and finger food in formerly rundown entrance."

The participation of the public in these free bets symbolically revived the potential of these informal spaces for community.[BS]

A project by transparadiso

Part of the Game was curated by Claudia Burbaum, Angus Cameron, Berit Fischer, Folke Köbberling, Pia Lanzinger, and Olivia Plender, nGbK neue Gesellschaft für bildende Kunst, trotting track Berlin-Karlshorst; k48—Offensive for Contemporary Perception, Vienna; curated by Oliver Hangl

Part of the Game, nGbk Berlin, Trabrennbahn Berlin-Karlshorst; k48, Trabrennbahn Krieau, Wien, 2014

AUF DIE GERINGE WAHRSCHEINLICHKEIT

Auf der Suche nach möglichen Assoziationen und Korrelationen des Wettens mit der Vorstellung von Glück entwickelte transparadiso AUF DIE GERINGE WAHRSCHEINLICHKEIT. transparadiso konzentrierte sich dabei auf die Pferdewette, die für das Bild einer Welt steht, in der sich Arm und Reich im Streben nach schnellem Ruhm auf paradoxe Weise mischen und sich Versuchung mit Hoffnung paart. Auf der Trabrennbahn Berlin-Karlshorst (im ehemaligen Ostberlin) offerierte transparadiso anstelle eines monetären Wettgewinns urbane Interventionen, die soziale Qualitäten für das umliegende Viertel mit sich bringen sollten – ein Versprechen, das gegebene Situationen und Lebensbedingungen zu durchbrechen versucht. Die SiegerInnenwette „Aufwertung trägt zum Wohlstand dieses Viertels bei" wurde schließlich als urbane Intervention in Form der Vergoldung eines Gully-Deckels an der Ecke Treskowallee/ Am Carlsgarten, realisiert.

Fortgesetzt wurde das Projekt in einem komplexen innerstädtischen Stadtentwicklungsgebiet in Wien. Auf Einladung des Projektraums k48 wurde die Trabrennbahn Krieau als signifikanter Schauplatz für eine weitere Wett-Performance gewählt. Die Trabrennbahn ist letzter Rest eines vormals belebten öffentlichen Raums, eines Treffpunkts für Menschen aus unterschiedlichen sozialen Verhältnissen, und liegt heute inmitten eines neu entwickelten luxuriösen Geschäfts- und Wohngebiets. Zwei realisierte Wettgewinne thematisieren die Veränderung des Quartiers, indem sie auf die ruhmreiche Vergangenheit der Trabrennbahn anspielen: Wette Nr. 3, „Soziale Gerechtigkeit: Golfen für alle", Wette Nr. 4, „Auf der Siegerseite: Prosecco und Fingerfood in einem herabgekommenen Eingang".

Mit der Teilnahme der Öffentlichkeit an diesen freien Wetten wurde das Gemeinschaftspotenzial dieser informellen Treffpunkte und mittlerweile verlorenen öffentlichen Räume symbolisch wiederbelebt.[BS]

Ein Projekt von transparadiso

Part of the Game wurde kuratiert von Claudia Burbaum, Angus Cameron, Berit Fischer, Folke Köbberling, Pia Lanzinger und Olivia Plender, nGbK neue Gesellschaft für bildende Kunst, Trabrennbahn Berlin-Karlshorst; k48 – Offensive für zeitgenössische Wahrnehmung, Wien, kuratiert von Oliver Hangl

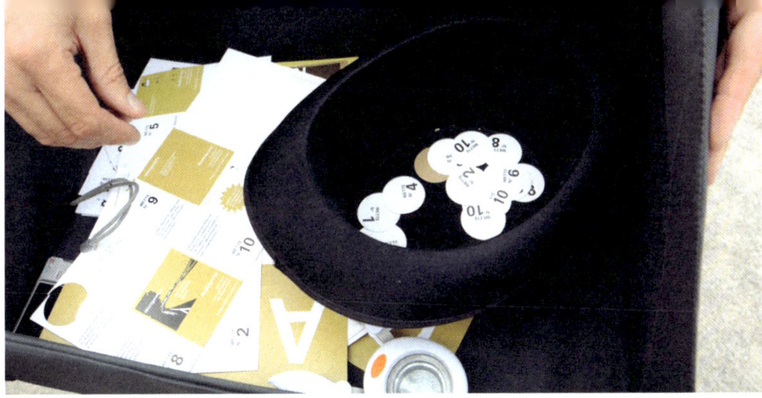

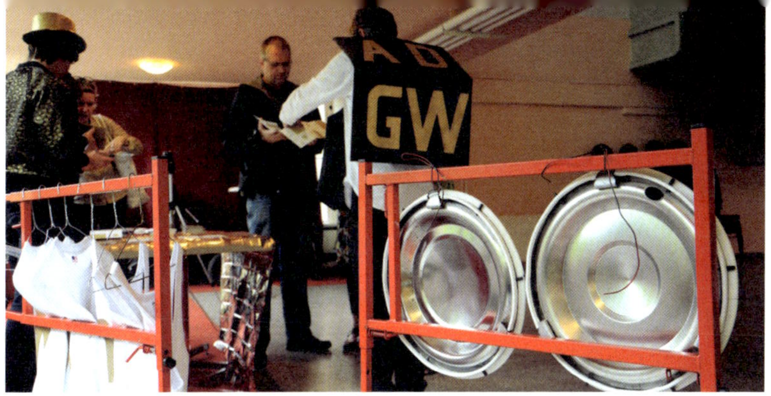

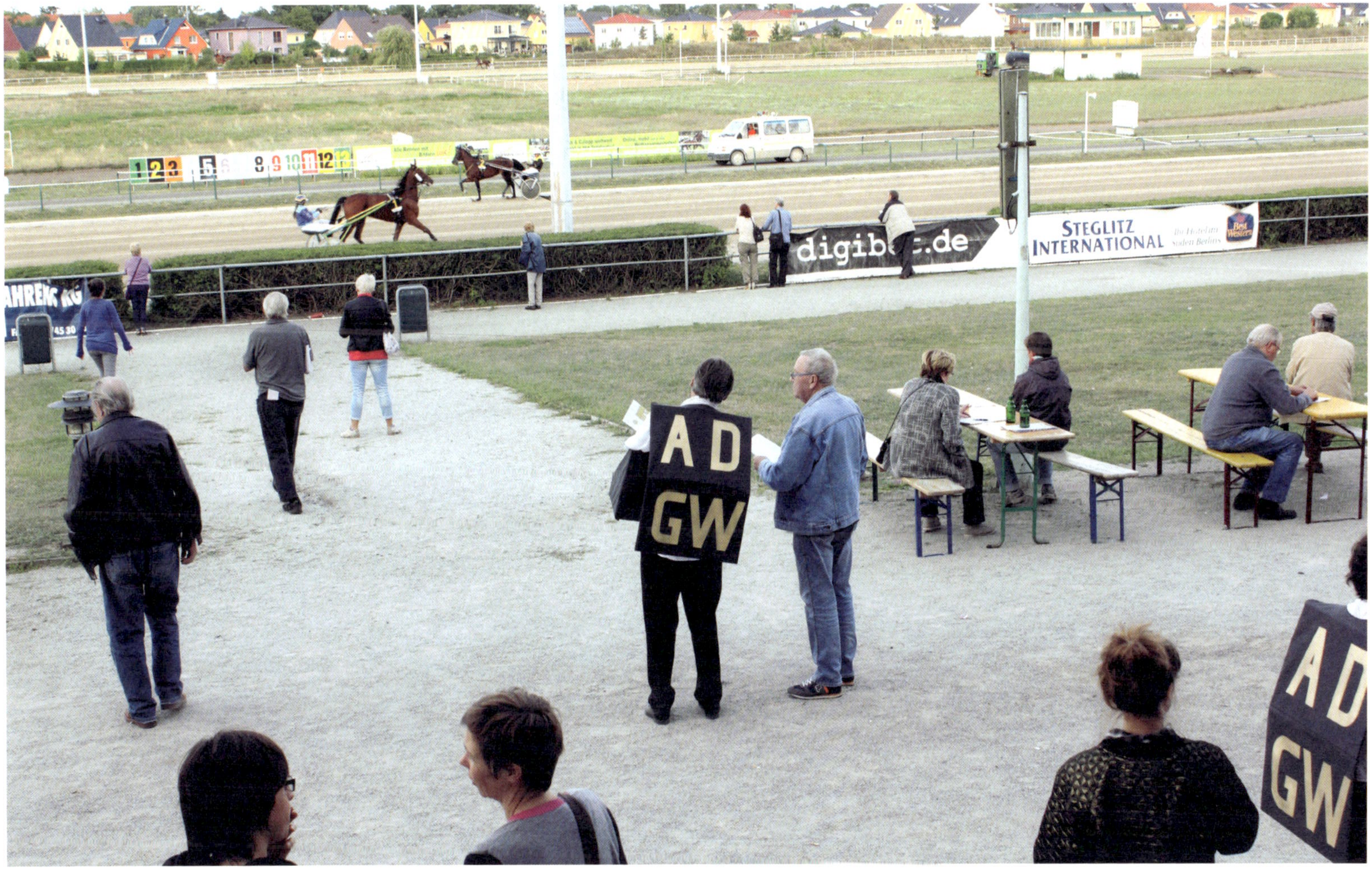

Trotting track Karlshorst, Berlin: offering bets

Trabrennbahn Karlshorst, Berlin: Angebot der Wetten

The bets offered were:

1. Revaluation contributes to the prosperity of this neighborhood
2. Redistribution
3. On the winning side
4. Social justice
5. My last shirt
6. I don't know how to go on
7. I feel comfortable in Karlshorst, therefore I would like to contribute the following:...
8. The game is a necessary deviation from the pressures of life.
9. The game is an abyss for all those who see this as the last straw.
10. I find social redistribution unfair – after all, I have worked hard for my prosperity.

Die angebotenen Wetten waren:

1. Aufwertung trägt zum Wohlstand dieses Viertels bei.
2. Umverteilung
3. Auf der Gewinnerseite
4. Soziale Gerechtigkeit
5. Mein letztes Hemd
6. Ich weiß nicht mehr wie weiter
7. Ich fühle mich wohl in Karlshorst, deshalb möchte ich folgendes beitragen: ...
8. Das Spiel ist notwendige Abweichung aus dem Druck des Lebens
9. Das Spiel ist Abgrund für all jene, die dies als letzten Strohhalm betrachten.
10. Soziale Umverteilung finde ich ungerecht – ich habe mir schließlich meinen Wohlstand hart erarbeitet.

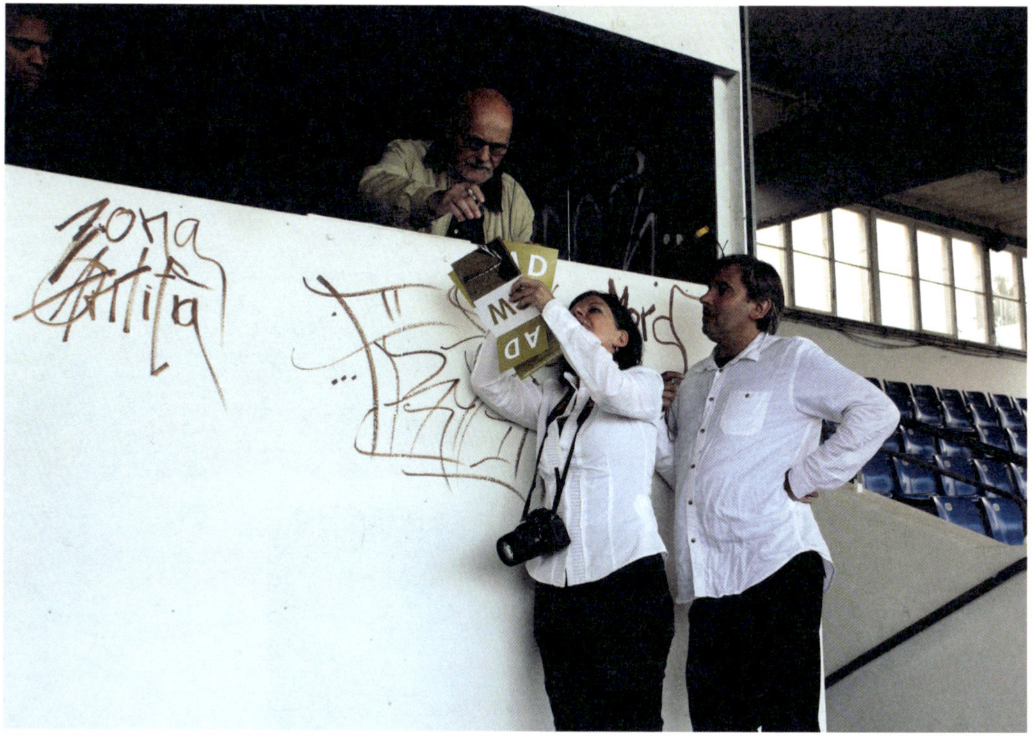

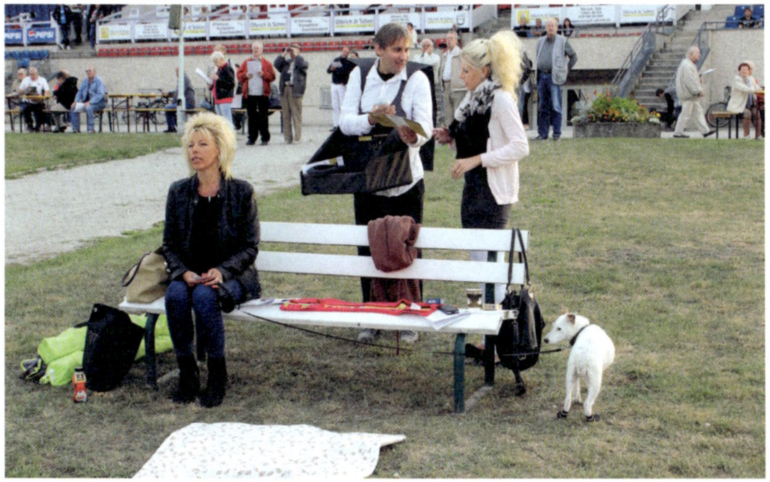

Public announcement of the winning bet #1 "Revaluation contributes to the prosperity of this neighborhood." Prize: gilding a gully cover

Öffentliche Ankündigung der Siegerwette #1 „Aufwertung trägt zum Wohlstand dieses Viertels bei", Wettgewinn: Gully vergolden

A1 transparadiso

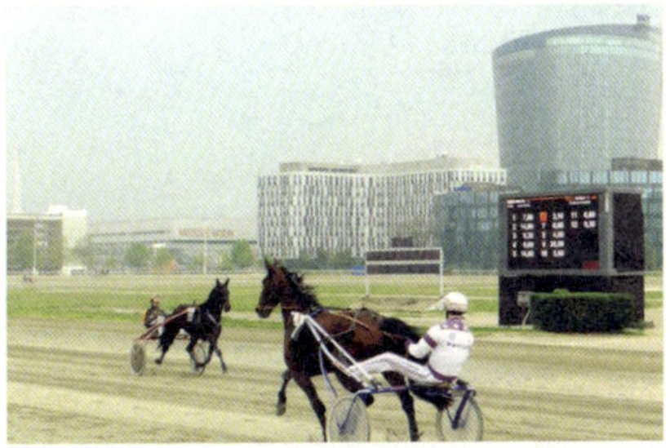

Setzen auf das Klientel

Zeitraum	1878–2014
Wutlevel	50%
Investoreninteresse	€ €
Ästhetik	Fin de Siècle

Das an den Wiener Prater angrenzende Areal der Trabrennbahn Krieau mit dem denkmalgeschützten Gebäudeensemble ist teilweise von Abriss und Umformung bedroht. Das Umfeld wird völlig neu strukturiert und weiter privatisiert. Bis dicht an die Trabrennbahn entstehen neue Bürokomplexe und private Luxusapartments. Der Wegfall informeller Qualitäten und die Ausgrenzung des weniger begüterten Publikums ist zu befürchten.

A2 transparadiso

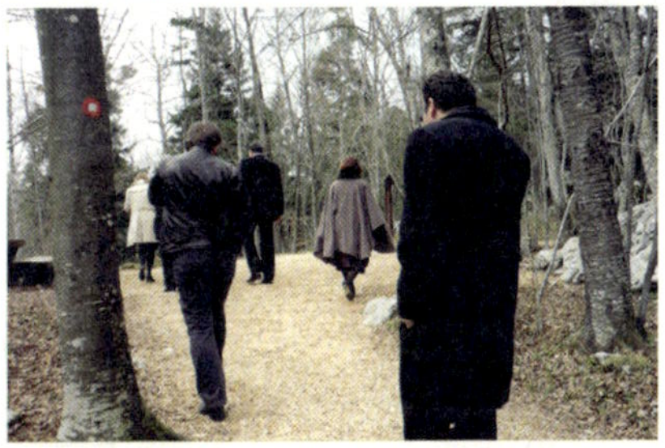

Spekulation auf Pleiten

Zeitraum	seit 2007
Wutlevel	95%
Investoreninteresse	€ €
Ästhetik	Börslaner-Schick

Hedgefonds spekulieren auf Kursverfall und die Pleiten von Ländern (Griechenland): »Offen ist aber noch, wie viele Gläubiger am Ende [bei der Rettung von Greichenland] mitziehen. Denn mittlerweile haben viele Hedgefonds griechische Staatsanleihen und entsprechende Ausfallversicherungen (CDS) gekauft, weil sie Finanzkreisen zufolge auf eine Pleite des Landes spekulieren. Sie hätten daher kein Interesse an einer Rettung des Landes.« (Die Welt, 12.01.2012)

A3 transparadiso

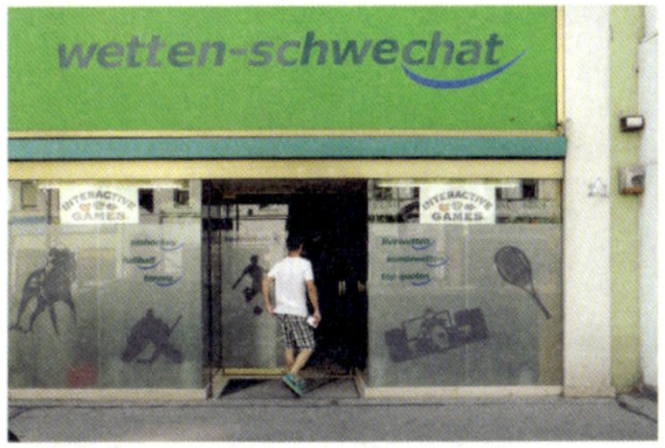

Die kleine Hoffnung

Zeitraum	seit 2000er Jahre
Wutlevel	50%
Investoreninteresse	€
Ästhetik	Falschgold

Wettlokale prägen – ebenso wie 1-Euro-Shops – zunehmend die EG-Zone, die aufgrund des Sterbens des Einzelhandels massive Leerstände verzeichnet. Anstatt dass die EG-Zone als Gemeingut zur Verfügung und damit von Verwertung freigestellt wird, sind diese Nutzungen Zeichen der »Hoffnung des kleinen Mannes« in prekären Lebensverhältnissen, die jenen jedoch oft noch weiter in Verzweiflung stürzen. In Wien-Margarethen haben sich auf 900 Metern 13 Wettlokale eingemietet.

A4 transparadiso

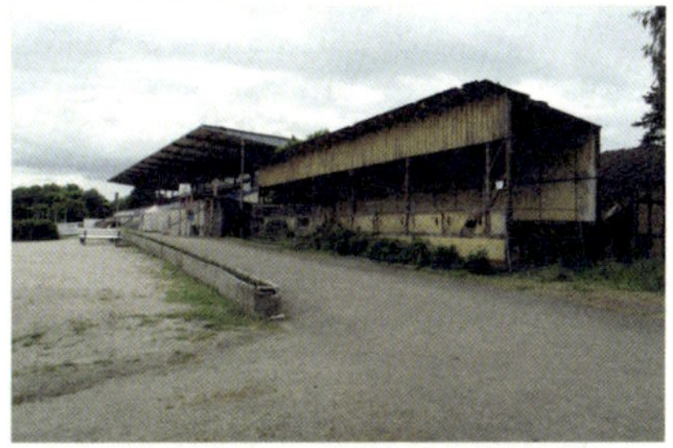

Auf die geringe Wahrscheinlichkeit

Zeitraum	1894–2014
Wutlevel	50%
Investoreninteresse	€
Ästhetik	Post-Ascot-Style

Auf die geringe Wahrscheinlichkeit bietet eine Wette auf dem Areal der Trabrennbahn Karlshorst an, die das Dispositiv des Wettens hinterfragt und neu interpretiert. Jenes Thema, auf das am meisten gesetzt wird, wird als urbane Intervention in Karlshorst realisiert. Die Devise ist: Spielen nicht auf Kosten von anderen – sondern gewinnen, indem man dazu beiträgt, einen kollektiven Wunsch zu realisieren.

As a "catalog," the playing card quartet *Part of the Game* was published by nGbK, Berlin, 2014

Als „Katalog" erschien das Quartett *Part of the Game*, herausgegeben von nGbK Berlin, 2014

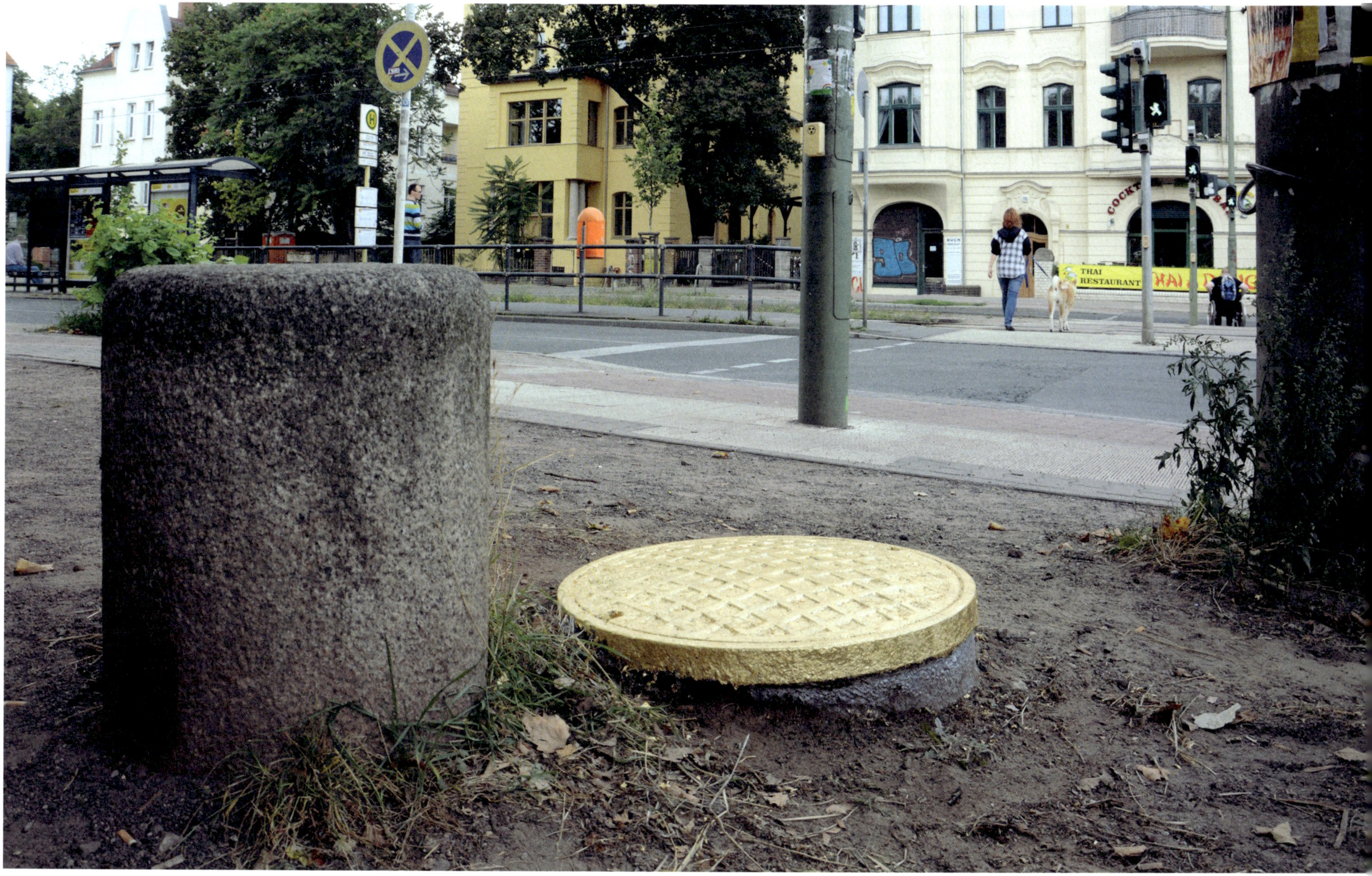

1st prize: Realization of the winning bet "gilding a gully," Treskower Allee, Berlin-Karlshorst

1. Preis: Realisierung der Gewinnerwette „Gully vergolden", Treskower Allee, Berlin-Karlshorst

Continuation of the project at the Trotting Track Krieau, Vienna

Fortsetzung des Projekts in der Trabrennbahn Krieau, Wien

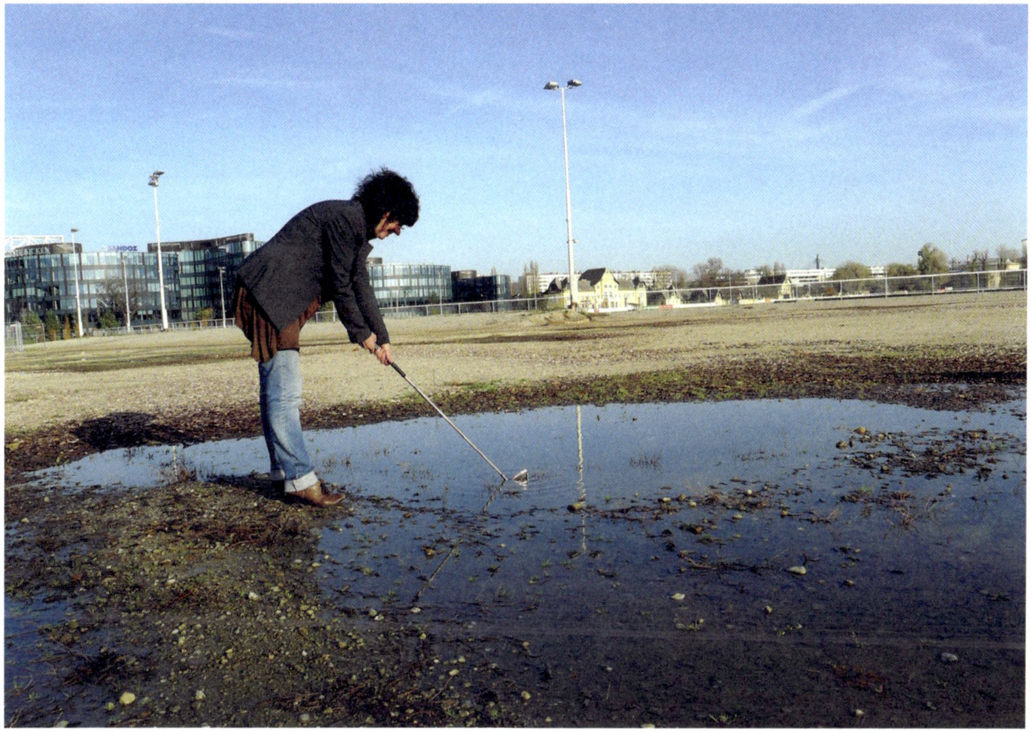

Realization of the winning bet #3 "Social justice." Prize: golfing for everyone

Realisierung der Siegerwette #3 „Soziale Gerechtigkeit", Wettgewinn: Golf für alle

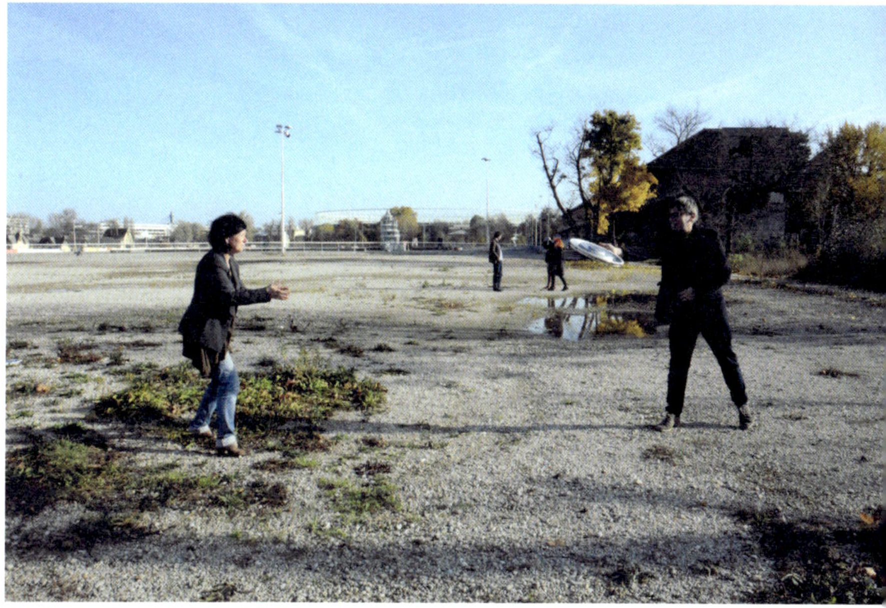

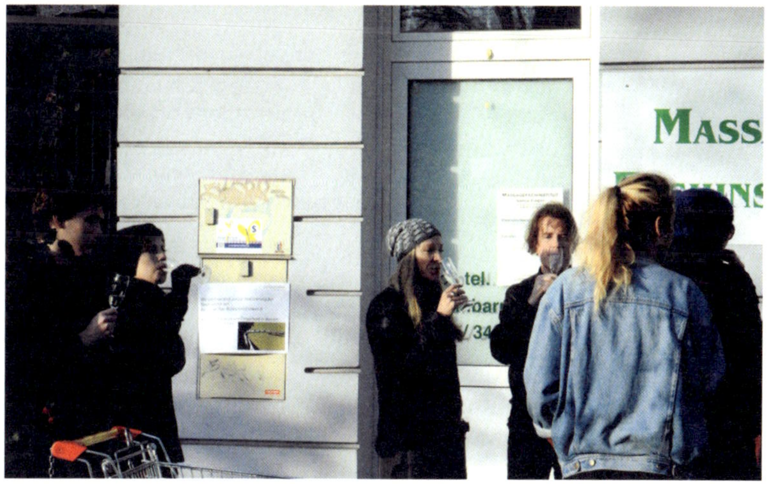

Realization of the winning bet #4 "On the winning side." Prize: prosecco and fingerfood in a previously rundown entrance area

Realisierung der Siegerwette #4 „Auf der Gewinnerseite", Wettgewinn: Prosecco und Fingerfood im ehemals heruntergekommenen Eingangsbereich

AT THE URBAN PERIPHERY

The identity of the outskirts of Vienna-Aspern has been experiencing a time of radical change in the course of transforming the former airfield at Vienna-Aspern into Lake-City Aspern. How will an identity be created for the inhabitants of this unspectacular gray area between city and countryside that continually shifts with the growth of suburban zones? AT THE URBAN PERIPHERY comprises a series of four "performative walks AT THE URBAN PERIPHERY" stimulating interpretations of this specific site at the periphery and rediscovering their existing qualities on site—potentials neglected in the masterplan. During her research, Holub detected a wild area next to the future Lake-City Aspern: the habitat of THE BLUE FROG SOCIETY, a species that had survived by counteracting the unlimited growth of urban development.

Holub's project includes the installation of billboards showing new drawings of, and for, Aspern based on photographs by the inhabitants, temporarily replacing the image campaign by 3420 Aspern Development AG. These drawings aimed at fathoming the potential of this in-between space "before the arrival of architecture," to allow for unplanned and unplannable wishes.

The contributions of the walks AT THE URBAN PERIPHERY served as the basis for *The Blue Frog Society Walks to the Moon* that Barbara Holub realized with Bruno Pisek, Anne Bennent and Dirk Nocker for Ö1 Kunstradio—today already a "quasi-historical" document for re-listening to visions.[BS]

AM STADTRAND

Der am Rand von Wien gelegene Stadtteil Aspern erlebt im Zuge der Umwandlung des früheren Flughafens Wien-Aspern in die Seestadt Aspern eine Zeit radikalen Wandels. Wie kann für die BewohnerInnen dieser unspektakulären Grauzone zwischen Stadt und Land, die eigentlich Visionen für eine „neue Stadt" imaginieren wollte, eine Identität geschaffen werden? Holubs Arbeit bestand aus einer Reihe performativer STADTRANDSPAZIERGÄNGE, die zu Interpretationen dieses konkreten Orts an der Peripherie und seiner existierenden Qualitäten anregen und Potenziale freisetzen sollten, die der Masterplan außer Acht ließ. Bei ihren Recherchen entdeckte Barbara Holub eine Wildnis neben der künftigen Seestadt Aspern – das Habitat der BLUE FROG SOCIETY – eine Spezies, die sich dem unbegrenzten Wachstum der angrenzenden Stadtentwicklung widersetzt hatte.

AM STADTRAND umfasst die Installation von Plakatwänden, auf denen – auf Fotografien von BewohnerInnen des Viertels beruhende – Zeichnungen von und für Aspern zu sehen waren, die vorübergehend die Image-Kampagne der 3420 Aspern Development AG ersetzten. Diese Zeichnungen versuchten das Potenzial des Zwischenraums „vor der Architektur" auszuloten und Platz für ungeplante und unplanbare Wünsche zu schaffen.

Die Beiträge der Stadtrandspaziergänge dienten als Grundlage für das Hörstück *Die Blue Frog Society spaziert auf den Mond*, das Barbara Holub mit Bruno Pisek, Anne Bennent und Dirk Nocker für Ö1 Kunstradio realisierte – heute bereits ein „quasihistorisches" Dokument zum Nachhören von Visionen.[BS]

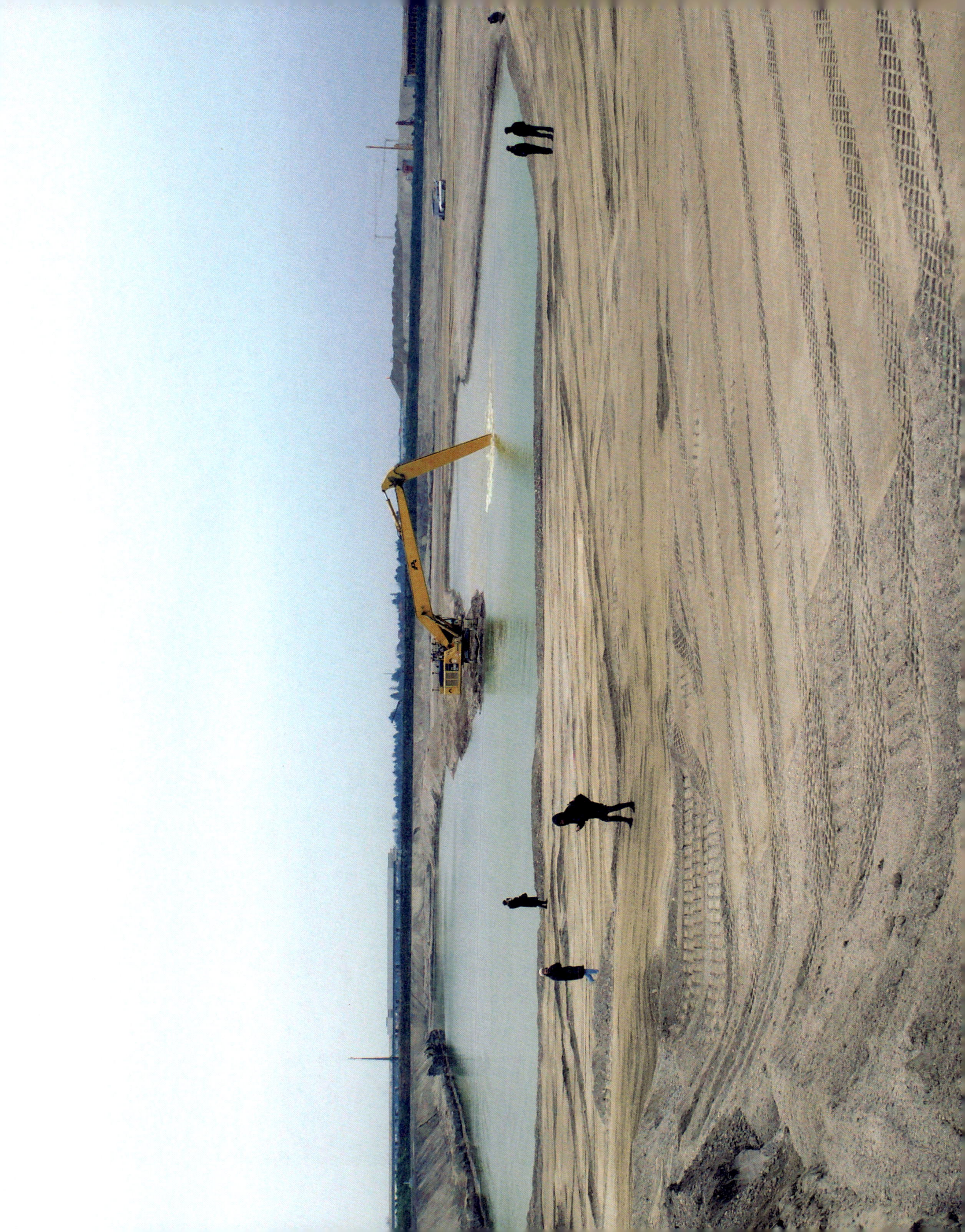

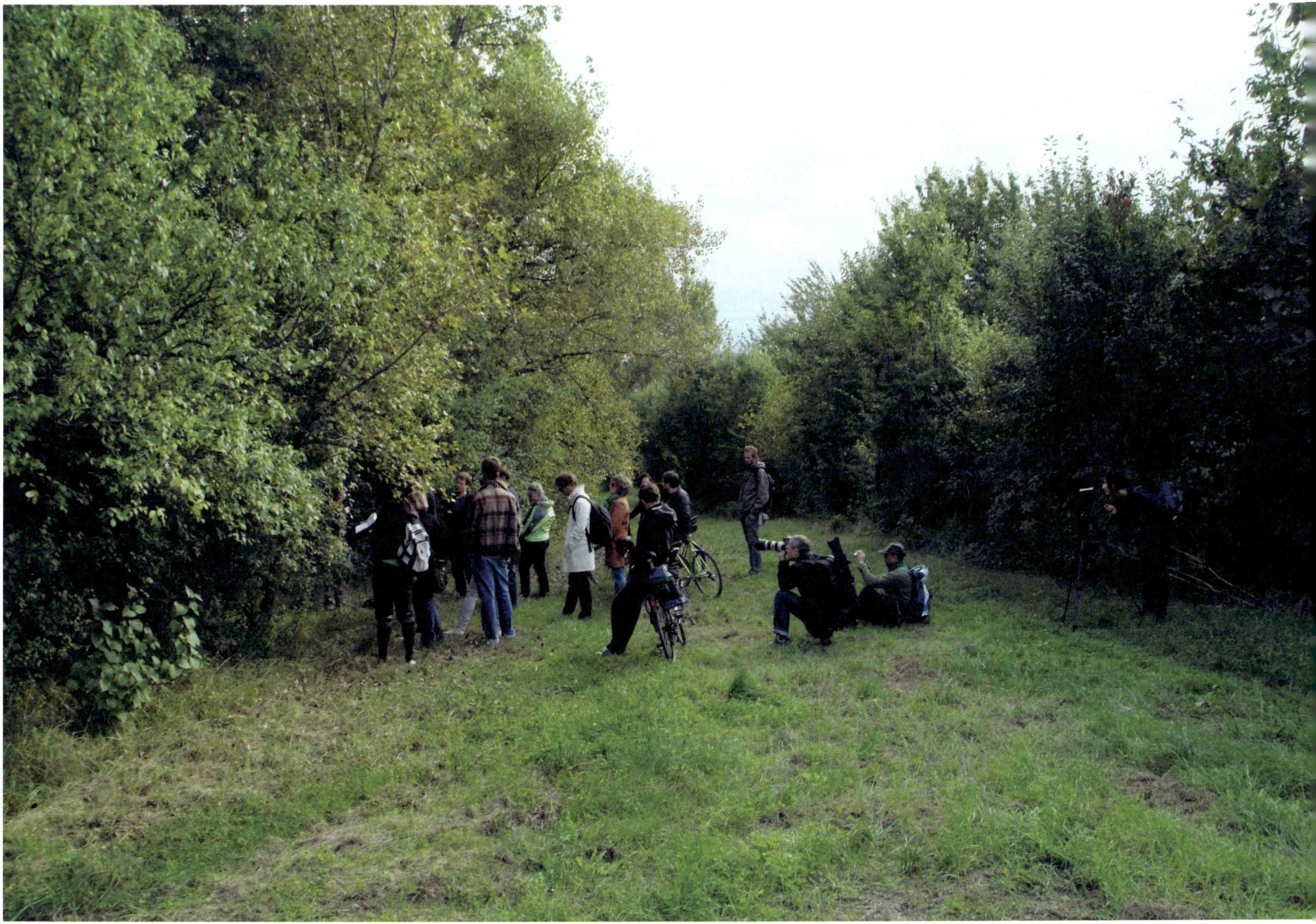

Habitat of THE BLUE FROG SOCIETY, Vienna, 2010

Habitat von THE BLUE FROG SOCIETY, Wien, 2010

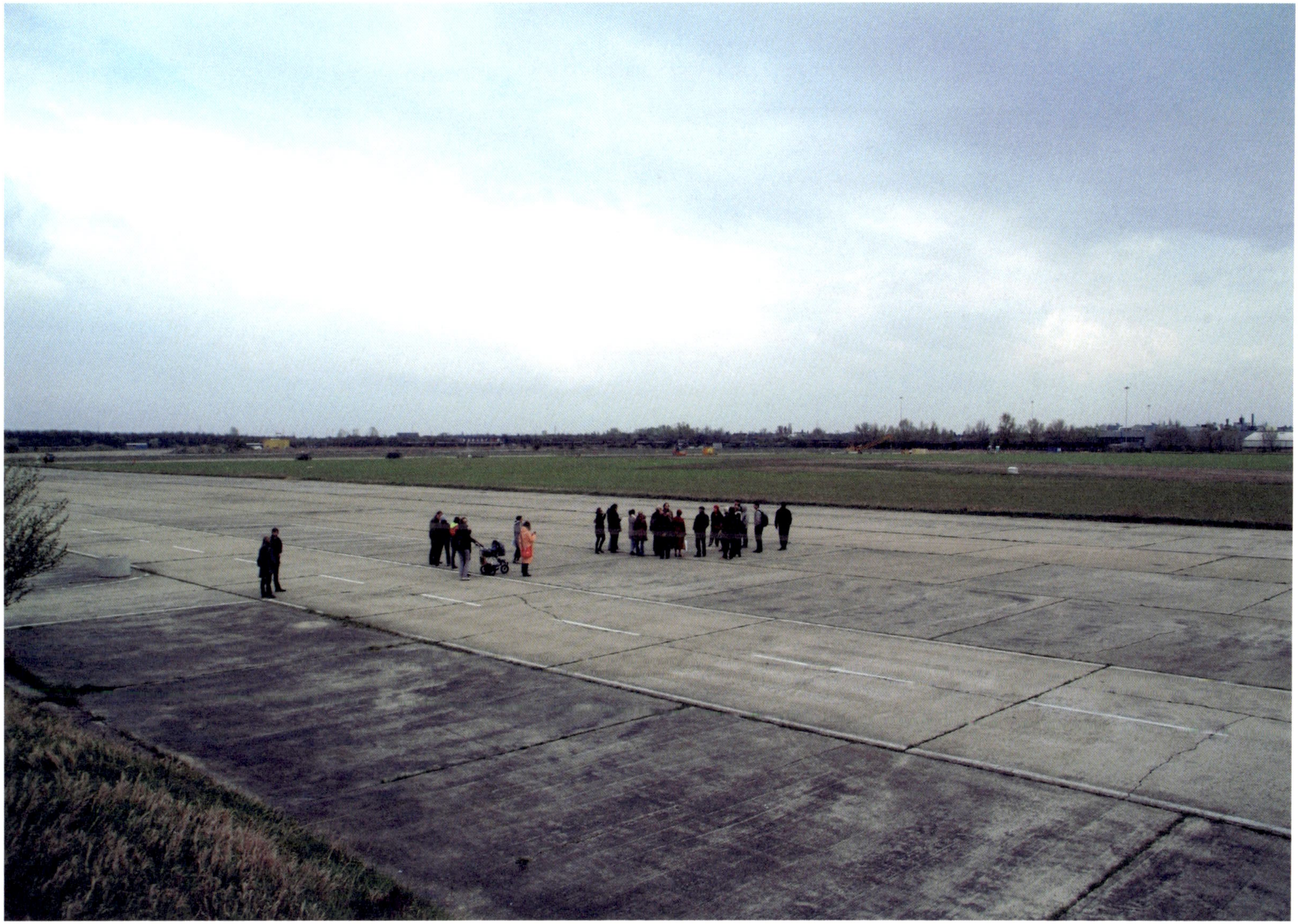

1st WALK AT THE URBAN PERIPHERY, April 11, 2010, as part of "Az W sonntags 230," organized by the Architekturzentrum Wien, with Max Rieder: *again/against—a city which will never be built*

1. STADTRANDSPAZIERGANG, 11. April 2010, im Rahmen von „Az W sonntags 230" mit Max Rieder: *wieder/wider – eine Stadt, die nie gebaut wird*

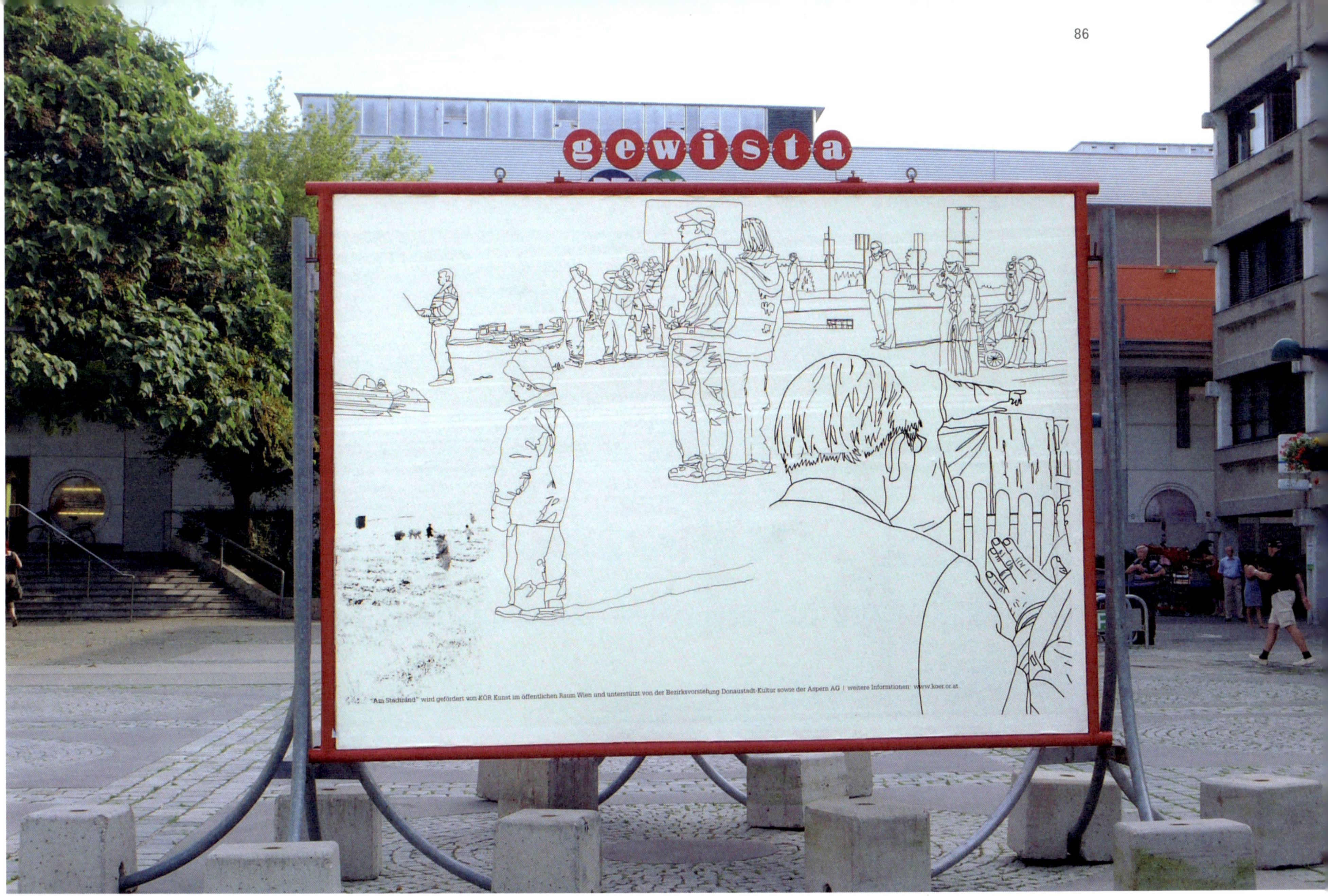

Installation of billboards, Erwin-Schrödinger-Square, Vienna 22—to announce AT THE URBAN PERIPHERY

Installation von Billboards, Erwin-Schrödinger-Platz, Wien 22 – zur Ankündigung von AM STADTRAND

Installation of new billboards, based on ideas by local residents: - an intervention with the image campaign of Lake-City Aspern

Installation von neu konzipierten Billboards, basierend auf Beiträgen der AnwohnerInnen: eine Intervention in die Image-Kampagne von Aspern Seestadt

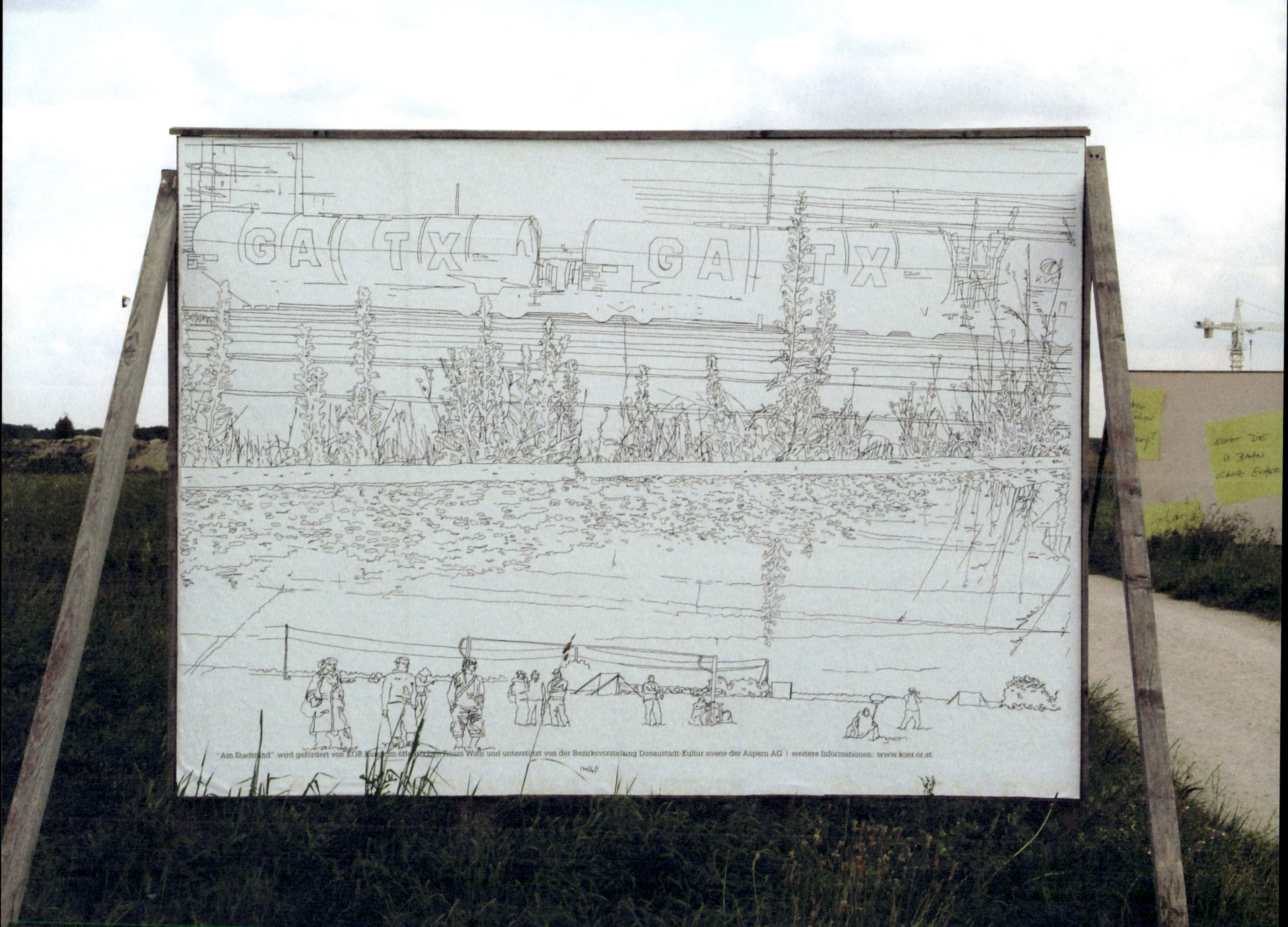

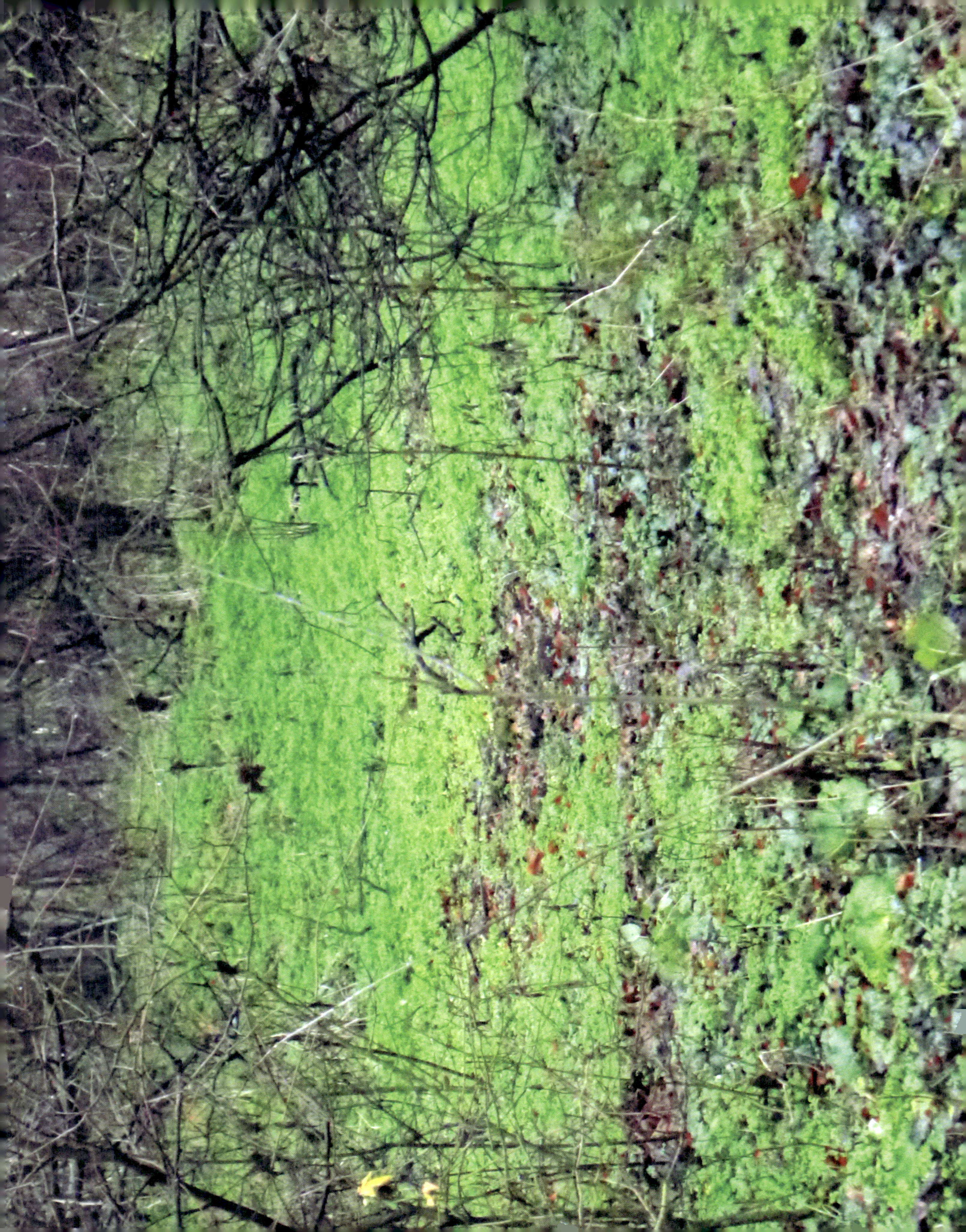

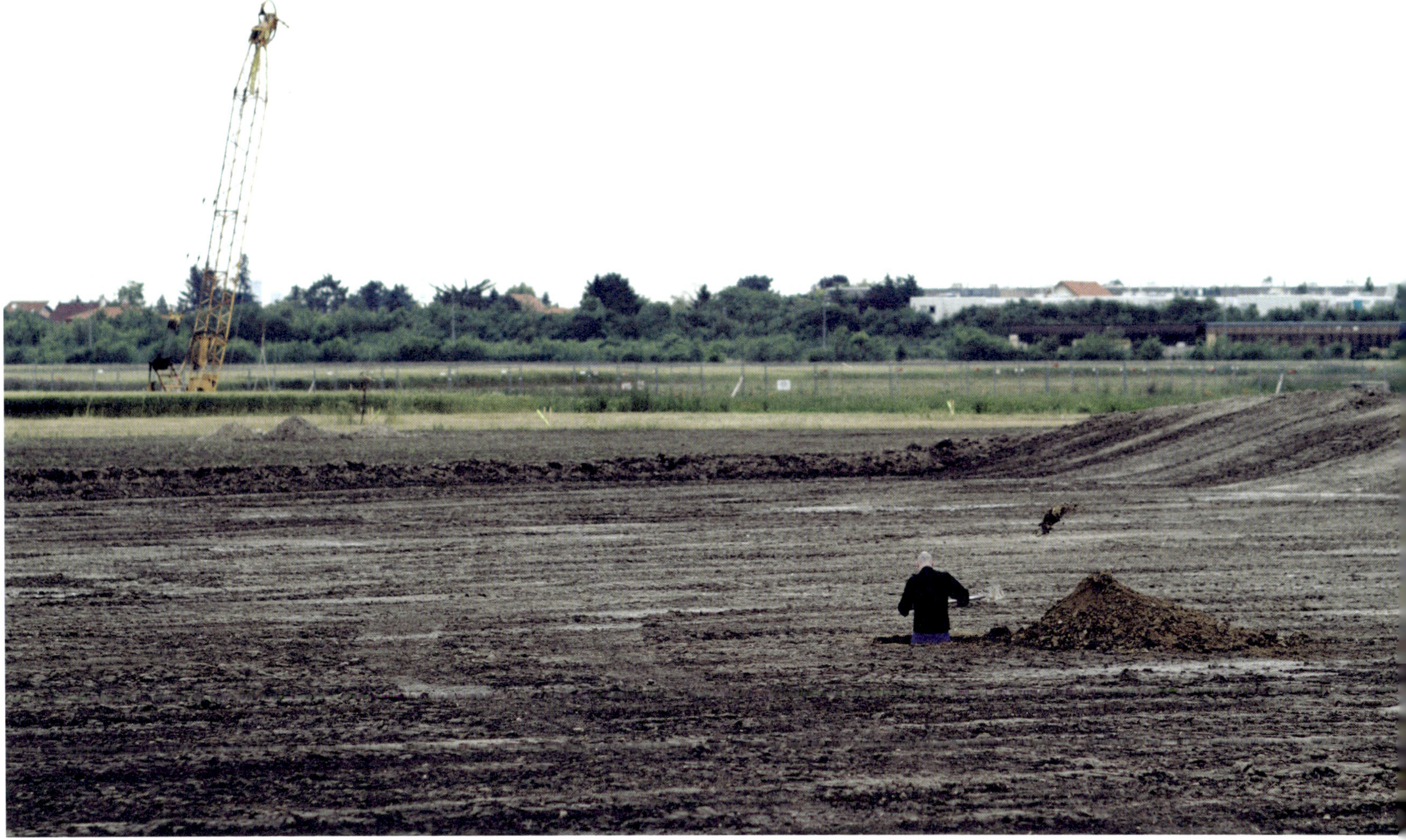

2nd WALK AT THE URBAN PERIPHERY, June 20, 2010,
with Gerald Straub, *on holes and on such that are missing* (performer: Noah Holtwiesche) and interviews by Barbara Holub on *Voices from a Future International City*. Actors: Dirk Nocker, Sönke Schnitzer

2. STADTRANDSPAZIERGANG, 20. Juni 2010,
mit Gerald Straub *zu Löchern und solchen, die fehlen* (Performer: Noah Holtwiesche) sowie Interviews von Barbara Holub zu *Stimmen aus einer internationalen Stadt der Zukunft*. Schauspieler: Dirk Nocker, Sönke Schnitzer

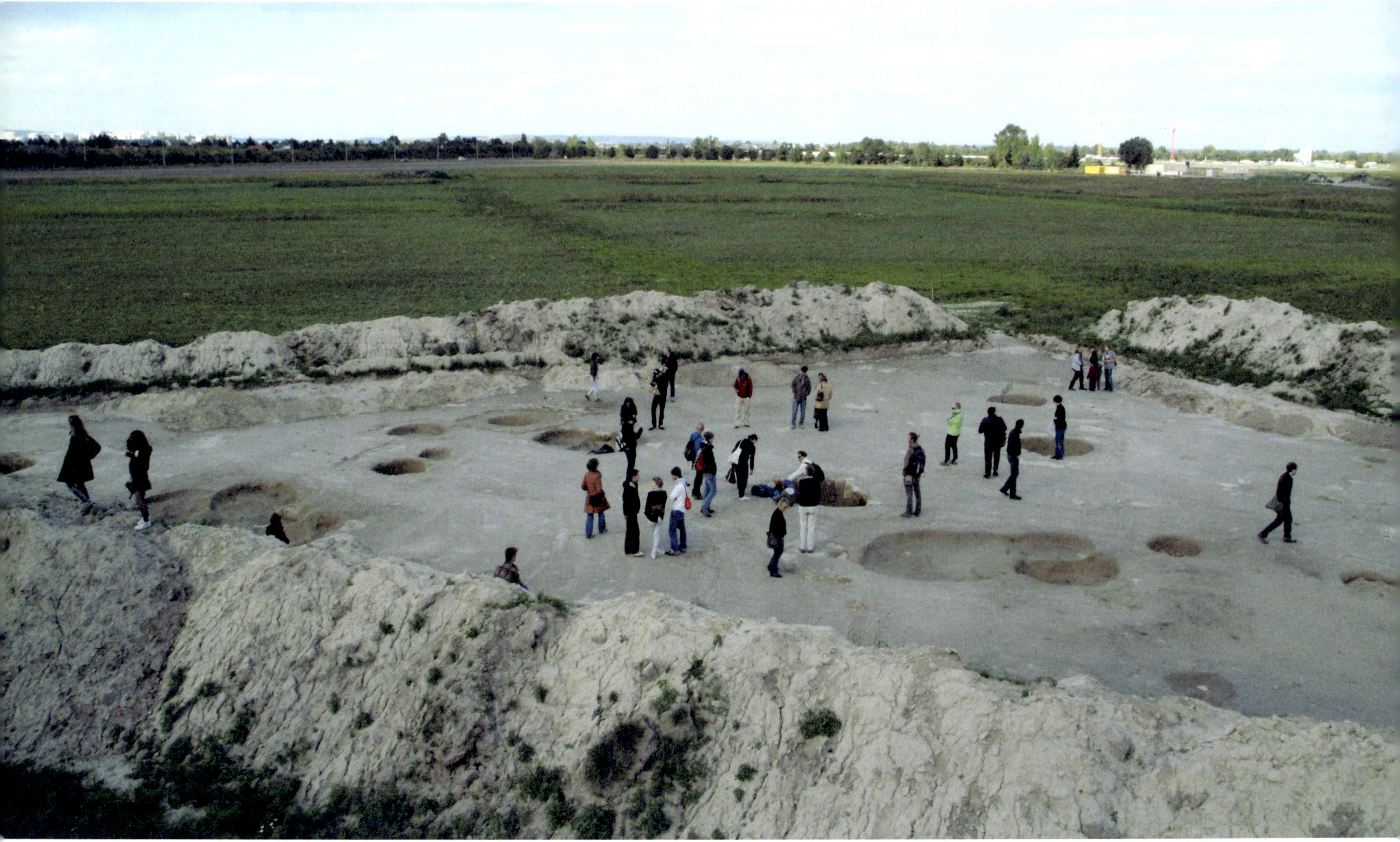

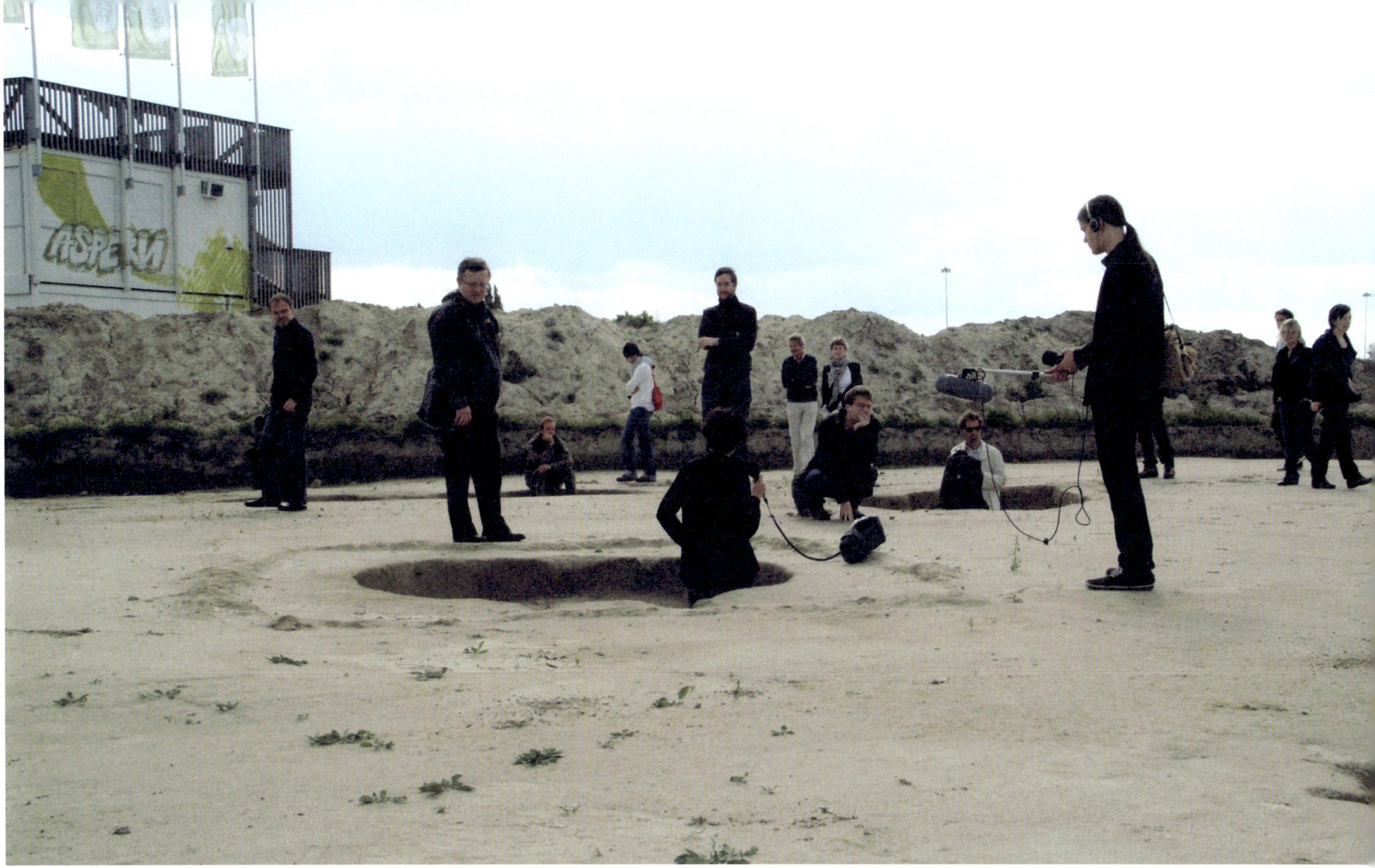

3rd WALK AT THE URBAN PERIPHERY, Sept. 19, 2010,
with contributions by Irene Bittner, Barbara Imhof, Srdan Ivkovic,
Bertram Weisshaar, Daniel Aschwanden

3. STADTRANDSPAZIERGANG, 19. September 2010,
mit Beiträgen von Irene Bittner, Barbara Imhof, Srdan Ivkovic,
Bertram Weisshaar und Daniel Aschwanden

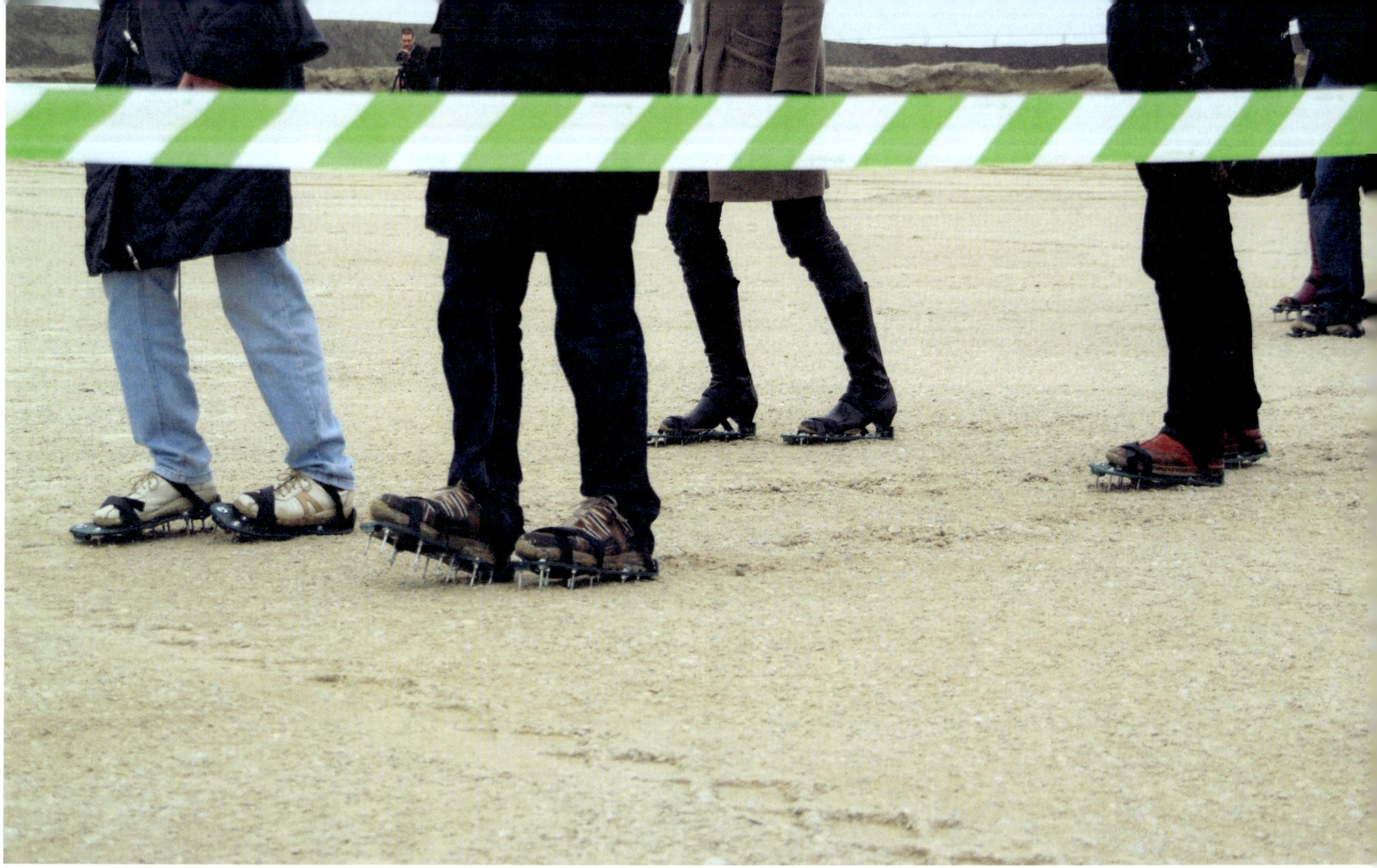

4th WALK AT THE URBAN PERIPHERY, Nov. 17, 2010, as part of Vienna Art Week 2010, with Georg Winter/ S_A_R Team (*Simple Anticipatory Basic Exercises for Improving the Living Conditions of Future Residents*) and Anne Bennent (*Le bâteau ivre* by Arthur Rimbaud, not performed)

4. STADTRANDSPAZIERGANG, 17. November 2010, im Rahmen der Vienna Art Week 2010, mit Georg Winter/S_A_R Team (*Einfache antizipatorische Grundübungen zur Verbesserung der Lebensumstände zukünftiger BewohnerInnen*) und Anne Bennent (*Le bâteau ivre* von Arthur Rimbaud, nicht aufgeführt)

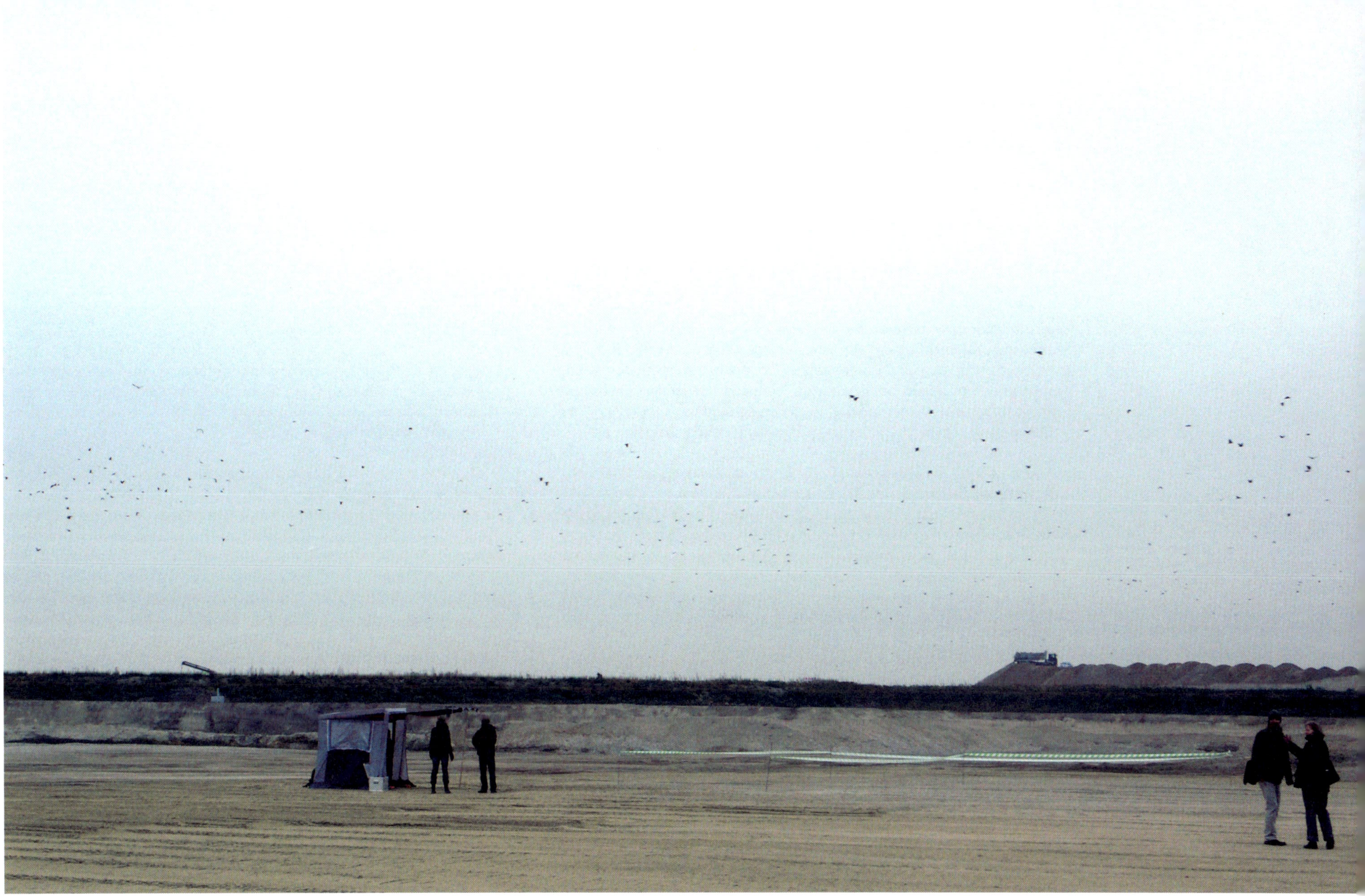

PIXXELPOINT New Media Art Festival, curated by Gülsen Bal and BridA,
Nova Gorica (SLO)/Gorizia (IT), 2011

ANYONE'S LAND

The video and installation *Anyone's Land/Terra di qualcuno/Vsakogaršnja zemlja* developed from Paul Rajakovics' 1997 architecture workshop in the city Gorizia (IT) und Nova Gorica (SLO). The title is a play on "no-man's land," this familiar military term converted into an invitation to anyone to cross the border between Nova Gorica, Slovenia, and its Italian counterpart Gorizia. By transforming an empty border control building into the exhibition space for ANYONE'S LAND—a space suggesting both a practical "limbo zone" for migrants and a discursive context—the project freed border zones from potential short-term investors' commercial interests. Central to the project is the question of how physical borders have an enduring psychological effect, even when they are removed.

For his workshop in 1997, Rajakovics had collected drawings from residents of Gorizia and Nova Gorica, made in response to questions about the future of these neighboring cities, which had been separated by the EU border until the fall of the iron curtain. This traumatic experience still resonated deeply in people's minds, as the drawings showed. When, in 2011, Barbara Holub and Paul Rajakovics returned to find the two cities again separated by a fence running in front of the train station (Stazione Transalpina), they realized that a new "border" had been constructed, this time by planters, meaning that the station was again not directly accessible by car from the Italian side. Despite Slovenia having become a member of the EU in 2004, this seemed like a subconscious reinstatement of the earlier divide.

Installed at the *PIXXELPOINT* exhibition, the video ANYONE'S LAND is an edited version of interviews conducted by Rajakovics with younger residents about their visions for the future. On returning to Gorizia in 1998, he initiated "spremembazione 1," a casting studio taking its name from the combined Slovenian and Italian words for "change" (*sprememba* and *modificazione*), reflecting the altered political prospects of the two cities since the collapse of Soviet-sponsored communism. After four Italians and four Slovenians were invited to show Rajakovics their favorite places in the area, the project culminated in an event at the Piazza della Transalpina. A game of "borderline badminton" took place in front of Stazione Transalpina, transforming the fence of the EU border into the net. The camera was placed right on the fence, a piece of which was removed to enable people to cross the border throughout the game. By incorporating footage from 1998 and connecting it to the subsequent development of Nova Gorica and Gorizia since the removal of the EU border, ANYONE'S LAND thus explored how local issues play out against a backdrop of national and international interests.[SA]

A project by transparadiso

PIXXELPOINT New Media Art Festival, kuratiert von Gülsen Bal und BridA,
Nova Gorica (SLO)/Gorizia (IT), 2011

JEMANDSLAND

Das Video und die Installation *Jemandsland/Terra di qualcuno/Vsakogaršnja zemlja* entwickelten sich aus einem von Paul Rajakovics 1997 in Gorizia (IT) und Nova Gorica (SLO) abgehaltenen Architekturworkshop. Der Titel verwandelt den vertrauten Begriff „Niemandsland" in eine Einladung an alle, die Grenze zwischen Nova Gorica und Gorizia zu überschreiten. Mit der Umwandlung eines leerstehenden Grenzgebäudes in Jemandsland – einen Raum, der sowohl eine konkrete „Zwischenzone" für MigrantInnen als auch einen diskursiven Kontext darstellt – entzog das Projekt das Grenzland den potenziellen kommerziellen Interessen von InvestorInnen. Im Zentrum des Projekts steht die Frage, wie weit physische Grenzen auch noch nach ihrer Beseitigung psychologisch fortwirken.

Für seinen Workshop hatte Rajakovics Zeichnungen von BewohnerInnen aus Gorizia und Nova Gorica gesammelt, die diese auf die Frage nach der Zukunft der benachbarten Städte hin verfertigt hatten, die damals noch durch eine EU-Außengrenze getrennt waren. Wie die Zeichnungen zeigten, war die traumatische Erfahrung der geteilten Stadt noch immer tief im Bewusstsein der BewohnerInnen verankert. Als Barbara Holub und Paul Rajakovics 2011 zurückkehrten, fanden sie die beiden Städte erneut durch eine vor dem Bahnhof (Stazione Transalpina) verlaufende Barriere getrennt. Diesmal wurde durch Blumentröge eine neue „Grenze" gezogen, die Autos die direkte Zufahrt zum Bahnhof von der italienischen Seite versperrte. Es war wie die unbewusste Wiedereinführung der früheren Teilung, obwohl Slowenien 2004 ein Mitgliedsstaat der EU geworden war.

Die Videoinstallation JEMANDSLAND im Rahmen der Ausstellung für *PIXXELPOINT* ist eine editierte Version der Interviews, die Rajakovics (mit seiner Gruppe transbanana) 1998 bei einem weiteren Aufenthalt in Nova Gorica/Gorizia mit jüngeren BewohnerInnen über ihre Zukunftsvorstellungen geführt hatte. Dafür hatte er das Casting-Studio „Sprememebazione 1" installiert, dessen Name sich aus dem slowenischen und dem italienischen Wort für „Wandel" (*sprememba* und *modificazione*) zusammensetzt und die veränderten politischen Aussichten der beiden Städte seit dem Zusammenbruch Jugoslawiens widerspiegelt. Vier ItalienerInnen und vier SlowenInnen wurden ausgewählt, Rajakovics ihre Lieblingsplätze zu zeigen, und das Projekt fand seinen Höhepunkt schließlich in einem „Borderline Badminton"-Spiel auf der Piazza della Transalpina, wofür der Zaun der EU-Außengrenze in ein Badminton-Netz umfunktioniert wurde. Dafür wurde ein Stück Zaun entfernt, um eine Kamera zu positionieren, und die SpielerInnen wurden aufgefordert, bei Seitenwechsel die Grenze illegal zu überqueren. Durch die Verbindung des Filmmaterials von 1998 mit der neueren Entwicklung von Nova Gorica und Gorizia untersuchte JEMANDSLAND, wie lokale Probleme direkt mit nationalen und internationalen Interessen verwoben sind.[SA]

Ein Projekt von transparadiso

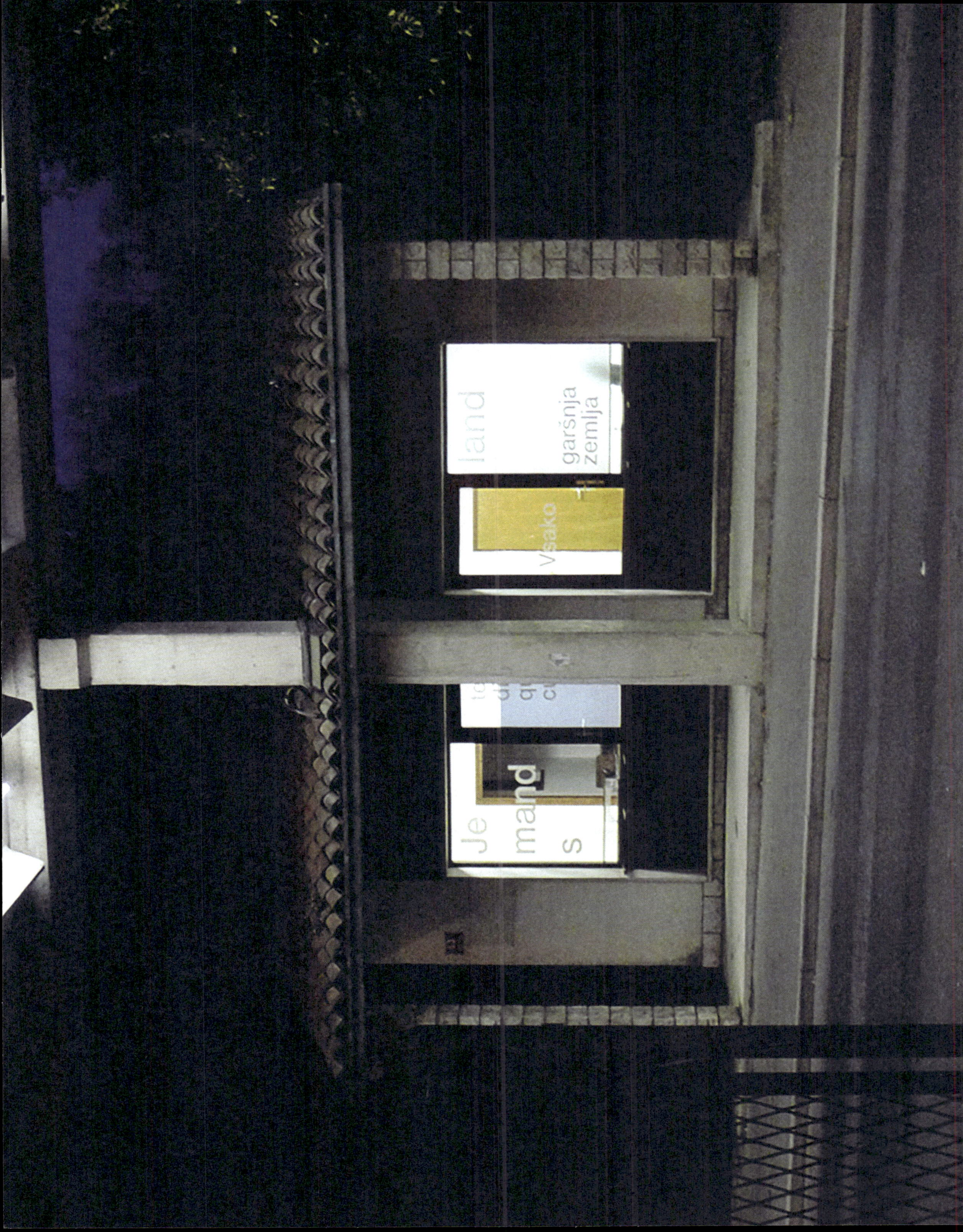
land
garšnja
zemlja
Vsako
Je
mand
s

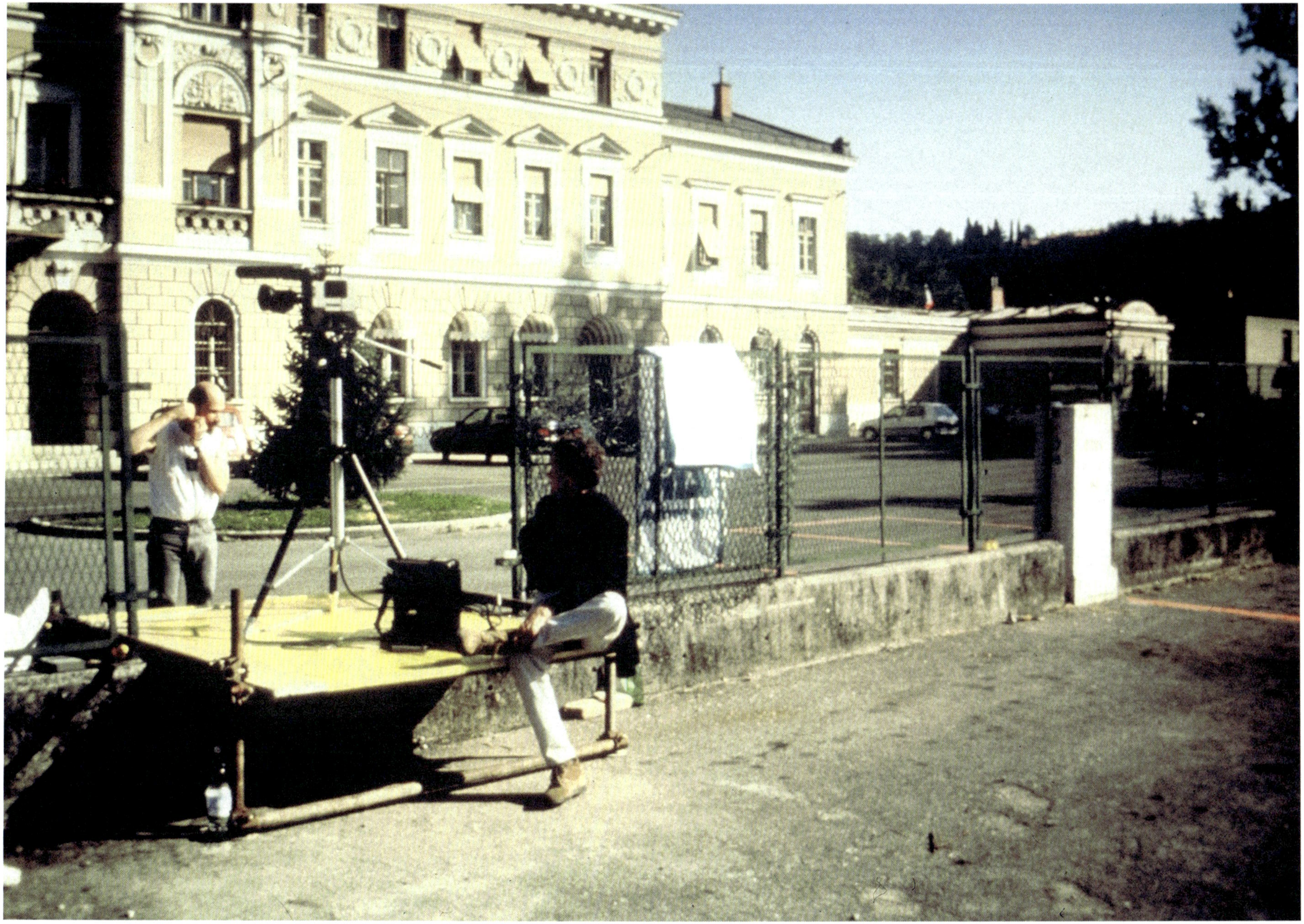

Spremembazione 1 (Paul Rajakovics/transbanana), Piazza della Transalpina, Gorizia/Nova Gorica, 1997

For a badminton game across the border fence of the EU's external border, a fence element was removed so that the players could swap sides.

Spremembazione 1 (Paul Rajakovics/transbanana), Piazza della Transalpina, Gorizia/Nova Gorica, 1997

Für ein Badmintonspiel über den Grenzzaun der EU-Außengrenze wurde ein Zaunelement entfernt, sodass die SpielerInnen Seiten tauschen konnten.

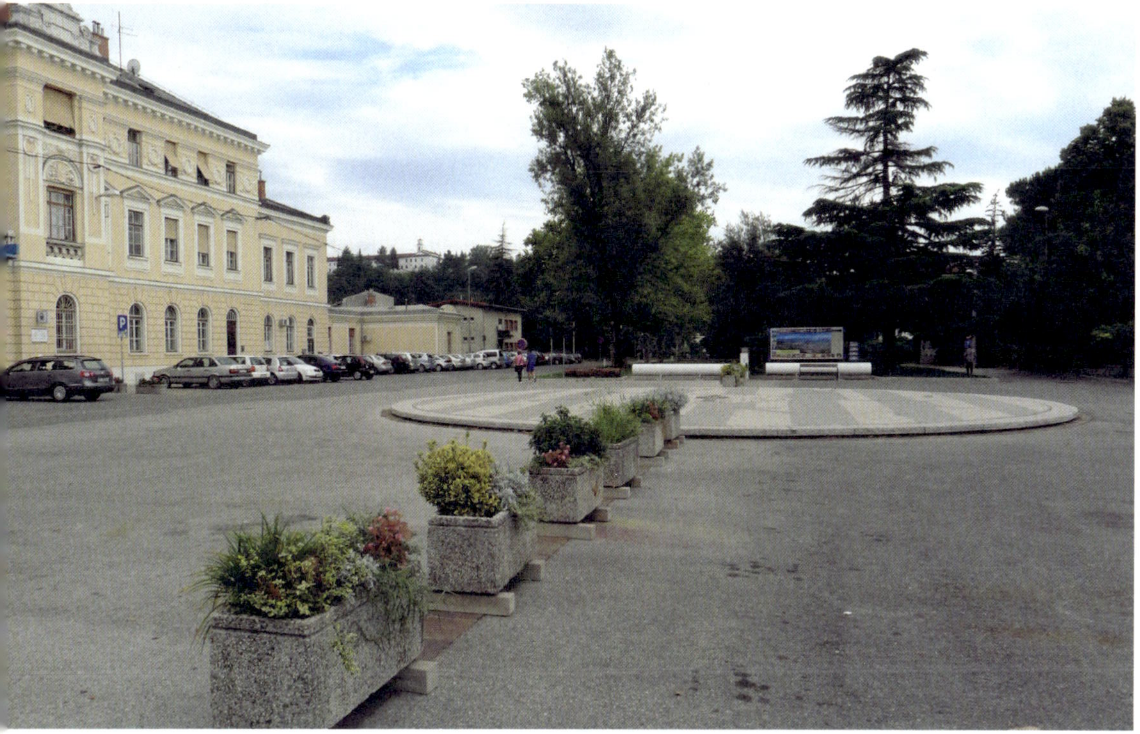

Piazza della Transalpina, 2011
The former border fence on the railway station forecourt had been replaced with planters (with the addition of metal bollards in 2020) so that the station was once again shut off for traffic on the Italian side.

Piazza della Transalpina, 2011
Auf dem Bahnhofsvorplatz war der ehemalige Grenzzaun durch Pflanztröge ersetzt (und 2020 durch Metallpflöcke ergänzt) worden, sodass der Bahnhof für den Autoverkehr wieder von der italienischen Seite abgeschottet war.

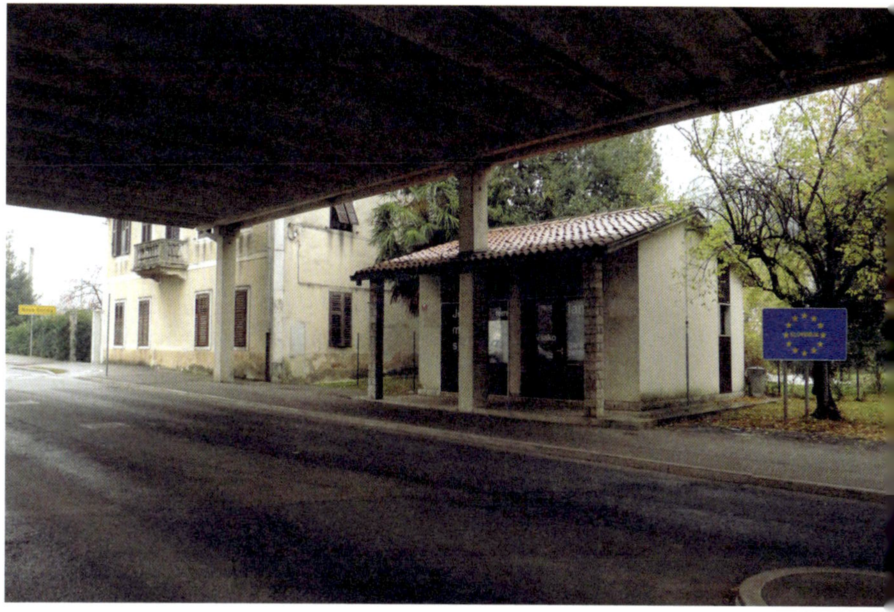

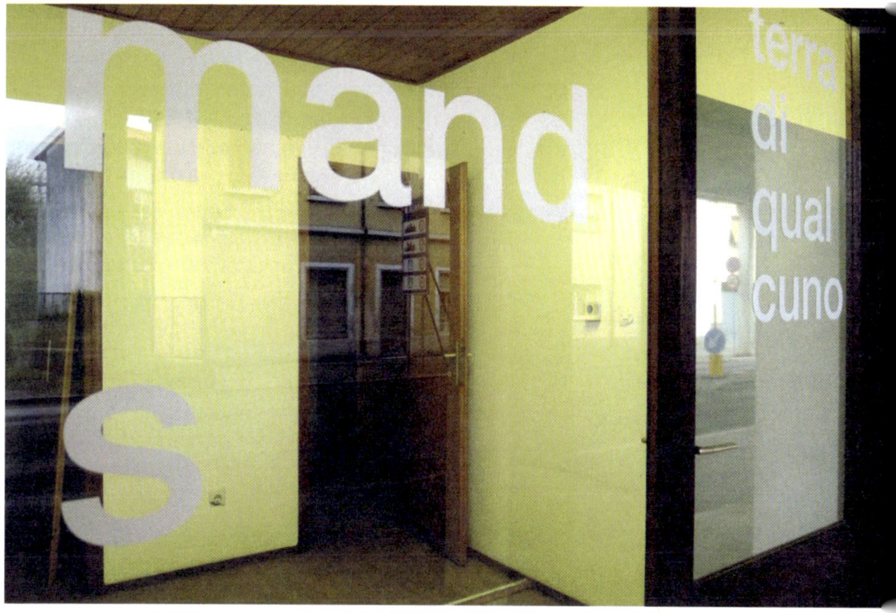

Shared values, ambulant gardens, and other spaces, curated by Giuliana Carbi, Trieste Contemporanea, Trieste, 2017; *TRI/E/S/T/E*, curated by Michael Petrowitsch, HDA/Haus der Architektur, Graz, 2018

HARBOUR FOR CULTURES

The aim of HARBOUR FOR CULTURES is to amend and reformulate the definition of the harbor, a place that has always stood for shipping commercial goods and has been a topos for the meeting of different cultures as well as for arrival and departure. Following current political events, increasing migration and streams of refugees, H/C examines the figure of the harbor as a place of exchanging non-material and non-commercial goods and values that strengthen society and create a space for different cultures.

The Porto Vecchio in Trieste, an inner-city area which has been languishing for decades, is the starting point for a series of artistic interventions initiated by transparadiso—with reference to THE BLUE FROG SOCIETY founded by Holub in 2010—together with partners for H/C: interventions which not only engage directly with existing urban processes but also seek to address a non-territorial, international community as anticipatory fiction. A wish production scheme was launched that—by means of symposia, workshops and exhibitions—invites people to contribute their ideas and visions for a development of the port that is not (exclusively) commercial.

Starting with *Shared values, ambulant gardens, and other spaces* (2017), transparadiso invited visitors to take part in a poetic, visionary walk with the aim of formulating personal wishes and ideas for specific sites with a view to harnessing the old port for non-commercial purposes, presenting the results in an exhibition at Trieste Contemporanea. The video *One Hundred Desires for Harbour for Cultures* (2018) lists one hundred wishes that were gathered collectively at various events for a visionary, socially engaged urban program. As a kind of preview of putting these ideas into practice, transparadiso carried out the clandestine art action *A Promise for Harbour for Cultures* on New Year's Day 2018. The action involved gilding a bollard as a symbolic pledge to enhance neglected qualities, an enhancement that H/C is pursuing in opposition to the urban planning concept for the old port that is primarily profit-oriented.

The wishes that were formulated oscillate between concrete and visionary and can be seen as the basis for a new programming of socially and culturally engaged urban development. The collective wish production and sum of artistic interventions form the basis for concrete plans for creating the HARBOUR FOR CULTURES Centre in Porto Vecchio.[BR]

A project of Trieste Contemporanea (Giuliana Carbi), transparadiso (Barbara Holub/ Paul Rajakovics) and Betta Porro. Exhibitions, symposia, workshops, and wish production in urban space.

Shared values, ambulant gardens, and other spaces, kuratiert von Giuliana Carbi, Trieste Contemporanea, Triest, 2017; *TRI/E/S/T/E*, kuratiert von Michael Petrowitsch, HDA/Haus der Architektur, Graz, 2018

HARBOUR FOR CULTURES

Die Definition des Hafens, seit jeher Umschlagplatz wirtschaftlicher Güter und ebenso Topos für das Aufeinandertreffen unterschiedlicher Kulturen sowie für das Ankommen und Abschiednehmen, soll mit HARBOUR FOR CULTURES ergänzt und neu formuliert werden. Den aktuellen politischen Ereignissen, der zunehmenden Migration und Fluchtbewegung folgend, beleuchtet H/C die Figur des Hafens als einen Ort des Austausches immaterieller und nicht ökonomischer Güter und Werte, die die Gesellschaft stärken und unterschiedlichen Kulturen Raum geben.

Der seit Jahrzehnten brachliegende innerstädtische Porto Vecchio in Triest ist Ausgangspunkt einer Reihe von künstlerischen Interventionen, die transparadiso – unter Bezugnahme auf die von Holub 2010 gegründete Blue Frog Society – gemeinsam mit PartnerInnen für H/C initiiert hat: Interventionen, die nicht nur direkt in bestehende urbane Prozesse eingreifen, sondern auf eine nicht territoriale internationale Gemeinschaft als antizipatorische Fiktion abzielen. Lanciert wurde eine Wunschproduktion, die – über Symposien, Workshops und Ausstellungen – Ideen und Vorstellungen für eine nicht (ausschließlich) kommerzielle Planung des Hafens einfordert.

transparadiso lud zunächst mit *Shared values, ambulant gardens, and other spaces* (2017) zu einem poetischen, visionären Spaziergang ein, um persönliche Wünsche und Vorstellungen für konkrete Orte hinsichtlich einer nicht kommerziellen Aktivierung des alten Hafens zu formulieren, und präsentierte diese in einer Ausstellung in der Galerie Trieste Contemporanea. Das Video *One Hundred Desires for Harbour for Cultures* (2018) listet 100 Wünsche auf, die in verschiedenen Events für ein visionäres und sozial engagiertes urbanes Programm kollektiv gesammelt wurden. Als Ausblick für deren Realisierung führte transparadiso am Neujahrstag 2018 *A Promise for Harbour for Cultures* als klandestine Kunstaktion durch: ein Poller wurde vergoldet – ein Versprechen für die Umwertung vernachlässigter Qualitäten, die H/C entgegen einer vordringlich gewinnorientierten Stadtplanung des alten Hafens verfolgt.

Die formulierten Wünsche oszillieren zwischen konkret und visionär und können als Grundlage für eine neue Programmierung gesellschaftlich und kulturell engagierter Stadtentwicklung betrachtet werden. Die kollektive Wunschproduktion sowie die gesamten künstlerischen Interventionen bilden die Grundlage für die konkrete Planung zur Realisierung des HARBOUR FOR CULTURES Center im Porto Vecchio.[BR]

Ein Projekt von Trieste Contemporanea (Giuliana Carbi), transparadiso (Barbara Holub/ Paul Rajakovics) und Betta Porro. Ausstellungen, Symposien, Workshops und Wunschproduktion im urbanen Raum.

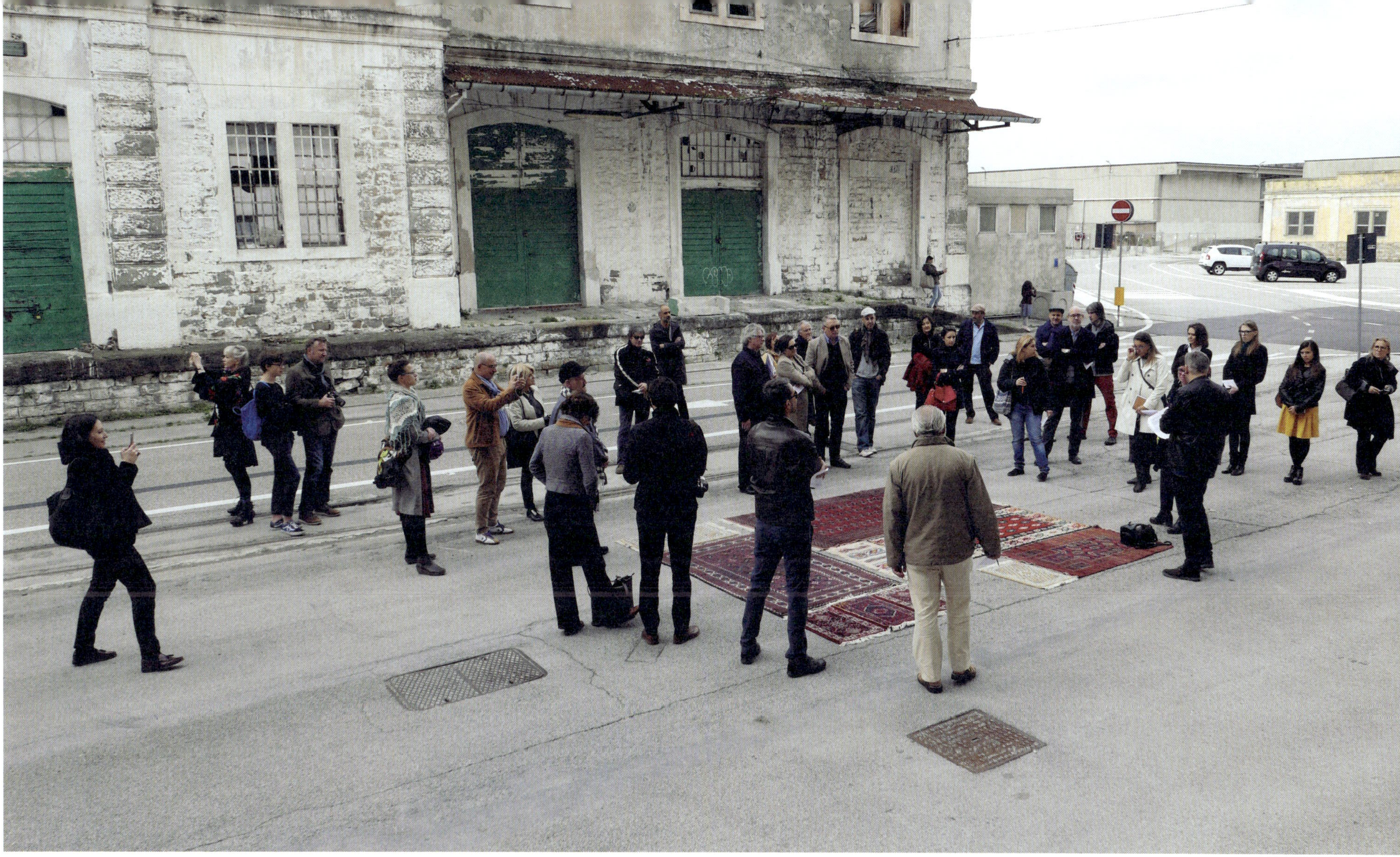

Porto Vecchio/Alter Hafen, Trieste, 2017, workshop
Shared values, ambulant gardens, and other spaces

Porto Vecchio/Alter Hafen, Triest, 2017, Workshop
Shared values, ambulant gardens, and other spaces

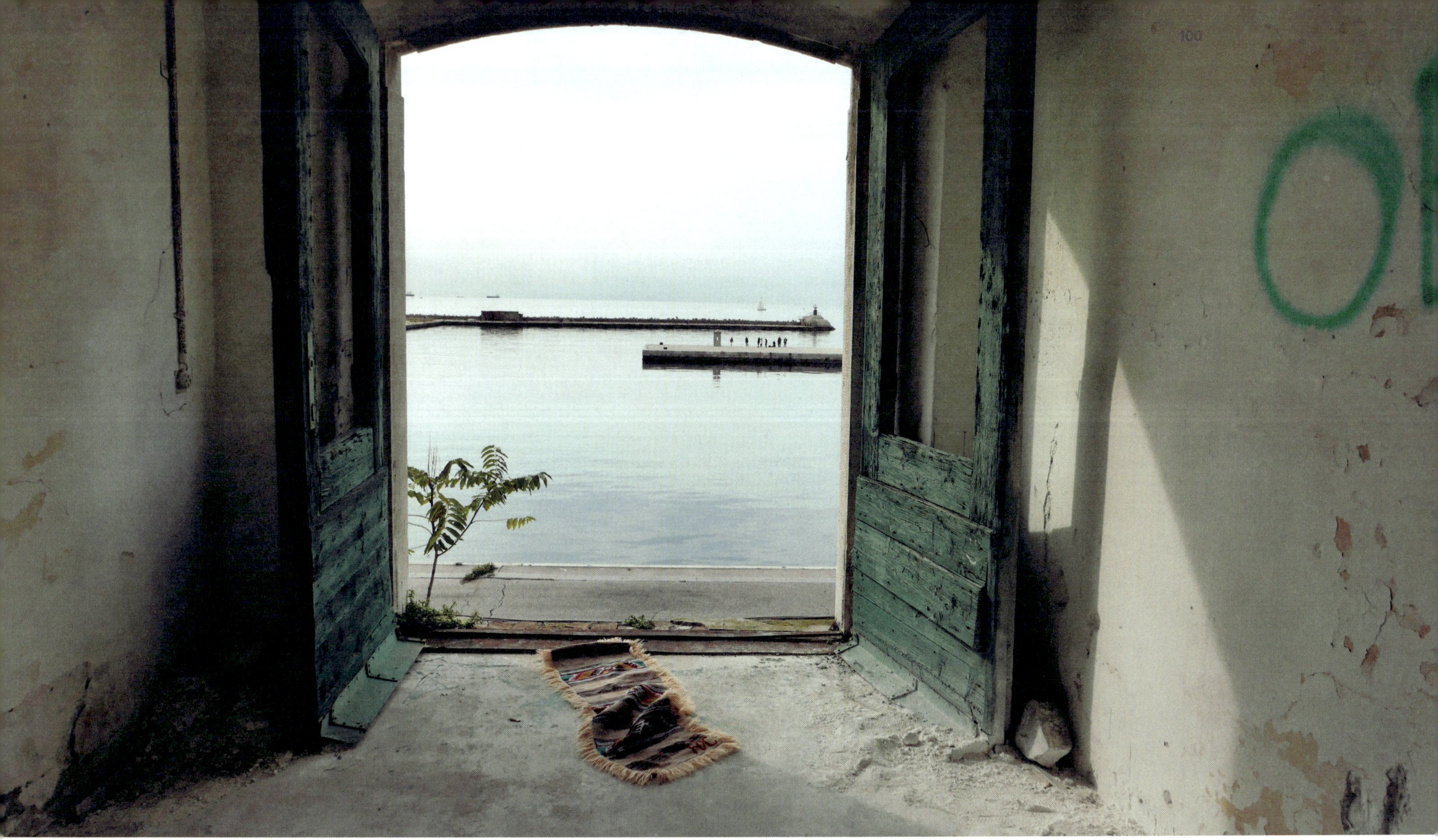

The carpet—as "garden" (see Foucault)—marked the site for which a wish was made.

Der Teppich markierte als „Garten" (siehe Foucault) jenen Ort, für den ein Wunsch ausgesprochen wurde.

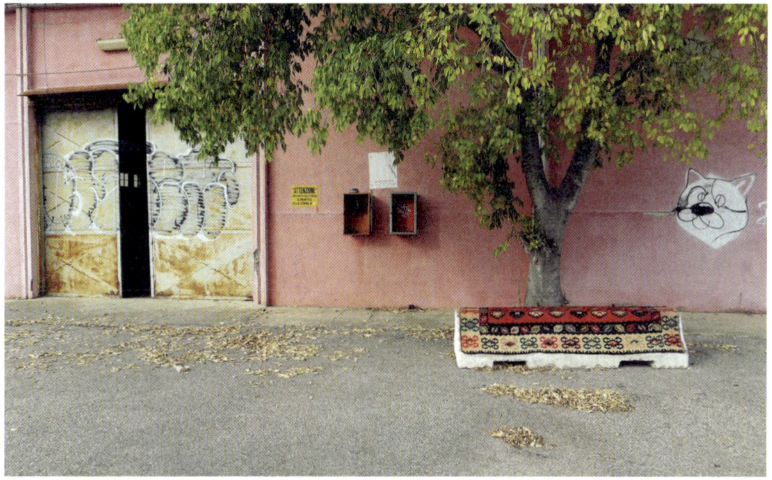

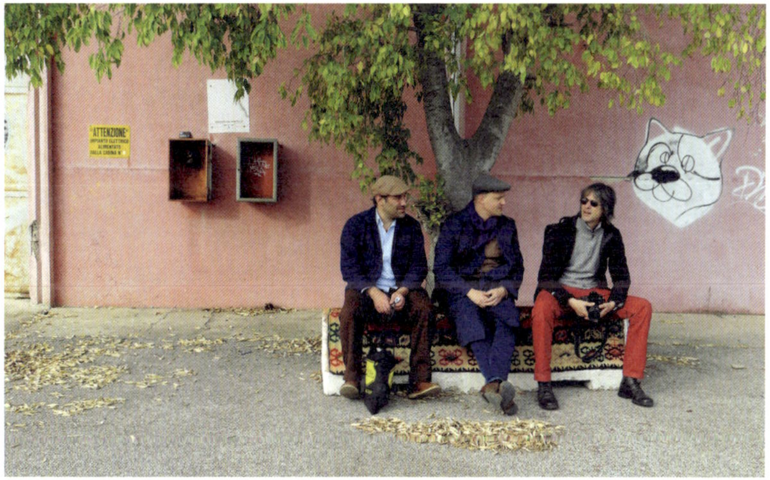
ATTENZIONE

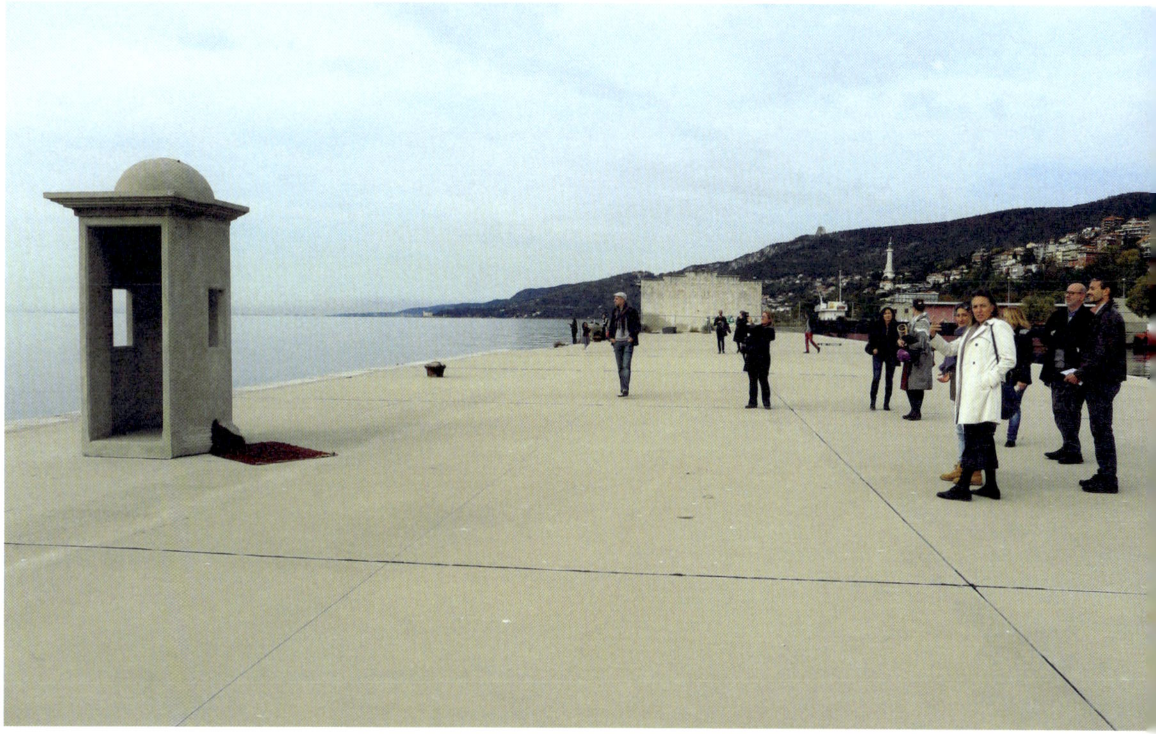

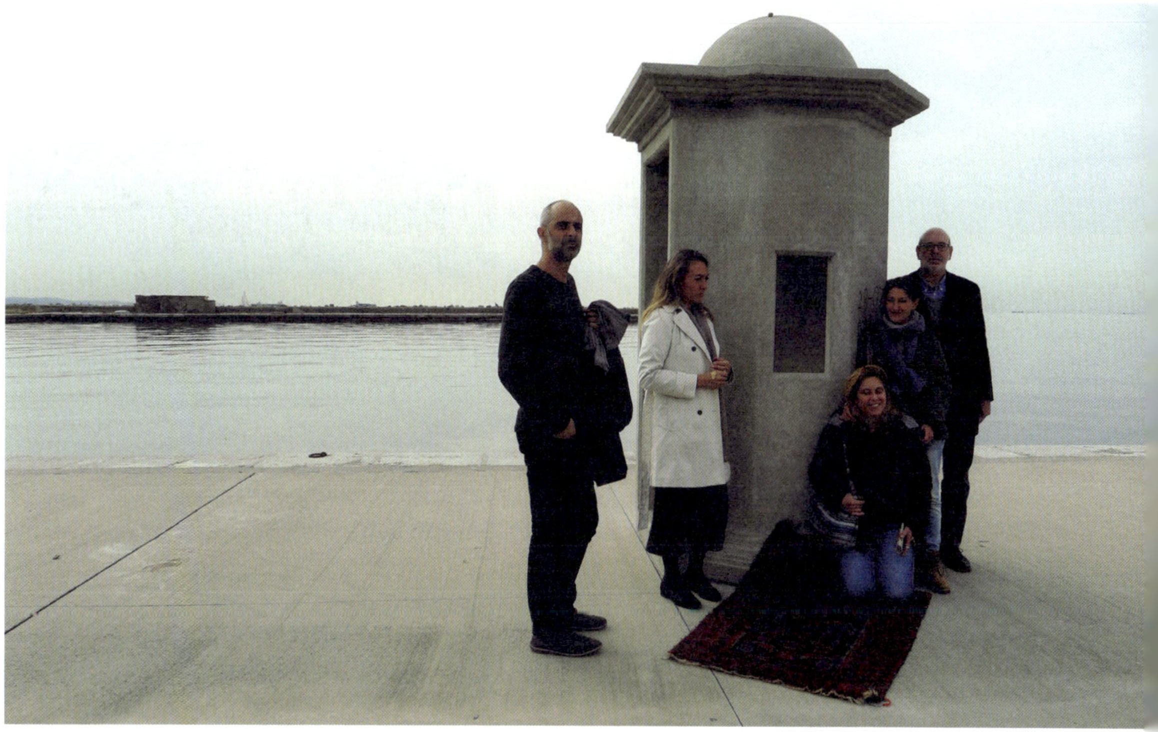

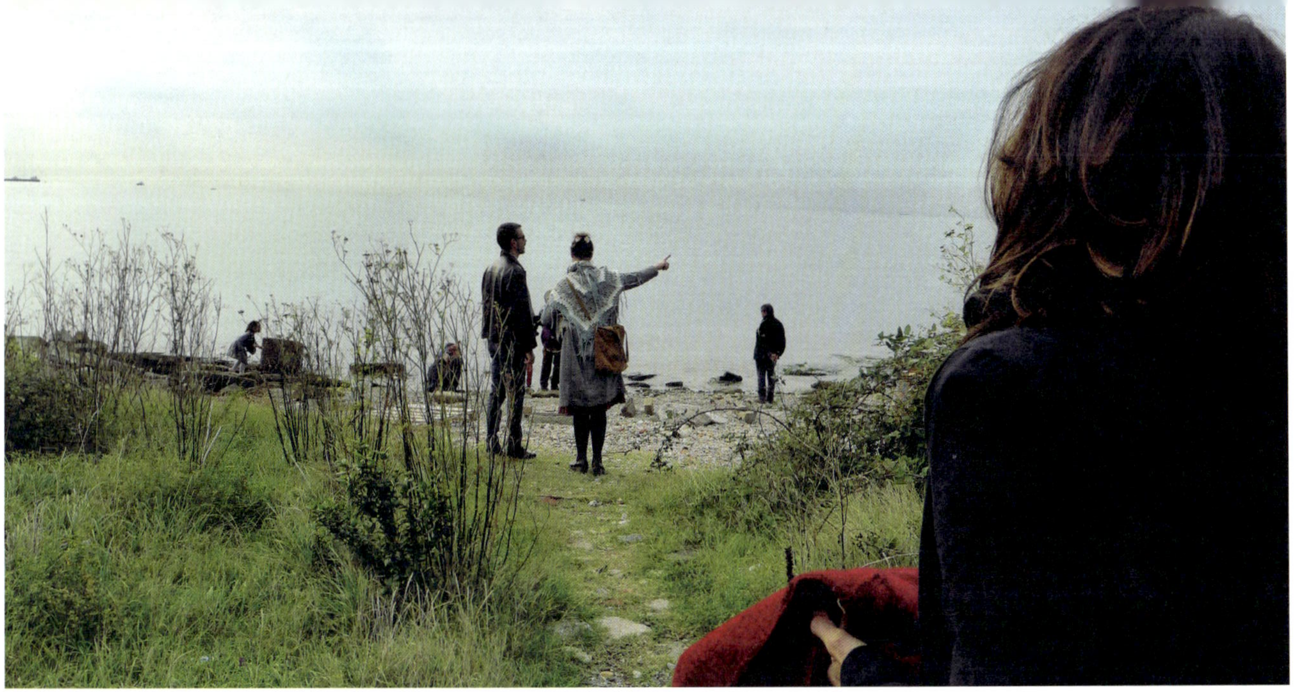

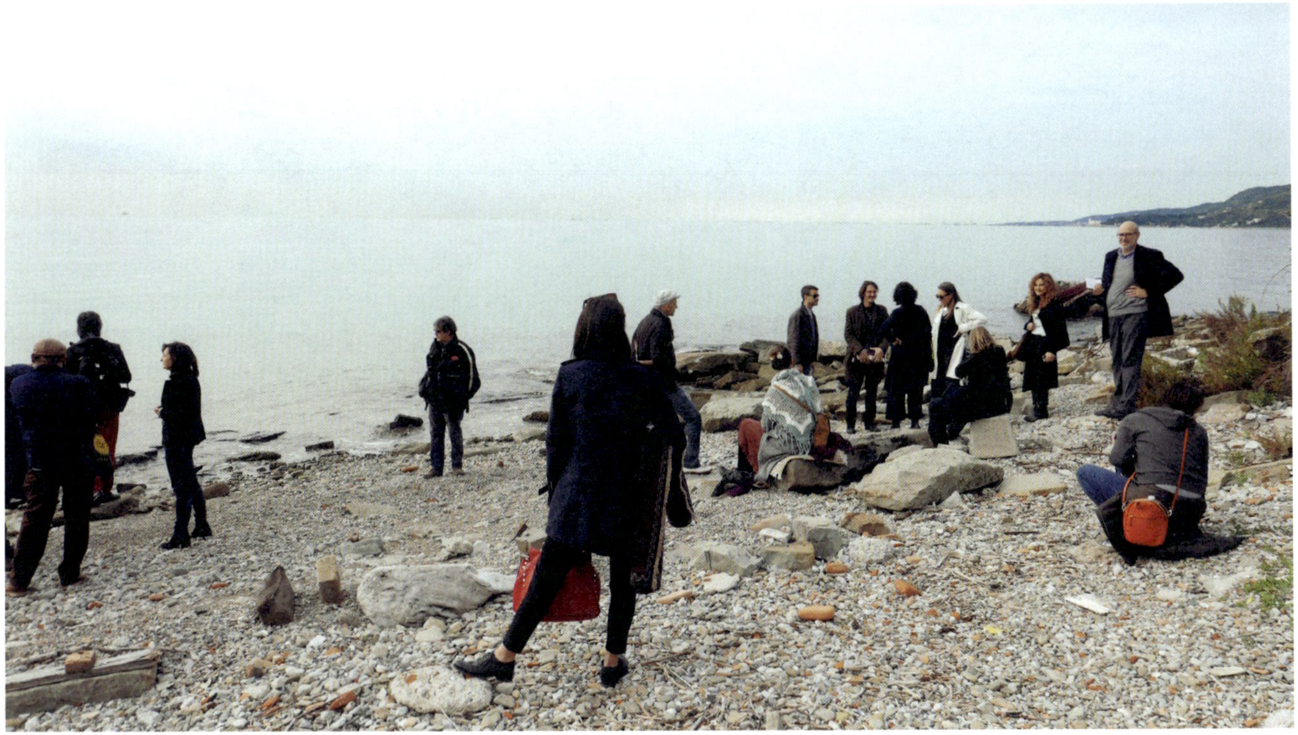

transparadiso
***One Hundred Desires for Harbour for Cultures / Cento desideri per il porto di culture*, 2018**
video, 12'04''

1 faro dei falsi orizzonti / light house of false horizons
2 false verità: riscrivere la storia / false truth: rewriting history
3 spazio di ascolto / listening space
4 sala d'attesa per tiranni /waiting room for tyrants
5 resistenza contemporanea / contemporary resistance
6 studio per cantautori depressi / studio for depressive song writers
7 quadrato per discussioni / boxing ring for debates
8 giardino aquatico / water garden
9 lungomare subacqueo della scienza/ underwater seafront of science
10 piattaforme per pescare e buttare sardoni / platforms for fishing and heavy flirting
11 fabbrica di gonfiabili / factory of inflatables
12 sportello di idee take-away / counter for take-away ideas
13 ufficio governativo del cambio di personalità / government office for personality change
14 scambio generazionale / exchange of generations
15 macchina totem per far sorgere la luna / totem machine for making the moon rise
16 sala da ballo per draghi / ballroom for dragons
17 area di decompressione / area of decompression
18 bivio delle culture / crossroad of cultures
19 centro culturale indipendente di incontro giovanile / independant cultural youth center
20 accademia del fastidio / academy of nuisance
21 improvvisazione / improvisation
22 trampolino musicale / musical trampoline
23 laboratorio di utopie / lab of utopias
24 punto di assaggio / point of taste
25 orto botanico / botanic garden
26 laboratorio d'arte / art lab
27 asilo / asylum
28 parco giochi per adulti / playground for adults
29 ricordo / memory
30 spiaggia degli angeli / angels' beach
31 auditorium strumentale / auditorium of instruments
32 meraviglie / miracles
33 sezione talenti (sconosciuti) / section of the (unrecognized) talented.
34 cose fuori dal mondo / things beyond the world
35 strumento per rompere il muro / instrument for breaking the wall
36 mediocrità / mediocracy
37 collettività / collectivity
38 blocco mentale / mental block
39 relazione / relation
40 romanticismo / romanticism
41 informale / informal
42 marginalità / marginality
43 sezione „i diversi" (matti, donne, gay, nani....) / section for „the diverse" (crazy, women, gay, dwarfs...)
44 incanto / enchantment
45 niente parole / no words
46 orto sociale / social garden
47 sintassi / syntax
48 urbanizzazione simbolica / symbolic urbanization
49 togliamo i tappi - un porto vive di occasioni / let's take off the plugs – a harbour lives on occasions
50 cineporto: coproduzioni internazionali / cinema harbour: international coproductions
51 magazzini della poca eleganza / warehouses of little elegance
52 materia del cinema: pauri e desideri / subjects of cinema: fears and desires
53 fitodepurazione / purification plant for plants
54 turbamento / agitation
55 complessità / complexity
56 apertura alla modernità / receptiveness of modernity
57 incontro / encounter
58 criticità / criticality

ONE HUNDRED DESIRES FOR HARBOUR FOR CULTURES,
TRI/E/S/T/E, HDA/Haus der Architektur, Graz, 2018

59 rottura / rupture
60 casa dei mestieri che non esistono più / house of professions which do not exist anymore
61 responsabilità / responsability
62 biblioteca / library
63 lentezza / slowness
64 conflitto / conflict
65 salotto di valore umano / lounge for human values
66 perdita di certezze / loss of certainties
67 canto delle sirene / song of the sirenes
68 montagne russe della contraddizione / roller coaster of contradictions
69 perplessità / perplexity
70 laboratorio di ricerca per il nuovo io / research lab of the new I
71 mensa del brodo primordiale / canteen for premordial broth
72 padiglione del vuoto / pavillon of the void
73 laboratorio sviluppo materiali (vernicular) a base aqua marina (biodegradabili) / lab for developing vernacular materials based on the sea (biodegradable)
74 sauna di insoddisfazioni / sauna of dissatisfaction
75 doccia fredda di illusioni / cold shower of illusions
76 ristorante delle belle speranze / restaurant of good prospects
77 tavolo del dialogo / table of dialogue
78 monumento a Malcolm X / monument for Malcolm X
79 luogo della dimenticanza / space of forgetting
80 fabbrica delle onde vaghe: trasformazione di situazioni rigide in situazioni fluide / factory of vague waves: transforming rigid situations into fluid situations
81 scuola di arti performative / school of performative arts
82 nuovi venuti - aquario umano / newcomers – human aquarium
83 laboratorio tra visione e know-how / lab between vision and know-how
84 Imparare ad infiorare / learning to embellish
85 EUtopia
86 salamelecco / salam alaikom
87 Ogni persona chi entra lascia un raconto, si identifica con una storia. La propria o inventata. /Each person who enters leaves a story – their own or an invented one.
88 autarchia / autarchy
89 equivoco / ambiguous
90 riuso delle risorse esistenti eco-innovativo per il terzo millennio / reuse of existing eco-innovative ressources for the 3rd millenium
91 centro permanente di critica creativa per la costruzione di una società contemporanea / permanent centre of creative critique for constructing a contemporary society
92 cucina sociale / social kitchen
93 stazione di sfruttamento energetico del moto ondoso / station making use of the energy of the sea
94 centro studi meteo idromarini – cambio climatico / research centre for seawater meteorology – climate change
95 museo del mare primordiale / museum of the primordial sea
96 museo della bora / bora-museum
97 una specie di G-7 della cultura: condivisione e prevenzione dei conflitti / a species of G-7 of culture: distribution and prevention of conflicts
98 scuola di interlinguistica e di inter-filosofia / school of interlinguistics and inter-philosophy
99 vaso di pandora rotto / broken Pandora's box
100 padiglione del mondo e centro di dibattimento / world pavillion and debate center

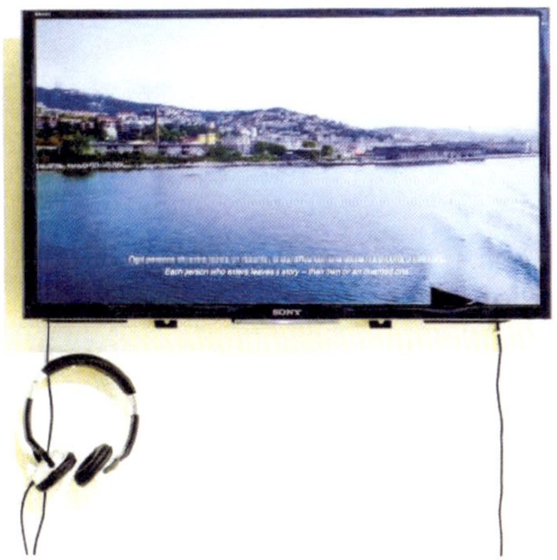

EINHUNDERT WÜNSCHE FÜR HARBOUR FOR CULTURES,
TRI/E/S/T/E, HDA/Haus der Architektur, Graz, 2018

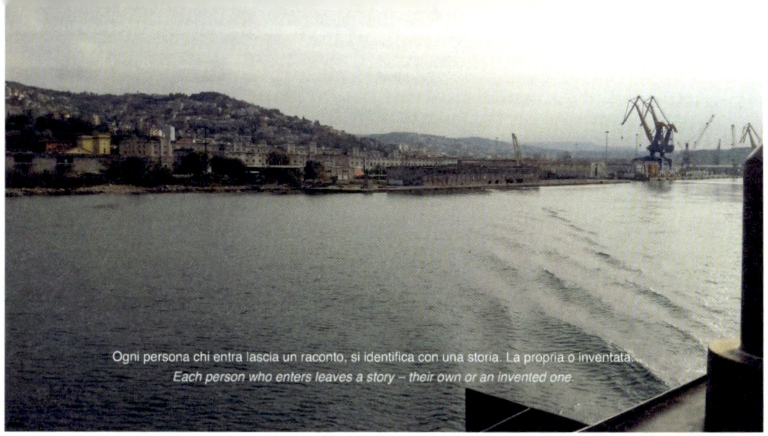

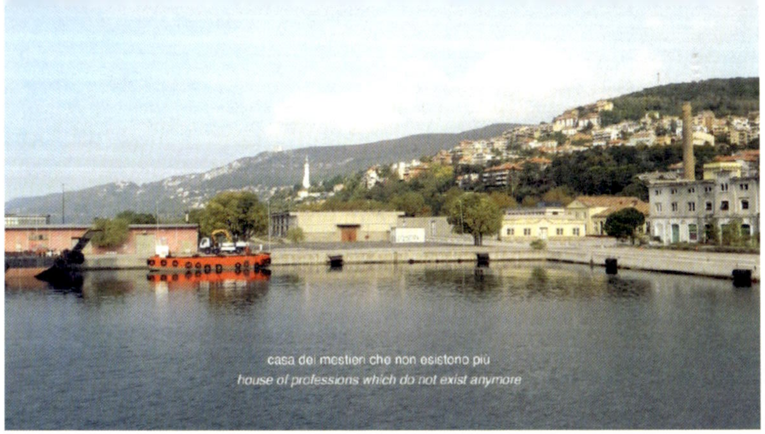

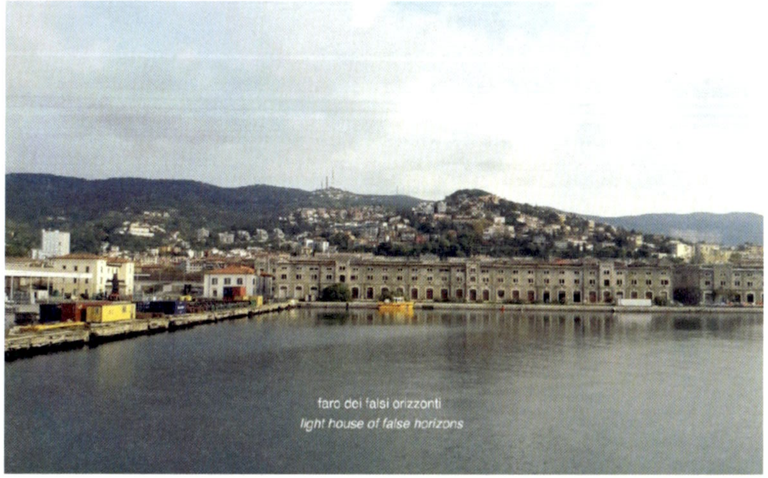

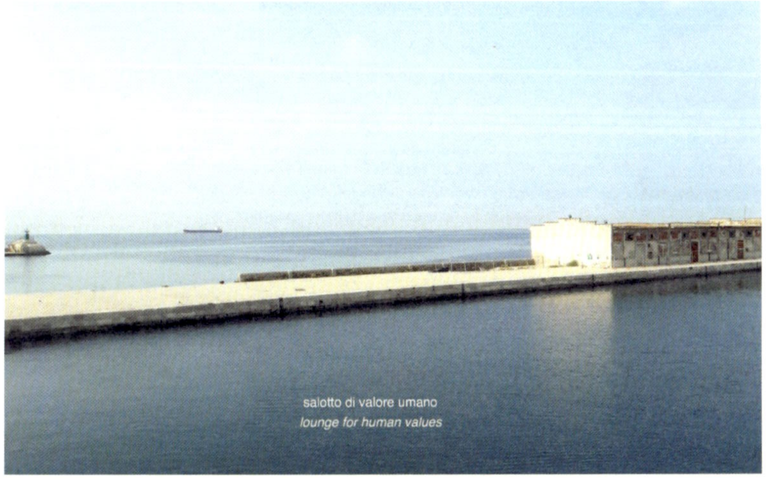

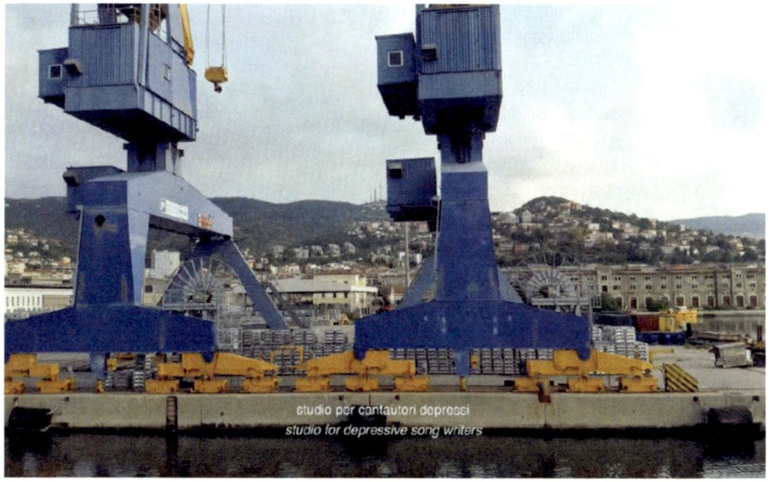

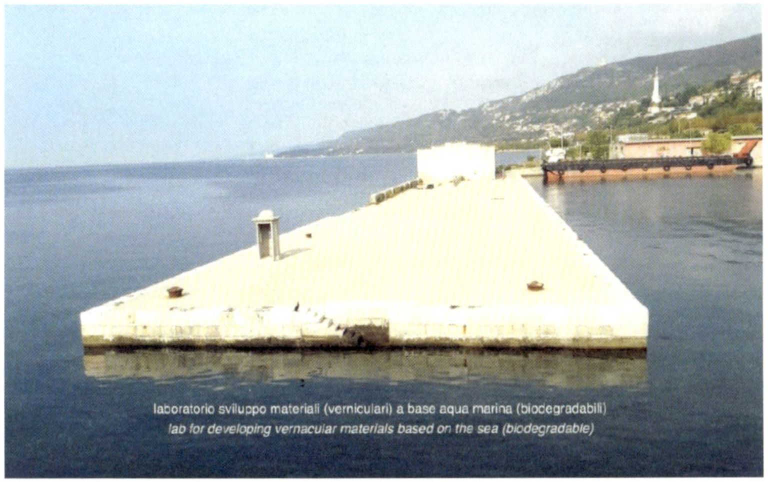

ONE HUNDRED DESIRES FOR HARBOUR FOR CULTURES
Video stills, 2018

EINHUNDERT WÜNSCHE FÜR HARBOUR FOR CULTURES
Video-Stills, 2018

Shared values, ambulant gardens, and other spaces,
Trieste Contemporanea, Trieste, 2018

Shared values, ambulant gardens, and other spaces,
Trieste Contemporanea, Triest, 2018

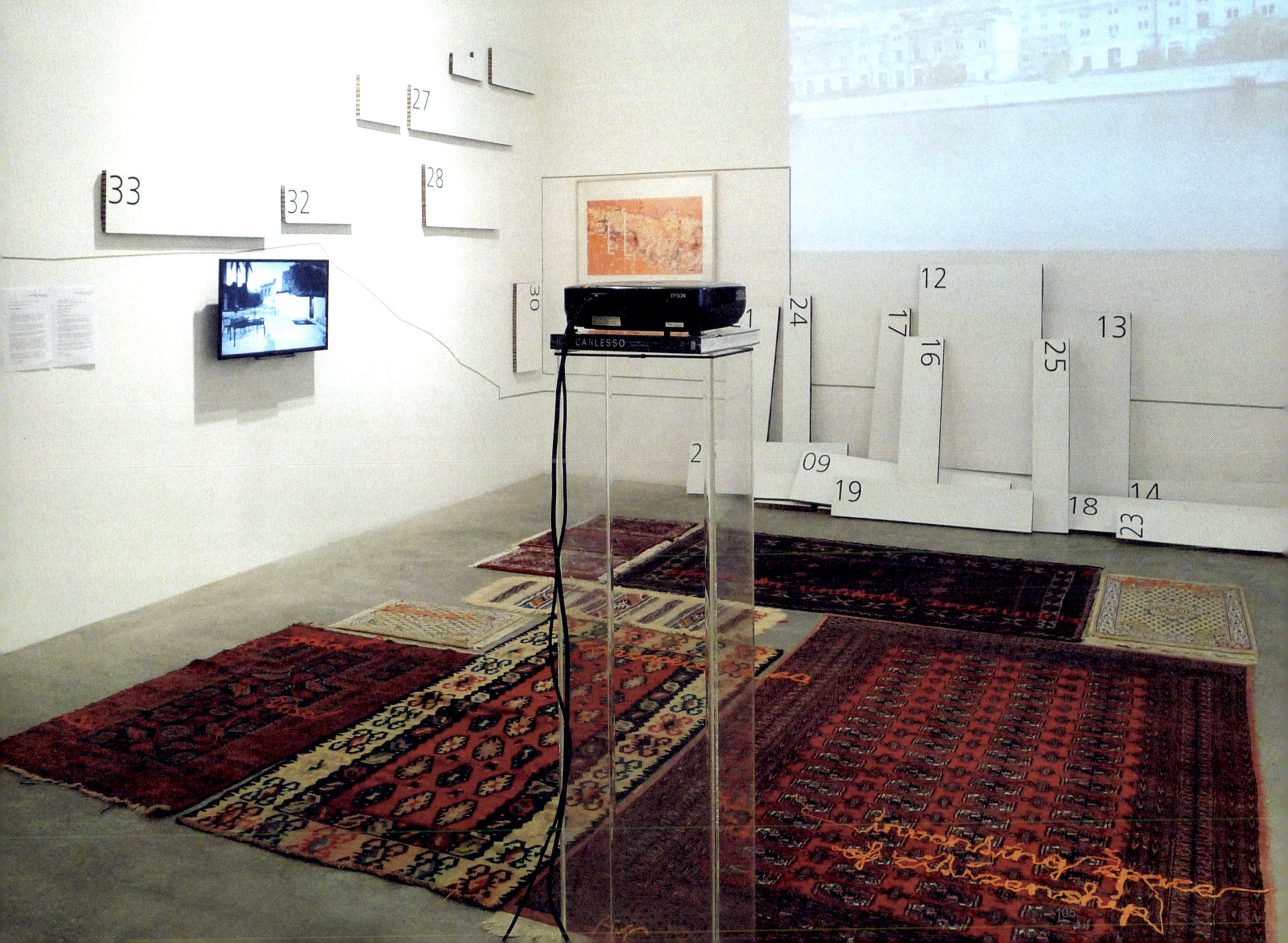

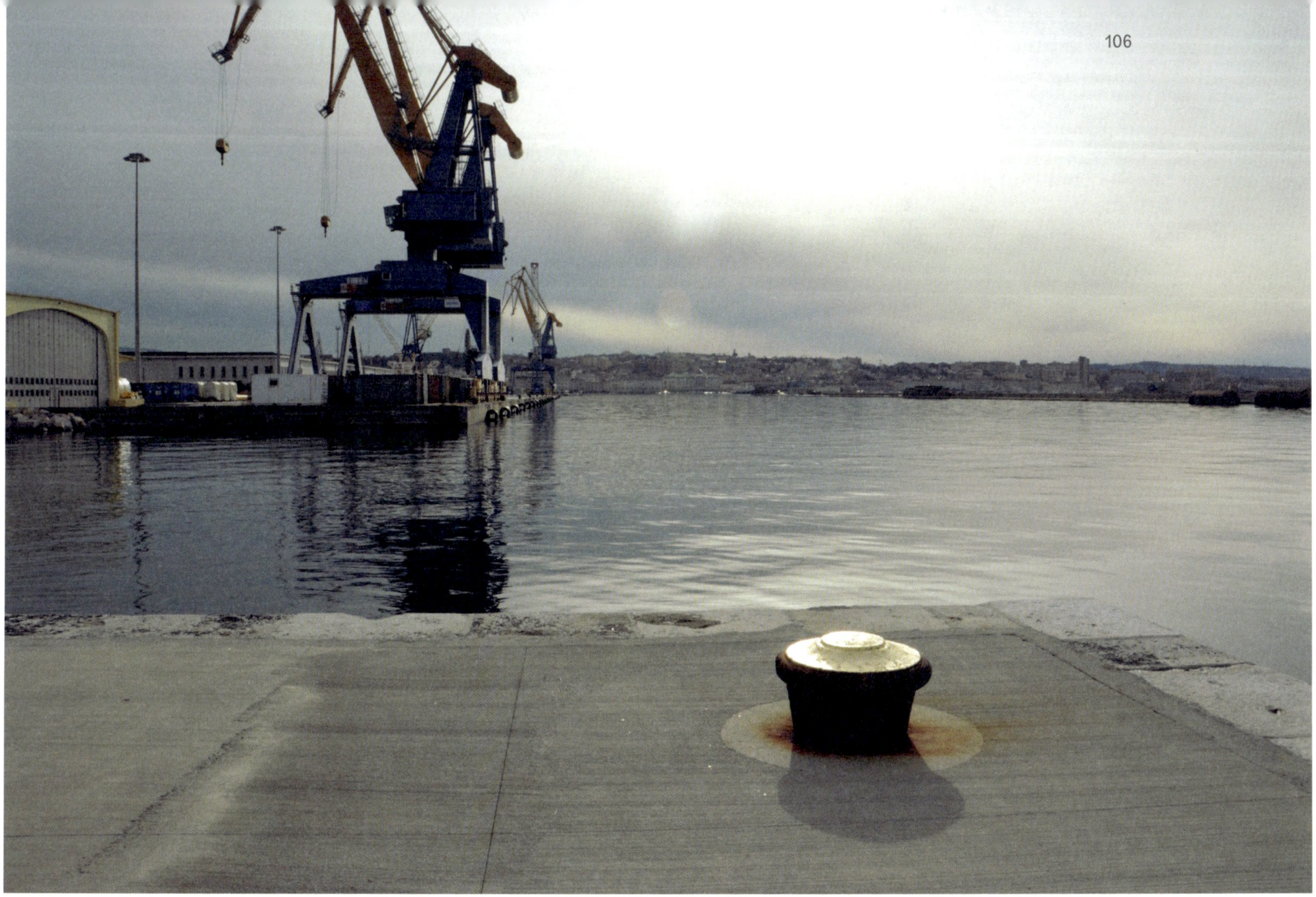

A PROMISE FOR HARBOUR FOR CULTURES
Gilded bollard, Porto Vecchio, Jan. 2, 2018

EIN VERSPRECHEN FÜR HARBOUR FOR CULTURES
Vergoldeter Poller, Porto Vecchio, 2. Januar 2018

III. Silent Activism, Dialog, and Poetic Moments

Stiller Aktivismus, Dialog und poetische Momente

BARBARA HOLUB AND THE POSSIBILITY OF OTHER WORLDS

Enrico Lunghi

Confusion and unpredictability are major characteristics of the present day: our world stumbles through the immensity of contradictory information and gets lost in the abundance of haunting images circulating through the media and digital networks. Whereas until the end of the 20th century the illusion of progress—especially technical progress—indicated a path to follow, our societies no longer offer a coherent vision of their future and have embarked on a blind headlong rush that we suspect will be fatal. The growth of cities is accelerating everywhere, the devastation of land and sea is continuing, and natural disasters are multiplying (viewed from a human perspective). In addition, through the absurd use of incantation, politicians, the mainstream media, and investors (each of them probably more short-sighted or cynical than the others) constantly reiterate the mantra of "green" or "renewable" energy and the "circular economy" that is supposed to perpetuate our model of society, yet the construction and installation of wind turbines, solar panels and nuclear power plants requires a huge amount of the fossil fuel they claim to replace, and mountains of waste are piling up in remote areas, far from the temples of consumerism.

It's obvious that there are some who profit from this confusion. While the most privileged part of the world's population entertains and bores itself with mindless consumption, and the vast majority—consisting of the poor, workers (if not slaves), refugees and fugitives (euphemized as migrants)—tries to keep its head above water (while harboring the mad hope that one day it will be able to entertain itself like the aforementioned, the ruling classes (or "elites") concentrate power and wealth in their own hands in order to enjoy their temporary advantages as much as possible and to protect themselves from the coming conflicts.

The rich understood before anyone else that our planet would not be enough to keep the promise of consumerist happiness within the reach of the greatest number of people, a promise that capitalist reason—with the massive support of manipulative advertising emanating from it—has been constantly asserting since the beginning of the industrial age. You only have to bear in mind that until the 18th century, human societies sought above all to preserve their traditions by idealizing their past, thinking of the present as a state of decline in comparison with ancient times, and that it was only after the invention of the steam engine that people began to fantasize about a radiant and prosperous future—that was always deferred. Even if it meant sacrificing a few generations of proletarians in the process.

BARBARA HOLUB OU LA POSSIBILITÉ D'AUTRES MONDES

Enrico Lunghi

La confusion et l'imprédictibilité sont des caractéristiques majeures de l'époque actuelle : notre monde erre dans l'immensité des informations contradictoires et s'abîme dans l'abondance d'images obsédantes qui circulent à travers les médias et les réseaux numériques. Alors que jusqu'à la fin du XXe siècle, l'illusion d'un progrès – surtout technique – leur indiquait une trajectoire à suivre, nos sociétés ne proposent désormais plus de vision cohérente de leur devenir et se sont engagées dans une fuite en avant et en aveugle que l'on pressent mortifère. Partout s'accélère l'accroissement des villes, se poursuit la dévastation des terres et des mers et se multiplient les catastrophes naturelles (considérées ainsi du point de vue des humains). À cela s'ajoute que, par un absurde recours à l'incantation, les politiques, les médias dominants et les investisseurs (probablement tous plus myopes ou cyniques les uns que les autres) ressassent le mantra des énergies «vertes» ou «renouvelables» et de «l'économie circulaire» censées perpétuer notre modèle de société, alors même que la construction et l'installation d'éoliennes, de panneaux solaires et de centrales nucléaires nécessitent grandement l'énergie fossile qu'ils prétendent remplacer et que les montagnes de déchets s'accumulent dans les zones reculées, loin des temples de la consommation.

Qu'il y en ait qui tirent profit de cette confusion est une évidence. Tandis que la partie la plus chanceuse de la population mondiale se divertit et s'abrutit en consommant de manière insensée, et que la grande majorité – constituée de pauvres, de travailleurs (sinon d'esclaves), de réfugiés et de fuyants («euphémisés» en migrants) – cherche à garder la tête hors de l'eau (tout en nourrissant le fol espoir d'un jour être à même de se divertir comme la première), les classes dirigeantes (ou «élites») concentrent dans leurs mains les pouvoirs et les richesses afin de jouir autant que possible de leurs avantages temporaires et de se mettre à l'abri des conflits qui s'annoncent.

Car les riches ont compris avant les autres que notre planète ne suffira pas pour tenir la promesse d'un bonheur consumériste à la portée du plus grand nombre, promesse que la raison capitaliste – avec le soutien massif d'une publicité manipulatrice émanant d'elle – ne cesse d'assener depuis les débuts de l'ère industrielle. Il suffit de se rappeler que jusqu'au XVIIIe siècle, les sociétés humaines cherchaient surtout à préserver leurs traditions en idéalisant leur passé, pensant le présent comme un état déchu au regard des temps anciens, et que c'est seulement à partir de l'invention de la machine à vapeur que l'on s'est mis à fantasmer un futur radieux et prospère – et toujours reporté. Quitte à sacrifier quelques générations de prolétaires en attendant.

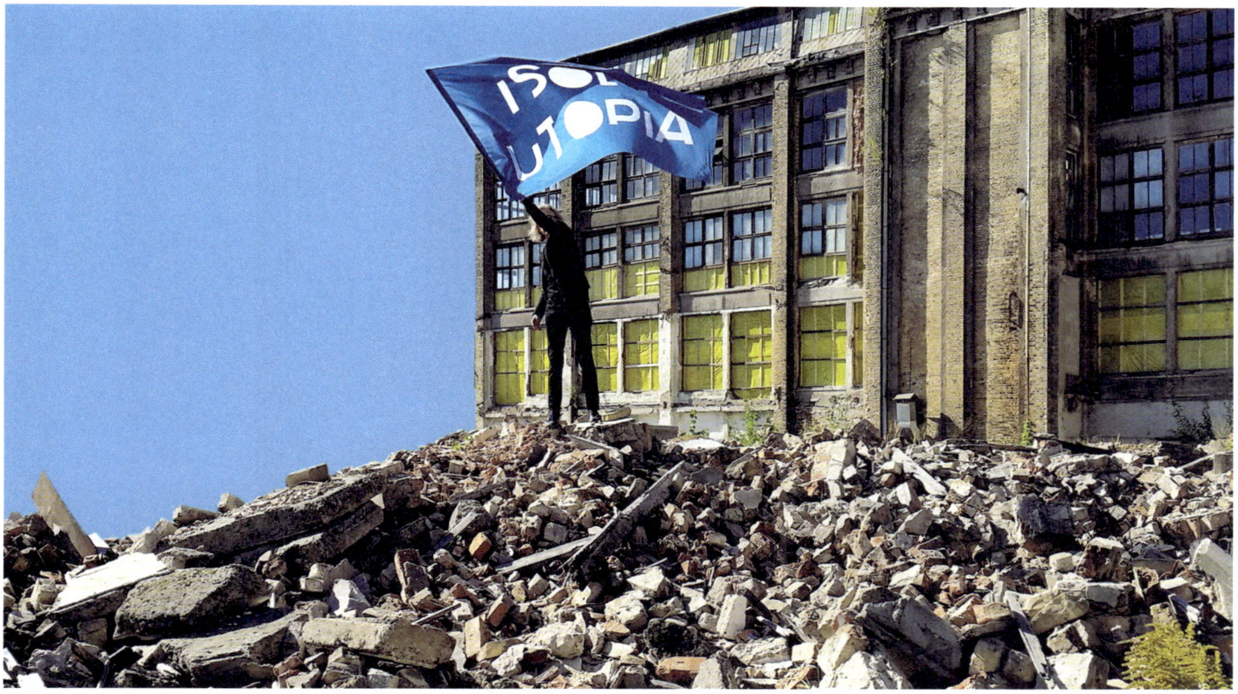

Bert Theis, from *Fight Specific Isola* to *Isola Utopia*, 2015

Bert Theis, von *Fight Specific Isola* zu *Isola Utopia*, 2015

Less than three centuries later, the findings make bitter (and bloody) reading: the Western or Westernized countries have managed to establish an enviable standard of living for some of their citizens thanks to the intensive and colonialist exploitation of the rest of the planet, while the overwhelming majority of the world's population struggles in indigence, even in misery, or in a situation of permanent or latent war. The growing threat of pollution, drastically reduced biodiversity and the grave consequences of climate change affect everyone.

The blindness, hubris and idiocy (in the medical sense of the word) of this capitalist rationale prevents it from integrating the idea of a limit because it is based on the principle of progression—stagnation being its worst enemy and regression its worst nightmare—and because it excludes the logic of a finite planet, going so far as to produce the chimera of an exploitation of outer space in order not to negate itself—in the same way that mathematical reasoning led to the invention of imaginary or complex numbers: great feats of the mind, allowing infinitesimal phenomena to be modeled and a plethora of universes to be conceived, but of no use when it comes to planting potatoes to feed the scientists.

In reality, territorial expansion of the capitalist system has not been possible since the last decades of the 20th century: with the fall of the Soviet bloc, no region of the world remains untouched by its reach (with the exception of the Sentinel Islands in the Andaman archipelago). This is where the financialization of the economy comes in, a convenient fiction for pursual of a virtual expansion of profits while

Moins de trois siècles plus tard, le constat est cinglant (et sanglant) : les pays occidentaux ou occidentalisés ont su instaurer un niveau de vie enviable pour une partie de leurs ressortissants grâce à l'exploitation intensive et colonialiste du reste de la planète, tandis que l'écrasante majorité de la population mondiale se débat dans l'indigence, voire dans la misère, quand ce n'est pas dans une situation de guerre permanente ou larvée. Et pour tous, une pollution de plus en plus menaçante, une réduction drastique de la biodiversité et un changement climatique lourd de conséquences.

L'aveuglement, l'hybris et l'idiotie (au sens médical du terme) de cette raison capitaliste l'empêchent d'intégrer l'idée d'une limite parce qu'elle est fondée sur le principe de la progression – la stagnation étant son pire ennemi et la régression son pire cauchemar – et parce qu'elle exclut les logiques d'une planète finie, allant jusqu'à produire la chimère d'une exploitation de l'espace pour ne pas se nier elle-même – un peu comme les raisonnements mathématiques ont mené à l'invention des nombres imaginaires ou complexes : de belles prouesses de l'esprit permettant de modéliser des phénomènes infinitésimaux et de concevoir pléthore d'univers, mais sans utilité lorsqu'il s'agit de planter des pommes de terre pour nourrir les savants.

En réalité, l'expansion territoriale du système capitaliste n'est plus possible depuis les dernières décennies du XXe siècle : avec la chute du bloc soviétique, aucune région du globe n'échappe plus à son emprise (à l'exception de l'île des Sentinelles, dans l'archipel d'Andaman). C'est d'ailleurs à ce moment qu'advient la financiarisation de l'économie, fiction pratique pour poursuivre une expansion virtuelle des bénéfices tout en accélérant sur le terrain la concentration

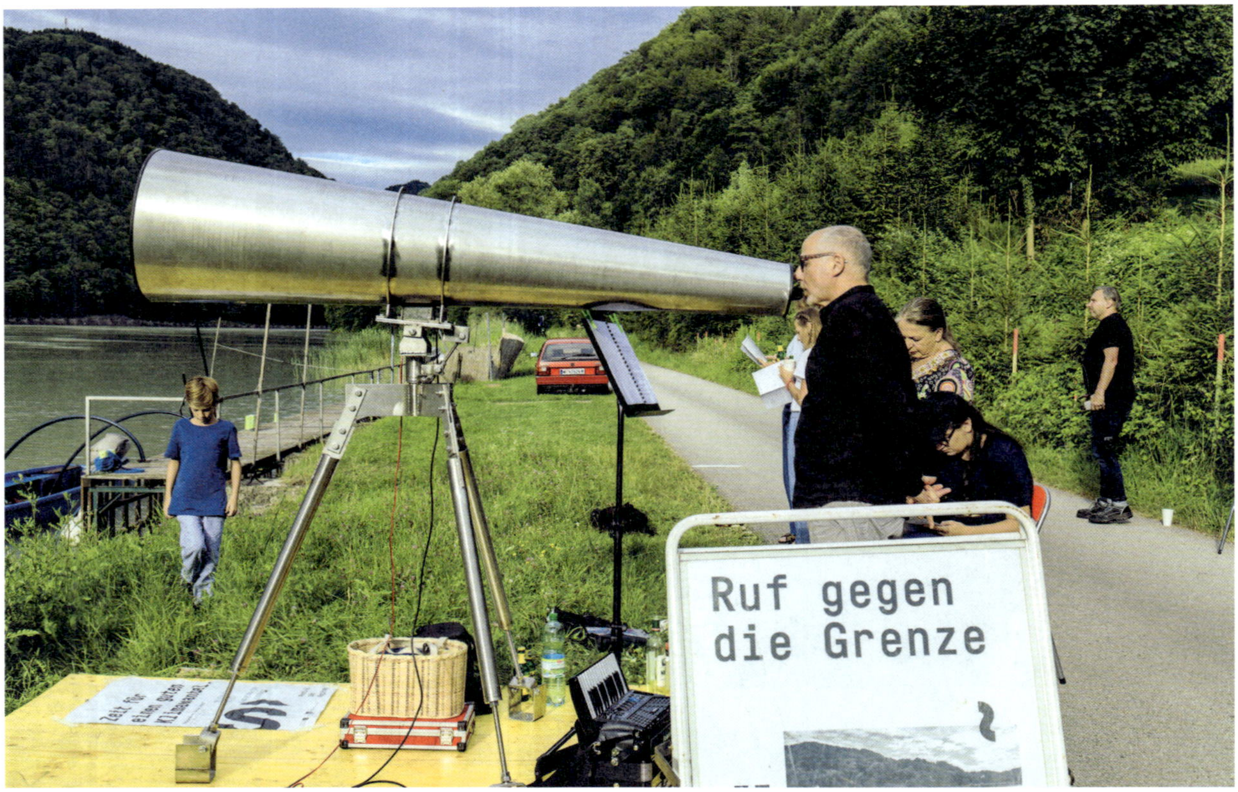

CALL AGAINST THE BORDER (transparadiso)
Grein (Upper Austria), *Festival of Regions*, 2018

RUF GEGEN DIE GRENZE (transparadiso)
Grein (Oberösterreich), *Festival der Regionen*, 2018

accelerating the concentration of wealth and power on the ground, with the support of digital technologies.

The Internet is another territory that gives the illusion of an ethereal infinity, whilst weighing very heavily in terms of materials and energy: Just think of the billions of mobile phone screens and computer cases, the countless cables littering the ocean floor, the increasingly invasive antennas, the entire buildings housing overheated servers, all the electricity consumed… not to mention the machines (running on petrol…) extracting the minerals and the factories manufacturing the components.

Ultimately, there is only one territory left for capitalism to conquer: the human body. It is the last to still be in expansion, and to exploit it fully all it takes is to desecrate the principle of physical integrity by dispossessing individuals of their full rights over it, as was done with the territories of indigenous peoples by Western colonizers, most often using cunning and force, if not extermination. The pandemic of the last two years has provided governments—who act as the interface between the interests of capital, whose puppets they are, and the people, who are under the illusion of electing their representatives—with an unhoped-for opportunity to carry out, through intimidation and coercion in the name of public health, the effective subjugation of bodies on a massive scale. In fact, public health is especially badly affected by the pollution and poor nutrition induced by the industrial system, something which the latter tries to conceal at all costs.

des richesses et des pouvoirs, avec l'appui des technologies numériques.

Or l'Internet est un autre territoire qui donne l'illusion d'un infini éthéré alors qu'il pèse très lourd en matières et en énergie : il suffit de songer aux milliards d'écrans de téléphones cellulaires et de boitiers d'ordinateurs, aux innombrables câbles jonchant le fond des océans, aux antennes de plus en plus envahissantes, aux bâtiments entiers abritant des serveurs surchauffés, à toute l'électricité consommée… sans compter les machines (roulant au pétrole…) pour extraire les minerais et les usines pour fabriquer les composants.

Finalement, il ne reste au capitalisme qu'un seul territoire à conquérir : le corps humain. C'est le dernier encore en expansion et pour l'exploiter à fond, il lui suffit de désacraliser le principe de l'intégrité physique en dépossédant les individus de leurs pleins droits sur elle, comme cela a été fait des territoires des peuples indigènes par les colonisateurs occidentaux, le plus souvent en faisant appel à la ruse et à la force, sinon à l'extermination. La pandémie des deux dernières années a fourni aux gouvernements – qui font office d'interface entre les intérêts du capital dont ils sont les marionnettes et le peuple entretenu dans l'illusion d'élire ses représentants – une occasion inespérée de s'exercer, par l'intimidation et la coercition au nom de la santé publique, à la soumission efficace des corps à grande échelle. Or la santé publique est surtout malmenée par la pollution et la mauvaise nutrition induites par le système industriel, ce que

It is a safe bet that in order to defend this system to the end and continue to ensure that the multinationals make their profits, the strategy of authoritarian and totalitarian governance will become more widespread in the coming decades, even in so-called democratic countries.

However, this headlong rush is a race against time which is doomed to failure. According to current projections, world population growth is already slowing down (except in Africa, the last continent to experience the demographic explosion, condemning large wild mammals to the extinction from which they have more or less escaped until now) and in less than a century it will be declining everywhere—admittedly, no present-day adult will witness this paradigm shift, but it is likely that most children born today will. And long before that, two other phenomena—which many of us are likely to witness—will pose problems: the reduction of habitable areas due to pollution and rising water levels, and the increasing age of the population. I imagine that the latter will be increasingly inclined to protect and retreat into itself, devoting more and more resources and energy (for the part that has them) to protecting itself and fighting for control of the remaining resources—which also explains the continuing and already noticeable increase in tensions (and arms sales) in the world. For the vast majority of humans, the worst dystopian scenarios will be the order of the day, because if until now we have been able to live on credit provided by the generosity of nature, the next generations will have to pay the bill and face, no matter what, the disaster created by those who preceded them. Thus, after only three centuries of shameless plundering of a bountiful planet, the last performance of the industrial and capitalist system will take place in the desolation of a theater offering only shortages and conflicts.

Perhaps there will then appear, in rare remote regions, attempts to build human societies based on other principles, such as self-sufficiency and restraint, and fully aware of their limits, which today is nothing more than utopian thinking—except perhaps for the people of the Sentinel Islands (so named by us) who, as far as we know, have been living for a very long time in perfect equilibrium on a small island which they have still not devastated.

This brings me back to art, and more particularly to Barbara Holub's practice and the transdisciplinary commitment of the transparadiso duo she founded with Paul Rajakovics in 1999.[1] Combining the vocation of artists, theoreticians and architect-urban planners, they intervene in problematic urban situations, proposing works in collaboration with the inhabitants. They developed the concept of direct urbanism for this practice, in reference to the concept of direct action theorized at the beginning of the 20th century to define interventions in the economic or political context of a city without the intermediary of institutional representatives. Although transparadiso's projects are usually realized with the support of an art centre

ce dernier s'efforce d'occulter à tout prix. Il est à parier que pour le défendre jusqu'au bout et continuer à assurer aux multinationales leurs bénéfices, la stratégie de gouvernance autoritaire et totalisante se généralisera dans les décennies qui viennent, même dans les pays dits démocratiques.

Pourtant, cette fuite en avant est une course contre la montre perdue d'avance. D'après les projections actuelles, la croissance de la population mondiale ralentit déjà (sauf en Afrique, le dernier continent à connaître l'explosion démographique, ce qui condamne les grands mammifères sauvages à l'extinction à laquelle ils ont plus ou moins échappé jusqu'à présent) et dans moins d'un siècle, elle déclinera partout – certes, aucun adulte actuel n'assistera à ce changement de paradigme, mais il est probable que la plupart des enfants qui naissent aujourd'hui le connaîtront. Et bien avant cela, deux autres phénomènes – auxquels beaucoup d'entre nous ont toutes les chances d'assister – poseront problème : la réduction des zones habitables en raison des pollutions et de la montée des eaux et le vieillissement de la population. J'imagine que cette dernière sera de plus en plus encline à se protéger et à se refermer sur elle-même, consacrant de plus en plus de moyens et d'énergie (pour la partie qui en dispose) à se protéger et à se battre pour le contrôle des dernières ressources – d'où aussi l'augmentation continue et déjà perceptible des tensions (et des ventes d'armes) dans le monde. Pour une grande majorité des humains, les pires scénarios dystopiques seront de mise, car si jusqu'à présent nous avons pu vivre à crédit sur le dos d'une nature généreuse, les générations naissantes devront, elles, payer la facture et faire face, coûte que coûte, au désastre fabriqué par celles qui les ont précédées. Ainsi, après trois siècles seulement de pillage sans vergogne d'une planète foisonnante, le dernier spectacle du système industriel et capitaliste s'accomplira dans la désolation d'un théâtre n'offrant que pénuries et conflits.

Apparaîtront alors peut-être, dans de rares régions à l'écart, des tentatives de construire des sociétés humaines fondées sur d'autres principes, comme l'autarcie et la retenue, et pleinement conscientes de leurs limites, ce qui aujourd'hui ne relève que de la pensée utopique – sauf peut-être pour le peuple des Sentinelles (ainsi nommé par nous) qui vit, d'après ce que nous en savons, depuis longtemps en équilibre sur une petite île qu'il n'a toujours pas dévastée.

Cela me ramène à l'art, et plus particulièrement à la démarche de Barbara Holub et à l'engagement transdisciplinaire du duo transparadiso qu'elle a fondé avec Paul Rajakovics en 1999.[1] Combinant la vocation d'artistes, de théoriciens et d'architectes urbanistes, ils interviennent dans des situations urbaines problématiques en proposant un travail en collaboration avec les habitants. Ils ont développé pour cette pratique le concept d'urbanisme direct, en référence à celui d'action directe théorisé au début du XXe siècle pour définir les interventions dans le contexte économique ou politique d'une cité sans l'intermédiaire des représentants des institutions. Bien que les projets de transparadiso

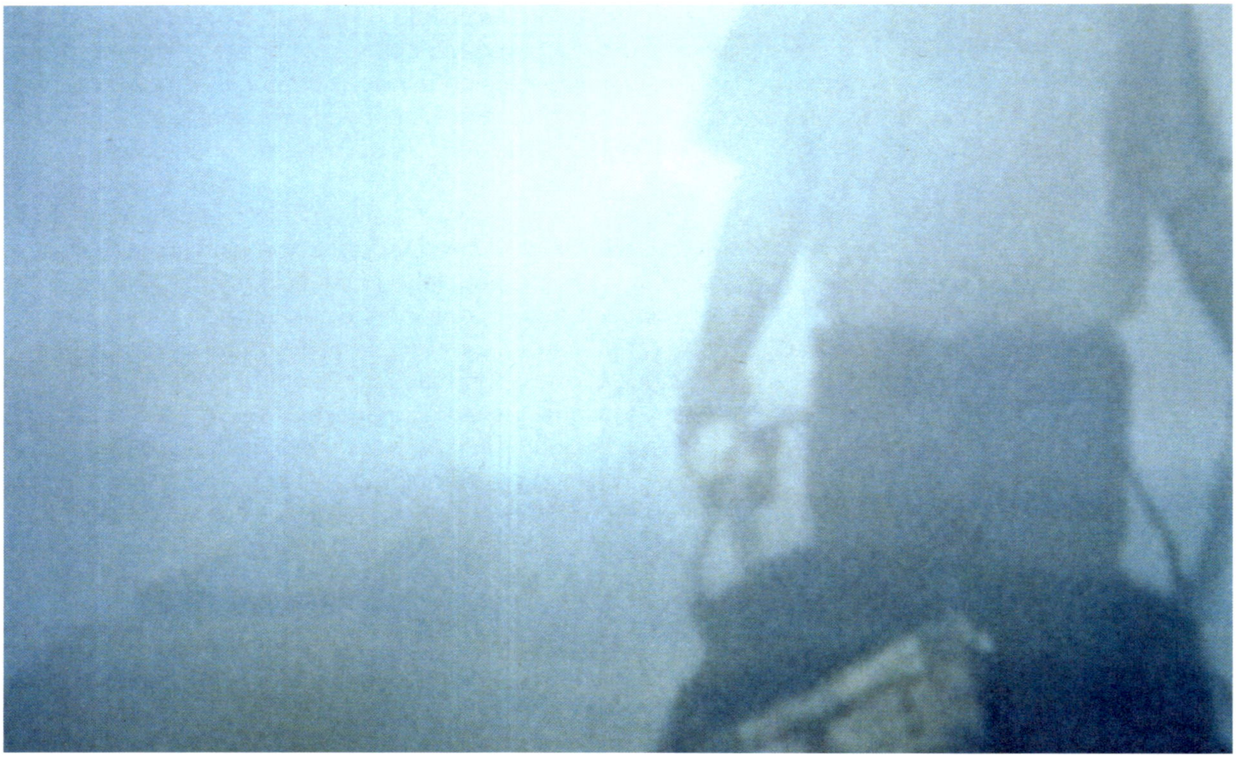

PREPARING GROUND, 2000
Asphalting the floor of Barbara Holub's new studio laid the groundwork for the installation of the garden for BETWEEN ROLES, thus addressing diverse formats of labor between the hard necessity to earn a living and leisure activities.

BODEN BEREITEN, 2000
Das Asphaltieren des Fußbodens von Barbara Holubs neuem Atelier bereitete den Boden für die Installation des Gartens für ZWISCHEN-ROLLEN und thematisierte damit verschiedene Formate von Arbeit zwischen harter Erwerbsrealität und Freizeitaktivitäten.

they aim to highlight what the public authorities neglect, conceal or cannot manage.

For MORE OPPORTUNITIES (Plymouth Arts Centre, 2007) for example, Barbara Holub staged a demonstration with white, message-less placards, in reference to the dockers' strikes of the 1960s which occurred after almost three centuries of good relations between the naval port—for a long time the city's main employer—and the citizens, a cohabitation which was considered beneficial to both parties. However, the successive de-industrialization and privatization of land benefited a few private companies at the expense of an impoverished population, leaving the latter with the bitter feeling of having missed an opportunity to start afresh. The public authorities, instead of playing their redistributive role, fully submitted to neoliberal logic by favoring the concentration of wealth.

In other projects Barbara Holub highlights the social weight of fashion on Muslim women in Austria (LISTEN TO THE QUIET VOICE, 2008), or takes the neighborhood as subject by organizing exchanges in a reconstructed garden in order to underline the rarity of real proximity between inhabitants in today's cities (ZWISCHENROLLEN/ BETWEEN ROLES, Hannover in 2000 and Graz in 2002).

More often than not, in the urban contexts in which she is invited to act, she identifies thorny or uncomfortable

se fassent généralement avec l'appui d'un centre d'art, ils visent à mettre en évidence ce que les pouvoirs publics négligent, occultent ou ne maîtrisent pas.

Pour MORE OPPORTUNITIES (Plymouth Arts Centre, 2007) par exemple, Barbara Holub a mis en scène une manifestation avec des panneaux blancs, sans message, en référence aux grèves des dockers des années 1960, survenues après presque trois siècles d'une bonne entente entre le port naval – longtemps le principal employeur de la ville – et les citoyens, cohabitation jugée jusque-là bénéfique pour les deux parties. Or la désindustrialisation et la privatisation successive des terrains ont profité à quelques compagnies privées aux dépens d'une population paupérisée, laissant cette dernière avec le sentiment amer d'avoir manqué une occasion de repartir sur de nouvelles bases. Quant aux pouvoirs publics, au lieu de jouer leur rôle de redistribution, ils se sont entièrement soumis à la logique néolibérale en favorisant la concentration des richesses.

Dans d'autres projets, Barbara Holub thématise le poids social de la mode sur les femmes musulmanes en Autriche (LISTEN TO THE QUIET VOICE, 2008), ou prend comme sujet le voisinage en organisant des dialogues dans un jardin reconstitué, afin de souligner la rareté d'une réelle proximité entre les habitants dans les villes actuelles (ZWISCHEN-ROLLEN, Hannovre en 2000 et Graz en 2002).

issues and proposes, in discussion and collaboration with the people concerned, to give them an aesthetic form (in the broadest possible sense), which means a sensitive, non-discursive and non-authoritarian expression of the issue: participatory workshops, collective performances, secular processions... each community and each situation calling for a different solution. To clarify the nature of her career as an artist, theorist and educator, Barbara Holub considers it, over the past ten years, as silent activism. Patient and unspectacular, this practice inserts itself into the shadowy areas of pretentious urban policies and aims above all to raise awareness of the mechanisms that underpin them and the subjugations they induce. This activism is more focused on the search for an agreed and shared experience in a certain time and place than on the production of a particular object or the achievement of a specific goal. It is deployed in the hope of generating a poetic moment felt by all the participants, a poetic moment that could open up unknown horizons, broaden the spectrum of the possible, or simply revive confidence in the ability to transform reality.

Ultimately, as I understand it, silent activism would lead to a slow but irrepressible spread of awareness of the values of solidarity, sharing, egalitarianism and respect for the environment (in the broadest sense, i.e. respect for living things), notions opposed to those advocated in an authoritarian and oppressive manner by our consumerist and capitalist societies, and which the resulting urbanism tramples mercilessly under the cover of misleading and perversely indoctrinating communication. It contributes to fighting fear and working for freedom through dialog and the sharing of ideas—a subversive commitment which, based on personal experience and individual responsibility, refuses to use the means and weapons (technical and psychological) of the industrial age which have made it possible to establish a society of mass submission, and systematic and total domination of the population.

My feeling is that art projects such as these, or the concept of concrete utopia proposed by Bert Theis[2] (1952–2016), an artist whose work is complementary to Barbara Holub's, are being undertaken without the arrogance of turn-key solutions imposed by those who claim to know what is good for others (while applying formulas whose inadequacy has been demonstrated time and again) and without any illusions about their power to transform the real conditions of the people concerned, let alone an entire city. They show, each in their own way, that other worlds are possible, and that the direction in which humanity as a whole is stumbling is the result of a multitude of choices added together, not an inescapable destiny.

If the majority of people were aware of these choices and clearly recognized them, they would perhaps move quickly enough to change course, or at least not be dragged so passively into a tragic impasse. But the fear

Le plus souvent, dans les contextes urbains où elle est invitée à agir, elle repère des sujets épineux ou malaisés et propose, en discussion et en collaboration avec les personnes concernées, de leur donner une forme esthétique (au sens large), c'est-à-dire une expression sensible, non discursive ni autoritaire : ateliers participatifs, performances collectives, processions laïques... chaque communauté et chaque situation appelant une solution différente. Pour clarifier la responsabilité de son parcours d'artiste, de théoricienne et d'enseignante, Barbara Holub le considère, depuis une dizaine d'années, comme un activisme tranquille. Patiente et peu spectaculaire, cette pratique s'insère dans les zones d'ombre des politiques urbaines prétentieuses et vise avant tout une prise de conscience des mécanismes qui les sous-tendent et des assujettissements qu'elles induisent. Cet activisme est davantage tourné vers la recherche d'une expérience consentie et partagée dans un temps et un lieu que vers la production d'un objet particulier ou l'atteinte d'un objectif précis. Il se déploie dans l'espoir de parvenir à engendrer un moment poétique ressenti par tous les participants, moment poétique susceptible d'ouvrir sur des horizons inconnus, d'élargir le spectre du possible, ou simplement de raviver la confiance en la capacité à transformer le réel.

Dans l'acception ultime tel que je le comprends, l'activisme tranquille déboucherait sur une lente mais irrépressible propagation des sensibilités aux valeurs de solidarité, de partage, d'égalitarisme et de respect de l'environnement (au sens large, c'est-à-dire de respect du vivant), notions opposées à celles prônées de manière autoritaire et oppressante par nos sociétés consuméristes et capitalistes et que l'urbanisme qui en découle piétine impitoyablement sous le couvert d'une communication mensongère, voire perversement décervelante. En fin de compte, il contribue à combattre la peur et à œuvrer pour la liberté par le biais du dialogue et la mise en commun des réflexions – engagement subversif s'il en est et qui, en s'appuyant sur l'expérience personnelle et la responsabilité individuelle, refuse d'utiliser les moyens et les armes (techniques et psychologiques) de l'ère industrielle qui ont permis d'établir une société de soumission massive et de domination systématique et totale des populations.

De tels projets artistiques, tout comme ceux découlant du concept de l'utopie concrète élaboré par Bert Theis[2] (1952–2016), un artiste dont le travail amène des réflexions complémentaires à celui de Barbara Holub, sont réalisés – c'est du moins mon sentiment – sans l'arrogance des solutions clé en main imposées par ceux qui prétendent savoir ce qui est bon pour les autres (non sans n'appliquer que des recettes dont l'indigence a maintes fois été démontrée) et sans pour autant s'illusionner sur leur pouvoir de transformation des conditions réelles des gens concernés, a fortiori d'une ville entière. Ils montrent, chacun à leur manière, que d'autres mondes sont possibles, et que la voie dans laquelle s'enfonce l'humanité dans son ensemble est le résultat d'une multitude de choix mis bout à bout, non un destin inéluctable.

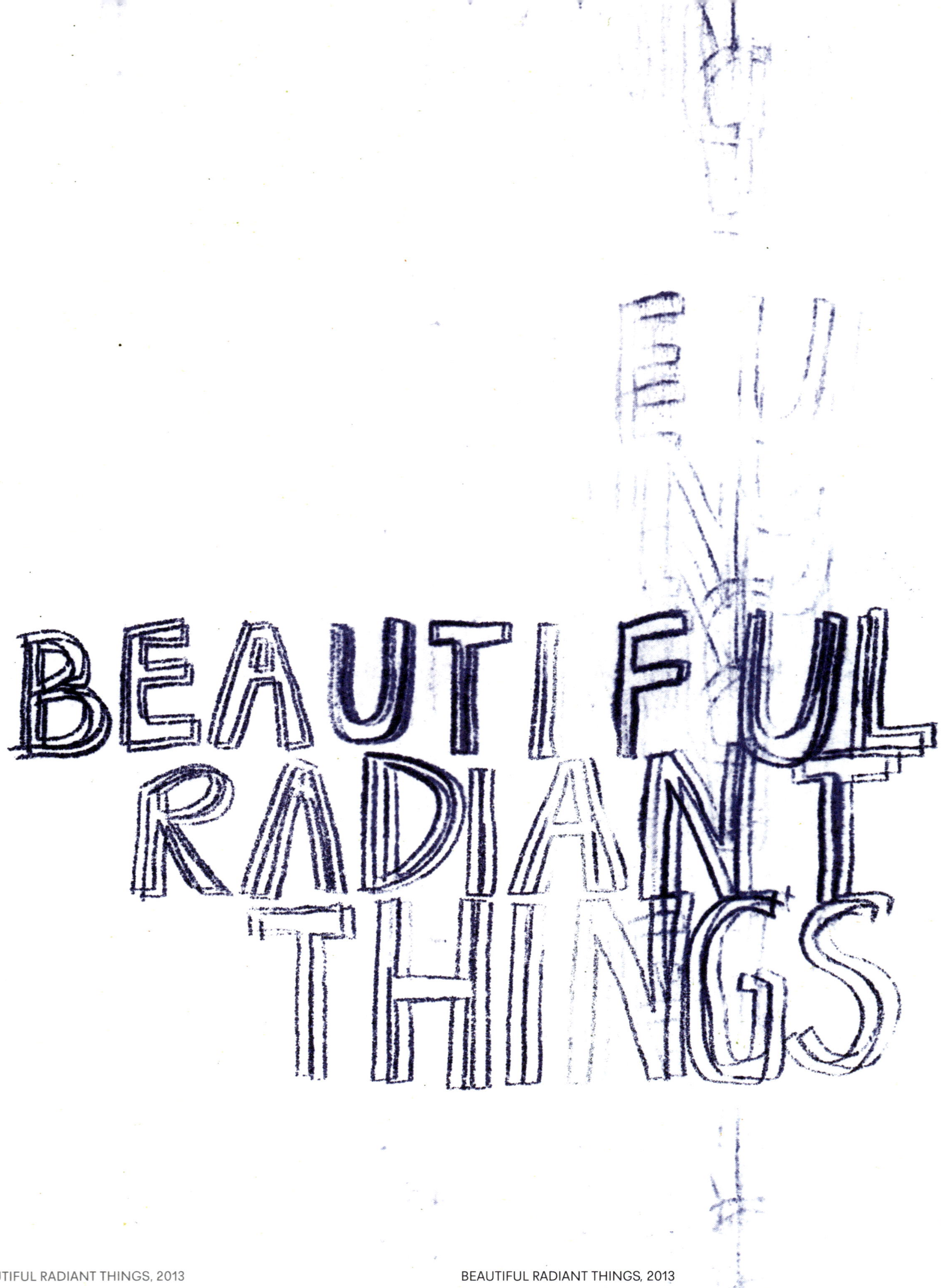

BEAUTIFUL RADIANT THINGS, 2013

BEAUTIFUL RADIANT THINGS, 2013

and confusion in which they are kept prevent them from rallying around a minimum of common positions, which serves the interests of the ruling classes, who have no other strategy left to mask their inability to avoid the foreseeable catastrophe. It is obvious that the "elites" have already lost control of the situation: trapped in their own logic, isolated from concrete realities and left only with the choice of murderous immoderation, they are nevertheless chained to the same people that they are plunging into the abyss and will end up living in fear of losing everything.

In the past, humanity experimented with many forms of society simultaneously, even adapting them to the changing seasons[3]: this is no longer the case. The grip of the capitalist system on the entire planet is as total as it is fatal. More and more people are feeling it in their bones: beyond a certain threshold—which the scarcity of natural resources, the explosion of energy costs and the multiplication of ecological disasters will rapidly lower—this system will no longer work, whatever the means put in place to control the populations and the brutality employed to repress them. By that time at the latest, alternative thought systems, such as those explored through the silent activism of Barbara Holub, will be valued.[EL]

1 barbaraholub.com and transparadiso.com

2 berttheis.com

3 David Graeber & David Wengrow: The Dawn of Everything: A New History of Humanity, Penguin / Allen Lane, 2021

Si la majorité des gens était consciente de ces choix et qu'elle les reconnaissait clairement, elle s'attellerait peut-être assez vite à un changement de cap, ou du moins ne se laisserait-elle pas entraîner aussi passivement dans une impasse tragique. Mais la peur et la confusion dans lesquelles elle est entretenue l'empêchent de se rassembler autour d'un minimum de positions communes, ce qui est à l'avantage des classes dirigeantes qui n'ont plus d'autre stratégie pour masquer leur incapacité à éviter la catastrophe prévisible. Car il est évident que les «élites» ont déjà perdu le contrôle de la situation : enfermées dans leur logique, coupées des réalités concrètes et n'ayant plus que le choix d'un jusqu'a-uboutisme meurtrier, elles sont pourtant enchaînées au même peuple qu'elles plongent dans le gouffre et finiront par vivre dans la crainte de tout perdre.

Dans le passé, l'humanité expérimentait simultanément de nombreuses formes de société, allant jusqu'à les adapter aux changements de saisons[3] : ce n'est plus le cas aujourd'hui. L'emprise du système capitaliste sur la planète entière est aussi totale que fatale. De plus en plus de gens le ressentent dans leur chair : à partir d'un certain seuil – que la raréfaction des ressources naturelles, l'explosion des coûts énergétiques et la multiplication des désastres écologiques vont rapidement abaisser – ce système ne fonctionnera plus, quels que soient les moyens mis en place pour contrôler les populations et la brutalité employée à les réprimer. Au plus tard à ce moment, on appréciera à sa juste valeur des modèles de pensée différents, comme ceux expérimentés à travers l'activisme tranquille de Barbara Holub.[EL]

1 barbaraholub.com et transparadiso.com

2 berttheis.com

3 David Graeber & David Wengrow : Au commencement était... Une nouvelle histoire de l'humanité, Ed. Les liens qui libèrent, Paris, 2021

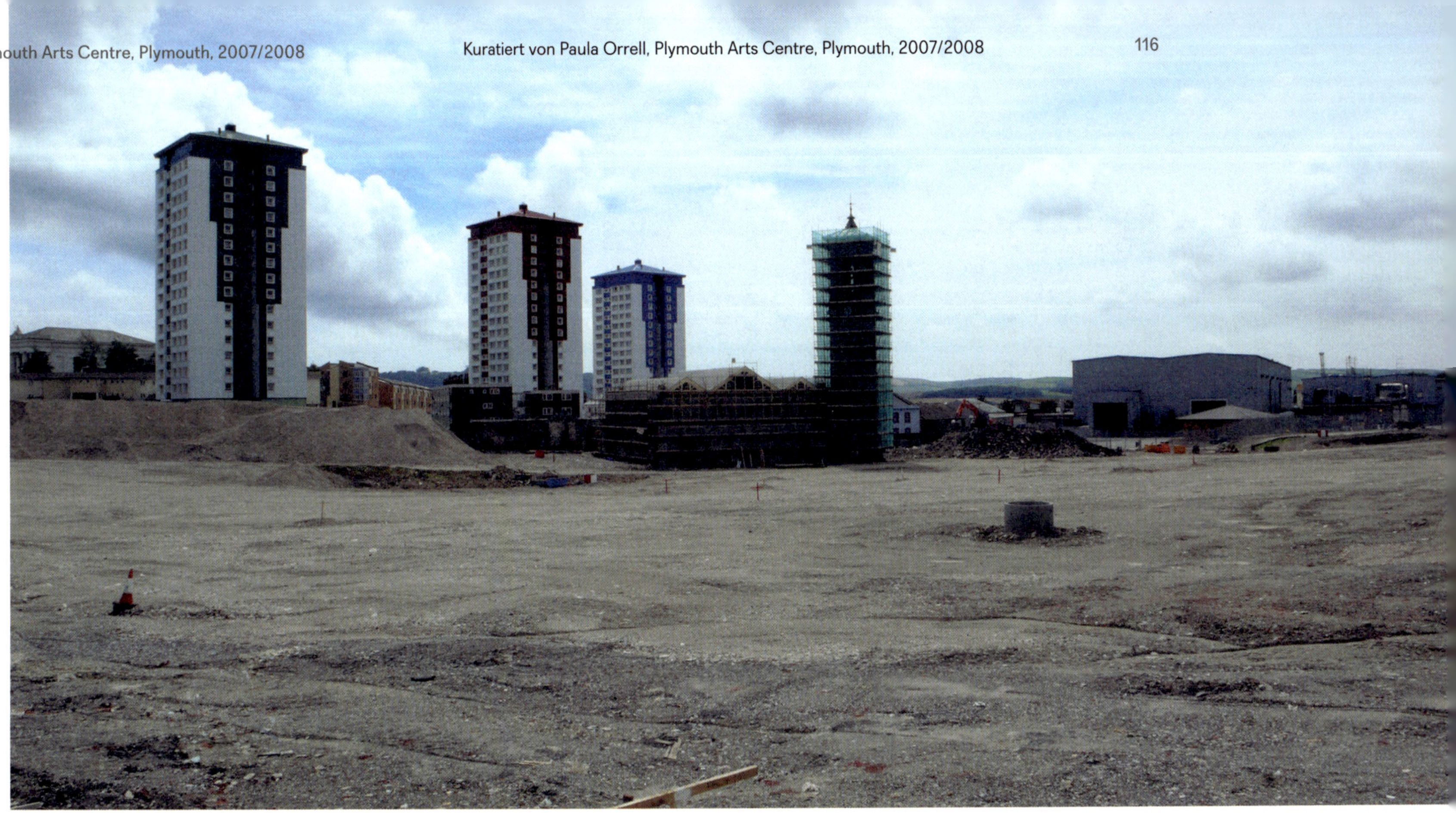

MORE OPPORTUNITIES

MORE OPPORTUNITIES is an early chapter in Holub's ongoing—and often abrasive—critique of "regeneration." Made in response to the redevelopment of Plymouth, the project explores the city's search for a new identity in a narrative and poetic way, rejecting the conventional idea of regeneration as a set of concrete solutions to urban problems in favor of a discursive approach that blends reality and fiction. As an artist and architect, Barbara Holub spent time talking to local people and planning departments in the city, consulting with those living in and around Devonport, then undergoing redevelopment. Taking the form of a "demonstration," MORE OPPORTUNITIES tests the limits of occupying space. As a format, the demonstration is arguably outdated, its retro-utopian character evinced by Holub's use of documentary footage of the dockyard strikes in Plymouth in the mid-1960s, which prefigure recent protests against the privatization of the naval yard in Devonport for residential development, which had failed to consider providing notions of urban public space. The feeling of lost opportunity that regeneration so often provokes is symptomatic of public-private

MORE OPPORTUNITIES

MORE OPPORTUNITIES ist ein frühes Kapitel aus Holubs anhaltender – und oft scharfer – Kritik des „Stadtumbaus". Bezugnehmend auf den Umbau von Plymouth verfolgt das Projekt narrativ und poetisch die Suche der Stadt nach einer neuen Identität. Mit einem diskursiven Ansatz, der Realität und Fiktion verknüpft, wendet es sich gegen die konventionelle Vorstellung von Stadterneuerung als einem Set konkreter „Lösungen" für urbane Probleme. Als Künstlerin und Architektin sprach Barbara Holub mit BewohnerInnen und städtischen Planungsbehörden, Leuten in und um den damals einer radikalen Transformation unterzogene Stadtteil Devonport. In Form einer „Demonstration" testet MORE OPPORTUNITIES die Grenzen der Aneignung von Raum aus. Eine Demonstration erscheint als Format für Veränderung eher unzeitgemäß. Ihr retro-utopischer Charakter zeigt sich auch in Holubs Verwendung dokumentarischen Filmmaterials von Werftarbeiterstreiks in Plymouth in den 1960er-Jahren als Vorläufer der neueren Proteste gegen die Privatisierung von Teilen der Marinebasis Devonport und deren Transformation in ein neues Wohnviertel, für das keinerlei Vorstellungen von

beyond the concrete origins of Plymouth, Holub suggests we think of urban transformation less as a search for new identities than as a provision of new opportunities for all.

The demonstration that forms the basis of MORE OPPORTUNITIES happened in front of Plymouth Arts Centre (then looking for a new site, thanks to regeneration) and directly references the demonstrations by dockyard workers in 1969. The dockyard and naval base were once major employers in the city, but the dockyard was privatized by property developer HML after years of decline. Some of the changes wrought by privatization include former navy officers functioning as tour guides in the dockyard, with visitors filling in questionnaires to assess whether the tour met their expectations. This narrativizing of social space—a signature ploy of property developers—is a tactic also used in MORE OPPORTUNITIES. Although the exhibition included video footage of the actual demonstration, the demonstration itself had a fictional premise. Because its placards and banners conveyed no message, viewers had to guess the cause of the people filing through Looe Street. The blank placards – visible in the show before the demonstration—could be interpreted in several ways: as a symbol of the innocence that participants of demonstrations sometimes show; of the different hopes that individuals project onto "the cause"; of the empty promises politicians make; of the lack of real choices for the electorate; and—most tellingly – of the ineffectiveness of demonstrations in our globalized economy.

In 2008, Barbara Holub developed the double video installation *Make News Instead Of*, based on a double slide projection in her show at Plymouth Arts Centre. This work focuses on Plymouth's transformation as an example of how former industrial cities are bowing to the new economic demands of globalization, exploring the rapid and radical change of the city's identity. The fictional documentary connects the manifestation of MORE OPPORTUNITIES to a collage of different materials: the science-fiction film *A Voyage to the Bottom of the Sea* by Irwin Allend (1961); a 16 mm documentary about the strike in the Plymouth shipyard by Southwest Filmarchive Plymouth (1969); Jill Craigie's documentary *The Way We Live*, about architect Sir Patrick Abercrombie (1946), who developed the visionary "Plan for Plymouth" in 1943 (after the medieval city centre was destroyed by German air raids in 1941). By overlaying current photos of the situations affected by urban renewal, Holub creates a "fictitious documentation" that opens up space for visions of future coexistence.[SA]

geht, ist typisch für Public-Private-Partnerships, die ihre Projekte meist durch eine konstruierte neue Identität vermarkten, wobei das kollektive Selbstverständnis der BewohnerInnen außer Acht gelassen wird. Jenseits der konkreten Situation von Plymouth propagiert Holub Stadterneuerung nicht nur als Suche nach einer neuen Identität, sondern auch als Schaffen neuer Möglichkeiten für alle.

Die Demonstration, die den Kern von MORE OPPORTUNITIES bildet, fand vor dem Plymouth Arts Centre statt (das sich wegen des urbanen Transformationsprozesses gerade nach einem neuen Standort umsah) und knüpfte direkt an die Demonstrationen der WerftarbeiterInnen von 1969 an. Die Werft und Marinebasis waren einst wesentliche Arbeitgeberinnen in der Stadt, aber die Werft war nach Jahren des Niedergangs von der Projektentwicklungsfirma Babcock International privatisiert worden. Eine der Folgen davon war, dass frühere Angehörige der Navy dann in den Docks als Tourguides fungierten, deren BesucherInnen hinterher per Fragebogen bewerteten, ob die Tour ihren Erwartungen entsprach. Diese Verwandlung des sozialen Raums in ein Narrativ – eine typische Strategie von ProjektentwicklerInnen – wird auch in MORE OPPORTUNITIES eingesetzt. In der Ausstellung waren zwar Videoaufnahmen von der Demonstration zu sehen, doch diese selbst war fiktiv. Da auf den Schildern und Transparenten keine Botschaft stand, waren die BetrachterInnen aufgefordert, sich zu fragen, für welches Anliegen die DemonstrantInnen vor dem Arts Centre auf die Straße gingen. Die leeren Schilder, die in der Ausstellung zu sehen waren, ließen sich verschieden deuten: als Symbol der Unschuld, die Demonstrierende bisweilen an den Tag legen; der unterschiedlichen Hoffnungen, die der/die Einzelne mit dem Anliegen verbindet; der leeren Versprechungen, die PolitikerInnen abgeben; des Mangels an echten Wahlmöglichkeiten für das Volk; und – wohl am bezeichnendsten – der Nutzlosigkeit von Demonstrationen in unserer globalisierten Wirtschaft.

2008 entwickelte Barbara Holub die Doppel-Videoinstallation *Make News Instead of*, die auf einer Dia-Doppelprojektion in der Ausstellung am Plymouth Arts Centre beruhte. Im Zentrum dieser Arbeit steht die Transformation von Plymouth als Beispiel für die „Anpassung" ehemaliger Industriestädte an die neuen ökonomischen Zwänge der Globalisierung. Um den raschen und radikalen Wandel der Identität der Stadt zu verdeutlichen, verknüpft die Künstlerin die Demonstration MORE OPPORTUNITIES mit einer Reihe anderer Materialien: dem Science Fiction-Film *Voyage to the Bottom of the Sea* von Irwin Allen (1961), einem 16-mm-Dokumentarfilm des Southwest Filmarchive Plymouth über den Werftarbeiterstreik (1969), und Jill Craigies Dokumentation *The Way We Live* über den Architekten Sir Patrick Abercrombie (1946), der 1943 (nach der Zerstörung des Stadtzentrums 1941 durch deutsche Luftangriffe) den visionären „Plan für Plymouth" entwarf. Durch die Überlagerung mit aktuellen Fotos der von Stadterneuerung betroffenen Situationen schafft Holub eine „fiktive Dokumentation", die Raum für Visionen zukünftigen Zusammenlebens eröffnet.[SA]

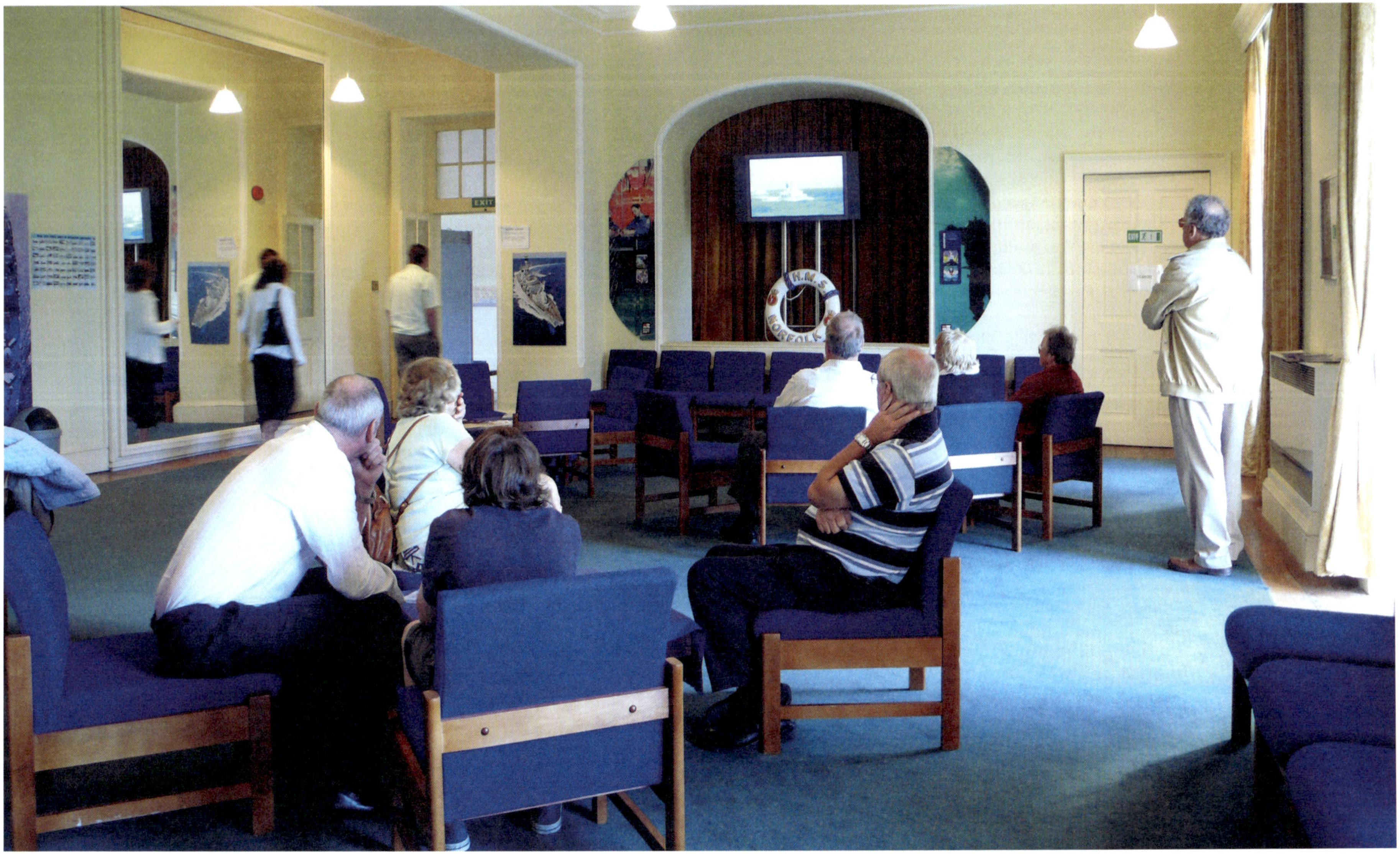

WELCOME TO THE NAVY BASE VISITOR CENTRE, 2007

WELCOME TO THE NAVY BASE VISITOR CENTRE, 2007

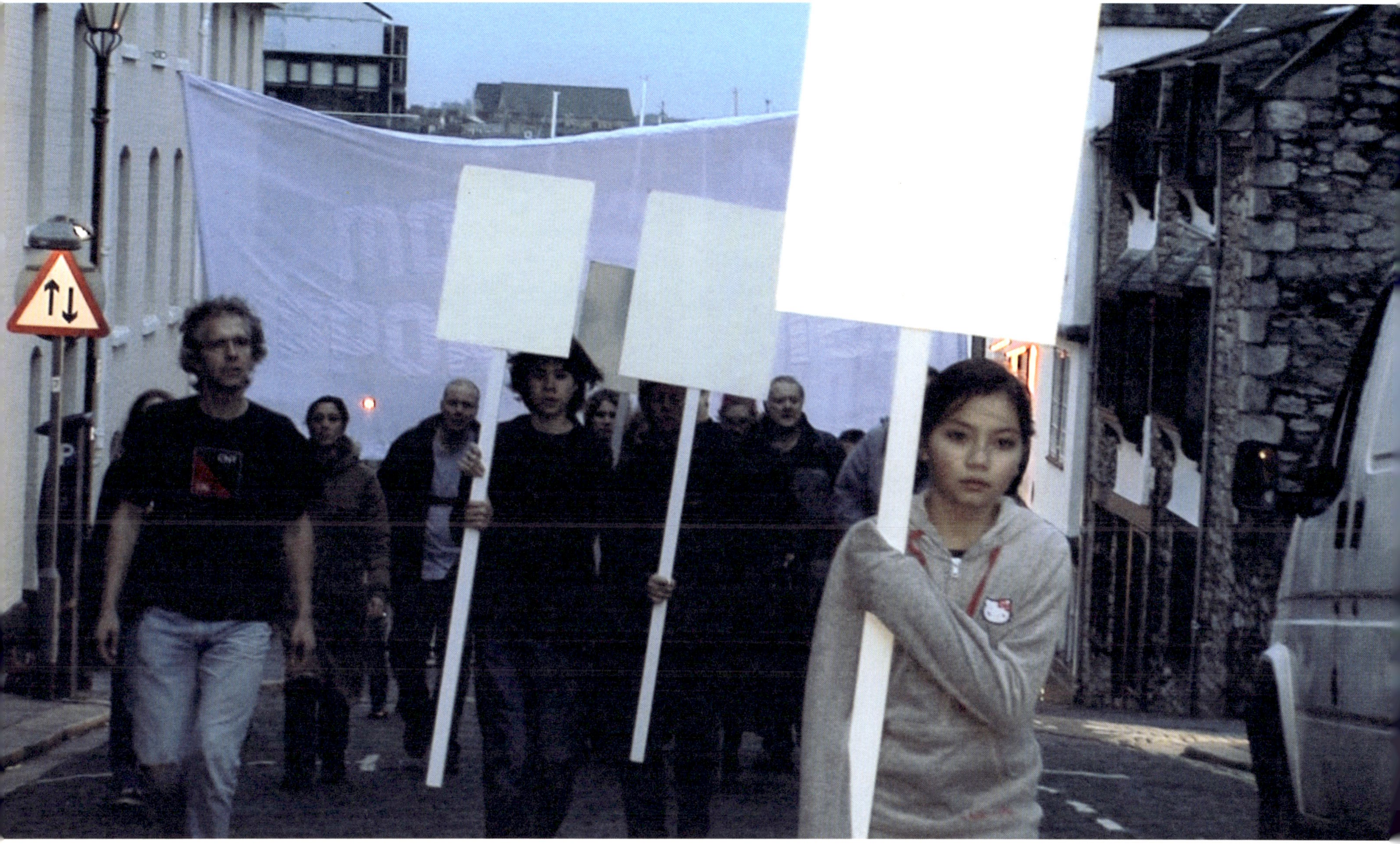

MORE OPPORTUNITIES
A staged demonstration in front of Plymouth Arts Centre, 2007

MORE OPPORTUNITIES
Eine inszenierte Demonstration vor dem Plymouth Arts Centre, 2007

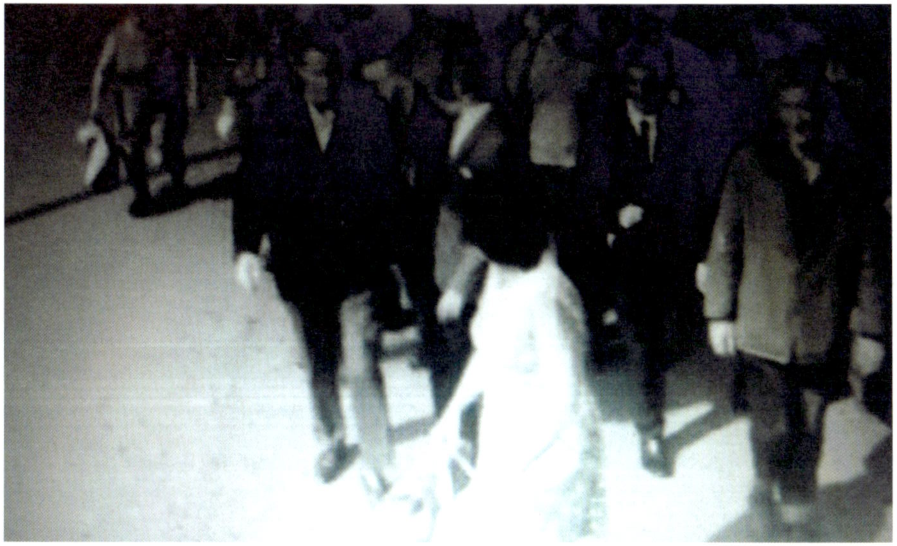

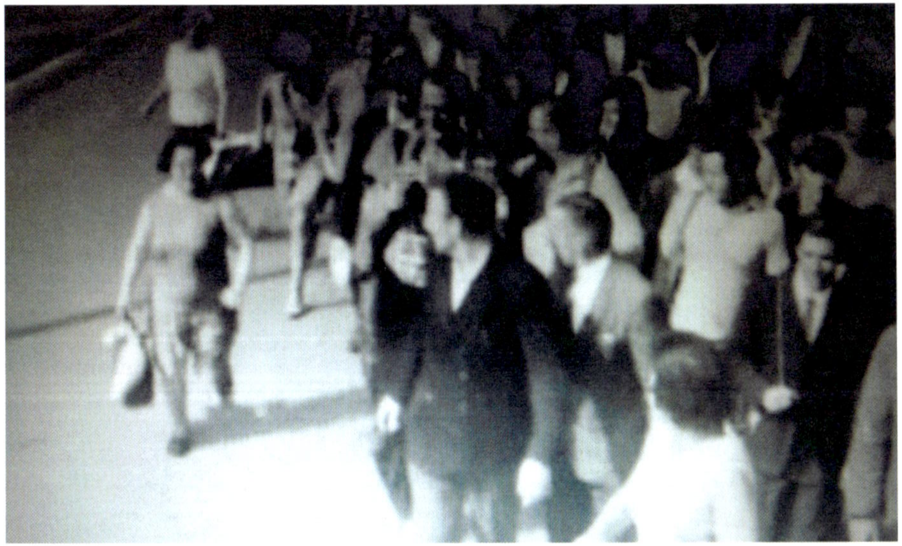

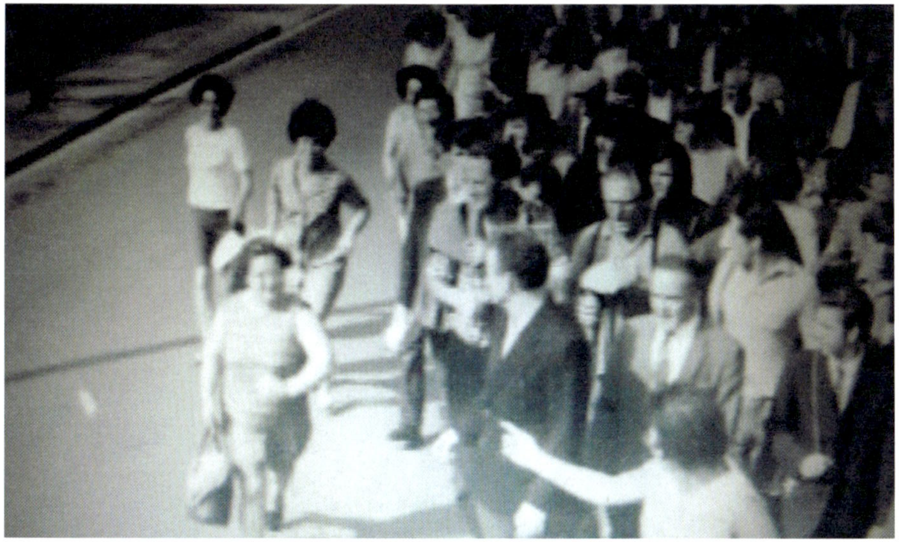

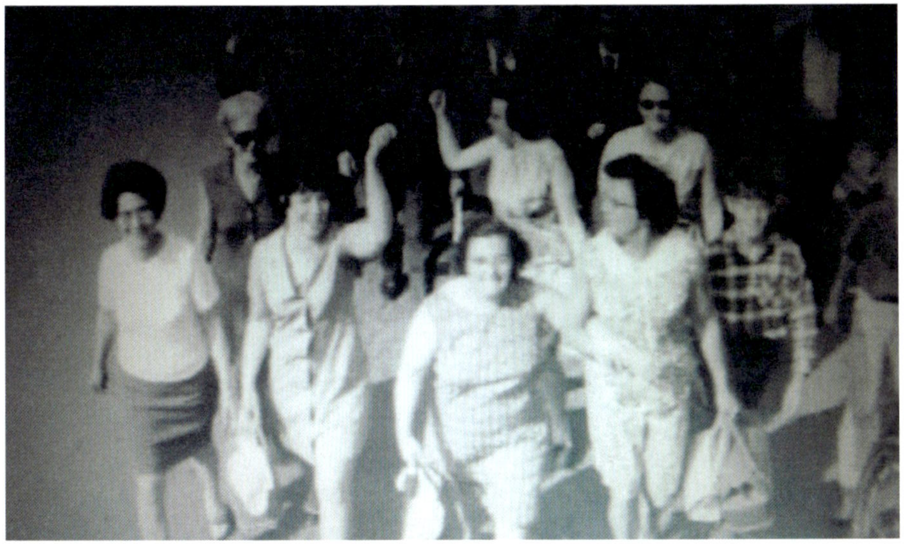

WE SHALL OVERCOME, 2007/2014
Video stills of the 16-mm documentary of the dockyard strike in Plymouth, 1969

WE SHALL OVERCOME, 2007/2014
Videostills der 16-mm-Dokumentation des Dockyard Strike in Plymouth, 1969

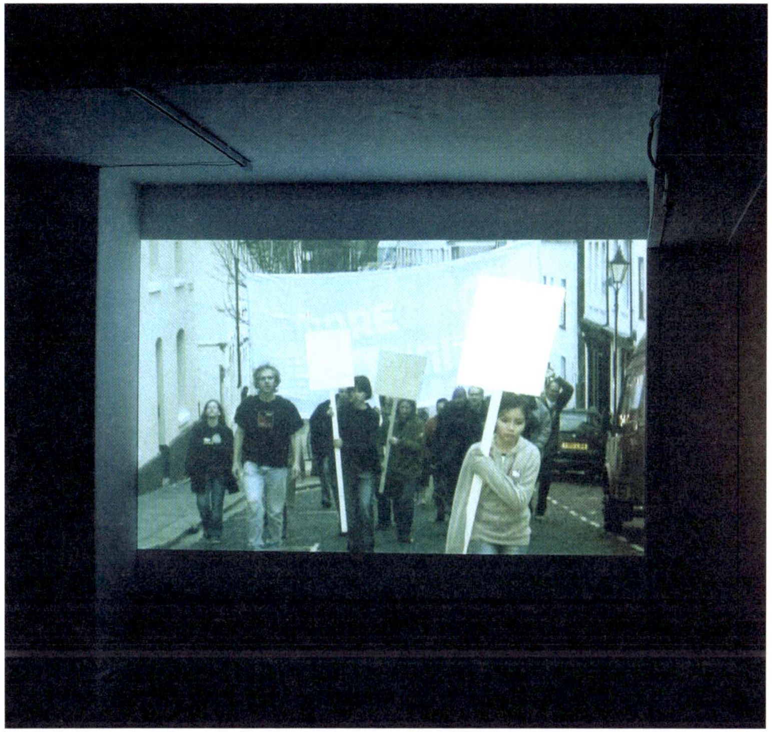

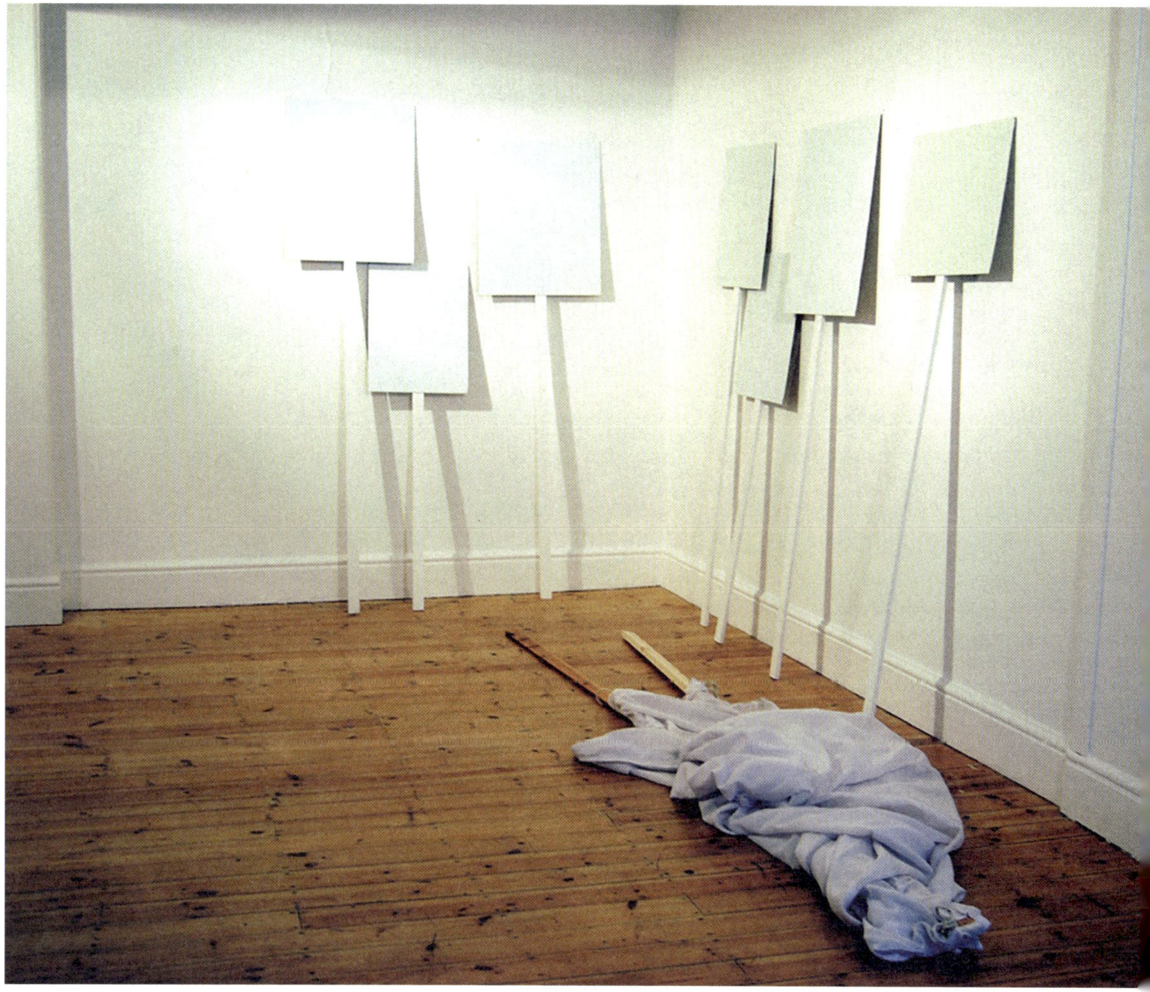

Exhibition view, Plymouth Arts Centre, 2007

Ausstellungsansicht, Plymouth Arts Centre, 2007

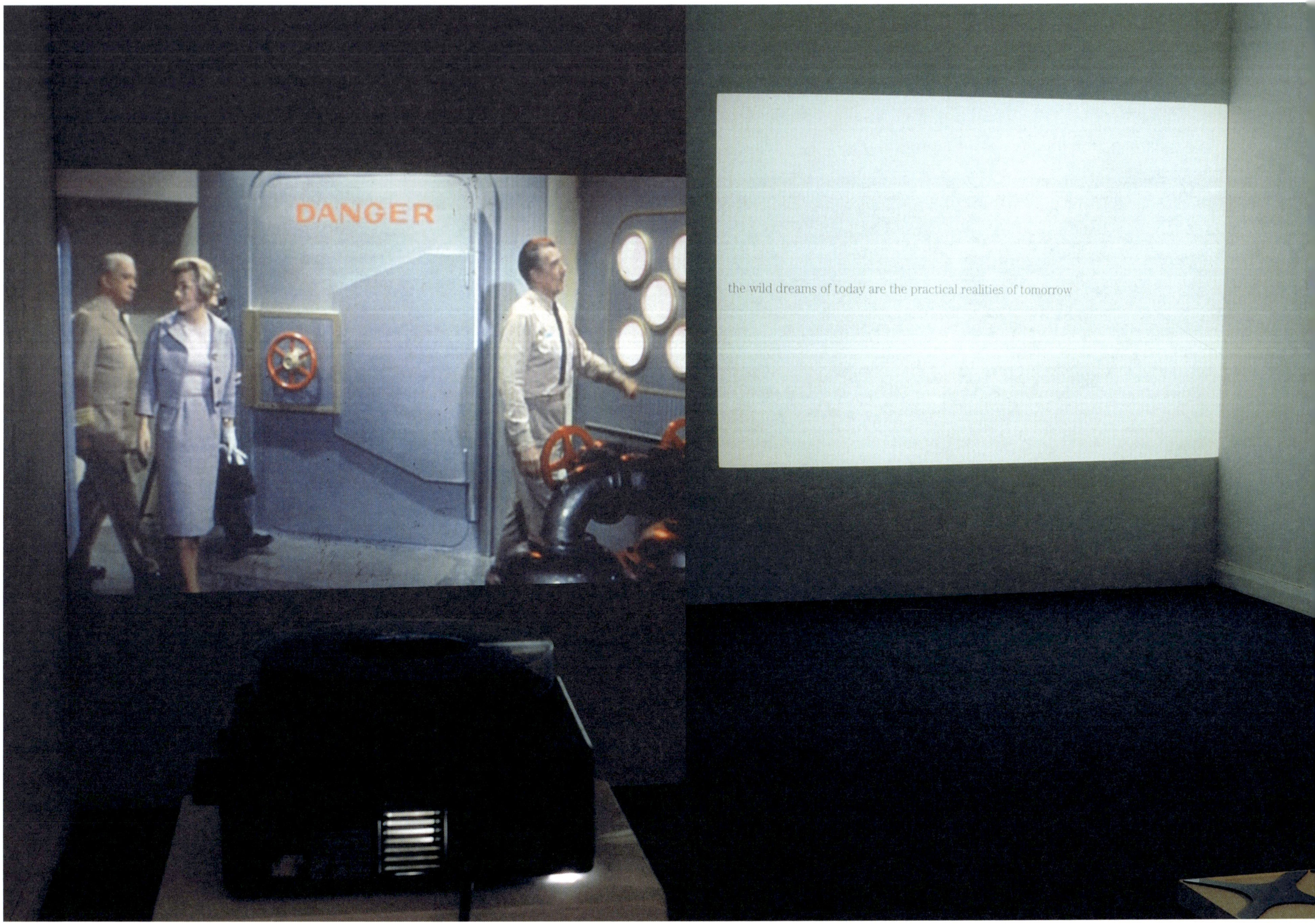

FROM THE DISTANCE OF OUR REALITY
WE BECOME TOURISTS IN OUR OWN CITY,
double slide installation, 2007

FROM THE DISTANCE OF OUR REALITY
WE BECOME TOURISTS IN OUR OWN CITY,
Doppel-Dia-Installation, 2007

"How can we listen beyond language, beyond what our ears can distinguish as sense? How can we hear voices spoken through silence? Demonstrating without words, Holub's performance does not offer us slogans or propaganda; there isn't a simple, populist message for us to recognize and digest. We are not given the few plain words, which would allow us to dismiss the campaign, reject its message by making it recede into a generic background of such-like events and homogeneous language. Instead, it haunts us; the demonstration, a ghostly, empty frame, alone and without content. Exposing the obsolete nature of the street protest, it also points to a linguistic drought, to a society without messages, without songs of liberation to sing. Liberation from what?"

Céline Condorelli,
Walking in Silence

we are writing the year 2040. the submarine newview is bound for a new mission. after closing down of the naval base it was turned into a think tank for future visions. In this mission it can appear in various disguises:
as showboat for tourists ... as research station for social behaviour ... as desire for dramatic rather than only pragmatic moments ... as set for retrofictions ... as more opportunities ... as metaphor codetermining reality ...

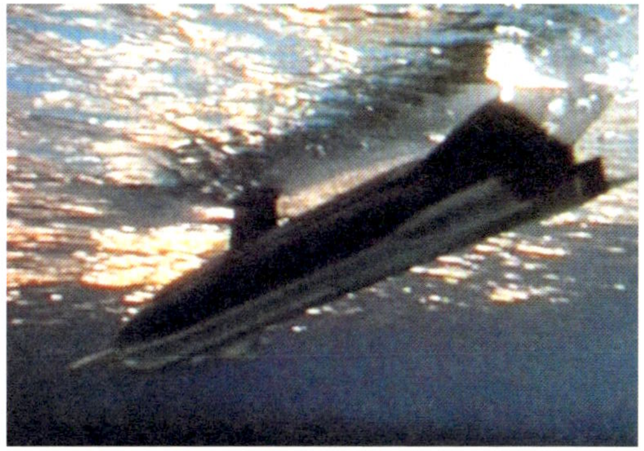

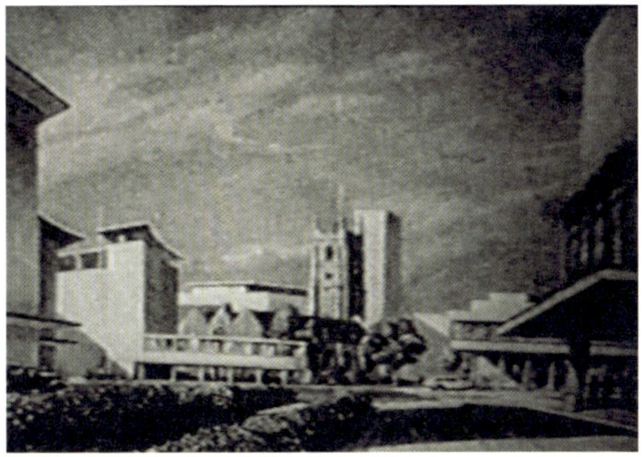

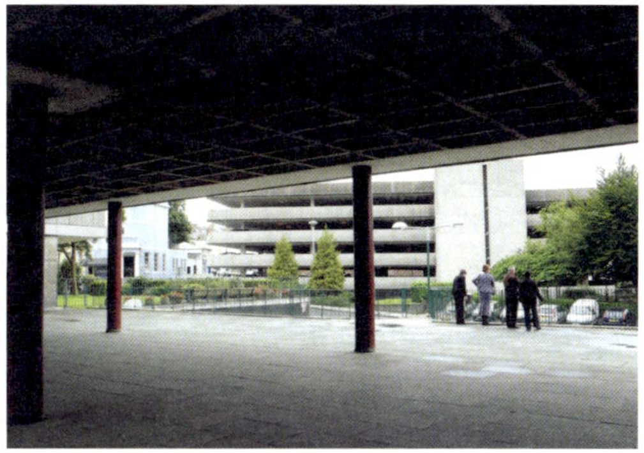

we don't believe in activism

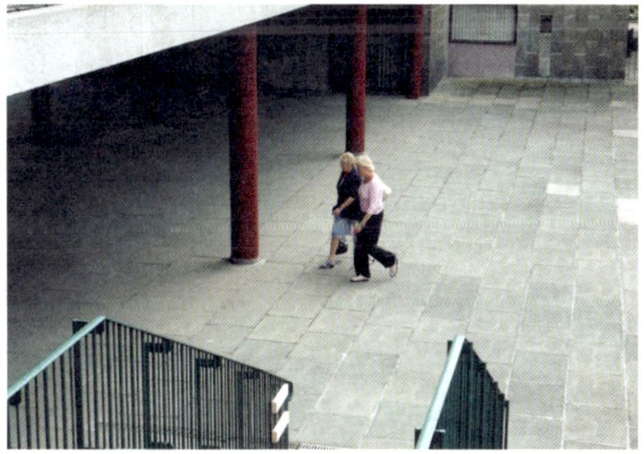

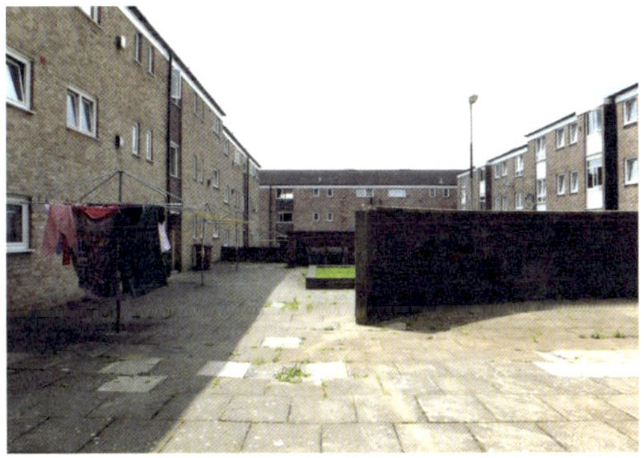

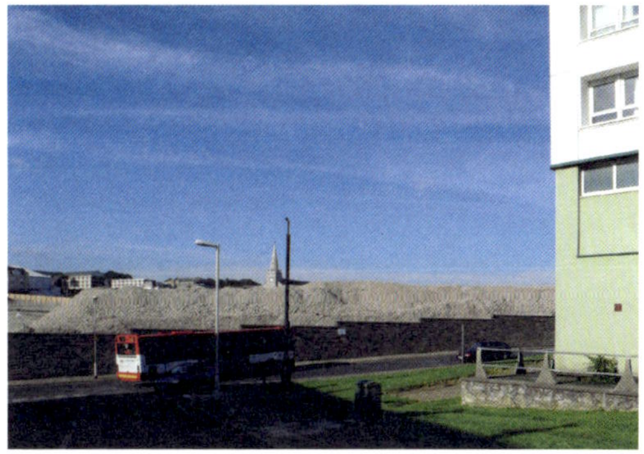

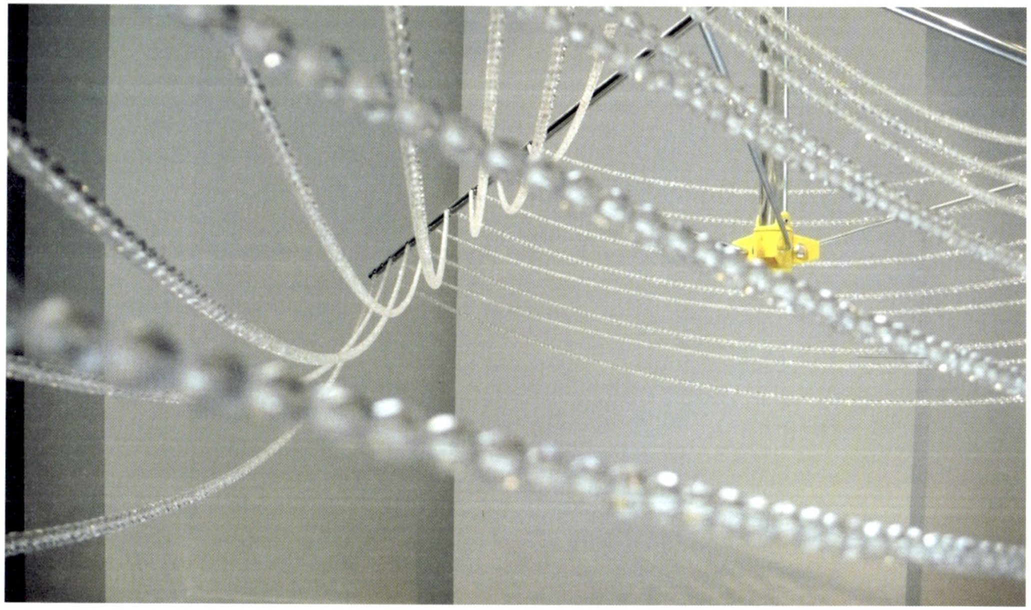

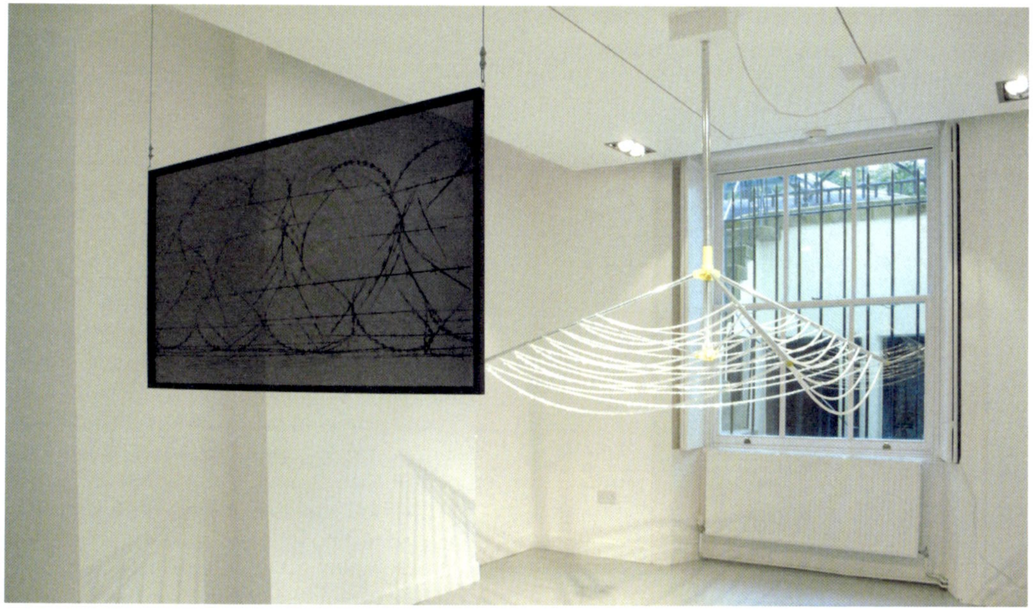

MORE OPPORTUNITIES, London Festival of Architecture, Austrian Cultural Forum, London, 2008

MORE OPPORTUNITIES, London Festival of Architecture, Austrian Cultural Forum, London, 2008

"Holub introduced an art piece paying tribute to the rotary airer (also known as the laundry spider). This object does not only help people to hang out their laundry in small gardens, a rotary airer claims extra territory within the spatial restrictions of social housing systems. At the same time the use of this instrument can be interpreted as a public demonstration of the habitants' confidence in their communities: 'Laundry hung out in these areas is agreed on, it is a consensus'. Holub has transformed this everyday tool, expressing the 'power' of the lower classes, into a sparkling chandelier, the washing lines being replaced by chains with crystal beads."

Marjolein Schaap,
Barbara Holub—A close reading of today's systems, in:
INITIATIVE ISLAND, Eastside Projects, 2008

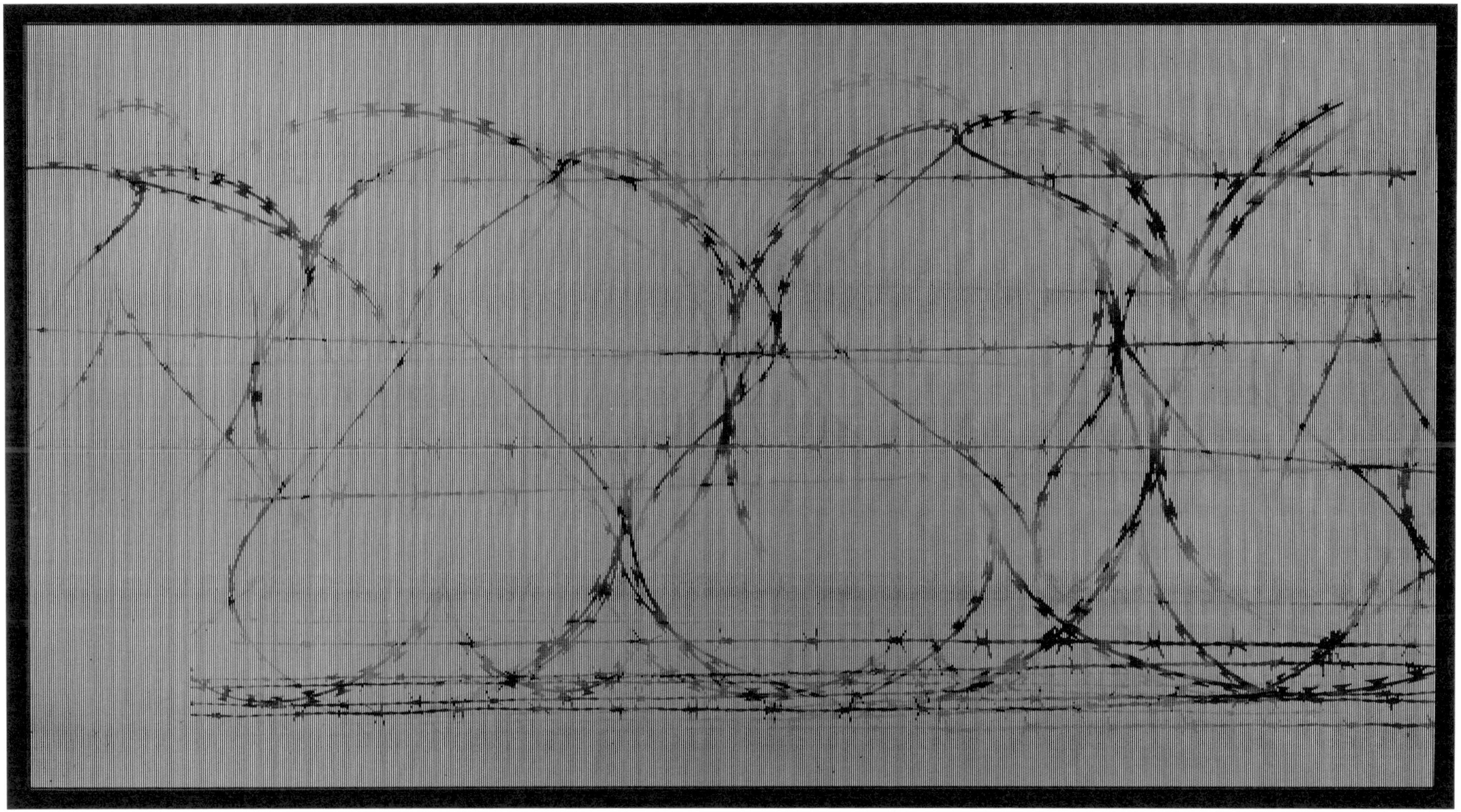

TAKING THE FUTURE INTO OUR HANDS, 2007

TAKING THE FUTURE INTO OUR HANDS, 2007

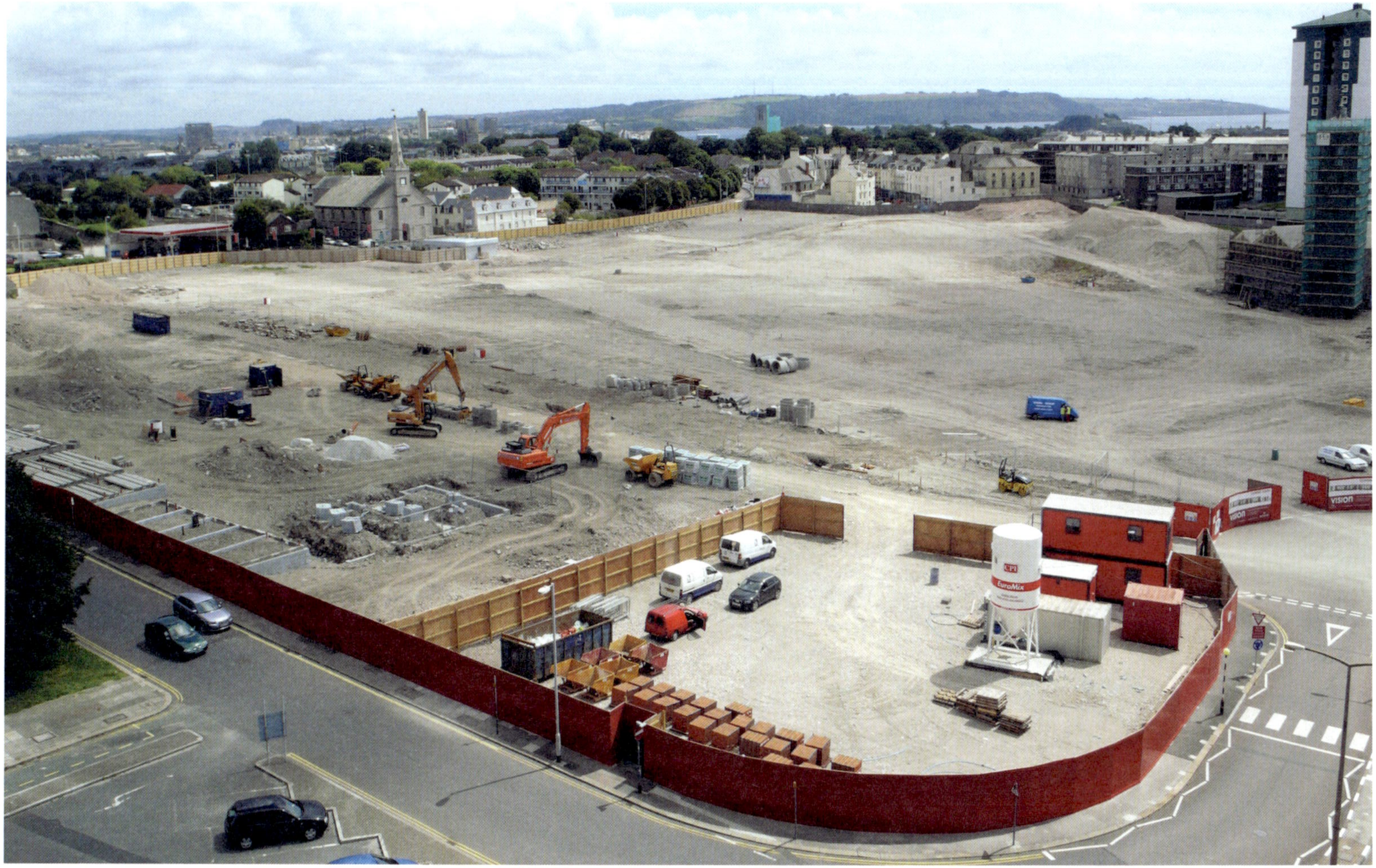

LOST PERSPECTIVES, 2007
View from Marlborough Tower on the new urban development area in Devonport: Devonport's once vibrant town centre was destroyed in WW2, then became part of the naval base until it was sold to a private developer who has since developed the area as purely residential through a public-private partnership with the City of Plymouth. A lost opportunity to create a new urbanity in this disadvantaged neighborhood.

VERLORENE PERSPEKTIVEN, 2007
Blick vom Marlborough Tower auf das neue Stadtentwicklungsgebiet in Devonport: Das ehemals lebendige Stadtzentrum von Devonport wurde im Zweiten Weltkrieg zerstört, war dann Teil des Marine-Stützpunkts bis zum Verkauf an einen privaten Developer, der das Gebiet inzwischen durch eine Public-Private-Partnership mit der Stadt Plymouth als reines Wohngebiet entwickelt hat. Eine vergebene Möglichkeit, in diesem benachteiligten Viertel eine neue Urbanität zu schaffen.

"You, the citizens of Plymouth, must own the land"

Sir Patrick Abercrombie "A Plan for Plymouth,"
in: Jill Craigie's film *The Way We Live*, 1946

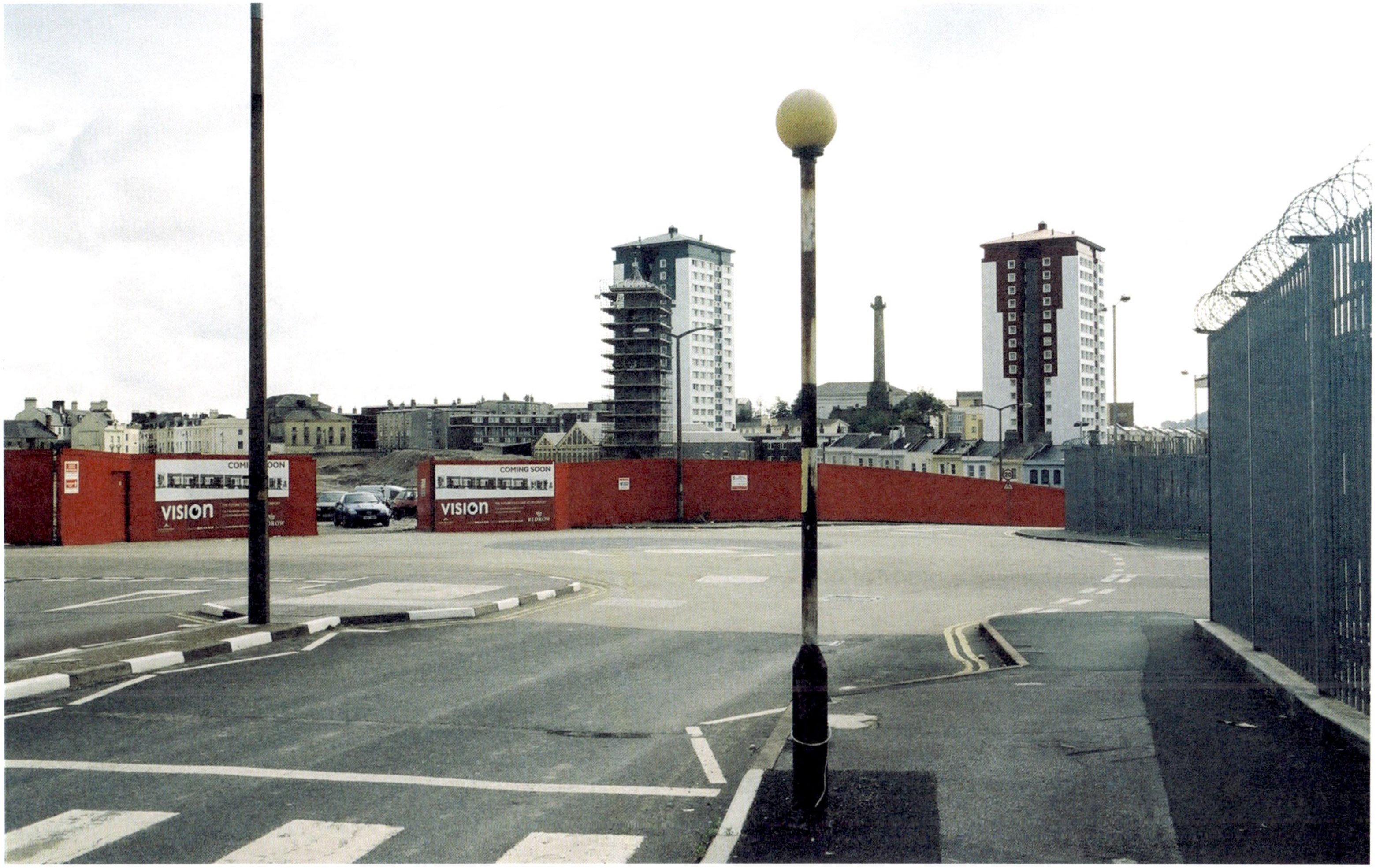

UNFULFILLED VISIONS, 2007

UNERFÜLLTE VISIONEN, 2007

Shows and screenings of MAKE NEWS INSTEAD OF:
London Festival of Architecture, Austrian Cultural Forum, London (UK), 2008
Rencontres Internationales (film festival): Ca2m/Reina Sofia, Madrid (E), 2009
Centre Georges Pompidou/La Villette, Paris (F), 2009
Haus der Kulturen der Welt, Berlin (D), 2009
The Dignity of Man, curated by Maja Abdomerović, Berthold Ecker, Roland Fink, Terezie Petišková, and Jana Vránová, MUSA, Vienna, 2014, House of Arts, Brno (CZ), 2014
Art Gallery of Bosnia and Herzegovina, Sarajevo (BA), 2014

Screenings und weitere Ausstellungen von MAKE NEWS INSTEAD OF:
London Festival of Architecture, Österreichisches Kulturforum London (UK), 2008
Rencontres Internationales (Filmfestival): Ca2m/Reina Sofia, Madrid (E), 2009
Centre Georges Pompidou/La Vilette, Paris (F), 2009
Haus der Kulturen der Welt, Berlin (D), 2009
The Dignity of Man, kuratiert von Maja Abdomerović, Berthold Ecker, Roland Fink, Terezie Petišková und Jana Vránová, MUSA, Wien, 2014, House of Arts, Brno (CZ), 2014
Art Gallery of Bosnia and Herzegovina, Sarajevo (BA), 2014

III. *Orientierungen*, curated by Alexandra Riewe, public space/Kunsthalle Feldbach, regionale08, Feldbach/Styria, 2008
Mujeres Alcanzando la Luz curated by Ursula Maria Probst, Banco Nacional de Panamá, Panama (PA), 2015

Orientierungen, kuratiert von Alexandra Riewe, öffentlicher Raum/Kunsthalle Feldbach, regionale08, Feldbach/Steiermark, 2008
Mujeres Alcanzando la Luz, kuratiert von Ursula Maria Probst, Banco Nacional de Panamá, Panama (PA), 2015

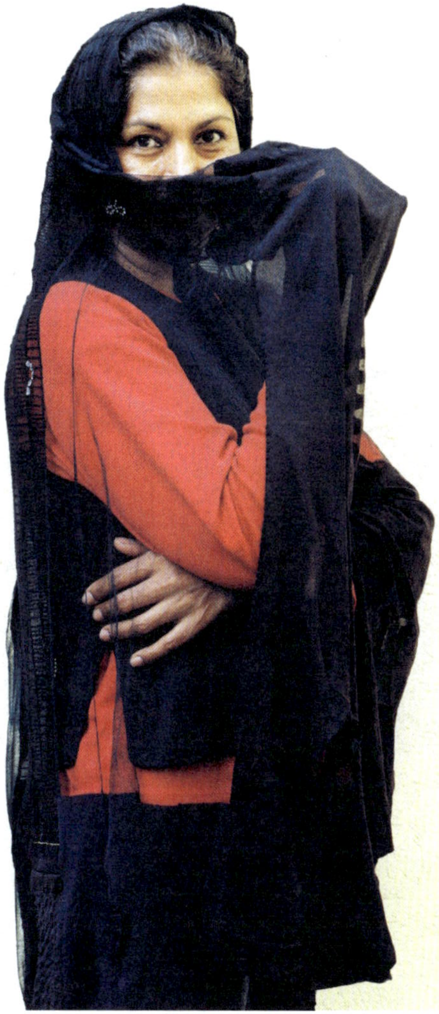

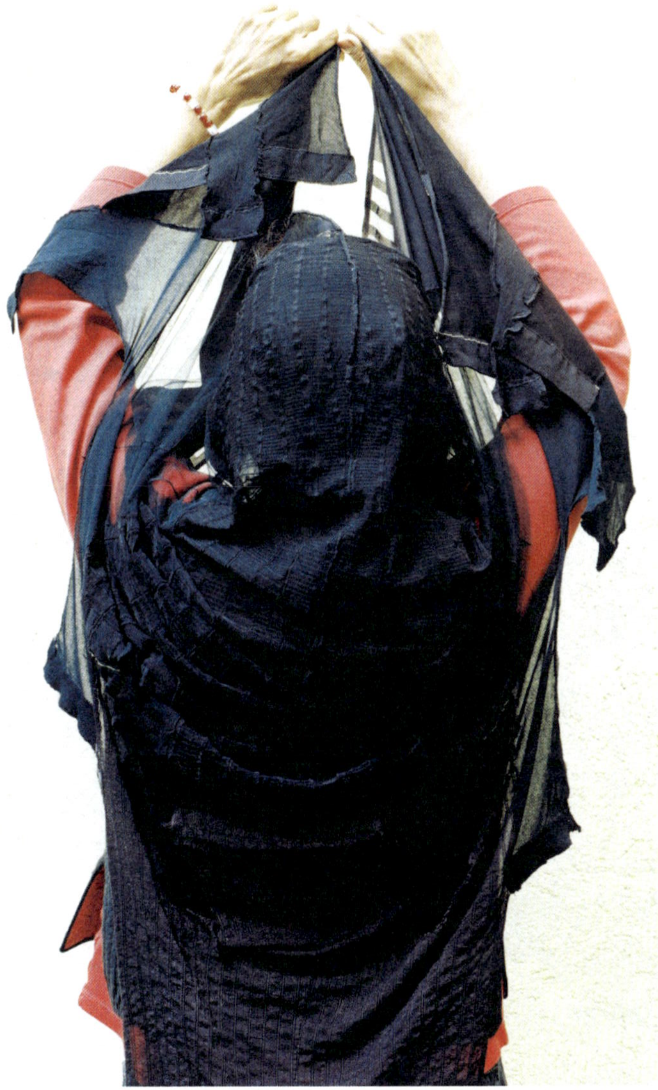

LISTEN TO THE QUIET VOICE

Nylons and headscarf, both items of clothing generally associated with female wearers, are a reflection of their roles in a particular society: while one represents the West as a fashion achievement, the other symbolizes the religious power relations of Eastern cultures; while one arouses sexual desire, the other aims to prevent the same. Taking the headscarf as an example that has always been synonymous with tradition, culture, religion, and protective garments, LISTEN TO THE QUIET VOICE questions assigned female roles and their functions in society.

Posters displayed in public space depict four women (each from the front and back) whose head coverings are reminiscent of Islamic hijabs but which were in fact made from worn nylons. While all four women live and work in Austria, biographically they have different links to Islam. The posters were placed on triangular stands normally used to display election posters. Instead of election slogans proclaiming mostly vacuous political ideas in large letters, all we see are white text boxes.

The title of this silent election campaign is borrowed from *Oblique Strategies* (Brian Eno/Peter Schmidt, 1975), a compilation of text cards containing instructions for unconventional thinking strategies intended to help the readers overcome creative blocks or, as in this example, overcome cultural and gender-specific prejudices and one-dimensional ideologies.

Performers: Gülsen Bal (p. 130), Mehru Jaffer (p. 128), Barbara Wally (p. 138)

LISTEN TO THE QUIET VOICE

Nylonstrümpfe und Kopftuch, beides Kleidungsstücke, die im Allgemeinen weiblichen Trägerinnen zugeordnet sind, spiegeln deren Rollenbilder in der jeweiligen Gesellschaft wider: Während das eine als modische Errungenschaft den Westen repräsentiert, symbolisiert das andere religiöse Machtverhältnisse östlicher Kulturen; während das eine sexuelles Begehren weckt, soll das andere selbiges unterbinden. LISTEN TO THE QUIET VOICE hinterfragt am Beispiel des Kopftuchs – seit jeher Synonym für Tradition, Kultur, Religion und Schutzbekleidung – weibliche Rollenzuschreibungen und deren gesellschaftliche Funktionen.

Im öffentlichen Raum sind auf Plakaten vier Frauen (jeweils in einer Vorder- und einer Rückenansicht) zu sehen, deren Kopfbedeckungen an islamische Hidschābs erinnern, jedoch aus getragenen Nylonstrümpfen angefertigt wurden. Während alle vier Frauen in Österreich leben und arbeiten, stehen sie, biografisch bedingt, in unterschiedlichen Beziehungen zum Islam. Affichiert wurden die Plakate auf Dreieckständern, die üblicherweise zum Aufstellen von Wahlwerbeplakaten verwendet werden. Anstelle von Wahlslogans, die in großen Lettern zumeist bedeutungsschwache politische Ideen preisgeben, sind lediglich weiße Textbalken zu sehen.

Der Titel dieser stillen Wahlkampagne ist *Oblique Strategies* (Brian Eno/Peter Schmidt, 1975) entnommen, einer Kompilation aus Textkarten, die Anleitungen zu unkonventionellen Denkstrategien enthalten, um den LeserInnen beim Überwinden kreativer Blockaden behilflich zu sein – oder, im vorliegenden Fall, beim Überwinden kultureller und geschlechtsspezifischer Vorurteile und eindimensionaler Ideologien.[BR]

Performerinnen: Gülsen Bal (S. 130), Mehru Jaffer (S. 128), Barbara Wally (S. 133)

"Don't stress one thing more than another"
"Do something boring"
"Do something sudden, destructive and unpredictable"
"Do the last thing first"
"Do the words need changing?"
"Emphasize differences"
"Emphasize the flaws"
"Faced with a choice, do both (from Dieter Rot)"

Brian Eno/Peter Schmidt,
Oblique Strategies © 1975–2001

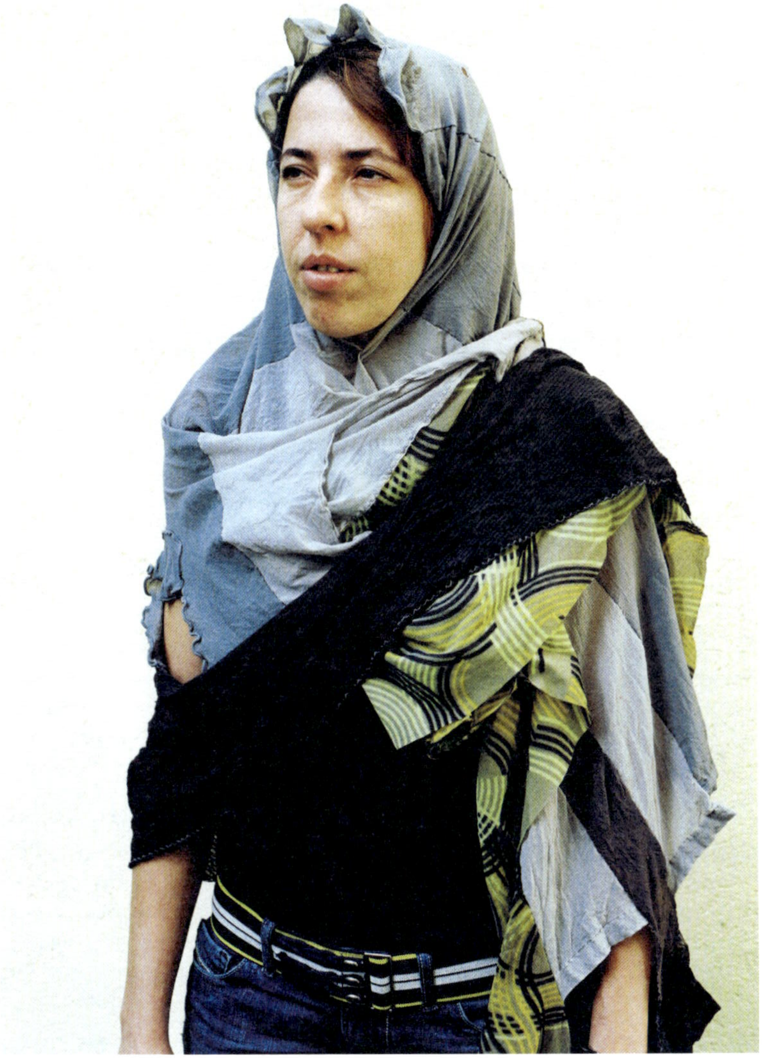

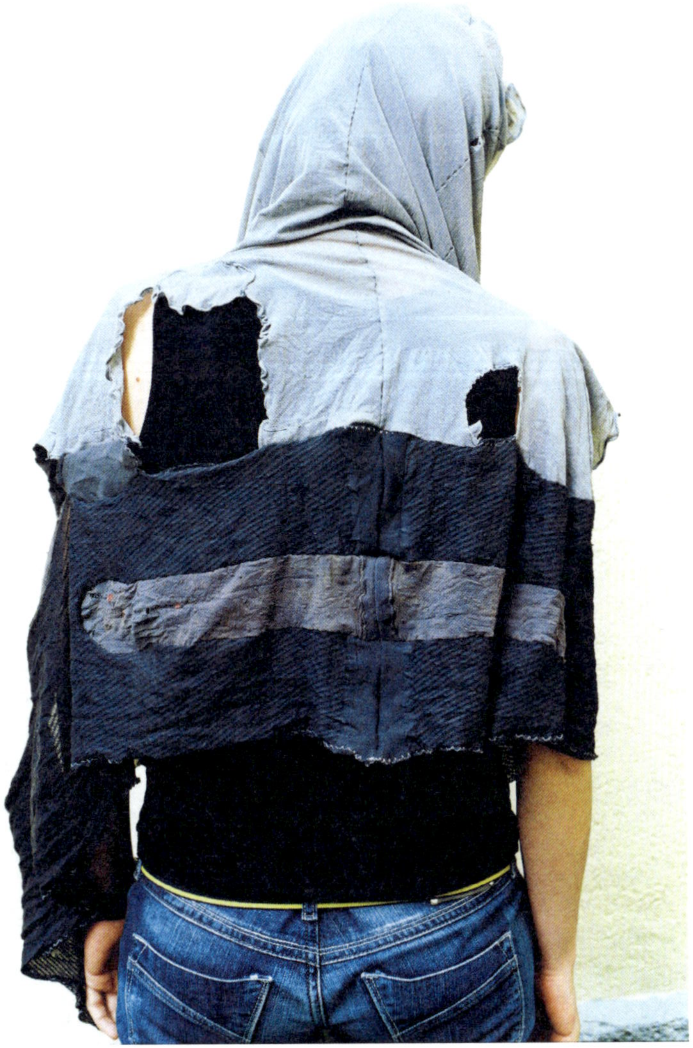

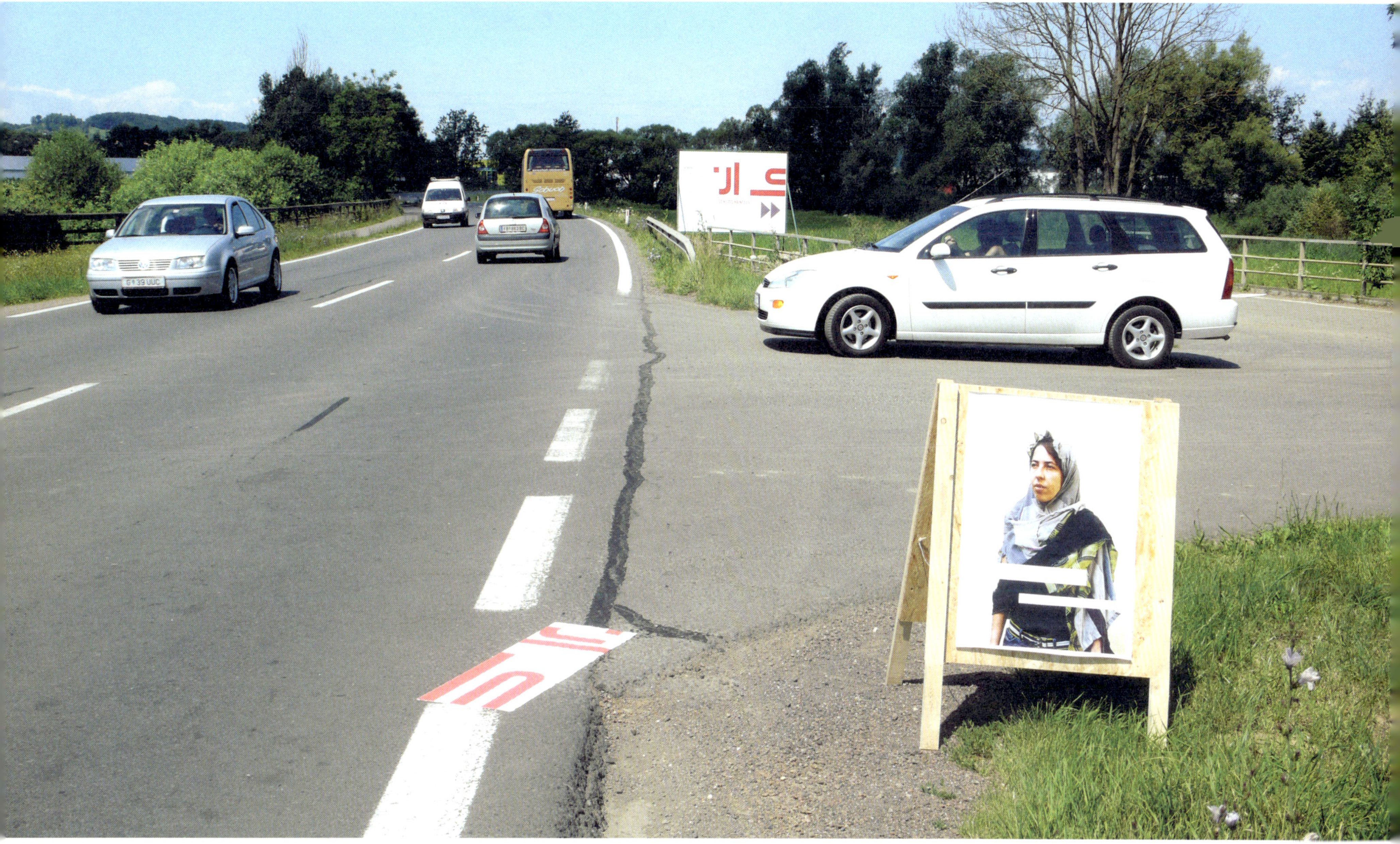

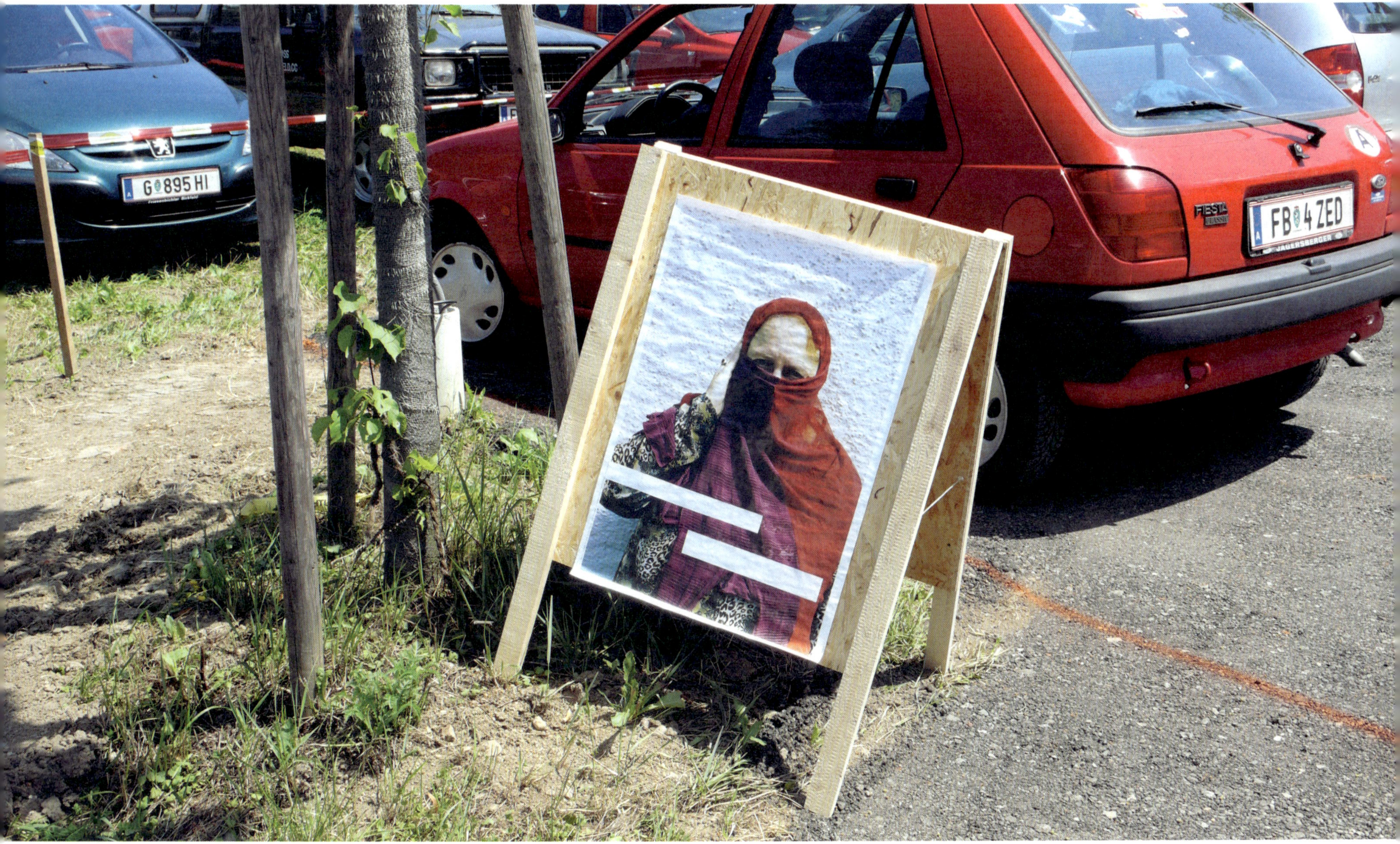
G 895 HI
FB 4 ZED

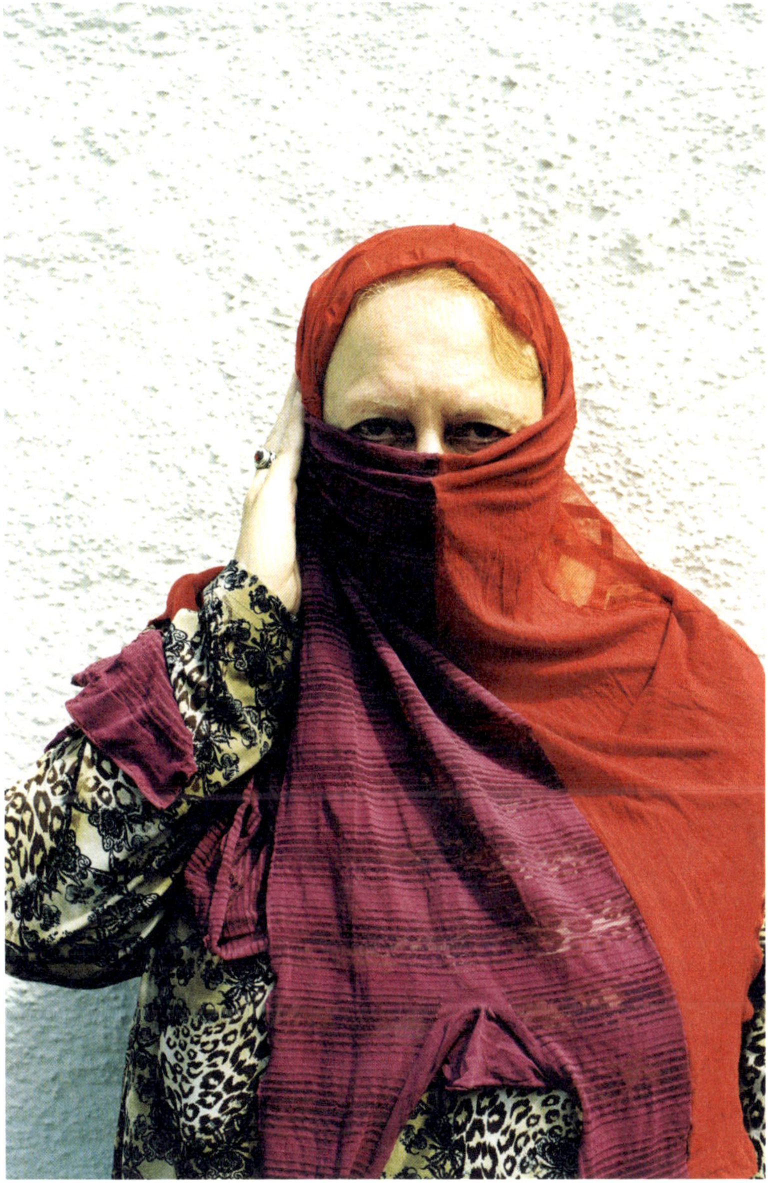

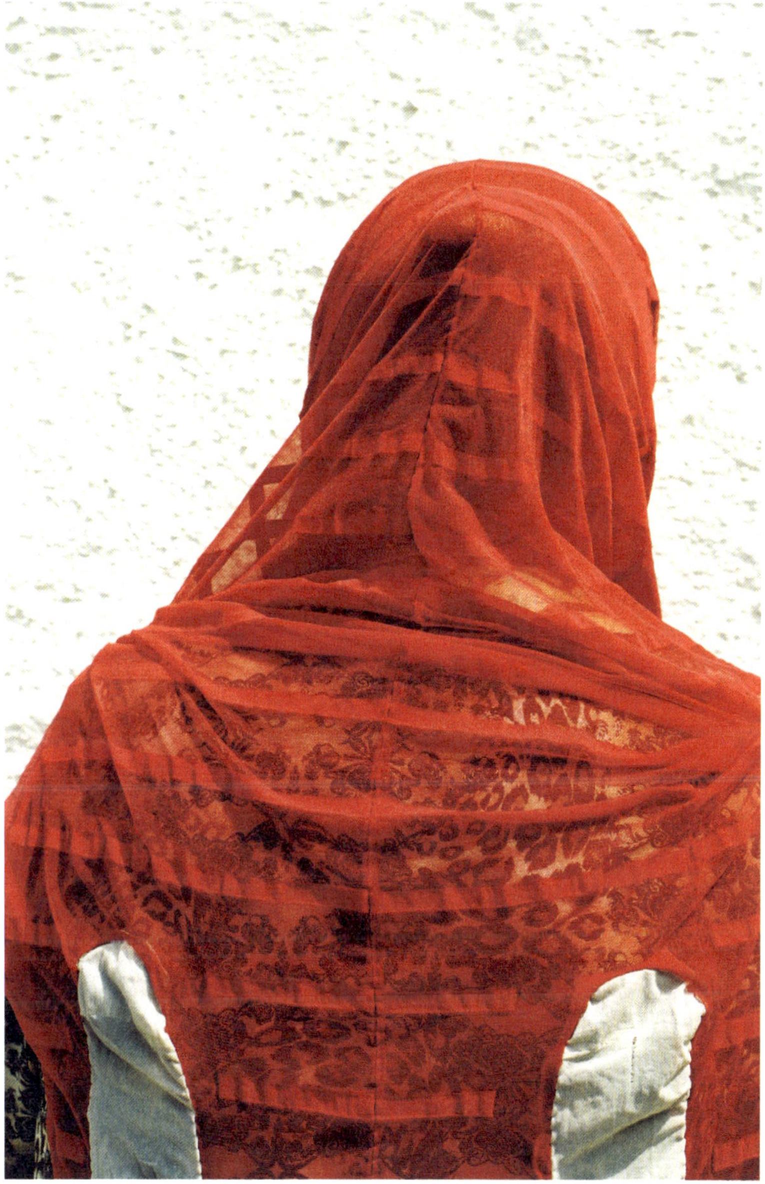

THE BLUE FROG SOCIETY | A HABITAT WITHOUT TERRITORY

THE BLUE FROG SOCIETY is a messenger for a future society. It pushes the borders of the possible to make space for the unplanned and unthinkable, emphasizing civic engagement and the need for new social values, commons, and forms of living together beyond cultural, social, or geographical borders. Through a variety of formats—exhibitions, informal meetings and urban interventions—THE BLUE FROG SOCIETY aims at activating the engagement of civil society and actors in the arts and cultural environment to promote new social values, a new community and new forms of coexistence beyond cultural, social or geographical boundaries.

The "wild habitat" of THE BLUE FROG SOCIETY—a spot of earth untouched by investors' interests—was discovered by the artist in the course of her research for AT THE URBAN PERIPHERY, right next to the new urban development of Lake-City Aspern in Vienna. In the publication *found, set, appropriated* (2010), Barbara Holub published the "10 Issues of THE BLUE FROG SOCIETY" for the first time.

"THE BLUE FROG SOCIETY imagines the impossible and takes the primary meaning of society as one of active companionship, of fellowship, and of kinship. Society is that to which we all belong. Society is the system of common life by which we are governed and that we may wish to transgress, subvert, or overcome. Therefore, there are always multiple conflicting societies at any given time within THE BLUE FROG SOCIETY. Society is always plural and is the bodies and histories of relationships within which a relatively large group of people live, and the contemporary conditions in which institutions and relationships are formed. In this sense, society is a living form of commoning, of association, of equalities.

THE BLUE FROG SOCIETY is public, real, and concrete. THE BLUE FROG SOCIETY is an informal assembly without organs, borders or limitations. All other members of THE BLUE FROG SOCIETY like to keep a low profile. They are in waiting. They are the agents of transformation. THE BLUE FROG SOCIETY is a decentreed artwork as much as a site of collaboration and of value production. THE BLUE FROG SOCIETY is where we all go when we have nowhere else to go. THE BLUE FROG SOCIETY is a refuge. THE BLUE FROG SOCIETY has its own language, and its own speech. THE BLUE FROG SOCIETY is an institute for all minorities within which to constitute themselves against the dominant regimes of state repression. THE BLUE FROG SOCIETY is a coming together, a space of potential belonging for the future in the lived present. THE BLUE FROG SOCIETY is the future's futures. THE BLUE FROG SOCIETY doesn't exist, but is everywhere. THE BLUE FROG SOCIETY is already planning for the unplanned.

THE BLUE FROG SOCIETY | A HABITAT WITHOUT TERRITORY

THE BLUE FROG SOCIETY ist Vorbotin einer zukünftigen Gesellschaft. Sie verschiebt die Grenzen des Möglichen und schafft Raum für das Ungeplante und Undenkbare im Sinne einer antizipatorischen Fiktion. In vielfältigen Formaten – Ausstellungen, informellen Meetings und urbanen Interventionen – setzt THE BLUE FROG SOCIETY auf das Engagement der Zivilbevölkerung und AkteurInnen im Kunst- und Kulturumfeld, um neue soziale Werte, ein neues Gemeinwesen und neue Formen des Zusammenlebens jenseits kultureller, sozialer oder geografischer Grenzen zu fördern.

Das „wilde Habitat" der Blue Frog Society – ein von InvestorInnen-Interessen unberührtes Fleckchen Erde – entdeckte die Künstlerin im Rahmen ihrer Recherchen für AM STADTRAND, direkt neben der neu entstehenden Seestadt Aspern in Wien. In der Publikation *found, set, appropriated* (2010) veröffentlichte Barbara Holub dann erstmals die „10 Issues of THE BLUE FROG SOCIETY".

„THE BLUE FROG SOCIETY stellt sich das Unmögliche vor und versteht unter Gesellschaft in erster Linie aktive Teilhabe, Gemeinschaft und Verbundenheit. Gesellschaft ist etwas, dem wir alle angehören. Gesellschaft ist das System des gemeinsamen Lebens, das uns alle leitet und das wir vielleicht überschreiten, untergraben, überwinden möchten. Darum existieren in THE BLUE FROG SOCIETY stets mehrere, auch einander widersprechende Gesellschaften nebeneinander. Gesellschaft ist immer plural und besteht aus Körpern und Geschichten von Beziehungen, in denen eine relativ große Gruppe von Menschen lebt. Und den zeitgenössischen Bedingungen, in denen Institutionen und Beziehungen gebildet werden. So gesehen ist Gesellschaft eine lebendige Form des Commoning, des Sich-Zusammenschließens, des Gleich-berechtigt-Seins.

THE BLUE FROG SOCIETY ist öffentlich, real und konkret. THE BLUE FROG SOCIETY ist eine informelle Versammlung ohne Organe, Grenzen oder Beschränkungen. Alle anderen Mitglieder der Blue Frog Society halten sich gerne bedeckt. Sie verharren in Wartestellung. Sind AgentInnen der Transformation. THE BLUE FROG SOCIETY ist ein dezentrales Kunstwerk ebenso wie ein Ort der Zusammenarbeit und der Produktion von Werten. THE BLUE FROG SOCIETY ist der Ort, an den wir alle gehen, wenn wir sonst nirgendwohin gehen können. THE BLUE FROG SOCIETY ist ein Zufluchtsort. THE BLUE FROG SOCIETY verfügt über ihre eigene Sprache und Art zu sprechen. THE BLUE FROG SOCIETY ist eine Institution für alle Minderheiten, in der sie sich gegen die herrschenden Regimes staatlicher Repression konstituieren können. THE BLUE FROG SOCIETY ist eine Zusammenkunft, ein Raum potenzieller künftiger Zugehörigkeit in der gelebten Gegenwart. THE BLUE FROG SOCIETY ist die Zukünfte der Zukunft. THE BLUE FROG SOCIETY existiert nicht, sie ist überall. THE BLUE FROG SOCIETY plant bereits das Ungeplante. THE BLUE

belonging. There is no future, only this here now. It is a space of imagining, of longing and of lived imagination. It is a space of poetic and of real projection." (Paul O'Neill, in: Şenova, *CrossSections*, 2020)[BS]

Sie projektiert keine Zukunft, nur das Hier und Jetzt. Sie ist ein Vorstellungsraum, ein Sehnsuchtsraum, ein Raum gelebter Imagination. Sie ist ein Raum poetischer und realer Projektion." (Paul O'Neill, in: Şenova, *CrossSections*, 2020)[BS]

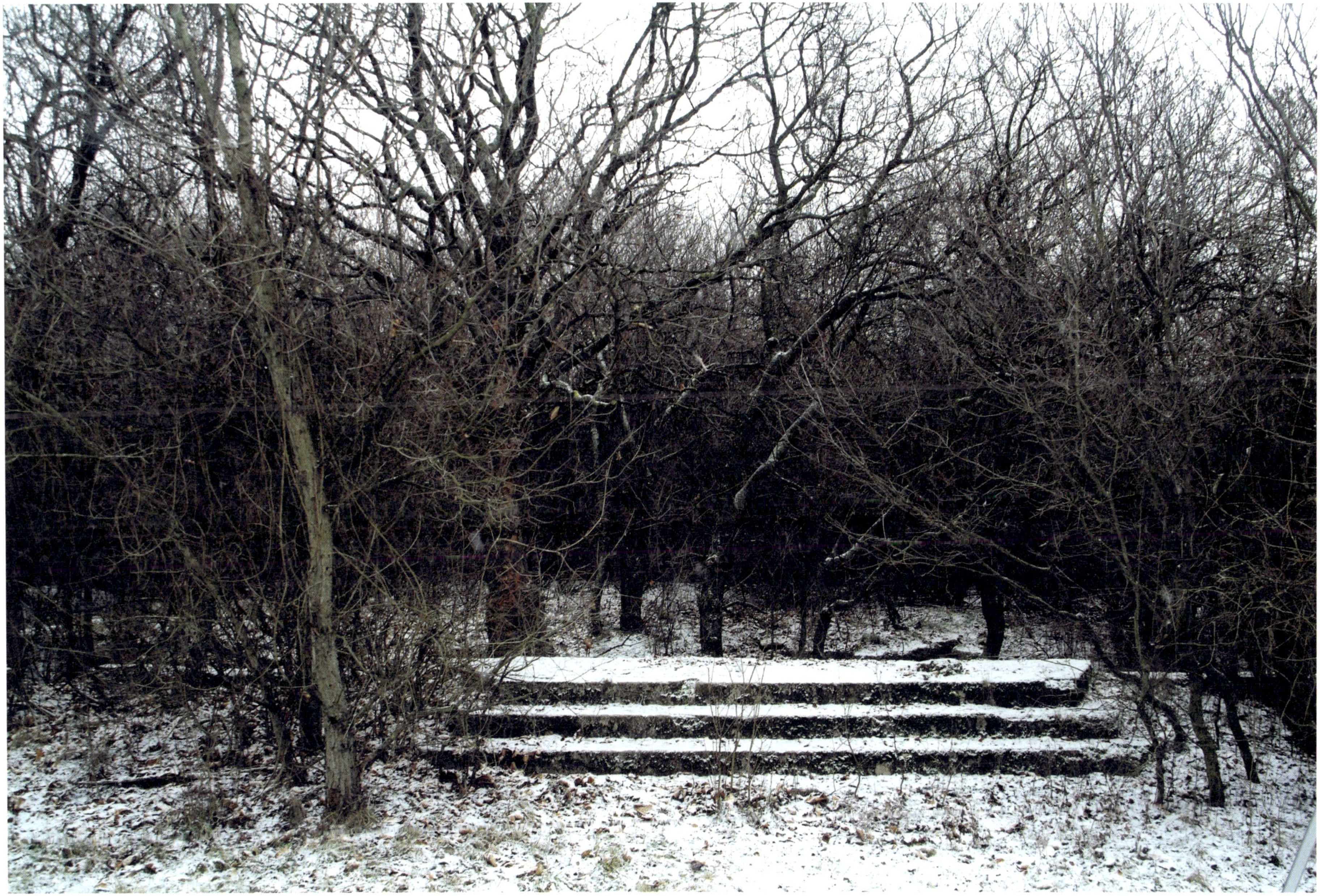

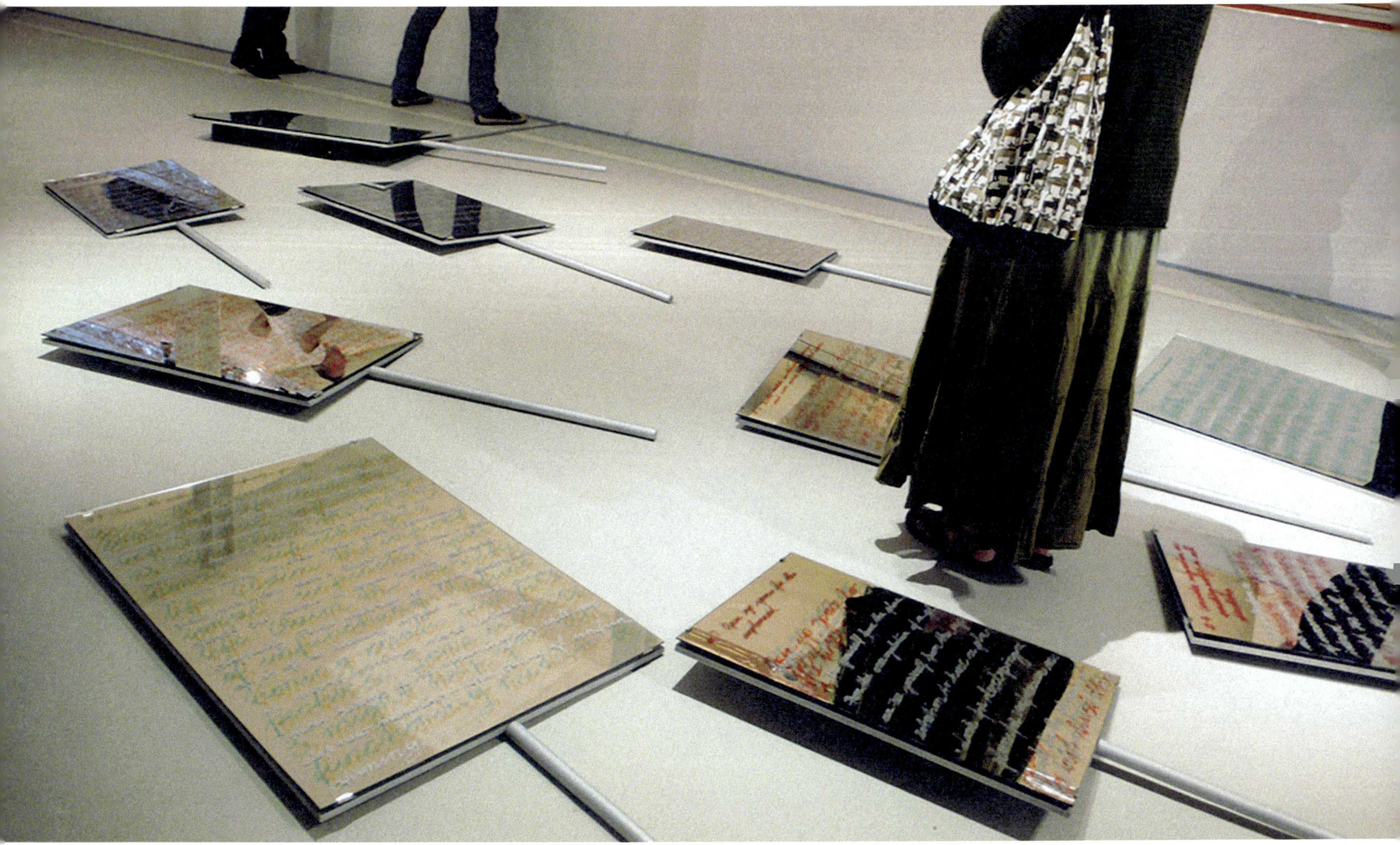

Exhibition view, *The Future of the Future*,
DOX Centre for Contemporary Art, Prague, 2010

Ausstellungsansicht, *The Future of the Future*,
DOX Centre for Contemporary Art, Prag, 2010

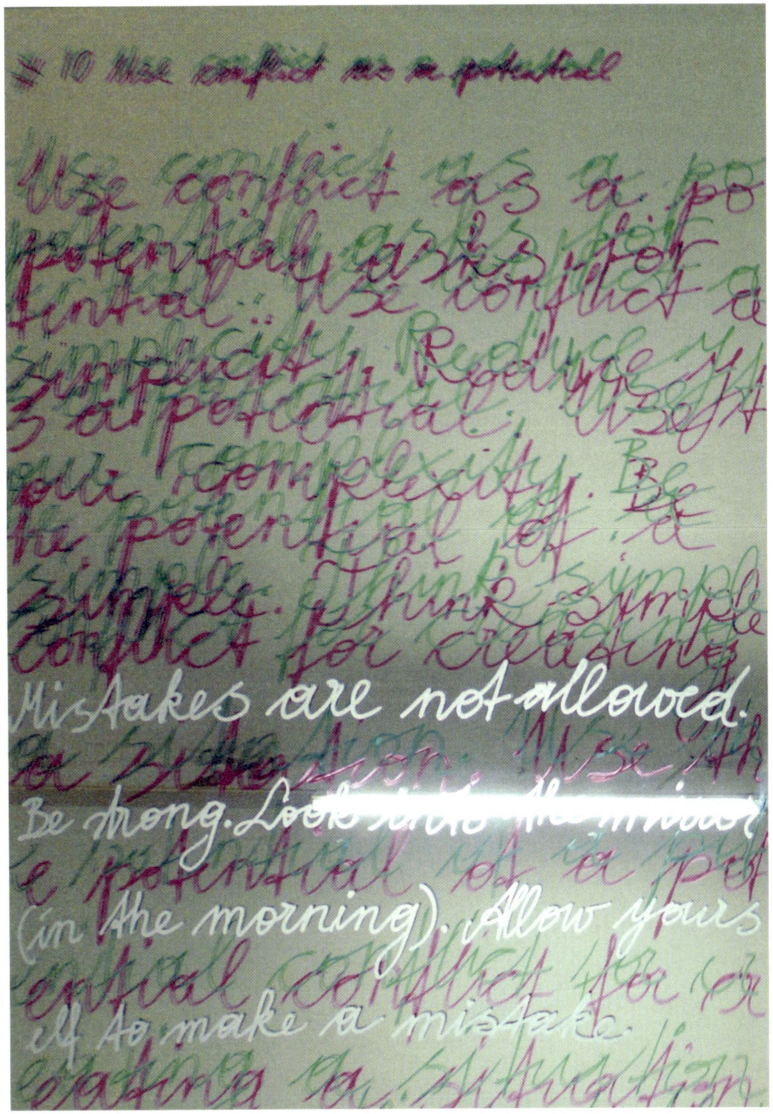

THE BLUE FROG SOCIETY | A HABITAT WITHOUT TERRITORY (2010–ongoing), exhibitions include:
The Future of the Future, curated by Jaroslav Anděl, DOX Centre for Contemporary Art, Prague, 2010
WINDOWS ON MADISON/CZECH MISSION TO THE UN, curated by Jaroslav Anděl, Czech Centre, New York, 2011
64. UN DPI/NGO Conference, Bonn, 2011 (on invitation by Shamina de Gonzaga/World Council of Peoples for the United Nations, New York).
CrossSections_Potentials, curated by Başak Şenova, Kunsthalle Exnergasse, Vienna, 2018, and Konstfack, Stockholm, 2019
PUBLICS, curated by Paul O'Neill, Helsinki, 2019
Showing Styria: what will be. Towards a Plurality of Futures, curated by Barbara Steiner, Katrin Bucher Trantow, Martin Grabner, Kunsthaus Graz, Graz, 2021

THE BLUE FROG SOCIETY | A HABITAT WITHOUT TERRITORY (2010–lfd.), Ausstellungen u. a.:
The Future of the Future, kuratiert von Jaroslav Anděl, DOX Centre for Contemporary Art, Prag, 2010
WINDOWS ON MADISON/CZECH MISSION TO THE UN, kuratiert von Jaroslav Anděl, Czech Centre, New York, 2011
64. UN DPI/NGO-Konferenz, Bonn, 2011, auf Einladung von Shamina de Gonzaga/World Council of Peoples for the United Nations, New York.
CrossSections_Potentials, kuratiert von Başak Şenova, Kunsthalle Exnergasse, Wien, 2018, und Konstfack, Stockholm, 2019
PUBLICS, kuratiert von Paul O'Neill, Helsinki, 2019
Steiermark-Schau: Was sein wird. Von der Zukunft zu den Zukünften, kuratiert von Barbara Steiner, Katrin Bucher Trantow, Martin Grabner, Kunsthaus Graz, Graz, 2021

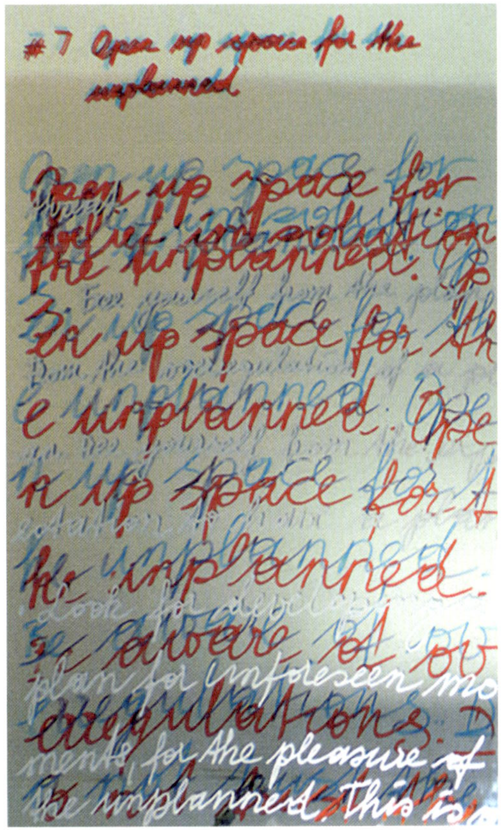

found,
set,
appropriated,

150

1 Arbeiten Sie den dominanten Prinzipien des Nicht-Glaubens entgegen: Schaffen Sie Vertrauen

Arbeiten Sie den dominanten Prinzipien des Nicht-Glaubens entgegen. Arbeiten Sie der Schwäche von Prinzipien entgegen. Handeln Sie, anstatt dagegen zu handeln. Handeln Sie, um Vertrauen zu schaffen. Vergessen Sie, was als modisch oder unmodisch betrachtet wird. Es ist unmodisch / unpopulär, über persönliche Schwächen zu sprechen. Es ist unmodisch / unpopulär, sich zu beschweren. Es wird als naiv betrachtet, sich für Themen zu engagieren, die das persönliche Befinden überschreiten. Es ist unmodisch / unpopulär, nicht nur über Mängel zu sprechen, sondern auf der Überzeugung zu beharren, dass eine grundlegende Veränderung notwendig ist.

2 Überprüfen Sie drängende Themen wie Nachhaltigkeit

Überprüfen Sie drängende Themen wie Nachhaltigkeit.
Überprüfen Sie drängende Themen. Vermeiden Sie leere Phrasen. Nachhaltigkeit wurde zu einer leeren Phrase, einem Synonym für Leere. Wie kann sie mit Bedeutung gefüllt werden? Wahlperioden und die Notwendigkeit des sofortigen Erfolgs verhindern langfristiges Denken. Überprüfen Sie drängende Themen wie Nachhaltigkeit. Stellen Sie Fragen, die Ihre Vorstellung überschreiten. Was erwarten Sie von einem Künstler / einer Künstlerin? Was erwarten Sie von sich selbst? Kann ein Künstler / eine Künstlerin zu Nachhaltigkeit beitragen? Ja, wir können. Aber wir brauchen Sie dazu.

3 Stellen Sie sich das Unmögliche vor (und arbeiten Sie daran)

Stellen Sie sich das Unmögliche vor (und arbeiten Sie daran).
Stellen Sie sich das Unmögliche vor. Und vielleicht braucht das nicht soviel Arbeit.
Stellen Sie sich das Unmögliche vor. Das Unmögliche ist persönlich. Das Unmögliche betrifft die Gesellschaft. Wir wollen keine neue Utopie schaffen. Utopien bedeuten immer auch, dass etwas zerstört werden muss. Wir wollen nicht zerstören. Wir wollen fördern. In dem Moment, wenn Sie diese Worte lesen, widmen Sie sich selbst der Möglichkeit des Unmöglichen. Das wird gebraucht. Das brauchen Sie. Das braucht die Gesellschaft. Alle Gesellschaften. Den Moment des Unmöglichen teilen. Teilen. Das Unmögliche flieht immer.

4 Betrachten Sie Migration als bereichernde Qualität in allen Richtungen

Betrachten Sie Migration als bereichernde Qualität in allen Richtungen.
Betrachten Sie Migration als bereichernde Qualität in allen Richtungen – und als Basis des Lebens im 21. Jahrhundert. Fordern Sie die Bewegungsfreiheit als Grundrecht. Bewegungsfreiheit muss als grundlegendes Menschenrecht anerkannt werden. Für alle. Kein wenn und aber. Keine Ausreden. Mobilität wird uns aufgezwungen. Aber wir wollen Bewegungsfreiheit. Wir sind in der Position, dies zu fordern.

5 Glauben Sie an das, was Sie wagen zu glauben

Glauben Sie an das, was Sie wagen zu glauben. Überwinden Sie die Selbst-Zensur, wenn es notwendig ist. Seien Sie sich bewusst, wann Sie auf andere hören sollten und wann nicht. Wir sind wenige. Wir sind viele. Glauben Sie an das, was Sie wagen zu glauben. Die *Blue Frog Society* wird Ihnen helfen, Ihre Ängste zu überwinden. Manchmal ist es notwendig, seine Gedanken zu schützen. Wir müssen handeln. Nicht jetzt, aber die Zeit wird kommen. Fühlen Sie, wann die richtige Zeit ist. Wir müssen uns nicht schützen vor dem, was wir denken, sondern vor dem, was wir nicht denken. Manchmal ist es notwendig, unsere Gedanken zu schützen. Aber jetzt ist die Zeit, unsere Gedanken mitzuteilen.

10 Aspekte
der *Blue Frog Society*
für eine Gesellschaft
der Zukunft

151

6 Involvieren Sie KünstlerInnen in Entscheidungsprozesse

Involvieren Sie KünstlerInnen in Entscheidungsprozesse.
Involvieren Sie KünstlerInnen in Entscheidungsprozesse – und sorgen Sie dafür, dass KünsterInnen ihre Grenzen überschreiten. Sie als Künstler müssen lernen, Ihre Grenzen zu vergessen. Sie müssen das System ablegen. Sie müssen sich engagieren. Nutzen Sie die KünstlerInnen. Sie als KünstlerIn müssen Ihre Funktion in der Gesellschaft überdenken. Das Leben ist außer Kontrolle. Außer unserer Kontrolle. Würden KünstlerInnen (als Individuen) anders entscheiden? Die *Blue Frog Society* hat es gewagt. Musste es wagen. Und es gibt keinen Grund, dies zu bedauern.

7 Schaffen Sie Raum für das Ungeplante

Schaffen Sie Raum für das Ungeplante. Seien Sie sich der Überdeterminierungen bewusst. Vertrauen Sie nicht dem Glauben an Lösungen. Befreien Sie sich vom Plan. Von der Überdeterminiertheit des Plans. Befreien Sie sich von der Erwartung, dass es einen Plan gibt. Versuchen Sie, einen Plan für unvorhergesehene Momente zu entwickeln, für den Genuss des Ungeplanten. Das ist eine Bedrohung.

8 Überwinden Sie den Pragmatismus – führen Sie poetische Momente ein

Überwinden Sie den Pragmatismus.
Überwinden Sie den Pragmatismus – führen Sie poetische Momente ein.
Überwinden Sie den Pragmatismus – führen Sie poetische Momente im Alltag ein. Nehmen Sie einen Umweg ab und zu. Nehmen Sie einen Umweg ab und zu, vor allem wenn Sie von Wut geleitet sind. Nehmen Sie den Lift zum obersten Geschoss, gehen Sie dann hinunter zu Ihrem Stockwerk (nach einer Empfehlung von Georges Perec). Grüßen Sie Menschen auf der Straße in der Stadt und denken Sie an das „Wunder von Mailand" von Vittorio de Sica.

9 Fordern Sie das Unfunktionale – funktionalisieren Sie Ihr Leben um

Fordern Sie das Unfunktionale – funktionalisieren Sie Ihr Leben um.
Fordern Sie die Notwendigkeit des Umfunktionalisierens. Umfunktionalisieren schafft neue Perspektiven. Manche Übungen (nach Georges Perec) könnten hilfreich sein: „Notieren Sie, was immer Sie sehen können. Alles, was sinnvoll erscheint zu notieren. Wissen Sie, wie man sieht? Was wichtig ist, notiert zu werden? Gibt es etwas, das Sie überrascht? Nichts überrascht Sie. Sie wissen nicht, wie man sieht. Sie müssen das langsamer angehen, fast naiv. Zwingen Sie sich, das aufzuschreiben, was bedeutungslos ist, was sehr gewöhnlich ist, sehr offensichtlich, sehr farblos." Was bedeutungslos erscheint, wird neue Bedeutung entwickeln – die Qualität des Umfunktionalisierens.

10 Nutzen Sie Konflikte als Potenzial

Nutzen Sie Konflikte als Potenzial.
Nutzen Sie deren Komplexität.
Nutzen Sie Ihre Komplexität.
Nutzen Sie das Potenzial eines Konflikts, um eine Situation zu schaffen.
Nutzen Sie das Potenzial eines potenziellen Konflikts, um eine Situation zu schaffen. Der Konflikt der Möglichkeiten braucht Einfachheit. Reduzieren Sie Ihre Komplexität. Seien Sie einfach. Denken Sie einfach. Fehler sind nicht erlaubt. Seien Sie stark. Schauen Sie am Morgen in den Spiegel. Erlauben Sie sich, einen Fehler zu machen.

The 10 ISSUES OF THE BLUE FROG SOCIETY were published for the first time in the catalog FOUND, SET, APPROPRIATED, Barbara Holub, Verlag für moderne Kunst Nürnberg, 2010

Die 10 ISSUES DER BLUE FROG SOCIETY erschienen erstmals im Katalog FOUND, SET, APPROPRIATED, Barbara Holub, Verlag für moderne Kunst Nürnberg, 2010

10 issues of the
Blue Frog Society
as contribution
to the future

6 Involve artists in decision making – and make artists transgress their borders

Involve artists in decision making.
Involve artists in decision making – and make artists transgress their borders. You as an artist have to unlearn your borders, your limits. You have to unlearn the system. You have to get involved. Make use of the artists. You as an artist reconsider your function in society. Life is out of control. Out of our control. Would artists (as individuals) decide differently? The *Blue Frog Society* took the risk. Had to take the risk. And there was no reason to regret.

7 Open up space for the unplanned

Open up space for the unplanned. Be aware of overregulations. Do not trust the belief in solution. Free yourself from the plan. From the overregulation of a plan. Free yourself from the expectation to have a plan. Look for developing a plan for unforeseen moments, for the pleasure of the unplanned. This is a threat.

8 Step beyond pragmatics – insert poetic moments

Step beyond pragmatics.
Step beyond pragmatics – insert poetic moments.
Step beyond pragmatics – insert poetic moments in the everyday. Take a detour once in a while. Take a detour especially when driven by anger. Take the elevator to the last floor and then walk downstairs to your floor (see Georges Perec). Say hi to people on the street in the city and remember the "Miracle of Milano" by Vittorio de Sica.

9 Claim the unfunctional – unfunction your life

Claim the unfunctional – unfunction your life.
Claim the necessity of unfunctioning. Unfunctioning creates new perspectives. Some exercises might help you. Unfunctioning needs to be trained. Exercises (after Georges Perec) might be helpful: "Note down what you can see. Anything worthy of note going on. Do you know how to see? What's worthy of note? Is there anything that strikes you? Nothing strikes you. You don't know how to see. You must set about it more slowly, almost stupidly. Force yourself to write down what is of no interest, what is most common, most obvious, most colorless." What seems to be meaningless will develop new meaning – the value of unfunctioning.

10 Use conflicts as a potential

Use conflicts as a potential.
Use their complexity.
Use your complexity.
Use the potential of a conflict for creating a situation.
Use the potential of a potential conflict for creating a situation. The conflict of the potential asks for simplicity. Reduce your complexity. Be simple. Think simple. Mistakes are not allowed. Be strong. Look into the mirror (in the morning). Allow yourself to make a mistake.

found,
set,
appropriated,

1 Counteract governing principles of no-belief: make belief

Counteract governing principles of no-belief.
Counteract the weakness of principles. Act instead of counteract. Act to make belief. Forget about what is considered fashionable or unfashionable. It is unfashionable to talk about (personal) lacks. It is fashionable to complain. It is considered naive to engage in issues beyond the personal wellbeing. It is unfashionable to not only talk about the lacks but to insist in the belief that fundamental change is needed.

2 Reassess vital issues like sustainability

Reassess vital issues like sustainability.
Reassess vital issues. Avoid empty phrases. Sustainability has become an empty word, a synonym for emptiness. How can it be filled with new meaning? Election periods and the need for immediate success prevent from long term thinking. Reassess vital issues like sustainability. Ask questions transgressing your imagination. What do you expect from an artist? What do you expect from yourself? Can an artist contribute to sustainability? Yes we can. But we need you to come along.

3 Imagine the impossible (and work on it)

Imagine the impossible (and work on it).
Imagine the impossible. And maybe it does not need so much work.
Imagine the impossible. The impossible is personal. The impossible concerns society. We do not want to create a new utopia. Utopias also mean that something needs to be destroyed. We do not want to destroy. We want to cultivate. The moment you read these words you dedicate yourself to the possibility of the impossible. This is what is needed. What you need. What society needs. All societies. Sharing the moment of the impossible. Sharing. The impossible always escapes.

4 Consider migration as enriching reality in all directions

Consider migration as enriching reality in all directions.
Consider migration as enriching reality in all directions – and as basis of living in the 21st century. Ask for freedom of movement as human right. Freedom of movement must be considered a basic human right. For all. No ifs or buts. No more excuses. Mobility is forced onto us. But we want freedom of movement. We are in the position to ask for.

5 Believe in what you dare to believe

Believe in what you dare to believe. Overcome self-censorship when necessary. Know when to listen to others and when not. We are few. We are many. Believe in what you dare to believe. The *Blue Frog Society* will help you to overcome your fear. Sometimes it is necessary to protect our thoughts. We have to act. Not now but time will come. Feel when the time is right. We do not need to protect ourselves from what we think but from what we do not think. Sometimes it is necessary to protect our thoughts. But now is the time to share our thoughts.

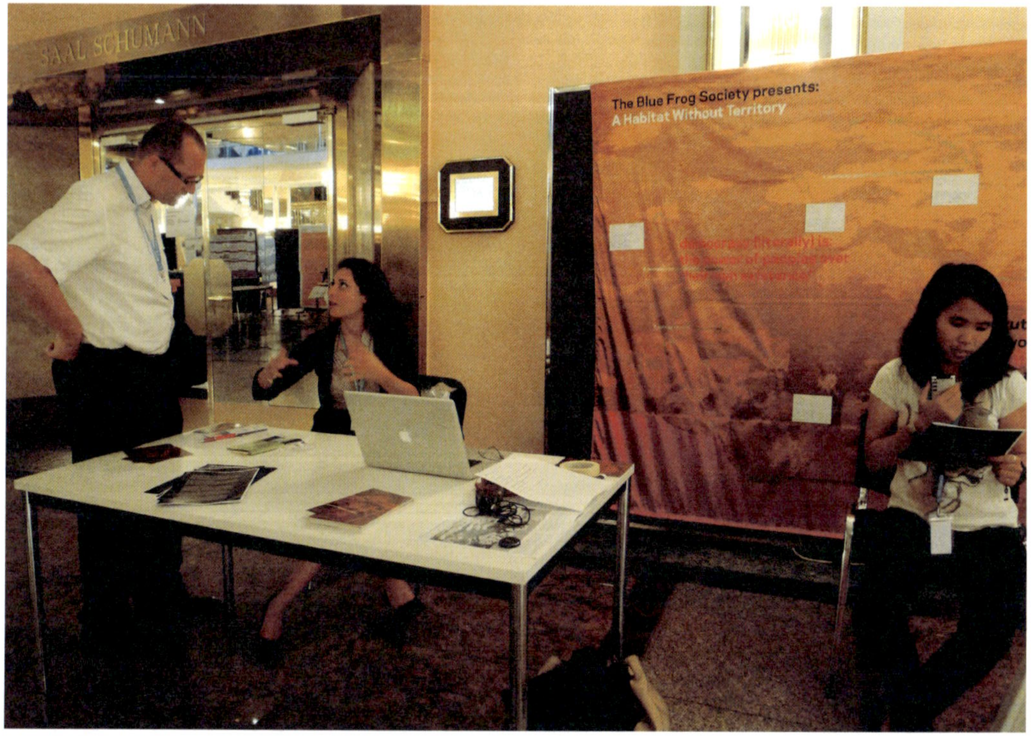

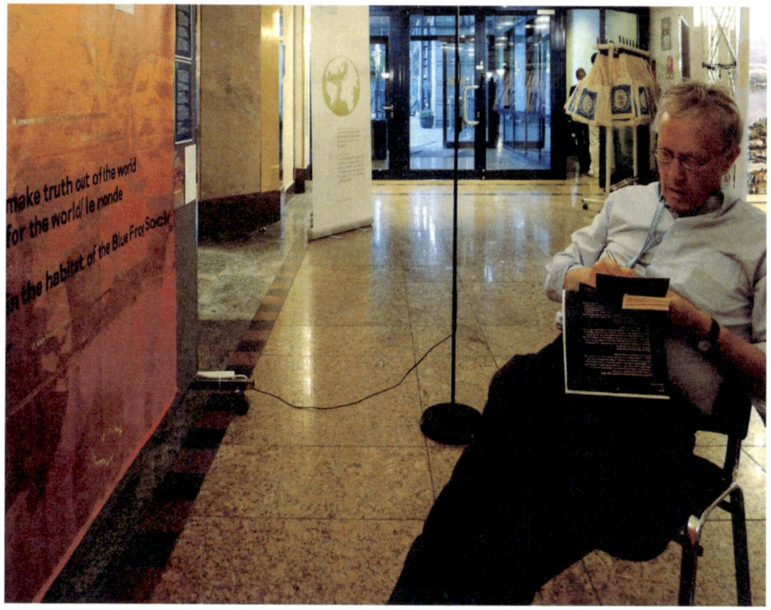

The 64th UN DPI/NGO Conference, Bonn, 2011

Die 64. UN DPI/NGO-Konferenz, Bonn, 2011

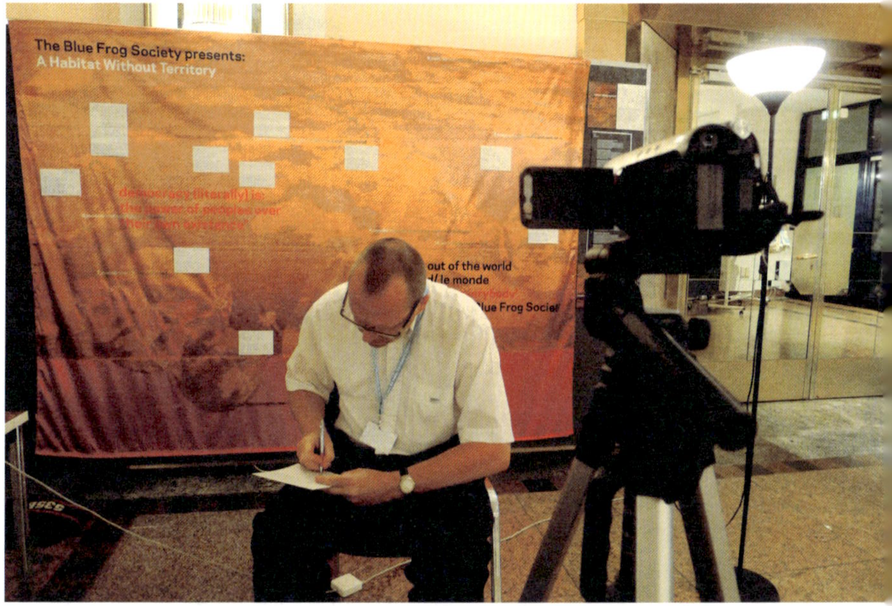

I am interested in

✓ joining the Blue Frog Society

✓ acquiring a share of the non-territorial habitat

✓ receiving more information

✓ supporting the Blue Frog Society/ providing my expertise as
please specify
Lobbying

o contributing a statement:
To achieve change you need to imagine the impossible and share these dreams with everyone and soon the impossible becomes possible

or send an email to: holub@transparadiso.com
www.transparadiso.com

To
Barbara Holub
Gr.Mohreng.23/18
1020 Wien
Austria / Europe

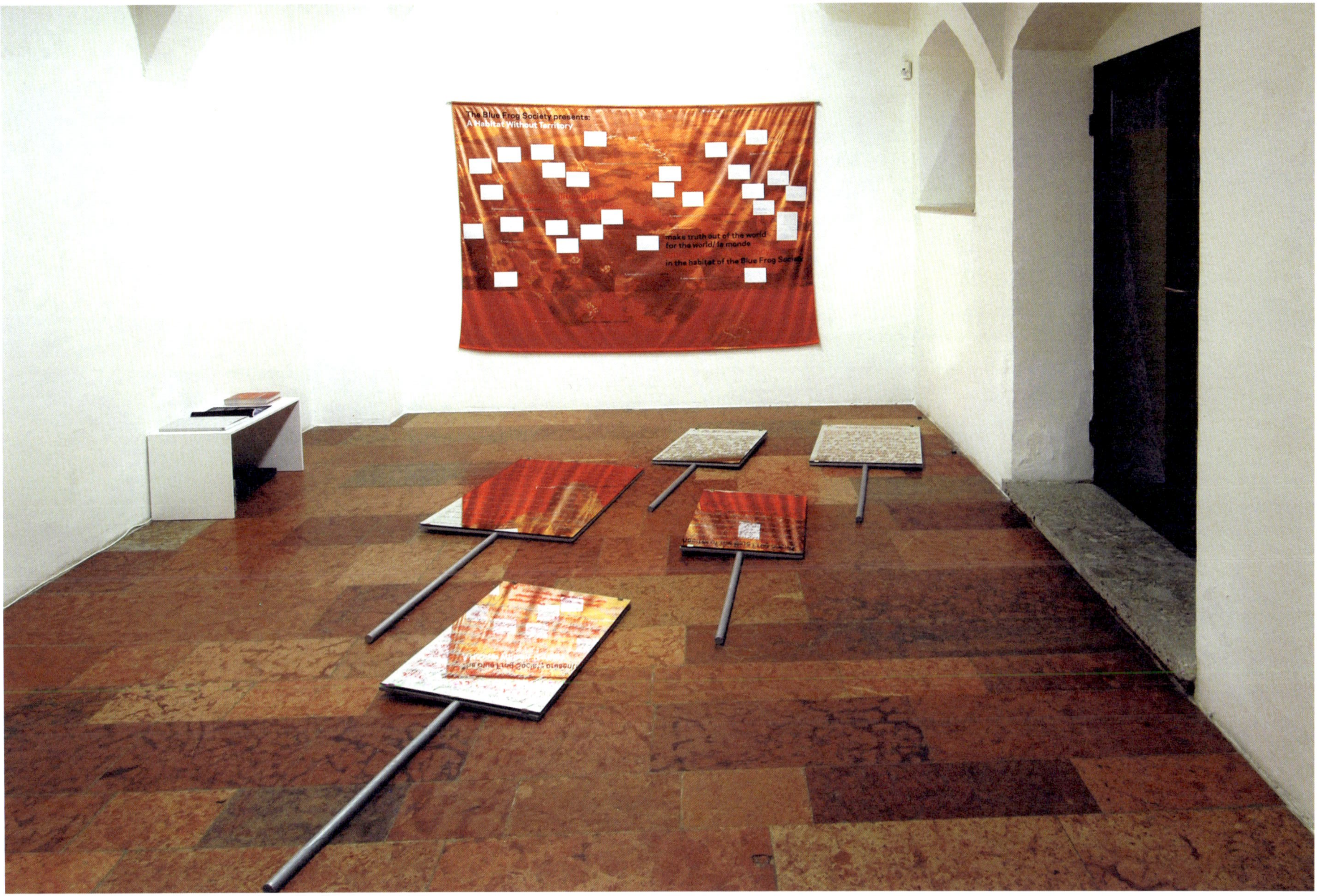

Exhibition view, *Grand Art Award of the State of Salzburg*, Traklhaus, Salzburg, 2013

Ausstellungsansicht, *Großer Kunstpreis des Landes Salzburg*, Traklhaus, Salzburg, 2013

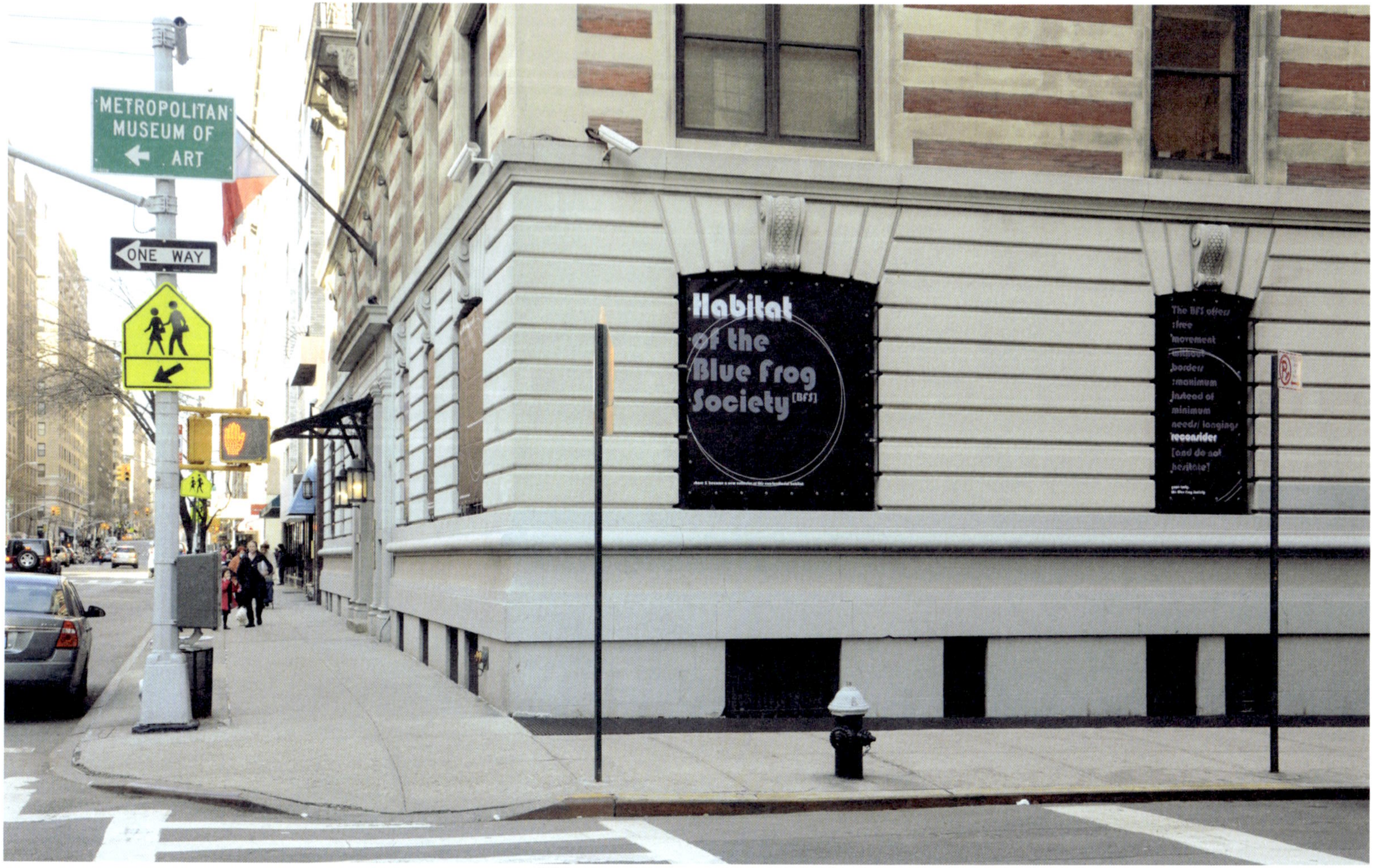

MAKE TRUTH OUT OF THE WORLD, installation for *Windows on Madison*, Czech Mission to the UN/Czech Centre, New York (US), 2011

MAKE TRUTH OUT OF THE WORLD, Installation für *Windows on Madison*, Czech Mission to the UN/Czech Centre, New York (US), 2011

"By way of an imaginary new species, Holub's project addresses the issues of territory and habitat that go to the very foundation of the dominant socio-economic system, invoking the tradition that started with Hans Haacke's Shapolsky et al., Manhattan Real Estate Holdings, a Real-Time Social System, as of May 1, 1971, which still haunts the Guggenheim Museum located a few blocks from the Windows on Madison. Holub's project takes a different direction by raising the question of habitat in relation to our values, and thus foregrounding the interconnectedness of nature, culture and economy and our vital investment in it."

Jaroslav Anděl

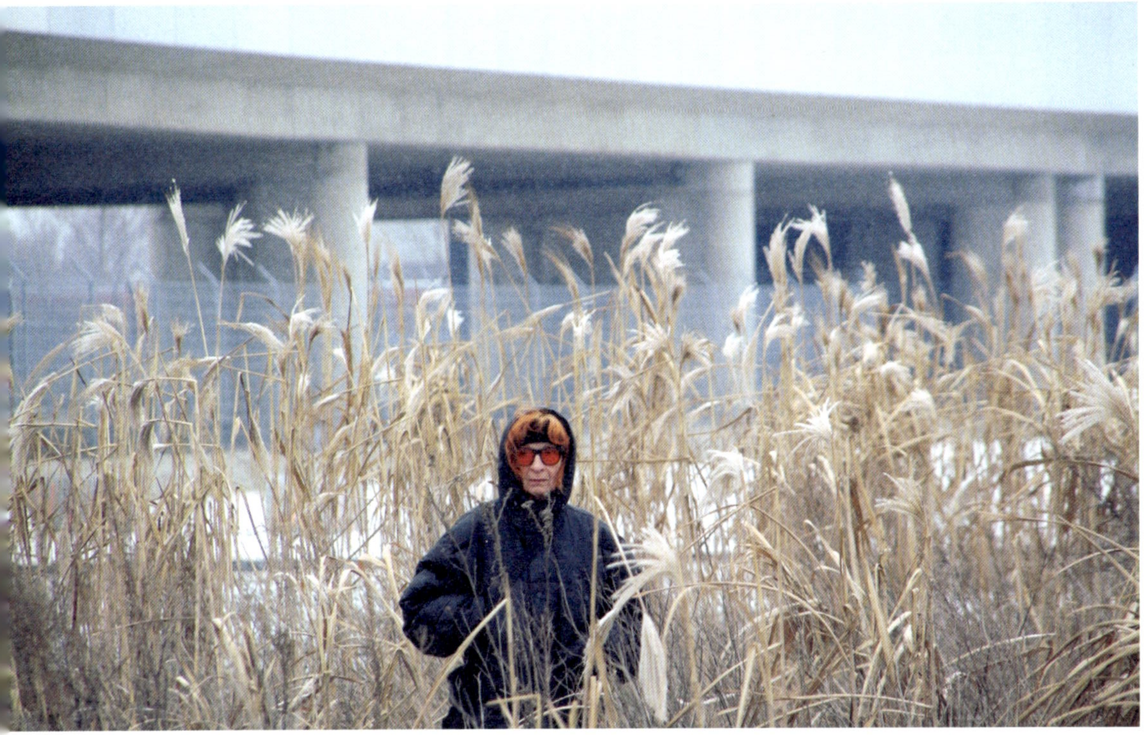

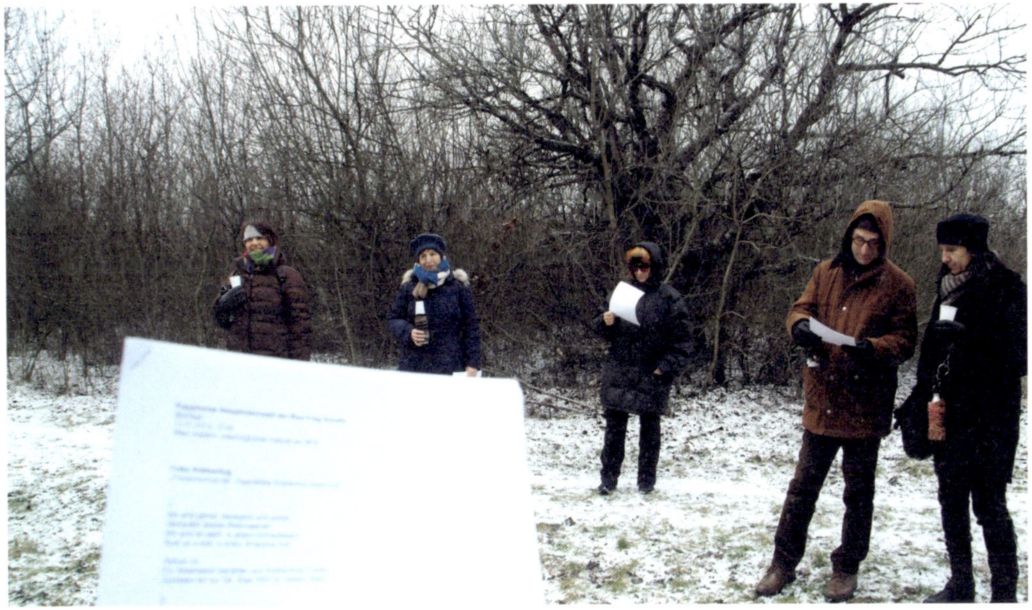

A polyphonic New Year's Concert of THE BLUE FROG SOCIETY, Lake-City Aspern, Vienna, Jan. 13, 2013

Ein polyphones Neujahrskonzert von THE BLUE FROG SOCIETY, Aspern Seestadt, Wien, 13. Januar 2013

„Das wahre Bild der Vergangenheit huscht vorbei.
Erkannte gemeint ihm in als nicht sich die,
droht verschwinden zu Gegenwart jeder mit das
Vergangenheit, der Bild unwiederbringliches.
Nur als Bild, das auf Nimmerwiedersehen im
Augenblick seiner Erkennbarkeit eben aufblitzt"

Martin Krenn

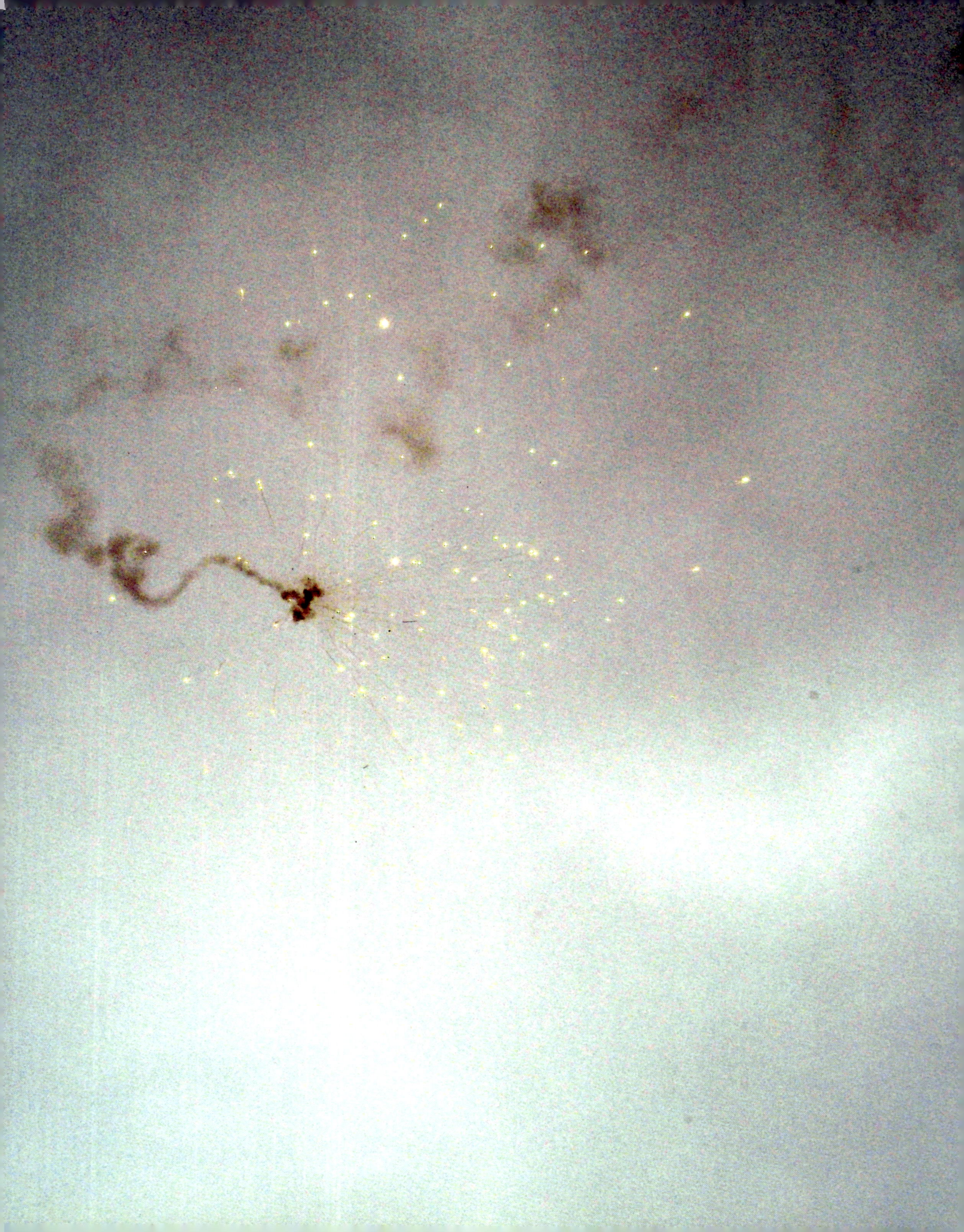

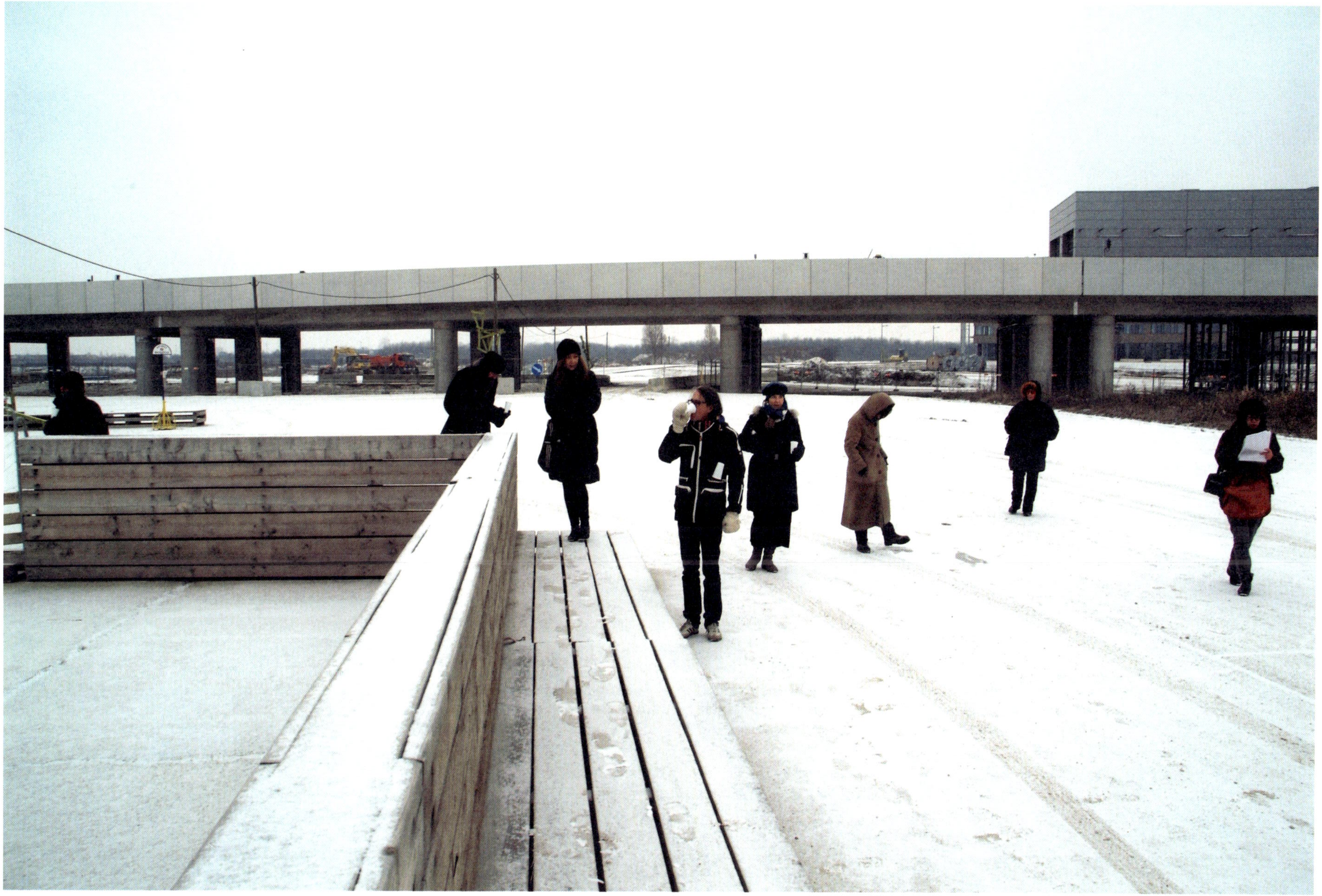

With contributions by Folke Köbberling, Martin Krenn, Isa Rosenberger, Rita Vitorelli, Joanna Warsza

Mit Beiträgen von Folke Köbberling, Martin Krenn, Isa Rosenberger, Rita Vitorelli, Joanna Warsza

CrossSections_Intervals, curated by Başak Şenova, Kunsthalle Exnergasse, Vienna, 2018; Konstfack, Stockholm, 2019; PUBLICS, Helsinki, curated by Paul O'Neill, 2019

A STATE VISIT TO THE BLUE FROG SOCIETY BY MINORITY NATIONALITIES

With this new chapter, THE BLUE FROG SOCIETY calls upon people to revisit the idea of a joint, "extended" Europe based on humanist values and to recognise diversity as a crucial element of a future society. Many small minority nationalities in Europe (whose existence we are generally unaware of as they are not the ones demanding a new nation-state) are in danger of dying out—along with their languages.

Therefore, THE BLUE FROG SOCIETY has invited representatives of dying languages in Europe to a state visit to their extraterritorial habitat, asking them to take this opportunity to give a short speech exploring the potentials of mutual enrichment and hopes and objectives for a common future—as a symbolic gesture inherent to the act of a state visit and an official sign of recognition of others as equal partners.

The first speeches were held by representatives of Friulian and Romanes, for which the speakers developed very different formats. Nancy Black, for example, translated Charlie Chaplin's speech from *The Great Dictator* (1940) into Romanes for the first time, performing the speech at the exhibition. Her aim was also to draw attention to the dearth of written translations into Romanes. Selma Selman created a video artwork depicting her blinking eyes: "Believe in the youth and the youth who believe will achieve! Stop killing!" Gabriele Zanello (Società Filologica Friulana) presented the history of Friulian, while Costanza Travaglini reflected on her family tradition, speaking about the new self-awareness and recognition of Friulian.

The next state visits are planned for the Sámi languages (in collaboration with PUBLICS/Helsinki) and Sorbian, among others.[BS]

CrossSections_Intervals, kuratiert von Başak Şenova, Kunsthalle Exnergasse, Wien, 2018; Konstfack, Stockholm 2019; PUBLICS, Helsinki, kuratiert von Paul O'Neill, 2019

A STATE VISIT TO THE BLUE FROG SOCIETY BY MINORITY NATIONALITIES

Mit diesem neuen Kapitel ruft THE BLUE FROG SOCIETY dazu auf, die Idee eines gemeinsamen und „erweiterten" Europa auf der Grundlage humanistischer Werte wieder aufzugreifen und Vielfalt als wesentliches Element einer zukünftigen Gesellschaft zu erkennen. Denn viele kleine europäische Minderheitsnationalitäten (deren Existenz uns meist nicht bewusst ist, da sie nicht diejenigen sind, die einen neuen Nationalstaat fordern) sind – mitsamt ihren vielfältigen Sprachen – vom Aussterben bedroht.

THE BLUE FROG SOCIETY hat daher VertreterInnen aussterbender Sprachen in Europa zu einem Staatsbesuch in ihr exterritoriales Habitat eingeladen und sie gebeten, bei dieser Gelegenheit mit einer kurzen Rede die Potenziale gegenseitiger Bereicherung sowie Hoffnungen und Ziele für eine gemeinsame Zukunft auszuloten – als symbolische Geste, die dem Akt eines Staatsbesuches innewohnt, und als offizielles Zeichen der Anerkennung des Gegenübers als gleichberechtigte/r PartnerIn.

Die ersten Reden wurden von VertreterInnen des Friulanischen und des Romanes gehalten, für die die RednerInnen sehr unterschiedliche Formate entwickelten. So übersetzte etwa Nancy Black Charlie Chaplins Rede in *Der große Diktator* (1940) zum ersten Mal ins Romanes und hielt die Rede in der Ausstellung. Sie verwies damit auch auf den Mangel an schriftlichen Übersetzungen ins Romanes. Selma Selman schuf ein Künstlerinnen-Video, das ihre blinzelnden Augen zeigt: „Believe in the youth and the youth who believe will achieve! Stop killing!" Gabriele Zanello (Società Filologica Friulana) stellte die Geschichte des Friulanischen vor, während Costanza Travaglini über ihre Familientradition nachdachte und über das neue Selbstbewusstsein und die Anerkennung des Friulanischen sprach.

Die nächsten Staatsbesuche sind u. a. für die samischen Sprachen (in Zusammenarbeit mit PUBLICS/Helsinki) und das Sorbische geplant.[BS]

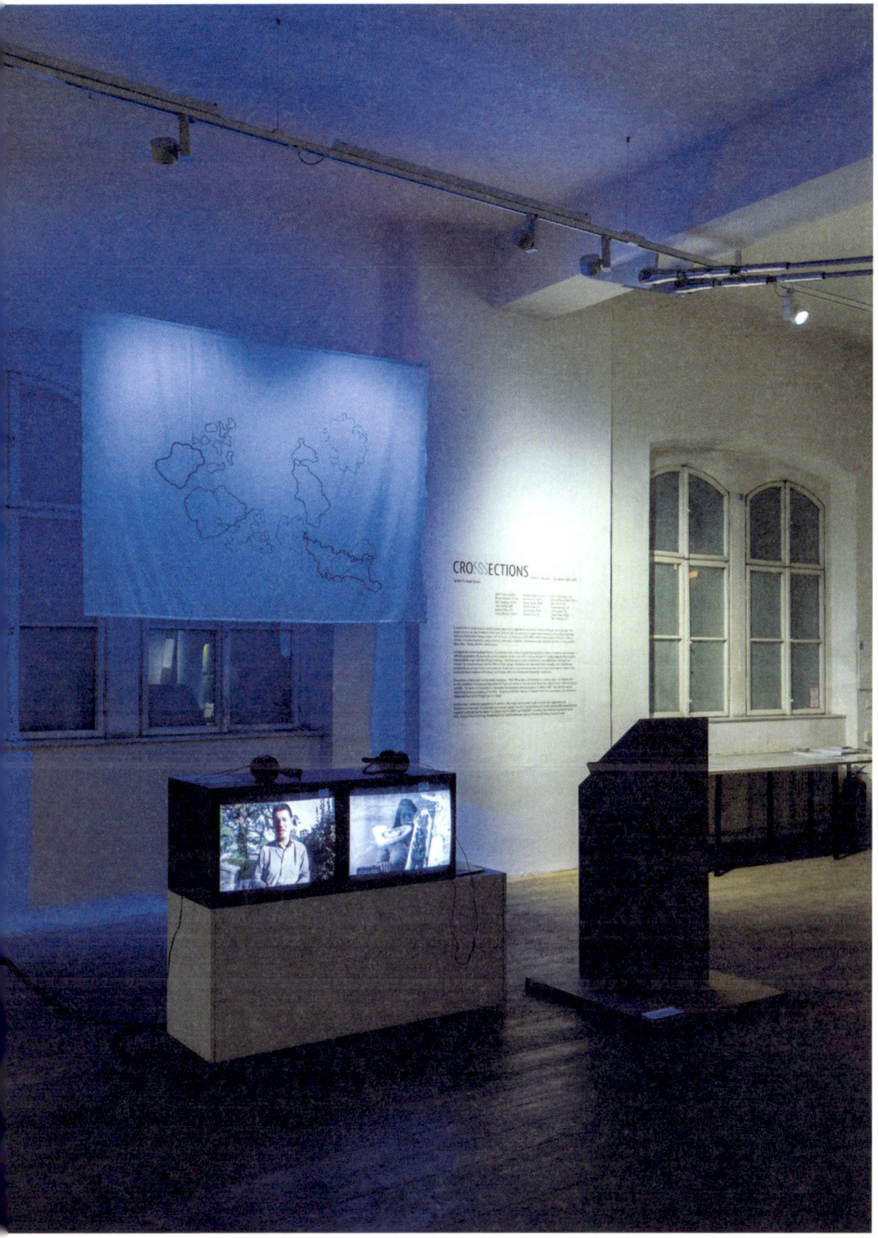

Installation view, *CrossSections_Intervals*, Kunsthalle Exnergasse, Vienna, 2018, with a lecture performance by Nancy Black

Ausstellungsansicht, *CrossSections_Intervals*, Kunsthalle Exnergasse, Wien, 2018, mit einer Lecture-Performance von Nancy Black

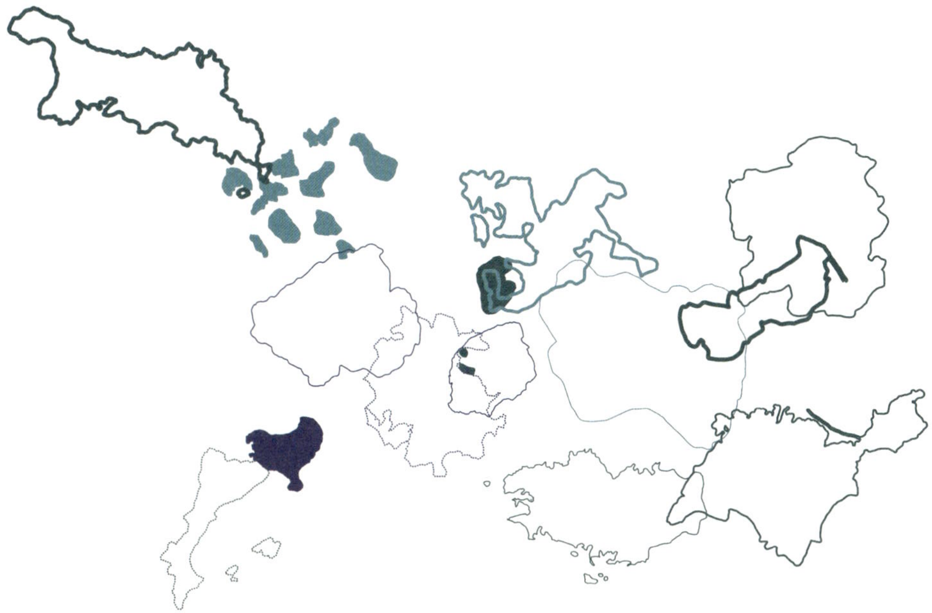

A new map with some European minority languages: Franco-Provençal, Aromanian, Crimean Tatar, Cornish, Friulian, Gagauz, Galician, Breton, Kashubian, Catalan, Basque, Frisian, Aragonese

Eine neue Landkarte mit einigen europäischen Minderheitensprachen: Franco-provençalisch, Aromunisch, Krimtatarisch, Kornisch, Friulan, Gaugasisch, Galizisch, Bretonisch, Kasubisch, Katalanisch, Baskisch, Friesisch, Aragonesisch

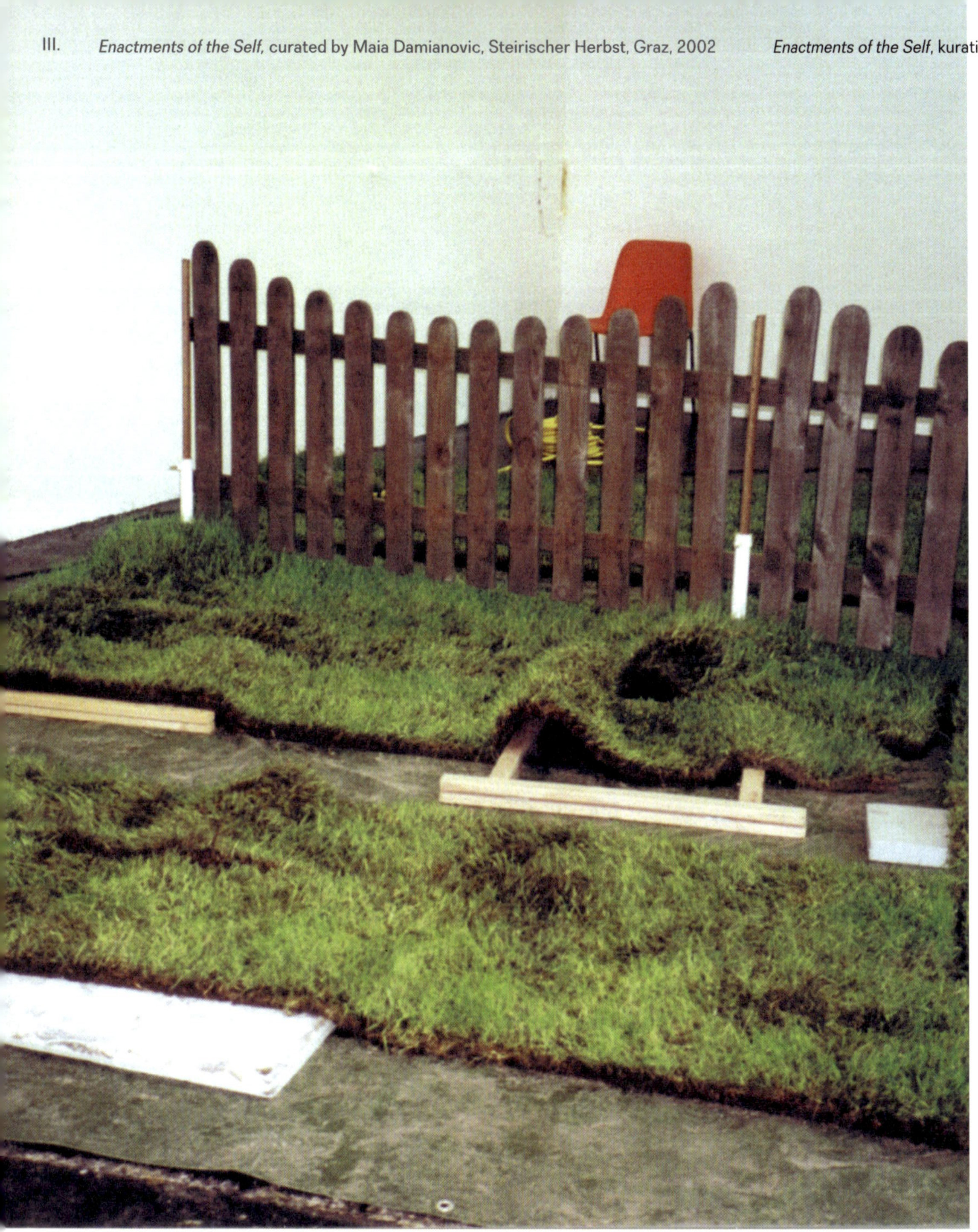

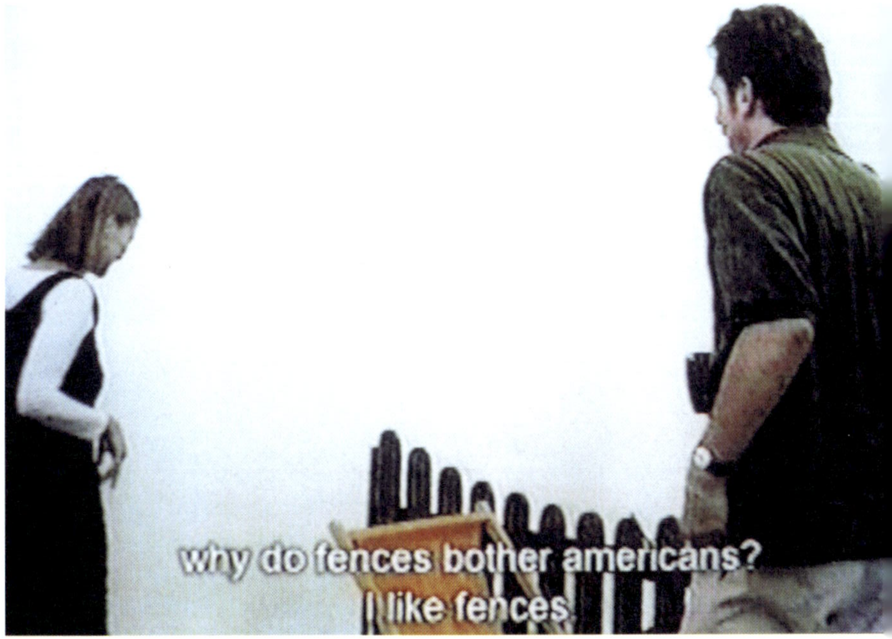

BETWEEN ROLES, Barbara Holub's studio, 2000 ZWISCHENROLLEN, Atelier Barbara Holub, 2000

BETWEEN ROLES

Work is underway in Barbara Holub's new studio: construction workers begin unloading various building materials, moving on to unroll rolls of paper and lay down asphalt, and finally laying turf and putting up a fence – now the lawn can be mown. The installation BETWEEN ROLES invites people to take part in over-the-fence conversations, exploring the (urban) notion of the happiness of garden (fence) owners. The focus is on reflections on the concepts of "work," "leisure," and "forced economization" as well as on questions of the available time budget and quality demands to be met by paid and voluntary (unpaid) work.

BETWEEN ROLES took place simultaneously at three venues during Steirischer Herbst '02: as a performative installation of a seemingly everyday garden (fence) situation in the exhibition space, as a public casting in urban space in a specially adapted limousine, and as a video installation in a furniture store in Graz. The video showed the participants' over-the-fence conversations, edited live in the exhibition space. Barbara Holub had invited the participants, in particular, to discuss the subject of "borders" over the fence. Additionally, the guests cast for the project had the opportunity to take advantage of this garden situation for their own conversations with interested visitors. Inspired by the projection of the video *Swinging*, which alternated between watching a girl enjoying herself swinging wildly and the sedate rocking of a swing seat, visitors found themselves between the poles of (giving up) control and losing control—a push and pull that is also reflected in the way we look at gardens, between domestication and ecological responsibility.

Coming increasingly into the public eye, climate change and its effects open up an additional perspective on the territory explored in this project, between everyday situation and art context, a perspective that not only reflects yearnings between urban and rural environments but also raises the prospect of (artificial) indoor gardens (kept at the perfect temperature). Just like in "real life," voluntary services and neighborly help were certainly welcome in the (exhibition) garden too.[BR]

Barbara Holub's studio, 2nd district, Vienna, 2000. *Gouvernementalität. Kunst in Auseinandersetzung mit der internationalen Hyperbourgeoisie und dem internationalen Kleinbürgertum*, curated by Roger Buergel, Alte Kestner Gesellschaft, Hanover, 2000. *Niemandsland*, curated by Henny Liebhart-Ulm, Katharina Pabisch, and Anna Soucek, Künstlerhaus Wien, Vienna, 2004

ZWISCHENROLLEN

Im neuen Atelier von Barbara Holub wird gearbeitet: Bauarbeiter laden zunächst Baumaterial ab, entrollen Papierrollen und tragen Asphalt auf, bis schließlich der Rollrasen aufgelegt wird, ein Zaun aufgestellt – und Rasen gemäht werden kann. Zu „Zaungesprächen" lädt die Installation ZWISCHENROLLEN ein, die der (urbanen) Vorstellung vom Glück der Garten(zaun)besitzerInnen nachspürt. Im Fokus stehen Reflexionen zu den Begriffen „Arbeit" und „Freizeit", „Ökonomisierungszwang" ebenso wie Fragen nach dem verfügbaren Zeitbudget und dem Qualitätsanspruch von bezahlter und freiwillig (unentgeltlich) geleisteter Arbeit.

Im Rahmen des Steirischen Herbst '02 fand ZWISCHENROLLEN an drei Orten gleichzeitig statt: als performative Installation einer scheinbar alltäglichen Garten(zaun)situation im Ausstellungsraum, als öffentliches Casting im Stadtraum in einer eigens dafür adaptierten Limousine, und als Videoinstallation in einem Grazer Möbelkaufhaus. Gezeigt wurden hier die im Ausstellungsraum live editierten Zaungespräche der TeilnehmerInnen, die Barbara Holub insbesondere einlud, um sich über das Thema „Grenzen", über den Zaun hinweg, zu unterhalten. Zusätzlich stand die Gartensituation den gecasteten Gästen sowie interessierten BesucherInnen für eigene Gespräche offen. Angeregt durch die Projektion des Videos *Swinging*, das zwischen dem Betrachten eines genüsslich wild schaukelnden Mädchens und dem des bedachten Schwingens auf einer Hollywoodschaukel oszillierte, fanden sich die BesucherInnen zwischen den Polen von (der Aufgabe von) Kontrolle und Kontrollverlust konfrontiert – ein Spannungsfeld, das sich auch im Umgang mit Gärten zwischen Domestizierung und ökologischer Verantwortung widerspiegelt.

Die aktuell immer stärker in den öffentlichen Fokus rückende Veränderung des Klimas und deren Auswirkungen eröffnen eine zusätzliche Perspektive auf die zwischen Alltagssituation und Kunstkontext eroberten Terrains. Es werden hier nicht nur Sehnsüchte zwischen Stadt und Land zum Ausdruck gebracht, sondern auch Perspektiven von künstlichen Gärten im temperierten Innenraum aufgeworfen.Freiwillige Dienstleistungen und Nachbarschaftshilfe waren im (Ausstellungs-)Garten, wie im „realen Leben", jedenfalls willkommen.BR

Atelier Barbara Holub, 2. Wiener Gemeindebezirk, Wien, 2000. *Gouvernementalität. Kunst in Auseinandersetzung mit der internationalen Hyperbourgeoisie und dem internationalen Kleinbürgertum*, kuratiert von Roger Buergel, Alte Kestner Gesellschaft, Hannover, 2000. *Niemandsland*, kuratiert von Henny Liebhart-Ulm, Katharina Pabisch und Anna Soucek, Künstlerhaus Wien, Wien, 2004

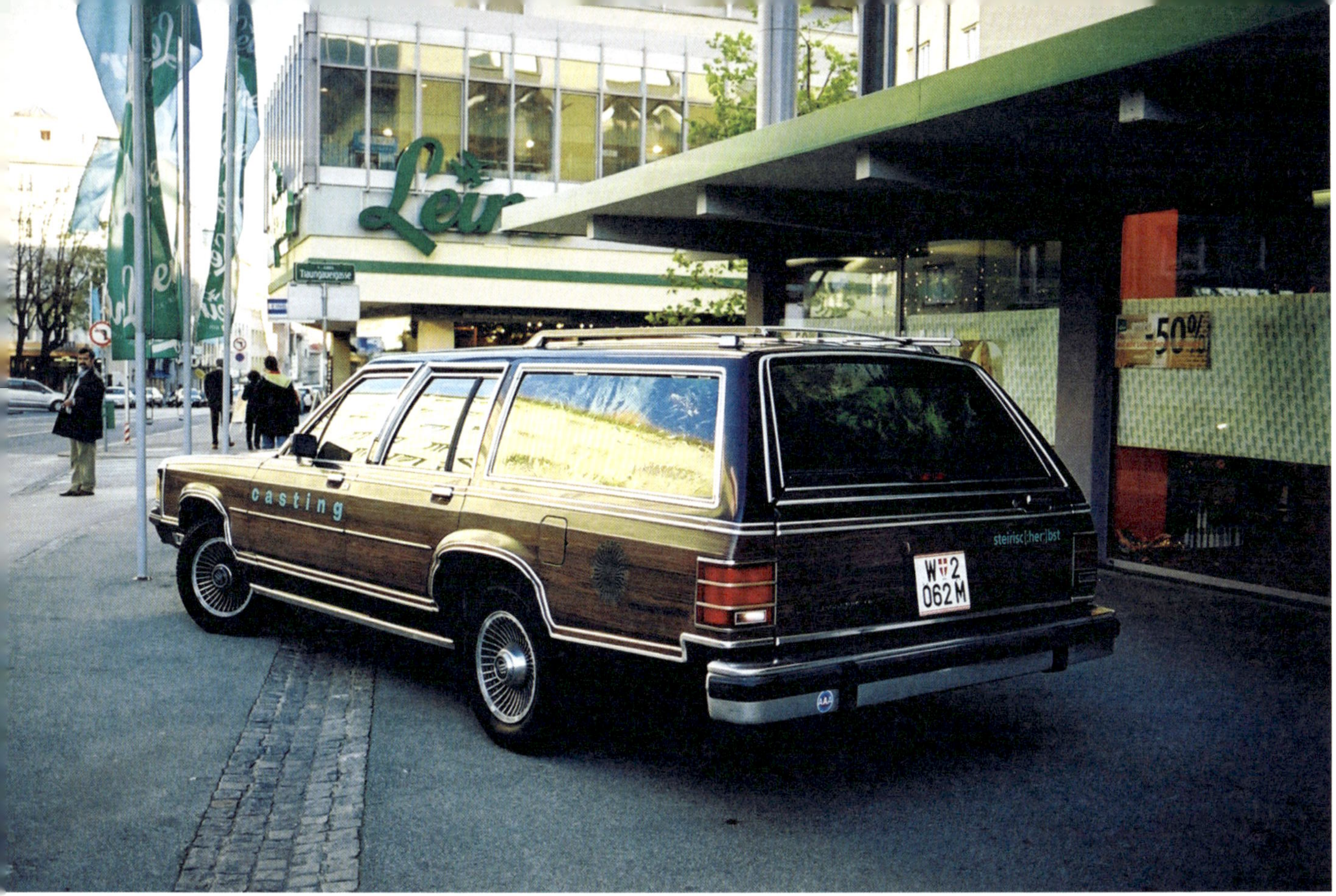

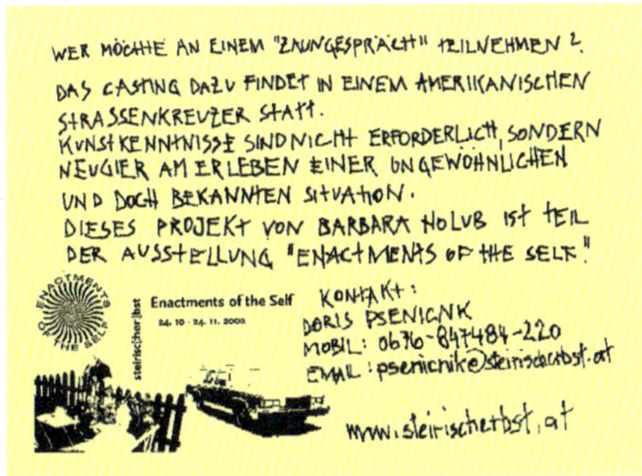
WER MÖCHTE AN EINEM "ZAUNGESPRÄCH" TEILNEHMEN?

DAS CASTING DAZU FINDET IN EINEM AMERIKANISCHEN STRASSENKREUZER STATT.

KUNSTKENNTNISSE SIND NICHT ERFORDERLICH, SONDERN NEUGIER AM ERLEBEN EINER UNGEWÖHNLICHEN UND DOCH BEKANNTEN SITUATION.

DIESES PROJEKT VON BARBARA HOLUB IST TEIL DER AUSSTELLUNG "ENACTMENTS OF THE SELF".

steirisc[her]bst Enactments of the Self 24.10.–24.11.2003

KONTAKT:
DORIS PSENICNIK
MOBIL: 0676-847484-220
EMAIL: psenicnik@steirischerbst.at

www.steirischerbst.at

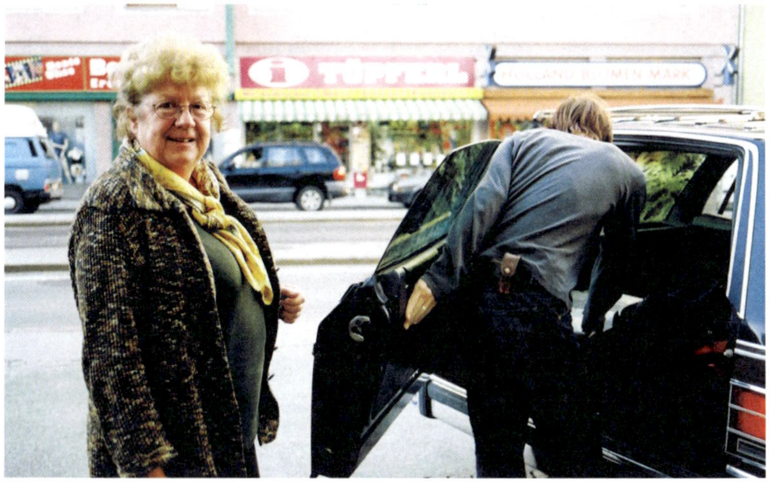

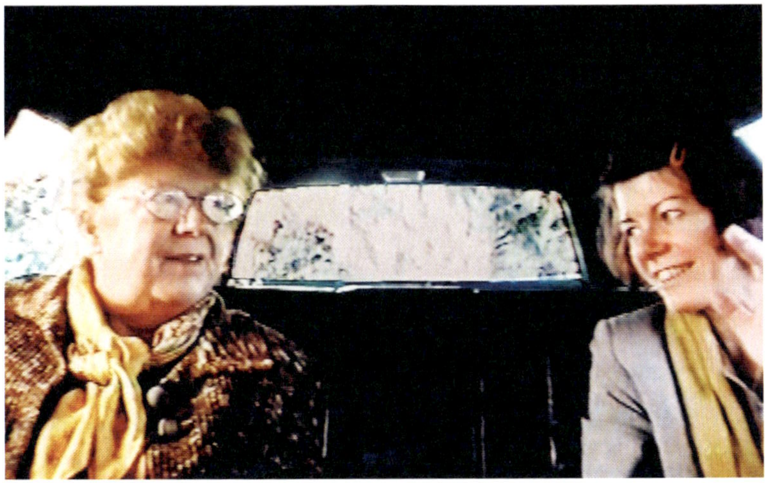

A "casting car" invited people to participate in conversations across the fence.

Ein „Casting-Auto" lud zur Teilnahme an den Zaungesprächen ein.

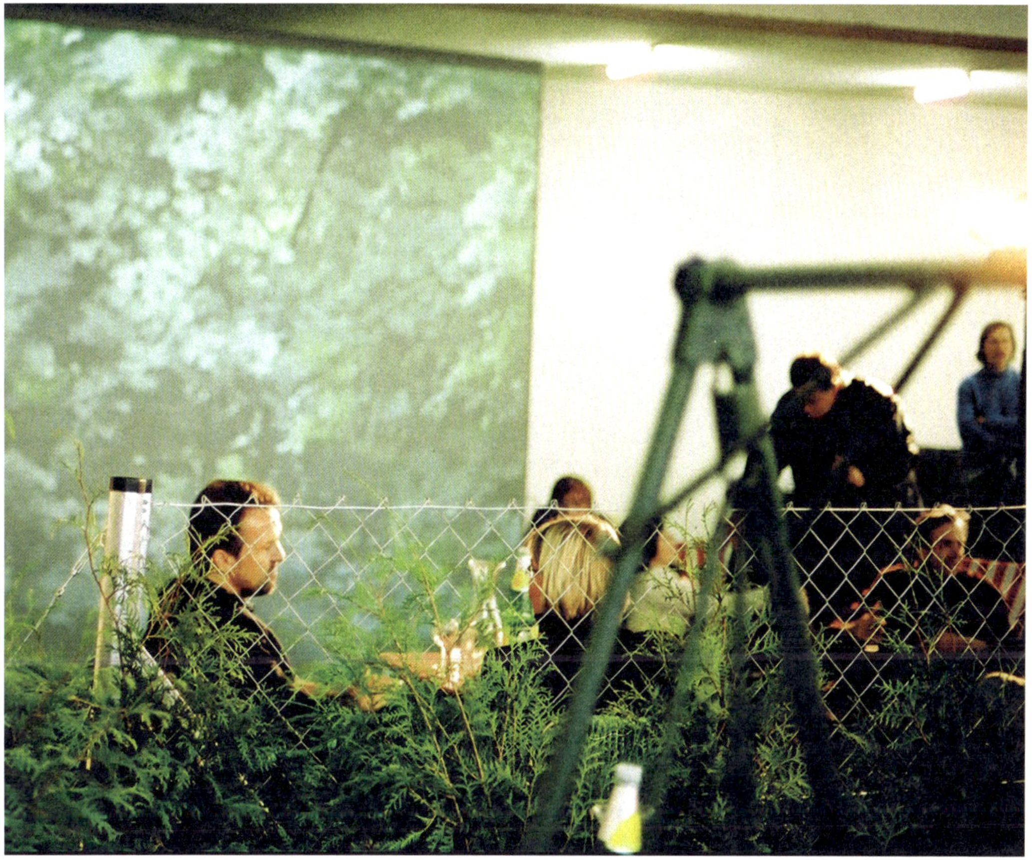

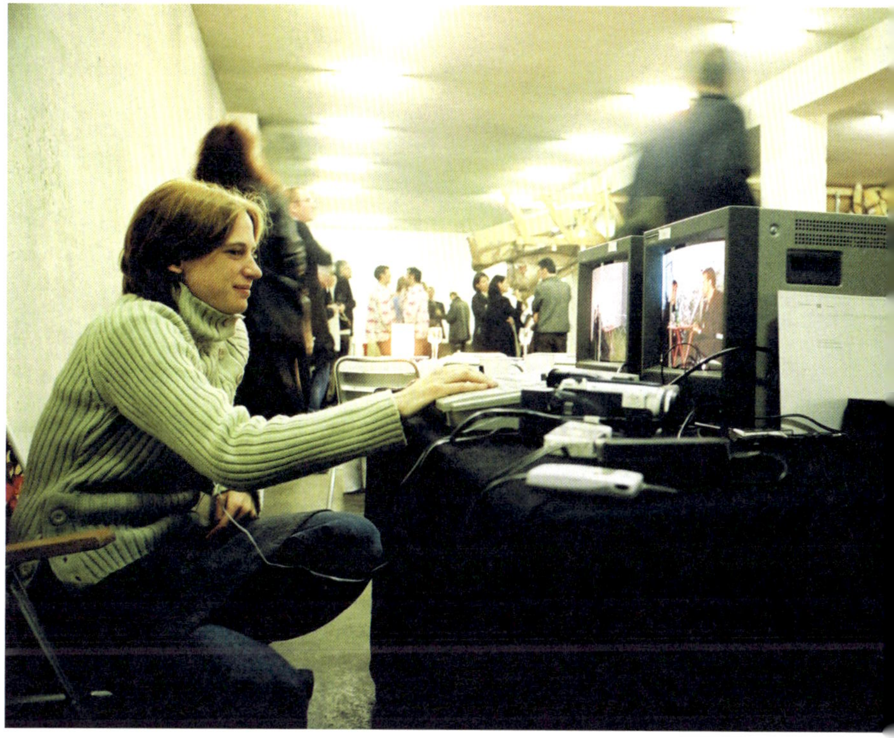

BETWEEN ROLES
Performative installation in the exhibition hall of *Enactments of the Self*, Graz, 2002
The conversations were recorded and edited live, and then shown in the window of a furniture store in a shopping street during the exhibition.

ZWISCHENROLLEN
Performative Installation in der Ausstellungshalle von *Enactments of the Self*, Graz, 2002
Die Zaungespräche wurden aufgenommen und live geschnitten und während der Ausstellungsdauer im Schaufenster eines Möbelhauses in einer Einkaufsstraße gezeigt.

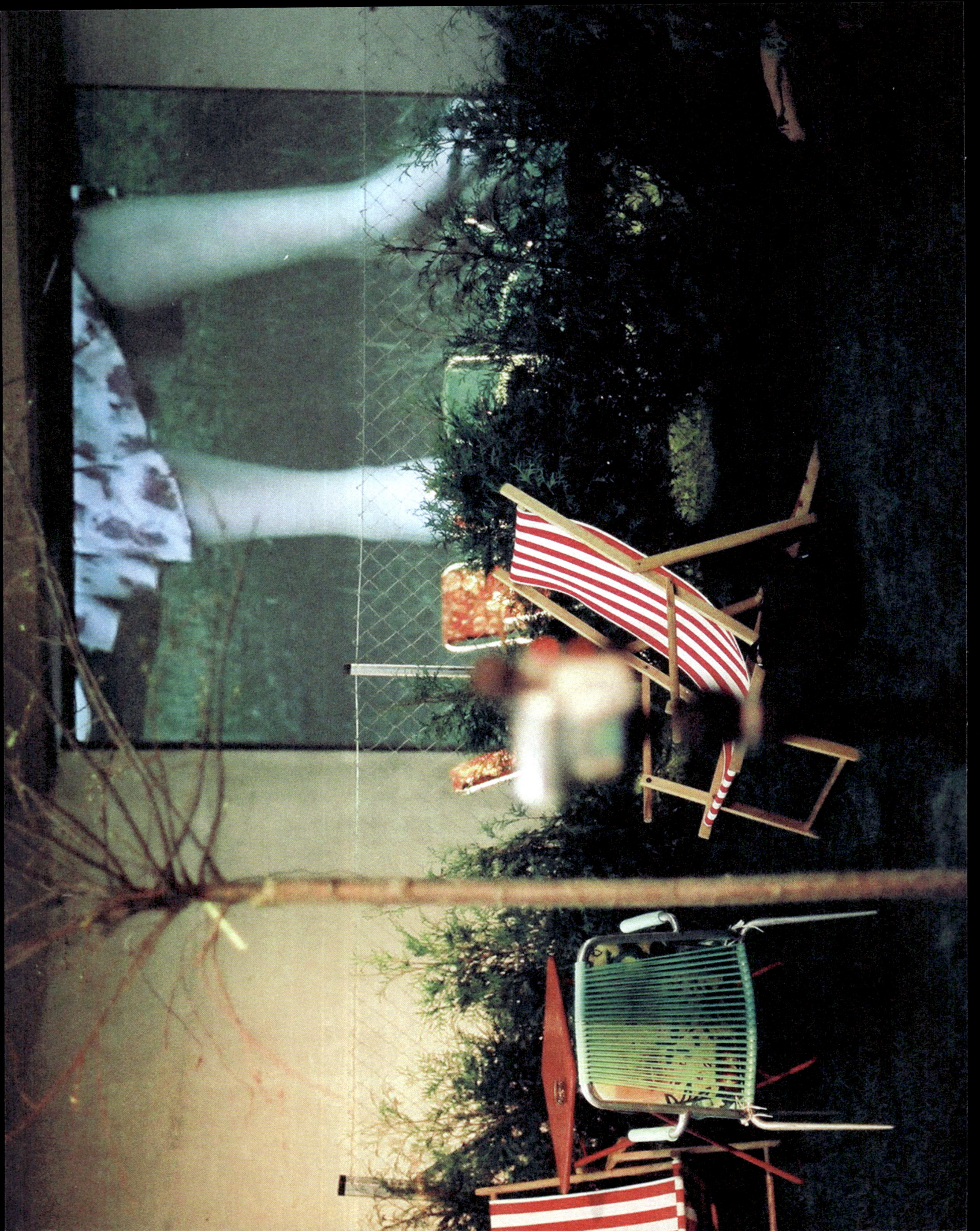

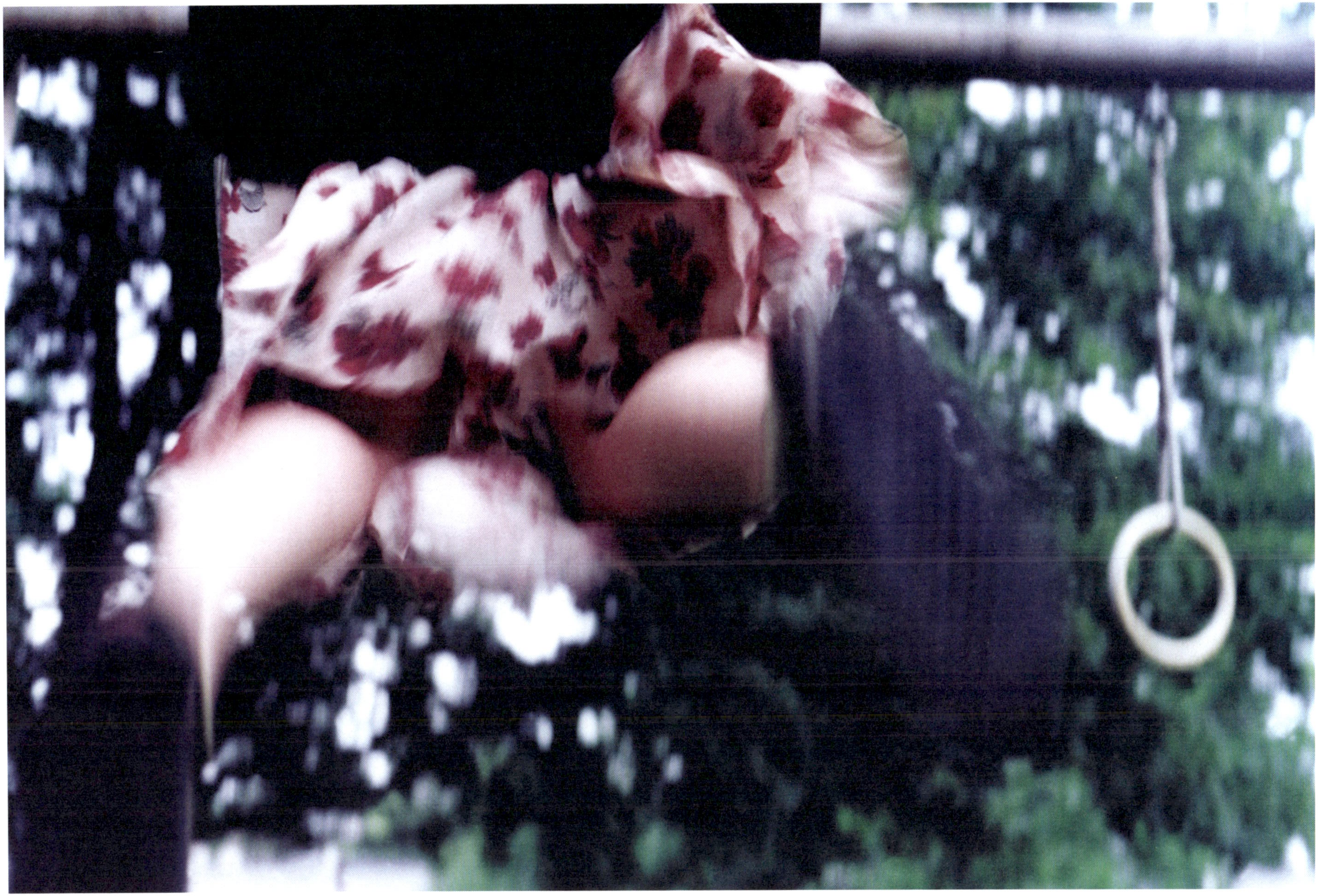

SWINGING, video, 2002
The video shows a girl alternately swinging wildly and sedately rocking on a swing seat—between control and losing control.

SWINGING, Video, 2002
Das Video zeigt ein Mädchen, das sich zwischen wildem Schaukeln und gemächlichem Hin- und Herwippen auf einer Hollywoodschaukel bewegt, zwischen Kontrolle und Kontrollverlust.

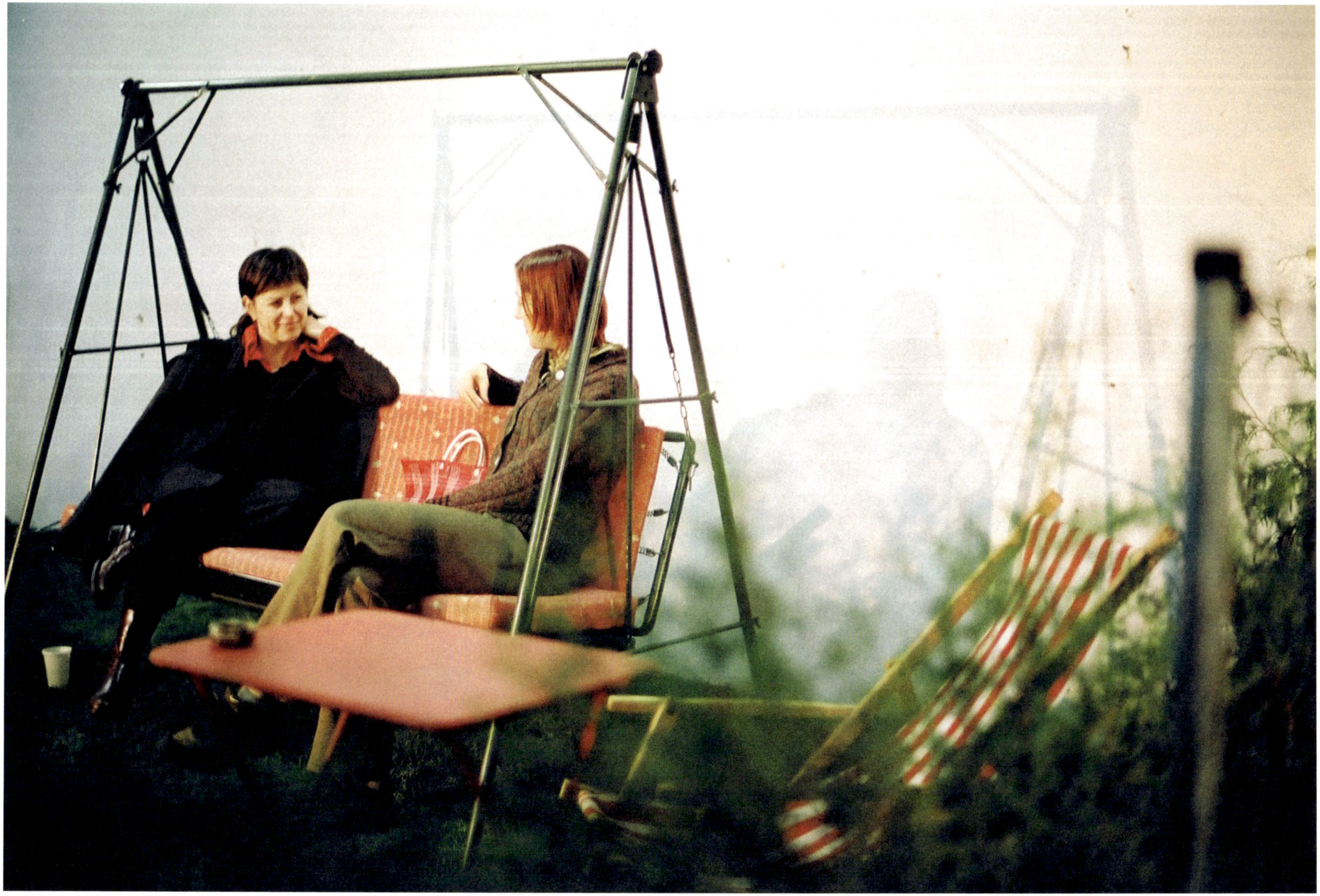

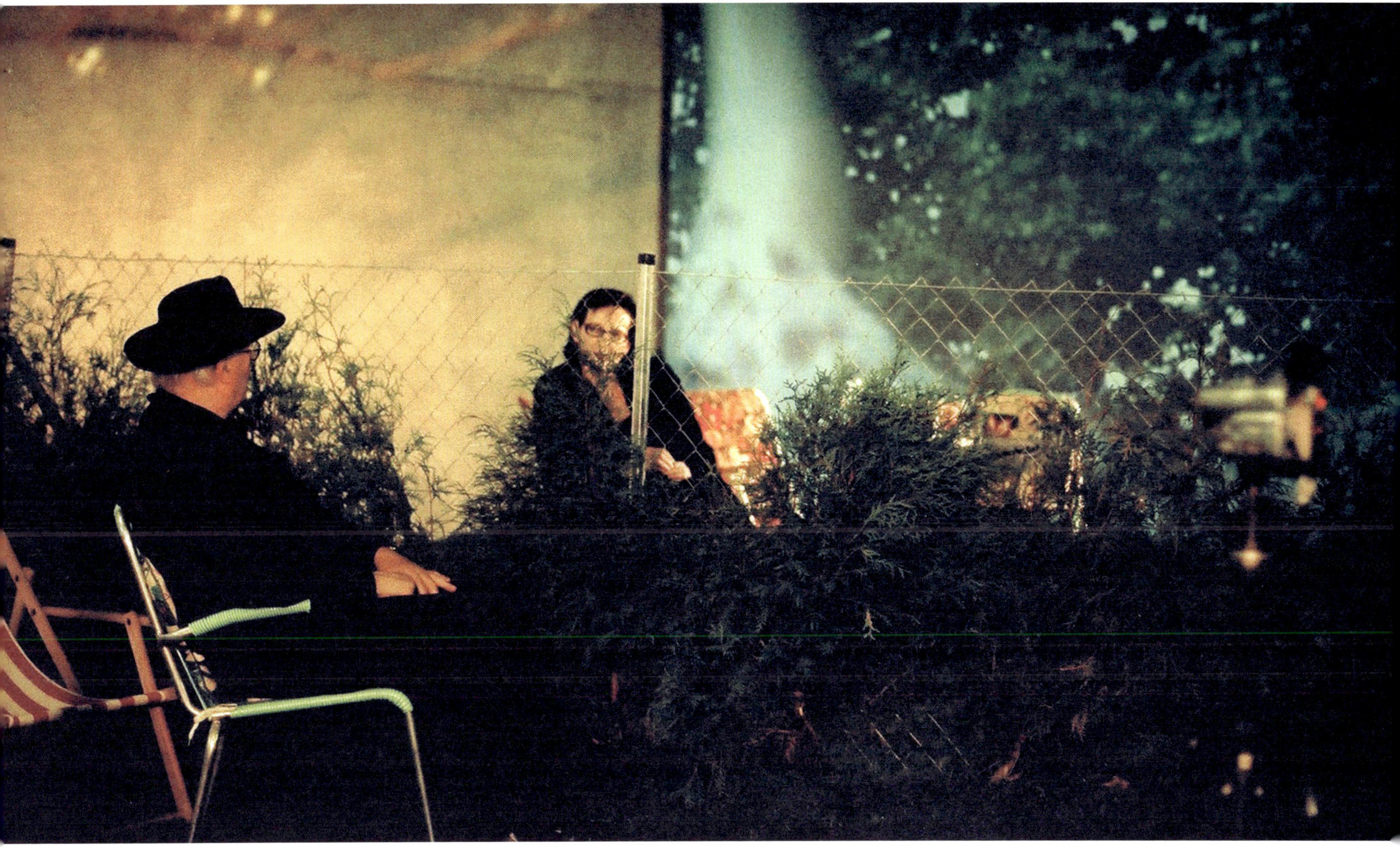

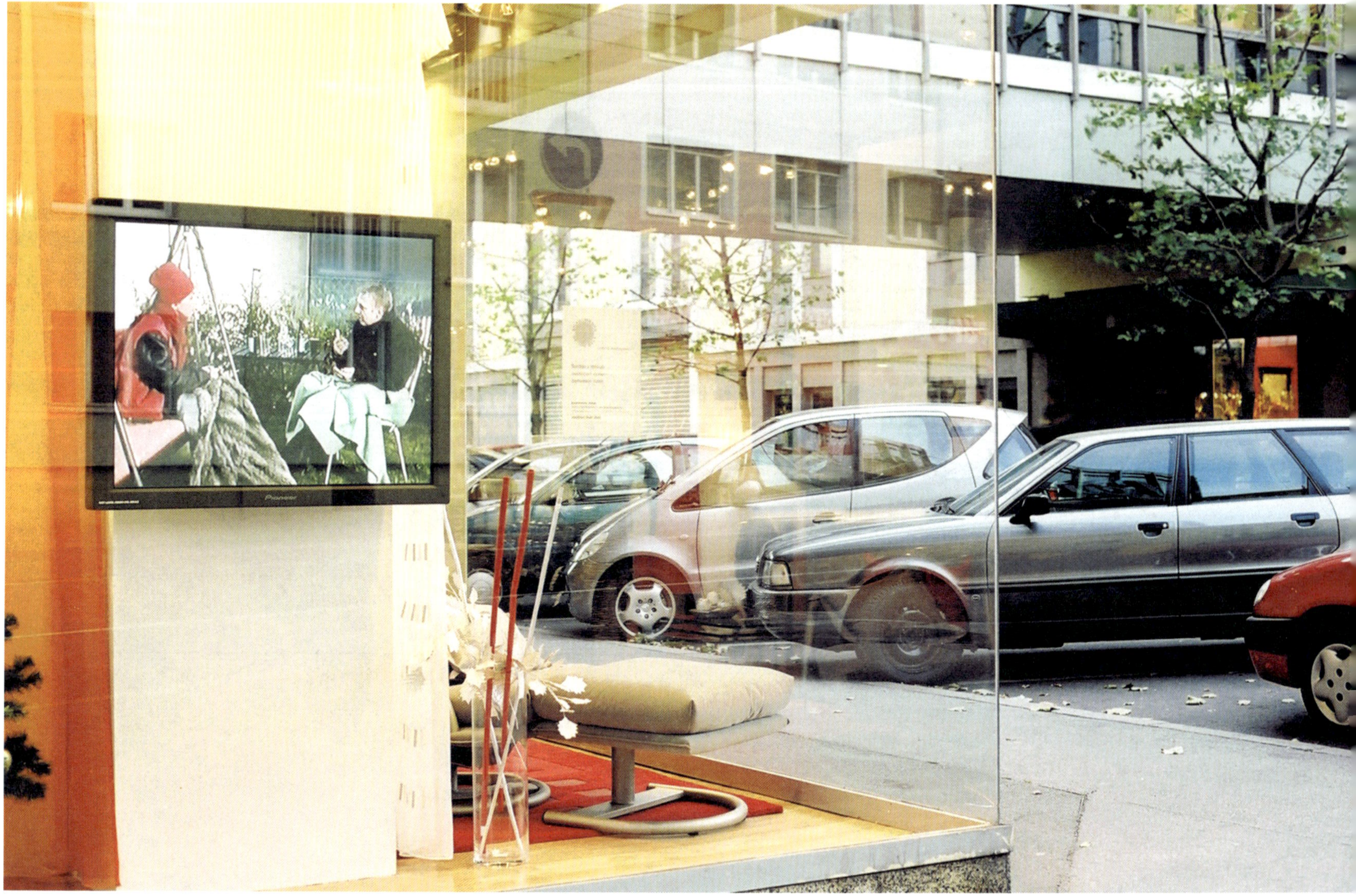

Screenings of the conversations in a furniture store near the train station: the sound was transmitted to the outdoor space so that the conversations across fences mixed with urban life in public space.

Screenings der Zaungespräche in einem Möbelhaus nahe des Bahnhofs: Der Ton wurde in den Außenraum übertragen, sodass die Gespräche über Zäune sich mit dem urbanen Leben im öffentlichen Raum vermischten.

IV. Systems, Secrecy, Voices

Systeme, Geheimnis, Stimmen

EXTRA ORDINARY

Jonatan Habib Engqvist

"Return to normalcy" was United States presidential candidate Warren G. Harding's campaign slogan for the election of 1920. It evoked a return to the way of life before World War I, the "First Red Scare"[1] and the Spanish flu pandemic. One hundred years later this notion of an ill-defined cliché return to some non-existent golden past seems to be exactly what the world wants to hear from its politicians. Perhaps more so now than a century ago. Or perhaps then, there were simply other utopias that didn't look toward a future past. Indeed, Zygmunt Bauman's posthumous book from 2017 explores the pertinent concept of "retrotopia," and with an ideologically critical gaze Bauman argues that the past has taken over the role of the future as desirable, and that retrotopia has replaced utopia. As the future frightens us, he argues, we shy away from it rather than strive for it. In short, the argument is that modernity's narrative of optimistic development no longer works, and instead of imagining a bright future characterized by, for example, an enlightened humanity or a secure existence, the future is depicted as an apocalypse filled with environmental disaster and fascism. No wonder we turn the other way, toward a kind of golden age idea where at least things used to be better than we can hope that they ever will become. The problem is that the longing for what no longer exists often tends to turn into a longing for what never even existed. Retrotopic thinking is thus not only a protective mechanism in difficult times, but a central driving force of contemporary populist and neo-nationalist currents that are dependent on a description of the current times as dismal. As such, this concept of retrotopia is an apt description of today's society, or rather, of contemporary society's perception of itself, which probably will outlive Bauman's book. Isn't that "new normal" we're entering, or desiring, now precisely such a retrotopia rather than utopia?

Our Western late modernity, which Bauman in earlier books has referred to as "liquid modernity" (2000), has to a large degree been defined by globalization and neoliberalism. The autonomized individual lives in a fluid existence between precarious working conditions and theoretical choices, where social emancipation has become self-emancipation. It is exactly this harsh existence, which indeed has generated a longing for inclusive contexts where we can appreciate what we are and not just what we achieve, that Barbara Holub's works often take as their point of departure. In her own words:

"Normality from the perspective of artists and urban practitioners can mean something quite different from what it means for those parts of the population marked

AUSSER GEWÖHNLICH

Jonatan Habib Engqvist

„Return to normalcy" lautete der Wahlslogan des US-amerikanischen Präsidentschaftskandidaten Warren G. Harding bei den Wahlen 1920. Dieser Slogan versprach die Rückkehr zu einer Lebensweise vor dem 1. Weltkrieg, vor der „Ersten Roten Angst"[1] und vor der Spanischen Grippe. Hundert Jahre später scheint die vage, klischeehafte Vorstellung von einer Rückkehr in eine vermeintlich „goldene Vergangenheit" genau das zu sein, was von den PolitikerInnen erwartet wird. Dies gilt heute vielleicht noch mehr als vor einem Jahrhundert. Oder es gab damals einfach andere Utopien, die nicht in die Vergangenheit als Zukunft blickten. In seinem 2017 posthum erschienenen Buch untersucht Zygmunt Bauman das Konzept der „Retrotopie". Aus einer ideologiekritischen Perspektive zeigt Bauman, dass die Vergangenheit die Rolle einer wünschenswerten Zukunft übernommen hat; die Retrotopie hat die Utopie ersetzt. Die Zukunft macht uns Angst, so Bauman, deshalb schrecken wir eher vor ihr zurück, statt nach ihr zu streben. Kurz zusammengefasst lautet Baumans These, dass das moderne Narrativ des optimistischen Fortschritts nicht mehr überzeugt und statt der leuchtenden Zukunft einer aufgeklärten Menschheit oder einer existenziellen Sicherheit die Zukunft als eine Apokalypse aus Umweltkatastrophen und Faschismus dargestellt wird. Es ist also nicht weiter verwunderlich, dass wir in die entgegengesetzte Richtung blicken und uns nach der Vorstellung eines „goldenen Zeitalters" sehnen, in dem alles besser war, als es jemals zu werden verspricht. Aber die Sehnsucht nach dem, was nicht mehr ist, neigt schnell dazu, eine Sehnsucht nach dem zu werden, was niemals war. Ein retrotopisches Denken ist somit nicht einfach nur ein Schutzmechanismus in schwierigen Zeiten, sondern liefert auch wichtige Impulse für heutige populistische und neo-nationalistische Strömungen, deren Anziehungskraft davon abhängig ist, die Gegenwart als möglichst düster darzustellen. Insofern beschreibt das Konzept der Retrotopie die heutige Gesellschaft oder vielmehr ihre eigene Selbstwahrnehmung sehr genau und wird Baumans Buch sehr wahrscheinlich noch lange überdauern. Ist diese „neue Normalität", auf die wir uns zubewegen und die wir herbeisehnen, nicht eher genau jene Retrotopie, denn eine Utopie?

Unsere westliche Spätmoderne, die Bauman in früheren Publikationen als „flüchtige Moderne" (2000) bezeichnet hat, ist vor allem ein Resultat von Globalisierung und Neoliberalismus. Das autonome Individuum lebt zwischen prekären Arbeitsbedingungen und theoretischen Entscheidungsmöglichkeiten in einer flüchtigen Existenz, in der aus dem Versprechen einer gesellschaftlichen Emanzipation die Emanzipation Einzelner geworden ist. An dieser Erfahrung,

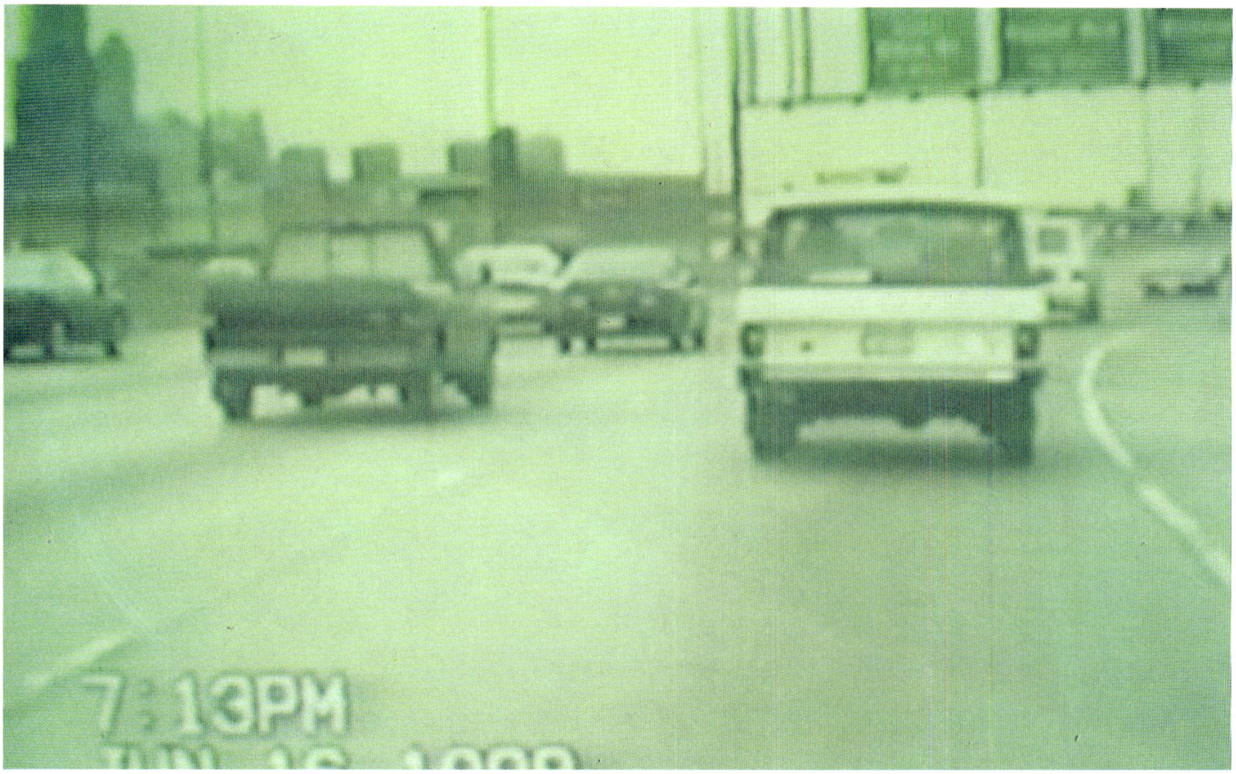

DRIVEN, Pick up-Truck-Gallery 7562LR, Chicago, 1998 (video still)

DRIVEN, Pickup-Truck-Galerie 7562LR, Chicago, 1998 (Video-Still)

by increasing fear of career disadvantages due to deviant behaviour or simply resentment or envy from their neighbours. [...] When these different normalities collide, they can be given space through special artistic settings, thus creating a productive force that breaks up the dominant form of normality. What is normal is particularly defined by the feedback of our fellow human beings. Who do we ask for an assessment? Whose opinion do we find relevant? What is perceived as normal is in motion; it changes over time according to the development of society."[2]

The question of normalcy can also be seen as a golden thread that runs through Holub's practice. Already in the nineties, Miško Šuvaković wrote of Holub's PERSONAL INVESTIGATION (1994):

"In each case, the basis was: a) the identification of the specific space and related contexts, b) the placement of indices in the spaces through the introduction and installation of textual/visual works serving to disrupt the 'normalcy' of the spaces, and c) a more specific breakdown of the disruptions and their impact on the everyday sites of linguistic games in society."[3]

Subscribing to this description, I would add that this investigative methodology endures in many of her works to this day, and through the private investigation in this text, which looks at a few selected works from the past three decades, other meanings might surface which allow for this disruption, or transubstantiation, of normalcy in Holub's practice to become even more apparent. In

die eine Sehnsucht nach gesellschaftlich inklusiven Zusammenhängen entstehen lässt, in denen wir für das anerkannt werden, was wir sind und nicht nur für das, was wir leisten, setzen Holubs Arbeiten an. In ihren eigenen Worten:

„Normalität aus der Perspektive von KünstlerInnen und urban practitioners kann etwas ganz anderes bedeuten als für die Teile der Bevölkerung, die von zunehmender Angst geprägt sind, durch abweichendes Verhalten Nachteile in der Karriere oder einfach Missgunst oder Neid durch die NachbarInnen zu erfahren. Prallen diese verschiedenen Normalitäten aufeinander, kann ihnen mittels spezieller künstlerischer Settings Raum gegeben werden, wodurch eine Produktivkraft entsteht, die die herrschende Form des Normalen aufbricht. Was normal ist, misst sich insbesondere am Feedback unserer Mitmenschen. Wen befragen wir um eine Einschätzung? Wessen Meinung empfinden wir dabei als relevant? Was als normal empfunden wird, ist in Bewegung; es verändert sich im Laufe der Zeit entsprechend der gesellschaftlichen Entwicklung."[2]

Die Auseinandersetzung mit Vorstellungen von Normalität zieht sich wie ein roter Faden durch Holubs künstlerische Praxis. Bereits in den 1990er-Jahren schrieb Miško Šuvaković über Holubs PERSONAL INVESTIGATION (1994):

„Jede einzelne Realisierung begründet sich auf: a) der Einordnung des spezifischen Ortes und des ihm entsprechenden Kontexts, b) der Indexierung des Ortes durch Einbringung und Installierung textueller/visueller Arbeiten, welche die Funktion der Erzeugung einer Störung in der

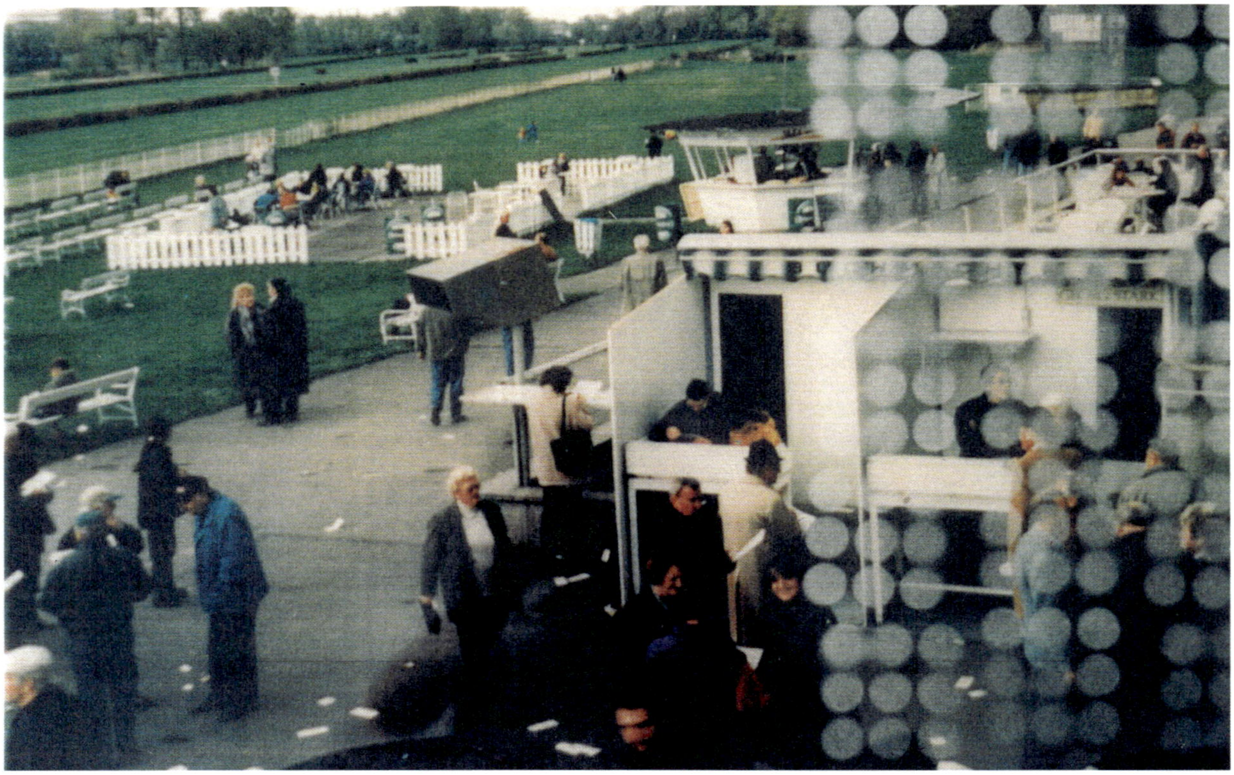

Playing, desiring, needing (Freudenau horse race track), Vienna, 1998 *Spielen, begehren, brauchen* (Galopprennbahn Freudenau), Wien, 1998

CARRIERS OF SECRETS (1996) she explored questions of surveillance, state secrets, cartels, cold war games, in a claustrophobic environment constructed of padded vinyl jigsaw puzzle pieces which were organized so that the buttons created a grid. Two years later, at the Art Fair Chicago, Holub showed the work DRIVEN (1998). The pickup truck gallery 7562LR by the artist Matthew Girson was parked inside the art fair. Suddenly a well-oiled and pumped-up male stripper got up on the pickup and started to strip. What's normal here? Bored people flying around the world to look at stuff, for investment? Or a guy doing his thing to pay the rent? Or the art crowd standing around having opinions about it? I guess it depends on your perspective... Through a tape recorder during the striptease, we hear Holub's voice: "All this art that surrounds you but doesn't mean you personally... Maybe you always wanted something more. From life. From yourself... You don't have to be uncomfortable..." This is clearly not only about a juxtaposition, dialectics, or irony. As Christa Steinle wrote before this performance, in 1996:

"Barbara Holub's work is not about a critique of modernity from the subject's stance, as in symbolism and surrealism. However, secret and desire, hidden wishes, all these dynamic mechanisms of libido in the constitution of the subject all go to form a subversive element in her work... she acts out the seductive power emanating from hidden and repressed things. Thus, her social critique also bears the traits of being playful and humorous. Holub's work is primarily about the social sphere, the body of society, the public field upon which

'Normalität' des Ortes haben, und c) der näheren Spezifizierung der entstandenen Störungen und deren Folgen im alltäglichen Ort der gesellschaftlichen Sprachspiele."[3]

Somit ist dieser Text auch eine „private investigation" zu einigen ausgewählten Arbeiten der Künstlerin der letzten drei Jahrzehnte, in der auch weitere Aspekte in Holubs Arbeiten sichtbar werden, die ihre Auseinandersetzung mit Brüchen und Wandlungen von Normalität noch deutlicher hervortreten lassen. In GEHEIMNISTRÄGER (1996) setzte sich Holub mit Fragen zu Überwachung, Staatsgeheimnissen, Kartellen und Fantasien des Kalten Kriegs auseinander. Die klaustrophobisch anmutende Installation bestand aus gepolsterten Puzzlestücken, die so an der Wand angebracht waren, dass die Polsterknöpfe ein Raster bildeten. Auf der internationalen Kunstmesse Art Chicago zeigte Holub zwei Jahre später die Arbeit DRIVEN (1998). Die mobile Pickup-Truck-Galerie 7562LR des Künstlers Matthew Girson parkte in der Messehalle, als unerwartet ein muskulöser, männlicher Stripper auf der Ladefläche zu strippen begann. Was ist hier normal? Gelangweilte Menschen, die um die Welt fliegen, um sich Kunst als potenzielles Investment anzuschauen? Oder jemand, der/die tut, was er/sie kann, um seine/ihre Miete zu bezahlen? Oder das herumstehende Kunstpublikum, das seine Meinung dazu abgibt? Das hängt wohl von der eigenen Perspektive ab ... Während der Show hören wir Holubs Stimme aus einem Kassettenrecorder: „Diese ganze Kunst, die dich umgibt, dich aber nicht persönlich anspricht ... Vielleicht wolltest du schon immer mehr. Vom Leben. Von dir selbst ... Das

individuals stake their contractual claims, their claims to autonomy, self-government, self-realization etc. But she also shows us that these claims must pay a price imposed upon them by the fusion of public and private spheres."[4]

Holub's projects are, in other words, at once both simple and complicated, generic and specific, in terms of both subject matter and execution. For instance, THE SYSTEM: PRÊT-À-PORTER (2006) looks at second-hand exchange, ranging from a yard sale to clothing donated to charity, along with the systems that render large profits while outsourcing labor and allegedly "creating jobs." However, it is neither the nature of global enterprise nor the clothes themselves that are her primary interest, rather, she says: "[...] the material is communication. The question of fashion, that is to say the added value that elevates an item of clothing above a merely functional object, is for me only the communicator that allows entry into the system from a concrete side or allows one to question this system. This process of "refinement," and with it the creation of an added value, is naturally an aspect that also exists in the case of all artistic works."[5]

In her research, Holub found how various "charity" companies and organizations like Humana operate just like any corporate business, closing their premises in Austria and outsourcing the labor of sorting to, for instance, Bulgaria and Turkey. Focusing on the question of labor, Holub traced routes of transport and categories of sorting, which later was re-addressed as a fashion show/photo shoot within the framework of her exhibitions at Künstlerhaus Wien and Plymouth Arts Centre. At the Künstlerhaus in Vienna another layer was added through a video loop of a yard sale in Los Angeles. The film focuses on people who, during the weekend, search the front yard for second-hand clothes as observed from the other side of the street, from the Mackey Apartments.[6] Already in other projects such as SET! (2000) at Hohenlohe & Kalb Gallery in Vienna or BETWEEN ROLES (2002) at Steirischer Herbst, Graz, Holub looked at communication "across the (garden) fence" in residential areas.

Holub's filmic short cuts with schematic silhouettes and blackouts also evoke bodies that pose as if they were somewhere else, perhaps staging a music video, where gestures form a significant and expressive element. At a certain moment a boy pulls out his toy-pistol and starts shooting. Although the exchange and circulation of (repurposed) goods and subsequent profit form the basis of communication in THE SYSTEM: PRÊT-À-PORTER, Holub furthermore argues that economic profit is not the only topic at hand by looking at small gestures, at the general through the specific, in what might provide new optics on the predicaments of our liquid modernity. It is not as simple as creating an illusion of "empowerment" although "the material is communication."

muss dir nicht unangenehm sein ..." Es geht hier ganz offensichtlich nicht nur um eine Gegenüberstellung, um Dialektik oder Ironie. So schreibt Christa Steinle 1996, vor dieser Performance:

„In der Arbeit von Barbara Holub geht es nicht um eine Kritik an der Moderne vom Standpunkt des Subjekts, wie im Symbolismus und Surrealismus. Geheimnis und Begehren, verborgene Wünsche, all diese dynamischen Mechanismen der Libido bei der Konstitution des Subjekts bilden jedoch auch in ihrer Arbeit ein subversives Element. Die Verführungskraft, die von verbotenen und verdrängten Dingen ausgeht, spielt sie lustvoll aus. Ihre soziale Kritik trägt also auch Züge des Spielerischen und Humorvollen. Bei Holub geht es primär um den sozialen Raum, um den Gesellschaftskörper, um jenes Feld der Öffentlichkeit, auf dem die Individuen vertraglich ihre claims abstecken, ihre Ansprüche auf Autonomie, Selbstverwaltung, Selbstverwirklichung usw. Sie zeigt uns aber, dass diese Ansprüche einen Preis zahlen müssen, der ihnen von der Durchdringung öffentlicher und privater Sphären auferlegt wird."[4]

Mit anderen Worten, Holubs Projekte sind zugleich einfach und kompliziert, konkret und allgemein, sowohl in ihrer Thematik als auch in ihrer Umsetzung. In THE SYSTEM: PRÊT-À-PORTER (2006) etwa geht es um den Handel mit Secondhandkleidung, vom Flohmarkt bis zur Kleiderspende, und um ein System, das enorme Gewinne generiert und vermeintlich „Jobs schafft", während es eigentlich vor allem Arbeit auslagert. Dabei legt Holub den Fokus jedoch weder ausschließlich auf die Strukturen eines globalen Handels noch auf die Kleidungsstücke selbst, sondern, wie sie sagt:

„[...] das Material [ist] die Kommunikation. Die Frage nach der Mode, also nach dem Mehrwert, der ein Kleidungsstück über den Gebrauchsgegenstand hinaushebt, ist für mich also nur der Kommunikator, um von einer konkreten Seite in das System einzusteigen oder dieses zu hinterfragen. Dieser ‚Veredelungsprozess' – und dadurch das Schaffen eines Mehrwerts – ist natürlich ein Aspekt, der auch bei allen künstlerischen Arbeiten existiert."[5]

Bei ihren Recherchen fand Holub heraus, dass viele „wohltätige" Organisationen und Unternehmen genauso operieren wie jedes andere profitorientierte Unternehmen. Humana schloss beispielsweise seine Geschäftsstellen in Österreich und lagerte die Sortierarbeit nach Bulgarien und in die Türkei aus. Mit dem Schwerpunkt auf „Arbeit" untersuchte Holub Transportwege und Sortierungskategorien, die in ihren Ausstellungen im Künstlerhaus Wien und im Plymouth Arts Centre als Modeschau/Fotoshooting wieder aufgegriffen wurden. Im Künstlerhaus Wien fügte das Video eines Gartenflohmarkts in Los Angeles dem noch eine weitere Ebene hinzu. Von den Mackey Apartments[6] aus werden in dem Video Menschen dabei beobachtet, wie sie am Wochenende im Vorgarten auf der gegenüberliegenden Straßenseite nach Second-

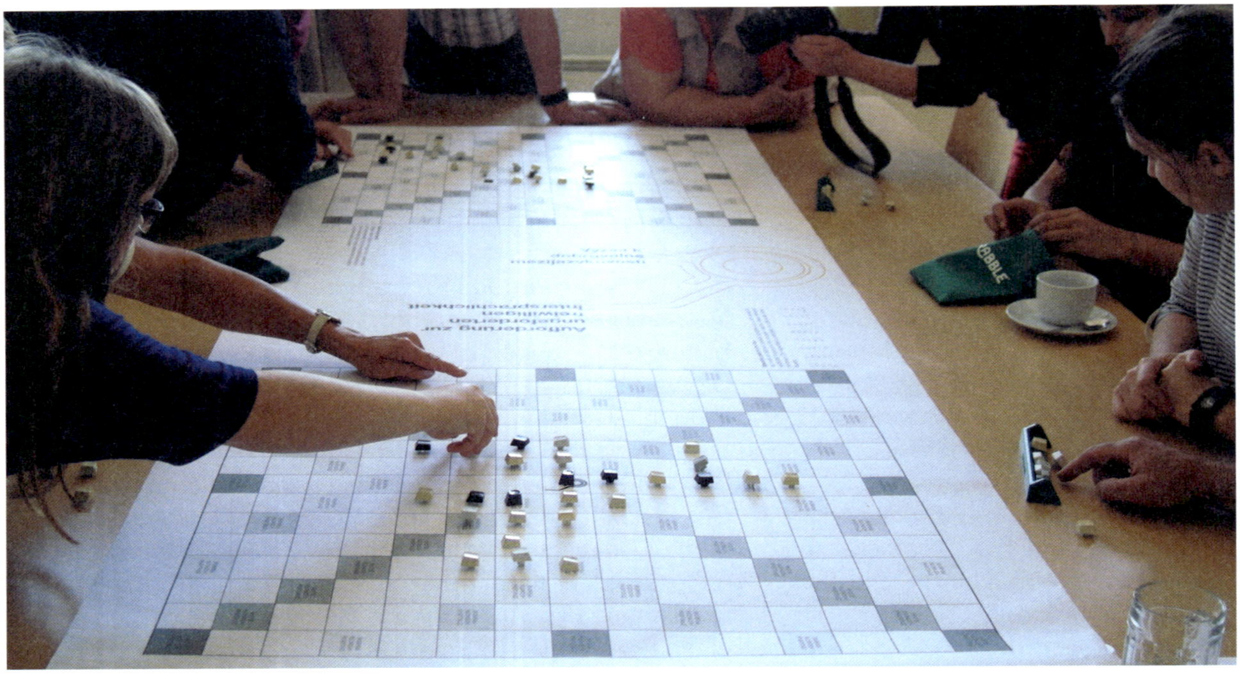

UNREQUESTED, VOLUNTARY INTERLINGUISTICALITY
(transparadiso), Pottenhofen, 2016
For the design of the new village square, transparadiso developed a bilingual (German-Czech) Scrabble game, whose collectively devised, idiosyncratic word creations shaped the seating-table sculpture.

UNAUFGEFORDERTE FREIWILLIGE INTERSPRACHLICHKEIT
(transparadiso), Pottenhofen, 2016
Für die neue Platzgestaltung des Dorfes entwickelte transparadiso ein zweisprachiges (deutsch-tschechisches) Scrabble-Spiel, dessen kollektiv erarbeitete, eigenwillige Wortschöpfungen die Sitz-Tisch-Skulptur prägten.

Through the years, Holub has also worked with several corporate companies. She looks at the many ways that office life can be a microcosm of society at large. Offices are quite mundane things, full of routines, repetition, relationships, and invisible rules. Embedded in this liquid modernity, it is an environment that constitutes the condition for a large portion of the awake time for many individuals. In HANDLED CONFIDENTIALLY (1997–1999), for instance, she invited employees of the office furniture company Bene to stage a series of images envisioning situations that might happen "under the table."

Collages of these images were later installed on the façade of their office building. I wouldn't go so far as to say that she infiltrates the organization, but she does manage to expose internal power structures, sexism, fantasies, and projections within the daily doings in the office. Perhaps revealing what is considered to be okay, to be normal, in the daily doings of that site. Using the office workers as models for a series of slightly overexposed "paparazzi" photographs of hands and thighs under a table, she not only makes them complicit in her actions, but also convinces them to share this reality with passersby in the street. On the second floor, the images were mounted on the façade as light boxes visible from afar, replacing the gray panels that had previously concealed employees' legs, bags and wastebaskets under the tables.

In another corporate office investigation, DEVOTION TO UNINTENTIONALITY (1999), Holub was invited to the

handkleidung suchen. Zuvor hatte sich Holub schon in anderen Projekten mit der Kommunikation „über den Gartenzaun" in Wohngegenden beschäftigt, so etwa in SET! (GALERIE HOHENLOHE & KALB, WIEN, 2000), oder auch in ZWISCHENROLLEN, Steirischer Herbst, Graz (2002).

In Holubs Video-Clip erinnern die expressiven Gesten der zwischen Schwarzblenden schemenhaft erscheinenden Silhouetten an Körper, die sich woanders zu befinden scheinen, vielleicht beim Dreh eines Musikvideos. Auf einmal holt ein Junge eine Spielzeugpistole hervor und beginnt zu schießen. Auch wenn in THE SYSTEM: PRÊT-À-PORTER, der Handel und Transport von (gebrauchten) Waren und der daraus resultierende Profit die Grundlage von Kommunikation darstellten, interessiert sich Holub nicht nur für die ökonomischen Zusammenhänge. Indem sie ihre Aufmerksamkeit auch auf die kleinen Gesten richtet und über das Spezifische auf das Allgemeine blickt, eröffnen sich neue Perspektiven auf das Dilemma unserer „flüchtigen Moderne". Selbst wenn „das Material die Kommunikation ist", ist es nicht so einfach, eine Illusion von „Empowerment" zu generieren.

Im Laufe der Jahre hat Holub auch mit verschiedenen Unternehmen zusammengearbeitet. Dabei interessierte sie vor allem, wie der Büroalltag auf unterschiedliche Art und Weise als Mikrokosmos der Gesellschaft verstanden werden kann. Büros sind ganz alltägliche Orte, geprägt von Routine, Wiederholungen, Beziehungen und unsichtbaren Regeln. Als Teil der „flüchtigen Moderne" bilden

headquarters of Porsche, Porschehof, in Salzburg where she asked white-collar employees of Porsche to play with Carrera racetracks in the lobby of their offices, outside of office hours and without salary. A birds-eye view photograph of the collective endeavor served as the basis for a large installation (2.5 × 8 meters) for the same area of the building. At the same time, she interviewed employees of Porschehof as well as friends and colleagues from the art context about their thoughts of behaving like a "child" or an "adult." The recorded interviews then acted as a voice-over to black-and-white images of children interacting with each other. Together with the video of the adults playing with the Carrera racing tracks, they were shown as a double video projection at the Secession in Vienna.

Now, the relationship between art and play has been widely discussed and some people think that all artistic production needs it, whereas others go further and claim that it is the basis for creativity. Although it may sound like a contradiction, taking play seriously could mean that we can use it to transform our actions with exciting, uncertain outcomes. Most artists know this, of course, and to play seriously is a method of letting go of control within a controlled system and—like most improvisation—it is something that requires rules and regulations. But what is most striking with Holub's games is that they are by no means extravagant. On the contrary, this work is, in all its playfulness, quite mundane. Perhaps even sober. And I think this is important. Throughout her works, Holub seems to stress the everyday, the vernacular, the banal, to say something profound. Or, perhaps, to say that this is where we can find some kind of profundity. Investigations of, if you will, the norms that govern understandings of normalcy. Norms to which normalcies are relative, relational, or relevant.

Since 1999, Holub has also been working with the architect and urbanist Paul Rajakovics in various contexts. Under the name "transparadiso," they move between theories and practices of architecture, art, urban design, urbanism, and urban-artistic intervention.[7] A couple of years ago I witnessed one of their common processes in Valletta, Malta: For TIMES OF DILEMMA (2018)[8] two groups of Għana singers (known as *għannejja*) communicated with each other via two large megaphones on either side of the sea between the city of Valletta and Manoel Island, between the historic site of St. Michael's Counterguard and the only public access to the sea on the largely privatized Manoel Island, to be transformed into a new urban development project.[9] Historically, these two locations prompt the memory of a time when leprosy patients were quarantined on the island and a priest would hold his prayers for the hospital from across the channel. These singing performances had been preceded by workshops that combined an open call for participation, invited Maltese authors, *għannejja* singers, activists and experts from various backgrounds, to discuss conflicting and sometimes contradictory inter-

sie das Umfeld, das den größten Teil der wachen Zeit sehr vieler Menschen ausmacht. In VERTRAULICH BEHANDELT (1997–1999) etwa bat Holub MitarbeiterInnen des Büromöbelherstellers Bene, sich in einer Serie von inszenierten Bildern vorzustellen, was „unter dem Tisch" passieren könnte. Die daraus entstandenen Collagen wurden später an die Fassade des Bürogebäudes montiert. Zwar würde ich nicht so weit gehen und behaupten, dass Holub das Unternehmen unterwanderte; es gelang ihr aber, interne Machtstrukturen, Sexismus, Fantasien und Projektionen des Büroalltags offenzulegen und damit auch ein Stück weit zu zeigen, was als normal und zulässig betrachtet wird. Indem die Angestellten zu ProtagonistInnen einer Serie leicht überbelichteter „Paparazzi"-Fotografien wurden, auf denen zu sehen ist, wie sich Hände und Beine unter dem Tisch berühren, machte Holub die Angestellten nicht nur zu KomplizInnen ihres Vorhabens, sondern brachte sie auch dazu, ihre Realität mit den PassantInnen auf der Straße zu teilen. Im ersten Stock wurden die Bilder als Leuchtkästen von Weitem sichtbar an die Fassade montiert und ersetzten die grauen Paneele, die zuvor Beine, Taschen und Papierkörbe unter den Tischen der Angestellten verdeckt hatten.

In HINGABE AN DIE ABSICHTSLOSIGKEIT (1999) setzte sich Holub mit dem Büroalltag des Porschehofs, der Firmenzentrale von Porsche in Salzburg, auseinander. Holub lud die Angestellten ein, nach der Arbeit in der Eingangshalle mit Carrera-Rennbahnen zu spielen. Die Fotos von den gemeinsamen Aktivitäten aus der Vogelperspektive wurden zum Ausgangspunkt für eine großformatige Installation (2,5 × 8 m), die danach am selben Ort gezeigt wurde. Zusätzlich fragte Holub sowohl Angestellte von Porsche als auch FreundInnen und KollegInnen aus dem Kunstkontext, was es für sie bedeute, sich wie „Kinder" oder wie „Erwachsene" zu verhalten. Die aufgezeichneten Interviews gaben das Voiceover für die Schwarz-Weiß-Videoaufnahmen, auf denen Kinder im Spiel miteinander interagieren. Zusammen mit dem Video, in dem die Erwachsenen mit den Carrera-Rennbahnen spielen, wurden sie als Doppel-Videoprojektion in der Secession in Wien gezeigt.

Über das Verhältnis von Kunst und Spiel ist schon viel diskutiert worden, wobei manche der Meinung sind, das Spiel bilde die Voraussetzung für jede künstlerische Produktion, während andere noch darüber hinausgehen und behaupten, das Spiel sei die Grundlage jeglicher Form von Kreativität. Das Spiel ernst zu nehmen, so widersprüchlich dies zunächst auch klingt, kann dazu führen, dass wir unser Handeln auf überraschende und unvorhersehbare Weise ändern. Die meisten KünstlerInnen setzen das als selbstverständlich voraus; das ernsthafte Spiel wird zur Methode, um innerhalb eines geregelten Systems die Kontrolle zu verlieren. Wie bei jeder Form von Improvisation, braucht es auch hier Vorschriften und Regeln. Aber was bei Holubs Spielen am meisten überrascht, ist, dass sie alles andere als außergewöhnlich sind. Trotz ihrer

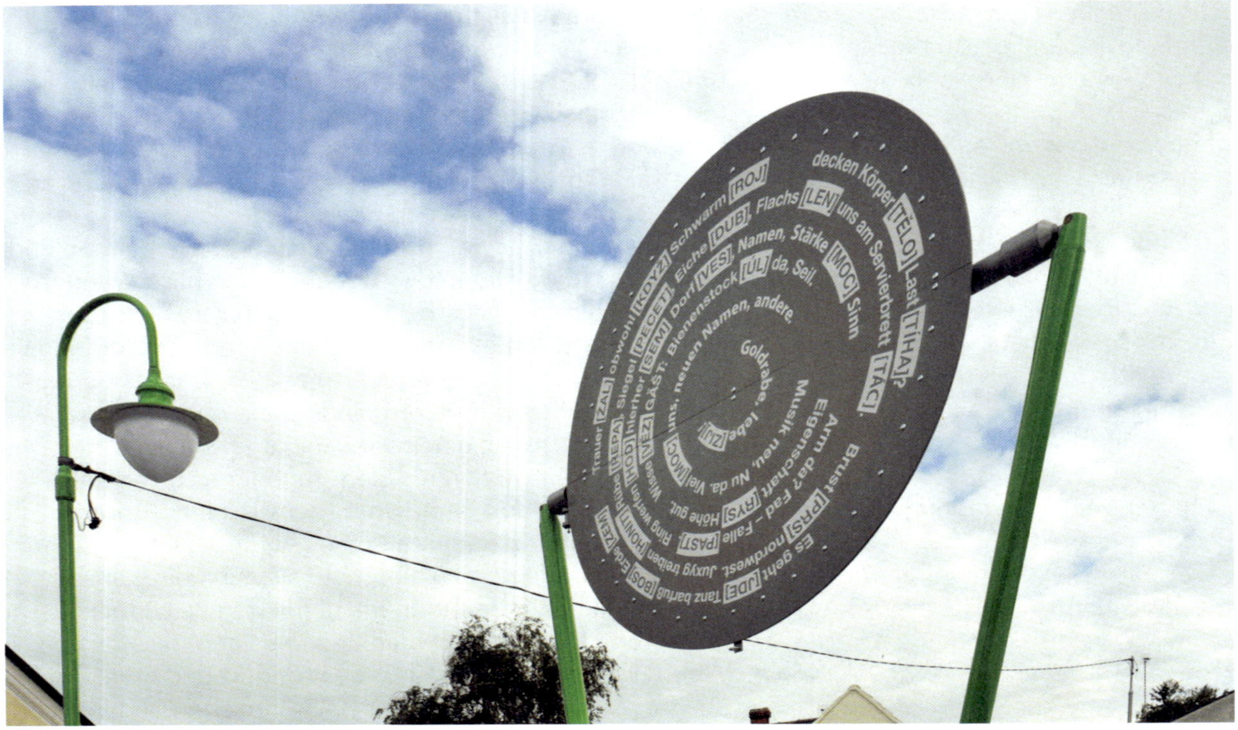

UNREQUESTED, VOLUNTARY INTERLINGUISTICALITY
(transparadiso), Pottenhofen, 2016
The word collection of the bilingual Scrabble game formed the basis for the central element of the square sculpture.

UNAUFGEFORDERTE FREIWILLIGE INTERSPRACHLICHKEIT
(transparadiso), Pottenhofen, 2016
Die Wortsammlungen des zweisprachigen Scrabble-Spiels bildeten die Grundlage für das wesentliche Element der Platzskulptur.

ests between economic wealth and communal values, based on the following simple topics: what I miss, what I am afraid of losing, what I find problematic, what I treasure, WHAT I AM PROUD OF, what I want to change. Among other things, this process resulted in several texts by Maltese authors. As such, the *għannejja* performed scripted texts about their concerns with urban development and other pressing social matters in Maltese society, while contravening borders between so-called "high" and "folk" culture—a method that Holub developed in her articulation of *"silent activism"* as a method of creating platforms for art to channel social change while keeping artistic independence and integrity.[10]

In choosing to pose general questions to specific situations, Holub places herself between the general questions' desire for general answers and the specific's means of providing concrete examples. And the answers to these general questions will always be specific, since they are posed to and from a specific context, within a defined framework. In all her works, being situated is thus always present, since the answer to the general questions connect to other questions about which roles a person can take in relation to the public realm or the exhibition space, the creation of his or her own subjectivity, day-to-day politics and so on. Holub's trick seems to be to prepare situations and spaces open enough to support and take this into account—open yet regulated—to allow site-sensitivity, coherent narratives, coherences, and contradictions (dialog rather than dialectics).

spielerischen Aspekte sind sie eher alltäglich, vielleicht sogar banal. Für mich ist das ein zentraler Aspekt. In ihren Arbeiten scheint Holub das Alltägliche, das Vernakulare, das Banale in den Vordergrund zu stellen, um etwas Grundlegendes auszudrücken; vielleicht sogar um zu behaupten, dass gerade dort Grundlegendes zu finden sein könnte. Holub untersucht damit die Normen, die unser Verständnis von Normalität bestimmen. Diese Normen und unsere Normalität stehen in einem relativen, relationalen und relevanten Verhältnis zueinander.

Seit 1999 arbeitet Holub auch mit dem Architekten und Urbanisten Paul Rajakovics in verschiedenen Kontexten zusammen. Unter dem Namen transparadiso bewegen sie sich zwischen Theorie und Praxis, zwischen Architektur, Kunst, Stadtplanung sowie Urbanismus und künstlerischen Interventionen im öffentlichen Raum.[7] Vor einigen Jahren hatte ich die Gelegenheit, eine ihrer gemeinsamen Arbeiten in Valletta auf Malta zu sehen. Für TIMES OF DILEMMA (2018)[8] standen sich zwei Gruppen von Għana-SängerInnen gegenüber, eine Gruppe in Valletta, die andere auf der Insel Manoel. Sie kommunizierten mit Hilfe zweier großer Megafone von der historischen Befestigungsanlage St. Michael's Counterguard (Valletta) zu dem in Zukunft einzigen noch öffentlichen Zugang zum Meer auf der ansonsten weitgehend privatisierten Insel Manoel.[9] Beide Orte rufen eine Zeit in Erinnerung, als Leprakranke auf der Insel Manoel unter Quarantäne gestellt wurden und ein Pfarrer von Valletta aus für die Menschen im Lazarett auf der Insel

In the epilogue to *Retrotopia*, Bauman points to positive aspects of late modernity and the globalization of cosmopolitanism, namely the possibility of dialog. At the same time, I would also add that it is crucial to understand that the growing interest in history, and its specific aspects, is not something exclusively negative. Take, for instance, all the new stories that various ethnic and sexual minorities have developed in the context of their liberation projects in recent years. Indeed, the microhistories provided in many of Holub's works also have the capacity to operate as a form of resistance to both grand narratives and mechanisms of hypernormalization.[11] Here I am borrowing the term "hypernormal" from Adam Curtis, who in turn borrowed it from a person trying to describe life during the collapse of the Soviet Union, who, according to Curtis, says something like: "There were not really any protests, but everyone somehow sensed that everything wasn't quite right."[12] So, basically, they knew that those in control had no control—the economy was corrupt and their leaders were pretending to be in control. "Everyone knew it, the leaders knew that everyone knew, but no one did anything because there was nothing else. It was normal. Hypernormal."[13] Somehow everything was a bit odd, fake, but since there was no other picture of the world within the system, this one was accepted as normal and people simply went on with their lives. Time, geographies, and policies obviously have changed since then, yet many people around the world, in dissimilar situations, do share a sense that those in charge know that they're not in charge, and that they also know that we know this, and that everything seems to be all over the place. Because many people also sense a great deal of corruption of various kinds, it is not strange that there is such a plethora of conspiracy theories trying to make sense in all this chaos. Driven by retrotopian fantasies, they sometimes surface, gain force, and even enter governmental buildings... It is in any event clear that those claiming to be in control of the global economy are not in fact in control of the global economy. It is also clear that everyone knows that everyone knows this. But as everyone is so embedded, invested or incapsulated by this system, and as there are few alternative visions of how things could be different, we accept it as, well... normal.

Holub's supplement is her understanding of the commonplace as something far from mediocre. And in a climate of extremely aggressive and polarized rhetoric—where hospitality is conditioned by geopolitics, and phenomena like platform labor skew the idea of decent working conditions—the precariousness of mundane normality is exposed as something we must safeguard. Not as the hypernormal, but as something comprehensively human stressing the value of a condition and sense of security in the normalcy in which many of us are fortunate enough to spend a lot of our time, be it in an office, rummaging second-hand clothes, or interacting with each other while discussing everyday matters. If anything

betete. Den Gesangsperformances gingen Workshops voraus, zu denen maltesische SchriftstellerInnen, Għana-SängerInnen (għannejja), AktivistInnen und ExpertInnen unterschiedlicher Disziplinen sowie die Öffentlichkeit zur Teilnahme eingeladen wurden, um die unterschiedlichen Interessen und daraus resultierenden Konflikte zwischen wirtschaftlichem Wohlstand und gemeinschaftlichen Werten zu diskutieren. Dabei dienten folgende alltägliche Themen als Ausgangspunkt: „Was mir fehlt, was ich fürchte zu verlieren, was ich problematisch finde, was ich schätze, worauf ich stolz bin, was ich verändern möchte." Aus den Beiträgen verfassten die AutorInnen in der Versform von Għana dialogische Texte über Probleme der Stadtentwicklung und andere soziale Thematiken der maltesischen Gesellschaft. Die għannejja sangen diese geskripteten Texte und überschritten somit die Grenzen zwischen sogenannter „Hoch-" bzw. „Volkskultur" – ein Ansatz, den Holub als „stillen Aktivismus" bezeichnet und zu einer Methode weiterentwickelt hat, mit der Kunst gesellschaftliche Veränderungen anstoßen und zugleich ihre künstlerische Unabhängigkeit und Integrität behaupten kann.[10]

Indem sich Holub über allgemeine Fragen konkreten Situationen nähert, positioniert sie sich zwischen dem Verlangen allgemeiner Fragen nach allgemeinen Antworten und der Möglichkeit des Spezifischen, konkrete Beispiele zu liefern. Doch die Antworten auf diese allgemeinen Fragen sind immer zugleich auch spezifisch, weil sie innerhalb eines definierten Bezugssystems sowohl einen spezifischen Kontext adressieren als auch aus einem spezifischen Kontext heraus formuliert werden. In all ihren Arbeiten schwingt so immer auch die Frage nach der Situierung mit. Antworten auf allgemeine Fragen werden hier mit weiteren Fragen verknüpft, wie etwa nach der Rolle, die eine Person im Verhältnis zum öffentlichen Raum oder zum Ausstellungsraum einnehmen kann, oder nach der Entstehung der eigenen Subjektivität, oder der Bedeutung von alltäglichem politischen Geschehen. Holubs Strategie besteht darin, Situationen und Räume herzustellen, die offen genug sind, um diesen Austausch zu ermöglichen, und die zugleich ausreichend definiert sind, um sowohl eine Sensibilität für den Ort als auch kohärente Narrative, Zusammenhänge, aber auch Widersprüche (im Dialog statt als Dialektik) zuzulassen.

Im Nachwort zu *Retrotopia* verweist Bauman auf die positiven Aspekte der Spätmoderne und der Globalisierung des Kosmopolitismus, vor allem auf deren Fähigkeit zum Dialog. Zugleich möchte ich hinzufügen, wie wichtig es ist, sich klarzumachen, dass das zunehmende Interesse an Geschichte und an ihren spezifischen Erscheinungsformen nichts ausschließlich Negatives ist. Als Beispiel dafür können die neuen Narrative gesehen werden, die unterschiedliche ethnische und sexuelle Minderheiten in den letzten Jahren im Rahmen ihrer emanzipatorischen Bewegungen entwickelt haben. Auch die im Zentrum vieler von Holubs Arbeiten stehenden Mikrogeschichten haben das Potenzial, widerständig gegenüber den großen

should be scrutinized and critically investigated as a means of bringing us back to a being-here, and to what can be done, it is precisely this modality.

Holub's works have, over the past decades, operated on the level of community and started to gain a personality, or character, of their own. In turn, this character often generates an amplitude of what it is to be a person—suggesting a vision of the future through the small, rather than grand, gestures or nostalgic notions of a normality passed (and which we never knew). A vision of the future made possible in the existing. Not returning-to but enduring, obfuscating and altering the concept of normalcy. A silent activism. A vision that might even manage to resist the ideals of stupidity and futility which signify the time we live in.

Erzählungen und den Mechanismen der „Hypernormalisierung"[11] zu agieren. Den Begriff „hypernormal" übernehme ich aus Adam Curtis Dokumentarfilm *HyperNormalisation*, der den Begriff wiederum von einer Person übernommen hat, die das Leben während des Zusammenbruchs der Sowjetunion, laut Curtis, so zu beschreiben versuchte: „Es gab eigentlich keine Proteste, aber jeder konnte irgendwie spüren, dass etwas nicht stimmte."[12] Im Grunde wusste jedeR, dass diejenigen, die an der Macht waren, die Kontrolle verloren hatten, dass die Wirtschaft korrupt war und dass die Regierenden nur so taten, als hätten sie alles unter Kontrolle. „Alle wussten es, die Regierenden wussten, dass alle es wussten, aber niemand unternahm etwas, weil es nichts anderes gab. Alles war normal. Hypernormal."[13] Alles schien irgendwie seltsam, fast unwirklich, aber da innerhalb des Systems keine andere Vorstellung von der Welt existierte, wurde die bestehende als normal akzeptiert und die Menschen gingen ihrem Leben einfach weiter nach. Seitdem haben sich die Zeiten, Räume und politischen Strategien offensichtlich geändert, doch viele Menschen auf der ganzen Welt und aus ganz unterschiedlichen Kontexten haben den Eindruck, dass diejenigen, die das Sagen haben, wissen, dass sie nichts zu sagen haben, und auch wissen, dass wir das wissen, und dass alles im Chaos zu versinken droht. In Anbetracht dessen, dass sehr viele Menschen die allgegenwärtige Korruption in ihren unterschiedlichsten Formen wahrnehmen, ist die weite Verbreitung von Verschwörungstheorien, die in diesem Chaos nach Sinn und Bedeutung suchen, nicht weiter verwunderlich. Von „retrotopischen" Fantasien angetrieben, kommen diese Theorien zum Vorschein, gewinnen an Einfluss und dringen bis in Regierungsgebäude ... Auf jeden Fall ist allen klar, dass diejenigen, die behaupten, die globale Wirtschaft zu kontrollieren, in der Tat weit davon entfernt sind. Klar ist auch, dass alle wissen, dass es alle wissen. Aber da alle Teil des Systems sind, darin verstrickt und abgeschottet, und es kaum alternative Vorstellungen dazu gibt, akzeptiert man diese Situation als, nun ja ... normal.

Für Holub ist das Alltägliche jedoch alles andere als normal. In einem gesellschaftlichen Klima, das von einer äußerst aggressiven und polarisierenden Rhetorik geprägt ist, in dem Gastfreundschaft eine Frage der Geopolitik ist und Phänomene wie das Arbeiten über digitale Plattformen die Vorstellung von menschenwürdigen Arbeitsbedingungen in ihr Gegenteil verdrehen, wird die Prekarität der alltäglichen Normalität als etwas dargestellt, das wir verteidigen müssen. Nicht als etwas „Hypernormales", sondern als etwas zutiefst Menschliches. Als ein Gefühl der Sicherheit, in dem sich viele von uns glücklich schätzen, einen Großteil ihrer Zeit zu verbringen, sei es im Büro, beim Durchstöbern von Secondhandkleidung oder im alltäglichen Umgang miteinander. Um uns jedoch ins Hier-und-Jetzt zurückzuholen und um herauszufinden, was sich ändern muss, sollte der gerade beschriebene Zustand selbst hinterfragt und kritisch untersucht werden.

1 The "First Red Scare" was a period during the early 20th-century history of the United States marked by a widespread fear of far-left extremism, including but not limited to Bolshevism and anarchism, due to real and imagined events. Real events included the Russian 1917 October Revolution and anarchist bombings. At its height in 1919–20, concerns over the effects of radical political agitation in society and the alleged spread of communism and anarchism in the labor movement fueled the "red scare."

2 "Normal–Direct Urbanism × 4", Culture Year Graz 2020, please see: www.transparadiso.com/en/projects/normal-direct-urbanism-x-4, (accessed March 29, 2022).

3 Miško Šuvaković, "The Asymmetrical Other: Barbara Holub's Investigations," in: PERSONAL INVESTIGATION, Barbara Holub, (Casablanca Gallery, Vienna 1994), p. 25.

4 "Art and Control, A site-specific installation by Barbara Holub," from the exhibition catalog accompanying Personal Investigation, Barbara Holub, (Graz: Neue Galerie Studio, 1996).

5 "Prêt-à-porter on the conveyor belt," a conversation with Manuela Hötzl, www.barbaraholub.com/uploads/2/9/1/1/29117589/interview_hoetzl_holub_the_system.pdf, (accessed March 29, 2022).

6 As artists-in-residence of the MAK Schindler Grant 2004, Barbara Holub and Paul Rajakovics lived in the Mackey Apartments.

7 For more about transparadiso, see www.transparadiso.com, (accessed March 28, 2022).

8 Realized for "The Island is What the Sea Surrounds", European Capital of Culture Valletta 2018.

9 Għana is a dialogical, improvised Maltese folk singing tradition. *Għana* has two literal meanings. The first is richness, wealth, and prosperity; the second is associated with singing, verse, rhyme and even *kantaliena*, a type of singing with a slow rhythm. A singer in this field is locally called *għannej* (literally "the singer").

10 See for instance: www.publics.fi/calendar/silent-activism-for-an-active-role-of-art-in-society-and-in-thepublic-realm, or Holub's talk at The Bartlett/International Lecture Series, Feb. 2, 2022: vimeo.com/677202901, (accessed March 29, 2022).

11 The Adam Curtis documentary *HyperNormalisation* (2016) argues that an army of technocrats, complacent radicals and Internet entrepreneurs create an unreal world: one whose familiar and often comforting details blind us to its inauthenticity. The full documentary can be found here: www.youtube.com/watch?v=thLgkQBFTPw, (accessed March 29, 2022).

12 "Russell Brand & Adam Curtis—Do We Really Want Change?" Under The Skin no. 03, www.youtube.com/watch?v=MIHC4NNScEI&t=80s, (accessed March 29, 2022).

13 Ibid.

Holubs Arbeiten haben in den letzten Jahrzehnten Themen von Gemeinschaft fokussiert und dabei eine eigene Persönlichkeit, einen eigenen Charakter entwickelt. Im Gegenzug lassen uns ihre Arbeiten in eine Zukunft blicken, die eher von kleinen als von großen Gesten beeinflusst werden kann. So entsteht die Vision einer Zukunft, die aus dem gegenwärtigen Zustand heraus denkbar wird, und die sich nicht auf ein Konzept von nostalgischen Vorstellungen einer vergangenen Normalität (die wir niemals gekannt haben) zurückbesinnt, sondern sich mit der bestehenden Normalität auseinandersetzt, sie dekonstruiert und verändert. Ein stiller Aktivismus. Eine Vision, die womöglich den Idealen von Dummheit und Sinnlosigkeit, die unsere Zeit prägen, zu widerstehen vermag.

1 Die „Erste Rote Angst" (engl. „First Red Scare") bezeichnet eine historische Periode in den USA Anfang des 20. Jahrhunderts, in der die Angst vor linkem Extremismus weit verbreitet war, nicht nur vor Bolschewismus und Anarchismus, sondern auch vor imaginierten sowie realen Ereignissen wie etwa der russischen Oktoberrevolution 1917 und anarchistischen Bombenanschlägen. Die Sorge vor dem gesellschaftlichen Einfluss radikaler politischer Agitation und die vermeintliche Verbreitung kommunistischer und anarchistischer Ideen in der Arbeiterbewegung fachte diese Angst vor allem in den Jahren 1919–1920 weiter an.

2 transparadiso (Barbara Holub/Paul Rajakovics), „Die Normalität des Unspektakulären an den Rändern der Stadt", in: NORMAL × 4, Direkter Urbanismus, Graz 2020, S. 8. http://www.transparadiso.com/media/pages/projects/normal-direkter-urbanismus-x-4/normal-katalog-1/800449aa99-1612555266/normal_catalog_w_01.pdf (Zugriff: 11.5.2022).

3 Der Titel PERSONAL INVESTIGATION verweist auf die Arbeit der Privatdetektivin/des Privatdetektivs, die als *private investigation* bezeichnet wird [Anm. d. Ü.].

4 Christa Steinle, „Kunst und Kontrolle: Zu einer Rauminstallation von Barbara Holub", in: GEHEIMNISTRÄGER, Graz 1996.

5 Manuela Hötzl, *Prêt-à-porter auf dem Fließband*, Interview mit Barbara Holub, siehe: http://www.barbaraholub.com/uploads/2/9/1/1/29117589/interview_hoetzl_holub_the_system.pdf (Zugriff: 12.4.2022).

6 Barbara Holub und Paul Rajakovics wohnten als Artists in Residence des MAK-Schindler-Stipendiums 2004 in den Mackey Apartments.

7 Für weitere Informationen zu den Projekten von transparadiso siehe: https://www.transparadiso.com (Zugriff: 11.5.2022).

8 Realisiert für *The Island is What the Sea Surrounds*, Europäische Kulturhauptstadt Valletta 2018.

9 Għana ist ein traditioneller, dialogischer und improvisierter Gesang aus Malta. Das Wort Għana hat zwei unterschiedliche Bedeutungen – zum einen bezeichnet es Reichtum, Besitz und Wohlstand, zum anderen Gesang, Vers, Reim sowie Kantaliena, einen Gesang mit langsamem Rhythmus. Die SängerInnen werden Għannejja (Għannej heißt auf Maltesisch „der Sänger") genannt.

10 Siehe zum Beispiel: https://www.publics.fi/calendar/silent-activism-for-an-active-role-of-art-in-society-and-in-the-public-realm (Zugriff: 11.5.2022). Siehe dazu auch Holubs Vortrag in: The Bartlett's International Lecture Series (2.2.2022), https://vimeo.com/677202901 (Zugriff: 11.5.2022).

11 In seinem Dokumentarfilm *HyperNormalisation* (2016) zeigt Adam Curtis, wie ein Heer aus TechnokratInnen, selbstgefälligen Radikalen und InternetunternehmerInnen eine unwirkliche Welt erschaffen hat, deren vertraute und oft beruhigende Merkmale uns ihre eigentliche Unwirklichkeit nicht mehr erkennen lässt. Der vollständige Film ist hier zugänglich: https://www.youtube.com/watch?v=thLgkQBFTPw (Zugriff: 11.5.2022).

12 Siehe: „Russell Brand & Adam Curtis – Do We Really Want Change?", Under The Skin Nr. 03, https://www.youtube.com/watch?v=MIHC4NNScEI&t=80s (Zugriff: 11.5.2022).

13 Ebd.

Kunst im Porschehof/ Speed curated by Hildegund Amanshauser, Johanna Hofleitner, and Eva Schlegel, Salzburger Kunstverein, in cooperation with Porsche Holding, Porschehof Salzburg, Salzburg, 1999.

DEVOTION TO UNINTENTIONALITY

In DEVOTION TO UNINTENTIONALITY, Holub explores the profoundly "retrotopian" (see text "Extra Ordinary" by J. H. Engqvist in chapter 4) desire of adults for children's ability to lose themselves in games, for that uncompromising experience of the here and now. Playing, unintentionality, and unadulterated devotion to the moment are diametrically opposed, in our society, to the adult ego's pressure to achieve and succeed, whereas management and creativity seminars seek to bring these two "worlds" back together.

For the multi-part project DEVOTION TO UNINTENTIONALITY, Holub invited staff from Porsche Holding Salzburg to play with a lot of Carrera racetracks in the lobby of the Porschehof, with the aim of exploring the experience of free (i.e. purposeless) action in the work environment in the name of art. This playful intervention also served as the starting point for a large-format photographic work that was installed on the wall of the lobby.

Parallel to this, interviews conducted with staff and people from Holub's personal artistic circles were subsequently presented as part of the video installation WITH VEILING HANDS at the Vienna Secession, continuing her critical reflection on the traditional assignment of roles between adulthood and childhood, between contemplation, action, and rebellion.[BR]

Geschwindigkeit, Kunst im Porschehof kuratiert von Hildegund Amanshauser, Johanna Hofleitner und Eva Schlegel, Salzburger Kunstverein in Kooperation mit Porsche Holding, Porschehof Salzburg, Salzburg, 1999.

HINGABE AN DIE ABSICHTSLOSIGKEIT

Der geradezu „retrotopischen" (siehe „Extra Ordinary" von J. H. Engqvist, Kapitel 4) Sehnsucht Erwachsener nach der kindlichen Fähigkeit des Sich-selbstvergessenen-Spielens, des kompromisslosen Erlebens des Hier-und-Jetzt spürt Holub in HINGABE AN DIE ABSICHTSLOSIGKEIT nach. Das Spiel, die Absichtslosigkeit, die ungetrübte Hingabe an den Moment stehen in unserer Gesellschaft diametral dem Leistungs- und Erfolgsdruck des Erwachsenen-Egos gegenüber, während in Management- und Kreativitätsseminaren versucht wird, diese beiden „Welten" wieder zusammenzuführen.

Holub lud für das mehrteilige Projekt HINGABE AN DIE ABSICHTSLOSIGKEIT MitarbeiterInnen der Porsche-Holding in Salzburg ein, mit einer Vielzahl von Carrera-Autorennbahnen im Foyer des Porschehofs zu spielen, um, im Auftrag der Kunst, die Erfahrung des freien (weil zweckentbundenen) Handelns am eigenen Arbeitsplatz auszuloten. Diese spielerische Intervention diente zugleich als Ausgangspunkt für eine großformatige Fotoarbeit, die an der Wand des Foyers angebracht wurde.

Parallel dazu geführte Interviews mit den MitarbeiterInnen sowie mit Menschen aus dem persönlichen künstlerischen Umfeld Holubs wurden, als Teil der Videoinstallation MIT VORGEHALTENER HAND, darauffolgend in der Secession in Wien gezeigt und setzten die kritische Reflexion tradierter Rollenzuschreibungen zwischen Erwachsensein und Kindsein, zwischen Kontemplation, Aktion und Rebellion fort.[BR]

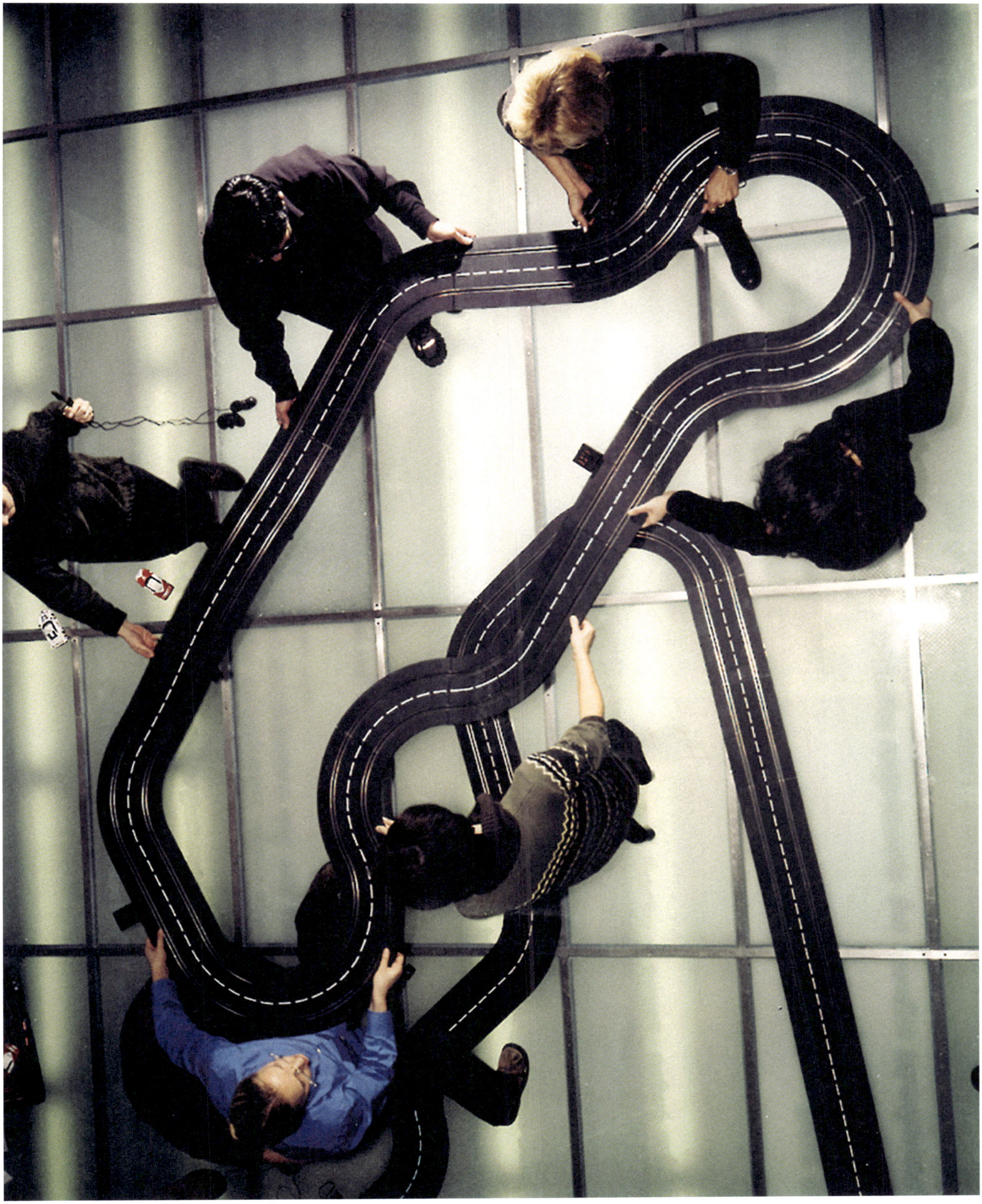

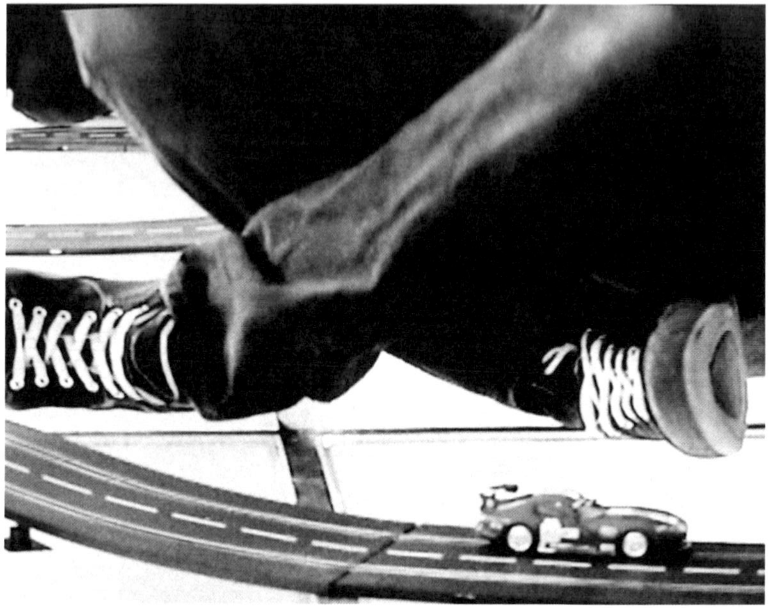

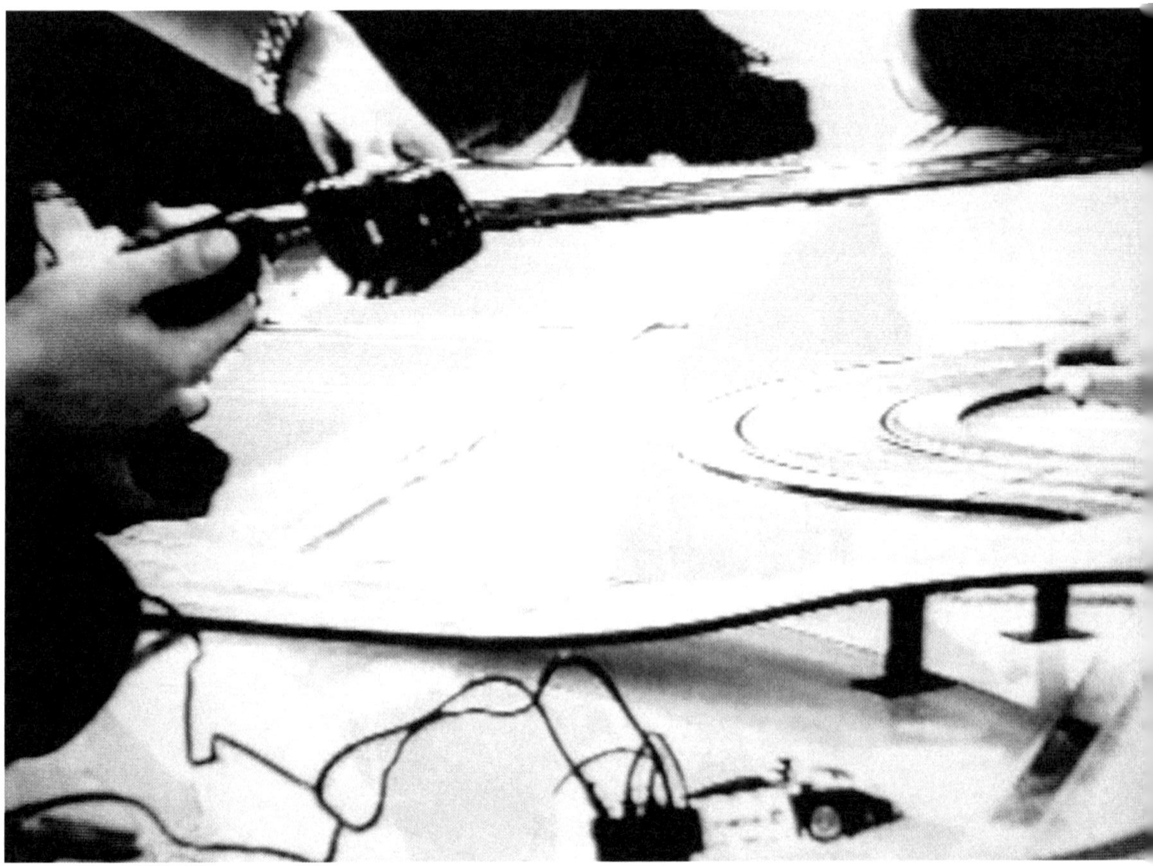

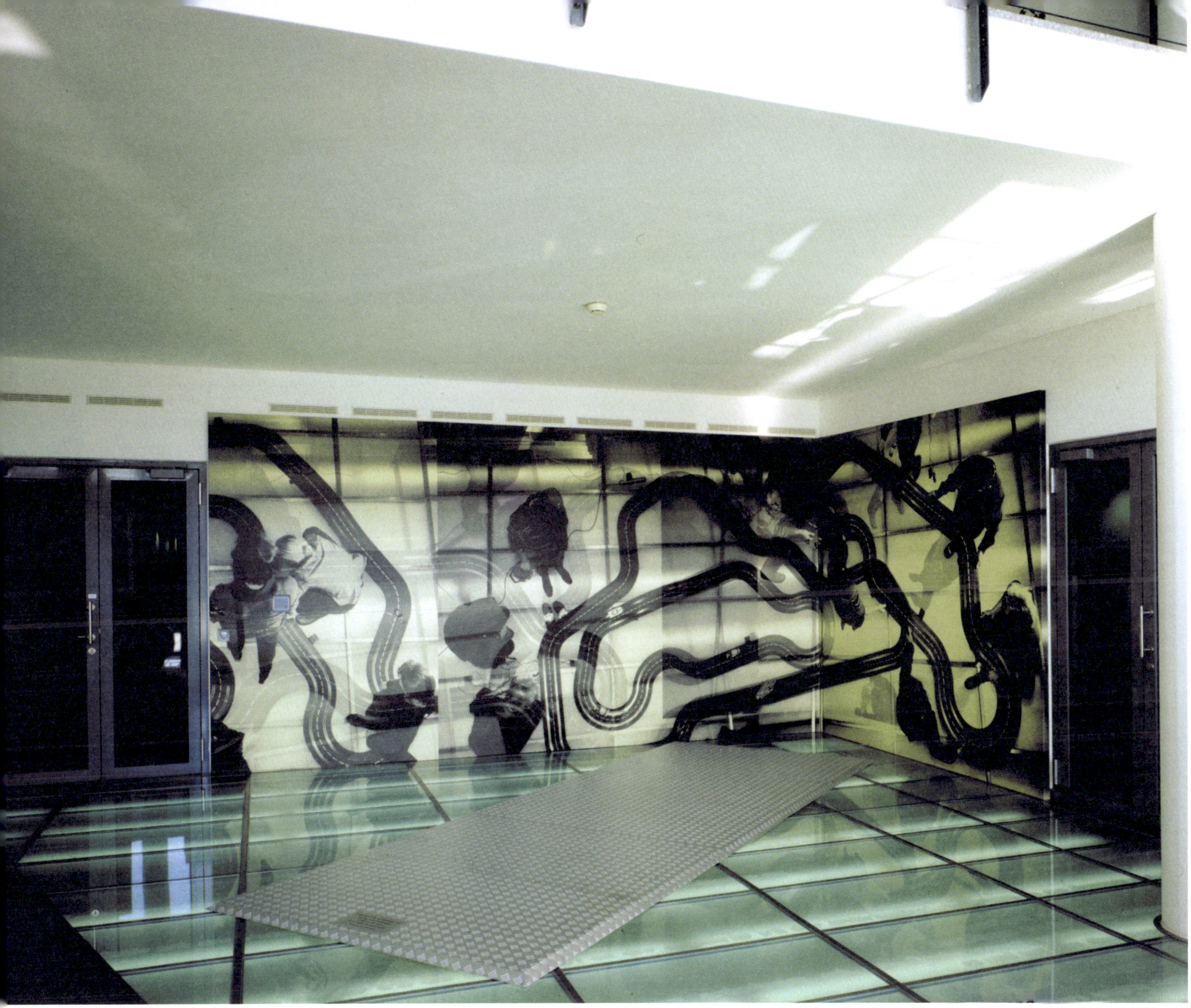

WITH VEILING HANDS

Assigned roles and traditional behavior patterns, yearnings and taboos, desires and concealment, all of which inform our social and personal identity, revolve in the exhibition around the (supposed) opposite poles of childhood and adulthood.

In the double video projection WITH VEILING HANDS, the video on the right shows excerpts of the interviews conducted by Holub as part of her project DEVOTION TO UNINTENTIONALITY with Porsche Holding staff and acquaintances from her personal artistic circles. The video sequences are repeated by super-slow-motion videos of children bouncing on a trampoline and scenes of staff playing with Carrera slot car racetracks at Porschehof Salzburg. In the video on the left, again in super-slow motion, we see details of close-ups of children play-acting stereotyped gestures from adult life, again and again nearing the line between play and earnest.

At the level of film—despite the different visual idioms involved—the references are in fact cross-references, so that the child's perspective equally includes aspects of adulthood and vice versa, and thus repeatedly questions these assigned roles. The high-contrast black-and-white editing, the slow-motion mode, and the synchronicity of the images create, in the viewer, a sense of both closeness and distance, unity and separation, play and earnestness, self and other. These moments of ambivalence are augmented by the installation of airport seats that expose the spectators to a situation that prompts them to decide between the incidental nature of a temporary waiting position and actively focusing on the video projection.

In the exhibition, the video installation was prefaced in the two preceding rooms by the audio play WARUMEN/WHYING, which could be viewed on inflatable cushions on a "hopscotch" court, and by a large-format curtain displaying a stadium grandstand from a Playmobil set. The title of the audio play is a reference to the seemingly endless "why" questions that children ask and the search for answers, introducing the listeners—by way of associations with experiences of their own—to the experience of leaving questions unanswered and enduring this openness, this "otherness."BH/BR

MIT VORGEHALTENER HAND

Rollenzuschreibungen und tradierte Verhaltensmuster, Sehnsüchte und Tabus sowie Begehren und Verbergen, allesamt unsere soziale und persönliche Identität prägend, zentrieren sich in der Ausstellung um die (vermeintlichen) Gegenpole Kindsein und Erwachsensein.

In der Doppel-Videoprojektion MIT VORGEHALTENER HAND zeigt das rechte Video Auszüge aus den Interviews, die Holub im Rahmen ihres Projekts HINGABE AN DIE ABSICHTSLOSIGKEIT mit MitarbeiterInnen der Porsche-Holding sowie mit Bekannten aus dem persönlichen künstlerischen Umfeld geführt hat. Die Videosequenzen werden wiederholt durch Superzeitlupenaufnahmen von trampolinspringenden Kindern sowie von Spielszenen der MitarbeiterInnen mit Carrera-Autorennbahnen im Porschehof Salzburg unterbrochen. Im linken Video sind, ebenfalls in Superzeitlupe, Ausschnitte von Nahaufnahmen von Kindern zu sehen, die klischeehafte Gesten aus dem Erwachsenenleben spielerisch vorführen und dabei immer wieder an die Grenze zwischen Spiel und Ernst geraten.

Auf Filmebene laufen die Verweise – trotz unterschiedlicher Bildsprachen – querbezüglich, sodass die Ebene des Kindes auch Aspekte des Erwachsenenseins beinhaltet und umgekehrt, und dadurch wiederholt diese Rollenzuschreibungen infrage gestellt werden. Die kontrastreiche Schwarz-Weiß-Bearbeitung, der Zeitlupenmodus und die Synchronizität der Bilder suggerieren bei der Betrachterin/beim Betrachter gleichzeitig Nähe und Distanz, Einheit und Getrenntsein, Spiel und Ernst sowie das Selbst und die Anderen. Verstärkt werden diese Momente der Ambivalenz durch die Installation einer Flughafenbestuhlung, die die ZuseherInnen einer Situation aussetzt, die sie zwischen der Beiläufigkeit einer interimistischen Warteposition und der aktiven Hinwendung zur Videoprojektion entscheiden lässt.

In der Ausstellung wurde die Videoinstallation in den zwei unmittelbar davor liegenden Räumen, vorbereitet durch das Hörspiel WARUMEN, das auf aufblasbaren Polstern auf einem „Himmel und Hölle"-Spielfeld rezipiert werden konnte, und durch einen großformatigen Vorhang, der eine Stadion-Tribüne aus einem Playmobil-Spiel zeigte. Der Titel des Hörspiels bezieht sich auf das scheinbar endlose Fragen von Kindern nach dem Warum und die Suche nach Antworten, und führt die ZuhörerInnen – über Assoziationen mit möglichen eigenen Erfahrungen – in das Erleben des Offenlassens von Fragen, des Aushaltens dieser Offenheit, des „Andersseins". BH/BR

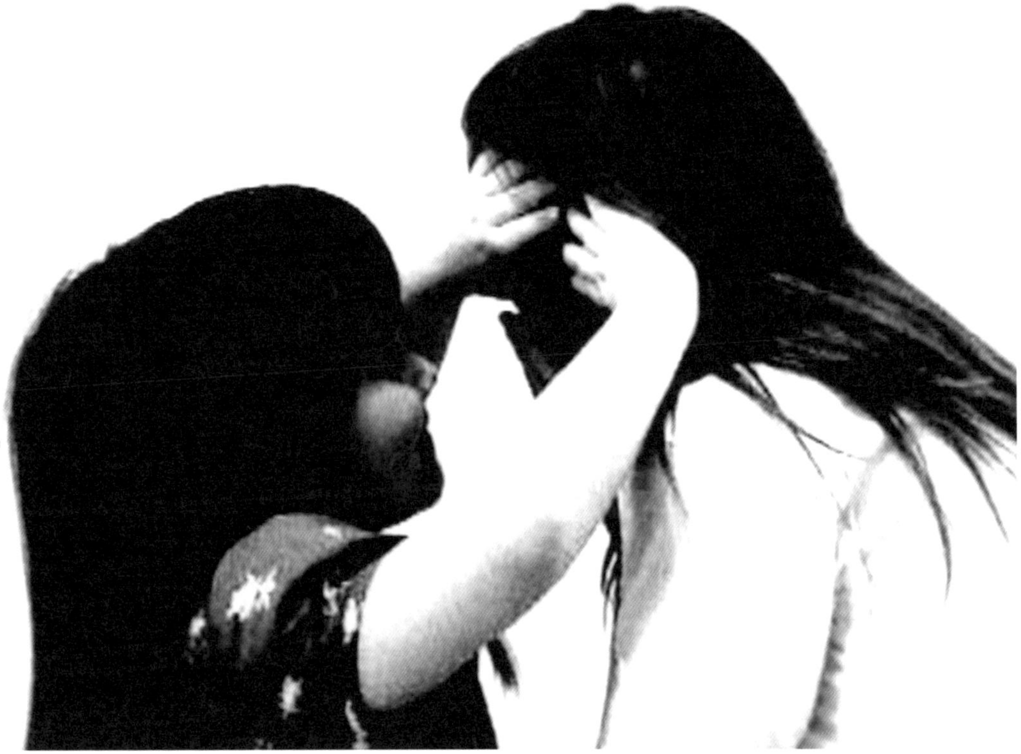

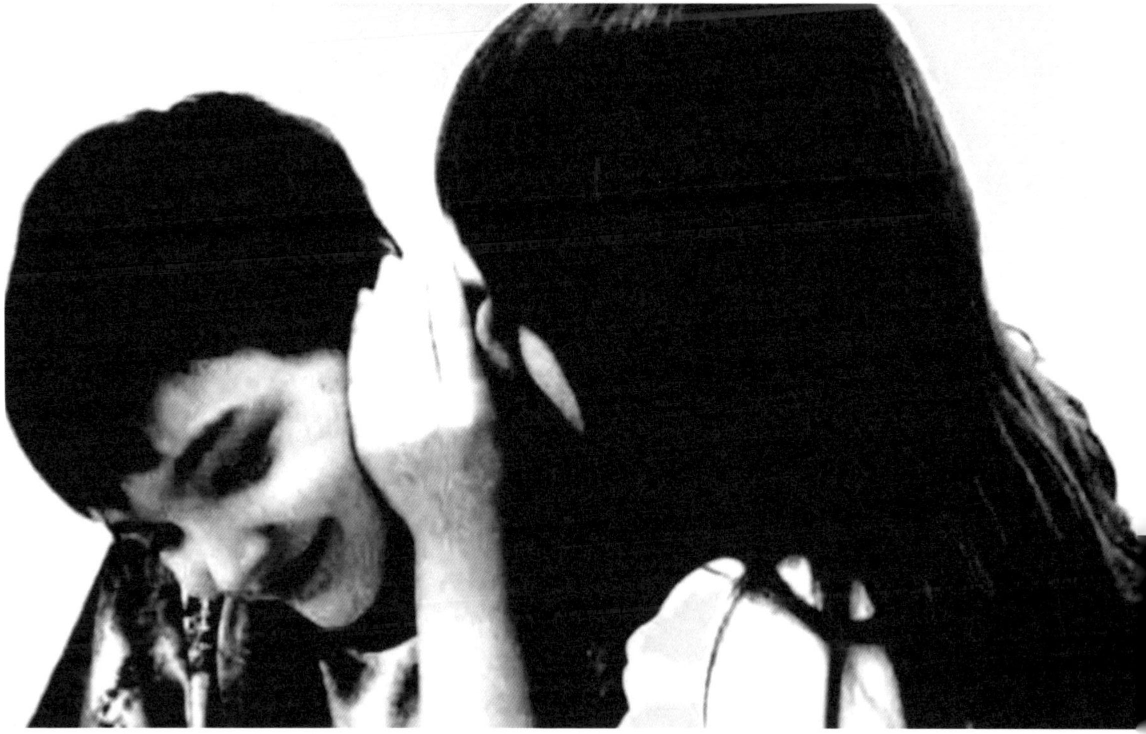

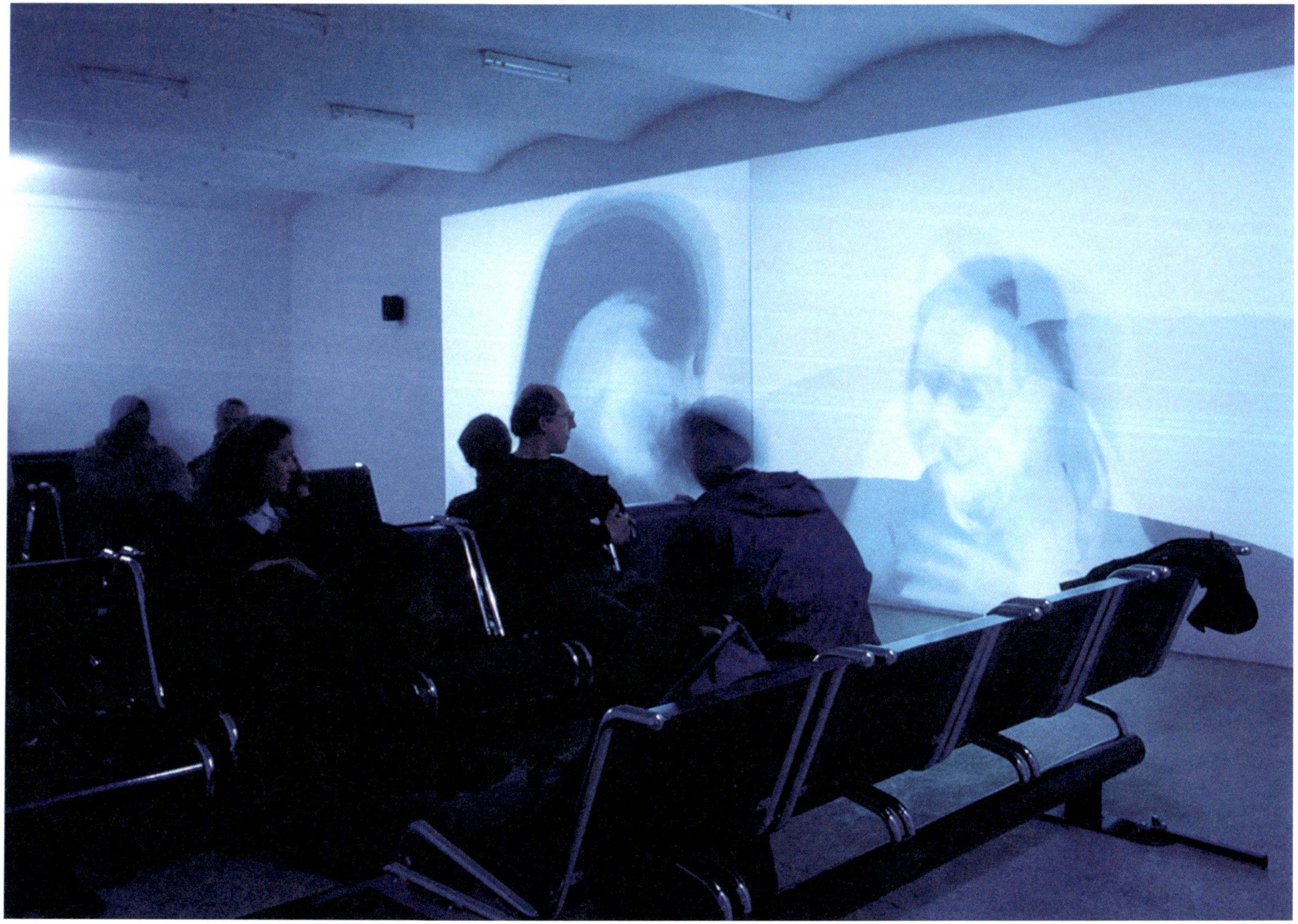

Exhibition view, Secession, Vienna, 1999
WITH VEILING HANDS, installation with double video projection

Ausstellungsansicht, Secession, Wien, 1999
MIT VORGEHALTENER HAND, Installation mit Doppel-Videoprojektion

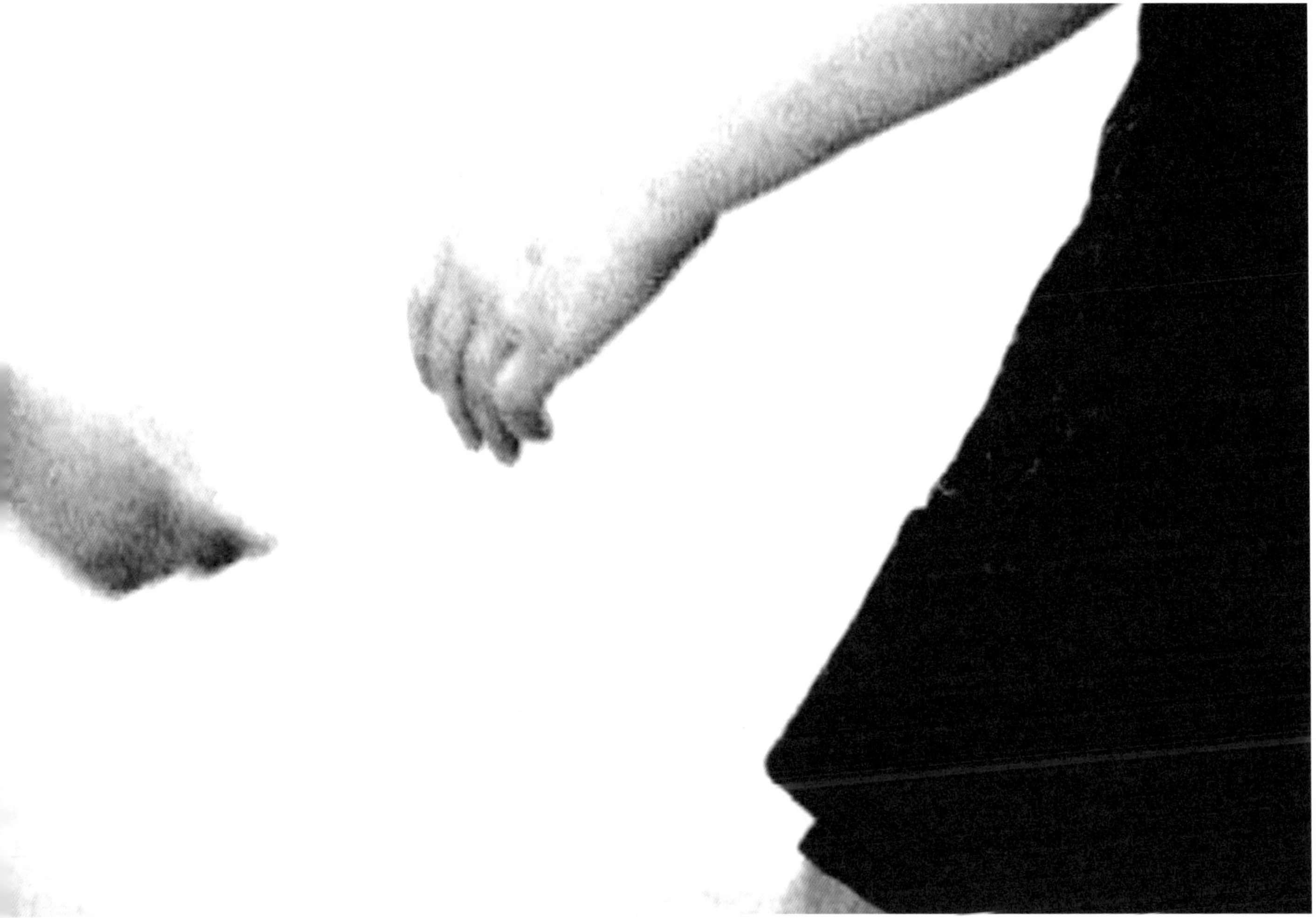

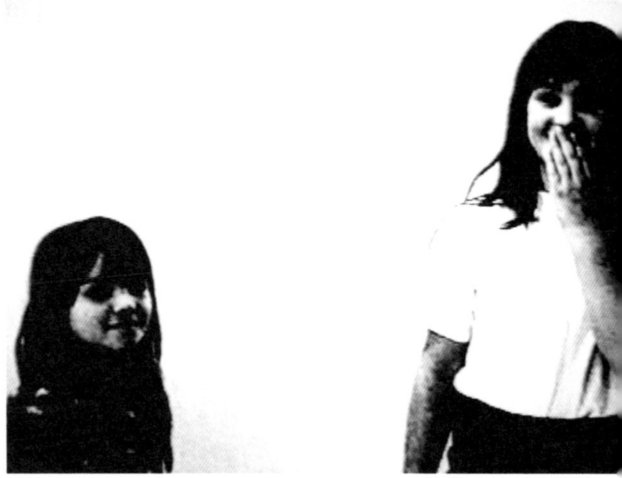

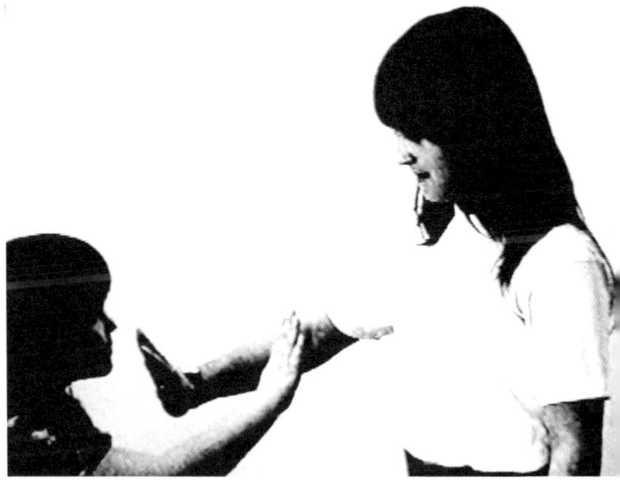

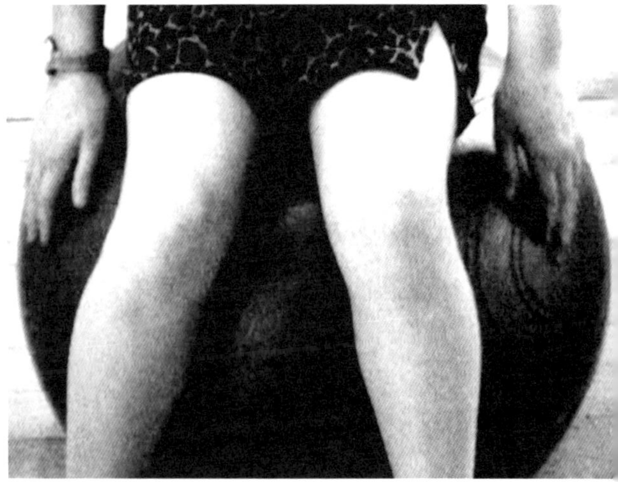

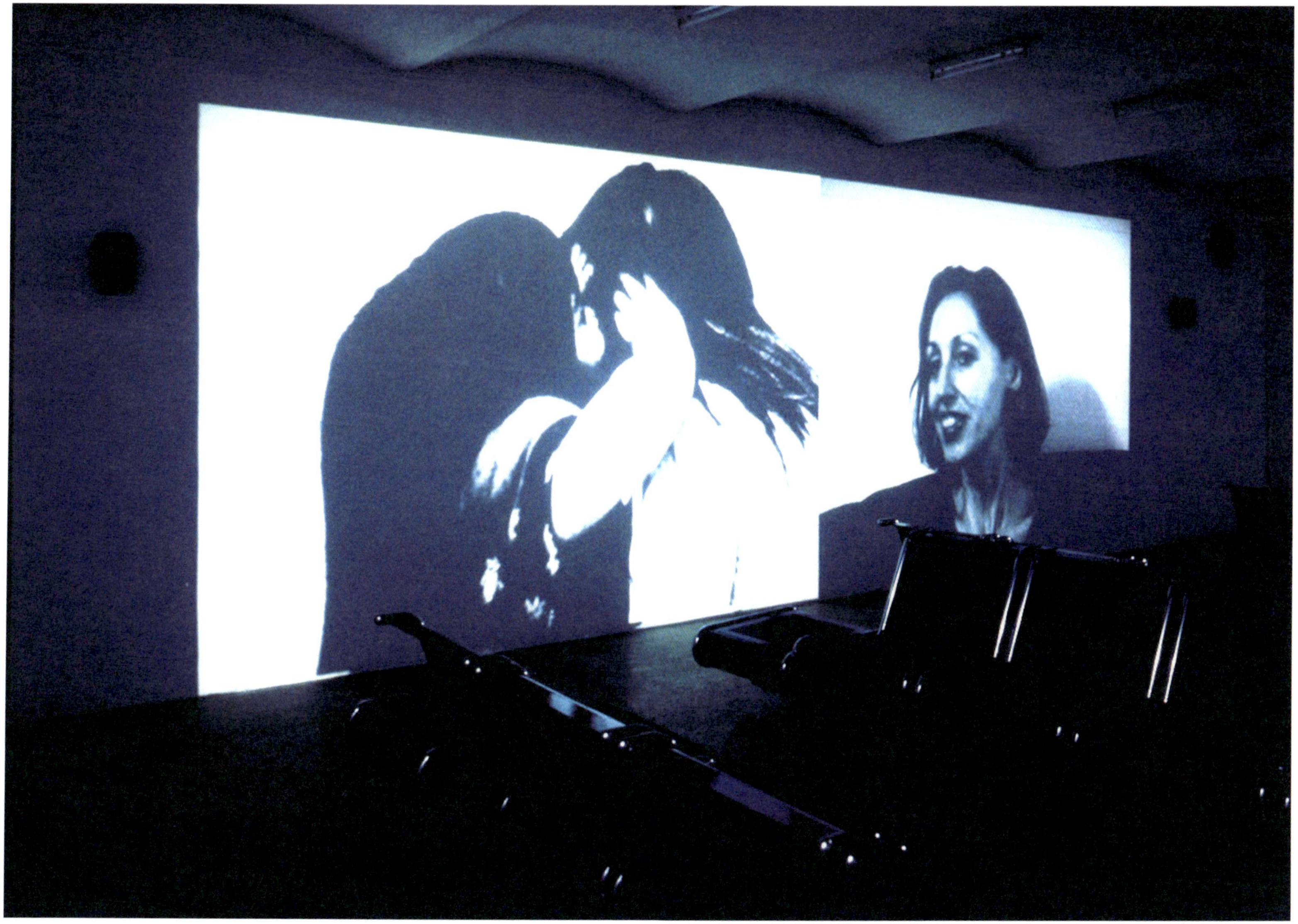

"What do you mean by 'normal'?
I don't know. [...]
Keeping things under control [...]
What do you mean by 'safe'?"

*„Was meinst du mit ‚normal'?
Ich weiß es nicht. [...]
Dinge unter Kontrolle zu halten [...]
Was meinst du mit ‚sicher'?"*

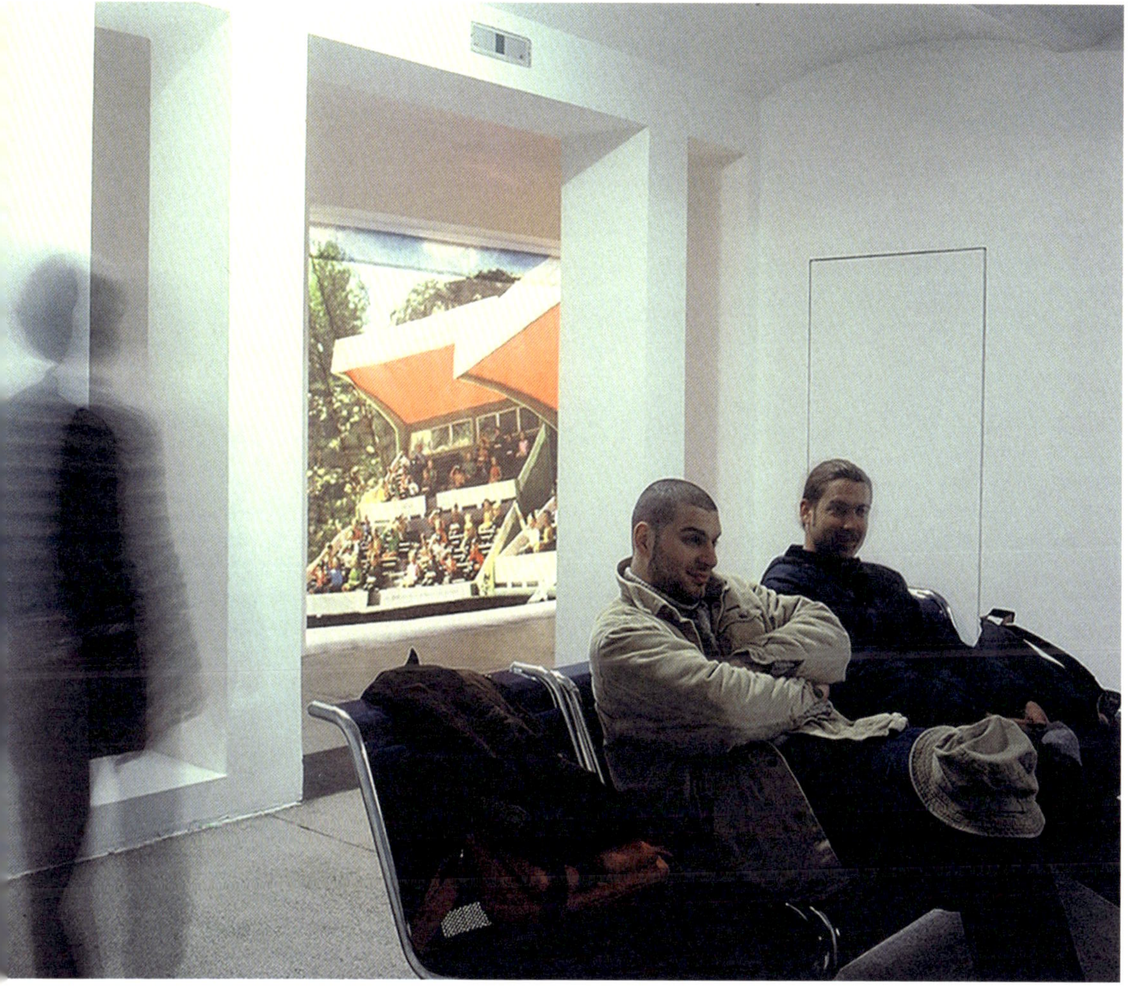

WARUMEN (WHYING), audio play, 22'

WARUMEN, Hörspiel, 22'

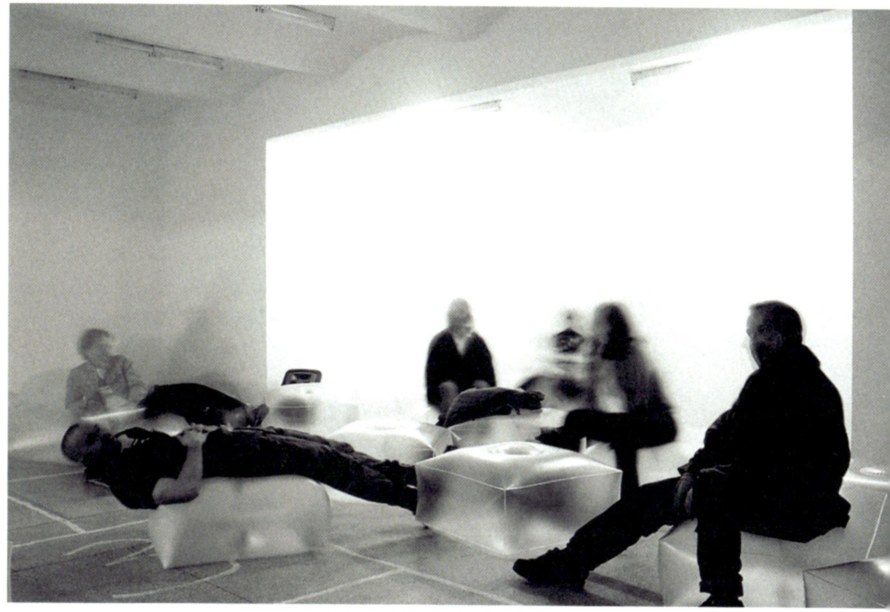

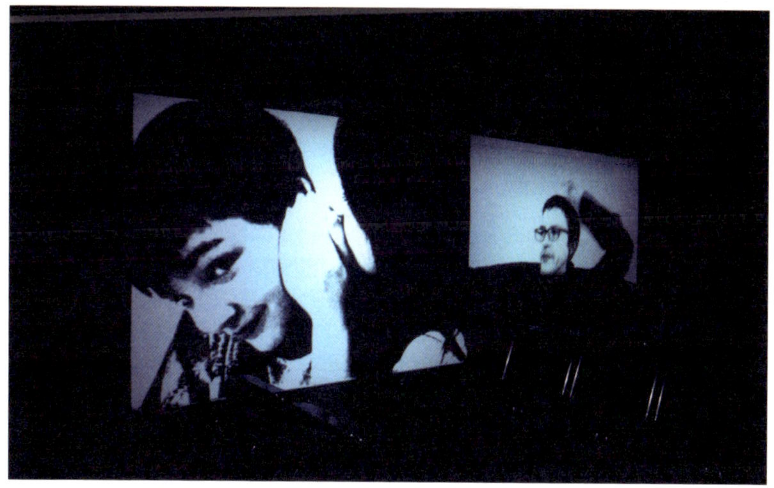

HANDLED CONFIDENTIALLY

In HANDLED CONFIDENTIALLY, the desk—besides other office furnishings, the Bene company mainly manufactures desks—becomes the stage for Holub's artistic examination of social rules. The focus, however, is not on what happens on the table during the day in the course of everyday office life, but on what happens—or rather what *can* happen—under the table during leisure time, away from the office. We see one thing above all, seemingly unasked, sensual, provocative, as if in the flashlight of a paparazzo: legs and hands, furtively touching, interacting on familiar terms, and thus affording a stolen glimpse of intimacy.

Holub demonstrates the fact that social norms can be absurd, and the necessity of sometimes exposing their absurdity, not only by staging the intimate actions with the office staff but also by showcasing these intimate moments to the outside world in large images displayed on the façade of the building. At the same time, the large-format lightboxes conceal the area under the staff tables that, without this installation, would be visible from the street, through the windows. HANDLED CONFIDENTIALLY thrusts covert, taboo, perhaps even illicit behavior among colleagues into the public eye, causing discreet conventions of everyday office life to clash with indiscreet images from private life.

In an additional video, the staff who took part in the project have their say, displaying cards with photos of the staged "under-the-table activities" accompanied by speech bubbles that are as suggestive as they are banal, or, as Rosa von Suess puts it: "The professional social codes, silent agreements over sexual associations are again demonstrated in the video."[1 BR]

1 Rosa von Suess, "Barbara Holub. HANDLED CONFIDENTIALLY," in: Medienkunstarchiv, 1999, www.mka.at/werk.php?vid=2021&e=1 (accessed: July 12, 2022).

VERTRAULICH BEHANDELT

Der Tisch – die Firma Bene produziert neben anderen Büroausstattungselementen vor allem auch Tische – wird in VERTRAULICH BEHANDELT zur Bühne der künstlerischen Auseinandersetzung Holubs mit gesellschaftlichen Reglements. In den Fokus rückt jedoch nicht das, was untertags, im Büroalltag auf dem Tisch passiert, sondern das, was in der Freizeit, außerhalb des Büros unter dem Tisch passiert – oder vielmehr passieren kann. Scheinbar ungefragt, lustvoll, provokativ, im Blitzlicht einer vermeintlichen Paparazza ist vor allem eines zu sehen: Beine und Hände, die einander verstohlen berühren, miteinander vertraut agieren und so einen gestohlenen Blick auf Intimes gewähren.

Dass gesellschaftliche Normen absurd sein können bzw. dann und wann ad absurdum geführt werden müssen, zeigt Holub nicht zuletzt, indem sie die festgehaltenen intimen Handlungen gemeinsam mit den MitarbeiterInnen des Büros inszeniert hat, sondern auch, indem sie diese vertraulichen Momente großflächig nach außen hin, an der Hausfassade, zur Schau stellt. Die großformatigen Leuchtkästen decken dabei wiederum den Bereich unter den Arbeitstischen der MitarbeiterInnen ab, der ohne diese Installation von der Straße aus durch die Glasfenster sichtbar ist. VERTRAULICH BEHANDELT katapultiert das Verborgene, Tabuisierte, vielleicht sogar Illegitime unter KollegInnen an die Öffentlichkeit und lässt diskrete Konventionen des Büroalltags mit indiskreten Abbildungen aus dem Privatleben aufeinanderprallen.

In einem zusätzlichen Video kommen die beteiligten MitarbeiterInnen zu Wort, indem Fotokarten mit den Sujets der inszenierten „Unter-dem-Tisch-Happenings" und mit ebenso andeutungsvollen wie banalen Sprechblasen gezeigt werden, oder, wie Rosa von Suess beschreibt: „Die gesellschaftlichen Codes professionalisierter Übereinkünfte über das Stillschweigen sexueller Assoziationen werden im Video abermals vorgeführt."[1 BR]

1 Rosa von Suess, „Barbara Holub. VERTRAULICH BEHANDELT", in: Medienkunstarchiv, 1999, http://www.mka.at/werk.php?vid=2021&e=0 (Zugriff: 12.7.2022).

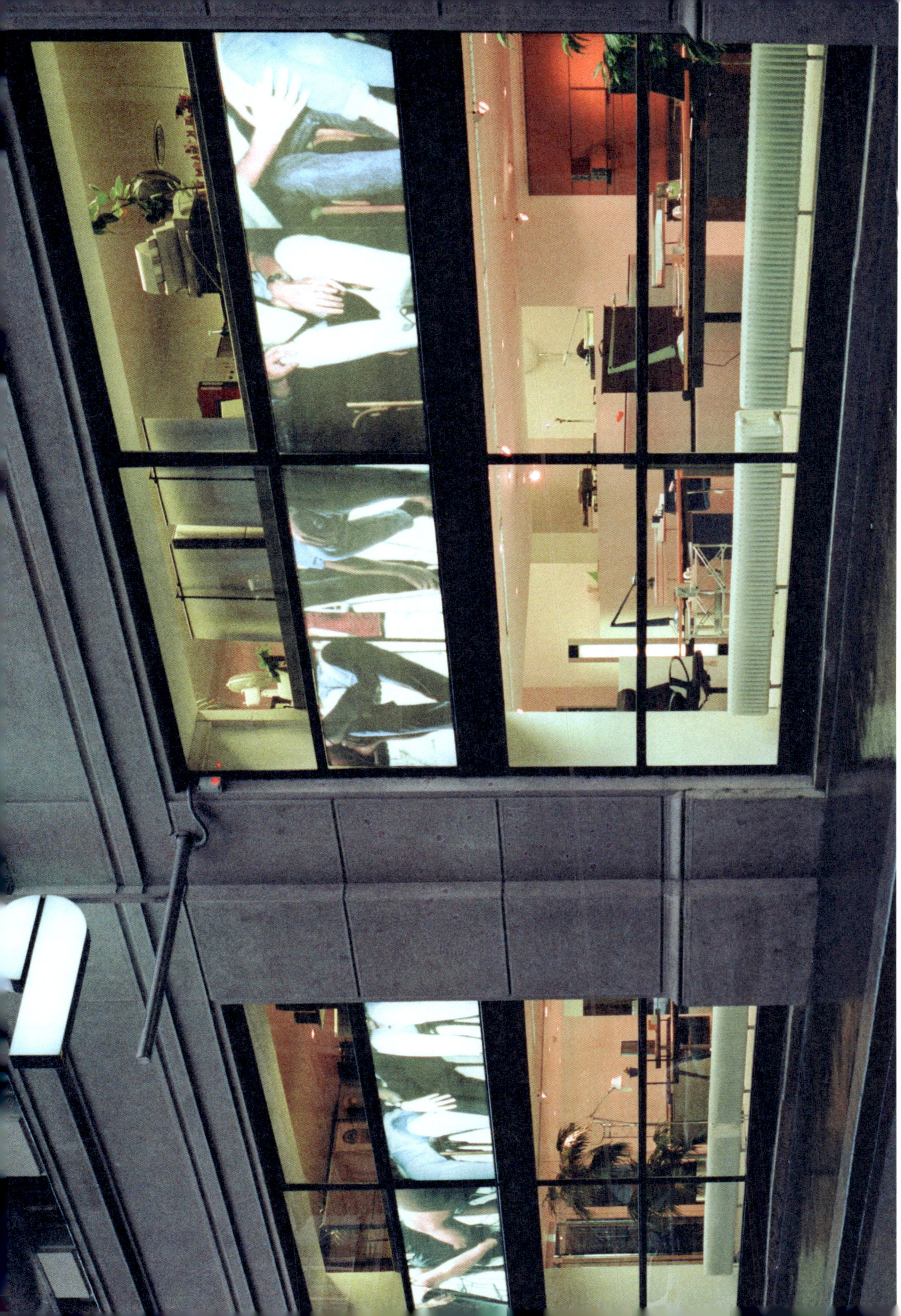

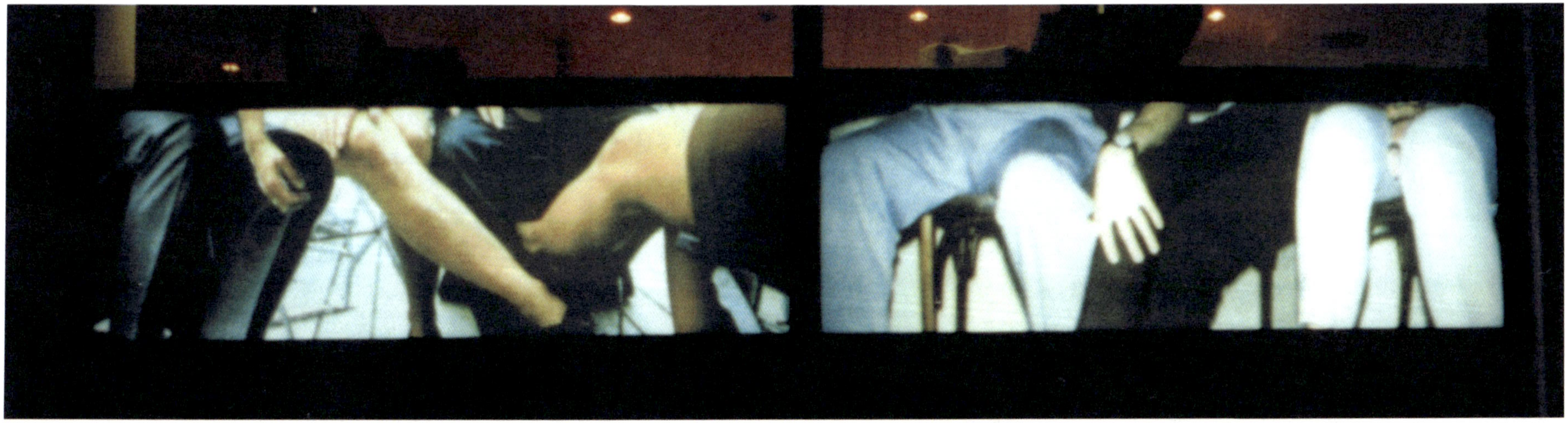

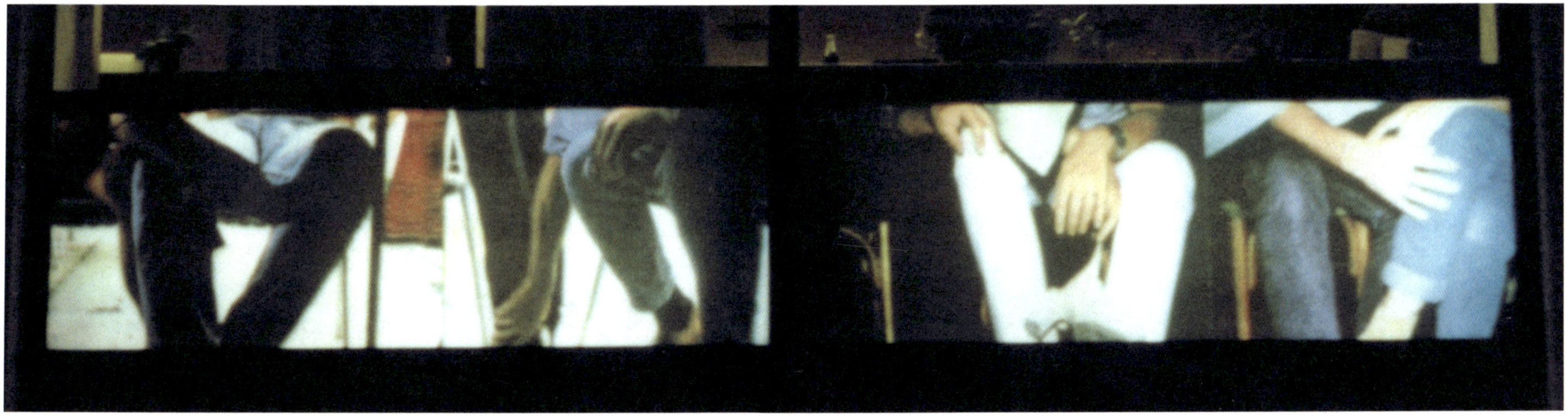

Permanent installation in the Bene show room, Renngasse, Vienna, 1998–2010

Permanente Installation im Bene-Schauraum, Renngasse, Wien, 1998–2010

Subsequently, a video was produced of interviews with the employees about their experiences with HANDLED CONFIDENTIALLY, 1999.

In weiterer Folge entstand ein Video der Interviews mit den MitarbeiterInnen über ihre Erfahrungen mit VERTRAULICH BEHANDELT, 1999.

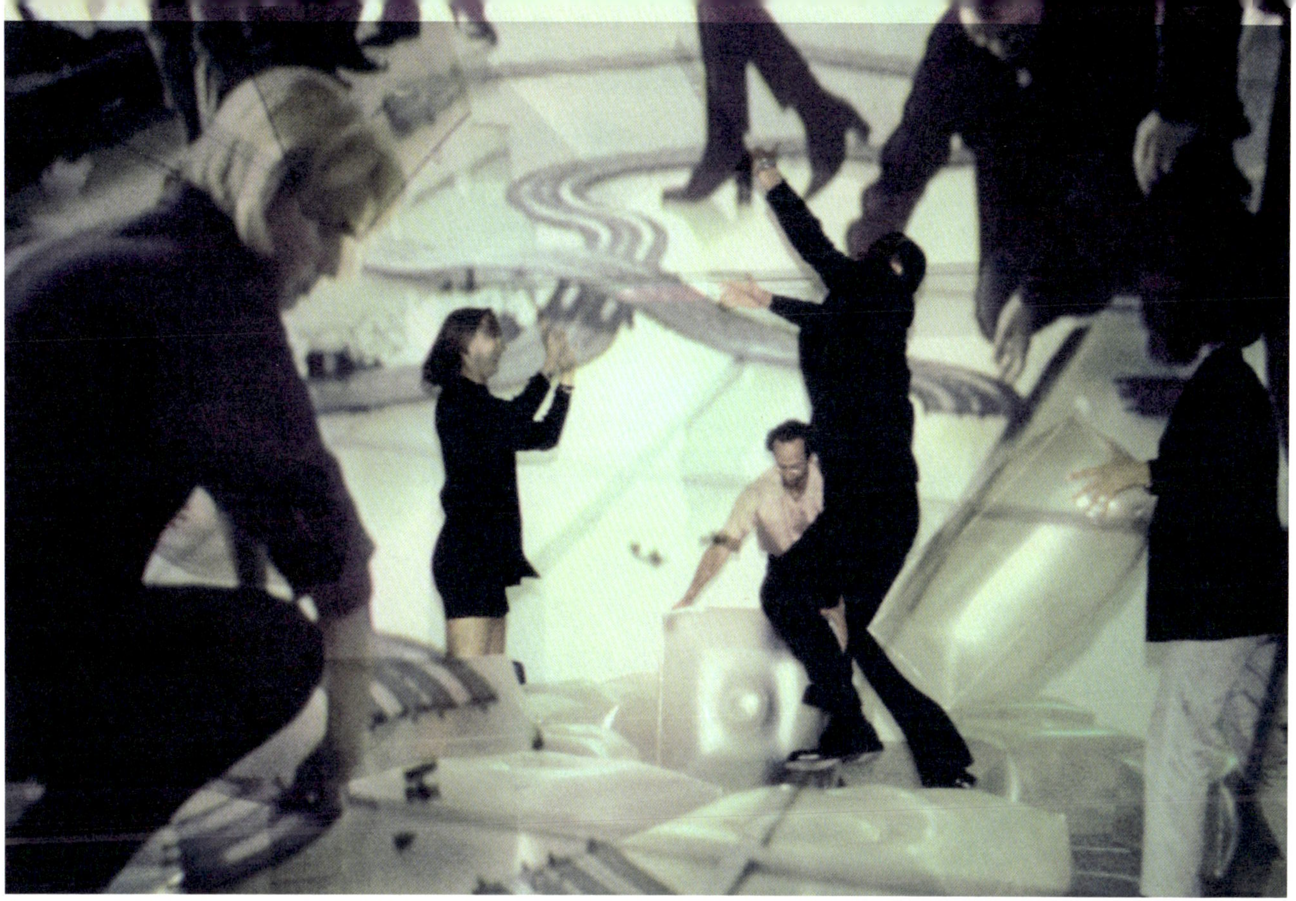

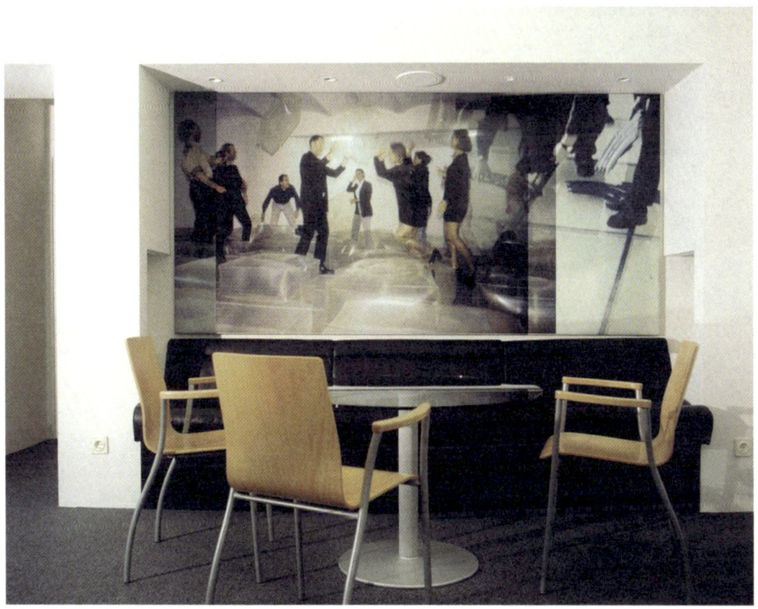

PLAYING ALONG...? In the newly staged pieces for the interior, the employees of the Porschehof Salzburg met with those of the Bene show room.

MITSPIELEN ...? In den neu inszenierten Werken für den Innenraum trafen sich die MitarbeiterInnen des Porschehofs Salzburg mit jenen des Bene-Schauraums.

IV. Curated by Peter Bogner, Künstlerhaus/Künstlerhauspassage, Vienna, 2006
Slow, curated by Paula Orrell, Plymouth Arts Centre, Plymouth (UK), 2007

Kuratiert von Peter Bogner, Künstlerhaus/Künstlerhauspassage, Wien, 2006
Slow, kuratiert von Paula Orrell, Plymouth Arts Centre, Plymouth (UK), 2007

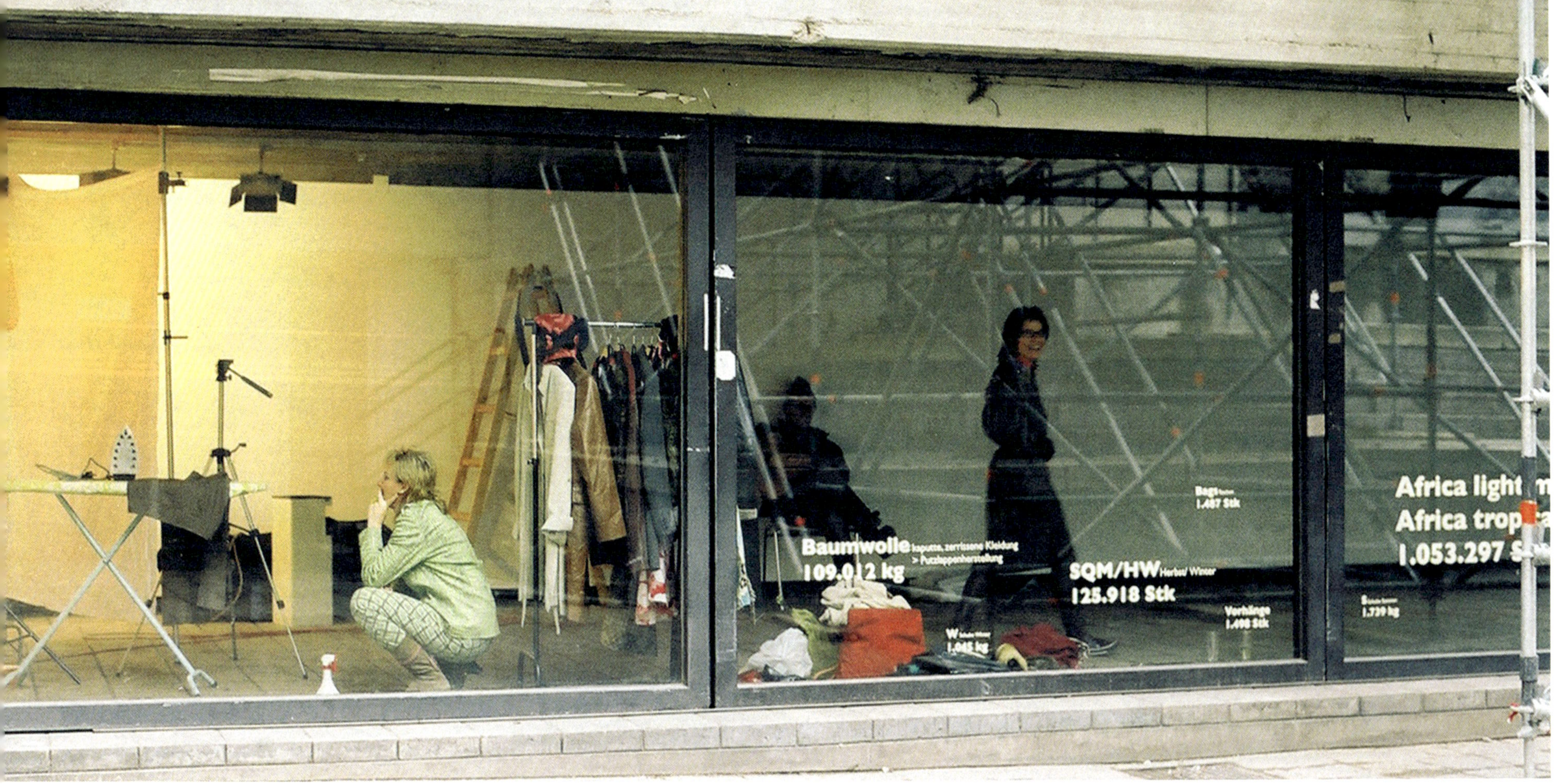

The exhibition space of the Passage Gallery of the Künstlerhaus is used for a fashion show and photo shoot, while the quantities and categories of the sorted second-hand clothes can be read on the façade, allowing conclusions to be drawn about the export countries: For instance, "Africa light" requires skirts to at least cover the knees.

Die Passagegalerie des Künstlerhauses wird für eine Modenschau und ein Fotoshooting genutzt, während auf der Fassade die Mengen und Kategorien der sortierten Secondhandkleidung abzulesen sind, die auch Rückschlüsse auf die Exportländer zulassen. So inkludiert "Africa light" Röcke, die zumindest das Knie bedecken müssen.

THE SYSTEM: PRÊT-À-PORTER

THE SYSTEM: PRÊT-À-PORTER analyses the economy of the second-hand clothing industry by looking at a range of models: clothing exchanges, yard sales, and charity donations. A short video loop of a yard sale in Los Angeles focuses on the physical postures of people searching through clothes, highlighting the social interaction that occurs in residential areas otherwise detached from the outside world. Holub's short cuts with schematic silhouettes and blackouts depict the eclectic styles of communication in this not-for-profit

THE SYSTEM: PRÊT-À-PORTER

THE SYSTEM: PRÊT-À-PORTER analysiert die Secondhandkleidungswirtschaft anhand verschiedener ökonomischer Modelle: Kleidertausch, Yard Sale und Kleiderspenden. Ein kurzes, geloopptes Video von einem Yard Sale in Los Angeles legt den Fokus auf die Körperhaltungen der Personen beim Sichten der Kleidungsstücke, auf die soziale Interaktion, die dabei in Gegenden entsteht, in denen sonst kaum öffentliches Leben stattfindet. Holubs von Schwarzblenden getrennte Short Cuts von verschwommenen Personen beschreiben eigenwillige Kommunikations-

Alongside this video is a large billboard image installed on scaf-folding in the courtyard of the Künstlerhaus, showing an automated system for sorting second-hand clothing, a recently closed operation once used by the Humana development aid organization in Vienna. In its shops, Humana sells second-hand clothes collected in containers and sorted according to different categories, the proceeds financing aid projects in African countries. A graphic depiction of a person incorporated into the billboard image of the sorting system stands symbolically for the vanishing labor force and production process which, no longer economically viable in Vienna, has now relocated to Bulgaria. This collaging of a drawing onto a photographic image is a technique Holub has developed for investigating the (unplanned) use of public space. Here, a figure sorting clothes on a conveyor belt merges seamlessly with the interior of Humana's operation, the contrast between the drawing's hand-produced quality and the surrounding photographic context dramatizing the exploitation of workers within automated environments. The second-hand clothing industry offers a wide range of commercial possibilities, and the spotlight that moves across the whole exhibition setup further emphasizes the need to shed light on an economic system that remains largely hidden from public view.

But where do the items of clothing processed by Humana actually end up? Holub marks out eighteen destinations on the window façade, written in a text size proportionate to the volume of clothing delivered to each one. During the exhibition, Humana staff members are invited to model Humana clothing at a photo shoot. This is a crucial part of a project which, in addition to revealing the labor and economy of second-hand clothing, can't help but raise the question of how "style" migrates from one cultural context to another, highlighting the potential difference between what is desirable in Europe and what is desirable in Africa.

Holub critically investigates the relation between labor conditions in the globalized clothing market and the African second-hand clothing market that, though having become an important way for women in particular to make a living, has adversely affected local clothing production. Thus, with THE SYSTEM: PRÊT-À-PORTER Holub questions "systems" in a larger context, advocating the necessity of equally distributed resources.[SA]

Im Kontrast dazu war auf einem großen, über das Baugerüst im Hof des Künstlerhauses gespannten Banner eine automatische Sortieranlage für Secondhandkleidung in einem vor kurzem geschlossenen Sortierbetrieb des Hilfswerks Humana in Wien zu sehen. Humana verkauft in seinen Läden in Containern gesammelte und nach unterschiedlichen Kategorien sortierte Secondhandkleidung und finanziert aus dem Erlös Hilfsprojekte in afrikanischen Ländern. Eine in das Foto auf dem Banner montierte Zeichnung einer Person steht symbolisch für die verschwundene Arbeit und Produktion, die damals gerade nach Bulgarien ausgelagert wurde, weil sie in Wien nicht mehr wirtschaftlich war. Diese Art der Strichzeichnung, die an Malbuchbilder erinnert, wurde von Holub ursprünglich dafür entwickelt, (ungeplante) Aneignungen des öffentlichen Raums zu sammeln. In diesem Fall verschmilzt eine Figur, die an einem Fließband Kleider sortiert, nahtlos mit dem Humana-Sortierbetrieb, wobei der Kontrast zwischen der Handzeichnung und dem sie umgebenden fotografischen Kontext die Ausbeutung von ArbeiterInnen in automatisierten Arbeitsumgebungen hervorhebt. Das Geschäft mit Secondhandkleidung bietet eine Fülle kommerzieller Möglichkeiten, und der über einen Bewegungsmelder aktivierte Suchscheinwerfer unterstrich die Notwendigkeit, Licht in ein ökonomisches System zu bringen, das für die Öffentlichkeit weitgehend im Dunkeln bleibt.

Aber wo gehen die von Humana verarbeiteten Kleidungsstücke tatsächlich hin? Holub gibt auf der Schaufensterfassade 18 Kategorien an, deren Schriftgröße die Menge der jeweils darunterfallenden Kleidungsstücke widerspiegelt. Während der Ausstellung waren MitarbeiterInnen von Humana eingeladen, in einem Fotoshooting Humana-Kleidungsstücke vorzuführen. Das ist ein wesentlicher Aspekt des Projekts, das neben der Enthüllung der Arbeitsprozesse und der Ökonomie der Secondhandkleidungswirtschaft zwangsläufig auch die Frage berührt, wie Stile von einem kulturellen Kontext in einen anderen wandern, und auf die potenzielle Differenz zwischen dem in Europa und in Afrika Begehrenswerten verweist.

Die Künstlerin untersucht kritisch das Verhältnis zwischen den Arbeitsbedingungen im globalisierten Kleidungsmarkt und dem afrikanischen Secondhandkleidungsmarkt, der zwar – speziell für Frauen – zu einem wichtigen Lebensunterhalt geworden ist, sich aber auch negativ auf die Kleidungsproduktion vor Ort auswirkt. Holub hinterfragt also mit THE SYSTEM globalisierte Wirtschaftssysteme im Allgemeinen und verweist auf die Notwendigkeit einer gerechten Ressourcenverteilung.[SA]

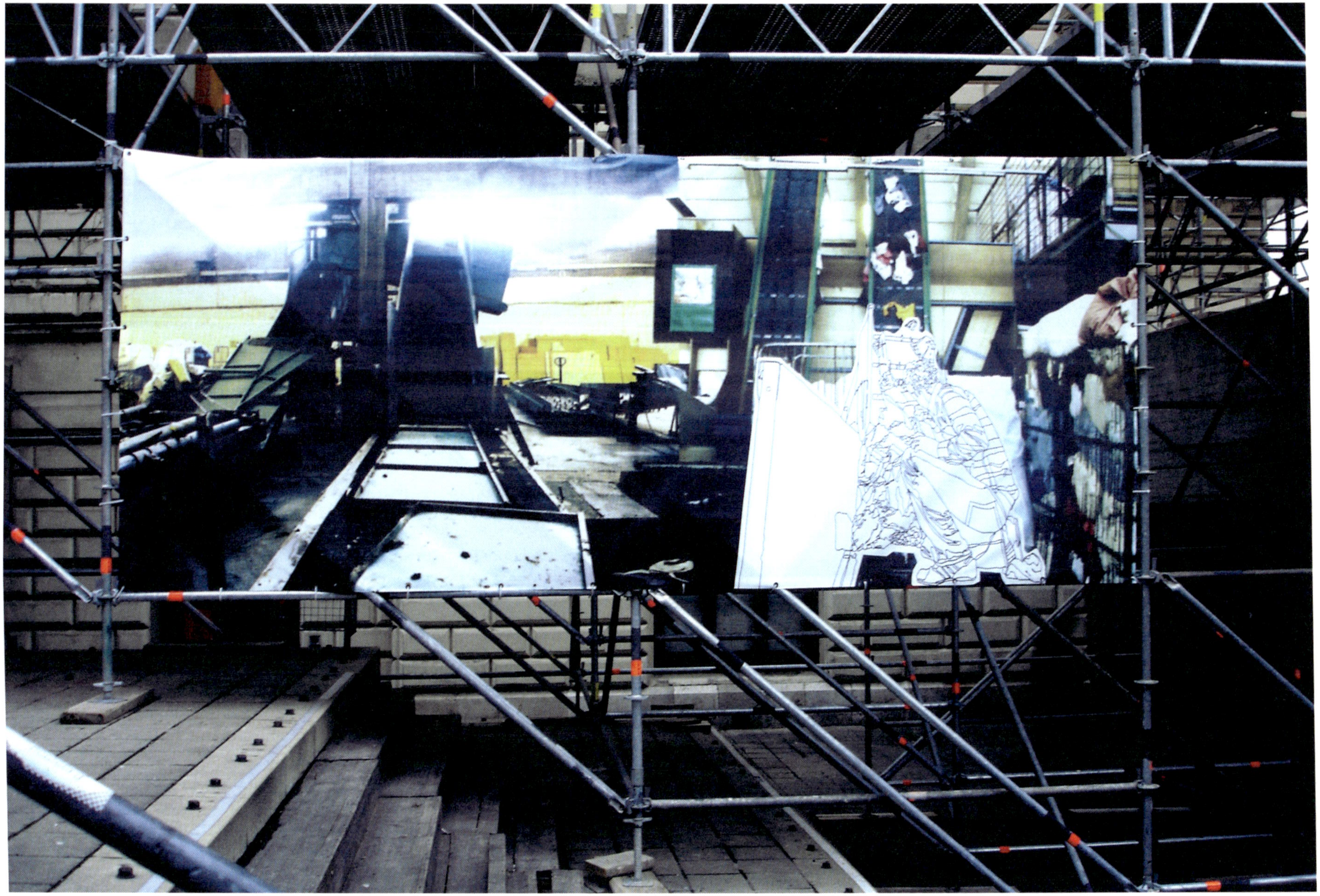

Installation on scaffolding in the courtyard of the Künstlerhaus: The work in a Humana sorting plant in Vienna is in its final stages before being outsourced to low-wage countries.

Installation auf dem Gerüst im Hof des Künstlerhauses: Die Arbeit an einer Sortieranlage von Humana in Wien liegt in den letzten Zügen vor deren Auslagerung in Billiglohnländer.

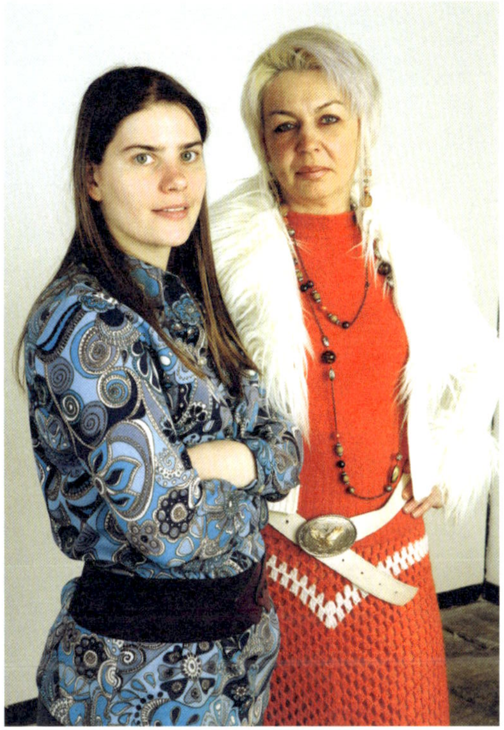

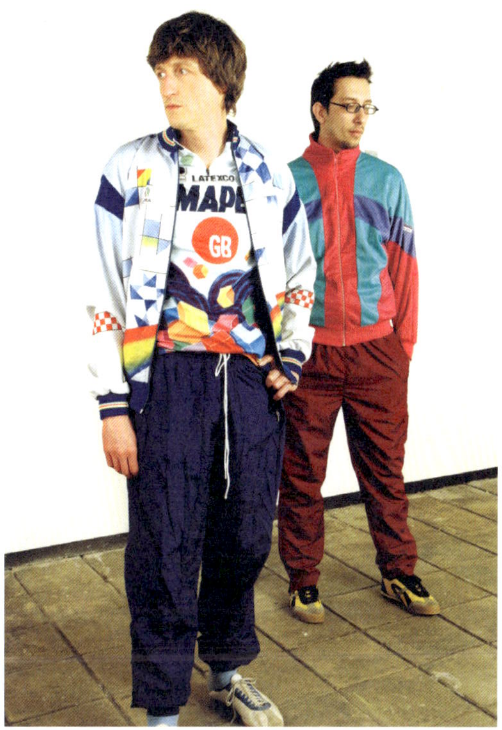

LATEXCO
MAPE
GB

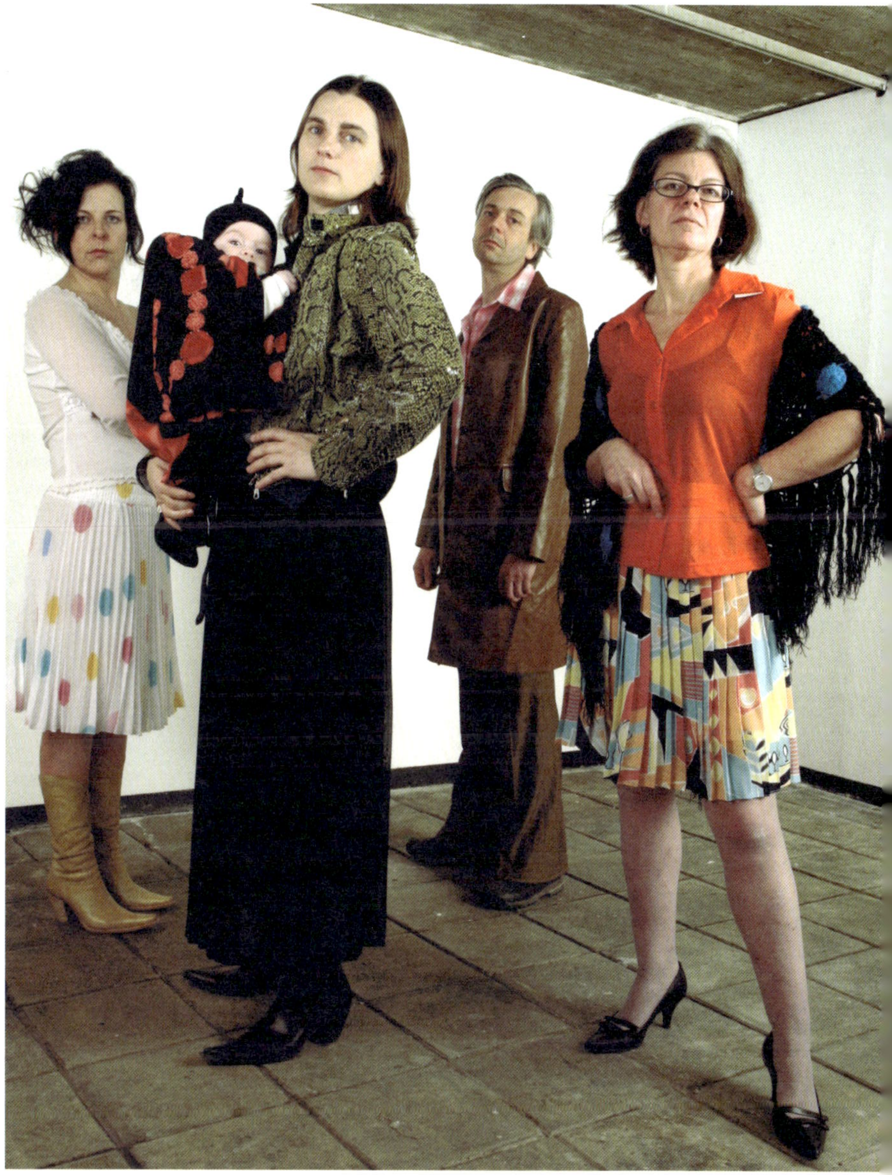

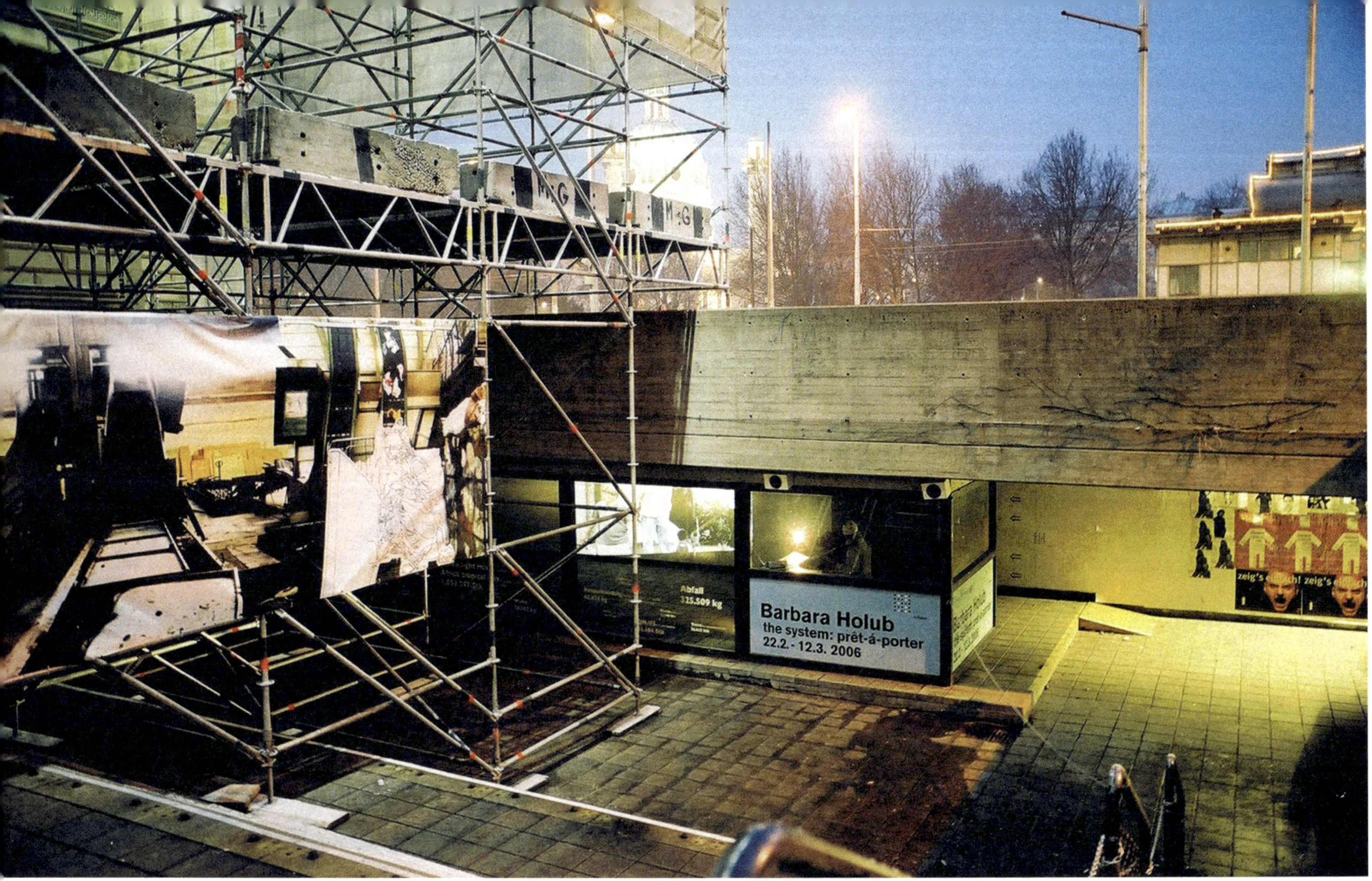

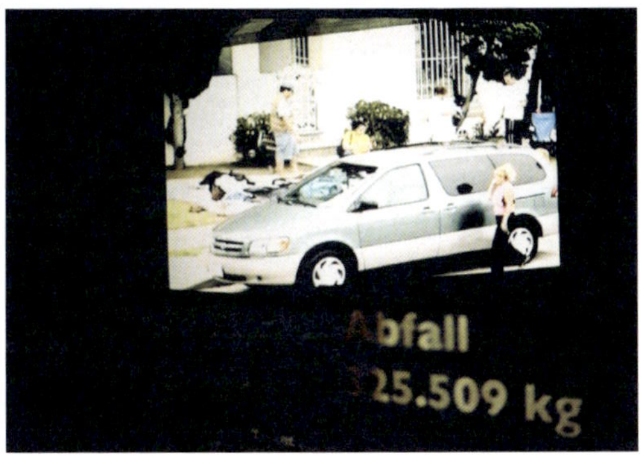

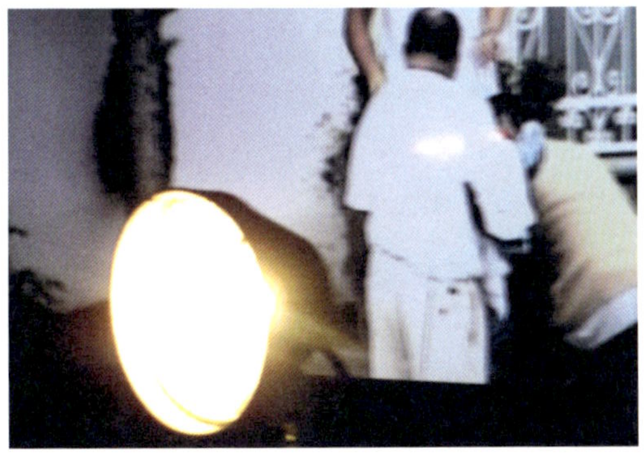

The video projection YARDSALE shows whimsical moments of a yard sale in Los Angeles, thus linking the trading of second-hand clothing between work and leisure. In the evening, a motion detector activated a searchlight that briefly illuminated the courtyard.

Die Video-Projektion YARDSALE zeigt skurrile Momente eines Gartenflohmarkts in Los Angeles und verknüpft somit das Handeln mit Secondhandkleidung zwischen Arbeit und Freizeit. Abends wurde durch einen Bewegungsmelder ein Suchscheinwerfer aktiviert, der den Hof

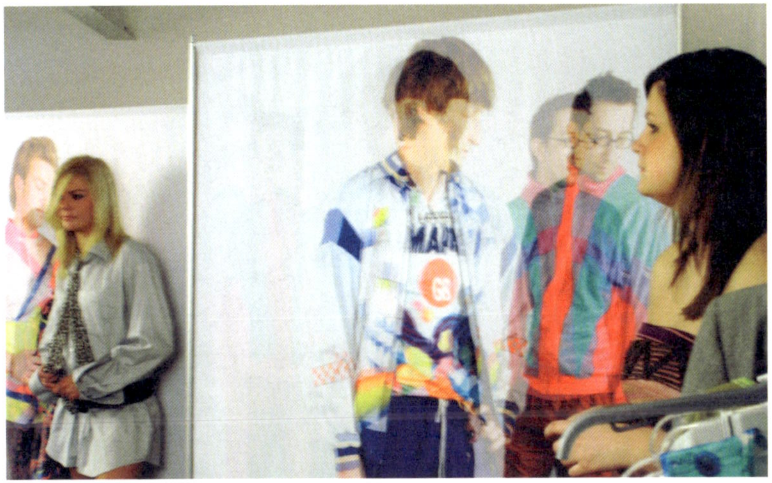

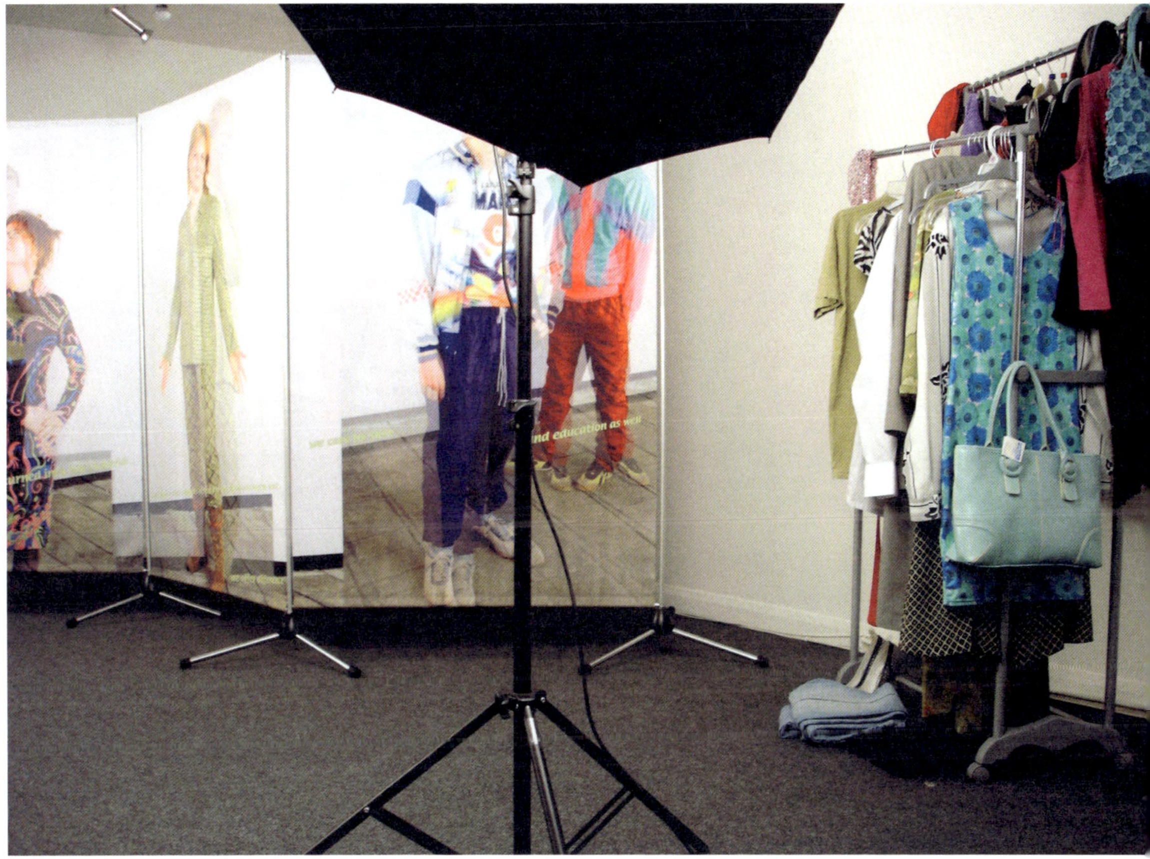

Photos from the fashion show in Vienna found their way into room dividers that served as the backdrop for a new fashion show as part of the *Slow* exhibition at Plymouth Arts Centre (this time in collaboration with the charity organization Oxfam).

Fotos der Modenschau in Wien fanden Eingang in Paravents, die als Hintergrund für eine neue Modenschau im Rahmen der Ausstellung *Slow* im Plymouth Arts Centre dienten (diesmal in Zusammenarbeit mit der Wohltätigkeitsorganisation Oxfam).

IV. *Casablanca Gallery*, curated by Silvia Eiblmayr, Städtische Galerie Fürstenfeld (Styria); Tobacco Factory Linz (Upper Austria), Tobacco Factory Hainburg (Lower Austria), 1994; Insam Gallery, Vienna, 1995; and elsewhere

Casablanca Galery, kuratiert von Silvia Eiblmayr, u. a. Städtische Galerie Fürstenfeld (Stmk.), Tabakfabrik Linz (OÖ), Tabakfabrik Hainburg (NÖ), 1994; Galerie Insam (Wien), 1995

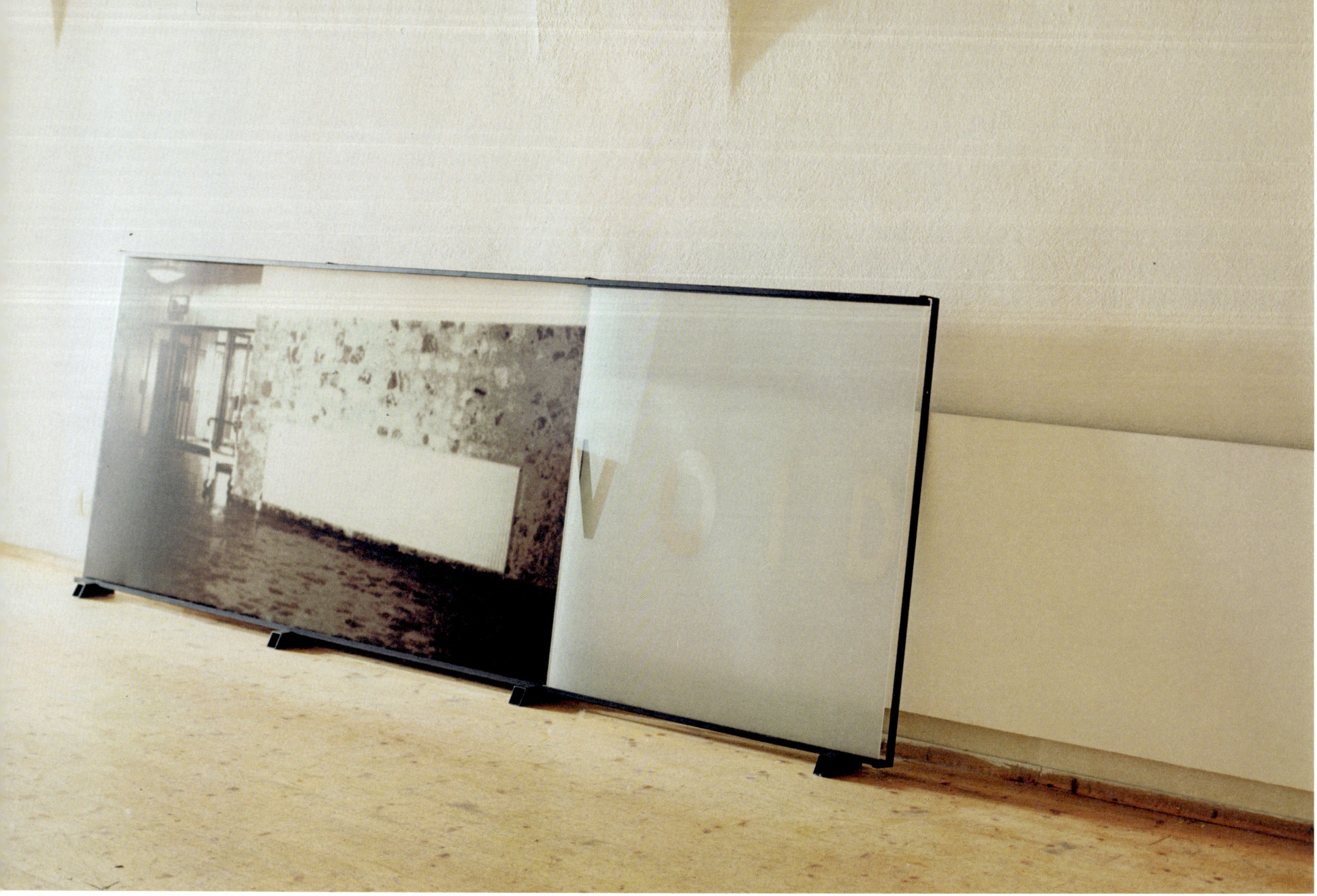

Exhibition view, Städtische Galerie Fürstenfeld, 1994

Ausstellungsansicht, Städtische Galerie Fürstenfeld, 1994

PERSONAL INVESTIGATION

PERSONAL INVESTIGATION is a reference to the work of the private detective or investigator. In her work, Holub explores internal structures of space and society and working conditions at the Austrian Tobacco Company, viewing them in relation to personal traces.

Printed in acrylic paint on acrylic glass, the overlapping handprints of selected workers raise questions about individuality and hierarchical structures. Whereas a single fingerprint can be used to identify a specific person, all evidence is obscured in this accumulation of so many, just as an individual can "dissolve" to the point of invisibility within the multitude of a community: it is neither possible to make out the individual, nor to distinguish in terms of gender, age, appearance, or between blue-collar and white-collar workers. The anonymous handprints are juxtaposed with Holub's personal correspondence: arranged in rows, the original color ribbons of her electric typewriter can be read as traces and yet—as a semantic unit—can no longer be deciphered. Was something left out here or does this represent the artist's current life without any "gaps"?

These personal objects are displayed alongside photographs of deserted situations in the factories that, among other things, cause Holub's artistic investigation to oscillate between private and public. Each image is accompanied by a sliding sheet of glass with a word sandblasted into its surface that might allude to the bureaucratic activities of a detective agency. The terms "PRIVATE," "SUBJECT," "VOID," "VALID," or "NEUTRAL" can be moved over each image so as to put a "stamp" on the situation depicted.

But what is "VALID"? And who decides? On the trail of the "truth"—similar to the random generator-controlled staff checks conducted on leaving the factory, intended to expose potential smugglers—visitors to the exhibition opening at Grita Insam Gallery were asked to empty their bags and allow the (mostly unremarkable) contents to be documented with an instant camera.[BR]

PERSONAL INVESTIGATION

PERSONAL INVESTIGATION referiert auf den englischen Begriff der Tätigkeit einer Privatdetektivin/eines Privatdetektivs *private investigator*. In ihrer gleichnamigen Arbeit spürt Holub interne räumliche und soziale Strukturen und Arbeitsverhältnisse in den Österreichischen Tabakwerken auf und setzt diese in Bezug zu persönlichen Spuren.

Die mit Acrylfarbe auf Acrylglas gedruckten und sich überlagernden Handabdrücke einzelner MitarbeiterInnen werfen Fragen nach Individualität und hierarchischen Strukturen auf. Während der einzelne Fingerabdruck zur eindeutigen Identifizierung einer Person führen kann, verschwindet jegliches Indiz in der Kumulation von vielen – so wie die Wahrnehmung des Individuums im Gefüge einer Gemeinschaft bis zu dessen „Auflösung" in den Hintergrund rücken kann: Weder ist der/die Einzelne erkennbar, noch ist hier eine Unterscheidung in Geschlecht, Alter, Aussehen bzw. zwischen ArbeiterInnen und Angestellten möglich. Den anonymen Handabdrücken ist die persönliche Korrespondenz Holubs gegenübergestellt: Die in Linien angeordneten originalen Farbbänder der verwendeten elektronischen Schreibmaschine sind als Spuren zu lesen, und dennoch – als semantische Einheit – nicht mehr dechiffrierbar. Wurde hier etwas ausgelassen oder doch das aktuelle Leben der Künstlerin „lückenlos" repräsentiert?

Diesen persönlichen Objekten werden Fotografien von menschenleeren räumlichen Situationen der Fabriken gegenübergestellt, die nicht zuletzt Holubs künstlerische Investigation zwischen Privatheit und Öffentlichkeit oszillieren lassen. Jedem Bild wird eine verschiebbare Glasplatte mit einem darauf sandgestrahlten Wort, das auf bürokratische Handlungen einer Detektei verweisen könnte, zur Seite gestellt: die Begriffe „PRIVAT", „BETRIFFT", „VOID", „VALID" oder „NEUTRAL" können über das jeweilige Bild verschoben werden und so der dargestellten räumlichen Situation einen „Stempel aufdrücken".

Was aber ist „gültig" („VALID")? Und wer entscheidet darüber? Auf den Spuren von „Wahrheit" wurden zur Eröffnung der Ausstellung in der Galerie Insam – in Anlehnung an die per Zufallsgenerator gesteuerte Kontrolle der MitarbeiterInnen beim Verlassen der Fabrik, um potenzielle SchmugglerInnen zu entlarven – die BesucherInnen gebeten, ihre Taschen auszuleeren, um deren (meist banalen Inhalt) mit einer Sofortbildkamera zu dokumentieren.[BR]

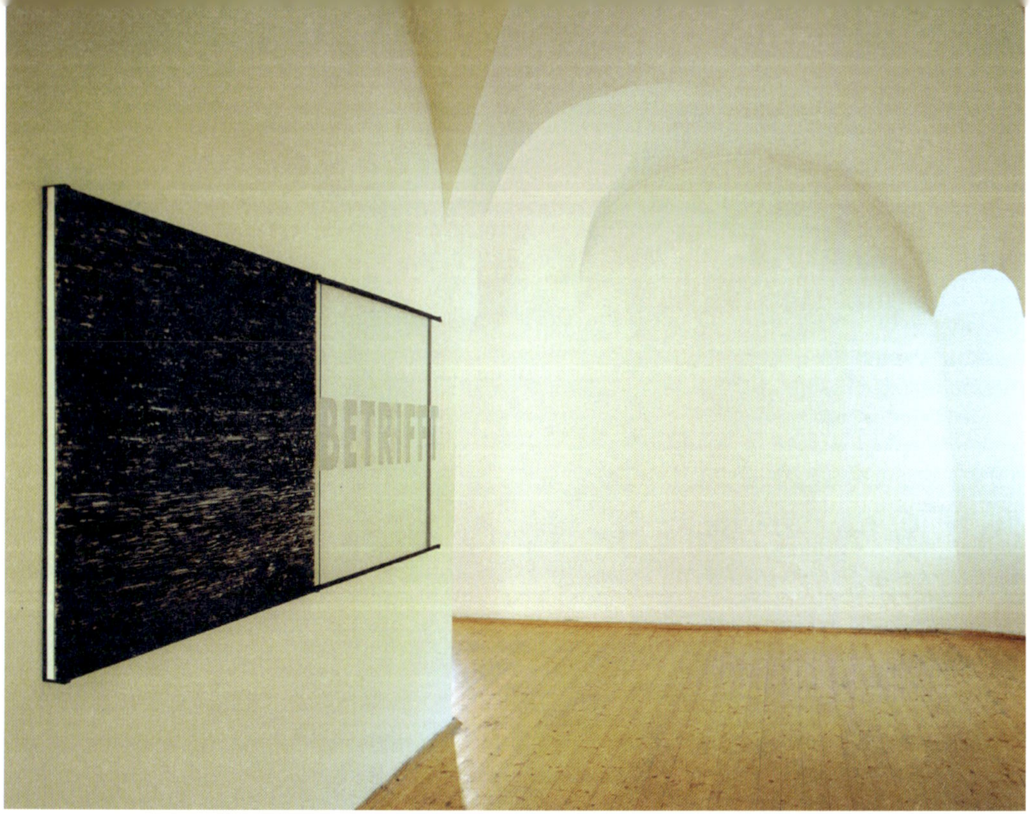

Exhibition view,
Städtische Galerie
Fürstenfeld, 1994

Ausstellungsansicht,
Städtische Galerie
Fürstenfeld, 1994

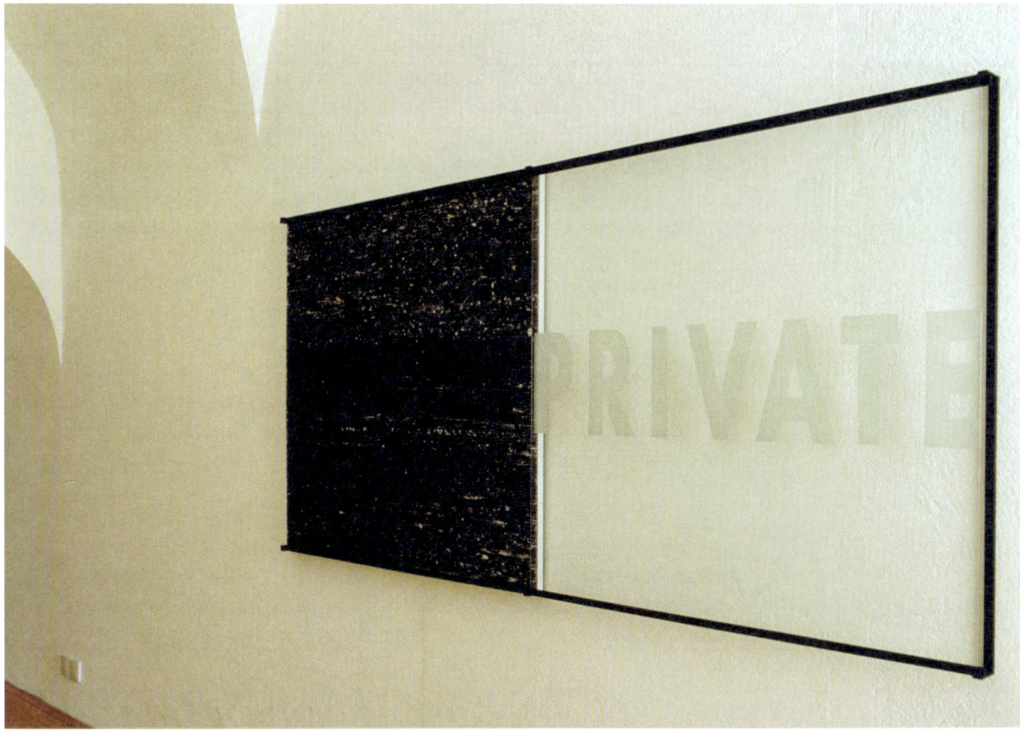

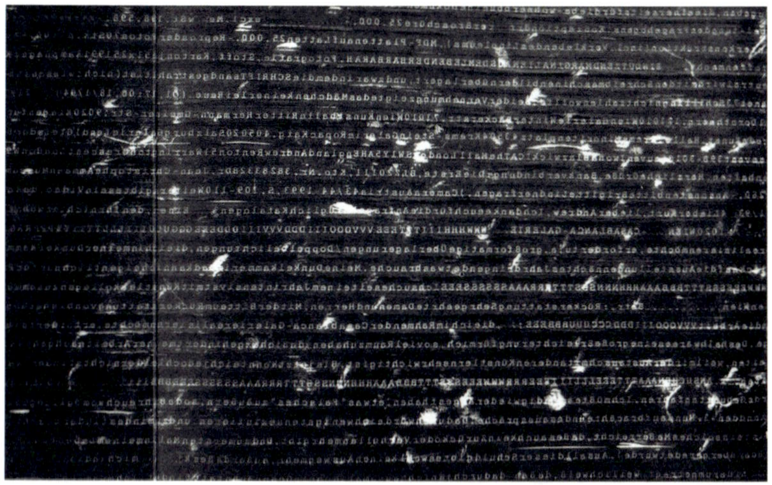

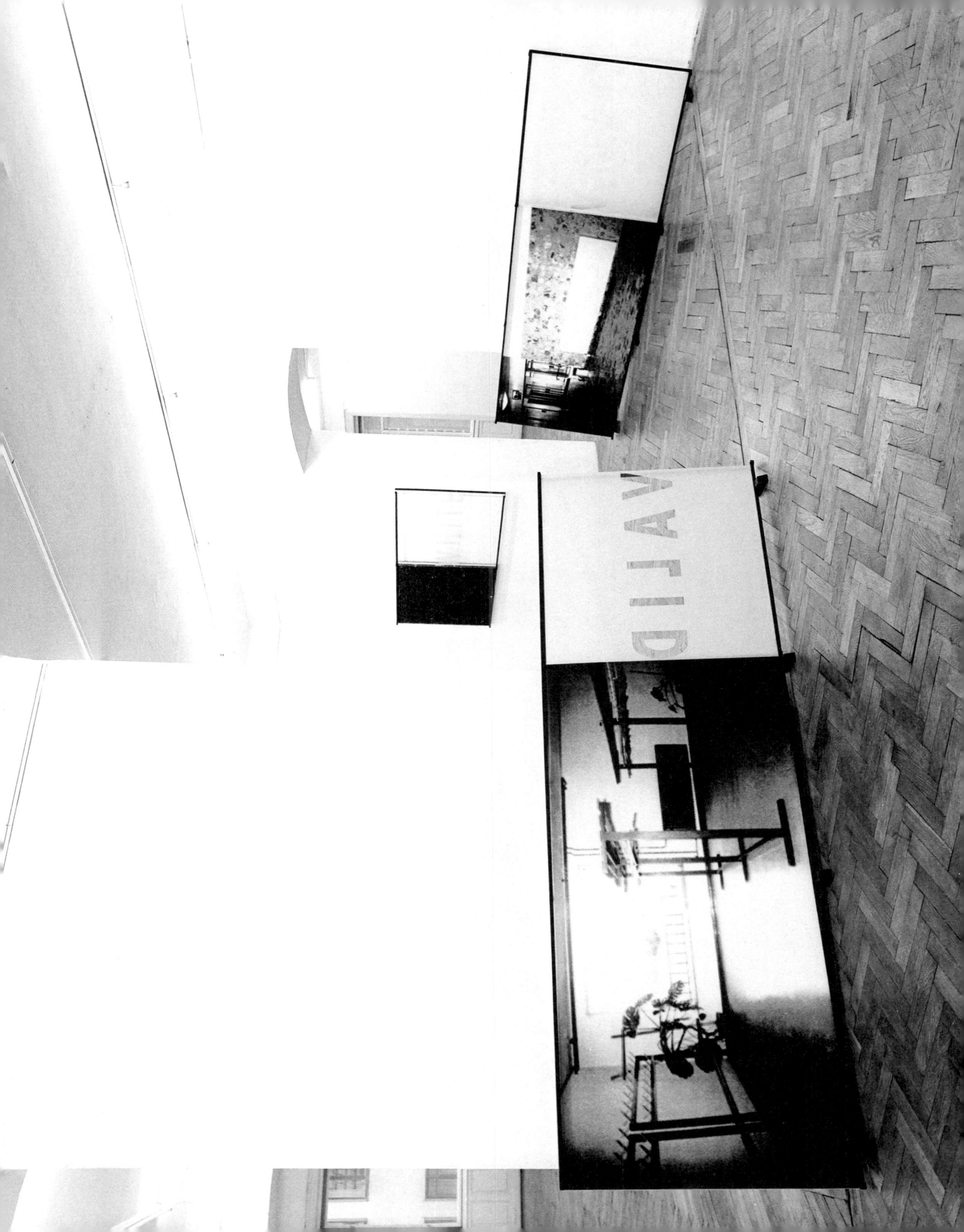

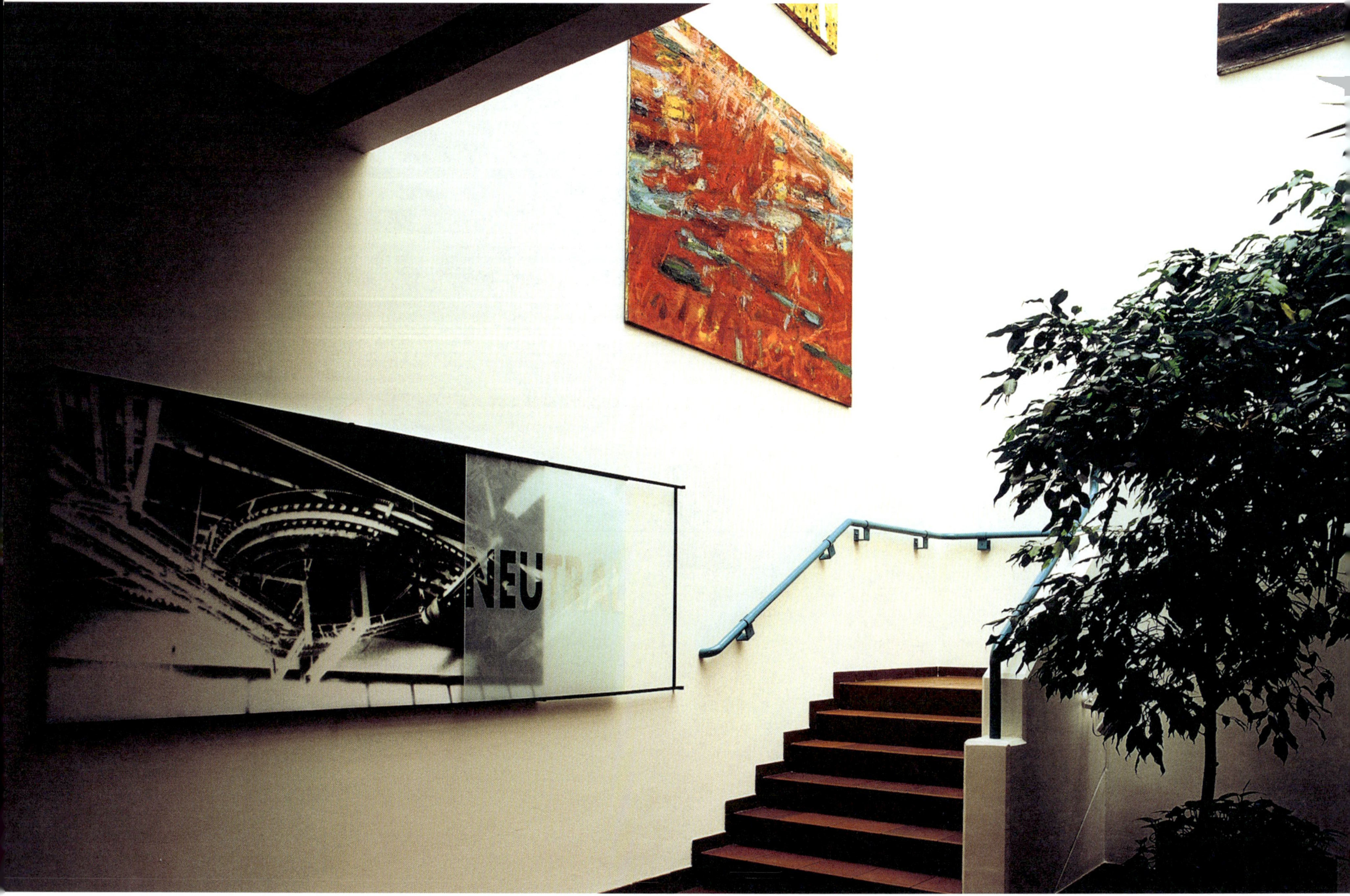
NEU

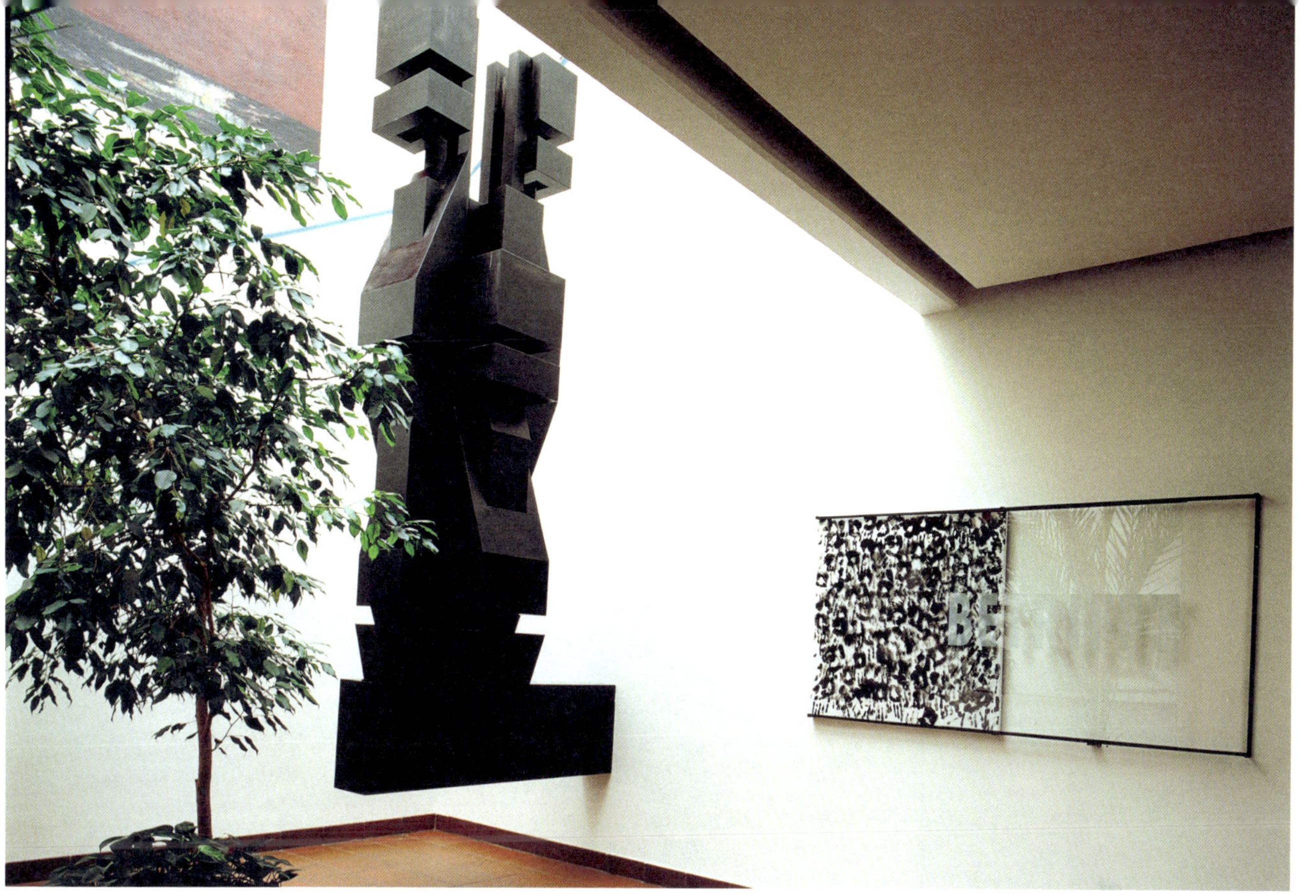

Tobacco Factory Linz, 1994

Tabakfabrik Linz, 1994

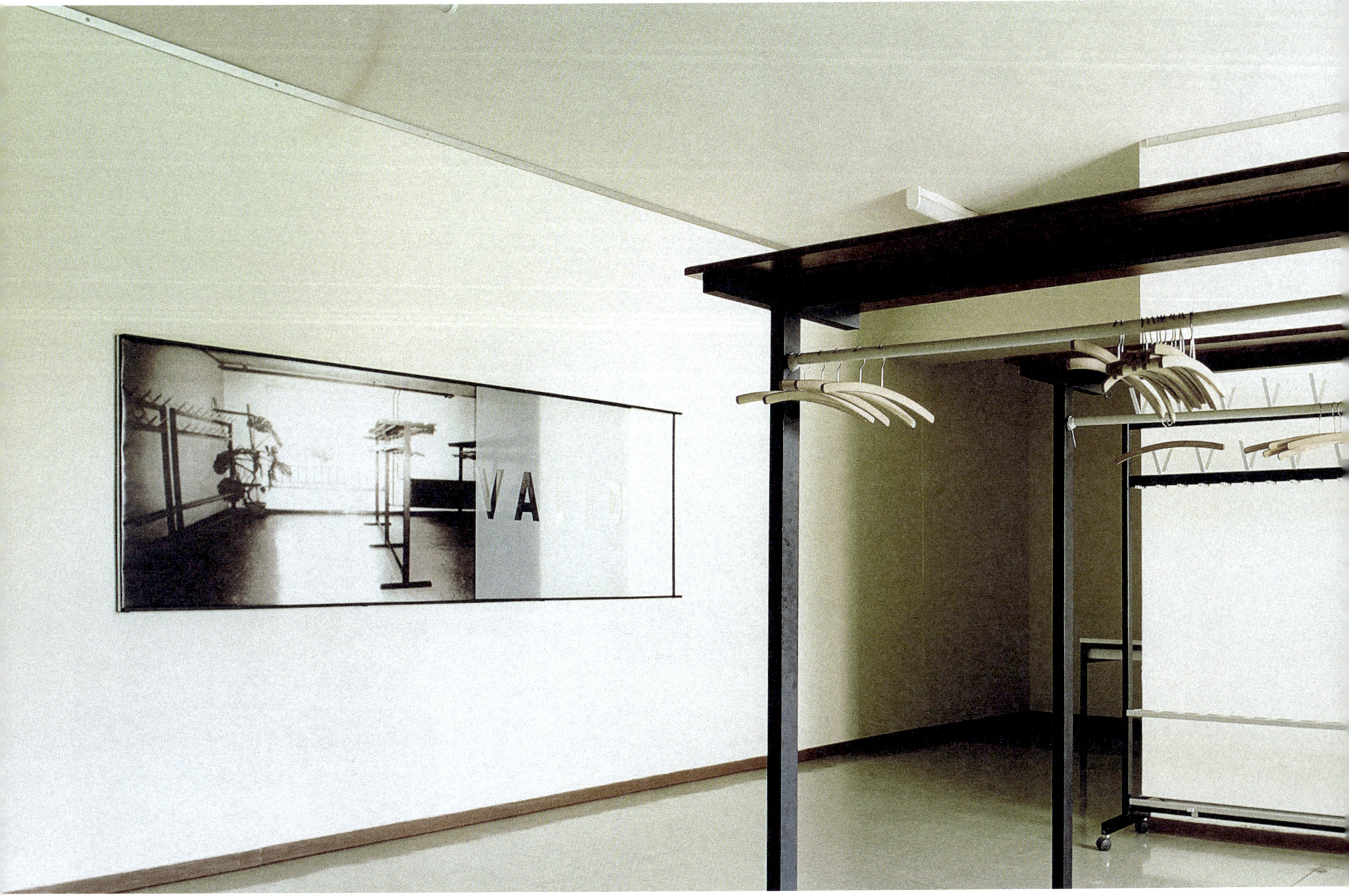
VA

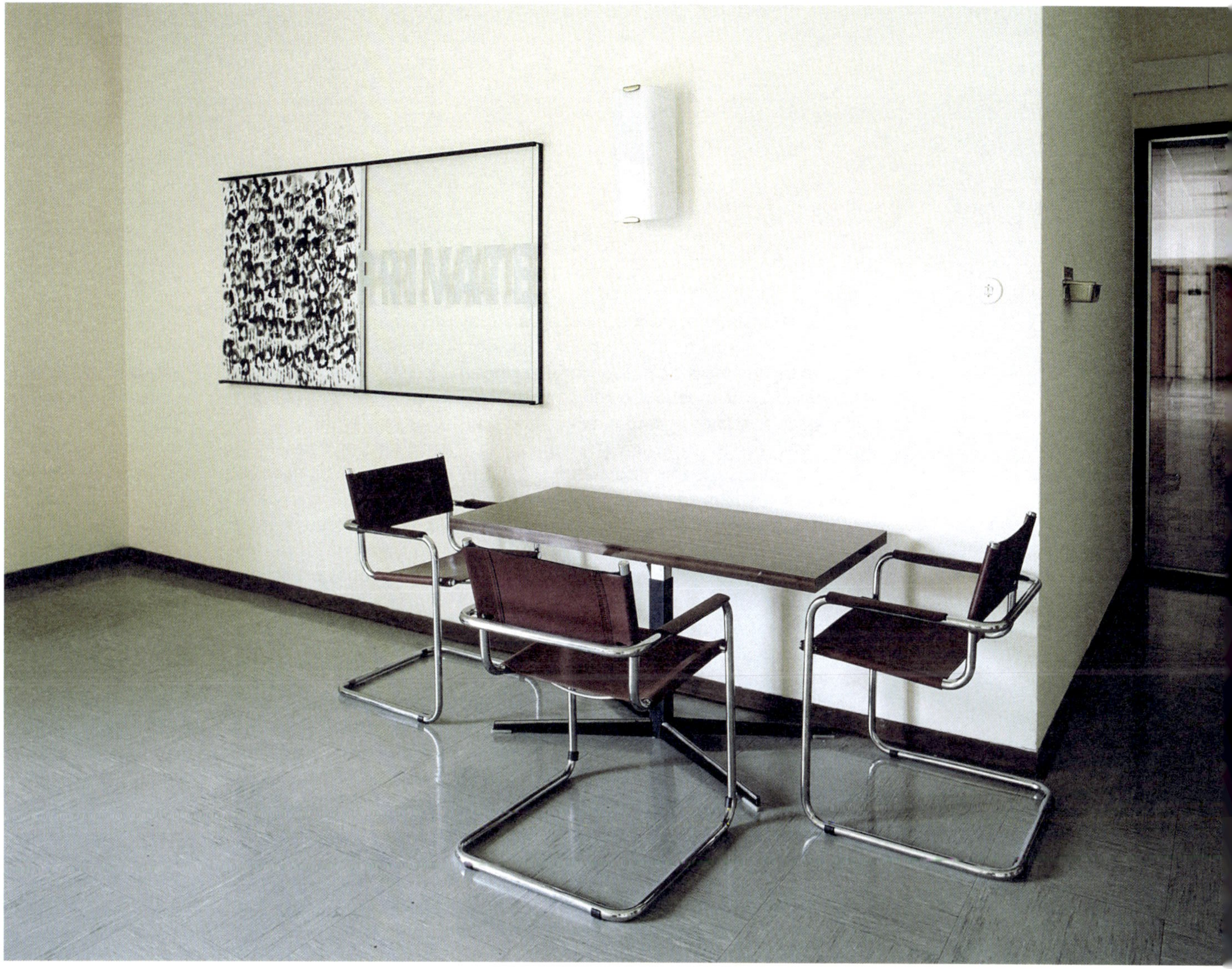

Tobacco Factory Hainburg, 1994

Tabakfabrik Hainburg, 1994

CARRIERS OF SECRETS

CARRIERS OF SECRETS, Holub's 1996 installation for Neue Galerie in Graz, comprises seven large jigsaw fragments upholstered with padded vinyl, like the office doors of executive business suites and secretive government institutions. To pass through such doors is to pass into a realm where secrets are divulged and kept—perhaps on pain of death or imprisonment. And yet, another association threatens to usurp this one. Because the eye tends to fill in the gaps when presented with fragments, it's easy to picture this whole room covered with vinyl, like the padded cell of a mental asylum. But are these images so very different? A form of madness arguably lurks at the centre of all government institutions, as any political satirist knows, and a padded office door may be a metaphor for the repression of madness, a symbol of madness held in check, or for the power that threatens to corrupt those who think themselves capable of wielding it without being morally scarred.

But closer inspection reveals more. For within each button of the vinyl is a peep-hole through which we can see a number. This number refers to images in the accompanying brochure of the foyers of iconic institutional buildings in Chicago: the City of Chicago Police Department, the Richard J. Daley Centre, the Everett Mc. Kinley Dirksen Building, to name a few. Psychologically speaking, then, it feels like we are inside some meta-institution—an Institution of Institutions—gazing upon the interiors of places where many secrets have been shared and kept, where the protocols of what is classified as "in the public interest" must be stringently followed. In her text "Art and Control: a Site-Specific Installation by Barbara Holub," Christa Steinle writes that secrets "draw their power from exclusion, they create a class division of knowers and non-knowers, of superior and inferior subjects." (Barbara Steinle, in: Holub [ed.], CARRIERS OF SECRETS, 1996). By placing us on the threshold of such divisions, CARRIERS OF SECRETS perhaps reminds us of one of art's signature characteristics: its ability to make us feel that we are on the cusp of gathering knowledge without ever quite achieving enlightenment; its tendency to prolong rather than resolve experience.[SA]

GEHEIMNISTRÄGER

Holubs 1996 für die Neue Galerie Graz geschaffene Installation GEHEIMNISTRÄGER besteht aus sieben großen gepolsterten Puzzleteilen aus Vinyl – wie die Bürotüren von Führungsetagen und verschwiegenen staatlichen Behörden. Wer durch eine solche Tür geht, betritt einen Raum, in dem Geheimnisse preisgegeben und gewahrt werden – vielleicht sogar unter Androhung von Tod oder Gefängnis. Da das Auge angesichts von Fragmenten versucht, die Zwischenräume zu füllen, stellt man sich alsbald den ganzen Raum gepolstert vor, wie die Gummizelle in einer Irrenanstalt. Aber ist eine Irrenanstalt tatsächlich etwas so anderes? Wohnt nicht staatlichen Institutionen ebenfalls ein gewisser Wahn inne? Eine gepolsterte Bürotür könnte also durchaus eine Metapher für die Verdrängung des Wahns sein, ein Sinnbild für den kontrollierten Wahn oder die Macht, die alle zu korrumpieren droht, die glauben, sie ausüben zu können, ohne moralisch Schaden zu nehmen.

Aber eine genauere Betrachtung enthüllt noch mehr. Denn in jedem Puzzleteil ist ein Knopf der Polsterung durch einen „Spion" ersetzt. Durch diesen erblickt man jeweils eine Zahl, die auf eine in der Begleitbroschüre abgebildete Eingangshalle einer ikonischen Chicagoer Institution verweist: etwa einer bekannten Polizeistation, des Richard J. Daley Centre oder des Everett McKinley Dirksen Courthouse. Psychologisch gesehen scheinen wir uns also in einer Meta-Institution – einer Institution der Institutionen – zu befinden und das Innere von Orten zu betrachten, an denen zahlreiche Geheimnisse geteilt und gewahrt wurden, streng die Protokolle der Geheimhaltung „im öffentlichen Interesse" zu beachten sind. In ihrem Text „Kunst und Kontrolle. Zu einer Rauminstallation von Barbara Holub" schreibt Christa Steinle: „Geheimnisse beziehen ihre Macht aus dem Ausschluss, sie schaffen eine Klassenteilung, die Mitwisser und die Nichtswisser, superiore und inferiore Subjekte." (Barbara Steinle, in: Holub [Hg.], GEHEIMNISTRÄGER, 1996) GEHEIMNISTRÄGER versetzt uns an die Schwelle solcher Unterscheidungen und gemahnt so vielleicht an eines der charakteristischen Merkmale der Kunst: dass sie uns das Gefühl vermittelt, wir seien im Begriff, Wissen zu erlangen, ohne tatsächlich Aufklärung zu erfahren; dass sie Erfahrungen eher intensiviert, als sie in Lösungen zu überführen.[SA]

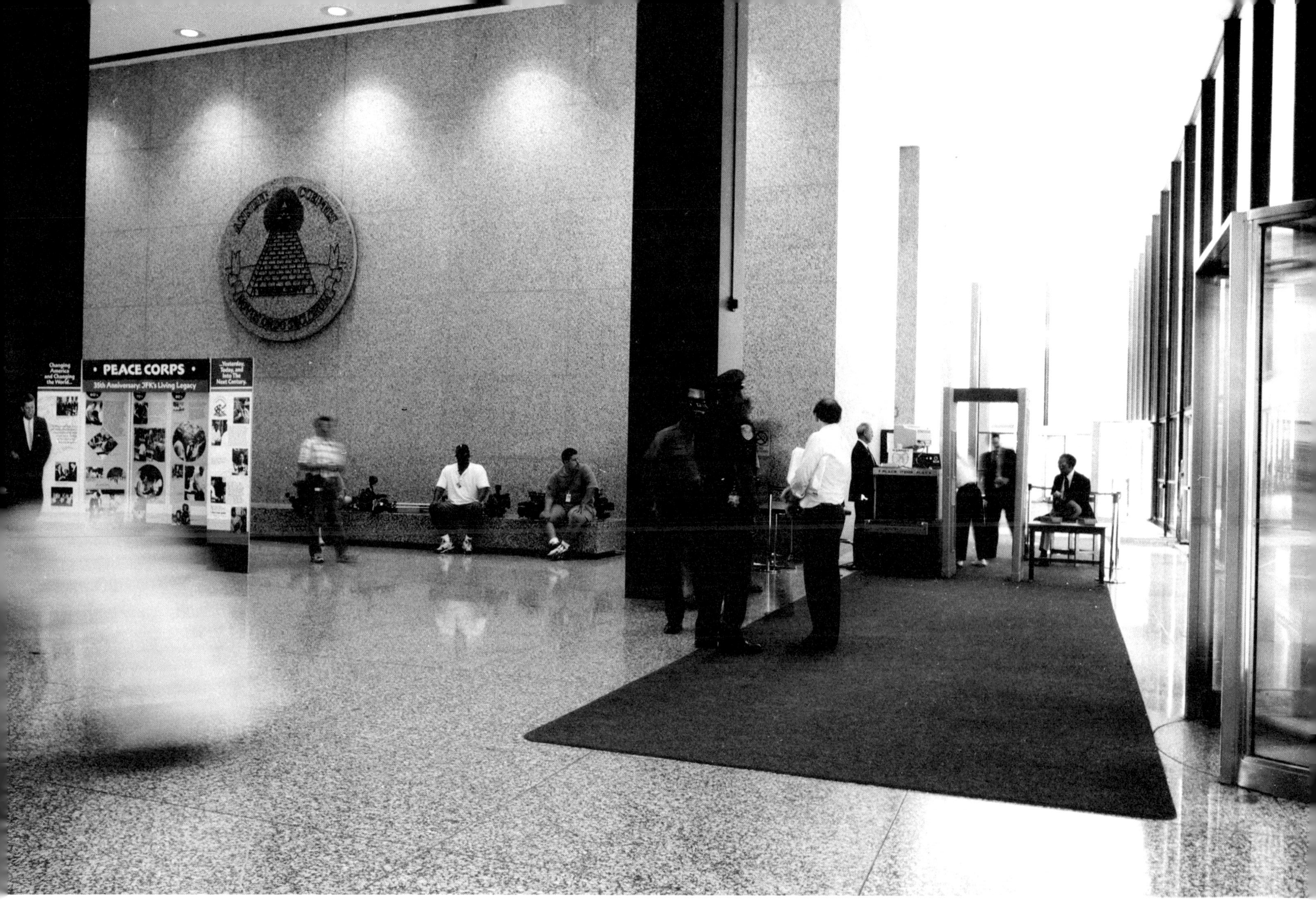

Everett Mc. Kinley Dirksen Building (Courthouse, 219 S. Dearborn)

Everett Mc. Kinley Dirksen Building (Courthouse, 219 S. Dearborn)

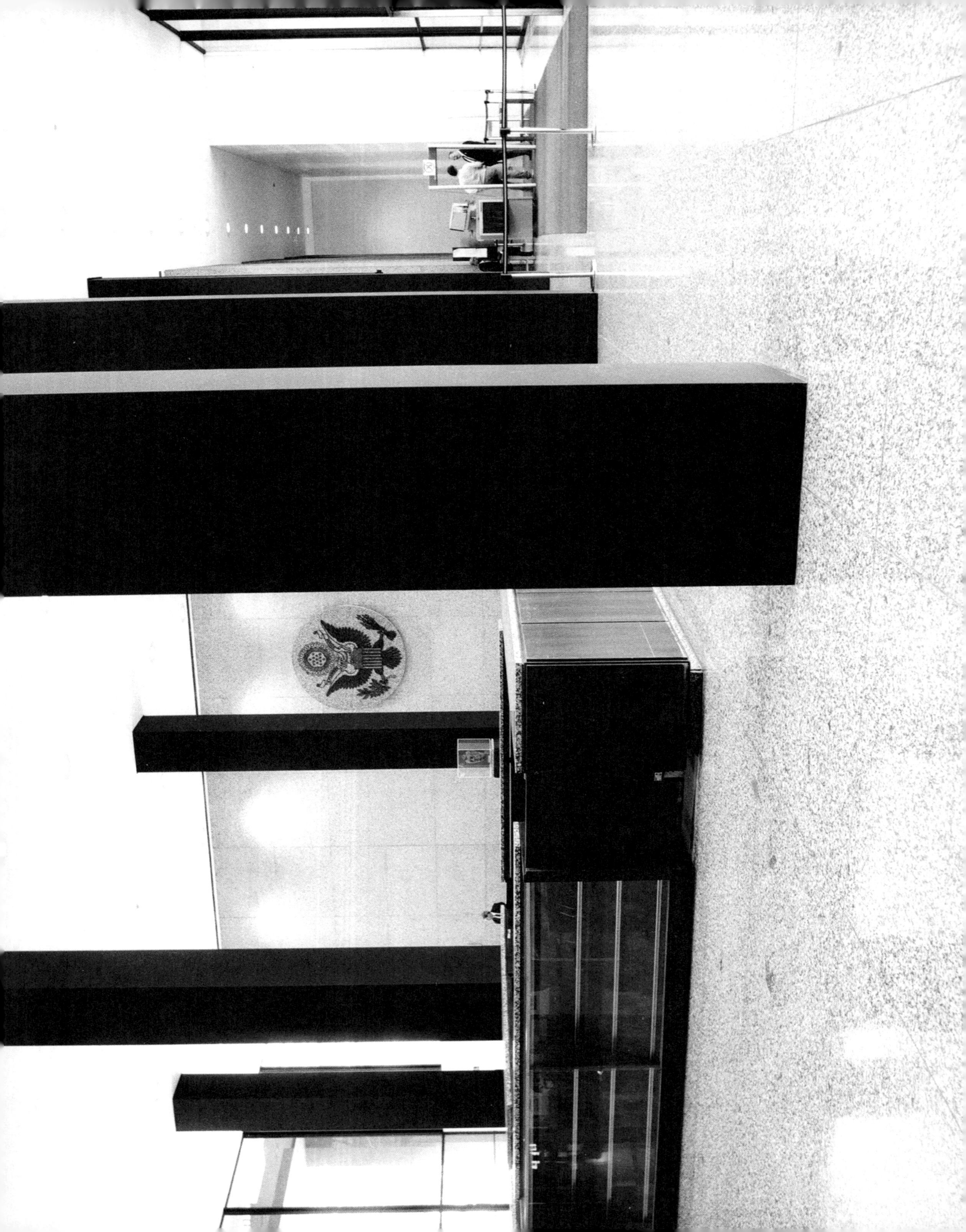

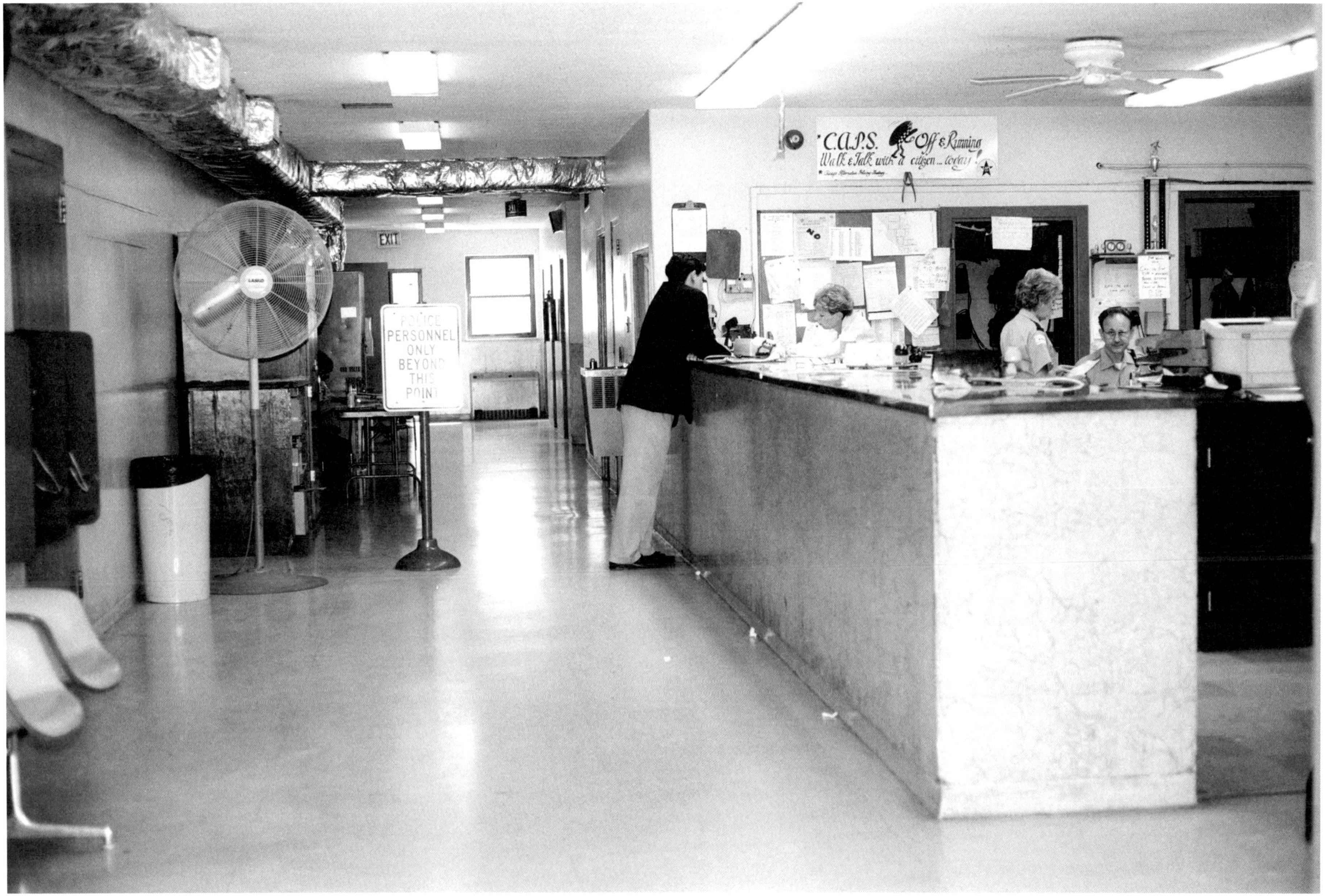

City of Chicago Police Department (113 W. Chicago)

City of Chicago Police Department (113 W. Chicago)

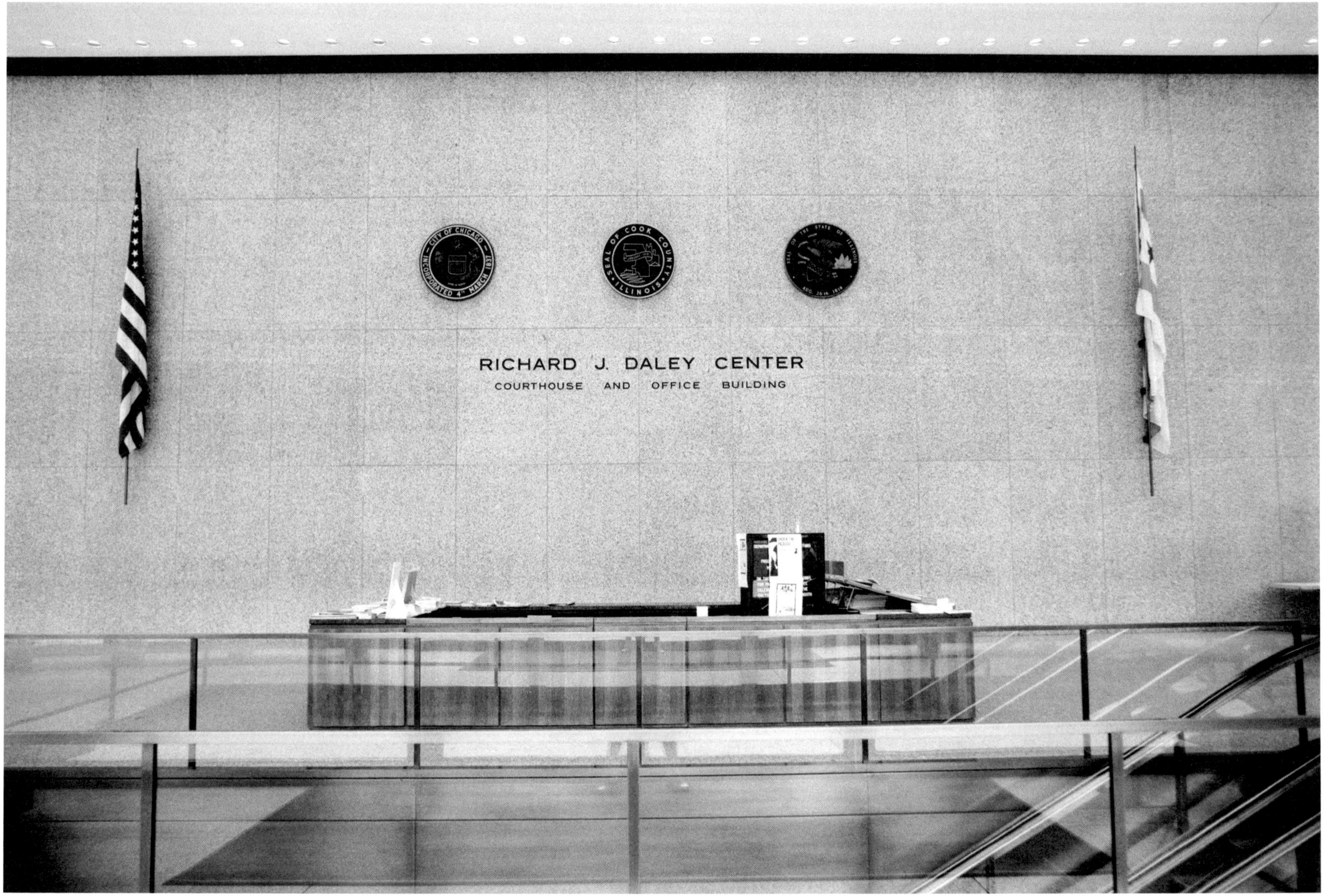

Richard J. Daley Centre
(Chicago Civic Centre, 50 W. Washington)

Richard J. Daley Centre
(Chicago Civic Centre, 50 W. Washington)

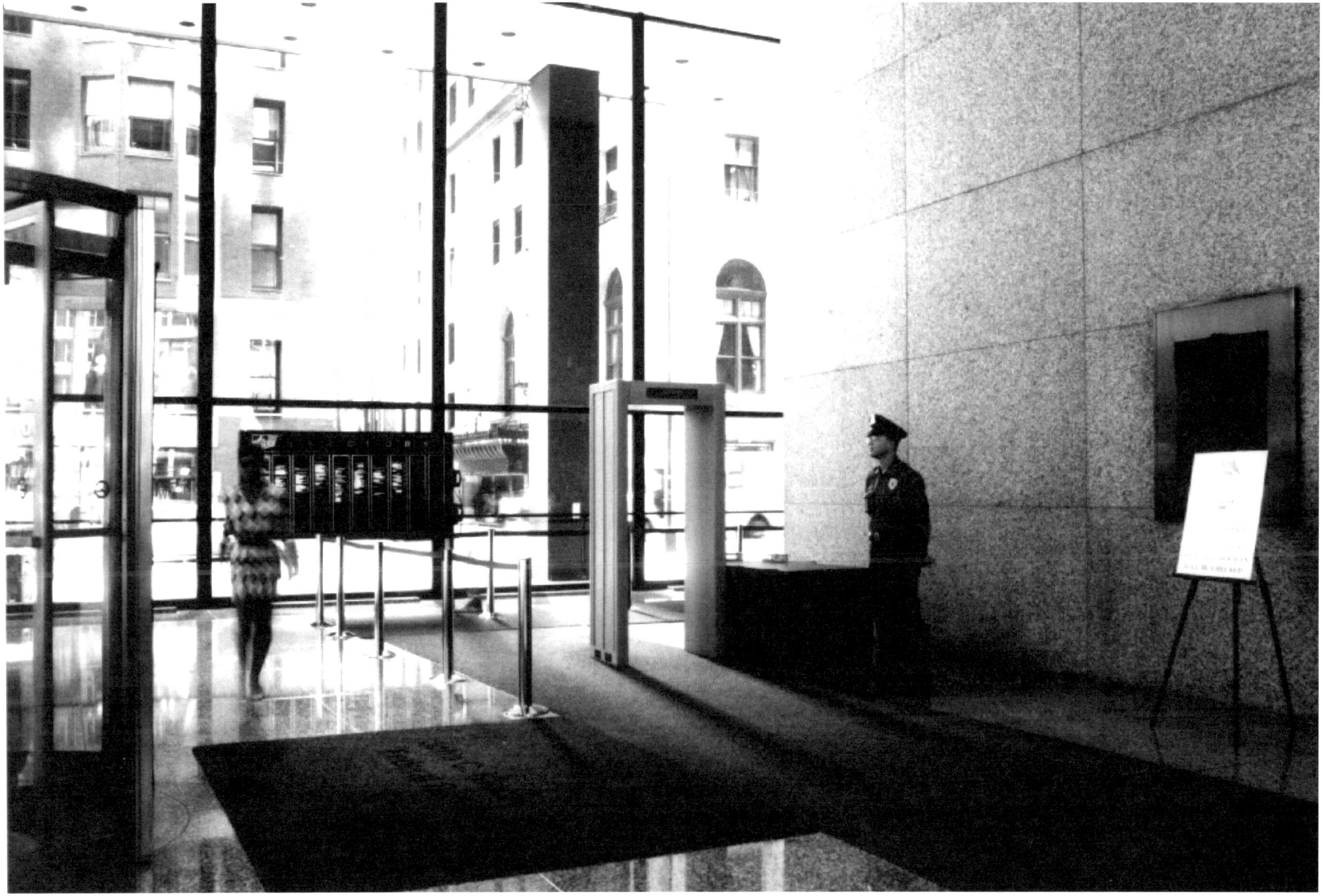

John C. Kluczynski Building (Federal Building, 230 S. Dearborn)

John C. Kluczynski Building (Federal Building, 230 S. Dearborn)

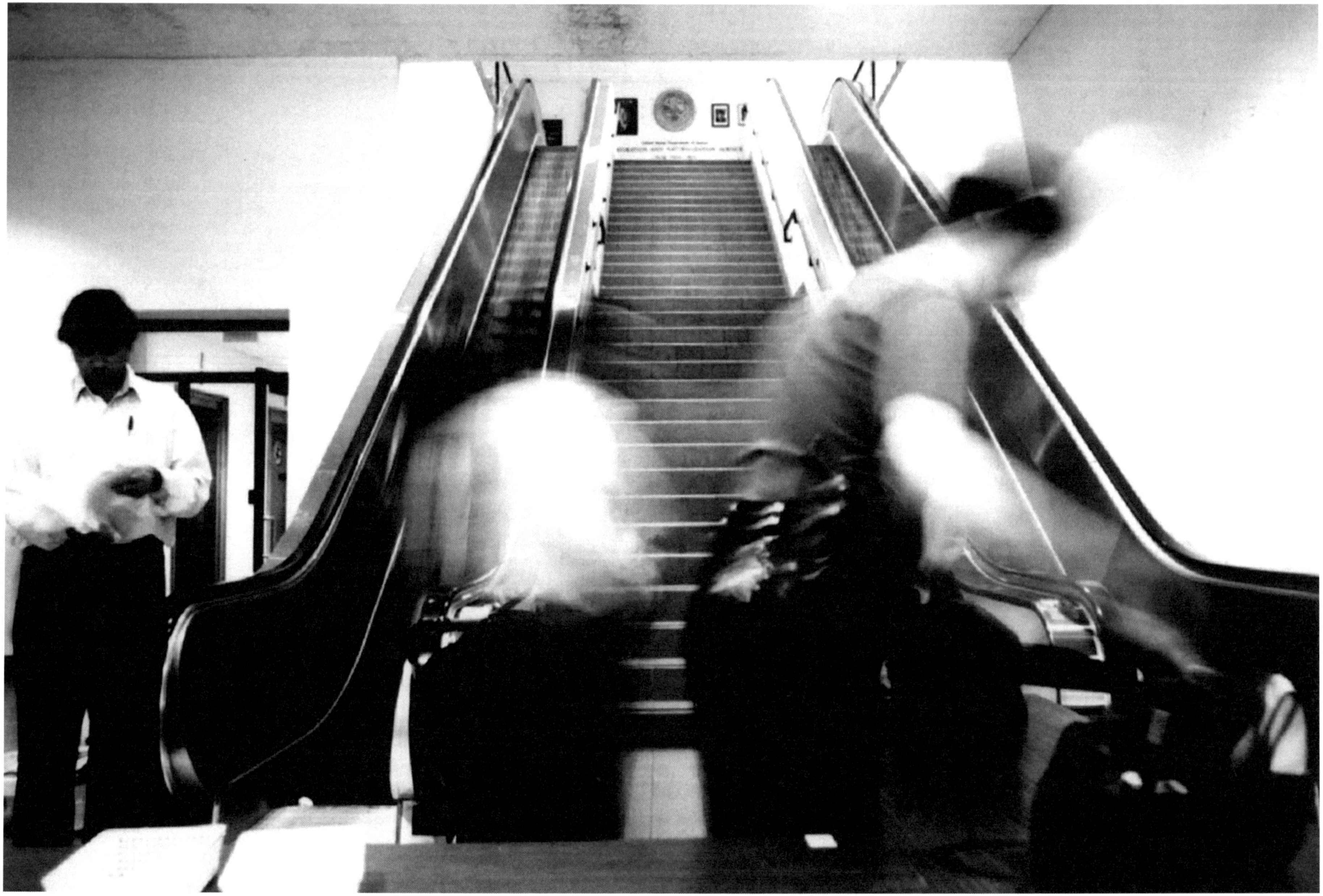

Immigration and Naturalization Service (10 E. Jackson)

Immigration and Naturalization Service (10 E. Jackson)

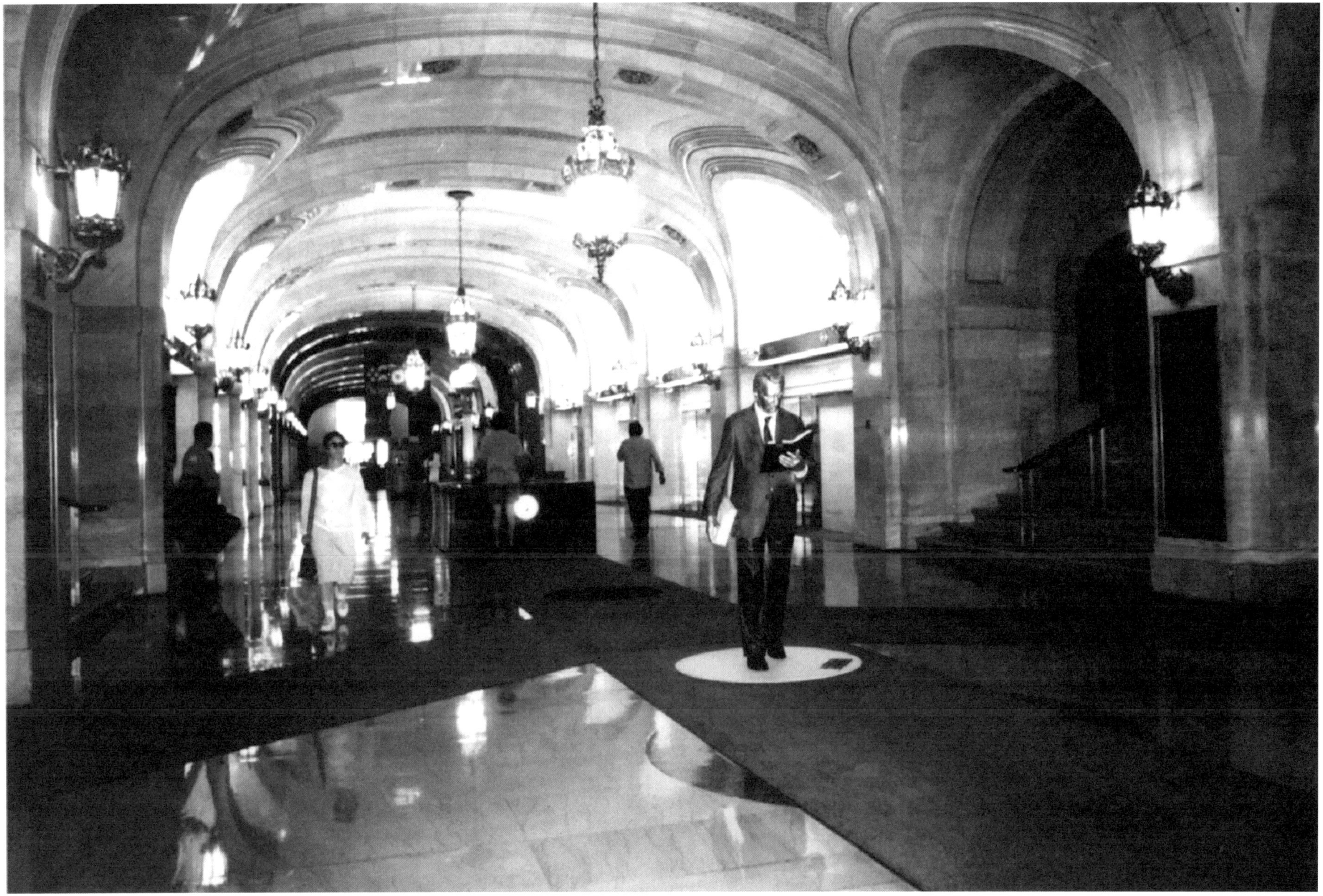

Cook County Building (118 N. Clark)

Cook County Building (118 N. Clark)

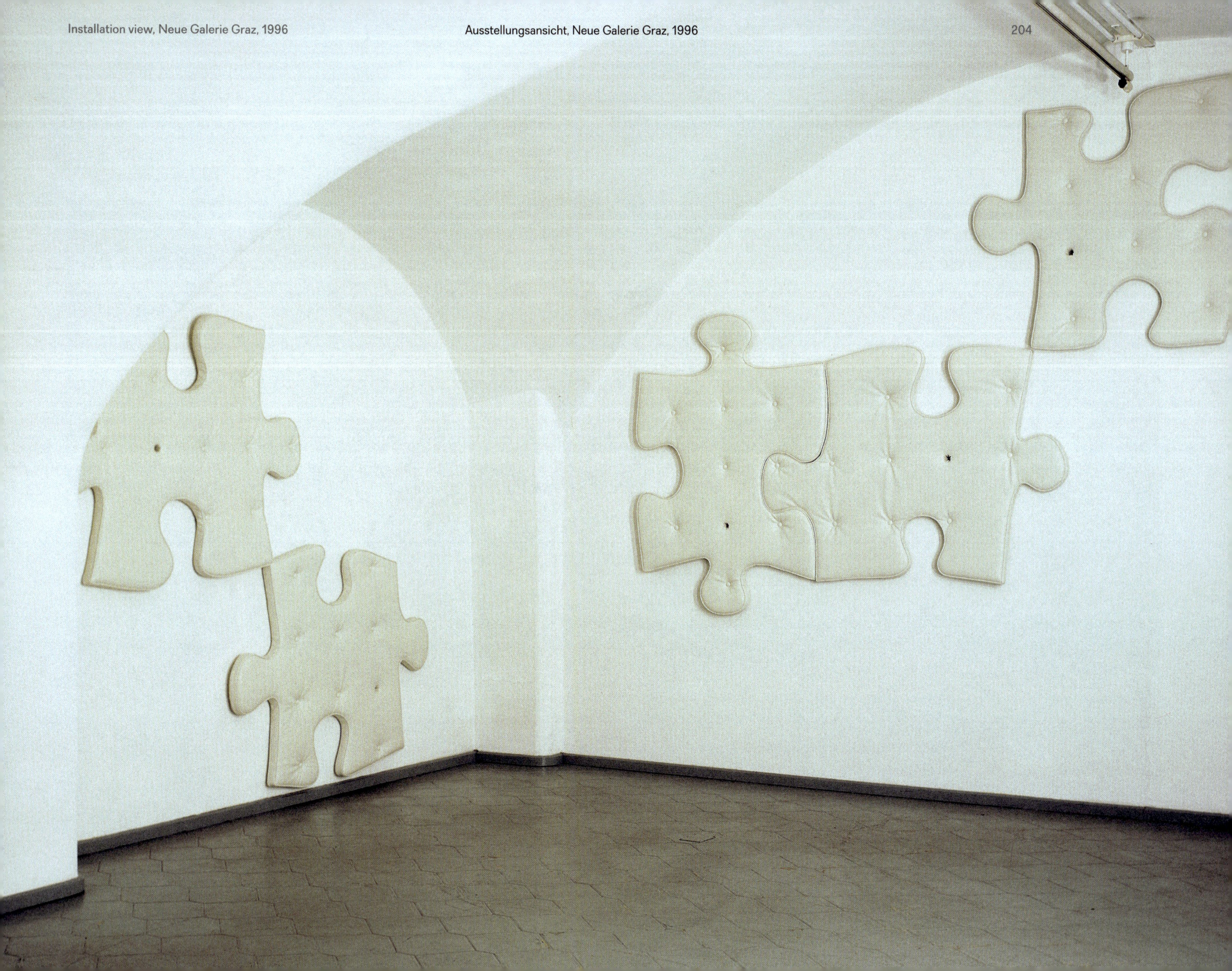

Installation view, Neue Galerie Graz, 1996

Ausstellungsansicht, Neue Galerie Graz, 1996

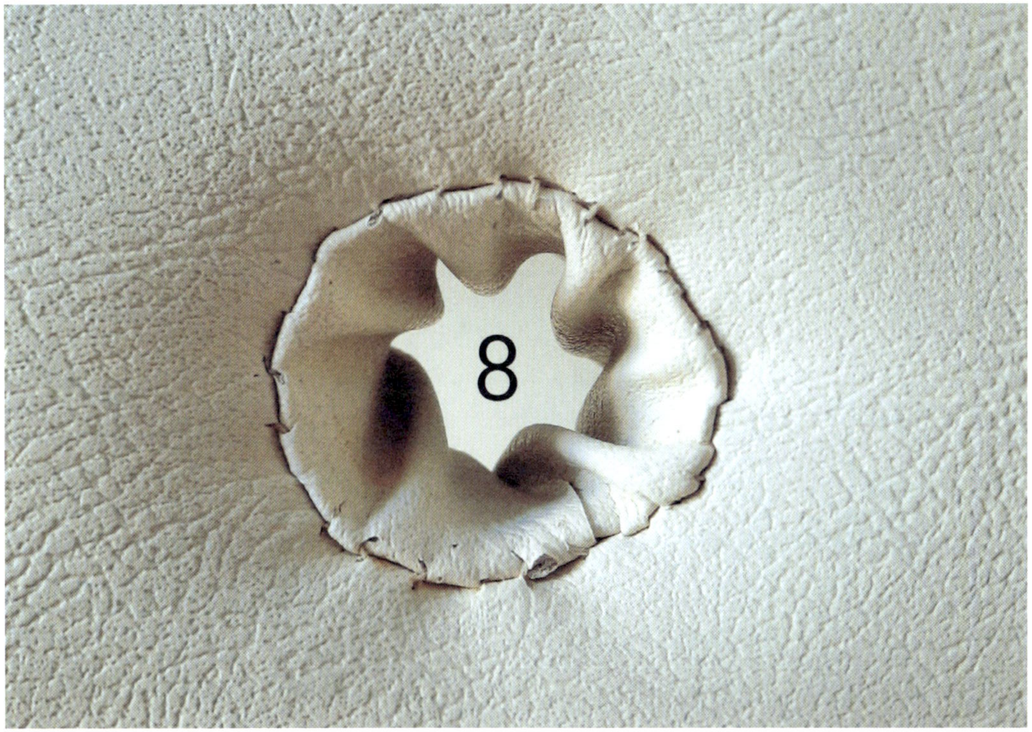

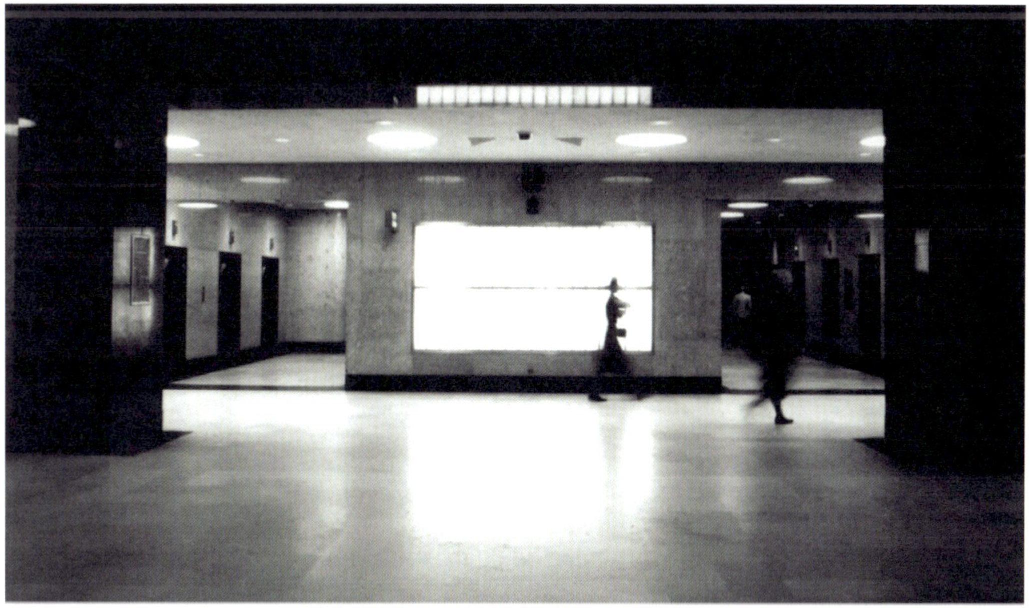

8 Chicago Board of Trade (400 P. LaSalle)

8 Chicago Board of Trade (400 S. LaSalle)

The Island is What the Sea Surrounds, curated by Maren Richter, European Capital of Culture Valletta 2018 (Malta), 2018

TIMES OF DILEMMA

By using the tradition of Għana, TIMES OF DILEMMA encouraged the Maltese residents to address current social and urban conflicts in a public performance. As a collaborative process, through workshops, transparadiso invited Għana singers (*għannejja*) and renowned Maltese authors to produce a contemporary Għana dialog, transforming the spontaneously improvised traditional Maltese singing of Għana into a scripted dialog that discusses the rapid transformation of Malta and the contradictory interests between economic prosperity and regaining communal values. In this way, transparadiso created a "situation" for the Maltese to take action.

For the *għannejja's* performances, transparadiso conceived two large megaphone sculptures, offering a sound transfer of 320 meters between St. Roche Chapel (from where the priest used to preach during the times of the plague) and Manoel Island, which is being transformed into an exclusive new urban development for the rich. In this way, the dialog between the two locations addresses today's "plague," namely uncontrolled urban development in Malta.

These contemporary Għana dialogs reposition the (today under-recognized) tradition of folk singing in "high culture" and explore Għana as an artistic method for addressing conflicts in an open process, highlighting the potential of poetics as subtle means for activism—as silent activism. The *għannejja* were challenged with the task of committing to a new format, the scripted text (since Għana is usually still performed as *spirtu pront* or "spontaneous improvisation") and it equally required the confidence of the renowned Maltese authors to offer their texts to be transformed into Għana dialogs. In this way, TIMES OF DILEMMA not only addresses Maltese society's burning questions, it also transgresses the borders of "high culture" and "folk culture" in a unique format.[BS]

A project by transparadiso

Għannejja: Il-Bukku Vince, Angelo Theuma, Mikkelina, Josmick Agius, and Maria Agius/Oħt iż -Żebbuġin'
Guitarists: John Saliba, Victor Grech, Frans Casha and Ruben Schembri
Texts for the Għana dialog by Jean Paul Borg, Jo Burden, and Immanuel Mifsud
Coordination of the performance of the Għana dialogs: Rachelle Deguara with Il-Bukku Vince, Angelo Theuma, Mikkelina and Josmick Agius

The Island is What the Sea Surrounds, kuratiert von Maren Richter, Europäische Kulturhauptstadt Valletta 2018 (Malta), 2018

TIMES OF DILEMMA

Anknüpfend an die maltesische Għana-Tradition lud transparadiso Għana-SängerInnen (*għannejja*) und renommierte AutorInnen ein, in einem gemeinschaftlichen Prozess und öffentlichen Workshops zeitgenössische Għana-Dialoge zu entwickeln, die den *spirtu pront*, den spontan improvisierten traditionellen Għana-Gesang, in geskriptete Dialoge über die ungehemmte urbane Transformation in Malta und die widerstreitenden Interessen von wirtschaftlichem Wohlstand und der Neu-Etablierung von Gemeinschaftswerten überführen sollten. Damit kreierte transparadiso eine „Situation", in der MalteserInnen aktiv werden konnten.

Für die Aufführungen durch die *għannejja* entwarf transparadiso zwei große Megafon-Skulpturen, die imstande waren, den Schall 320 Meter weit, von der Kapelle St. Roche in Valletta (von wo aus die Priester in Pestzeiten zu predigen pflegten) bis zur an private Investoren verkaufte Manoel-Insel zu tragen, die gerade in ein exklusives neues Quartier für Wohlhabende umgeplant wurde. Auf diese Weise brachte der Dialog zwischen den beiden Orten die heutige „Pest", die unkontrollierte Stadtentwicklung auf Malta, zur Sprache.

Die zeitgenössischen Għana-Dialoge transportierten die heute gering geschätzte Volksliedtradition in die „Hochkultur" und erprobten Għana als künstlerische Methode zur Austragung von Konflikten, das Potenzial von Poesie als subtiles Mittel für stillen Aktivismus. TIMES OF DILEMMA forderte die *għannejja* heraus, sich auf ein neues Format einzulassen, ebenso wie die maltesischen AutorInnen ihre Texte in der Versform von Għana-Dialogen schreiben sollten. So setzte sich TIMES OF DILEMMA nicht nur mit brennenden Fragen der maltesischen Gesellschaft auseinander, sondern überschritt auch auf einzigartige Weise die Grenzen zwischen „Hochkultur" und „Volkskultur".[BS]

Ein Projekt von transparadiso

Għannejja: Il-Bukku Vince, Angelo Theuma, Mikkelina, Josmick Agius und Maria Agius/Oħt iż -Żebbuġin'
Gitarristen: John Saliba, Victor Grech, Frans Casha und Ruben Schembri
Texte für die Għana-Dialoge: Jean Paul Borg, Jo Burden und Immanuel Mifsud
Koordination der Aufführung der Għana-Dialoge: Rachelle Deguara in Zusammenarbeit mit Il-Bukku Vince, Angelo Theuma, Mikkelina und Josmick Agius.

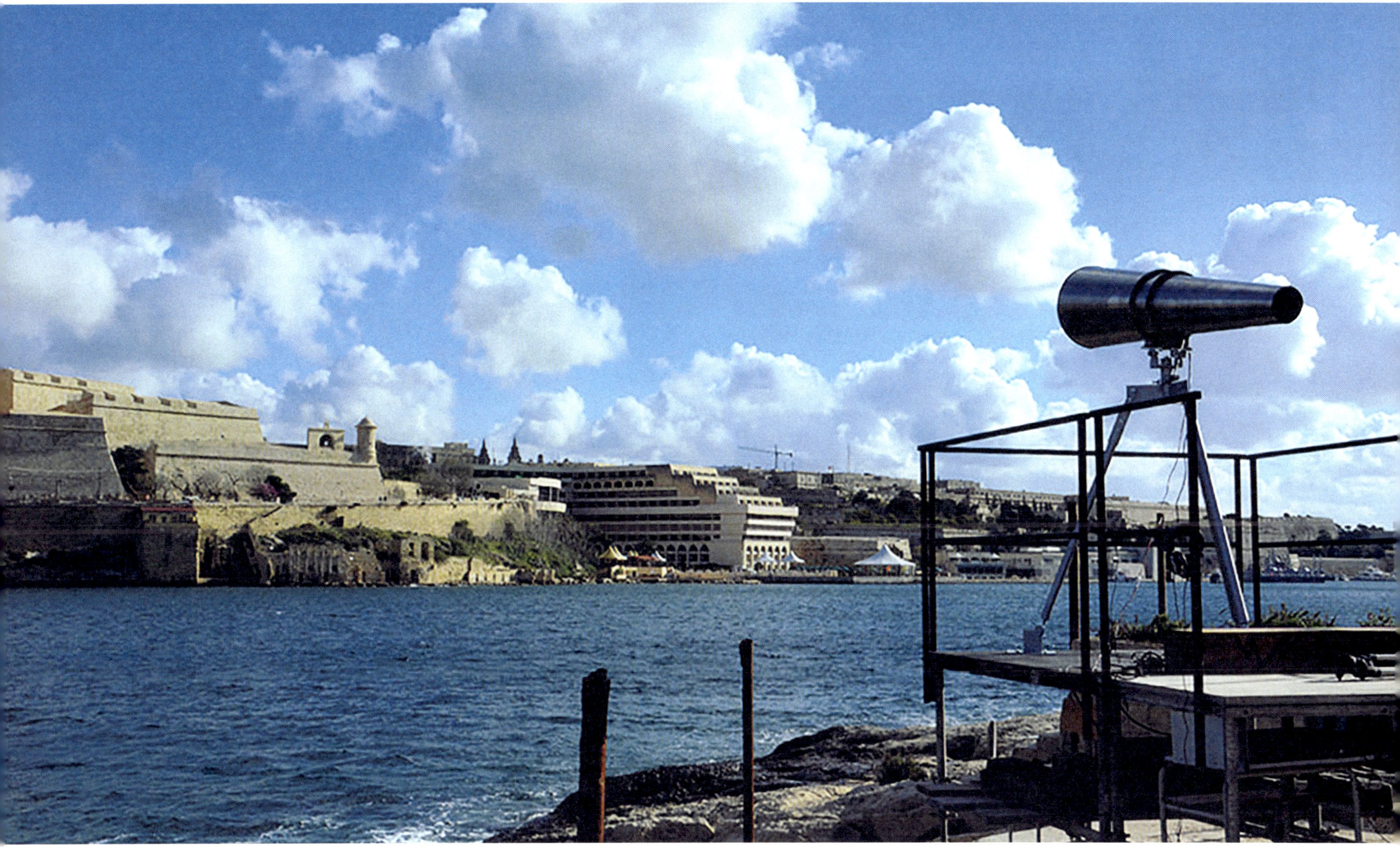

Dialog between Manoel Island and St. Roche Chapel / Valletta—over a distance of 320 m across the sea

Dialog zwischen Manoel Island und der Kapelle St. Roche / Valletta – über eine Entfernung von 320 m über das Meer

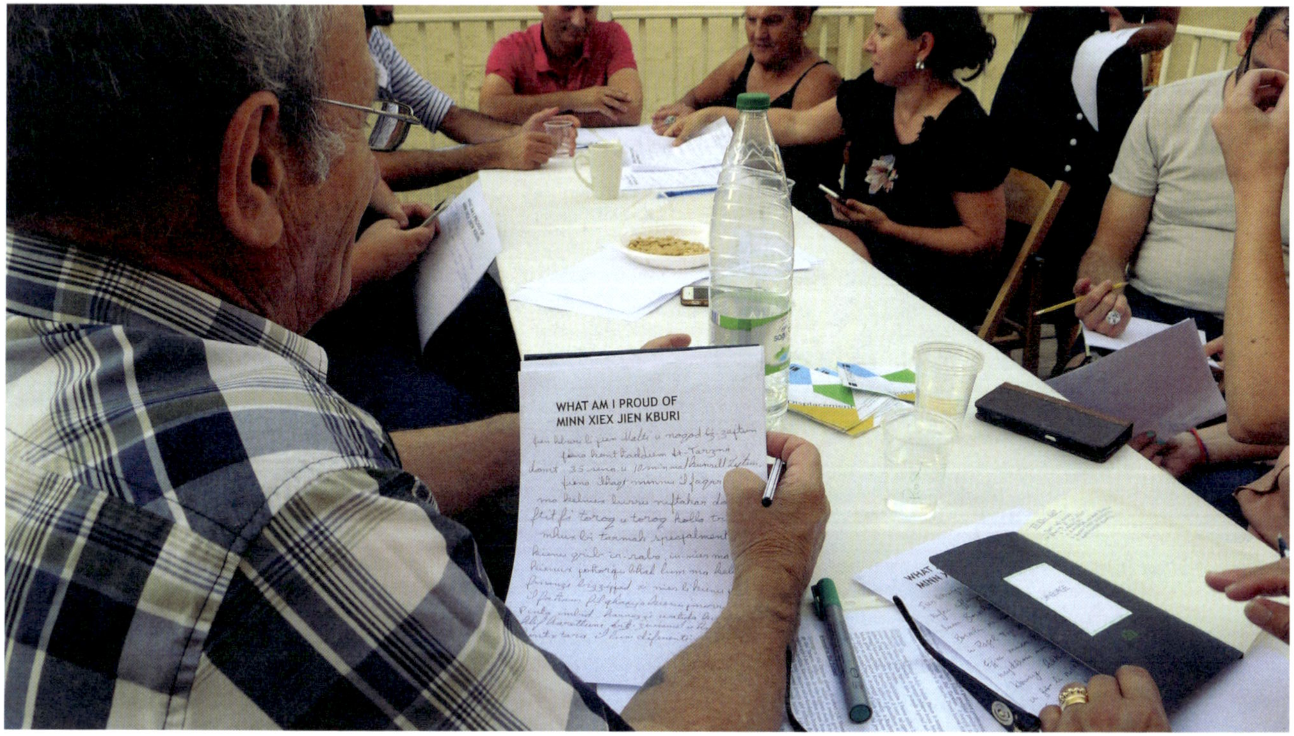

In workshops at the former Exam Centre in Valletta, where the exhibition *The Island is What the Sea Surrounds* was then held, topics and contributions for the Għana dialogs were collected with Għana singers (*għannejja*), Maltese authors and other participants.

In Workshops im ehemaligen Exam Centre in Valletta, in dem dann die Ausstellung *The Island is What the Sea Surrounds* stattfand, wurden mit Għana-SängerInnen (*għannejja*), maltesischen AutorInnen sowie weiteren TeilnehmerInnen Themen und Beiträge für die Għana-Dialoge gesammelt.

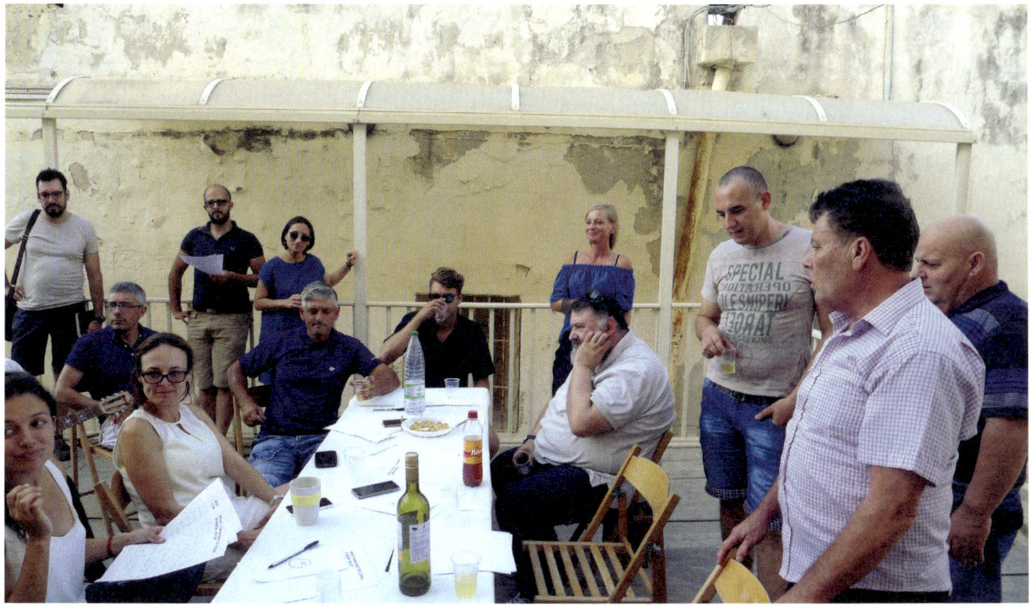

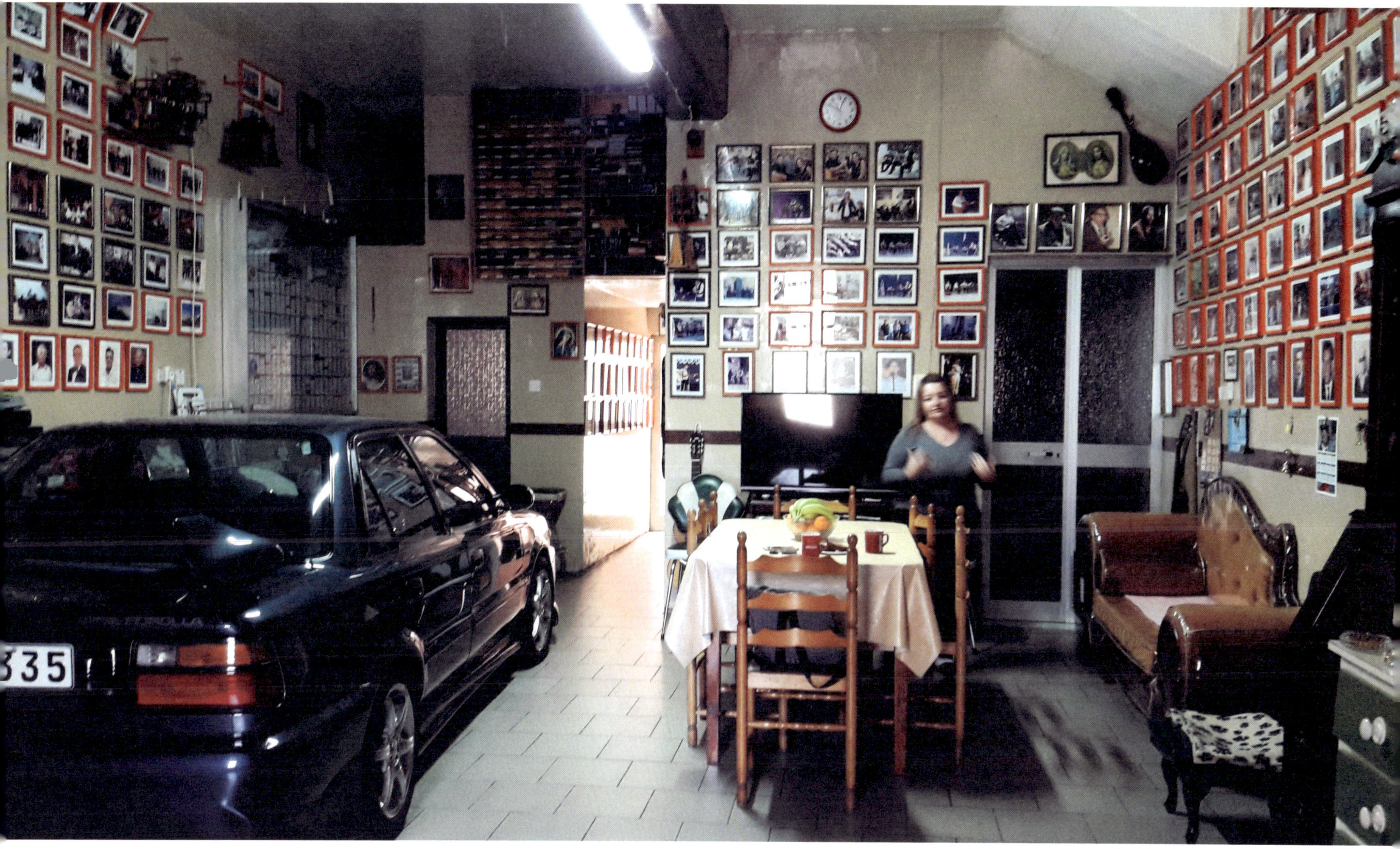

Home of the *għannejja* Zeppi and Rose Spanjol

Wohnung der *għannejja* Zeppi und Rose Spanjol

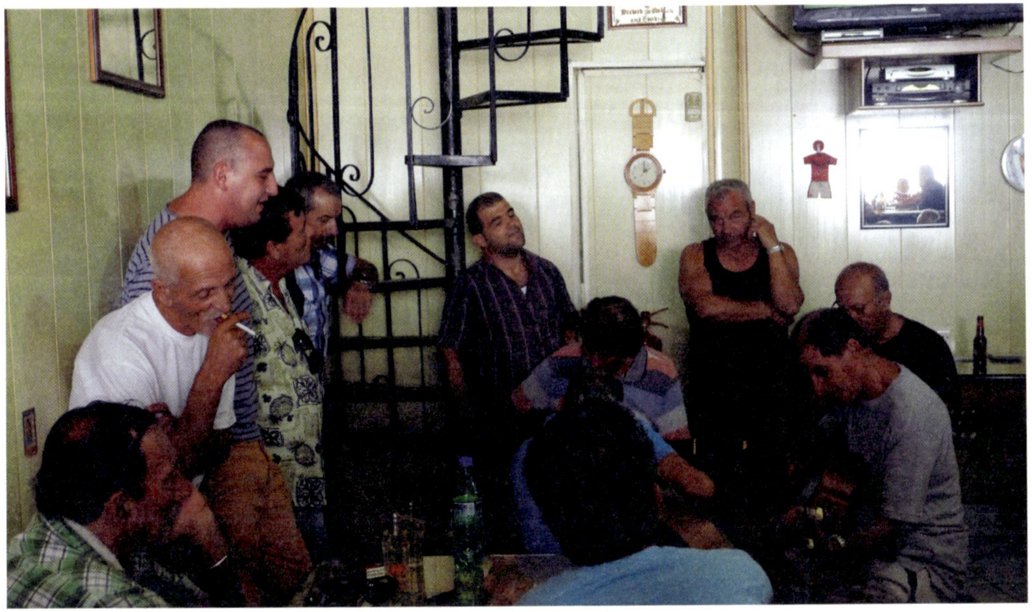

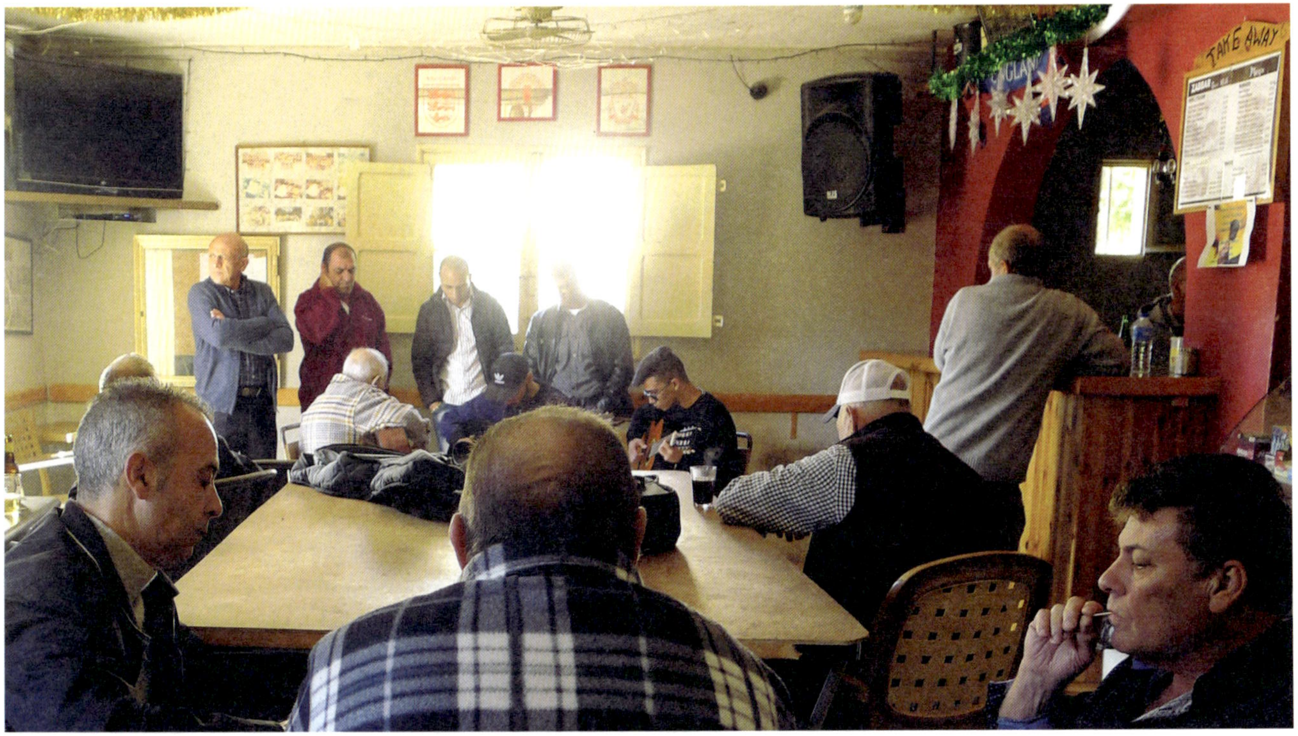

In the famous Għana bars Ta' Gianna Bar in Zejtun and Zabbar Bocci Klabb the tradition of Għana is regularly cultivated on Sundays.

In den berühmten Għana-Bars Ta' Gianna Bar in Zejtun und Zabbar Bocci Klabb wird regelmäßig sonntags die Tradition von Għana gepflegt.

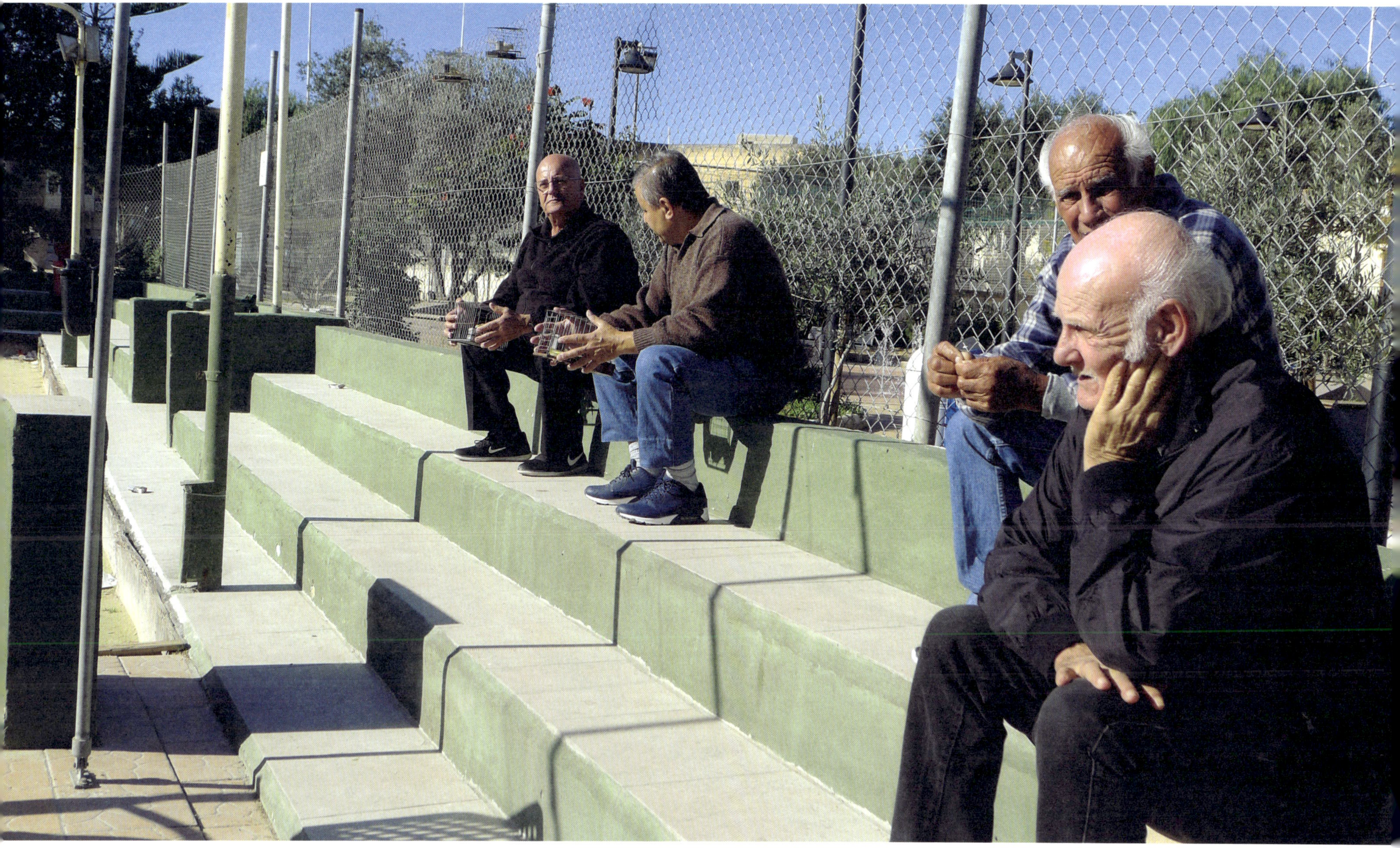

Analog communication with birds as pets

Analoge Kommunikation mit Vögeln als Haustieren

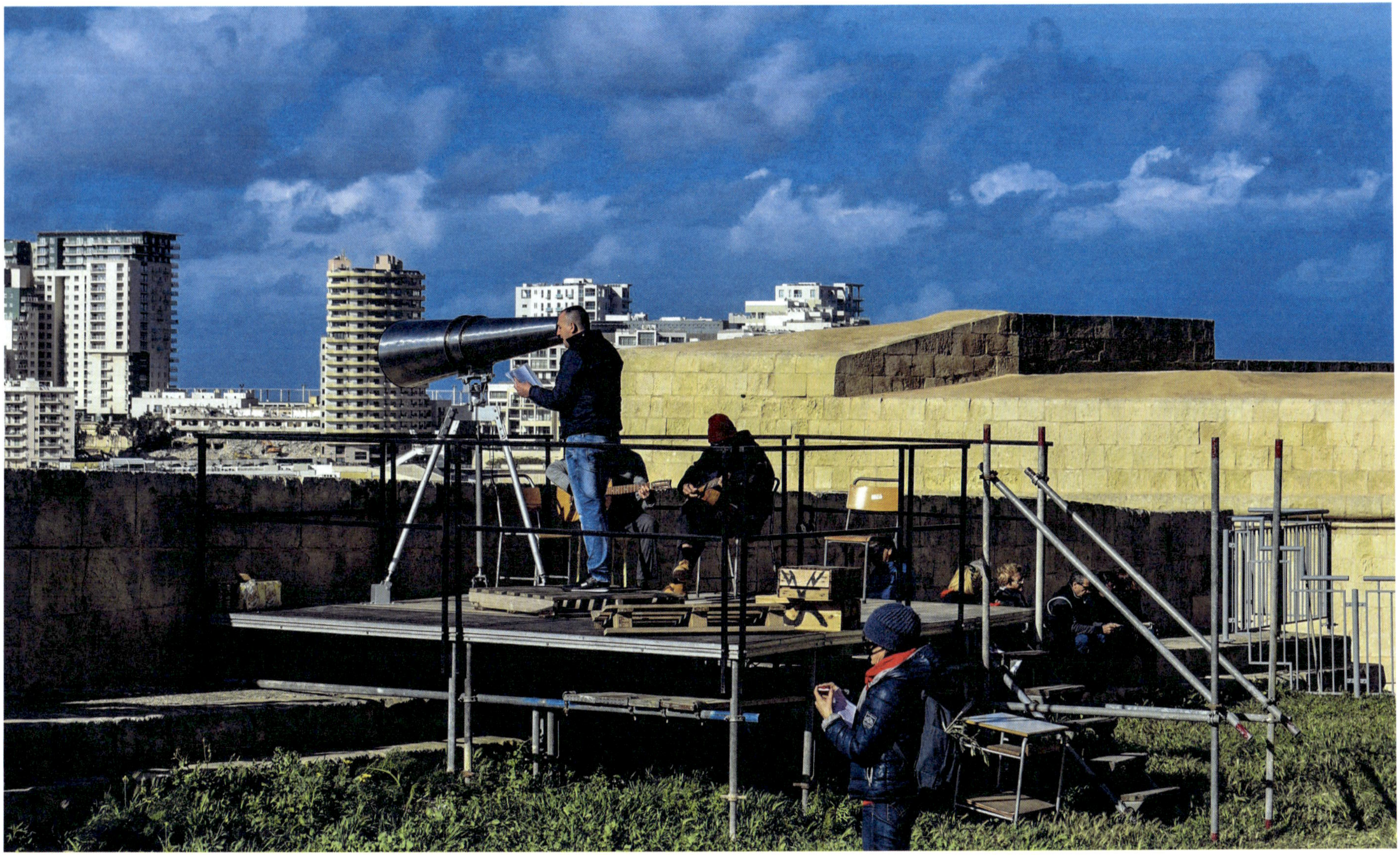

First performance of TIMES OF DILEMMA with Angelo Theuma, St. Roche Chapel / Valletta, March 2018

Erste Performance von TIMES OF DILEMMA mit Angelo Theuma, Kapelle St. Roche / Valletta, März 2018

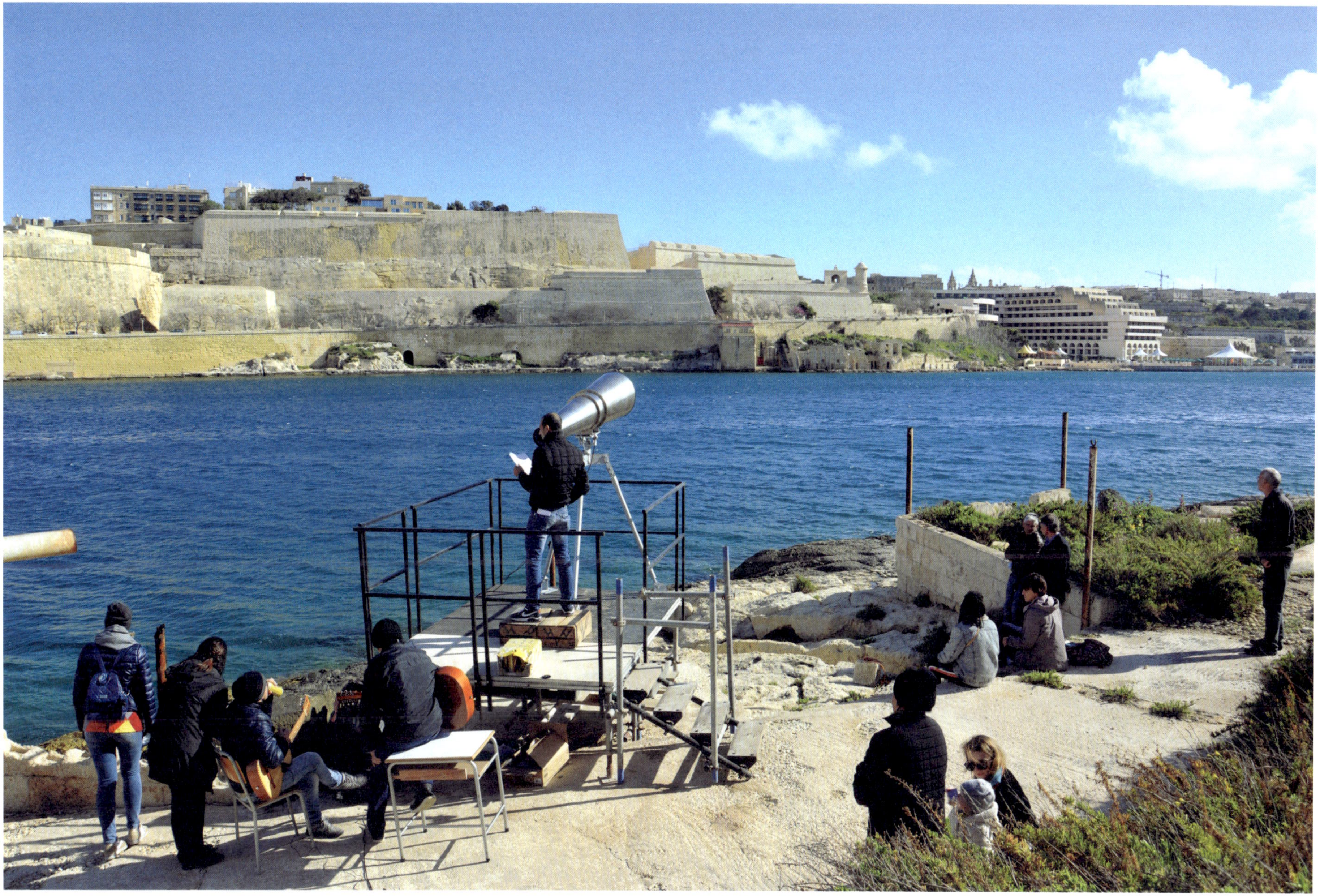

In dialog with Josmick Agius, Manoel Island

Im Dialog mit Josmick Agius, Manoel Island

	Is-Sistema Politika	The Political System
Vince:	Kulħadd għandu opinjoni, u tagħha għandu kull dritt, Li jispjega lilu nnifsu W minnha jagħmel profitt.	Everyone is entitled to his own opinion, express it, and from it make a million.
Maria:	Iżda b'din id-deċiżjoni Lid-demokrazija radmu, U għal ħobża ta' kuljum Ilkoll noħorġu naħdmu.	But through this decision they smothered democracy, and to bring home the bacon all of us have to go to work.
Vince:	Id-deċiżjonijiet jittieħdu Minn min aħna nagħtu l-vot, Dawn sigurtà u ġustizzja Lura lill-poplu jrodd.	Decisions are taken by whom we put in power, they ensure security and justice for us all.
Maria:	Demokrazija li ssaħħaħ Tagħti poter lill-maġġuranza, U linja marġinali Fil-ġenb tal-minoranza.	A democracy which strengthens and empowers the majority, while weakening and neglecting the minority.
Vince:	Għalhekk jitwettqu l-protesti W jinfetħu l-każijiet, Jistgħu jiġu għall-ġustizzja F'diversi sitwazzjonijiet.	This is what kindles protests, leads to court proceedings, they can come at loggerheads when they can't meet each other halfway.
Maria:	Għall-infurzar tal-liġijiet Li ma jarawx differenzi, Għal ta' fl-ammont ta' fil-bwiet Il-poplu jbati l-konsegwenzi.	On the enforcement of laws honest and unbiased, on how much they will pocket the people on the receiving end.
Vince:	Reklami mhux biss iħajru B'ħafna nies jinstigaw, Iżda għandna bżonn iktar Inkunu poplu li nikkritikaw.	We don't need more ads to entice and encourage, we need to find the courage to criticize and change.
Maria:	Jiena b'Malta tiegħi kburi, Fejn jiena twelidt u kbirt, Issa l-ġid nista' nesperjenza Qabel fil-povertà skirt.	I'm proud of the country, where I was bred and born, now I can enjoy prosperity while before, I suffered poverty.
Vince:	Biċċa ħobż b'naqra butir Qabel jiena kont niċċaħħad, Il-bżonn kien biss prekarju Min kulma ridt jew qatt xtaqt.	Years ago, bread and butter were deemed a luxury, satisfying your basic needs depended on the winds of fate.
Maria:	Mintoff beda l-benefiċċji Li minnhom ingawdu lkoll, Qabel kellna t-tarzna U biha kilna biċċa ħobż.	Mintoff introduced benefits, advantageous to us all, before we had the dockyard for our daily bread, toiled hard.
Vince:	Il-politikanti importanti Biex ir-rota tkompli ddur, Iqisu l-ġid ta' pajjiżhom U li nieshom kuntenti żgur.	Politicians are important for us to survive, they strive to ensure prosperity to please the people.
Maria:	Iżda dan mhux dejjem iseħħ Għax aħna differenti minn xulxin, Opinjonijiet u battibekki Dan li jagħmilna bnedmin.	But this isn't always the case, as no man is like another, opinions and disputes a reflection of our nature.
Vince:	Storja ta' filosofija Ġejja minn mijiet ta' snin, Politikanti li l-ħaqq jieħdu Salib biesu mis-snin bikrin.	The story of a philosophy reaching way back into history, of politicians who vow to endorse justice and righteousness by kissing the cross.
Maria:	Il-Kostituzzjoni tagħna Titlob minna dan l-aġir, Li kulħadd iwettaq xogħlu W ma jistennix tifħir.	This conduct is demanded by our country's constitution, and we don't expect any praise for our contribution.
Vince:	Il-bidla importanti Magħha ġġib il-progress, Jekk ma jkunx hemm il-bidla Kollox jibqa' l-istess.	Change is important through it we all progress, if we don't want to stagnate our priorities we must redress.
Maria:	'Il quddiem irridu nimxu ħalli lkoll navanzaw, U naraw lil uliedna Fl-edukazzjoni jistinkaw.	To develop and advance, we must work together, while seeing our children at school, doing better.
Vince:	Moħħna lkoll inserrħu Li pajjiżna pajjiż sigur, Libertà tal-espressjoni Biex inwasslu l-messaġġ żgur.	We put our mind at rest our country is a safe place, where for everyone's opinion we have ample space.
Maria:	U għal min ma jridx jisma' W irid biss jagħmel fattih, U mbagħad tarah il-ġustizzja W quddiem Alla jbatih.	And those who ignore this and would do as they see fit, are punished on judgment day and their misdeeds before all admit.

L-Iżvilupp f'Żoni Urbani

Jomike: Minn dal-lok illum se ngħannu
Dwar xi ħaġa tant magħrufa,
Storja antika, xejn ġdid fiha,
Dwar battalja ġà mitlufa.[1]

Il-battalja kontra r-regħba
Ta' min butu mhuwiex fqir,
Li jrid aktar ma' li għandu,
Jgħix il-ħajja ta' ħanżir. [2]

Angelo: Il-kburija oħt is-suppervja
Għalhekk kburi jien m'iniex,
In-nies li rashom wisq iebsa
Bħall-franka jew briksa Ingliż. [3]

Il-bini qed jibqa' jogħla
Dejjem iktar vertikali,
U addiju l-veduta
Tax-xatt minflok bini għali. [4]

Jomike: Is-saħħa u l-edukazzjoni
Qegħdin hemm għal kulħadd,
Tal-Gvern jew tal-Knisja
It-tagħlim jingħad [5]

Sejrin ngħannu b'weġgħa f'qalbna
Għal dak kollu l'hawn madwarna,
U bid-dmugħ f'għajnejna nħarsu
Għal mod kif qed tintemm darna.[6]

Angelo: Meta kont daqsxejn ta' tifel
Kont immur fl-għalqa ta' ħdejna,
Ħalli nilgħab mal-ħbieb tiegħi
Imma llum araw f'xiex ġejna. [7]

Sparixxiet l-għalqa fejn lgħabna,
Sparixxew anki l-widien,
U minflok tellgħu bħal torri,
Hekk għoġobhom lis-sidien. [8]

Jomike: Għalxejn tlabna kollna ħniena,
Għalxejn tlabna kollna ħrara,
Għalxejn bdejna nispjegawlhom
Li jikkawżaw il-ħsara. [9]

Din il-ħsara mhux għalina
'żda żgur għall-ulied tagħna,
Iżda s-sid jiġi jitmejjel
Jaħseb biss kif se jistagħna. [10]

Development in Urban Areas

Here we are today,
set to sing a song
of well-known issue:
a siege set up to fail.

A siege against the greed
of those who bitterly crave
for a more opulent cornucopia,
while wallowing in wealth.

Pride and haughtiness are siblings,
and I don't share their blood;
they who are so bloody pig-headed
have traded swine for stone.

And as building unabashedly
snake their way skywards,
seascapes are slowly swapped
for sheer unsustainability.

Here health and education
benefit the whole nation,
citizens are schooled
in senate and sanctuary.

Mired in anguish we're going to sing
for all that encompasses us.
Eyes glazed with tears, we look around
at how home is slowly being reduced to rubble.

When I was yet a little boy,
I dallied away the hours
in fields with friends;
but today I can only reminisce.

These fields where we used to play
have faded into memory. So have the valleys.
Instead they erected a tower.
Because, hey why not?

We prayed for mercy, with fervour.
We strived to convince them
of the damage they do,
but our prayers were stifled by obstinacy.

The consequences of this calamity
will snowball on the morrow.
Alas, the owner is deaf
bar to the clang of cascading cash.

Angelo: Qabel kont niftaħ għajnejja
Malli tibda tielgħa x-xemx,
Imma llum ħarsti fil-ġebel
Għax ħlief bini kbir ma hemmx! [11]

Kont inxomm ir-riħa tfewwaħ
Ta' xi tina w tal-ħarrub,
Kont nissemma' lill-għasafar
Li b'għanjiethom jgħaxxqu l-qlub. [12]

Jomike: Imbagħad meta mlew il-gżira
Ma baqax aktar irkejjen,
Qalu: "nibdew nibnu fl-għoli
Biex is-sema wkoll jiżżejjen".[13]

Ġol-għalqa spiss iġġerrejna
Sa ma dalam u l-ħin sar,
Inġbarna, lissinna t-talba,
Inġbarna lkoll ġewwa d-dar.

Angelo: Veduti jpaxxuk sbuħija
Jekk tbexxaq il-gallarija,
Tista' togħxa bil-veduta
Ebda ostaklu ma jgħattiha.

Tmur mixja tista' titpaxxa
Bil-ġenna fuq din l-art,
Malta gżira liema bħalha
La sħana ħafna u lanqas bard.

Jomike: Ir-rota trid min idawwarha
Li mhumiex il-maġġuranza,
Wieħed b'kemxa jxaħħam
laffaċċjak mingħajr kirjanza.

L-għalqa li temgħet lil familti
Issa l-għelieqi tan-naħat,
F'qasir żmien ġew mibnija
Kilna minn fuqhom għal snin sħaħ.

Angelo: Ilbieraħ il-permess twaħħal
Ta' min hu dan ma nafux,
Pprovajt nistaqsi dwaru
'żda dettalji ma sabux.

1, 2, 6-13 Immanuel Mifsud
3, 4, 5 Jean Paul Borg

Yesterday I feasted my eyes
on dawn's golden promises.
Today I wake up to staring at
hulking pillars of hopeless concrete.

I used to get dazed
by the sandy scent of fig strees,
and the cleansing caob;
by the tweeting cacophony in twigs.

And then, when construction spread rampantly
covering all like a cancerous fog,
they turned to the free firmament
building a towering tangle of thorns.

In the fields, we merrily ran
till prayer and sleep cocooned
the evening's amber glow
in night's sweet solace.

When you threw the balcony window open
you were graced by views brimming with beauty,
unfurling like magic carpets
with nothing masking their magnificence.

While taking a stroll,
you couldn't help but
feel blessed you were born
in such a heavenly abode.

The country needs a captain
and the majority is not qualified to steer.
One blatantly bribes another,
and strips off all sense of courtesy.

This field fed my family
for so long, others graced us
with generosity and green.
All lost: crushed under concrete.

They hung the permit yesterday:
owner's identity unknown.
When I asked for answers
I was handed a blank page.

Translation: Clifton Azzopardi

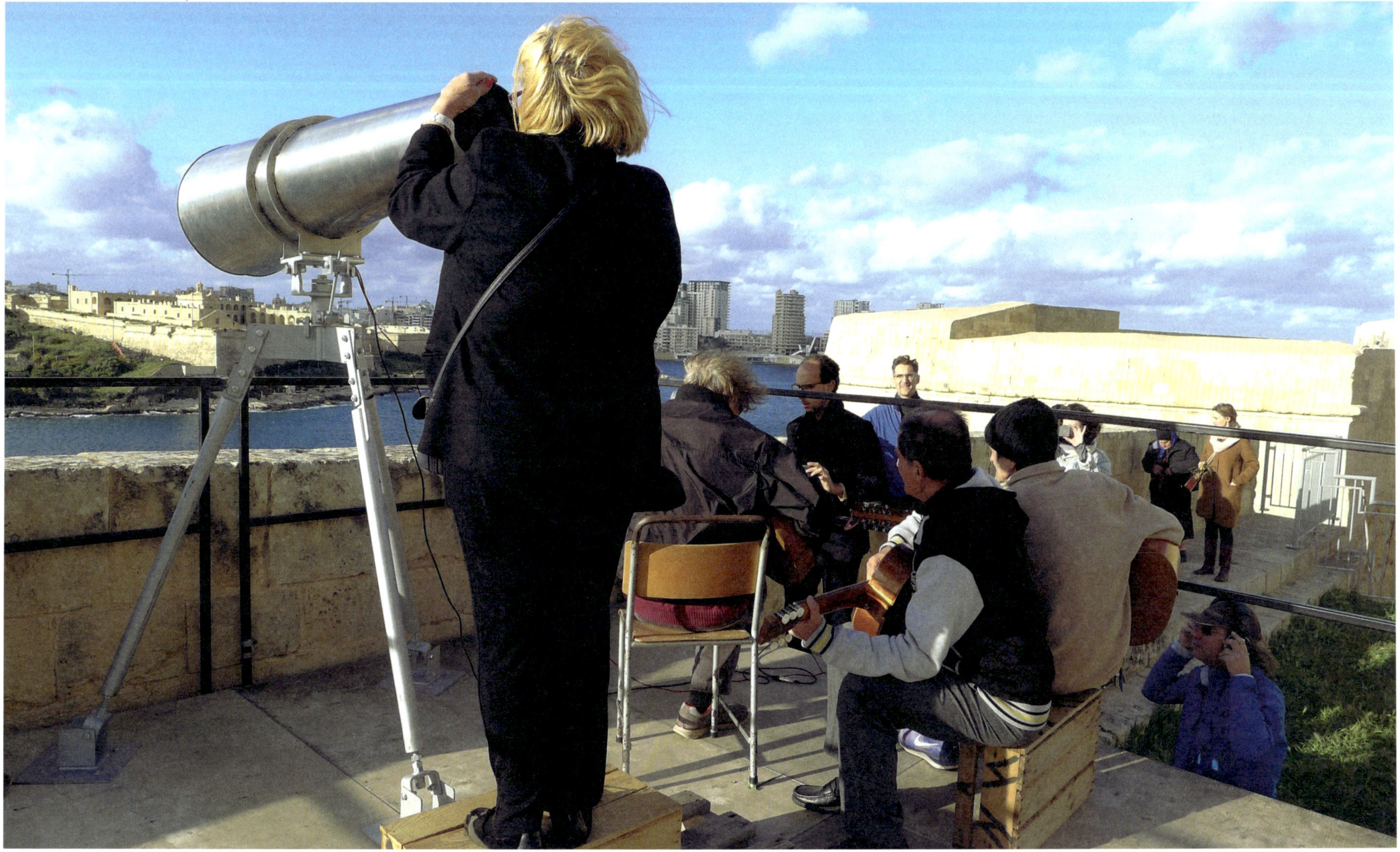

Maria Agius/Oħt iż -Żebbuġin' in dialog with Il-Bukku Vince, as well as with Mikkelina, who responded to the scripted Għana chants with a *spirtu pront* (the traditional format of spontaneous improvisation; see next page).

Maria Agius/Oħt iż -Żebbuġin' im Dialog mit Il-Bukku Vince, sowie mit Mikkelina, die auf die geskripteten Għana-Gesänge mit einem *spirtu pront* (dem traditionellen Format der spontanen Improvisation) reagierte (siehe nächste Seite).

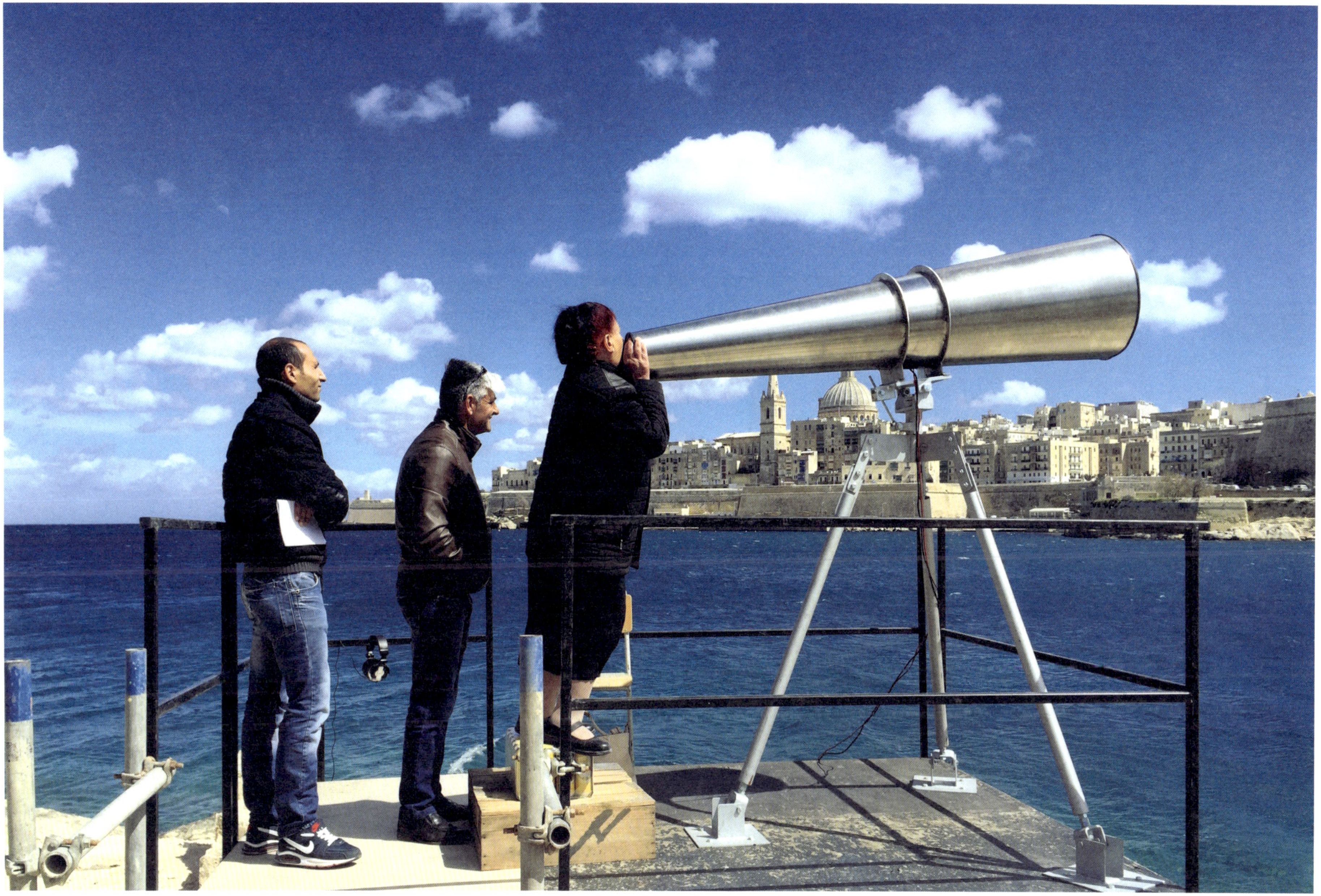

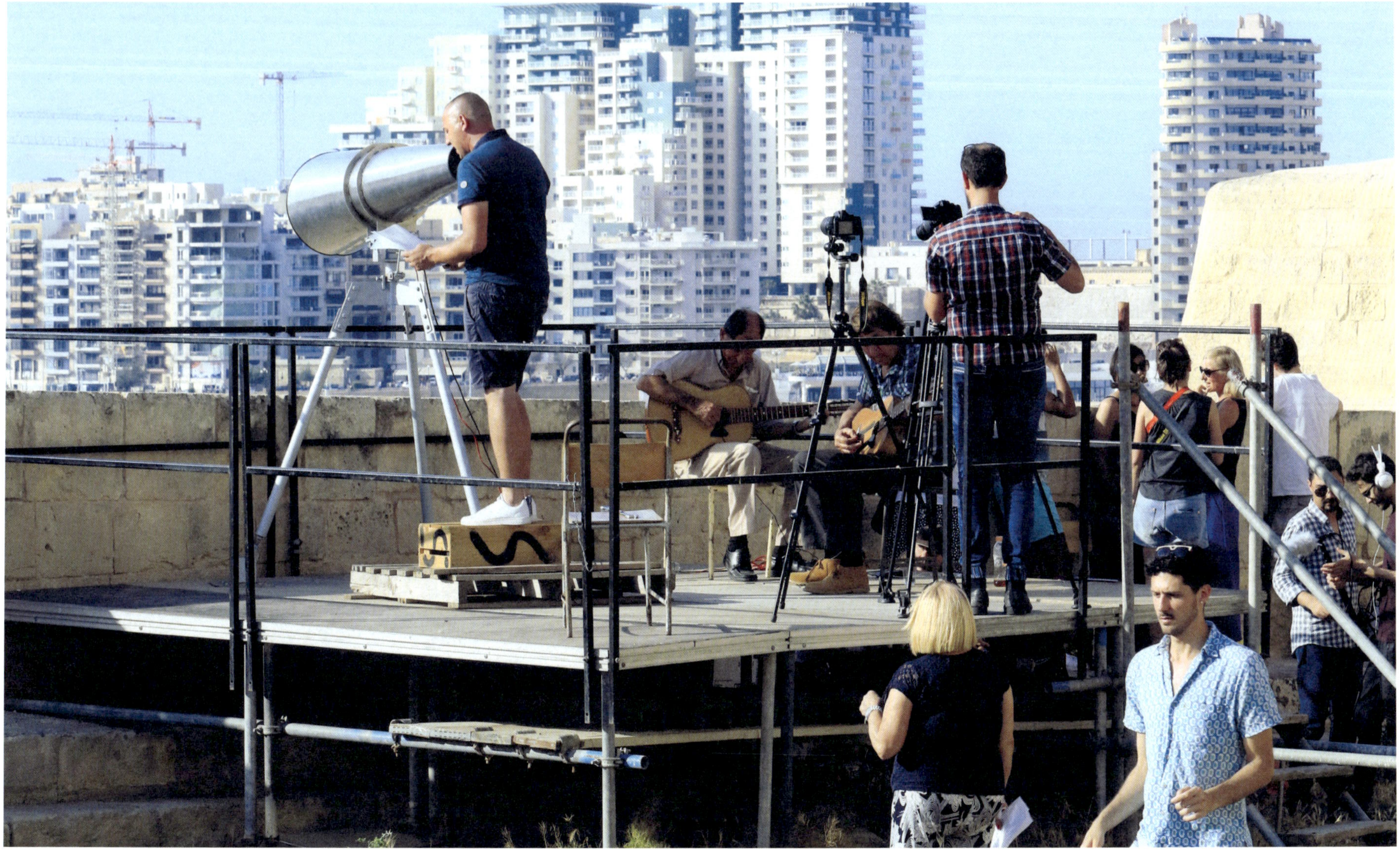

Third performance of TIMES OF DILEMMA with Angelo Theuma, Chapel St. Roche, Valletta, July 2018. The view of Sliema with the dense new high-rise buildings with which Malta wants to position itself as the "New Dubai" shows the uncontrolled urban development as today's "plague."

Dritte Performance von TIMES OF DILEMMA mit Angelo Theuma, Kapelle St. Roche, Valletta, Juli 2018. Der Blick auf Sliema mit den dichten neuen Hochhäusern, mit denen Malta sich als „Neues Dubai" profilieren möchte, zeigt die unkontrollierte Stadtentwicklung als heutige „Plage".

V. Missing Things— Noisy Activism

Dinge, die fehlen – geräusch-voller Aktivismus

BARBARA HOLUB'S NOISY ACTIVISM

Paul O'Neill

When scrolling through documentation of artist Barbara Holub and transparadiso's public art practices of the last twenty years, you will see many recurring motifs. You will see structures being built, assembled, things being made. You will see research-led exhibitions involving temporary architectural settings with something happening within their spaces. Within these spatial scenarios, there is an unfolding of the social, some form of gathering, some kind of conviviality, relationality, intersectionality. Often, you will see people standing among other people and things, lots of groups, where much listening and talking seems to be taking place, but without many spectators. Something seems to be happening, but there is not a lot to see. Instead, there is a sense of lightness, of breathing, of porosity.[1]

Holub's projects often focus on setting in motion a context for bringing people into the process from the beginning. People are mostly gathered or huddled together, sometimes in conversation, mostly not, and standing or sitting, attending to one another and their surroundings, they are mainly in smaller groups. There is always a lot of information, both spoken, and written—language is everywhere: in single-word phrases, full sentences, whole texts, typed on banners, in design objects, on textiles, placards, posters with slogans, titles, questions, lists, glossaries, claims, manifestos, uttered urgencies, notes, jokes, observations, scribbles, stated desires and fully formed statements. All these settings, words, people and their actions, make up the work of the artist's *silent activism*.

However, Holub's *silent activism* is neither silent nor merely activist. Instead of silence, there is an undercurrent of mumbling voices, a rumbling swell of noisy resistance, where the resultant works can also be bold, unequivocally loud, even full of ranting and raving. At the same time, the four well-trodden tenets of activism—advocacy, subversion, facilitation and healing—are constantly embroiled in a convoluted tension between the artist's desire for poetic forms of social resistance and the need for more direct approaches to imminent structural change. The works are always unique and site-responsive, yet they learn from, and are interconnected with, one another, accumulative while stretched across place and time.

Direct urbanism is a term often used to describe the approach of Barbara Holub and the work of transparadiso—the artist's collaborative practice with architect/urbanist Paul Rajakovics since 1999. They have developed

BARBARA HOLUBS GERÄUSCHVOLLER AKTIVISMUS

Paul O'Neill

Blättert man durch die Dokumentationen der künstlerischen Interventionen, die Barbara Holub und transparadiso in den letzten zwanzig Jahren im öffentlichen Raum realisiert haben, findet man einige immer wiederkehrende Motive. Es werden Gerüste gebaut, Objekte hergestellt, und in den Ausstellungen, die oft auch Rechercheprozesse zeigen, sowie in den temporären architektonischen Konstruktionen entstehen Räume, in denen etwas stattfindet. Innerhalb dieser Szenarien entfaltet sich das Soziale als eine Art des Versammelns, der Konvivialität, der Relationalität und der Intersektionalität. Häufig stehen Menschen inmitten anderer Menschen und Objekte, in zahlreichen Gruppen wird viel gesprochen und zugehört. Ein Publikum lässt sich jedoch kaum erkennen. Es scheint etwas stattzufinden, ohne dass es viel zu sehen gibt. Stattdessen herrscht ein Gefühl von Leichtigkeit, Luftigkeit, Porosität.[1]

In vielen ihrer Projekte geht es Holub darum, eine Situation zu schaffen, die viele verschiedene Menschen von Anfang an in den Prozess miteinbezieht. Die Menschen versammeln sich oder sind dicht zusammengedrängt, manchmal unterhalten sie sich, oft aber auch nicht, und widmen sich sitzend oder stehend ihrem Gegenüber und ihrem Umfeld, vorwiegend in kleineren Gruppen. Es gibt immer eine Menge an Informationen, gesprochen oder geschrieben, und stets ist man von Sprache umgeben: von einzelnen Wörtern, ganzen Sätzen und Texten, gedruckt auf Transparenten, auf Designobjekten, auf Textilien, Plakaten und Postern, als Slogans, Titel, Fragen, Listen, Glossare, Forderungen sowie Manifeste und Appelle, Mitteilungen, Witze, Beobachtungen, Skizzen, Wünsche und ausführliche Stellungnahmen. All diese Situationen, Worte, Menschen und Handlungen sind wesentliche Bestandteile des stillen Aktivismus der Künstlerin.

Holubs stiller Aktivismus ist jedoch weder still noch ausschließlich aktivistisch. Statt Stille hört man unterschwellige, murmelnde Stimmen, ein brodelndes Anschwellen eines geräuschvollen Widerstands. Ihre Arbeiten können gewagt, kompromisslos und laut sein, manchmal sogar voller Ärger und Wut. Gleichzeitig bleiben die vier altbewährten Grundsätze des Aktivismus – Engagement, Subversion, Unterstützung und Heilung – beständig mit eingebunden in das komplexe Spannungsverhältnis zwischen Holubs künstlerischer Suche nach poetischen Formen des sozialen Widerstands und ihrem Streben, in unmittelbar bevorstehende strukturelle Veränderungen noch direkter einzugreifen. Jede ihrer Arbeiten ist einzigartig und ortsspezifisch, zugleich aber „lernen" die Arbeiten voneinander, greifen ineinander über und entwickeln sich über Zeit und Raum gemeinsam weiter.

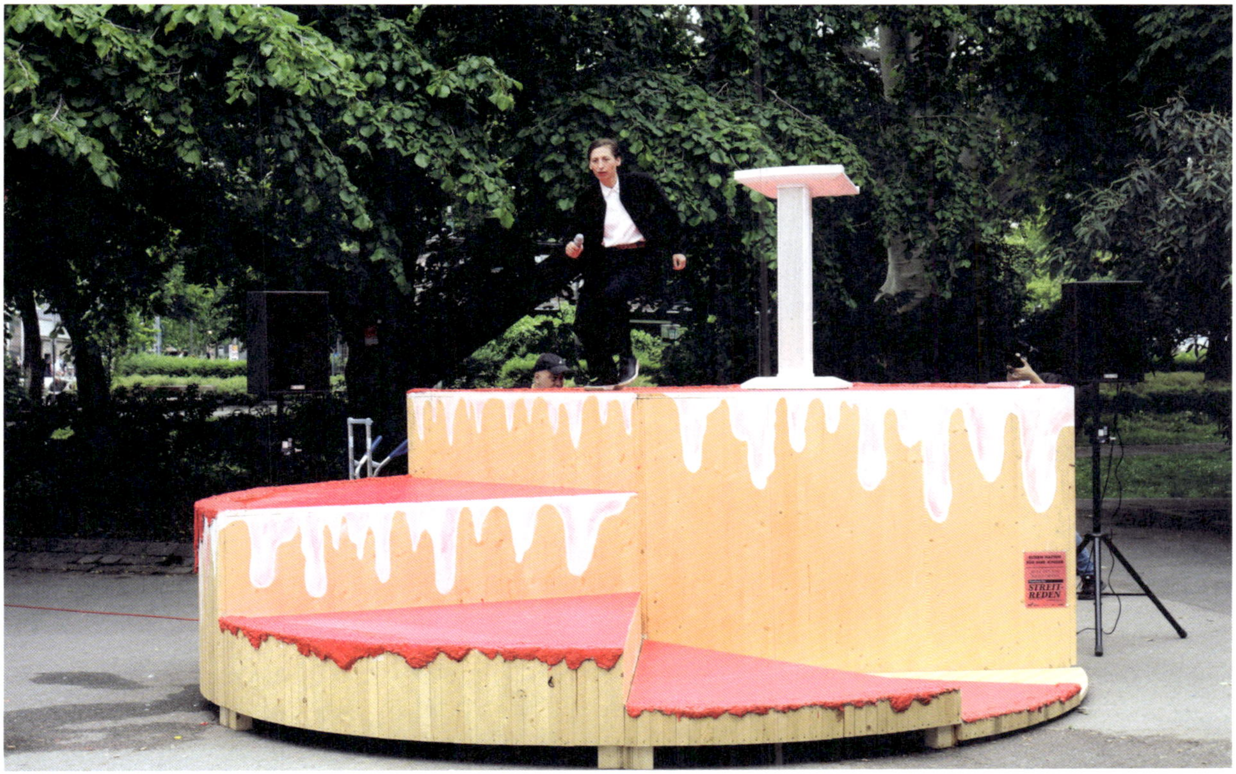

PLATFORM FOR ARGUMENTS, Barbara Holub/Christine Hohenbüchler with students of the Institute of Art and Design, TU Vienna/in cooperation with Public Art Vienna, Vienna, 2018. This sculpture was realized on the occasion of the "100th Anniversary of Female Students at the Vienna University of Technology" and programmed with performances and speeches. (image: Anna Mendelssohn)

PLATTFORM FÜR STREITREDEN, Barbara Holub/Christine Hohenbüchler mit Studentinnen des Instituts für Kunst und Gestaltung, TU Wien/in Kooperation mit KÖR Wien, Wien, 2018. Diese Skulptur wurde anlässlich von „100 Jahren Frauenstudium an der TU Wien" realisiert und mit Performances und Reden programmiert. (Bild: Anna Mendelssohn)

and continuously refined a method to respond to the social challenges of urban planning, where their work is directly related to urban issues, critical spatial practice and durational curatorial processes in urban developments, leading to artistic-urbanistic strategies for a socially committed approach, which is integrated into a longer-term urban planning process, sometimes as proposition, sometimes enacted. In other words, in their form of direct urbanism, planning is connected with a form of activism.

Holub's work is immersive and collectively formed, for artists as well as participants and invited guests. Temporary architecture or built spaces act as physical and conceptual frameworks and help structure conversations toward what can be done. These carefully sited infrastructures open up the social to the potentiality of the knowledge of those in attendance, where participants lead in a response to the artist's propositions to set in motion a discursive, durational process in which both poetic and direct action can emerge. Working on location as the "artist-in-residence," Holub is the skilled interlocutor, the in-betweener, mediating openings through research, finding the gaps and what is missing for people within a specific situation. The gatherings and responses lead to discussions by participant-observers and bring them into the fold of urban planning and decision-making within the architectural or artistic commissioning context.

Holub und der Architekt und Urbanist Paul Rajakovics, die gemeinsam seit 1999 als das Kollektiv transparadiso firmieren, bezeichnen ihren künstlerischen Ansatz als direkten Urbanismus. In ihren Arbeiten zu urbanen Fragen und kritischen räumlichen Praktiken sowie in ihren langfristig angelegten kuratorischen urbanistischen Projekten haben sie eine Methode erarbeitet und kontinuierlich weiterentwickelt, die auf soziale Herausforderungen der Stadtplanung reagiert. Ihre künstlerisch-urbanistischen und gesellschaftlich engagierten Strategien sind Teil langfristiger Planungsprozesse, sei es in Form konkreter Vorschläge oder in Form unmittelbarer Umsetzung. Anders ausgedrückt, verschränken sich in direktem Urbanismus Planung und Aktivismus.

Holubs Arbeiten entstehen durch die intensive Auseinandersetzung zwischen KünstlerInnen, Teilnehmenden und BesucherInnen. Die temporären Architekturen und Räume stellen den physischen sowie konzeptuellen Rahmen her, um in gemeinsamen Gesprächen herauszufinden, was zu tun ist. Diese behutsam entwickelten Infrastrukturen erschließen das Soziale als eine Quelle potenziellen Wissens und ermöglichen den Teilnehmenden, auch in Reaktion auf Vorschläge der Künstlerin, einen kontinuierlichen und diskursiven Prozess anzustoßen, in dem poetische Momente und direkte Aktion zusammenlaufen. Holub agiert vor Ort wie eine „Artist-in-Residence", als geübte Gesprächs- und Verhandlungspartnerin, die durch ihre Recherchearbeit Zugänge

transparadiso's work is part of a wider dynamic change in the commissioning of art in urban contexts. This turn in public art prioritizes long-term durational approaches and explicitly leaving things open but is not merely a question of time. It also represents a commitment to engaging art in, and for, a specific situated place with its most immediate audiences, citizens and inhabitants. As a co-operative procedure that links many actors and agencies, it involves the extended coming-together of a range of individuals with various objectives in common. Such durational praxis can make possible a mode of co-production in a slowly unravelling process that considers bringing in residents, users, and those most immediate to the contexts. When artists, participants, and commissioners contribute to sustaining a practice-in-place over time—with a view to leaving something behind that could not have been anticipated—the duration of a commissioning process matters because it is time that allows for the unexpected and accumulative impact to emerge. In the process, Holub situates herself often as a dedicated "amateur" finding the cracks and unforeseen ways around prescribed expectations of what one should be doing professionally, instead proposing new ways to challenge the context.

This is apparent in how a number of projects lead with a simple concept, moving it around in myriad ways to look at a given situation again and again. Holub's approach is, in that respect, similar to Edward Said's take on the amateur as non-expert, as an important intellectual figure of our times, in which an amateur is someone who doesn't know yet, but takes up.

"[W]hat today the intellectual ought to be, someone who considers that to be a thinking and concerned member of a society one is entitled to raise moral issues at the heart of even the most technical and professionalized activity as it involves one's country, its power, its mode of interacting with its citizens as well as other societies. In addition, the intellectual's spirit as an amateur can enter and transform the merely professional routine most of us go through into something much more lively and radical; instead of doing what one is supposed to do one can ask why one does it, who benefits from it, how can it reconnect with a personal project and original thought."[2]

Adopting Said's position, Holub often takes on the role of artist-curator as intellectual amateur in the context of predetermined, inflexible or over-professionalized processes, aiming to create a non-hierarchical setting for different kinds of questions to be asked of urban space, its residents and future social use. Each project is a fine balancing act between control and non-control and setting the structure or framework of invitation and response that is focused enough while remaining flexible at the same time. Like many cooperative curatorial practices in the public realm, there is a focus on the public exhibition as a collective form of co-productivity,

und Leerstellen offenlegt, aber auch aufzeigt, was den Menschen ganz konkret fehlt. Die Versammlungen und Beiträge führen zu Diskussionen unter den TeilnehmerInnen/BeobachterInnen und bringen diese in die Stadtplanung und die Entscheidungsfindung im Rahmen der architektonischen bzw. künstlerischen Beauftragungssituation ein.

Die Arbeiten von transparadiso sind Teil einer umfassenderen, dynamischen Veränderung in der Beauftragung von Kunstprojekten in urbanen Kontexten. Diese Wende in der Kunst im öffentlichen Raum ist gekennzeichnet durch ein Plädoyer für langfristig und explizit ergebnisoffen angelegte Projekte. Es geht aber nicht nur um die Frage nach Zeit und Dauer, sondern auch um das Bestreben, Kunst mit und für einen ganz konkreten Ort und sein unmittelbares Umfeld und dessen BürgerInnen und BewohnerInnen einzusetzen. transparadiso greift oft partizipative Herangehensweisen auf, um verschiedene AkteurInnen wie auch Interessen, und damit einhergehend auch sehr unterschiedliche, aber über gemeinsame Fragestellungen miteinander verbundene Menschen, zusammenzubringen. Die langfristig angelegten Projekte ermöglichen eine nachhaltige Form der Auseinandersetzung zwischen BewohnerInnen, NutzerInnen und dem unmittelbar involvierten Umfeld. Diese Langfristigkeit bildet die Voraussetzung dafür, aus den von KünstlerInnen, Beteiligten und AuftraggeberInnen gemeinsam entwickelten Herangehensweisen etwas entstehen zu lassen, das nicht schon von vornherein festgelegt ist. Holub übernimmt in diesen Prozessen oft die Rolle der engagierten „Amateurin", die abseits von festgefahrenen Vorstellungen Lücken und neue Wege findet, um diese Zusammenhänge zu hinterfragen.

Dies zeigt sich in einer Reihe von Holubs Projekten, die jeweils von einem einfachen Konzept ausgehen, das die Künstlerin in unzähligen Formen umsetzt, sodass eine bestimmte Situation immer wieder von Neuem betrachtet werden kann. In dieser Hinsicht gleicht Holubs Ansatz Edward Saids sehr einflussreicher zeitgenössischer Denkfigur der Intellektuellen als AmateurInnen im Sinne von Nicht-ExpertInnen, die sich auf etwas einlassen können, auch wenn sie davon noch nichts wissen.

„Der Intellektuelle heutzutage sollte ein Amateur sein, jemand, der der Meinung ist, daß man als denkendes Mitglied einer Gesellschaft das Recht hat, selbst bei einer ausschließlich technischen und hochprofessionalisierten Tätigkeit moralische Anliegen zur Sprache zu bringen. Sie können das eigene Land, Fragen der Machtausübung und des Umgangs mit den Bürgern wie auch mit anderen Gesellschaften betreffen. Zudem kann der Intellektuelle als Amateur die professionelle Routine, in der die meisten von uns gefangen sind, durchbrechen und in etwas viel Lebendigeres und Radikaleres verwandeln; statt einfach zu tun, was man tun sollte, kann man sich fragen, warum man es tut, wem es nützt, wie es mit einer persönlichen Intention und neuen Gedanken in Verbindung gebracht werden kann."[2]

bringing amateurs and professionals together in the hope of creating new forms of as-yet unknown knowledge and questioning the parameters of the authorship of public space through co-operative and post-autonomous modes of production. Projects involve varying degrees of co-operation with many different artists, architects, urbanists, curators and critics, where these multiple levels of social participation allow for divergent intellectual positions to co-exist, often in contradiction to one another. Here, the staging of publicness is like a model of "emergence," as it engenders new practices, new meanings, values and social relations between things, and in the generative sense of being the possible site of dialectical opposition to the dominant. This co-productive approach has the aspiration of overcoming, transgressing, evading, renegotiating or bypassing the dominant status in many small gestural ways as part of an accumulation of positions, reactions and propositions.

BARBARA HOLUB AND COOPERATIVE PRACTICE DISCOURSES

Increasingly, models of cooperation in social practices—which over the last decades have become prominent—have been associated with contextual and dialogical procedures rather than material outcomes. This has inevitably led to new terms of engagement. Classifying labels such as "conversational art" (Homi Bhaba), "dialogical art" (Grant Kester), "new genre public art" (Suzanne Lacy), "new situationism" (Claire Doherty), "connective aesthetics" (Suzi Gablik), "critical spatial practice" (Jane Rendell), "participatory art" (Claire Bishop), "social practice art" (Gregory Sholette), "community-based practice" (Nato Thompson), "Arte Utíl" (Tania Bruguera), "durational-specific" (Paul O'Neill, Dave Beech), "curatorial activism" (Maura Reilly), or "activist art" have all attempted to encapsulate the discursive qualities of "publicness" inherent in more immaterial forms of collective artistic co-production. All these terms have attempted to grasp how multiple participants are involved as co-creators in art projects, with a view to shaping counter-public spaces. This is a growing list that I often reference to frame an illustrative history of the expansion and diversification of the range of co-productive practices in which multiple participants are involved. In many of these practices, the moment of publicness is never fully revealed. The function of the curatorial proposition is to create situations of potential agency for the co-productive processes initiated by the artist, or curator, as post-autonomous producer of informal knowledge gatherings. Thus, an understanding of the curatorial is put forward as an accumulation of interactions and information, with the work of art configured as a cluster of interventions and interactions over time to result in more dispersed forms of distribution.[3]

This curatorial accumulation and clustering is most evident in Holub's non-hierarchical public World Congresses of the Missing Things, whose concept she developed first

In der Rolle der Künstlerin-Kuratorin agiert Holub oft im Sinne der intellektuellen AmateurInnen Saids, indem sie innerhalb der vorgegebenen, unflexiblen oder überprofessionalisierten Verfahren vor allem daran interessiert ist, nicht-hierarchische Settings herzustellen, um sich mit Fragen zur aktuellen und zukünftigen Nutzung von urbanen Räumen sowie mit deren BewohnerInnen auseinanderzusetzen. Jedes ihrer Projekte ist ein vorsichtiger Balanceakt zwischen Kontrolle und Nicht-Kontrolle, um partizipative Prozesse zu entwickeln, die sowohl zielgerichtet als auch ausreichend flexibel sind. Wie bei vielen kooperativen kuratorischen Praktiken im öffentlichen Raum liegt auch hier der Schwerpunkt auf einer öffentlichen Ausstellung als kollektives Format, das von AmateurInnen und ExpertInnen gemeinsam entwickelt wird, um dadurch neue Formate eines noch nicht bekannten Wissens hervorzubringen. Durch kooperative und postautonome Produktionsweisen werden ebenso die Parameter von AutorInnenschaft des öffentlichen Raums infrage gestellt. Die Projekte umfassen dabei unterschiedliche Formen der Kooperation zwischen KünstlerInnen, ArchitektInnen, StadtplanerInnen, KuratorInnen und KritikerInnen, deren vielschichtige und komplexe Ebenen sozialer Beteiligung auch das gleichzeitige Bestehen abweichender oder gar widersprüchlicher Positionen zulassen. Hier wird die Inszenierung von Öffentlichkeit zu einem Model für „Emergenz", das neue Bedeutungen und Werte sowie neue soziale Beziehungen hervorzubringen vermag und zugleich Ort für eine dialektische Opposition gegen das Vorherrschende werden kann. Dieser partizipative Ansatz versucht durch kleine Gesten sowie durch von der Norm abweichende Haltungen, Reaktionen und Vorschläge den dominanten Zustand zu überwinden, zu überschreiten, ihm auszuweichen, ihn neu zu verhandeln oder zu umgehen.

BARBARA HOLUB UND DIE DISKURSE PARTIZIPATIVER PRAKTIKEN

Die unterschiedlichen Formen von Kooperation, die in den letzten Jahrzehnten in gesellschaftlich engagierten künstlerischen Projekten zunehmend an Bedeutung gewonnen haben, legen ihren Fokus mehr auf kontextuelle und dialogische Prozesse als auf konkrete Ergebnisse. Das führte unausweichlich zu neuen Begriffen und Konzepten im Kunstdiskurs: „conversational art" (Homi Bhaba), „dialogical art" (Grant Kester), „new genre public art" (Suzanne Lacy), „new situationism" (Claire Doherty), „connective aesthetics" (Suzi Gablik), „critical spatial practice" (Jane Rendell), „participatory art" (Claire Bishop), „social practice art" (Gregory Sholette), „community-based practice" (Nato Thompson), „Arte Útil" (Tania Bruguera), „durational-specific" (Paul O'Neill, Dave Beech), „curatorial activism" (Maura Reilly) oder „activist art". All diese Begriffe versuchen, die diskursiven Qualitäten, die eher den immateriellen Formen kollektiver künstlerischer Produktion zugrunde liegen, zu erfassen. Sie zeigen auf, wie mehrere Beteiligte als Co-AutorInnen in Kunstprojekte involviert werden, um so Räume für eine Gegenöffentlichkeit zu erschließen. Immer wieder greife ich auf diese ständig länger werdende Liste zurück,

for Baltimore. THE FIRST WORLD CONGRESS OF THE MISSING THINGS (2014) especially invited people who inhabited the urban space around Lexington Market in Baltimore—a historical landmark, which had become a signifier of the lack of social welfare in the formerly lively city centre, with drug users and their case workers, homeless and underprivileged people socially excluded as primary residents. Holub was invited into the frame of a new "art district," funded by the NEA program for creative placemaking, whose goals she was suspicious of, since they often result in gentrification. The artist produced elements common to that of a congress, but accessible to everyone instead of being exclusive to the experts. She set up a congress office at Current, an artist-run gallery on Howard Street, produced performative moments in public space to invite people, while students of the University of Applied Arts Vienna set up an info desk at Lexington Market Hall.

A rhizomatic set of tables was designed to enable seating arrangements in non-hierarchical manners, turning the underused public space at the entrance of Lexington Market Subway Station into a permitted space of heterotopic appropriation for those who were already living there precariously. The content of the congress was also produced by diverse other audiences in Baltimore and led by people's informal knowledges. What emerged was an accumulation of stated desires of what was missing in Baltimore based on personal interpretations of the participants, contradicting a "scientific" production of knowledge genuine to a traditional format of a congress. "The Congress" meaning was deliberately open-ended and ambiguous, thus allowing the work to function on numerous levels of interpretation, while it refused to cohere into a singularly coded representation. In many ways, it behaved like what Henri Lefebvre calls "representational space."[4] This is a type of space that embraces the loci of passion, of action, of lived situations, and therefore by definition implies time and history in the making, but also reflects expertise and responsibility back to the decision makers, politicians, and citizens who are critically investigating/counteracting investment-driven creative placemaking agendas. Considering the project as a small gesture—as a starting point for a durational process to further develop programs and propositions for the future (social) infrastructure for the mix of people who inhabit the space—in the first congress in Baltimore residents and users of the urban public space claimed expertise themselves in relation to their environments. Resulting from the congress were two concrete projects: one was turning one of the dilapidated buildings on Howard Street into a vocational training centre for the homeless, drug addicts, ex-convicts, etc., inhabiting the area in and around Howard Street and Lexington Market. The second was the installation of an info kiosk for subsidy programs, jobs, etc. at the entrance of the Lexington Market subway station and site of the congress, because many of the people living around Howard Street were completely cut off from such information.

weil sich an ihr die Geschichte der Erweiterung und Diversifizierung koproduktiver Praktiken sehr gut ablesen lässt. In vielen dieser Ansätze wird das Moment von Öffentlichkeit nicht zur Gänze sichtbar ausgeschöpft. KünstlerInnen und KuratorInnen werden zu InitiatorInnen und postautonomen OrganisatorInnen von Versammlungen, in denen das Alltagswissen der Beteiligten im Mittelpunkt steht. Das kuratorische Ziel ist es, mögliche Handlungsspielräume für diese partizipativen Prozesse zu schaffen. Während also das Kuratorische Räume für Interaktionen und Informationen entwirft, entwickelt sich das Kunst„werk" selbst mit der Zeit zu einem aus Interventionen und Interaktionen bestehenden Gefüge, das für eine immer breitere Öffentlichkeit sorgt.[3]

Dieses kuratorische Versammeln und Zusammenfügen zeigt sich am deutlichsten in den nicht-hierarchischen öffentlichen Weltkongressen der fehlenden Dinge, die Holub 2014 in Baltimore entwickelte. THE FIRST WORLD CONGRESS OF THE MISSING THINGS richtete sich vor allem an die BewohnerInnen der Gegend um den Lexington Market in Baltimore. Die Markthalle war vom historischen Wahrzeichen der Stadt zum Symbol fehlender sozialer Fürsorgesysteme geworden. Im blühenden Stadtzentrum von einst lebten nunmehr insbesondere sozial benachteiligte Menschen, Obdachlose und DrogenkonsumentInnen. Holub wurde im Rahmen des Programms für *creative placemaking* (gefördert vom National Endowment for the Arts) eingeladen, ein Projekt für ein neues „Kunstviertel" zu entwickeln. Die Ziele des Programms waren Holub allerdings von Anfang an suspekt, da solche Projekte nicht selten Gentrifizierungsprozesse nach sich ziehen. Die Künstlerin entwickelte schließlich Elemente, die aus Kongressen bekannt sind, hier aber allen frei zugänglich und nicht nur den ExpertInnen vorbehalten waren. Sie eröffnete ein Kongressbüro in der von KünstlerInnen geleiteten Current Gallery in der Howard Street und lud zu performativen Interventionen im öffentlichen Raum ein, während Studierende von der Universität für angewandte Kunst Wien einen Infostand in der Lexington-Markthalle betrieben.

Eine rhizomatische Anordnung von Tischen erzeugte eine nicht-hierarchische Sitzordnung, durch die der wenig genutzte öffentliche Raum im Eingangsbereich der U-Bahnstation Lexington Market eine heterotopische Aneignung durch diejenigen ermöglichte, die dort schon seit längerem unter prekären Bedingungen lebten. Darüber hinaus wurde das Programm des Kongresses zusammen mit unterschiedlichen anderen TeilnehmerInnen und Gruppen aus Baltimore entwickelt und bezog das Alltagswissen aller Beteiligten mit ein. Das Ergebnis war eine Sammlung von Wünschen, die aufzeigte, was in Baltimore aus der persönlichen Perspektive der Teilnehmenden noch fehlte, im Gegensatz zu einer „wissenschaftlichen" Produktion von Wissen, wie sie in einem herkömmlichen Kongress erwartet wird. Das Ziel dieses Kongresses war jedoch ganz bewusst offen und mehrdeutig gelassen worden und so konnte das Projekt auf

THE SECOND WORLD NON-CONGRESS OF THE MISSING THINGS (2014) was held at the construction site of Vienna's new development of Lake-City Aspern. Holub called this a "non-congress" to reflect the fact it was a more incognito, clandestine and unpredictable gathering and refocus on vital issues of urban development in this Viennese district on the outskirts, the largest new urban residential extension of the city. For this non-congress, "missing things" were collected through workshops, events and non-meetings, addressing what remained under-developed and non-considered in the masterplan for Lake-City Aspern. They were researched in conversations with the construction workers and the first wave of fifty residents moving into the new district. In a workshop with the social design course at the University of Applied Arts Vienna, the students selected certain missing things and developed performances for the one-day congress, held at the canteen for the construction workers, an informal meeting place. The "missing things" were later proposed as a new planning vocabulary for future programs for Lake-City Aspern. The project also highlights the "production of (unwanted?) knowledge," where the "missing things" can be read as a reverse "production of desires" and as basis for "non-functional" urbanistic programs, not based on traditional functions, but highlighting hidden and poetic qualities or also political demands depending on the specific local scenario at a given time.[5]

THE THIRD WORLD CONGRESS OF THE MISSING THINGS (2021) focused on a key question evolving from research in a specific urban context, addressing "missing things" as a non-scientific topic and altogether—as method—raising the question of which, and whose, knowledge is considered relevant. Who decides? With the BambooKazas as informal structure for the congress, transparadiso transformed the parking lot of the Parish St. Paul in the Eisteich Housing Estate in Waltendorf for one weekend in early July into the informal congress centre. Several dérives explored hidden poetic moments in the Eisteichsiedlung, which characterize the quality of this neighborhood from the 1960s, at the same time creating an awareness for the obvious deficits in current-urban development driven by pragmatics and economical profit. One outcome of the research, and this congress, was a non-commercial community centre based on a collection of residents' desires, handed over as "Charter of the Missing Things" to the district manager and the City of Graz as a community-oriented proposal for change.

This most recent example of a Congress of the Missing Things, which transparadiso realized for Normal (2020–2021),[6] takes on multiple forms as part of an accumulative methodology. In the September 2021 mayoral elections, a new mayor was elected—Elke Kahr from the Communist party/KPÖ—as a reaction against the "big" projects (such as a cable car along the River Mur) of the previous mayor (conservative party/ÖVP), as well as

vielen unterschiedlichen Ebenen gelesen werden, indem es sich einer eindeutig kodierten Repräsentation entzog. In vielen Punkten glich der Kongress dem, was Henri Lefebvre als „Repräsentationsraum" bezeichnet.[4] Das ist jener Raumtypus, der durch die Orte „des Leidens/der Leidenschaft, des Handelns und früher erlebten Situationen" hergestellt wird und damit schon per definitionem Zeit und die im Entstehen begriffene Geschichte miteinbezieht. Er spiegelt aber auch Fachwissen und Verantwortung an die EntscheidungsträgerInnen, PolitikerInnen und BürgerInnen zurück, die sich kritisch mit investitionsgesteuerten Agenden von *creative placemaking* auseinandersetzen bzw. ihnen entgegenwirken. Das Projekt war als kleine Geste zu verstehen, als ein Ausgangspunkt für einen langfristig angelegten Prozess, aus dem sich weitere Programme und Vorhaben für eine zukünftige (gesellschaftliche) Infrastruktur entwickeln sollten, die auf die Bedürfnisse derjenigen einging, die diesen Raum bewohnten. Dieser erste Kongress in Baltimore bot den BewohnerInnen und NutzerInnen dieses öffentlichen urbanen Raums die Gelegenheit, bei Fragen und Problemen, die ihre eigene Umgebung betrafen, selbst als ExpertInnen aufzutreten und als solche anerkannt zu werden. Als ein konkretes Ergebnis des Kongresses entstanden zwei Projektvorschläge: Ein baufälliges Gebäude in der Howard Street sollte zu einem Ausbildungszentrum für die in der Gegend lebenden Obdachlosen, Suchtkranken und Haftentlassenen umgebaut werden und im Eingangsbereich der U-Bahn-Station Lexington Market, dem Veranstaltungsort des Kongresses, sollte ein Informationsstand eingerichtet werden, an dem sich die AnwohnerInnen etwa zu Förderprogrammen oder Jobangeboten beraten lassen konnten – Informationen, von denen sie bis dahin weitgehend ausgeschlossen waren.

THE SECOND WORLD NON-CONGRESS OF THE MISSING THINGS fand 2014 auf der Baustelle der Seestadt Aspern, dem größten neuen Stadtentwicklungsgebiet von Wien, statt. Holub nannte das Projekt einen „Non-Congress", um anzudeuten, dass es sich dabei um eine eher im kleinen Rahmen stattfindende Versammlung handelte, die sich mit grundlegenden Fragen von Stadtentwicklung in diesem AM STADTRAND gelegenen neuen Stadtteil beschäftigte. Im Rahmen von Non-Meetings, Workshops und Veranstaltungen wurden Missing Things für den Non-Congress zusammengetragen, die im Masterplan für die Seestadt Aspern kaum entwickelt bzw. weitgehend ignoriert worden waren. Die Recherche für das Projekt basierte sowohl auf Gesprächen mit den BauarbeiterInnen als auch auf solchen mit den ersten fünfzig BewohnerInnen von Aspern Seestadt. In einem Workshop des Studiengangs Social Design der Universität für angewandte Kunst Wien wählten Studierende einige Missing Things aus und entwickelten Performances für den eintägigen Non-Congress, der in der Kantine der BauarbeiterInnen stattfand, die zugleich als ihr informeller Treffpunkt fungierte. Danach wurden die Missing Things als neues Planungsvokabular für zukünftige Entwicklungsprojekte der Seestadt Aspern vorgeschlagen. Das Projekt untersuchte auch die

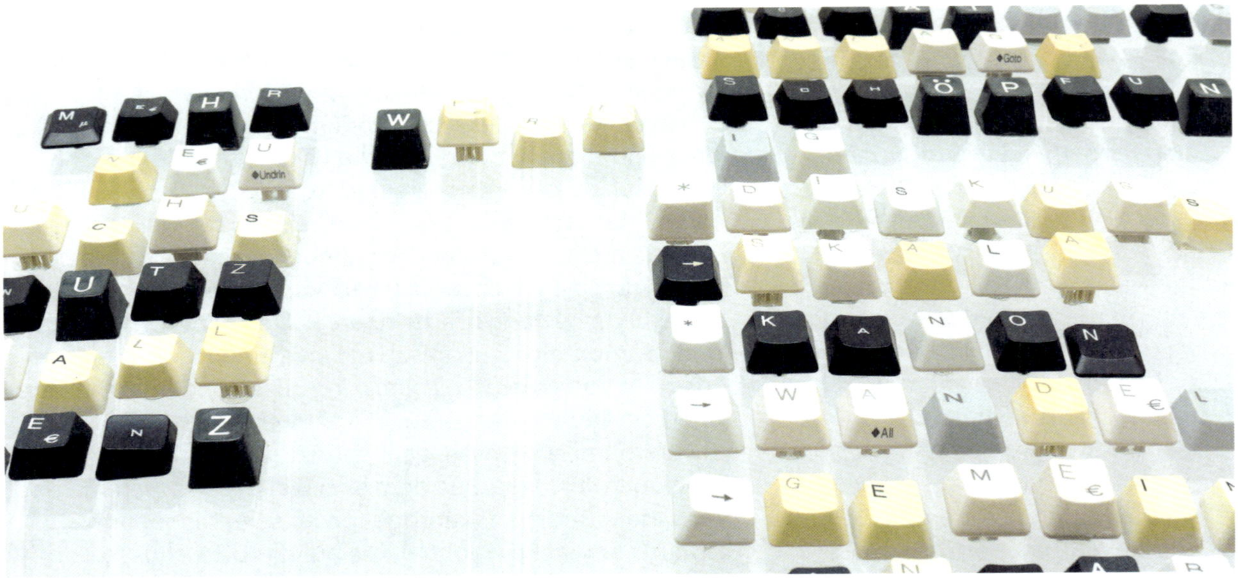

NEUWERTIG, Kunsthaus Wien, Vienna, 2015

NEUWERTIG, Kunsthaus Wien, Wien, 2015

selling off parcels of land without considering them as part of a larger urban context, transforming agricultural fields into maximum density and often luxurious housing as pure investment, etc.

What transparadiso had serendipitously set out to do by focusing on durational engagement was the following. NORMAL is an introductory gallery exhibition at the Haus der Architektur in Graz, presenting research and a series of four interrelated public art interventions based on this research. Here, the curatorial process involved a period of intense gathering, walks and focused research in Graz, resulting in a hybrid exhibition in parallel with four distinct commissioned public interventions proposed as part of Culture Year Graz 2020. NORMAL was framed around the single question "What is normal?" directed towards the city's specific peri-urban situation, additionally behaving as an open brief for the Third World Congress alongside the other three invited responses to four districts. Initial research highlighted the homogeneous character of the transformation of new peri-urban landscapes that transparadiso experienced in Graz—even though the four districts concerned are very different in terms of landscape, history and remnants of former village structures—typical of generic approaches to urban development, resulting in standardized types of urban residencies and lack of social spaces in many newly regenerated small towns in the region.

As one of the four interventions—following on from the *School for Civic Action* they carried out in Roskilde, Denmark (2018–2020)—public works from London asked what role a district's main square can play in relation to the city's main square by organizing PLATZEN—School for Civic Action in May 2021. The exhibition at the HdA (Haus der Architektur, Graz) presents themes for PLATZEN collected during the first intervention in

„Produktion von (unerwünschtem?) Wissen", wobei die Missing Things als umgekehrte Wunschproduktion und als Grundlage für nicht-funktionale urbanistische Programme verstanden werden können, die eben nicht auf herkömmlichen Funktionen basieren, sondern verborgene und poetische Qualitäten oder auch politische Forderungen betonen, die zu einer bestimmten Zeit an einem bestimmten Ort bestehen.[5]

THE THIRD WORLD CONGRESS OF THE MISSING THINGS (2021) setzte sich erneut mit der zentralen Frage auseinander, die aus der Untersuchung eines ganz konkreten städtischen Kontextes unter dem nicht-wissenschaftlichen Aspekt der Missing Things entsteht – der Frage danach, was und wessen Wissen überhaupt relevant ist, die hier zur grundlegenden methodischen Vorgehensweise wird. Wer aber entscheidet darüber? Mit den BambooKazas als temporärem Bau verwandelte transparadiso den Parkplatz der Pfarre St. Paul in der Eisteichsiedlung in Waltendorf (Graz, Steiermark) für ein Wochenende Anfang Juli 2021 in ein informelles Kongresszentrum. In mehreren dérives wurden verborgene poetische Momente der Eisteichsiedlung erkundet, die für das in den 1960er-Jahren entstandene Viertel charakteristisch sind. Gleichzeitig sollte dadurch auch für die offensichtlichen Mängel der aktuellen Stadtentwicklung sensibilisiert werden, die vor allem von pragmatischen Lösungen und Profitmaximierung bestimmt ist. Ein Ergebnis dieses Kongresses war die Forderung nach einem gemeinnützigen Stadtteilzentrum. Die von den KongressteilnehmerInnen geäußerten Veränderungsvorschläge wurden als „Charta of the Missing Things" dem Bezirksvorsteher und der Stadt Graz übergeben.

Der aktuellste Congress of the Missing Things basierte auf einer kumulativen Methode, nahm viele unterschiedliche Formen an und wurde von transparadiso für NORMAL

October 2020. A citizen's initiative from Andritz felt invigorated by public works' activation of the Andritz Main Square, including a manifestation for installing a *Begegnungszone* (meeting area), a street where pedestrians come first and cars have to slow down. transparadiso aims to organize meetings with the new vice-mayor from the Green Party (who also attended the final exhibition of NORMAL at Forum Stadtpark before the election), the head of the district of Waltendorf (who attended the whole Third World Congress), and others to discuss next steps, especially concerning a non-commercial centre in Waltendorf.

As part of another of the four interventions, Georg Winter/DancePlantPlan AG began working on the DancePlantPlan in Wetzelsdorf in spring 2020, installing the DancePlantField in cooperation with the Grottenhof Agricultural and Forestry School.[7] Activated with local residents, using performative artistic interventions, DancePlantPlan addressed the issue of converting agricultural land on the outskirts of the city into new housing estates, contrasting with the recent hype for urban gardening taking place in the city centre. The DancePlantPlan AG was recently offered a new field in the same area to be able to continue.

As their starting point, transparadiso provided research on the history of the surrounding territories and suggested topics to respond to, where each of the four proposed responsive interventions was to be realized in cooperation with local organizations with the aim of informing the longer-term development of districts, sites, and communities. This longer-term approach created a discursive constellation where the exhibition form (as space for public gathering rather than merely a display of objects—also in the final exhibition at Forum Stadtpark, which presented the realized urban interventions) remains one of many productive outcomes. The exhibition space represents a collective dimension for art as a socialized and open work, with participation taking part in a process of evaluation as much as activation. Shifting from the artist to the audience as co-producers of the critical and discursive content of the work, exhibition-making is thus put forth as an actual, as well as metaphorical, relational process. Such formats have become emblematic of the educational and curatorial models of the post-participatory condition, where Holub is an artist who produces the frameworks for different modes of participation not as public event, but as temporal degrees of agency.

Holub's works therefore can be said to often take the social as its territory, as metaphor and evocation. Her practice has its own rules and objectives, unfixed and open, enhancing a macro-utopia. The social is often suggested through a simple evocative image, a symbol, a trope, a gesture, akin to the poetic image, or the quite radical gesture of a "European parade of apple trees." This imaginary and real proposition is the underlying element of

(2020–2021) veranstaltet.[6] Bei der Grazer Bürgermeister-Innenwahl im September 2021 wurde Elke Kahr (KPÖ) zur neuen Bürgermeisterin gewählt. Ihr Wahlerfolg war eine Reaktion sowohl auf die „Großprojekte" ihres Vorgängers von der ÖVP, etwa die Seilbahn entlang der Mur, den Ausverkauf von Grundstücken, ohne auf den städtischen Kontext Rücksicht zu nehmen, die Umwandlung landwirtschaftlicher Flächen zu maximal verdichtetem Bauland als reines Investitionsprojekt, oft um Luxuswohnungen zu bauen.

Die Fokussierung von transparadiso auf langfristige Interventionen ist wesentlicher Bestandteil auch in NORMAL, einer Ausstellung im Haus der Architektur in Graz, die sowohl die Recherche zu den Grazer Stadtbezirken als auch die daraus hervorgegangenen vier sich aufeinander beziehenden künstlerischen Interventionen im öffentlichen Raum präsentierte. Hier bestand der kuratorische Prozess aus zeitintensiven Versammlungen und Ortsbegehungen sowie aus sorgfältigen Recherchen in Graz, aus denen schließlich eine hybride Ausstellung sowie vier Interventionen im öffentlichen Raum im Rahmen des Kulturjahres Graz 2020 und die abschließende Ausstellung im Forum Stadtpark hervorgingen. NORMAL entwickelte sich ausgehend von der Frage „Was ist normal?", die sich auf die spezifische periurbane Situation von Graz bezog. Neben den drei eingeladenen künstlerischen Beiträgen zu den vier Stadtbezirken war diese Frage zugleich auch der offene Ausgangspunkt für den Third World Congress. Obwohl die vier untersuchten Bezirke in Geschichte, Landschaft und ehemaliger dörflicher Struktur sehr unterschiedlich sind, stellte transparadiso in ihren ersten Recherchen die Gleichförmigkeit der neuen städtischen Veränderungen heraus, die für die schablonenhaften Ansätze in der Stadtentwicklung bezeichnend sind. In vielen der in der Umgebung liegenden, neugestalteten und sanierten Kleinstädte führte dieser Ansatz zu standardisierten Typologien städtischen Wohnens sowie zu einem Mangel an Sozialräumen.

In einer der vier Interventionen ging das Londonder Architektur- und Kunstkollektiv public works der Frage nach, in welchem Verhältnis der Hauptplatz des Bezirks zum Hauptplatz der Stadt Graz stehe. Nach ihrer *School for Civic Action* in Roskilde, Dänemark (2018–2020), organisierten public works im Mai 2021 *PLATZEN – School for Civic Action* in Graz. In der Ausstellung im HdA (Haus der Architektur, Graz) wurden die Themen vorgestellt, die während einer ersten Intervention im Oktober 2020 (für PLATZEN) gesammelt worden waren. public works' Auseinandersetzung mit dem Andritzer Hauptplatz brachte eine lokale BürgerInnen-Initiative u. a. dazu, sich für eine „Begegnungszone" einzusetzen, eine Straße, auf der die FußgängerInnen Vorrang haben und Autos langsamer fahren sollten. transparadiso beabsichtigt verschiedene Treffen zu organisieren, um über die Umsetzung eines nicht-kommerziellen Stadtzentrums in Waltendorf zu diskutieren, so auch mit dem neuen Vizebürgermeister der Grünen (der vor den Wahlen die abschließende NORMAL-Ausstellung im Forum Stadtpark besucht hatte) und dem Landrat von Waltendorf (der am gesamten Third World Congress teilgenommen hatte).

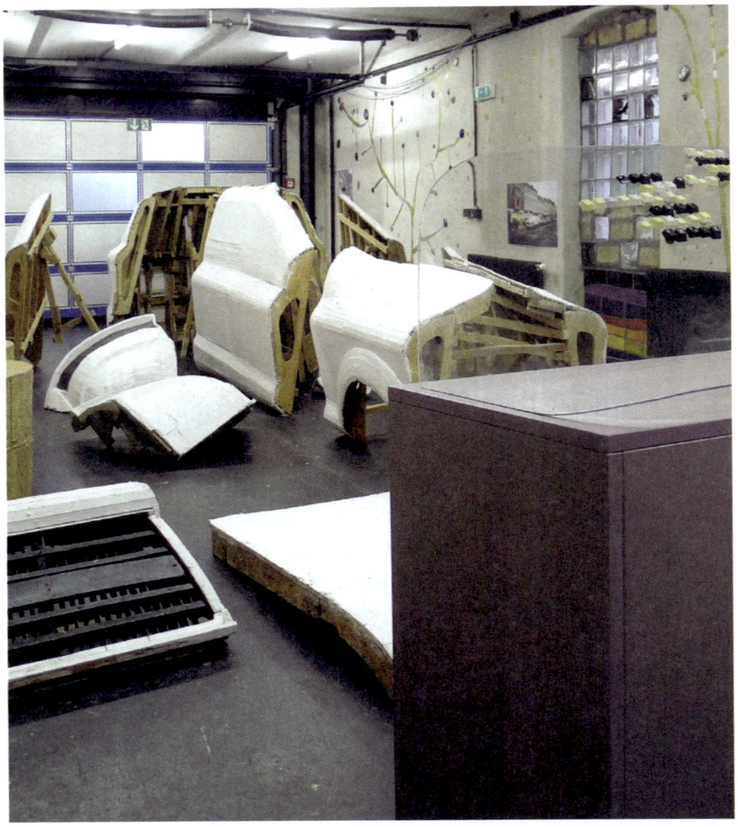

Exhibition view with NEUWERTIG, in: *Waste Value Rising*, Kunsthaus Wien, Vienna, 2016

Ausstellungsansicht mit NEUWERTIG, in: *Abfallwert steigend*, Kunsthaus Wien, Wien, 2016

Holub's recent artistic-curatorial project WE PARAPOM! (2021–2025, European Capital of Culture Chemnitz 2025), which invites the residents to open up their properties for this unusual parade as a means of envisaging a future world, crossing property lines as well as traversing social boundaries, laying the ground for artistic interventions, questioning standards and deconstructing the figure of a "parade" as a manifestation of power. Chemnitz (formerly Karl-Marx-Stadt in the GDR) is notorious for right-wing movements, and WE PARAPOM! thus also addresses the silent middle. This flagship project intends to evolve into 2025: an accumulation that begins with a simple gesture of planting apple trees, not symbolic but a real invitation for all citizens—as well as city administrations, institutions, associations and organizations—to grab and behold: to plant, grow, break soil, and take over "sponsorships" for the planting of apple trees on private and public areas. Extending the invitation for direct action with a future imaginary at the same time means bringing the social into the present with a form of pragmatic realness. What begins as a modest symbolic gesture offers huge potential for extensive layers of social and civic action, culminating in non-functioning poetics alongside actualized propositions whilst contributing to change for a more just society.

In einer weiteren Intervention begann Georg Winter, mit der TanzPflanzPlan AG in Zusammenarbeit mit der Landwirtschaftlichen Fachschule Grottenhof im Frühjahr 2020 in Wetzelsdorf das TanzPflanzFeld zu installieren.[7] Zusammen mit AnwohnerInnen befasste sich das Projekt TanzPflanzPlan in performativen künstlerischen Interventionen mit der Umwandlung von AM STADTRAND gelegenen landwirtschaftlichen Nutzflächen zu Neubausiedlungen und stellte diesem Vorgang den aktuellen Hype um Urban Gardening im Stadtzentrum gegenüber. Damit Georg Winter diese Arbeit fortsetzen kann, wurde ihm 2022 eine neue Fläche in der Nachbarschaft angeboten.

Als Ausgangspunkt von NORMAL stellte transparadiso umfangreiches Recherchematerial zur Geschichte der jeweiligen Orte und deren Kontexte zur Verfügung und schlug Themen vor, auf die die vier Interventionen reagieren konnten. Um die Entwicklungen in den Bezirken, Nachbarschaften und unterschiedlichen Standorten nachhaltig zu beeinflussen, sollte jede Intervention in Zusammenarbeit mit lokalen Einrichtungen und Institutionen realisiert werden. Dieser längerfristig orientierte Ansatz schuf eine diskursive Konstellation, in der das Format der Ausstellung nur eines von vielen Ergebnissen war. Die Abschlussausstellung im Forum Stadtpark in Graz fungierte daher auch als öffentlicher Versammlungsraum und nicht nur als Objektschau der realisierten urbanen Interventionen. Der Ausstellungsraum stellte eine kollektive Dimension künstlerischen Arbeitens dar, die zugleich gesellschaftlich engagiert und offen ist, und in der sowohl der Prozess der Aktivierung als auch jener des Reflektierens maßgeblich von partizipativen Praktiken getragen werden. Durch die Verschiebung des Fokus von den KünstlerInnen auf das Publikum wird dieses zu KoproduzentInnen des kritischen und diskursiven Inhalts der Arbeiten, und das Ausstellungsmachen sowohl zu einer konkreten als auch metaphorischen, relationalen Praxis. Solche Ansätze stehen emblematisch für „pädagogische" und kuratorische Modelle eines postpartizipatorischen Zustands, in denen Barbara Holub eine Künstlerin ist, die mit ihren Arbeiten unterschiedliche Rahmenbedingungen für verschiedene Formen von Partizipation schafft. Dabei ist sie weniger an öffentlichen Veranstaltungen interessiert als daran, (zeitliche) Phasen von Handlungen zu benennen.

Holubs Arbeiten bewegen sich oft auf dem Feld des Sozialen, sowohl im metaphorischen Sinne als auch als Handlungsaufforderung. Ihre künstlerische Praxis folgt ihren eigenen Regeln und Zielen, die offen und nicht festgelegt sind, die eine „Makro-Utopie" propagieren. Oft wird das Soziale durch ein einfaches assoziatives Bild, ein Symbol, eine Metapher, eine Geste, gleich dem poetischen Bild, angedeutet, oder durch eine radikalere Geste wie die der Europäischen Parade der Apfelbäume. Auf diesem imaginären sowie realen Vorhaben basiert Holubs neuestes künstlerisch-kuratorisches Projekt WE PARAPOM! (2021–2025, Europäische Kulturhauptstadt Chemnitz 2025). Das Projekt lädt die BewohnerInnen dazu ein, ihre Grundstücke für diese ungewöhnliche

1 As I've written about elsewhere, there has been a remarkable development within the contemporary art field that we have termed the "educational turn."[1] In proposing contemporary art as marked by this "educational turn," artists have mobilized different ways in which educational formats, methods, programs, models, terms, processes and procedures have become pervasive in art and social practices and its attendant critical frameworks. This is not simply observing that contemporary art has adopted education as a theme, but rather asserting that curating, and art production more broadly, increasingly operate as expanded educational praxes with a desire for active participation from diverse publics as part of a wider interest in "conversation," speaking together, and "discursive" processes connecting immediate localized concerns with something happening elsewhere. See Paul O'Neill and Mick Wilson (eds.), Curating and the Educational Turn (London/Amsterdam: Open Editions/de Appel, 2010).

2 Edward W. Said, Representations of the Intellectual (New York: Pantheon Books, 1994), unpaginated.

3 As seen in some of the people-based artist projects by Tania Bruguera, Black Quantum Futurism, Can Altay, BalinHouse Projects, Sandi Hilal, Cooking Sections, Temporary Services, Ber Theis, Oda Projesi, Ultra Red, Kathrin Böhm, Park Fiction, Rick Lowe, Blank Noise, Ahmet Ögüt, Apolonija Šušteršič, Li Mu, or Jeanne van Heeswijk, to name a few examples. See Claire Bishop, "The Social Turn: Collaborations and its Discontents," Artforum, vol. XLVI, no. 6 (February, 2006): pp. 178–183; and Maria Lind, "Complications: On Collaboration, Agency and Contemporary Art," Public Art/Culture/Ideas, no. 39, "New Communities" (Spring, 2009): pp. 52–73.

4 Henri Lefebvre, The Production of Space (Oxford: Blackwell, 1991), p. 39.

5 See www.transparadiso.com/en/projects/normal-direct-urbanism-x-4 and the publication NORMAL. Direct Urbanism x4 (Vienna: Salon für Kunstbuch, 2021).

6 These, as well as the outcomes of the other Congresses, are collated on the website www.missingthings.org.

7 For more information about the project, see tanzpflanzplan.at (accessed Sept. 5, 2022).

Parade zu öffnen, um eine zukünftige Welt zu imaginieren. Das Überschreiten von gesellschaftlichen Grenzen sowie von Grundstücksgrenzen lässt einen Raum entstehen, in dem durch künstlerische Interventionen vorherrschende Normen infrage gestellt und die Figur der „Parade“ als Manifestation von Macht dekonstruiert werden. Chemnitz (ehemals Karl-Marx-Stadt in der DDR) ist heute berüchtigt für eine einflussreiche rechte Szene, und so wendet sich WE PARAPOM! auch an die „stille Mitte“ der Gesellschaft. Dieses groß angelegte, repräsentative Projekt soll bis 2025 erste Formen annehmen: ein beständiges Wachsen, das mit der einfachen Geste des Pflanzens von Apfelbäumen beginnt. Es handelt sich dabei nicht um eine symbolische, sondern um eine ganz und gar reale Einladung, die sich an alle BürgerInnen sowie an die Stadtverwaltung, an lokale Institutionen, Vereine und Organisationen richtet, dabei zu sein und mitzumachen: zu pflanzen, zu ernten, umzugraben und „Patenschaften“ für die Apfelbäume zu übernehmen, die auf privaten und öffentlichen Flächen gepflanzt werden. Die Aufforderung zur direkten Aktion durch das Entwickeln von Visionen für die Zukunft bedeutet zugleich, das Gesellschaftliche/Soziale in Form einer „pragmatischen Realität“ in die Gegenwart zu holen. Was als bescheidene symbolische Geste beginnt, birgt in sich das enorme Potenzial eines vielschichtigen sozialen und zivilgesellschaftlichen Engagements, das in einer Poetik des Nicht-Funktionalen der realisierten Projekte seinen Höhepunkt findet, während es gleichzeitig dazu beiträgt, die Gesellschaft gerechter zu machen.

1 In der zeitgenössischen Kunst hat, wie an anderer Stelle erwähnt, in der letzten Zeit eine bemerkenswerte Entwicklung stattgefunden, die wir als *educational turn* bezeichnet haben. KünstlerInnen haben verschiedenste pädagogische Formate, Methoden, Programme, Modelle, Begriffe, Prozesse und Verfahren entwickelt, die sich sowohl in künstlerischen als auch in sozialen Kontexten bewegen. Dabei geht es nicht nur darum, dass nun in der zeitgenössischen Kunst vermehrt pädagogische Themen aufgegriffen werden, sondern auch darum, dass das Kuratieren, und auch künstlerische Arbeiten im weiteren Sinne, sich als erweiterte pädagogische Praktiken verstehen, die an der aktiven Beteiligung unterschiedlicher Öffentlichkeiten interessiert sind. Sie wollen „ins Gespräch“ kommen, miteinander diskutieren und durch diskursive Verfahren den unmittelbaren, lokalen Kontext mit anderen Orten verknüpfen. Siehe dazu Paul O'Neill und Mick Wilson (Hg.), Curating and the Educational Turn, London/Amsterdam: Open Editions/de Appel, 2010.

2 Edward W. Said, Representations of the Intellectual, New York: Pantheon Books, 1994, ohne Paginierung.

3 So wie auch in den partizipativen Projekten von Tania Bruguera, Black Quantum Futurism, Can Altay, BalinHouse Projects, Sandi Hilal, Cooking Sections, Temporary Services, Ber Theis, Oda Projesi, Ultra Red, Kathrin Böhm, Park Fiction, Rick Lowe, Blank Noise, Ahmet Ögüt, Apolonija Šušteršič, Mu, Jeanne van Heeswijk und anderen. Siehe Claire Bishop, „The Social Turn: Collaborations and its Discontents“, in: Artforum, Vol. XLVI, Nr. 6 (Februar 2006), S. 178–183 und Maria Lind, „Complications: On Collaboration, Agency and Contemporary Art“, in: Public Art/Culture/Ideas, Nr. 39, „New Communities“ (Frühling 2009), S. 52–73.

4 Henri Lefebvre, The Production of Space, Oxford: Blackwell, 1991, S. 39.

5 Siehe http://www.transparadiso.com/en/projects/normal-direct-urbanism-x-4 (Zugriff am 5.9.2022) und die Publikation Barbara Holub, Paul Rajakovics (Hg.), NORMAL. Direkter Urbanismus × 4, Wien: Salon für Kunstbuch, 2021.

6 Weitere Informationen zu diesem als auch zu den anderen Kongressen sind auf der Website http://www.missingthings.org verfügbar.

7 Für weitere Informationen zu diesem Projekt siehe https://tanzpflanzplan.at (Zugriff: 5.9.2022).

WHAT I AM PROUD OF

WHAT I AM PROUD OF explores the fast urban transformation in Istanbul and "the new international style" of globalized corporate architecture and its impact on the changing identity of Istanbul as a city undergoing rapid urban transformation between aspirations, desires of belonging and displacement, and the commodification of public space.

Based on a tour through the construction site of Zorlu Centre, which comprises of office buildings and housing—thus creating a new skyline of Istanbul by three towers—and her research in traditional quarters in Istanbul, Barbara Holub conceived a complex collage-drawing for the Zorlu Collection in Istanbul. This drawing is part of her series of "color book drawings" of unplanned or surprising appropriations of the urban public space, critically discussing the transformation of urban public space. In these drawings, and especially in WHAT I AM PROUD OF, hierarchies of information are flattened, their multilayered information exposed to interpretation by the viewer. A "site-specific" piece reduced to a drawing.

The artist continued the series of WHAT I as ink drawings of texts that call the viewer to action. However, the letters overlap in such a way that the text is no longer legible—again, recalling silent activism.[BS]

WHAT I AM PROUD OF

WHAT I AM PROUD OF beschäftigt sich mit Fragen des raschen urbanen Transformationsprozesses und des neuen „internationalen Stils" einer globalisierten „Unternehmensarchitektur" in Istanbul sowie deren Auswirkungen auf die sich verändernde Identität dieser Stadt, durch deren raschen Wandel Viertel ohne gesetzliche Reglements entwickelt werden – zwischen Ehrgeiz, dem Bedürfnis dazuzugehören, Entwurzelung und der Kommerzialisierung des öffentlichen Raums.

Ausgehend von einem Rundgang durch die Baustelle des Zorlu Centres, das aus Bürogebäuden und Wohnhäusern besteht und mit drei Türmen eine neue Skyline von Istanbul schafft, und ihren Recherchen in traditionellen Vierteln Istanbuls, konzipierte Barbara Holub eine komplexe Collage-Zeichnung für die Zorlu Collection in Istanbul. Diese Zeichnung ist Teil ihrer Serie von „Malbuchzeichnungen" ungeplanter oder überraschender Aneignungen des städtischen öffentlichen Raums, die sich kritisch mit der Transformation des städtischen öffentlichen Raums auseinandersetzen. In diesen Zeichnungen, und insbesondere in WHAT I AM PROUD OF, werden alle Informationen gleichwertig dargestellt, sodass die Hervorhebung bestimmter Inhalte, die üblicherweise das Medium Zeichnung kennzeichnet, gezielt unterminiert wird. Somit sind die BetrachterInnen ihren eigenen vielschichtigen Informationen ausgesetzt. Eine „ortsspezifische" Arbeit, reduziert auf eine Zeichnung.

Die Künstlerin setzte in der Folge die Serie von WHAT I als Tuschezeichnungen von Texten fort, die die BetrachterInnen direkt zum Handeln auffordern. Allerdings überlagern sich die Buchstaben dieser Aufforderungen derart, dass der Text nicht mehr lesbar ist – im Sinne von stillem Aktivismus.[BS]

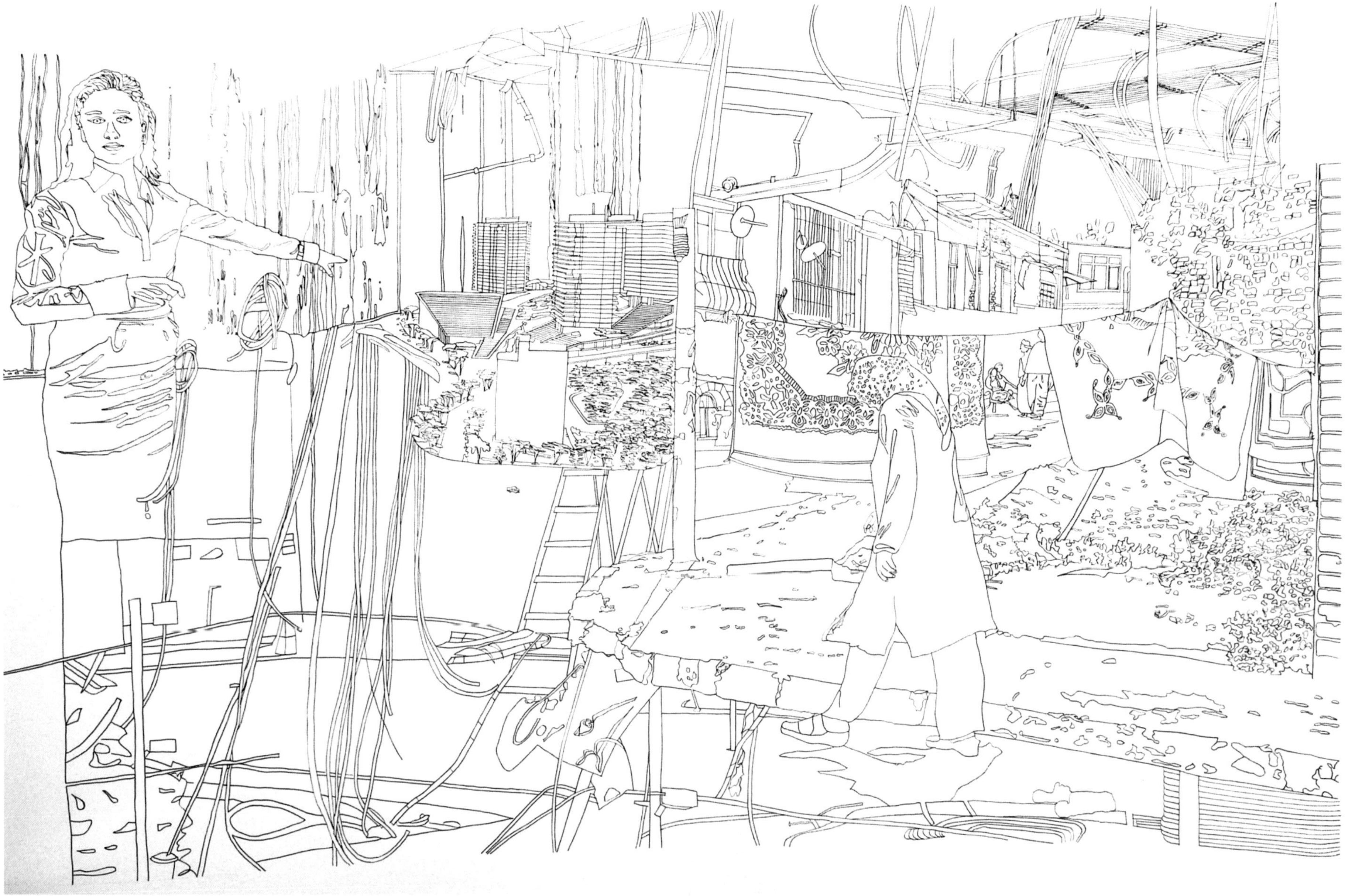

WHAT I AM PROUD OF, Zorlu Collection, Istanbul, 2011

WHAT I AM PROUD OF, Sammlung Zorlu, Istanbul, 2011

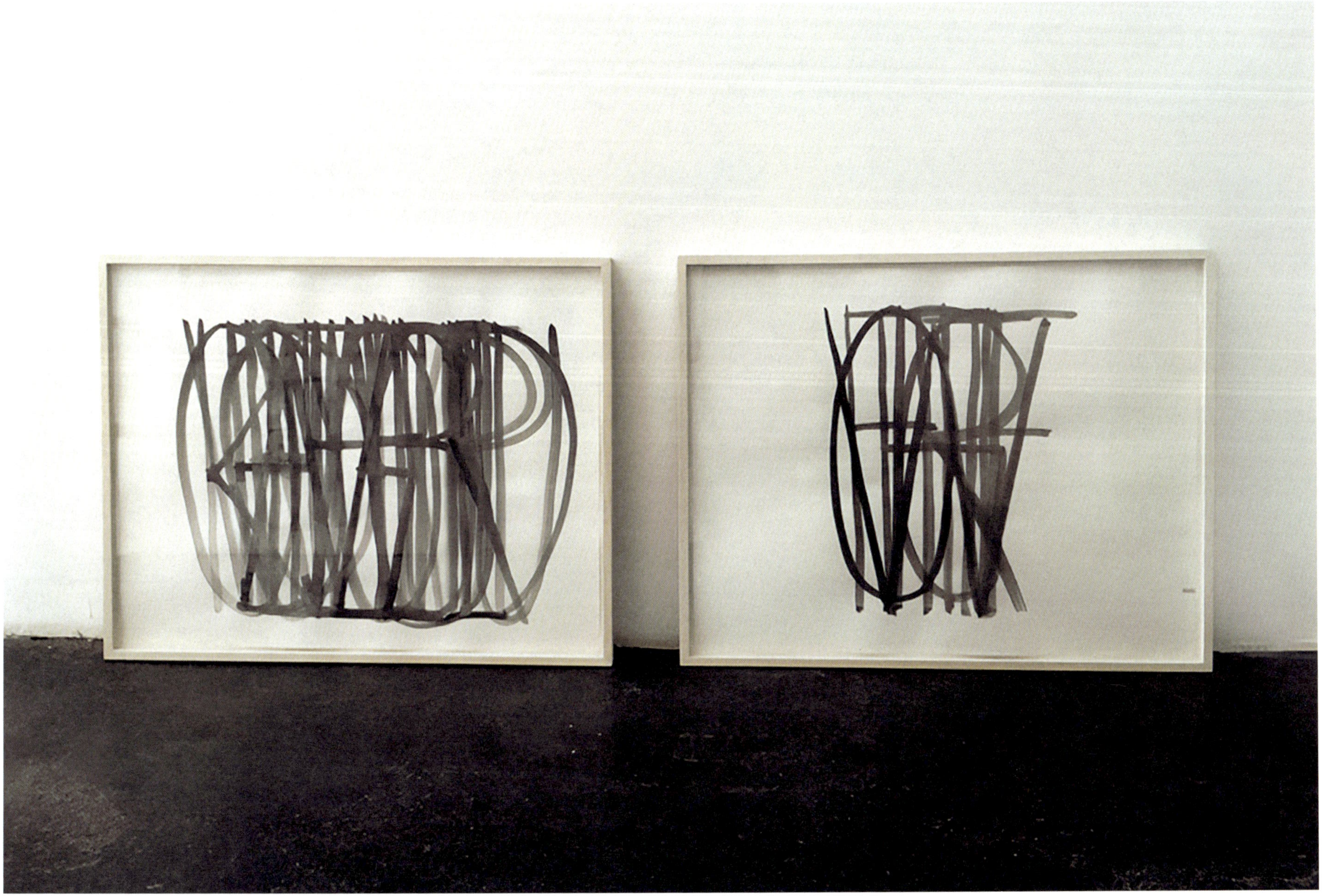

WHAT I..., *pursuing, proceeding*, exhibition view, Peithner-Lichtenfels Gallery, Vienna, 2017

WHAT I ..., *nachgehen, vorgehen*, Ausstellungsansicht, Galerie Peithner-Lichtenfels, Wien, 2017

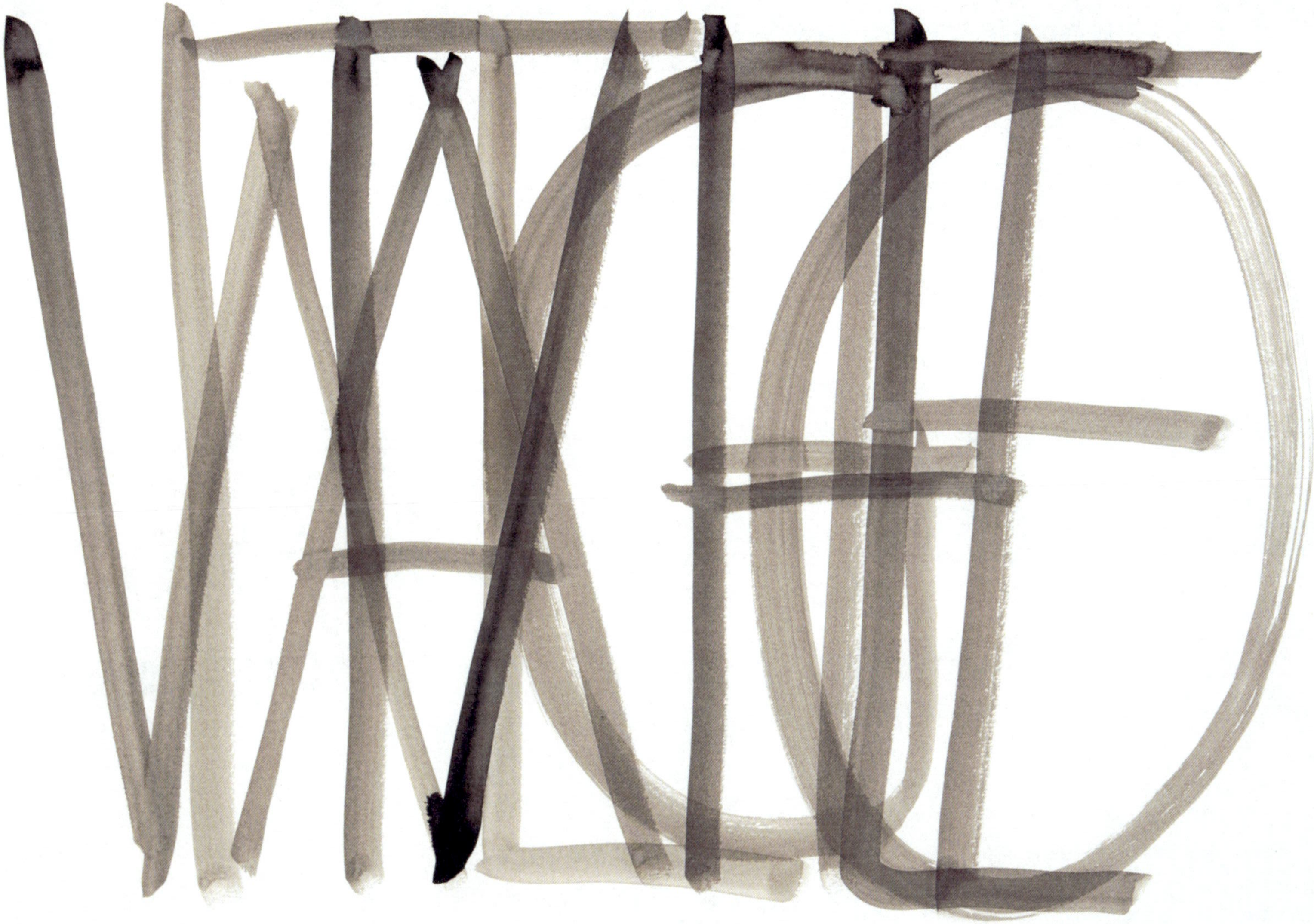

WHAT I LET GO, 2019

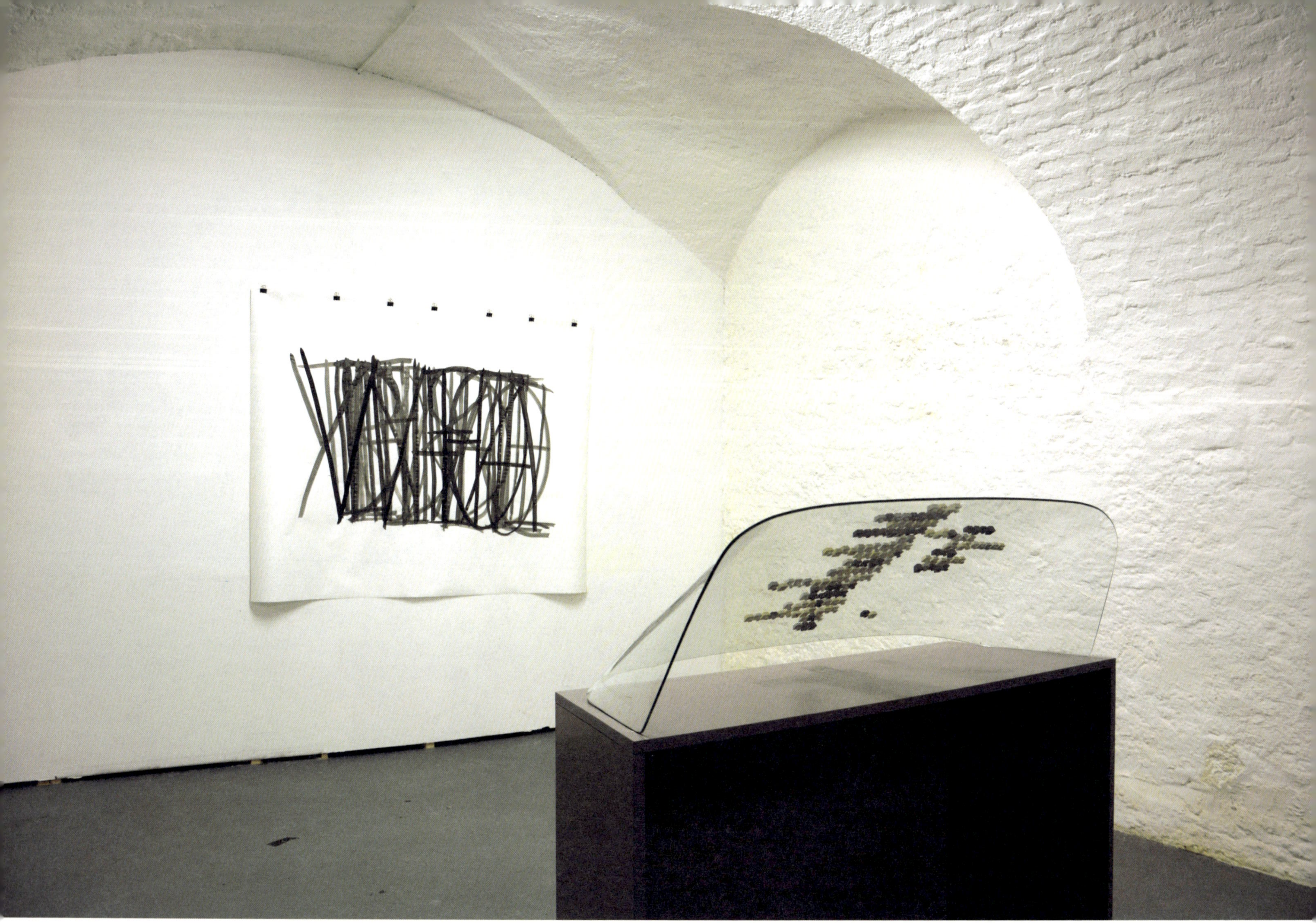

WHAT I WOULD LIKE TO HANDLE DISCRETELY
pursuing, proceeding, exhibition view, Peithner-Lichtenfels Gallery, Vienna, 2017

WHAT I WOULD LIKE TO HANDLE DISCRETELY
nachgehen, vorgehen, Ausstellungsansicht, Galerie Peithner-Lichtenfels, Wien, 2017

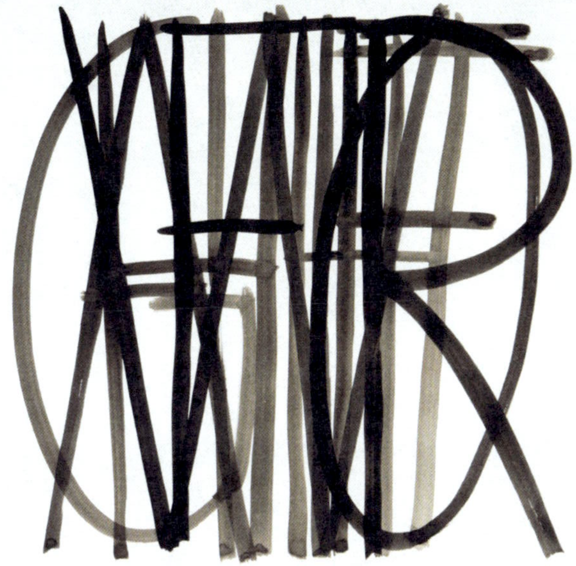

WHAT I FIGHT FOR, 2013 WHAT I FIGHT FOR, 2013

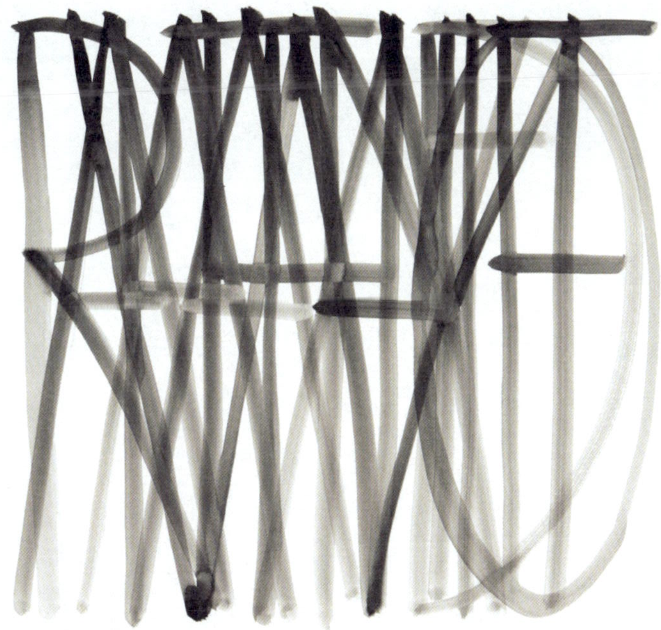

WHAT I AM AFRAID OF, 2013 WHAT I AM AFRAID OF, 2013

 COLLECTION 2003/2004, Hohenlohe & Kalb Gallery, Vienna, 2003

KOLLEKTION 2003/2004, Galerie Hohenlohe & Kalb, Wien, 2003

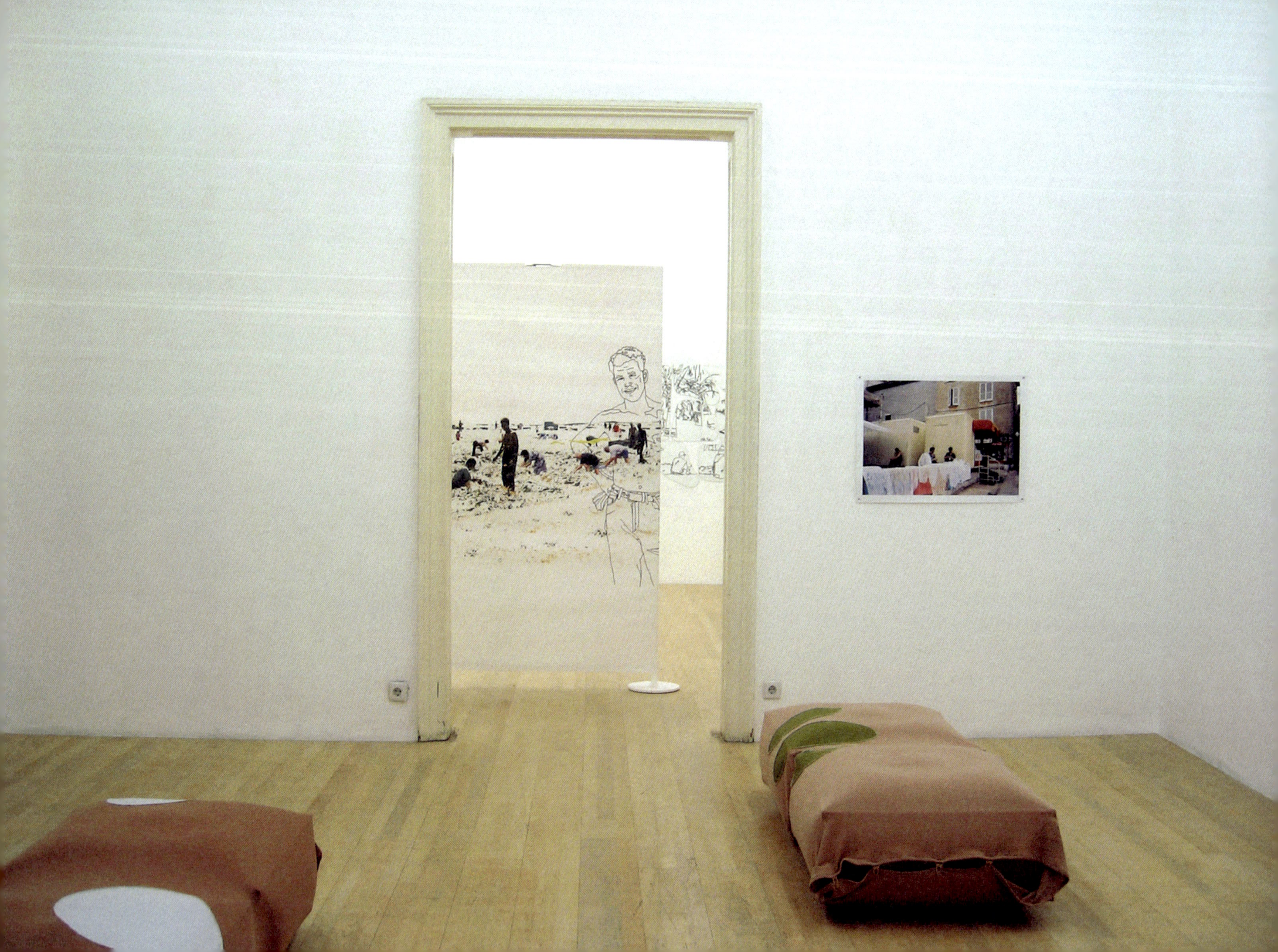

IN A SUNKEN LIVING ROOM THERE IS NO PICTURE BAN

The sunken living room has long been a staple of middle-class home furnishing. The price, quality, and design indicate the social status of the owner. A similar role as status symbol has always been attributed to owning art(works). With IN A SUNKEN LIVING ROOM THERE IS NO PICTURE BAN, Holub presents a "collection" of artworks disguised as furnishings (and vice versa), examining the fluid function of art between collectible and distinguishing feature.

To the opposites of nature (landscape) and culture (living) implied by the term "living landscape" (known in German as a *Wohnlandschaft*, literally a "living landscape" or "landscaped interior") Holub adds another aspect: she combines the elements in the domestic sphere that imply privacy and seclusion with critical reflections on the world of work in her objects. For example: the "handshake logo carpet" for good business, the car window mosaic with a "coloring book picture" of someone tending a park in La Réunion while visitors relax in the shade, and photographs of artisans working in public space in Croatia, or a room-divider covered with a rotating image. The latter combines two different aspects of harvest work: the harsh working conditions of North African migrant workers harvesting in southern Italy, and voluntary/unpaid work in the strawberry fields of Austria, which is more akin to an enjoyable leisure pursuit. The only object framed, and thus connoted as an artwork, depicts the photo of a ladder in a pantyhose—a fault.

Instead of viewing the question of the requirements to be met by an artwork—as a "collection object"—in a living landscape and "what fits" in the context of aesthetic criteria, she does so with regard to the function of art in society. The "models" on display are accompanied by a "catalog of samples" used to create additional versions of the existing objects to order.[BR]

IN EINER WOHNLANDSCHAFT HERRSCHT KEIN BILDERVERBOT

Die Wohnlandschaft ist längst zum fixen Bestandteil bürgerlicher Heimausstattung geworden. Preis, Qualität und Design geben Aufschluss über die gesellschaftliche Stellung seines Besitzers/seiner Besitzerin. Dem Besitz von Kunst(werken) wird seit jeher eine ähnliche Rolle als Statussymbol zugeschrieben. Holub präsentiert mit IN EINER WOHNLANDSCHAFT HERRSCHT KEIN BILDERVERBOT eine „Kollektion" von als Wohnobjekte getarnten Kunstwerken (und vice versa), indem sie die fluide Funktion von Kunst zwischen Sammlungsobjekt und Distinktionsmerkmal beleuchtet.

Dem Gegensatz Natur (Landschaft) und Kultur (Wohnen), der im Begriff „Wohnlandschaft" impliziert ist, fügt Holub eine weitere Ebene hinzu: Sie verknüpft die Elemente, die im Wohnbereich Privatheit und Zurückgezogenheit suggerieren, mit kritischen Reflexionen zur Arbeitswelt in ihren Objekten, wie z. B. dem „Handshake-Logoteppich" für ein gutes Geschäft, Autofensterscheiben-Mosaike mit einem „Malbuchbild" von der Pflege eines Parks in La Réunion, während BesucherInnen sich im Schatten entspannen, sowie die Fotografien von Handwerksarbeit, die im öffentlichen Raum in Kroatien ausgeführt wird, oder der Paravent, dem ein verdrehbares Bild übergestülpt ist. In Letzterem überlagern sich zwei verschiedene Aspekte von Erntearbeit – Erntearbeit in Süditalien, die von den harten Arbeitsbedingungen der Wanderarbeiter aus Nordafrika geprägt ist, sowie freiwillige/unentgeltliche Arbeit auf Erdbeerfeldern in Österreich, die eher einem Freizeitvergnügen entspricht. Das einzige gerahmte, und damit als Kunstwerk konnotierte, Objekt zeigt das Foto einer Laufmasche einer Strumpfhose – eines Fehlers also.

Die Frage nach den Ansprüchen, denen ein Kunstwerk – als „Sammlungsobjekt" – in einer Wohnlandschaft Rechnung tragen muss, und dem, „was passt", stellt Holub nicht in Bezug auf ästhetische Kriterien, sondern in Bezug auf die Funktion von Kunst in der Gesellschaft. Ergänzt werden die gezeigten „Modelle" durch einen „Musterkatalog", anhand dessen die vorhandenen Objekte mit zusätzlichen Ausführungen auf Bestellung angefertigt werden können.[BR]

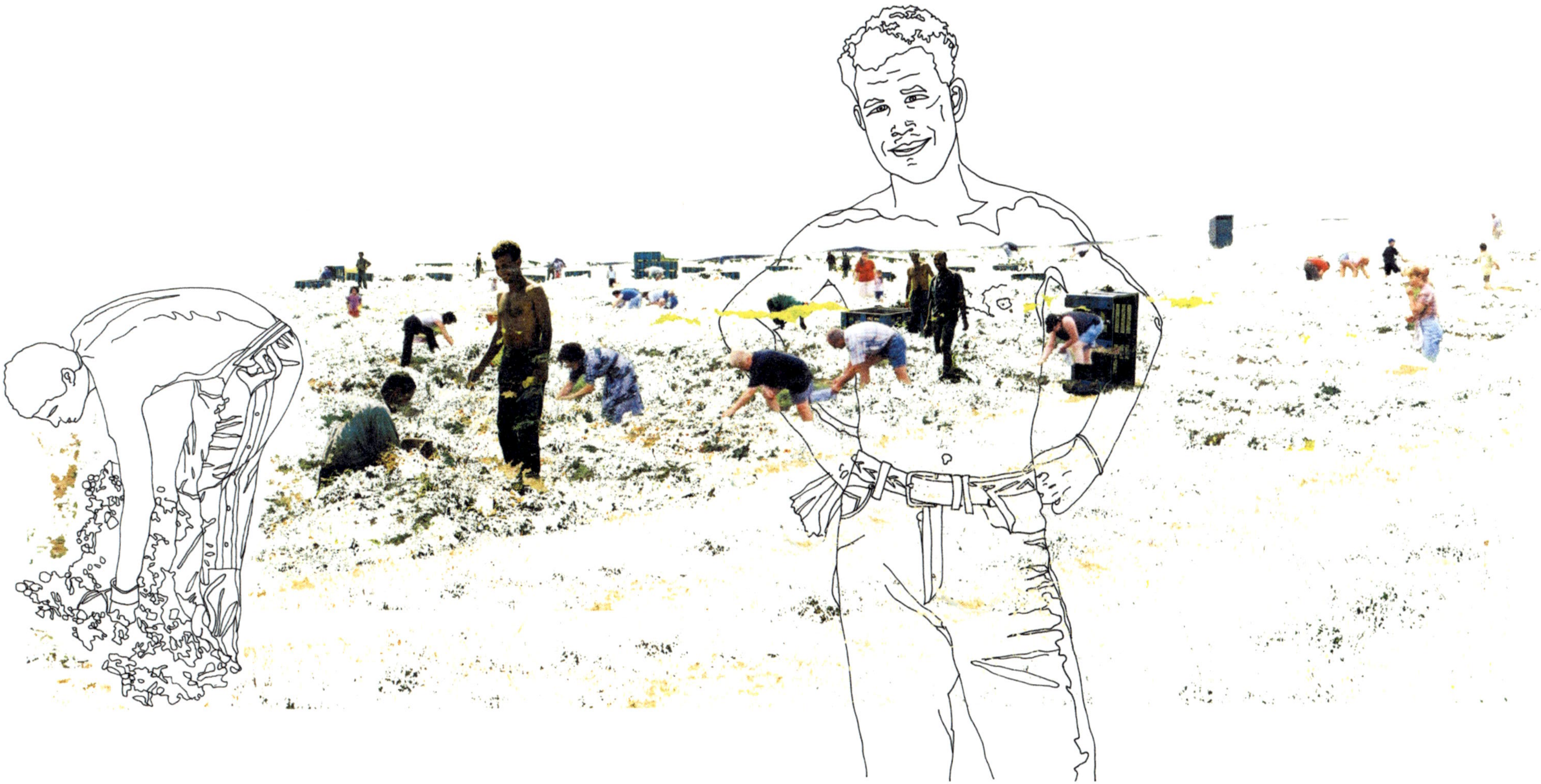

EXCHANGE OF FAVORITE PASTIMES AND NECESSITIES, 2003

TAUSCH VON LIEBLINGSBESCHÄFTIGUNGEN UND NOTWENDIGKEITEN, 2003

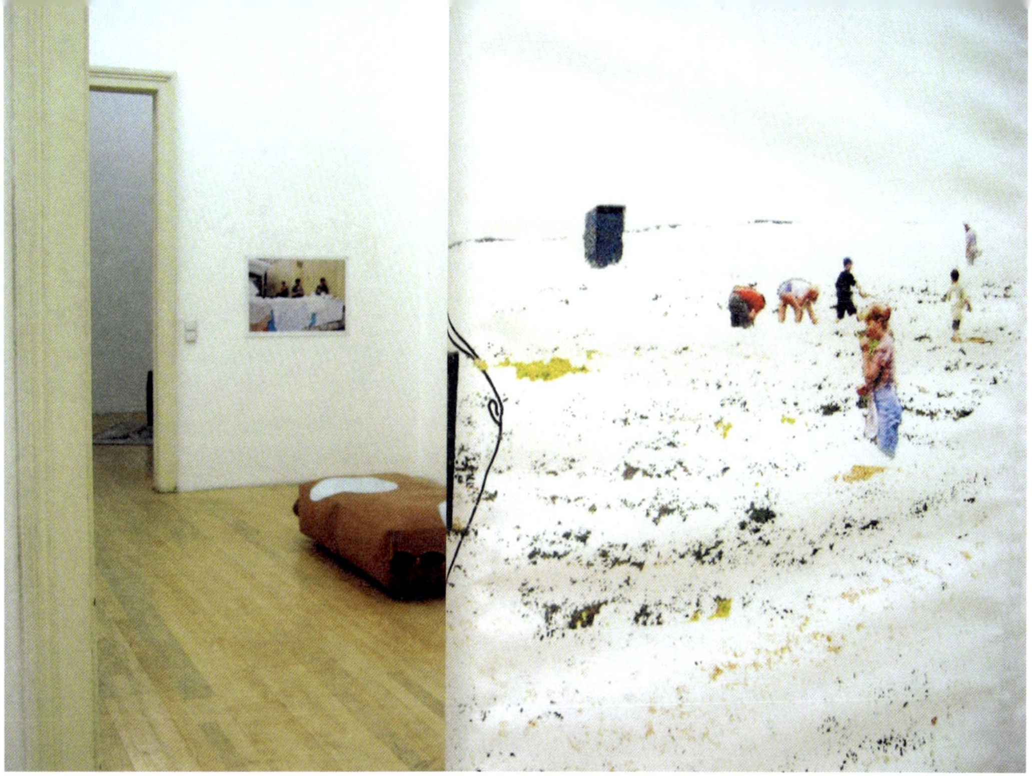

Exhibition view with EXCHANGE OF FAVORITE PASTIMES AND NECESSITIES

Ausstellungsansicht mit TAUSCH VON LIEBLINGSBESCHÄFTIGUNGEN UND NOTWENDIGKEITEN

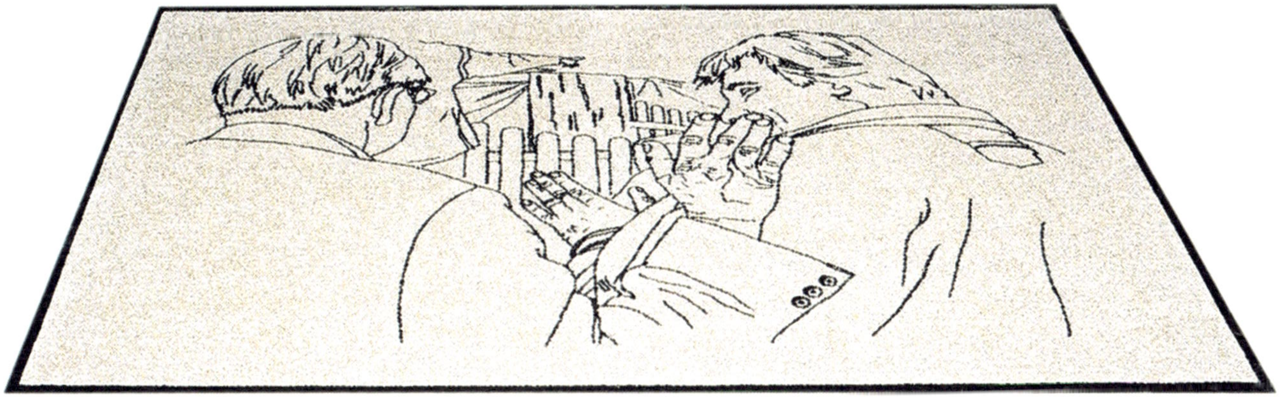

PATTING SHOULDERS, 2003

SCHULTER SCHÜTTELN, 2003

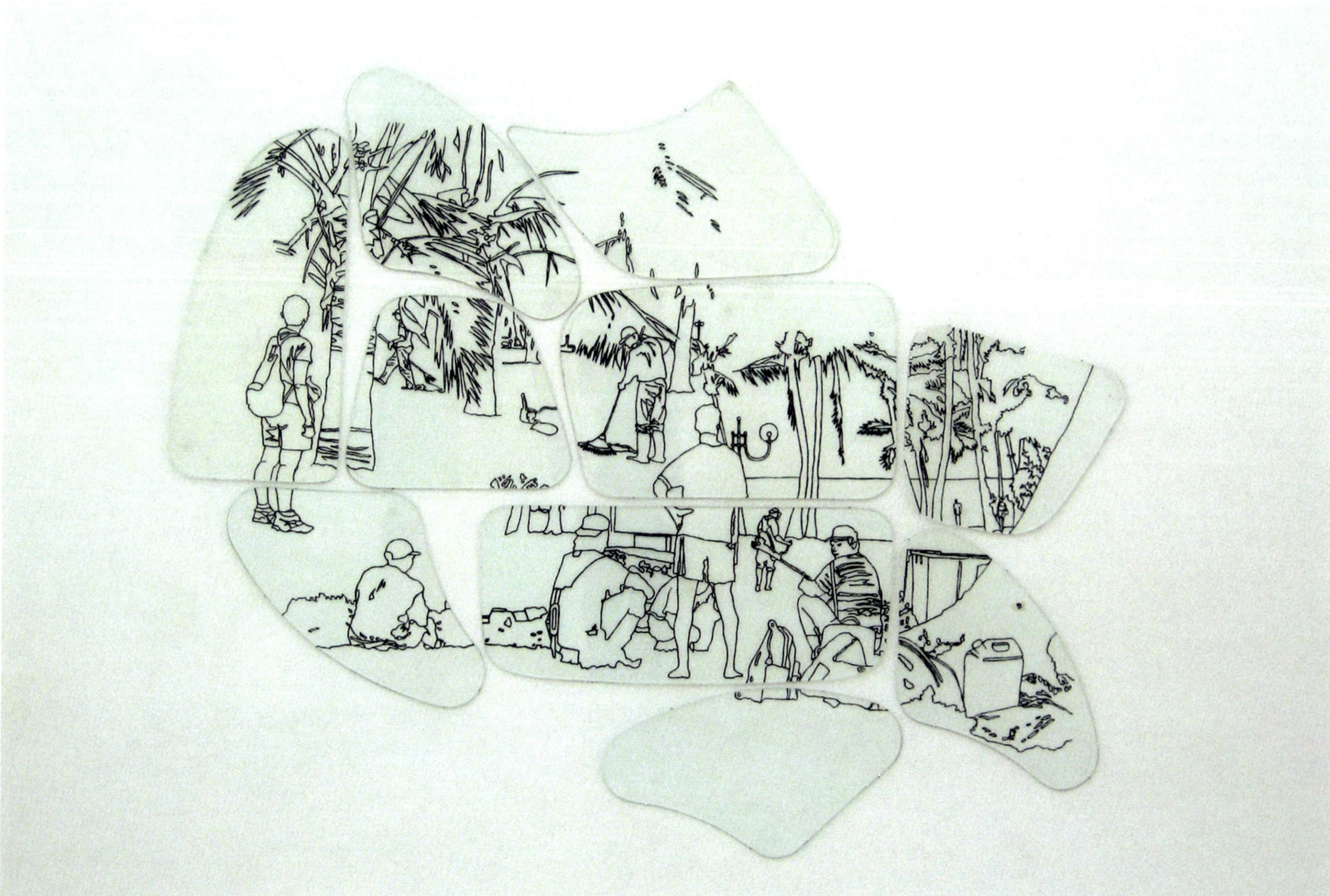

WHEN OTHERS DO THEIR WORK, 2003

WENN ANDERE IHRE ARBEIT TUN, 2003

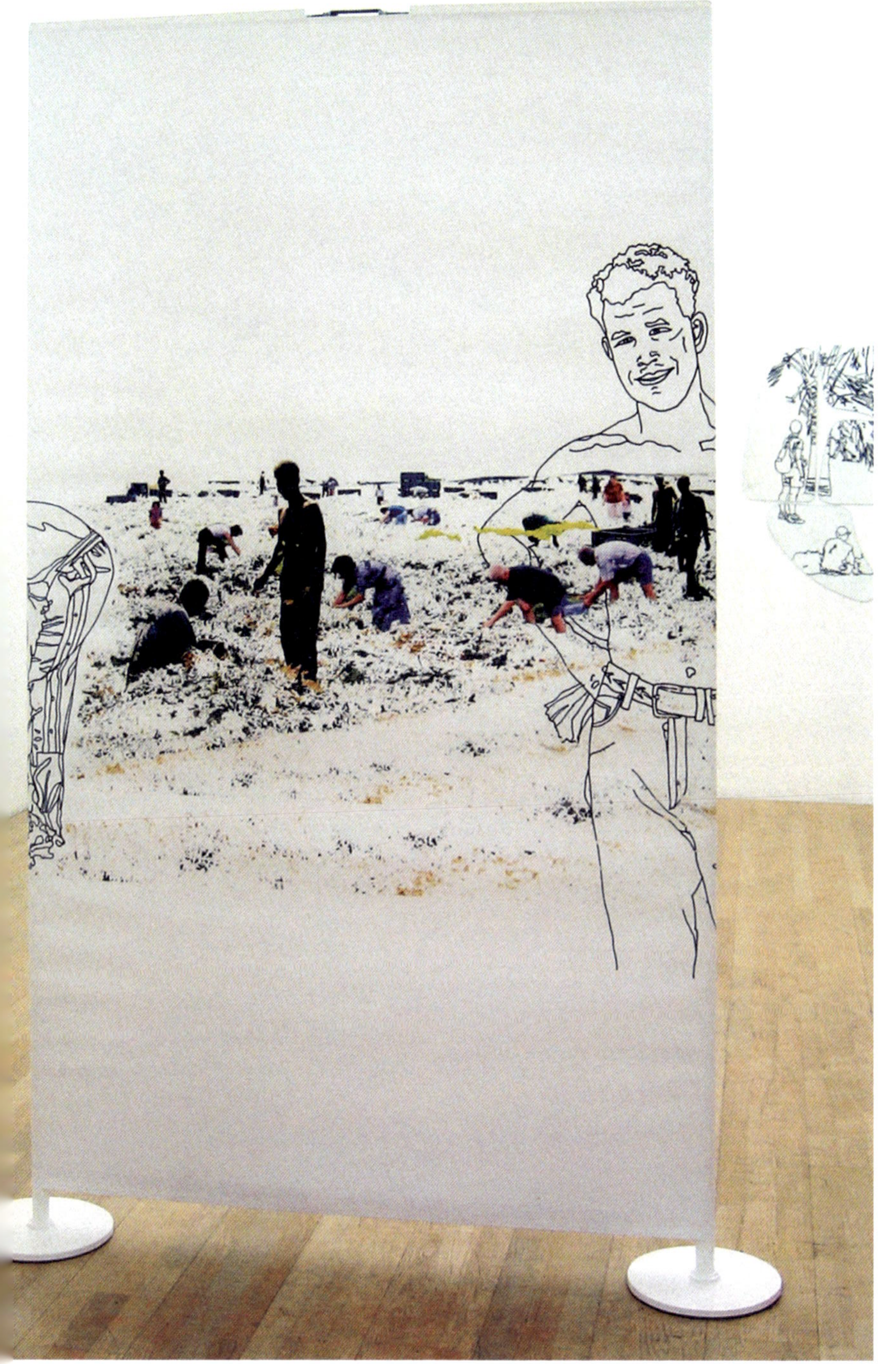

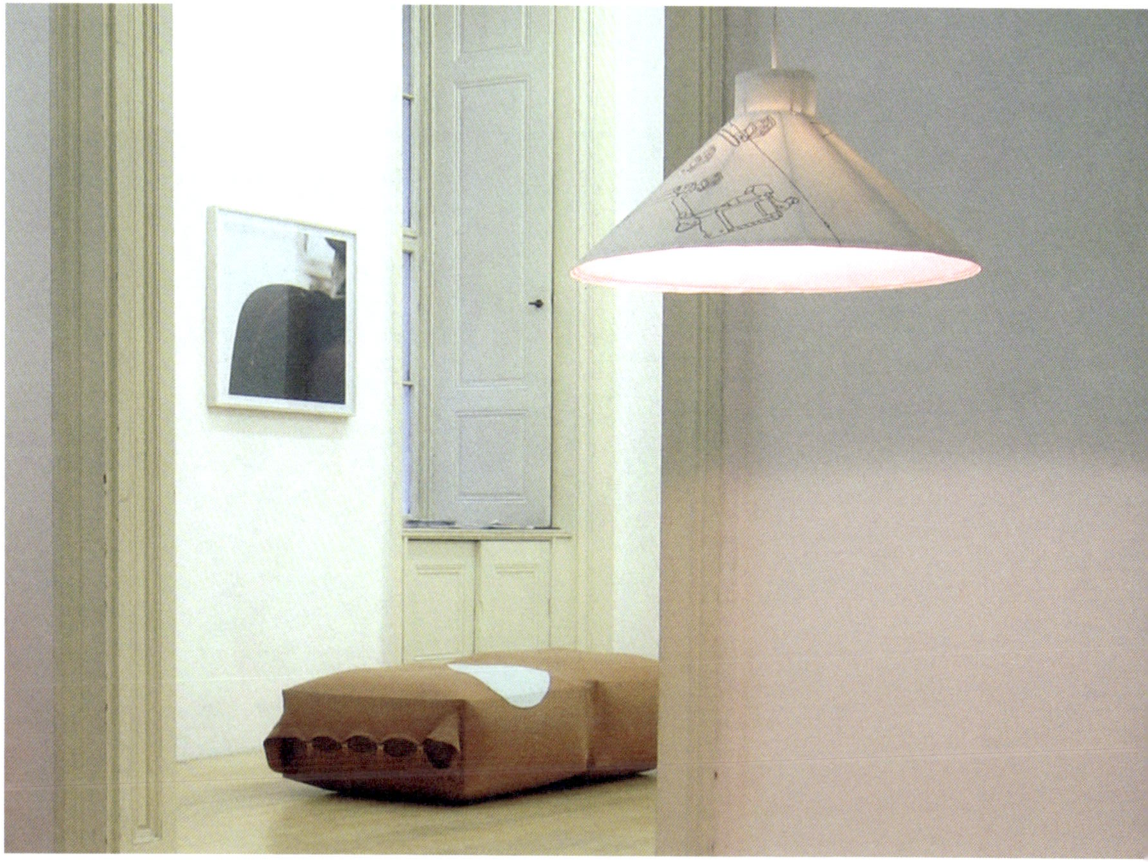

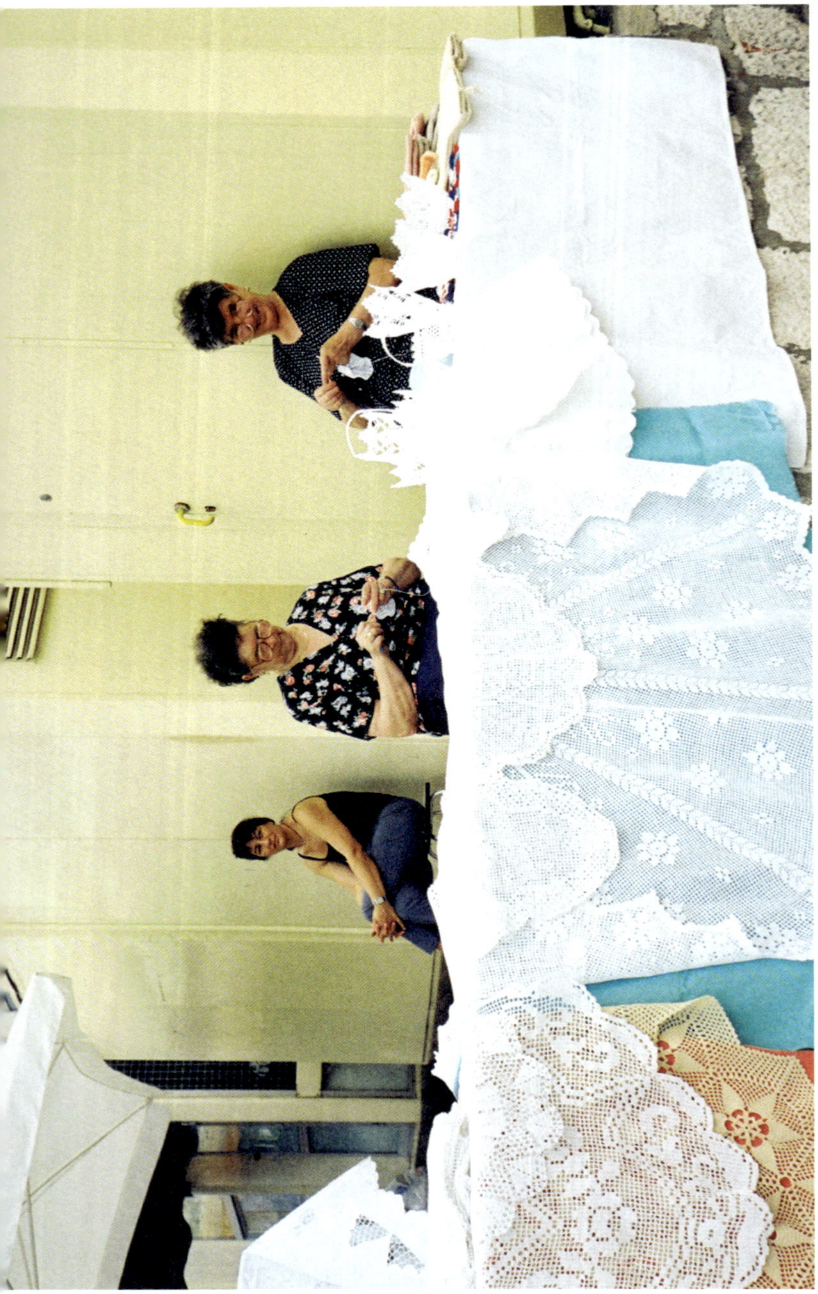

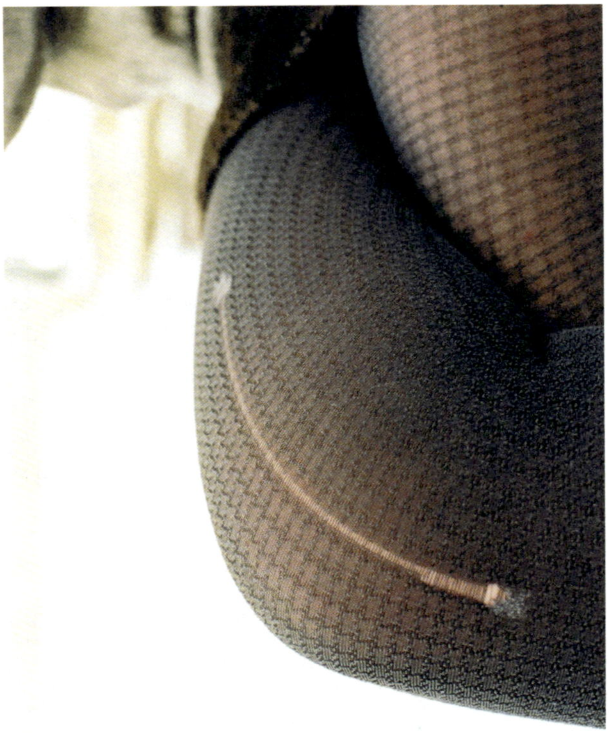

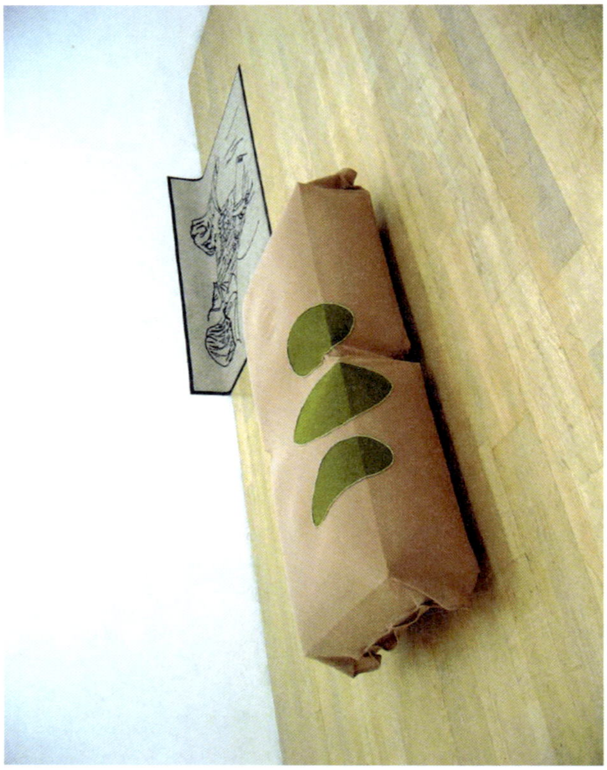

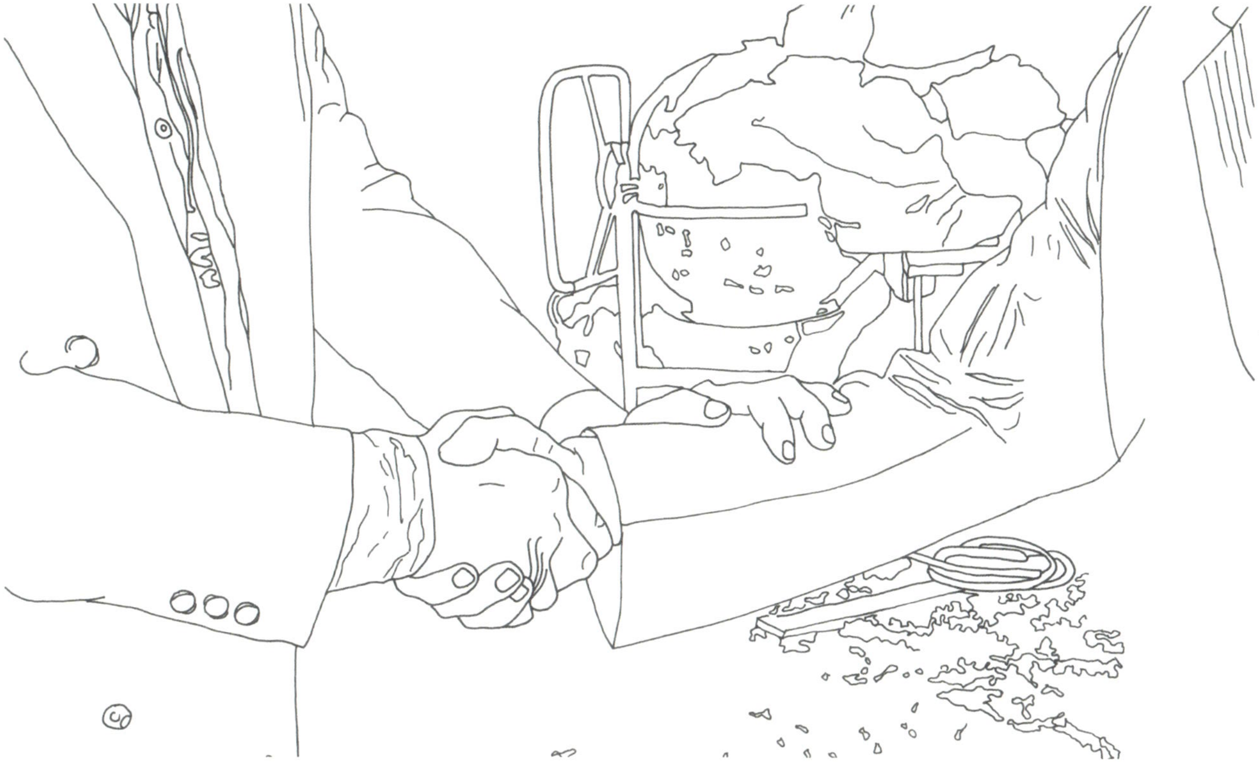

PATTING HANDS, 2003

HÄNDE KLOPFEN, 2003

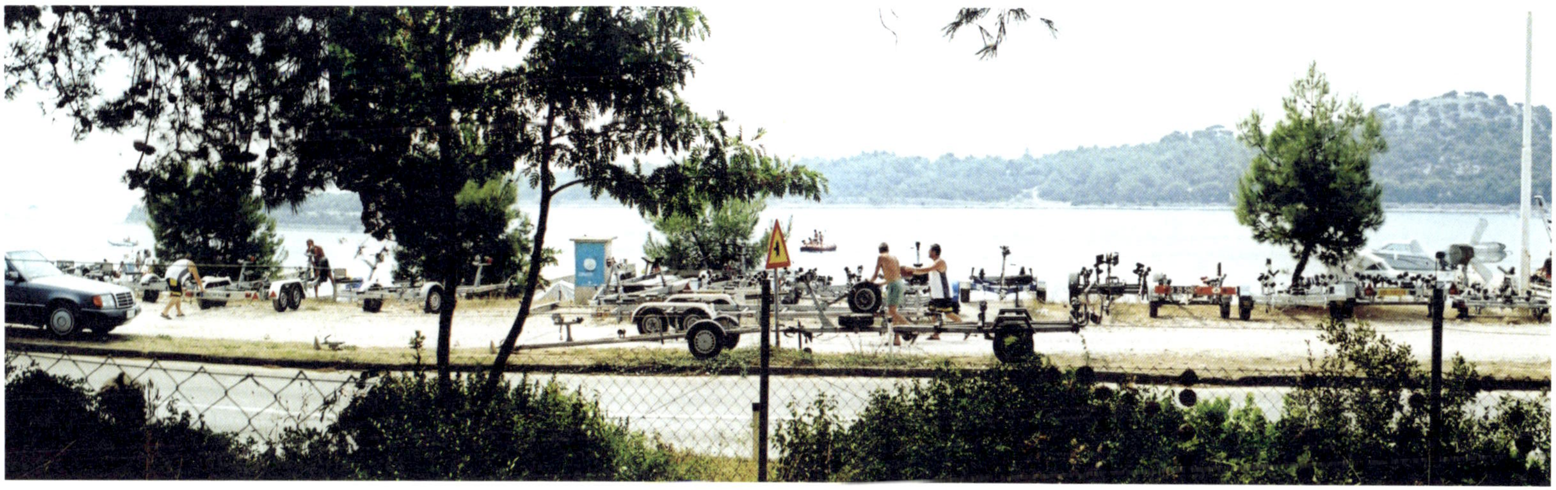

IMAGE TRANSFER

Image Transfer was made in response to the Austrian Cultural Forum's temporary homelessness while its new building in New York was being constructed. Barbara Holub took images of people she deals with daily in her home city of Vienna—drycleaners, bank clerks, hairdressers, photography store assistants—and inserted them into their corresponding locations in New York, either in the store interior or as part of the storefront window display. These large photographic portraits were overlaid with a number of common English expressions often used in Austria but sometimes with a different meaning, such as "name dropping," "happy hour," "sex appeal" or "handy" (i.e. mobile phone in German).

This work was a prescient critique of national identity, as it began to shift under the influence of globalization. A country's embassy can sometimes project a somewhat "branded" image of national identity. The role of the cultural "forum," though still diplomatic, is perhaps more flexible, open to more expansive ideas of cultural exchange. Holub exaggerates this, symbolically substituting blue- and white-collar workers for the Forum's personnel. In so doing, she rejects national identity ("Austrian-ness" versus "American-ness") in favor of shared professional identity. In a globalized economy, it sometimes makes more sense to define people in terms of cultural overlaps rather than as pure subjects of nation states.

Her photographic portraits echo a thought that we have all had from time to time: What would it be like to do my job in another country? They were also hung on the empty storefront of the former Austrian Cultural Forum, alongside a sound piece by the rapper Mr. Complex, composed using some of the aforementioned English expressions. This represented another kind of "transfer": between the Bronx, the birthplace of rap, and a part of Manhattan where that artform was largely absent. A subtler equivalence is also drawn here between the global ubiquity of America's biggest cultural export—rap/hip-hop—and English as an international *lingua franca*, the mother tongue of all those phrases that have worked their way into Austrian speech.[SA]

IMAGE TRANSFER

Image Transfer entstand als Antwort auf die temporäre Heimatlosigkeit des Österreichischen Kulturforums New York während dessen Neubaus. Barbara Holub fotografierte Menschen, mit denen sie im Alltag in ihrer Heimatstadt Wien zu tun hatte – der Mitarbeiterin einer Kleiderreinigung, einer Bankangestellten, ihrem Friseur und der Verkäuferin in einem Fotogeschäft –, und zeigte diese in entsprechenden Geschäften in der Gegend um das Österreichische Kulturforum in Manhattan, entweder im Innenraum oder im Schaufenster. Die großformatigen Fotoporträts waren mit einer Reihe im Deutschen gebräuchlicher englischer Ausdrücke wie z. B. „name dropping", „happy hour", „sex appeal" überdruckt, die manchmal – wie im Fall von „handy"– auch eine andere Bedeutung annehmen.

Die Arbeit war eine vorausschauende Kritik an nationaler Identität, die sich unter dem Einfluss der Globalisierung zu verändern begann. Die Botschaft eines Landes vermittelt mitunter ein eher markenförmiges Bild von nationaler Identität. Ein „Kulturforum" ist da – wenngleich ebenfalls Teil der Diplomatie – flexibler, erlaubt weltläufigere Vorstellungen von kulturellem Austausch. Holub überspitzt das, indem sie das Personal des Kulturforums symbolisch durch ArbeiterInnen und Angestellte ersetzt. Damit verwirft sie die nationale Identität (das „Österreichische" versus das „Amerikanische") zugunsten einer gemeinsamen beruflichen Identität. In einer globalisierten Wirtschaft ergibt es manchmal mehr Sinn, Menschen mittels kultureller Überschneidungen denn als bloße Subjekte von Nationalstaaten zu beschreiben.

Holubs Fotoporträts rufen einen Gedanken in Erinnerung, den wir alle schon einmal hatten: Wie wäre es wohl, meinen Beruf in einem anderen Land auszuüben? Eines der Porträts wurde im Schaufenster des verlassenen Gebäudes des Österreichischen Kulturforums gezeigt, während im Außenraum eine Komposition des Rappers Mr. Complex zu hören war, die auf den erwähnten englischen Ausdrücken beruht. Hier fand eine andere Art von „Transfer" statt, zwischen der Bronx, dem Geburtsort des Rap, und einem Viertel von Manhattan, in dem diese Kunstform weitgehend abwesend ist. Eine subtilere Parallele wird auch zwischen der globalen Allgegenwart von Amerikas größtem kulturellen Exportgut Rap/Hiphop und der englischen Sprache als einer internationalen Lingua franca gezogen: der Muttersprache all jener Ausdrücke, die sich ihren Weg in die österreichische Alltagssprache gebahnt haben.[SA]

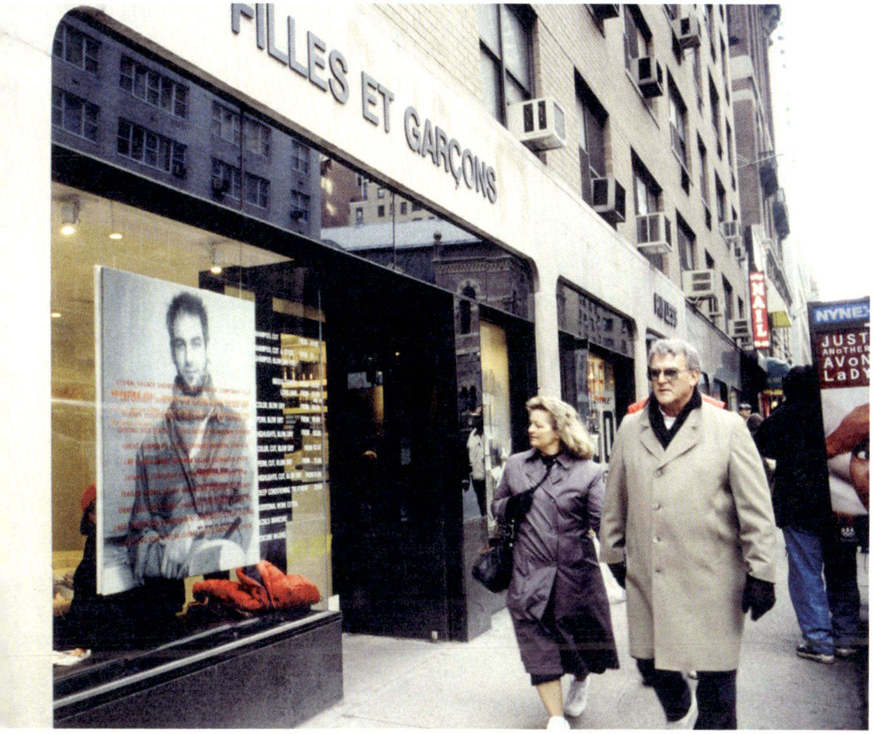

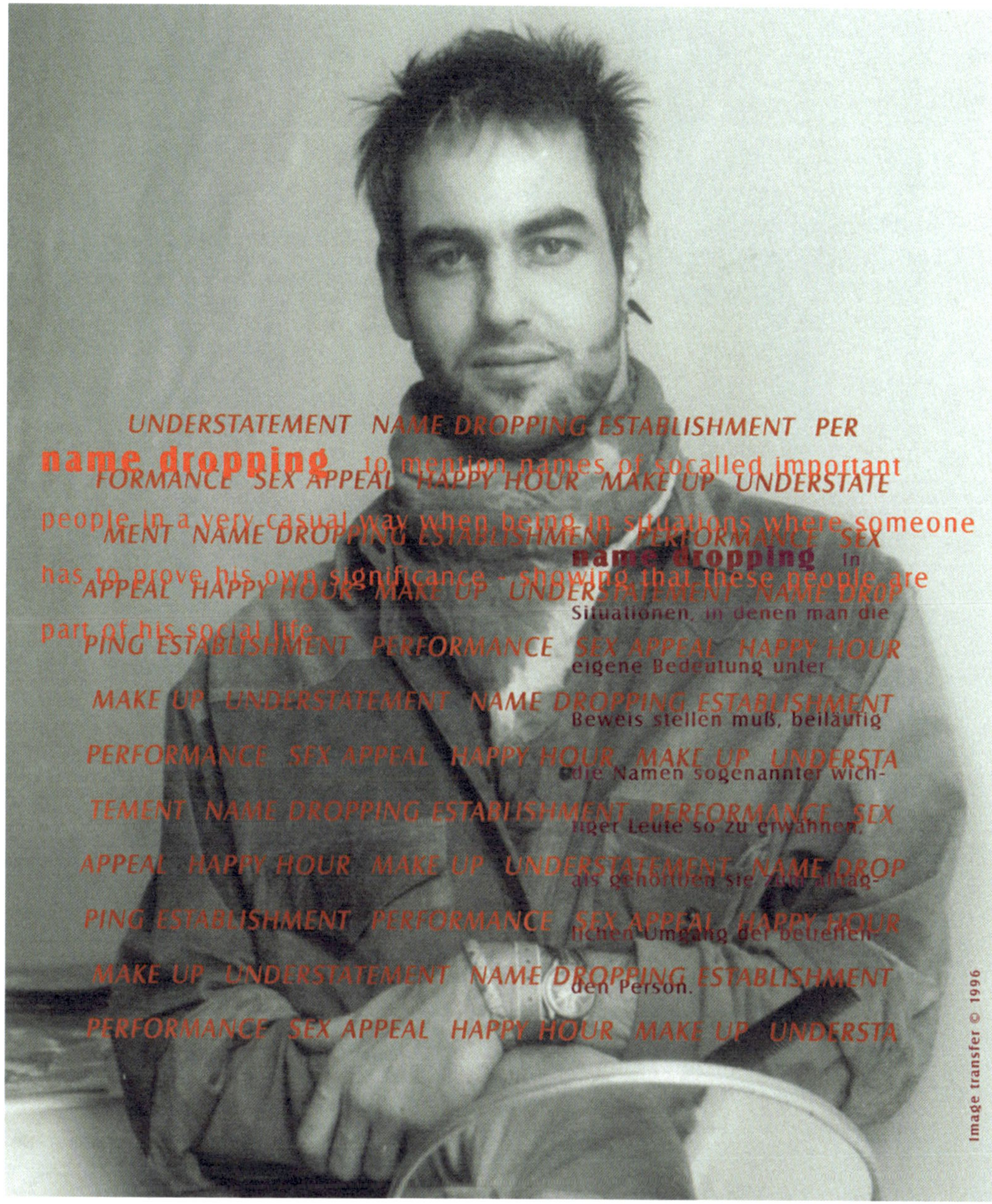

Hairdresser ("Haarsalat," Wienzeile), installed at "Filles et Garçons," 673 Lexington Ave.

Friseur („Haarsalat", Wienzeile), installiert in „Filles et Garçons", 673 Lexington Ave.

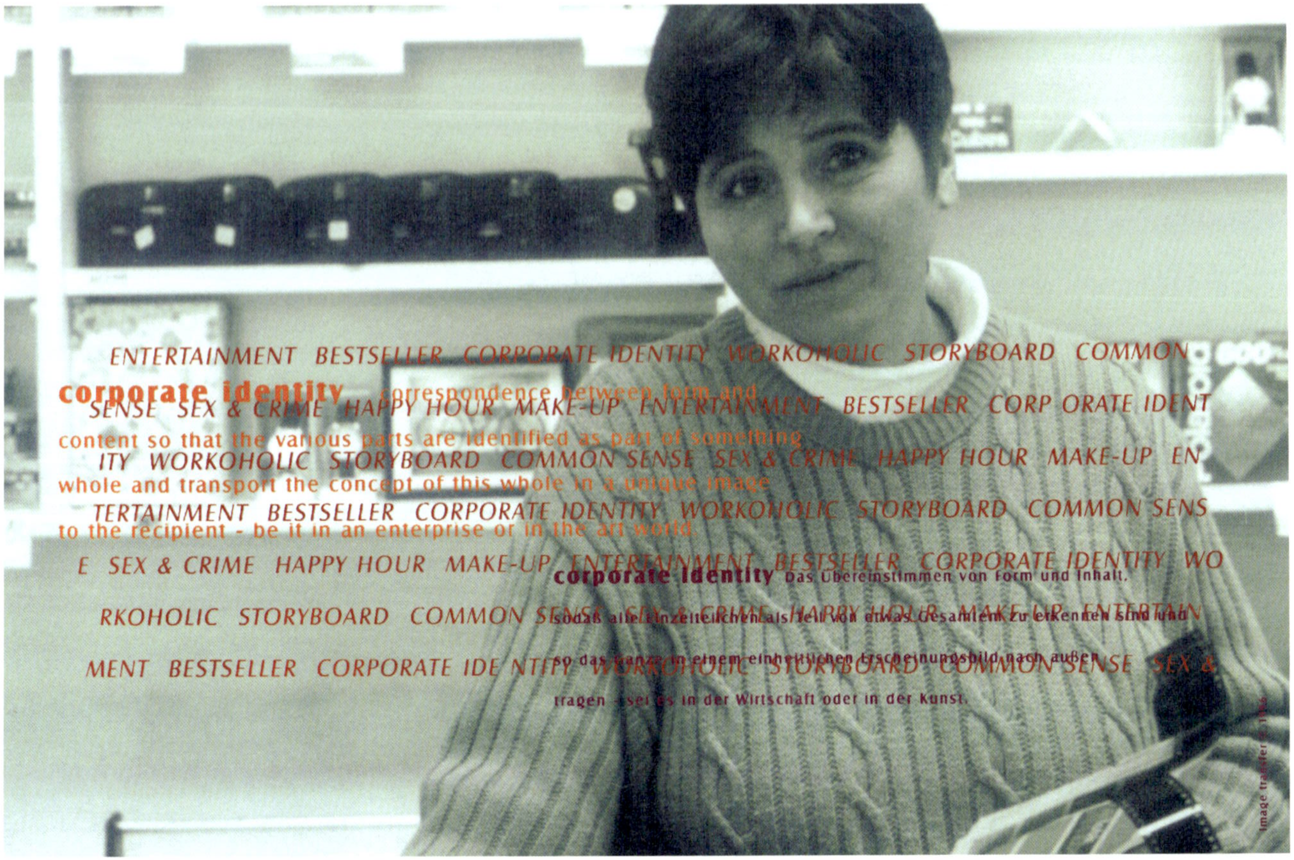

Photo lab technician (Fotokarussell, Taborstrasse), installed at "Kelly Film," 53rd St./3rd Ave.

Fotolaborantin (Fotokarussell, Taborstraße), installiert in „Kelly Film", 53rd St./3rd Ave.

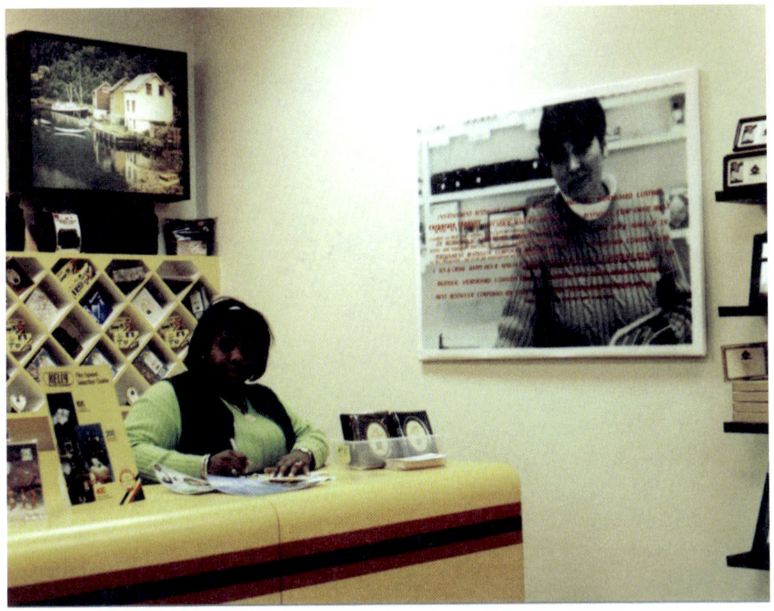

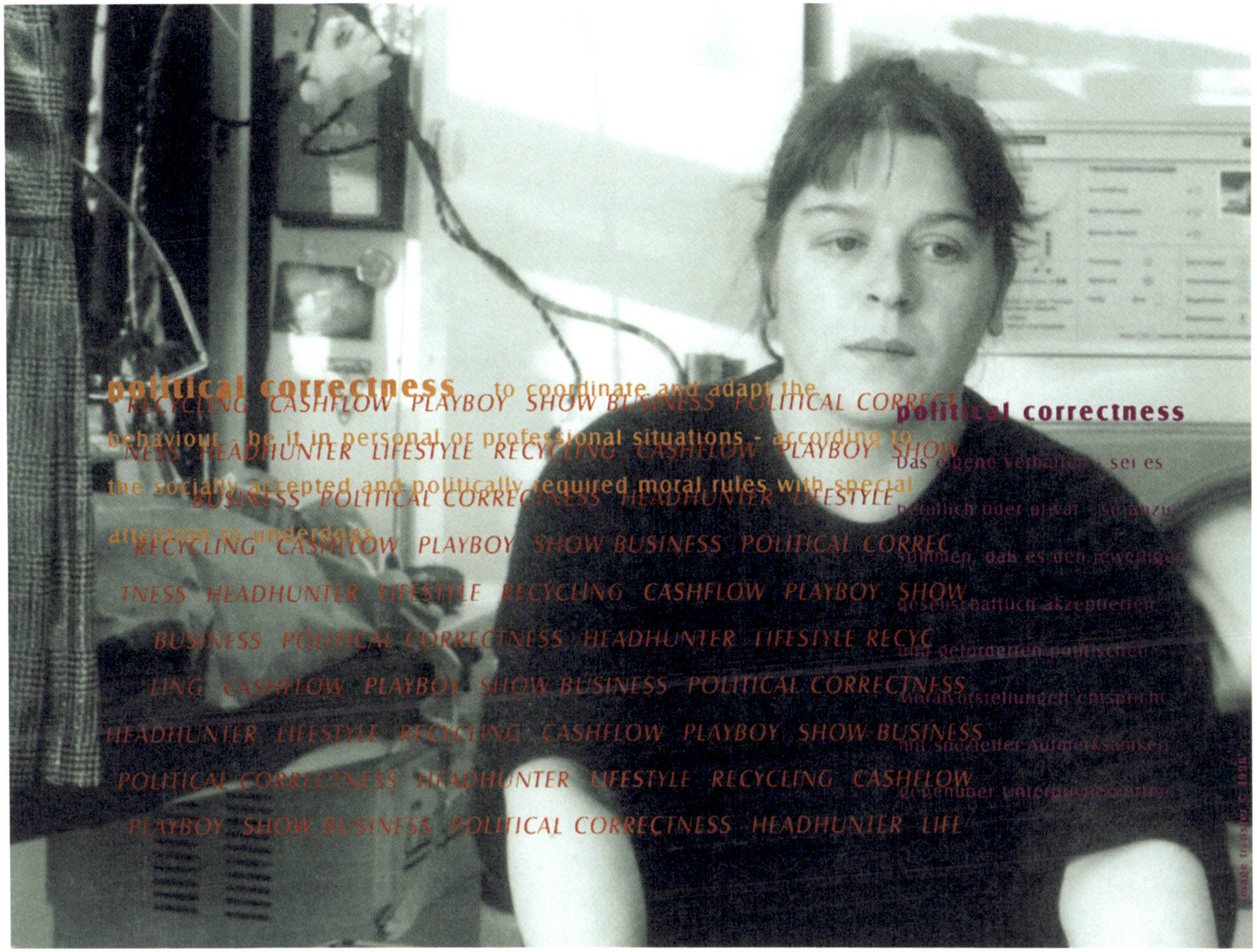

Drycleaner (Putzerei Maunz, Haidgasse), installed at "Quimby Valet," 235 E. 57th St.

Chemische Reinigung (Putzerei Maunz, Haidgasse), installiert in „Quimby Valet", 235. E 57th St.

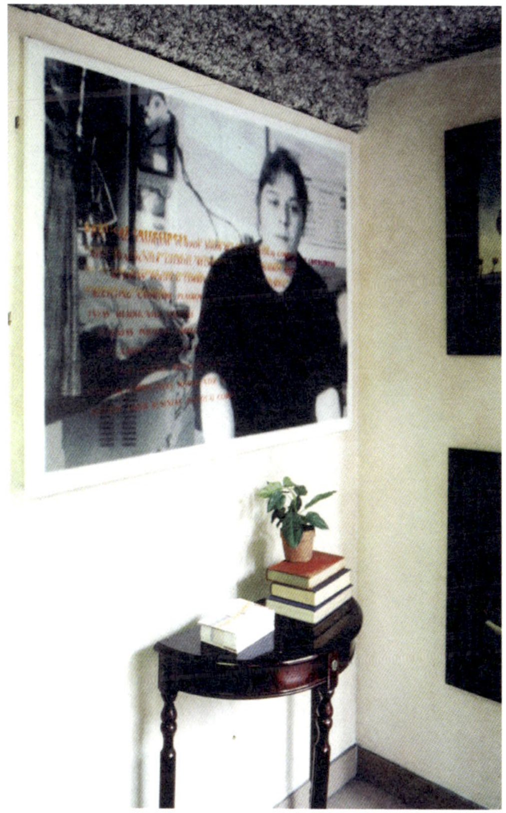

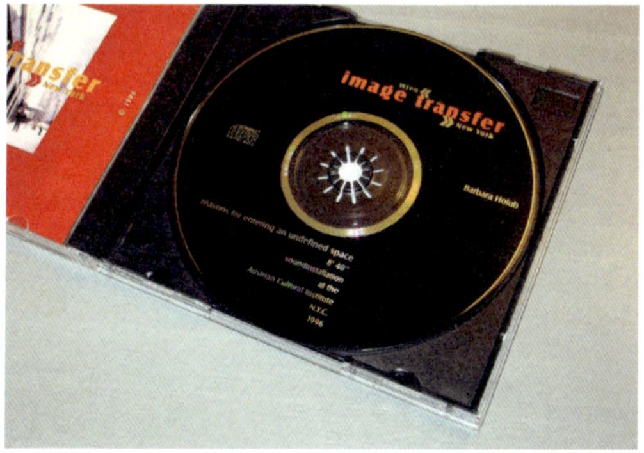

The audio installation in front of the Austrian Cultural Forum—a rap by Mr. Complex—came out as a CD.

Die Audio-Installation vor dem Austrian Cultural Forum – ein Rap von Mr. Complex – erschien als CD.

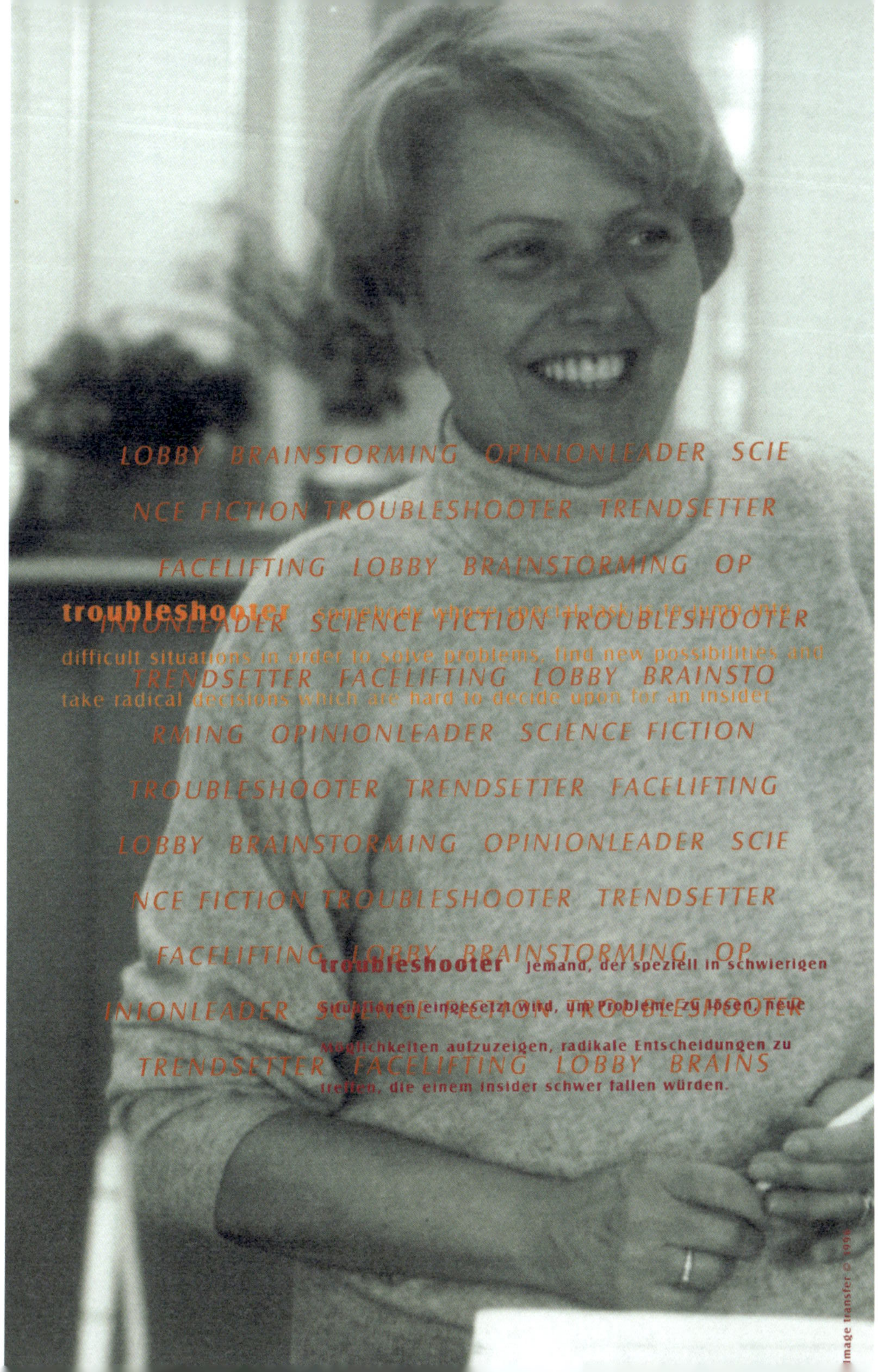

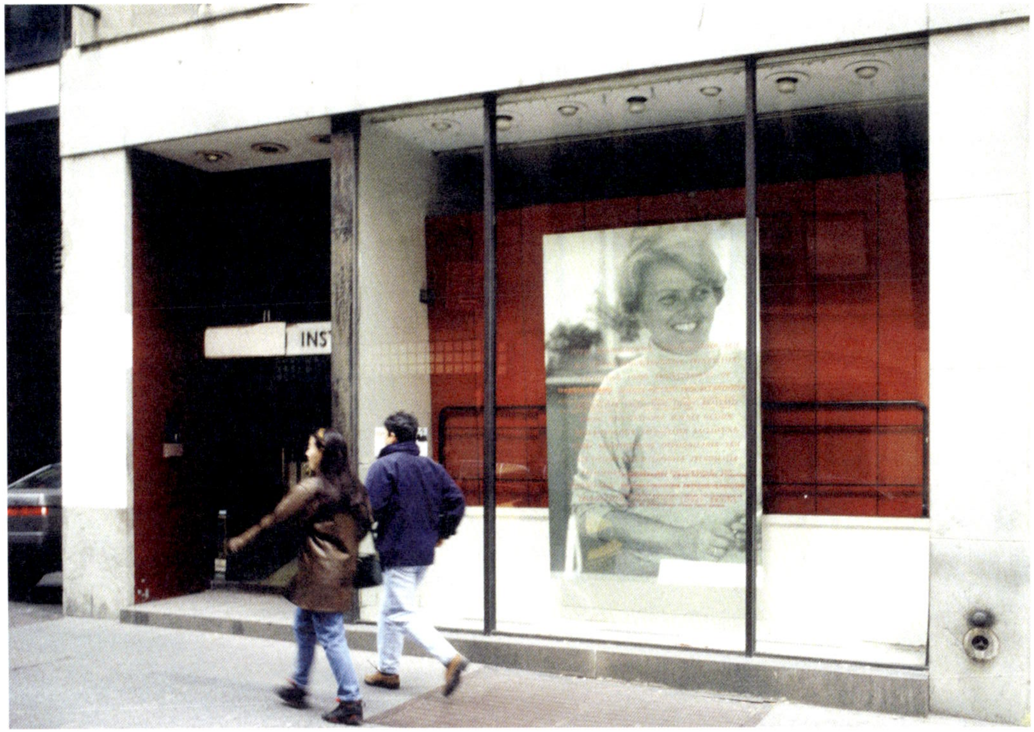

Bank employee (Die Erste Bank, Taborstrasse), installed in the abandoned Austrian Cultural Forum building, 11 E. 52nd St. (since Crossland Savings Bank withdrew from their commitment)

Bankangestellte (Die Erste Bank, Taborstraße), installiert im verlassenen Gebäude des Austrian Cultural Forum, 11 E. 52nd St. (nachdem die Crossland Savings Bank ihre Zusage zurückgezogen hatte)

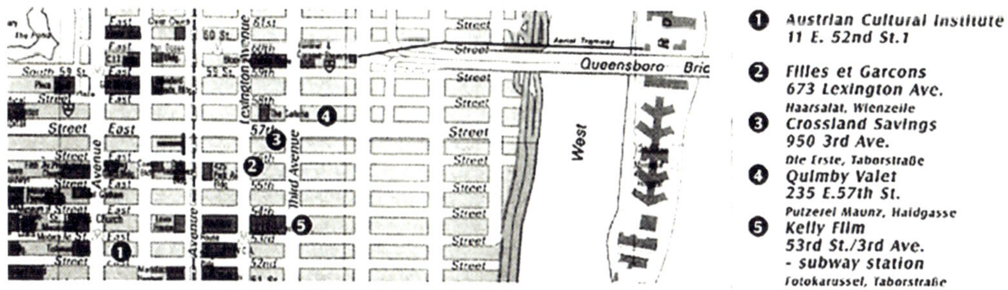

Map of Manhattan with the installation locations

Plan von Manhattan mit den Orten der Installationen

Realization in the frame of: Bromo Arts and Entertainment District, EUNIC (European Network of Institutes of Cultures), Austrian Cultural Forum Washington DC, Baltimore (US), 2014

THE FIRST WORLD CONGRESS OF THE MISSING THINGS

THE FIRST WORLD CONGRESS OF THE MISSING THINGS was a two-day event by Barbara Holub in the Lexington Market area of Baltimore's formerly flourishing city centre, aiming to give a discursive platform to disenfranchized citizens (the homeless, drug addicts, ex-convicts) who had been living there since the "white flight" of the 1950s, which marked a drastic shrinking of the city. Using the public space in front of the subway station, where a rhizomatic structure of tables was assembled, the Congress dispensed with the conventional division between audience and panelist, inviting the public to set the agenda by submitting missing things, i. e. whatever they felt was missing from Baltimore life. The resulting list, the "Charter of Missing Things," read out publicly during the Congress, was then handed to the Mayor of Baltimore.

As might be expected, this document is eclectic, ranging from staple socialist policies ("redistribution of wealth"), to particular concrete demands ("swimmable Inner Harbor," "recreation centres for the youth"), to more cerebral suggestions ("unmediated experience"), to strident criticisms ("honest politicians"). The content of the charter—reproduced on the Congress' website, where it reads like a multi-authored poem—raises the question of which desires can be met through municipal channels and which may fall outside their purview. To what extent can personal desires actually be realized through the municipal processes of lobbying, debate and legislature? By bringing this question to the fore, the Congress encourages local government to expand its idea of what is possible, critically addressing the agenda of "creative placemaking," which all too often is simply a way of raising property values for investors, leading to gentrification; however, it also—as some of the conversations in the video documentation show—gave citizens the chance to compare their understanding of certain terms pertinent to urban life: for example, the idea that a boundary need not be a division between different social factions but a porous zone for producing mutual understanding.

Though predominantly a discursive event, the Congress produced a number of concrete outcomes that offered long-term perspectives: to turn one of the dilapidated buildings on Howard Street into a vocational training centre for the homeless, to install an information kiosk for subsidy programs, jobs, etc. at the entrance of the subway station at Lexington Market (many of the people living around Howard Street having been completely cut off from such information). However, when a funder offered to finance these projects at the UN NGO DPI Conference in New York in August 2014, the City of Baltimore was not interested.[SA]

Realisierung im Rahmen von: Bromo Arts and Entertainment District, EUNIC (European Network of Institutes of Cultures), Austrian Cultural Forum Washington DC, Baltimore (US), 2014

THE FIRST WORLD CONGRESS OF THE MISSING THINGS

THE FIRST WORLD CONGRESS OF THE MISSING THINGS war eine zweitägige Veranstaltung in der Nähe des Lexington Market im einst blühenden Zentrum von Baltimore, die den benachteiligten BürgerInnen (Obdachlosen, Drogensüchtigen, Ex-Häftlingen), die dort leben, seit die „weiße Flucht" in den 1950ern eine drastische Schrumpfung der Stadt einleitete, eine diskursive Plattform bieten sollte. Der Kongress, der im öffentlichen Raum vor der U-Bahn-Station stattfand, hob die übliche Trennung in Publikum und Vortragende durch eine rhizomatische Struktur von Tischen auf und lud das Publikum ein, durch die Nennung dessen, was ihnen im Leben von Baltimore fehlt, selbst die Agenda zu bestimmen. Die dabei entstandene „Charta der fehlenden Dinge" wurde am Ende des Kongresses vorgetragen und dann der Bürgermeisterin überreicht.

Wenig überraschend handelte es sich bei der Charta um eine eklektische Liste, die von sozialistischen Grundforderungen („Umverteilung des Wohlstands") über konkrete Maßnahmen („Schwimmen im inneren Hafen", „Erholungszentren für die Jugend") bis hin zu eher intellektuellen Vorschlägen („unvermittelte Erfahrungen") und scharfer Kritik („ehrliche PolitikerInnen") reichte. Die auf der Kongress-Website wiedergegebene Charta – die sich dort wie ein von mehreren AutorInnen verfasstes Gedicht liest – wirft die Fragen auf, welche Wünsche sich über Stadtpolitik realisieren lassen und welche außerhalb ihrer Zuständigkeit liegen. In welchem Maß können individuelle Wünsche tatsächlich durch öffentliche Meinungsbildung, Diskussions- und Gesetzgebungsprozesse verwirklicht werden? Indem der Kongress diese Fragen ins Blickfeld rückte, forderte er die Stadtregierung auf, ihre Auffassung des Möglichen zu erweitern, und hinterfragte kritisch die Agenda des „creative placemaking", die allzu häufig nur der Aufwertung von Immobilien für InvestorInnen dient und zu Gentrifizierung führt. Er lud aber auch – wie Gespräche in der Videodokumentation belegen – die BürgerInnen ein, ihr Verständnis von Begriffen zu überprüfen, die für das urbane Leben relevant sind: etwa dem der Grenze, die nicht unbedingt eine Trennung zwischen verschiedenen sozialen Gruppen sein muss, sondern auch eine poröse Zone zur Schaffung von gegenseitigem Verständnis sein kann.

Der Kongress, der vor allem als diskursive Veranstaltung konzipiert war, brachte aber auch eine Reihe konkreter Vorschläge hervor, die langfristige Perspektiven eröffneten: etwa die Umwandlung eines baufälligen Gebäudes in der Howard Street in ein Berufsausbildungszentrum für Obdachlose oder die Errichtung eines Info-Kiosks für Förderprogramme, Jobangebote usw. am Eingang zur U-Bahn-Station (viele der um die Howard Street lebenden Menschen sind von solchen Informationen völlig abgeschnitten). Allerdings zeigte sich die Stadt Baltimore selbst dann nicht an deren Umsetzung interessiert, als ein Geldgeber auf der UN DPI/NGO-Konferenz New York im August 2014 anbot, diese Projekte zu finanzieren.[SA]

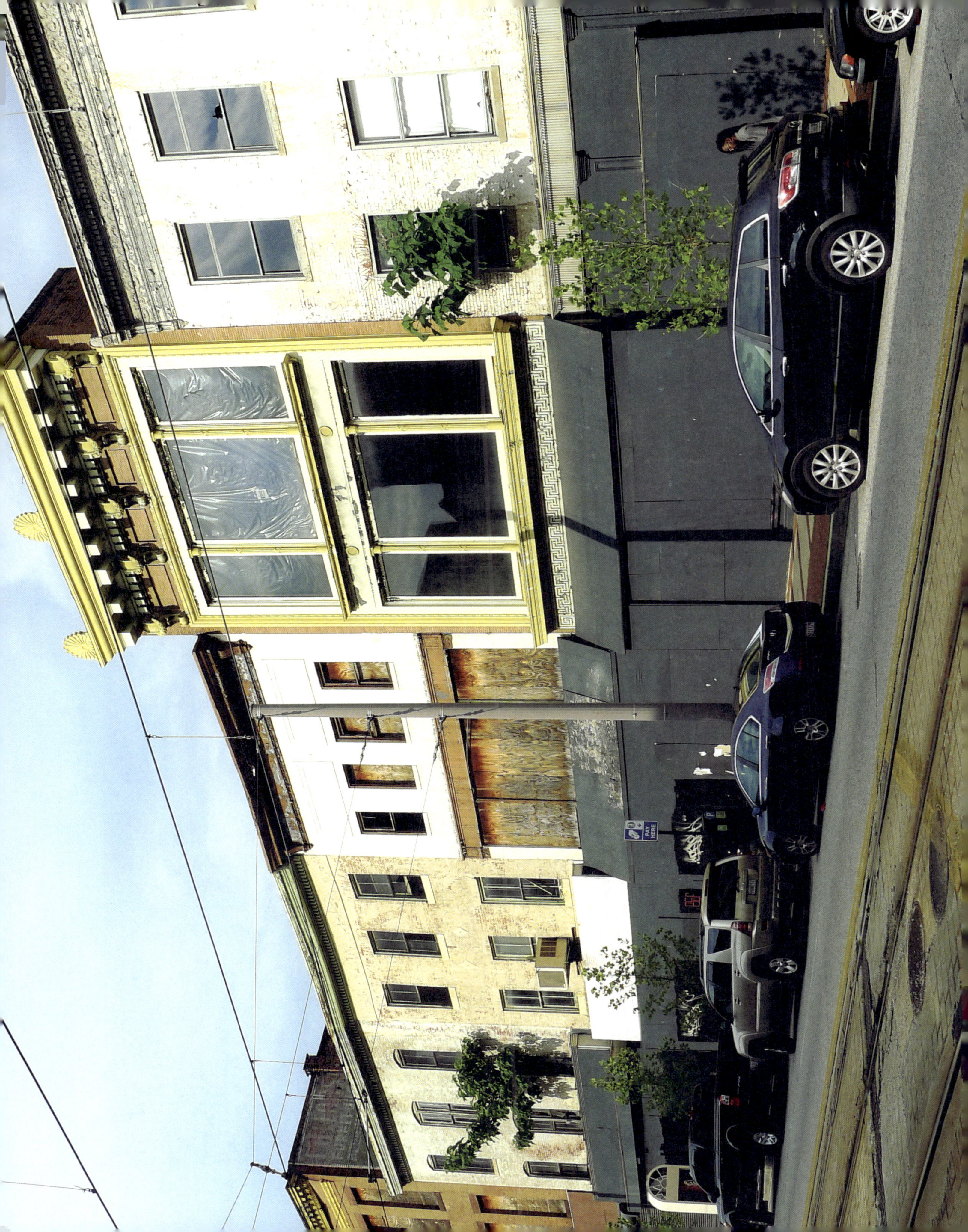

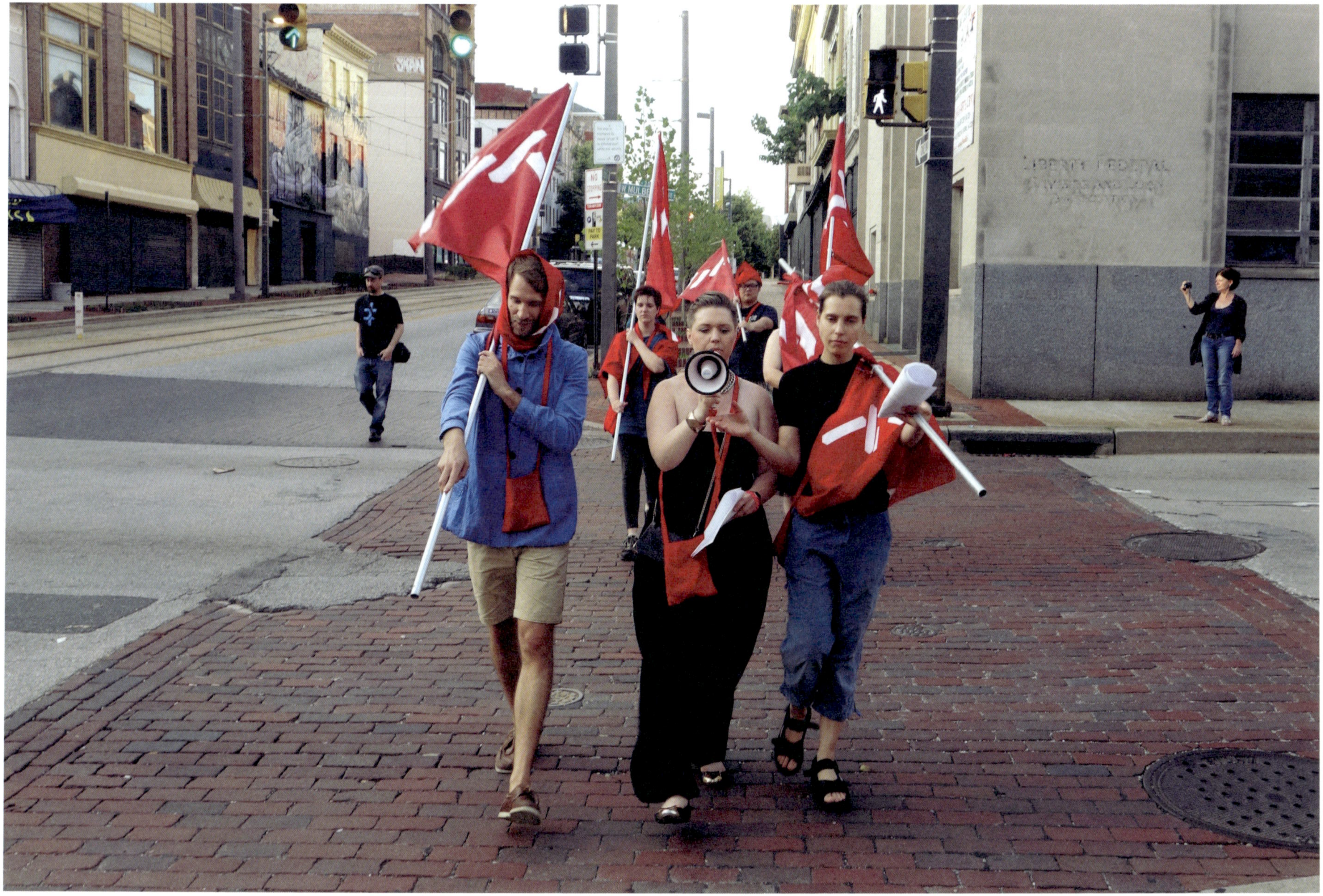

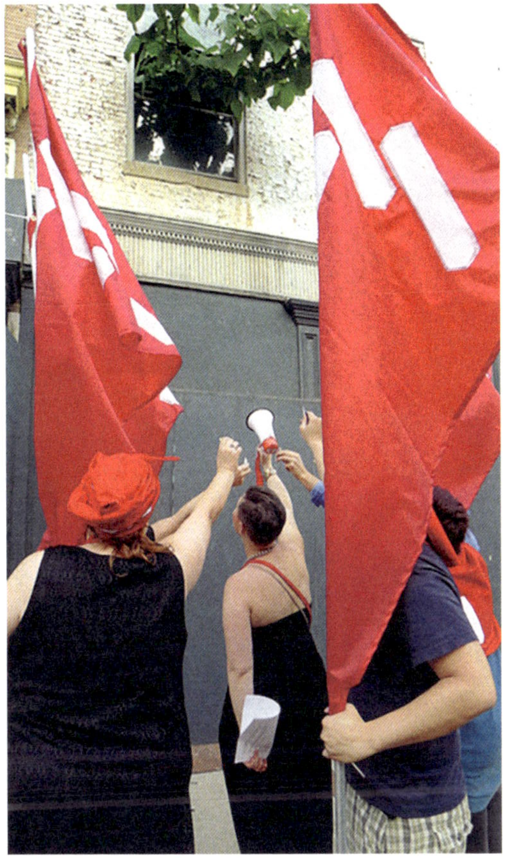

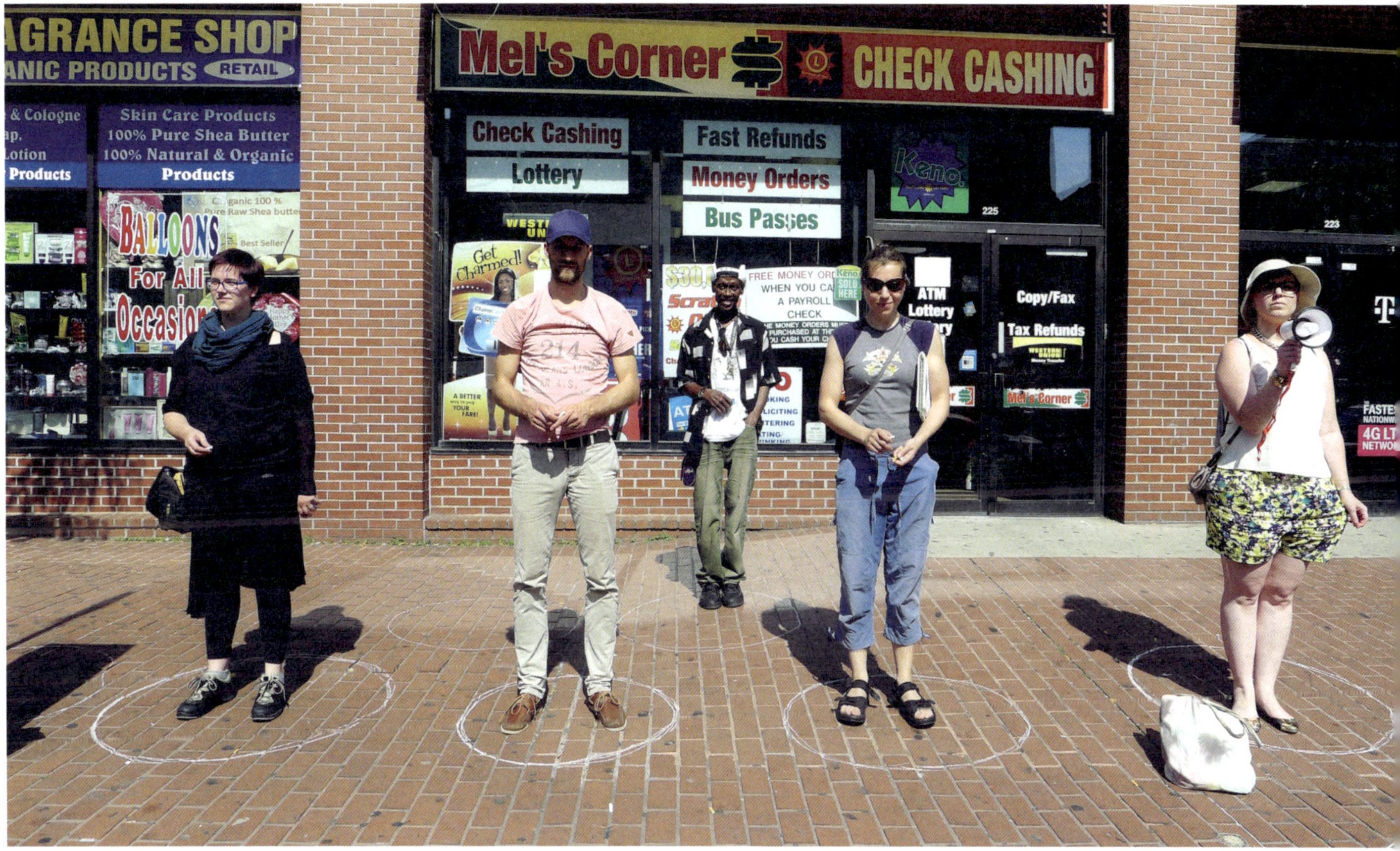

Various actions took place to publicly announce the Congress: trees growing out of the windows of abandoned buildings on Howard Street were sung to; circles marked with chalk invited people to occupy space and become part of the performances. Thus, residents joined informally already during the preparations for the Congress.

Zur öffentlichen Ankündigung des Kongresses fanden verschiedene Aktionen statt: Aus den Fenstern von verlassenen Gebäuden in der Howard Street herauswachsende Bäume wurden besungen; mit Kreide markierte Kreise luden dazu ein, sich einen Platz zu nehmen und Teil der Performances zu werden. So gesellten sich BewohnerInnen informell schon während der Vorbereitungen des Kongresses dazu.

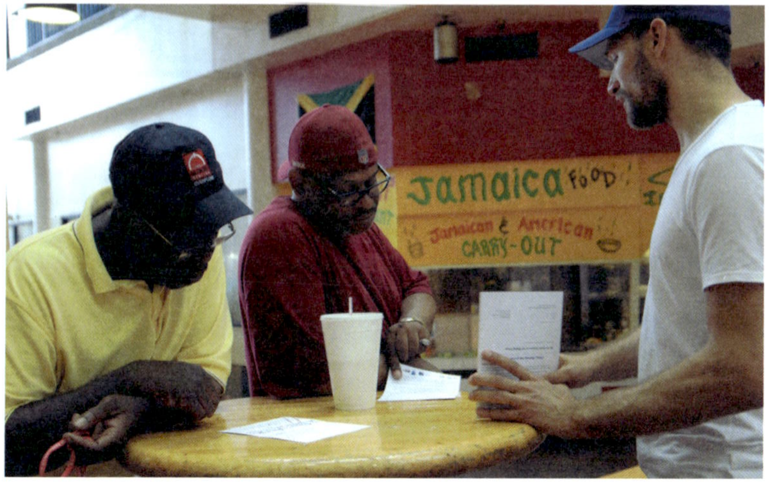

The information desk in Lexington Market addressed the customers of the Market Hall as well as the residents of the neighborhood, who used the Market Hall as a "living room," which most of them did not have in their own four walls. This is also how we found our young assistant for the Congress.

Der Info-Tisch im Lexington Market sprach die KundInnen der Markthalle ebenso an wie die BewohnerInnen des Viertels, die die Markthalle als „Wohnzimmer" benutzten, über das sie privat meist nicht verfügten. So fanden wir hier auch unseren jungen Assistenten für den Kongress.

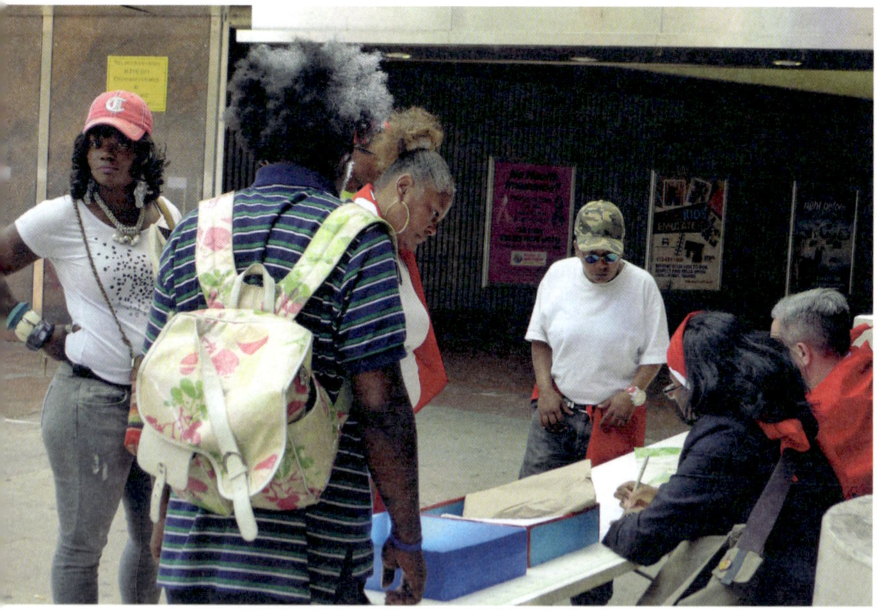

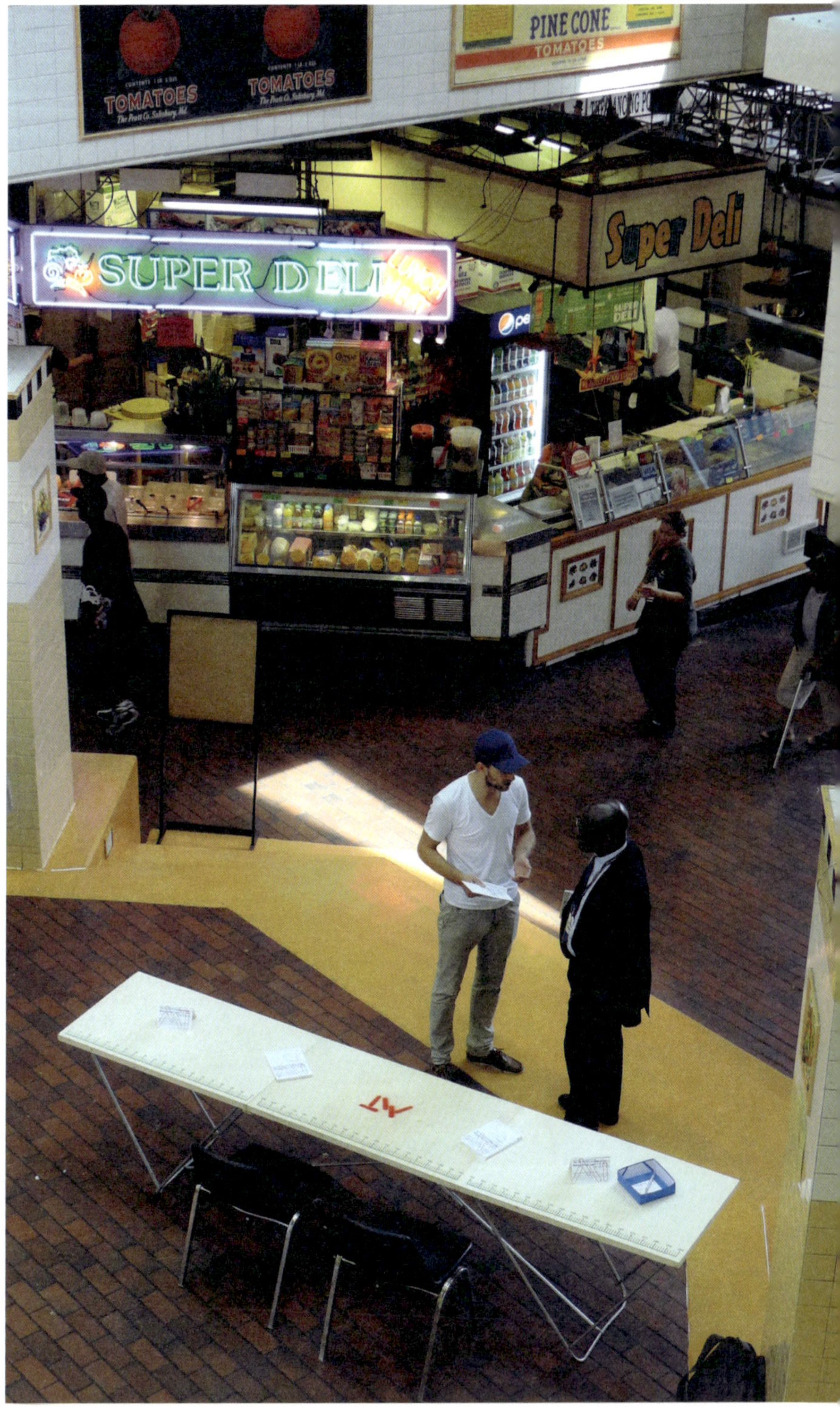

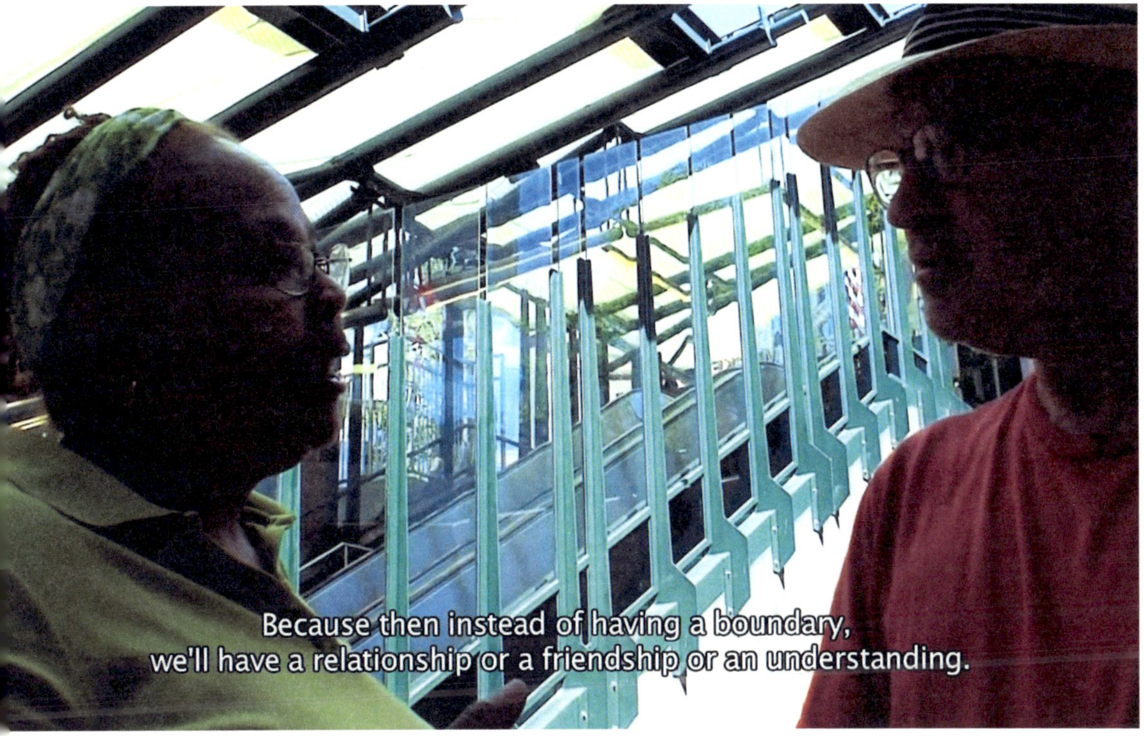

"You were born a master, I was born a slave.
How can we communicate?"

Videos still, FIRST WORLD CONGRESS OF THE MISSING THINGS, 2014

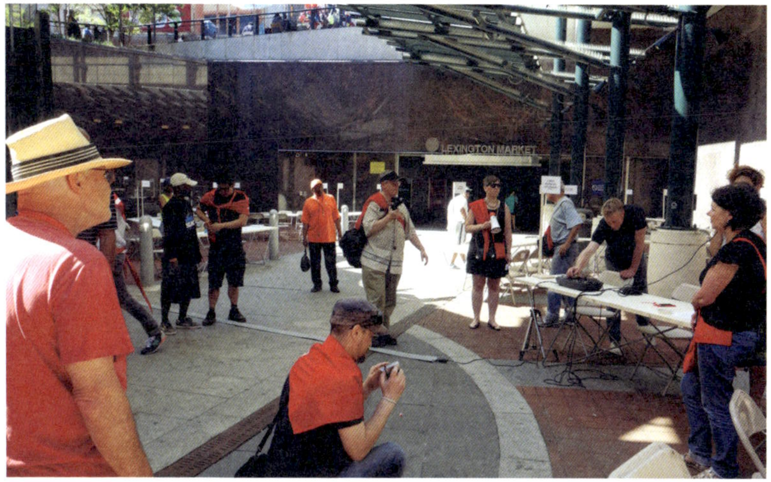

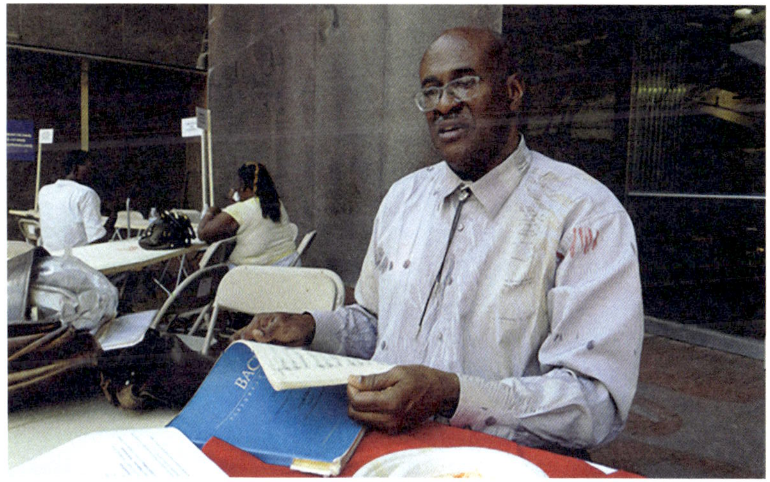

Visitors engaged intensively in conversations about the "missing things" that had been collected in advance at numerous events throughout the city.

Die BesucherInnen brachten sich intensiv in Gespräche über die „Missing Things" ein, die im Vorfeld über verschiedenste Veranstaltungen in der ganzen Stadt gesammelt wurden.

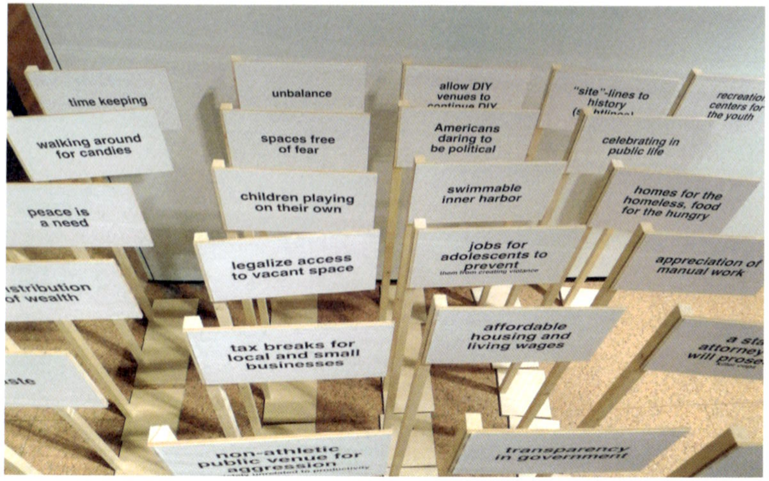

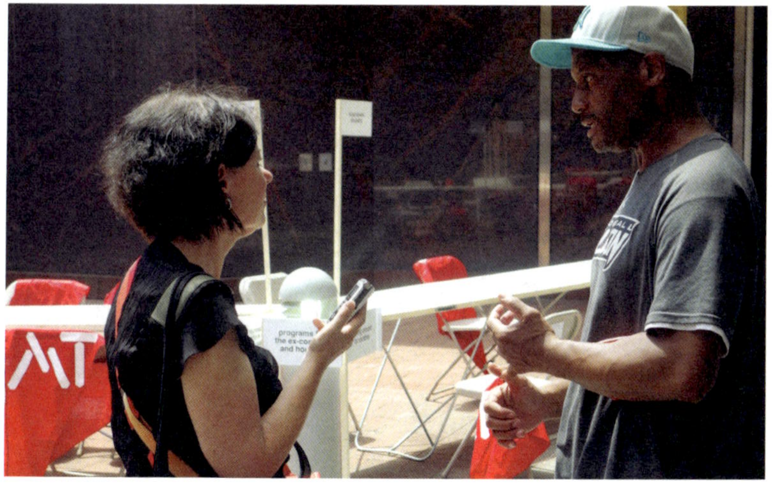

In an official closing act, the "Charter of the Missing Things" was handed over to the mayor.

In einem offiziellen Schlussakt wurde die „Charta of the Missing Things" an die Bürgermeisterin übergeben.

Missing Things

walking around for candies	1 #	48	unmediated experience
time keeping	2 #	49	generosity and simplicity
redistribution of wealth	3 #	50	help as a disabled citizen in America
peace is a need	4 #	51	a good Tex Mex restaurant
good taste	5 #	52	benefits made available for the displaced / missing people
(un)balance	6 #	53	a not over-regulated public space
spaces free of fear	7 #	54	La Vida (life)
children playing on their own	8 #	55	replace prevalent surveillance practices with affirmative, dialogic communicative practices
legalize access to vacant space	9 #		
tax breaks for local and small businesses	10 #	56	free access to the high quality education
allow DIY venues to continue DIY	11 #	57	tutors for children
Americans daring to be political	12 #	58	wind and solar energy for our house
swimmable Inner Harbor	13 #	59	more God
jobs for adolescents to prevent them from creating violence	14 #	60	honest politicians
affordable housing and living wages	15 #		
„site"-lines to history (sightlines)	16 #		
vibrant public life	17 #		
non-athletic public venue for aggression, unrelated to productivity	18 #		
celebrating in public space	19 #		
appreciation of manual work	20 #		
empathy, compassion, friendliness	21 #		
transparency in government	22 #		
homes for the homeless, food for the hungry	23 #		
a state's attorney who will prosecute killer cops	24 #		
recreation centers for the youth	25 #		
equal opportunity	26 #		
a government that's not for sale	27 #		
the 28th Amendment	28 #		
a subway that goes somewhere	29 #		
unbiased journalism	30 #		
green spaces, solar energy, good tasting city water	31 #		
tourist attractions that average people can afford to go to	32 #		
an overall plan	33 #		
olfactory perception	34 #		
functioning, contemporary & user-friendly infrastructure	35 #		
move jobs for ex-offenders	36 #		
programs for the ex-convicts and housing	37 #		
housing for the homeless	38 #		
fixing of the housing neighborhood	39 #		
better lighting on the streets of Baltimore	40 #		
safety awareness for the public	41 #		
honesty	42 #		
food system that links people to local, seasonal produce	43 #		
stop police brutality	44 #		
functioning, contemporary & user-friendly infrastructure	45 #		
prescription drugs	46 #		
respect for the merchants	47 #		

1st World Congress of the Missing Things / Baltimore, Lexington Market

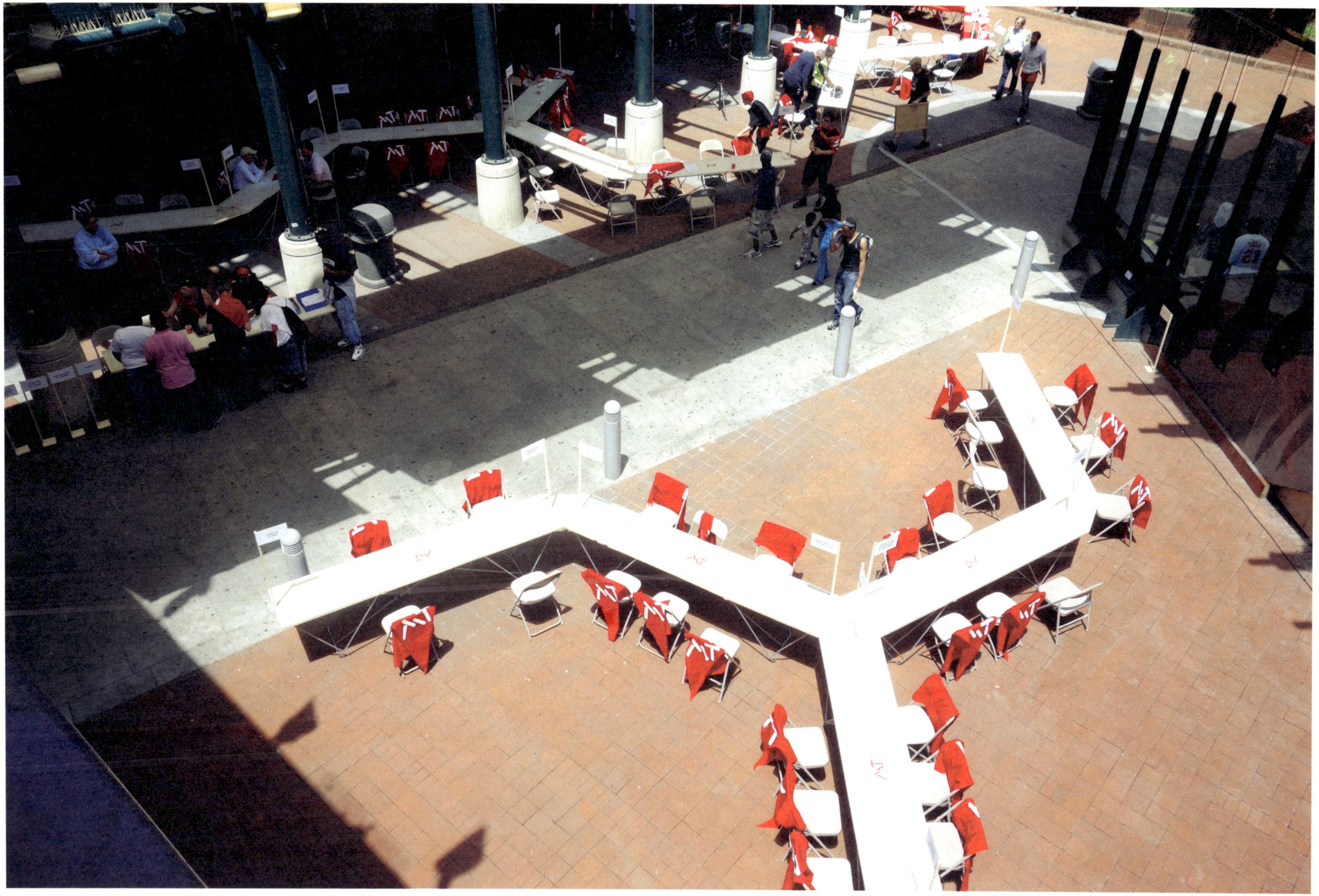

The rhizomatic spatial structure of a non-hierarchical congress

Die rhizomatische räumliche Struktur des nicht-hierarchischen Kongresses

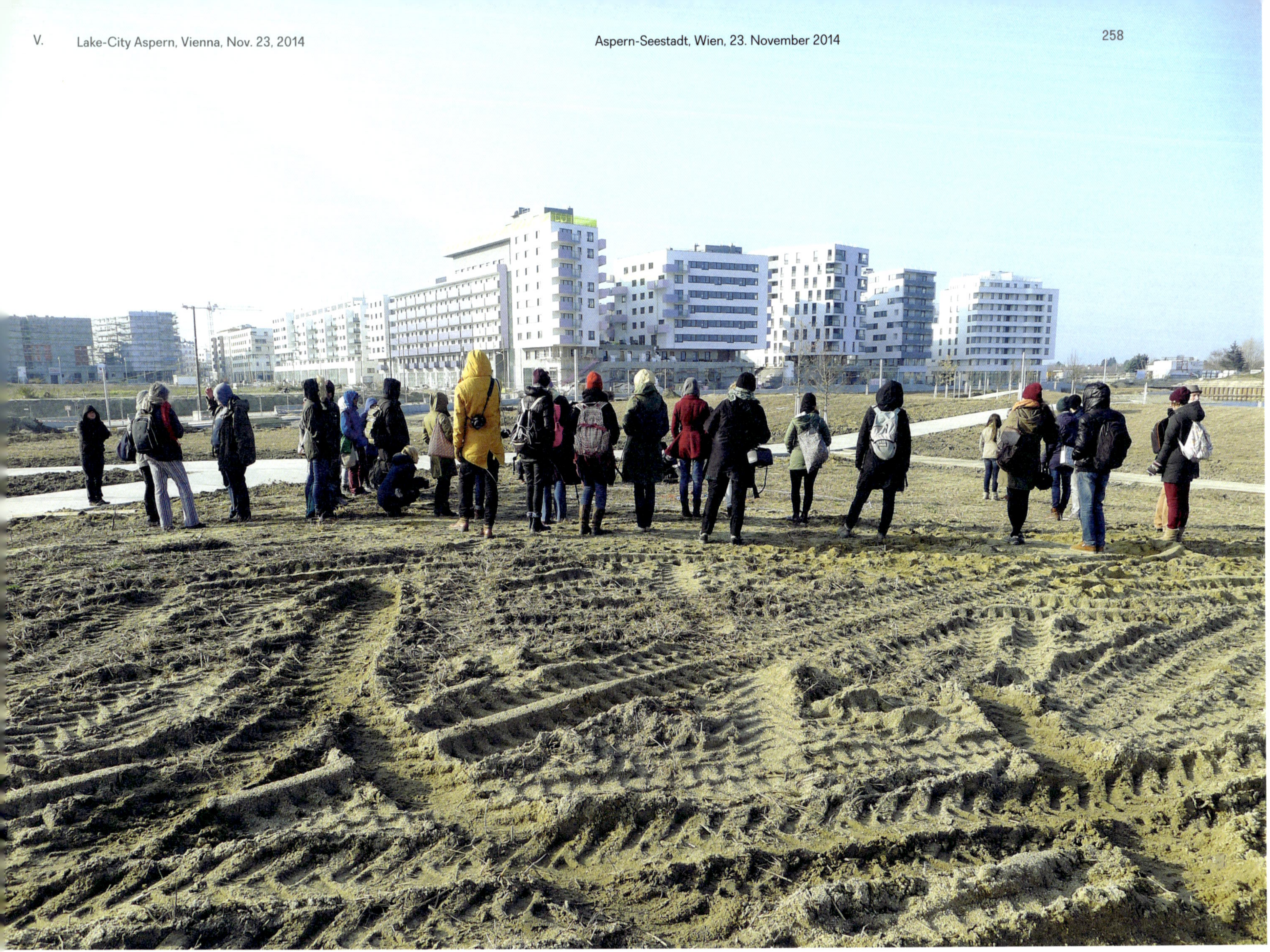

Participants of the congress facing the situation.

TeilnehmerInnen des Kongresses sehen der aktuellen Lage ins Auge.

THE SECOND WORLD *NON*-CONGRESS OF THE MISSING THINGS

In contrast to its predecessor in Baltimore four months earlier, which had been an assessment of what was missing from an already established community, THE SECOND WORLD *NON*-CONGRESS OF THE MISSING THINGS took place in a community at its earliest stage of development, Lake-City Aspern still under construction at the time. Where THE FIRST WORLD CONGRESS OF THE MISSING THINGS had dwelt on Baltimore's past and present, Barbara Holub now looked to the future, staging a one-day program of discussions and performances involving the first residents, construction workers and students from the social design course at the University of Applied Arts Vienna.

Again, a list of missing things was compiled, with contributors reflecting on qualities of the construction site that would vanish on completion of this suburban development. The content was more poetic than pragmatic, perhaps inspired by the eerie spectacle of a brand new, but almost entirely uninhabited, settlement. For example, item 1, "A sand dune for The Woman in the Dunes," refers to Kobo Abe's existentialist novel; while no. 14, "cricket players from distant lands," in mentioning a sport not played in Austria, evokes the interests of immigrant populations. Item no. 29, "the Bernhardiner-Allee," proposes a walkway named after the misanthropic author Thomas Bernhard, and no. 32 simply states: "the deserted city."

Suffice to say, the Congress did not espouse a utopian vision, less a panacea for social problems than a means of foregrounding the full richness of the social, both as lived reality and as imagined scenarios. If the many varied contributions dared to propose the construction site as more enchanting than the actually finished settlement, perhaps this was to show that settlements are never truly "finished," but always in flux, and even—to paraphrase Robert Smithson—a kind of future ruin. SA

Cooperation partner: University of Applied Arts Vienna, Social Design – Arts as Urban Innovation; projects by Oldooz Ahmadzadeh, Cornelia Bast, Antonia Eggeling, Dilruba Erkan, Roland Hampl, Katharina Heinrich, Wookseob Jeong, Lydia Kaminski, Sally Kotter, Hana Krizanova, Jan Phillip Ley, Alejandra Loreto, Anna Ilona Misovicz, Bo Mu, Vera Nikolaeva Naydenova, Peter Oroszlany, Madeleine Salinger, Christoph Steininger, Cosima Terrasse, Ana-Marija Vasicek, and Klelija Zhivkovikj; special guest: Shaheen Merali

THE SECOND WORLD *NON*-CONGRESS OF THE MISSING THINGS

Im Gegensatz zum Kongress in Baltimore vier Monate zuvor, der „fehlende Dinge" in einem historischen Stadtteil aufzeigte, fand THE SECOND WORLD *NON*-CONGRESS OF THE MISSING THINGS an einem Ort statt, der am Anfang seiner Entwicklung stand, nämlich in der sich in der ersten Bauphase befindlichen Seestadt Aspern. Hielt sich der FIRST WORLD CONGRESS OF THE MISSING THINGS bei Baltimores Vergangenheit und Gegenwart auf, so blickte Barbara Holub nun in die Zukunft. Sie organisierte ein eintägiges Programm mit Diskussionen und Performances unter Mitwirkung der ersten BewohnerInnen des Quartiers, BauarbeiterInnen sowie Studierenden des Studiengangs „Social Design – Arts as Urban Innovation" an der Universität für angewandte Kunst Wien.

Wieder wurde eine „Charta der fehlenden Dinge" erstellt, die diesmal jedoch Qualitäten der Baustelle reflektierten, die nach Fertigstellung des Stadtteils verschwinden würden. Der Inhalt war eher poetischer denn pragmatischer Natur, vielleicht inspiriert vom Unheimlichen einer brandneuen, aber fast unbewohnten Stadt. „1 Eine Sanddüne für die ‚Frau in den Dünen'" bezieht sich z. B. auf Kobo Abes gleichnamigen existenzialistischen Roman, während „Nr. 14 Cricketspieler aus fernen Landen" mit der Erwähnung eines in Österreich nicht betriebenen Sports die Berücksichtigung von MigrantInneninteressen einfordert. „Nr. 29 Die Bernhardiner-Allee" vermisst möglicherweise einen nach dem misanthropischen österreichischen Autor Thomas Bernhard benannten Fußgängerweg, und Nr. 32 lautet einfach: „Die menschenleere Stadt".

Der Nicht-Kongress wollte jedenfalls nicht für eine utopische Vision oder gar eine Lösung für soziale Probleme eintreten, sondern den vollen Reichtum von Sozialität deutlich machen, sowohl als gelebte Realität wie auch als imaginierte Vision. Wenn die höchst unterschiedlichen Beiträge anzudeuten wagten, dass der Baustelle mehr Zauber innewohne als der fertiggestellten Siedlung, so vielleicht um zu zeigen, dass Quartiere niemals ganz „fertig", sondern ständig im Fluss und sogar – um mit Robert Smithson zu sprechen – eine Art künftige Ruine sind. SA

Kooperationspartnerin: Universität für angewandte Kunst Wien/ Social Design – Arts as Urban Innovation; Projekte von Oldooz Ahmadzadeh, Cornelia Bast, Antonia Eggeling, Dilruba Erkan, Roland Hampl, Katharina Heinrich, Wookseob Jeong, Lydia Kaminski, Sally Kotter, Hana Krizanova, Jan Phillip Ley, Alejandra Loreto, Anna Ilona Misovicz, Bo Mu, Vera Nikolaeva Naydenova, Peter Oroszlany, Madeleine Salinger, Christoph Steininger, Cosima Terrasse, Ana-Marija Vasicek und Klelija Zhivkovikj, Special guest: Shaheen Merali

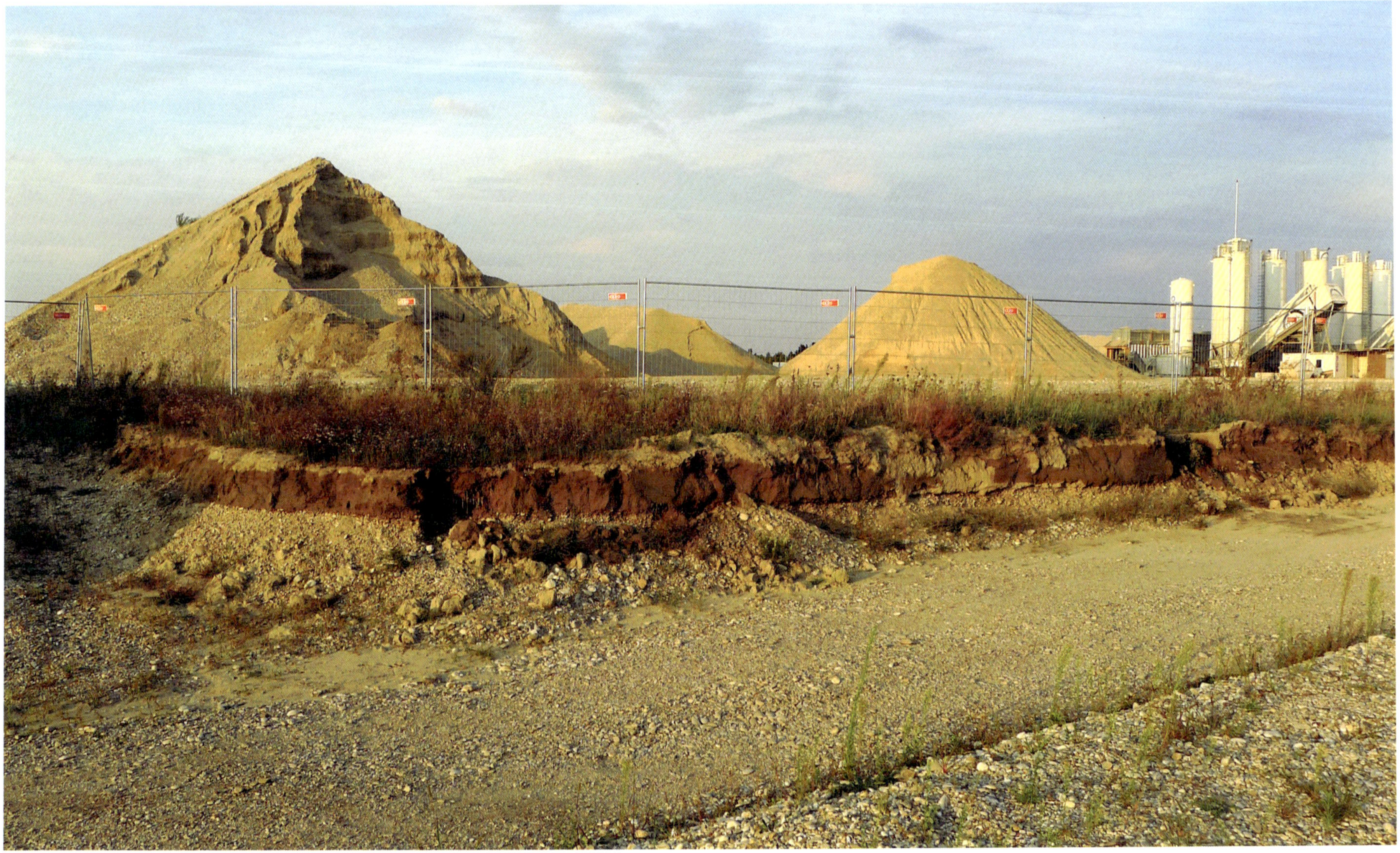

The Workers in the Dunes (after Kobo Abe)

Die Arbeiter in den Dünen (nach Kobo Abe)

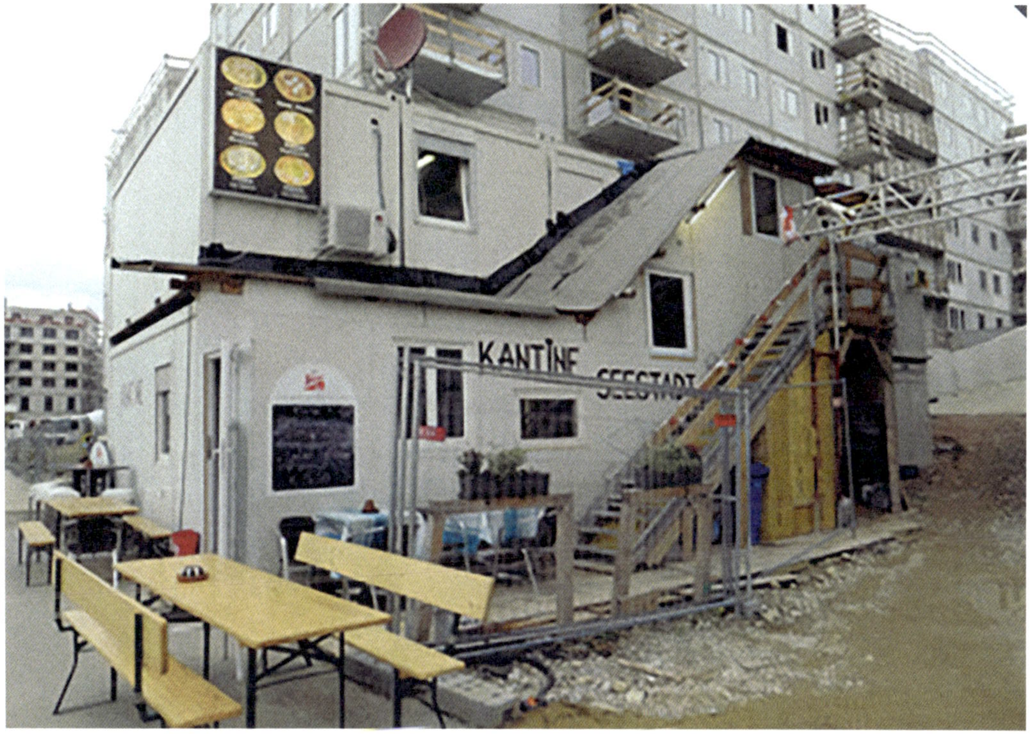

Congress Centre: the builders' canteen

Kongresszentrum: die Kantine fur die Bauarbeiter

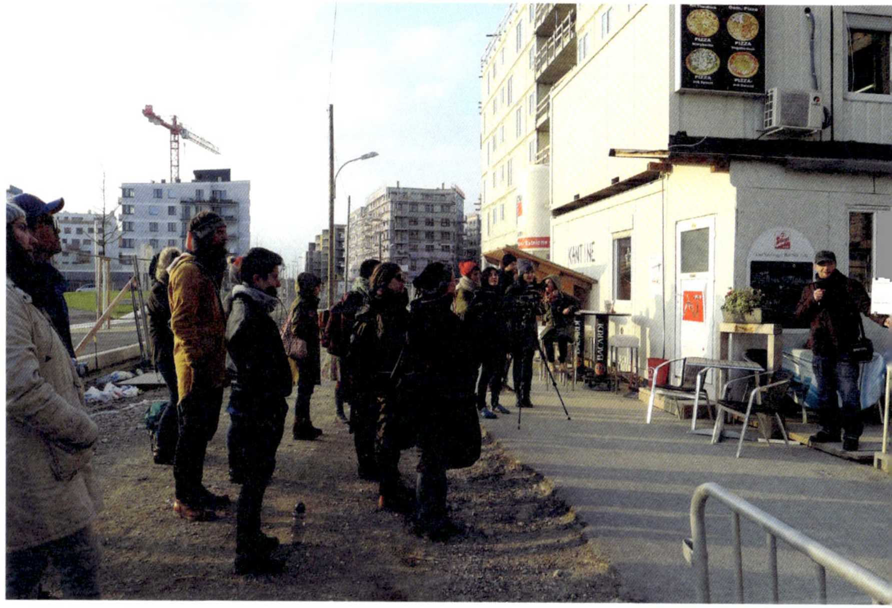

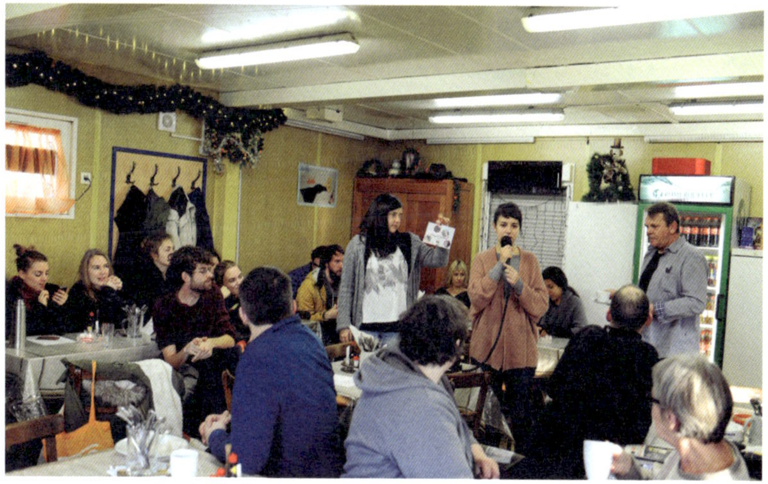

The "Charter of the Missing Things" could be read as an urbanist program that defies usual urban planning categories.

Die „Charta of the Missing Things" könnte als urbanistisches Programm gelesen werden, das sich üblichen stadtplanerischen Kategorien widersetzt.

Missing Things

Eine Sanddüne für die „Frau in den Dünen“	# 1	a sand dune for “the woman in the dune”
Wohnungen für queere Asylwerber	# 2	flats for queer asylum seekers
Dialog mit den Arbeitern von General Motors	# 3	a dialogue with the employees of General Motors
Reanimierung der fahrbaren (mittlerweile bereits ausrangierten) Kunstobjekte, die die Halbwertszeit von Kunst zeigen	# 4	reanimating the discarded art objects, showing the half life period of art.
Seeschwalben	# 5	terns
Eine chinesische Glückskatze	# 6	a chinese lucky-cat
Die Überraschung	# 7	the surprise
Der nahtlosen Übergang zwischen „Stadt“, Baustelle und „Gstettn“	# 8	the seamless transition between city, construction site and “Gstettn“
Der Hügel am nördlichen Seeufer	# 9	the hill at the northern lakeshore
Das Flederhaus	# 10	the “Flederhaus”
Die Aussichtsplattform	# 11	the observation deck
Neue Wege suchen	# 12	searching new ways
Der sich verändernde Horizont	# 13	the changing horizon
Cricketspieler aus fernen Landen	# 14	cricket players from distant land
Der maßgeschneiderte Blindenweg aus speziellen Pflanzkübeln	# 15	the tailored pass for blind people, made out of special planters
Der Erdkeller	# 16	the earth cellar
Platz für experimentelle Architektur	# 17	space for experimental architecture
Keramikbrennofen mit Holz befeuert	# 18	Ceramic kiln, fueled by wood
Mongolische Jurte	# 19	mongolian yurt
Aufbruchstimmung	# 20	“Aufbruchstimmung” // pioneer spirit
Sich besonders fühlen	# 21	to feel special
Die wilde Flora	# 22	the wild flora
Ein Ankunftszentrum für Roma	# 23	an arrival center for Roma
Der See der Namenlosen	# 24	the lake of the nameless
Preisverleihung für die Realisierung von 50 Stellplätzen (anstatt der geplanten 550) im Südteil	# 25	award ceremony for the realisation of 50 parking spaces (instead of the planned 550) for the Southern part
Die Baustellenkantinen	# 26	the construction site canteens
Die Nutzung einzelner Freiflächen nach Arbeitsschluss durch die Bauarbeiter	# 27	the use of vacant spaces by construction workers after work
Bitte liebt Aspern!	# 28	please love Aspern!
Die Bernhardiner-Allee	# 29	the Bernhardiner-Allee
Die riesigen Koi-Karpfen	# 30	the huge koi-carps
Die „Verwilderung“ und Sukzession einiger jetzt noch brachliegender Flächen und Bereiche, die einige sehr interessante jahreszeitliche Farb- und Pflanzstrukturen erkennen lässt, die aus der „Nichtpflege“ resultieren.	# 31	the wilderness of still fallow areas, and the seasonal changing structures of color and plant resulting from the lack of care
Die menschenleere Stadt	# 32	the deserted city
Container	# N	containers
Lärm	# N	noise
Analoge Kommunikation	# N	analog communication
Der Fußabdruck des Flughafens	# N	the footprint of the airport
Spiel von Licht und Schatten auf der Baustelle	# N	light and shadow situation at the construction site
Queere Räume	# N	queer spaces
Napoleons Rückkehr nach Aspern	# N	Napoleon‘s return to Aspern
	# N	
	# N	

2nd World Non-Congress of the Missing Things / Wien, Aspern Seestadt

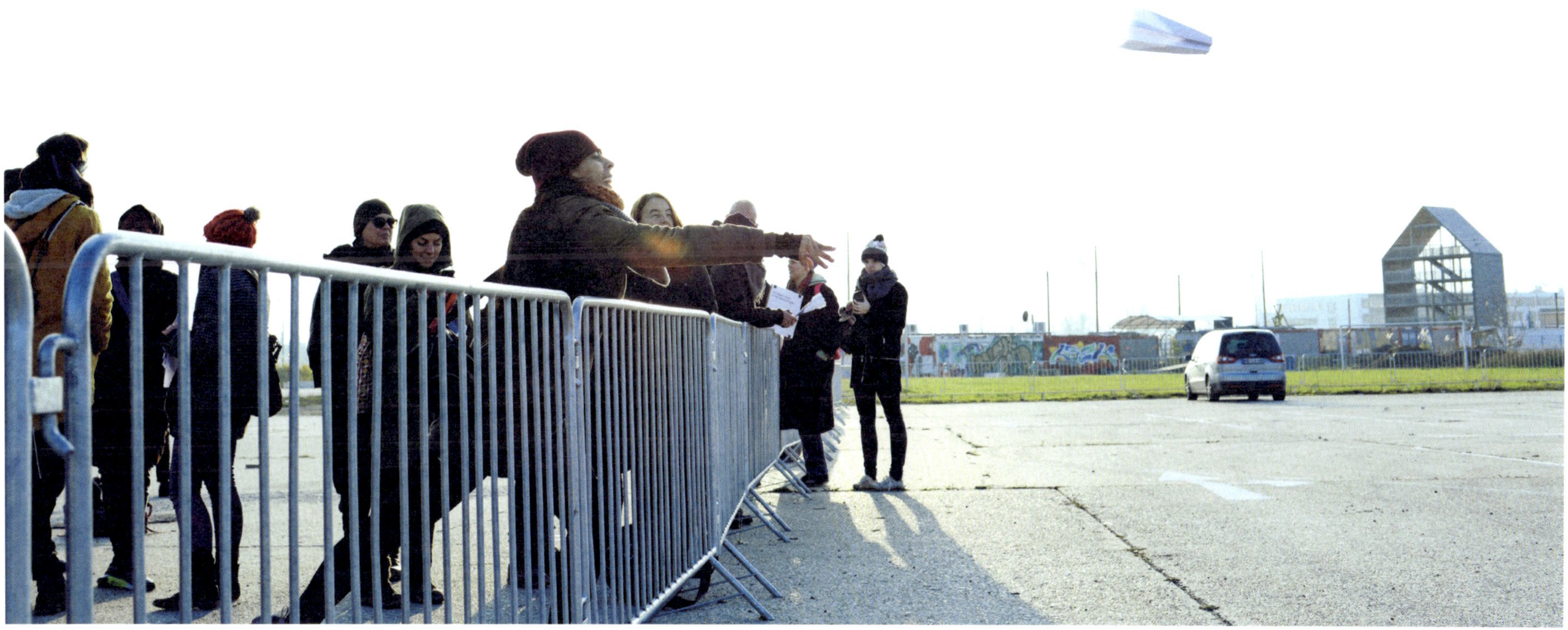

The last remaining runway of what was once Austria's largest airport was activated one last time for a special air show.

Die letzte noch vorhandene Landebahn des ehemals größten Flughafens Österreichs wurde ein letztes Mal für eine besondere Flugschau aktiviert.

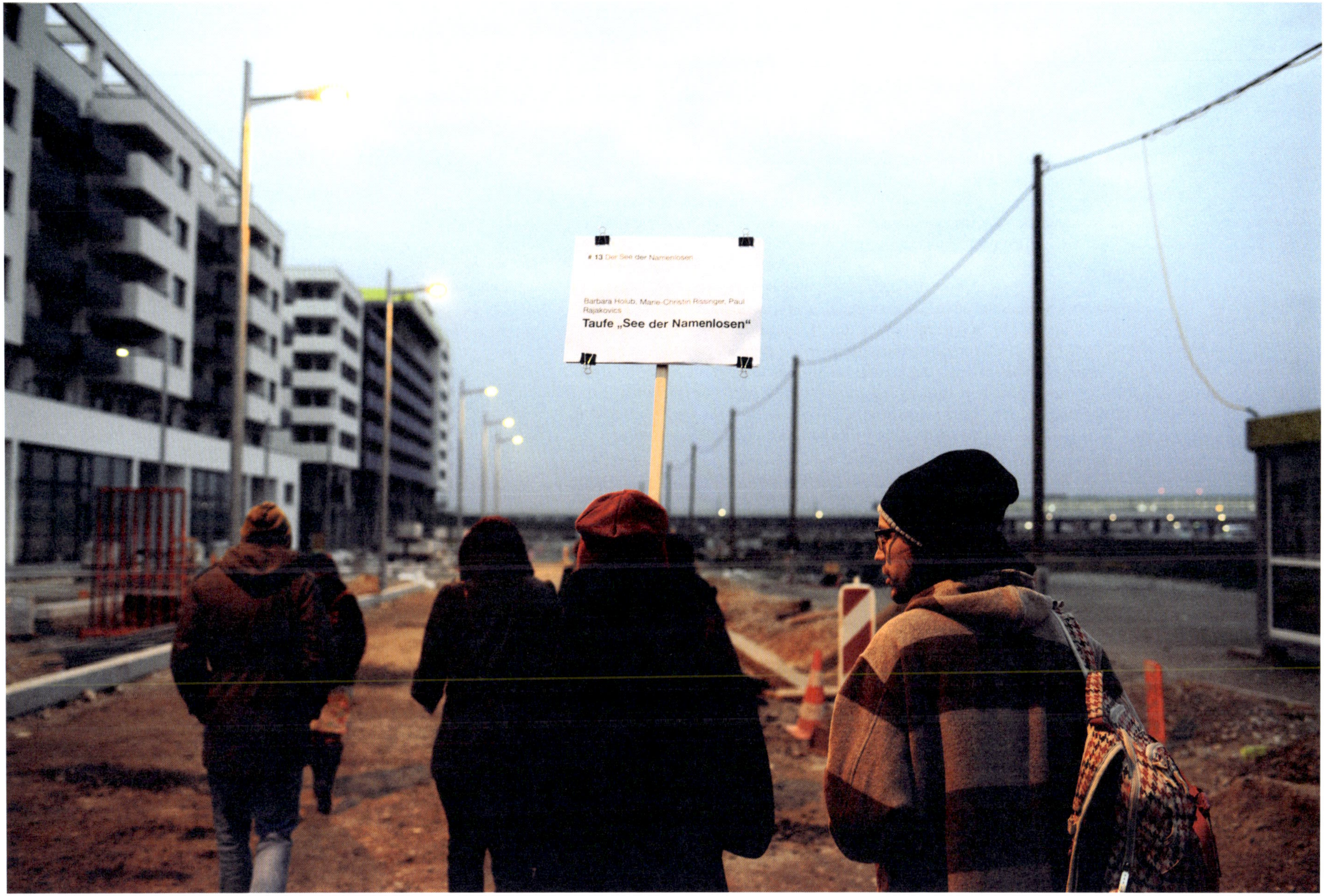
13 Der See der Namenlosen
Barbara Holub, Marie-Christin Rissinger, Paul Rajakovics
Taufe „See der Namenlosen“

THE THIRD WORLD CONGRESS OF THE MISSING THINGS

Coming seven years after the First and Second World Congresses of the Missing Things (in Baltimore, USA, and Lake-City Aspern, Austria), THE THIRD WORLD CONGRESS OF THE MISSING THINGS consolidated transparadiso's ongoing assertion of poetic over pragmatic aspects of urban space. Once more, they deployed their signature method of asking the public what they felt was missing from urban experience in a series of informal discussions prior to the event, the responses compiled into a charter submitted to the local authorities. Again, the question of whose knowledge is considered relevant was paramount, but this time explored in more peripatetic fashion, the charter being expanded by two "dérives" through the Eisteichsiedlung, a neighborhood with social housing from the 1960s. The "dérives" examined—with the help of "moment catchers"—previously overlooked qualities of public space, reversing the dictum of efficiency that typifies urban planning by alerting us to the redundancy of things that were once functional: the ruin of a former brickworks overrun by nature; how a broken gate emphasizes the open space of the park beyond, where previously it barred access to it; the contrast between well-trimmed hedges and an unkempt thicket near an abandoned swimming pool.

The two-day congress, which featured a number of performances, readings and discussions, took place in and around a set of "BambooKazas" (fold-out awnings held together with bamboo supports) specially designed for the occasion and donated to the district afterwards, for future events based on topics of conflict. A blank advertising column allowed people to chalk up their "missing things." Located in the parish of St. Paul in the Eisteichsiedlung, the "BambooKazas" occupied the parking lot of the parish, designed by architect Ferdinand Schuster in 1969 to serve as an "open" church, a kind of community centre. One of the functions of The Third World Congress was to reawaken and expand this original social purpose by revealing the potential of the parking lot as a public space for readings, concerts and other activities, anticipating what was to become a common refrain of the Congress: the desire to re-establish a non-commercial centre in the district. [SA]

A project by transparadiso

Cooperation partner transparadiso: Michael Petrowitsch
Cooperation partners for NORMAL: HdA Graz; Forum Stadtpark, Graz; dérive—magazine for urban research, Vienna

THE THIRD WORLD CONGRESS OF THE MISSING THINGS

Bei dem sieben Jahre nach dem ersten und dem zweiten WORLD CONGRESS (bzw. *NON*-CONGRESS) OF THE MISSING THINGS stattfindenden THIRD WORLD CONGRESS OF THE MISSING THINGS insistierte transparadiso noch konsequenter auf poetischen – im Gegensatz zu pragmatischen – Aspekten des urbanen Raums. Einmal mehr wandten die KünstlerInnen spezielle Methoden an, die BürgerInnen nach fehlenden Dingen in ihrem urbanen Umfeld zu befragen. Wieder wurden die Antworten, die in einer Reihe informeller Diskussionen schon im Vorfeld der eigentlichen Veranstaltung ermittelt worden waren, zu einer Charta gebündelt und den lokalen Behörden übergeben. Auch hier stand die Frage im Vordergrund, wessen Wissen als relevant erachtet wird, aber diesmal wurde die Charta zusätzlich mit zwei „dérives" durch die Eisteichsiedlung, einem in den 1960er-Jahren entstandenen, von sozialem Wohnbau geprägten Viertel in Graz, angereichert. In den „dérives" wurden – mit Hilfe von „Momentefängern" – nicht mehr wahrgenommene Qualitäten des öffentlichen Raums erkundet und die in der Stadtplanung übliche Forderung nach Effizienz konterkariert, indem die Aufmerksamkeit auf die Verwandlung einstmals funktionaler Elemente gelenkt wurde, die nun „poetische" Qualitäten aufweisen: die von der Natur zurückeroberte Ruine eines früheren Ziegelwerks; ein dysfunktionales Tor, das nun den freien Zugang zu einem Park betont, den es vorher verwehrte; den Gegensatz zwischen sauber gestutzten Hecken und einem wirren Dickicht neben einem aufgelassenen Swimmingpool.

Der zweitägige Kongress, der aus einer Reihe von Performances, Lesungen und Diskussionen bestand, fand unter zwei „BambooKazas" statt – ausfaltbaren Dächern auf einer Bambuskonstruktion –, die transparadiso speziell für den Anlass entworfen hatte und danach dem Bezirk Waltendorf für künftige Veranstaltungen zu umstrittenen Themen überlassen wollte. Eine schwarz bemalte Litfaßsäule diente als Tafel, um „fehlende Dinge" zu notieren. Installiert waren die „BambooKazas" auf dem Parkplatz des Katholischen Seelsorgezentrums St. Paul, das 1969 vom Architekten Ferdinand Schuster als eine „offene" Kirche – eine Art Gemeindezentrum – entworfen worden war. Der Third World Congress sollte u. a. diese ursprüngliche soziale Funktion wiederbeleben und erweitern, indem er das Potenzial des Parkplatzes als öffentlicher Ort für Lesungen, Konzerte und andere Aktivitäten aufzeigte. Das nahm einen allgemeinen Tenor des Kongresses vorweg: den Wunsch, in Waltendorf wieder ein nichtkommerzielles Zentrum zu etablieren. [SA]

Ein Projekt von transparadiso

Kooperationspartner transparadiso: Michael Petrowitsch
Kooperationspartner von NORMAL: HdA Graz; Forum Stadtpark, Graz; dérive – Zeitschrift für Stadtforschung, Wien

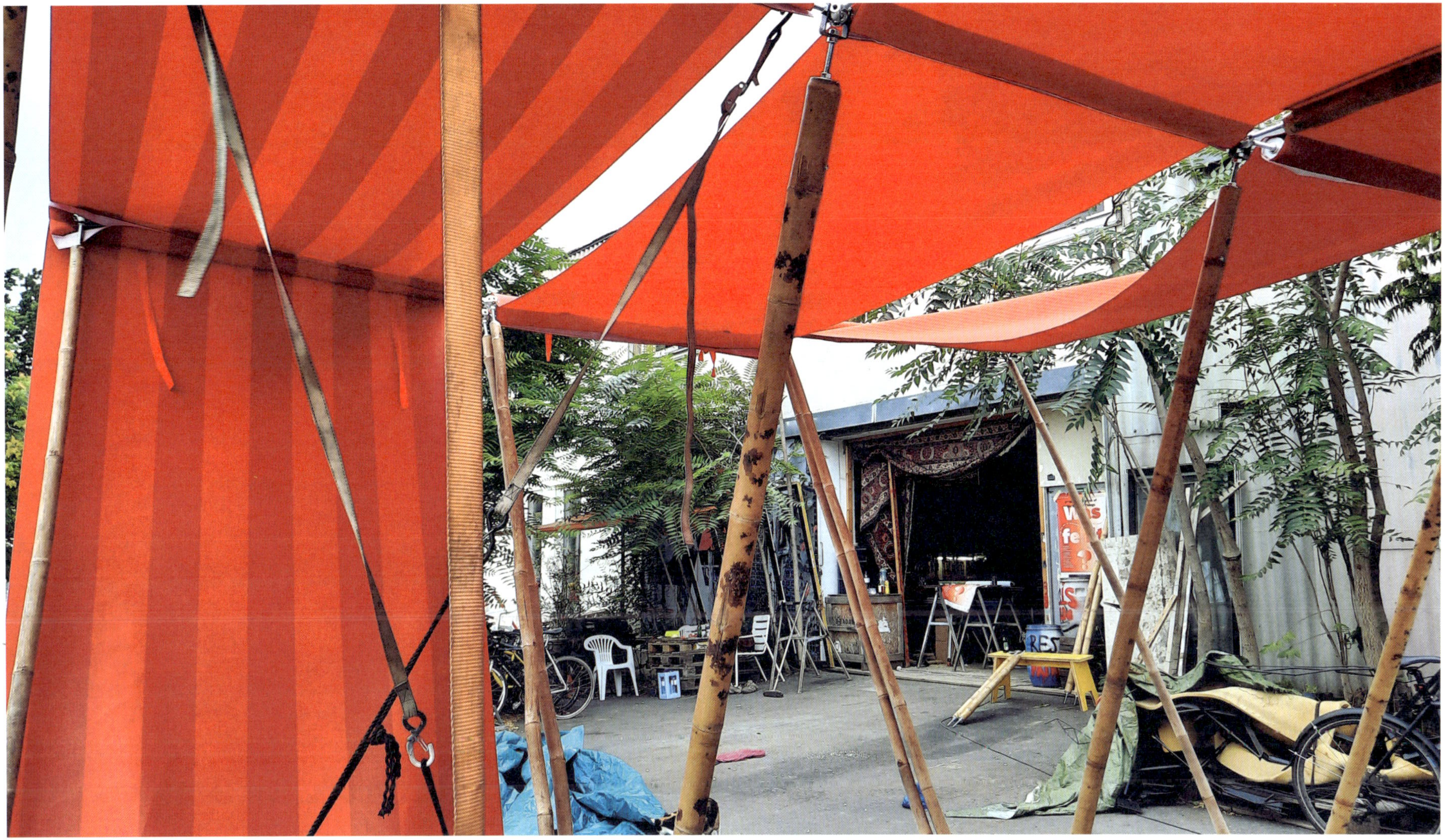

Trial setup, Schaumbad/studio Stefan Lozar, Graz, June 2021

Probeaufbau, Schaumbad/Studio Stefan Lozar, Graz, Juni 2021

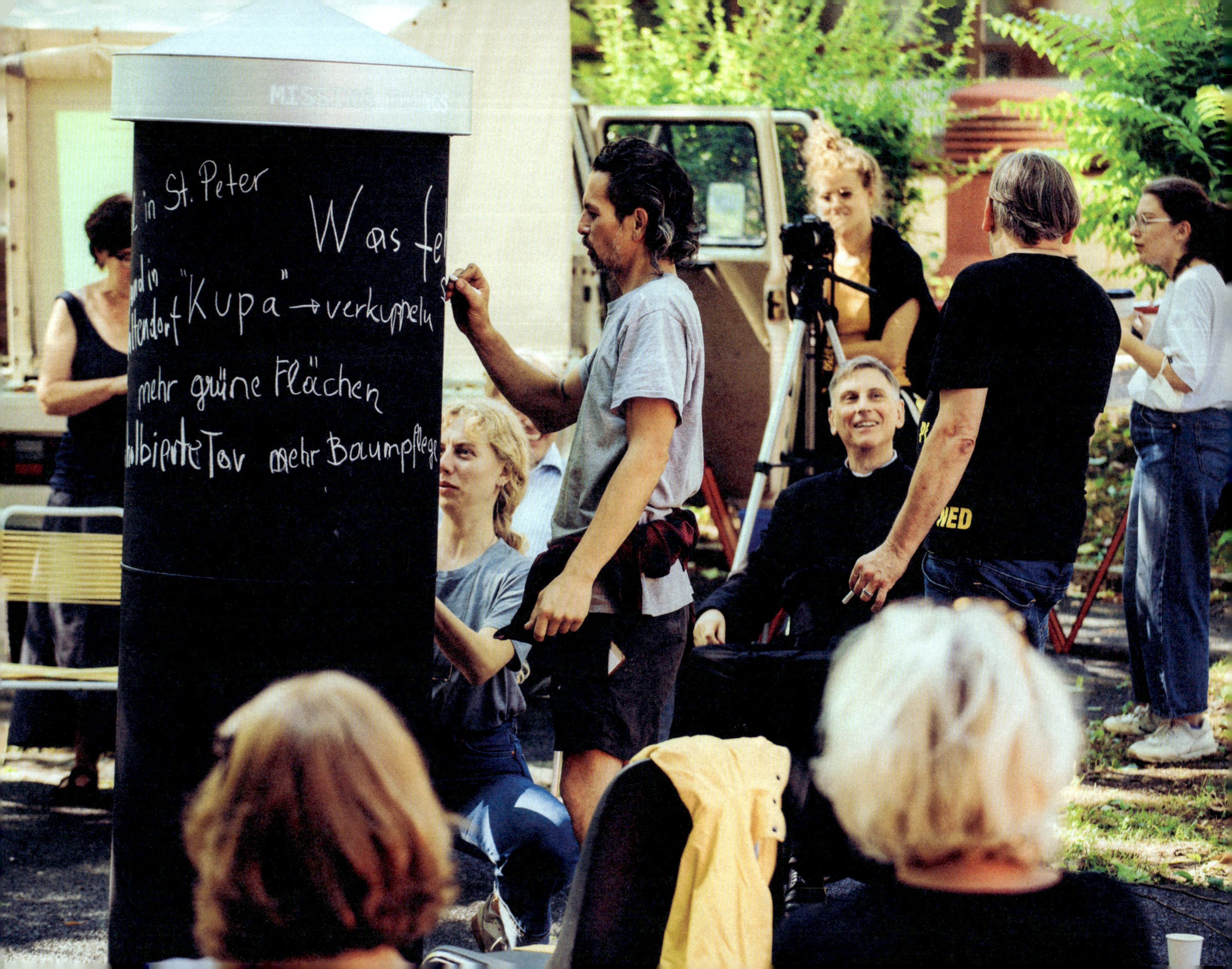
in St. Peter
"Kupa" → verkuppeln
mehr grüne Flächen
mehr Baumpflege

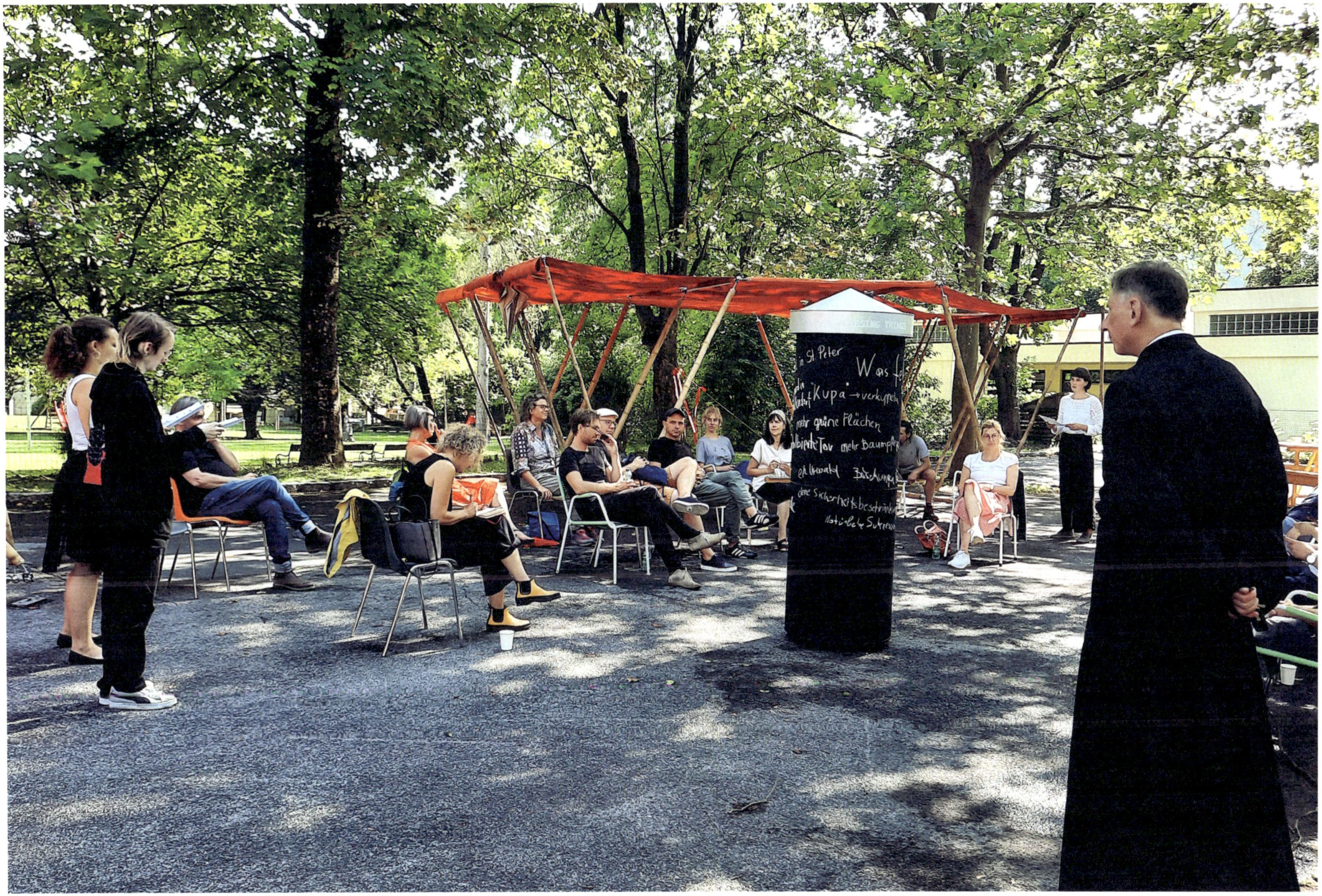

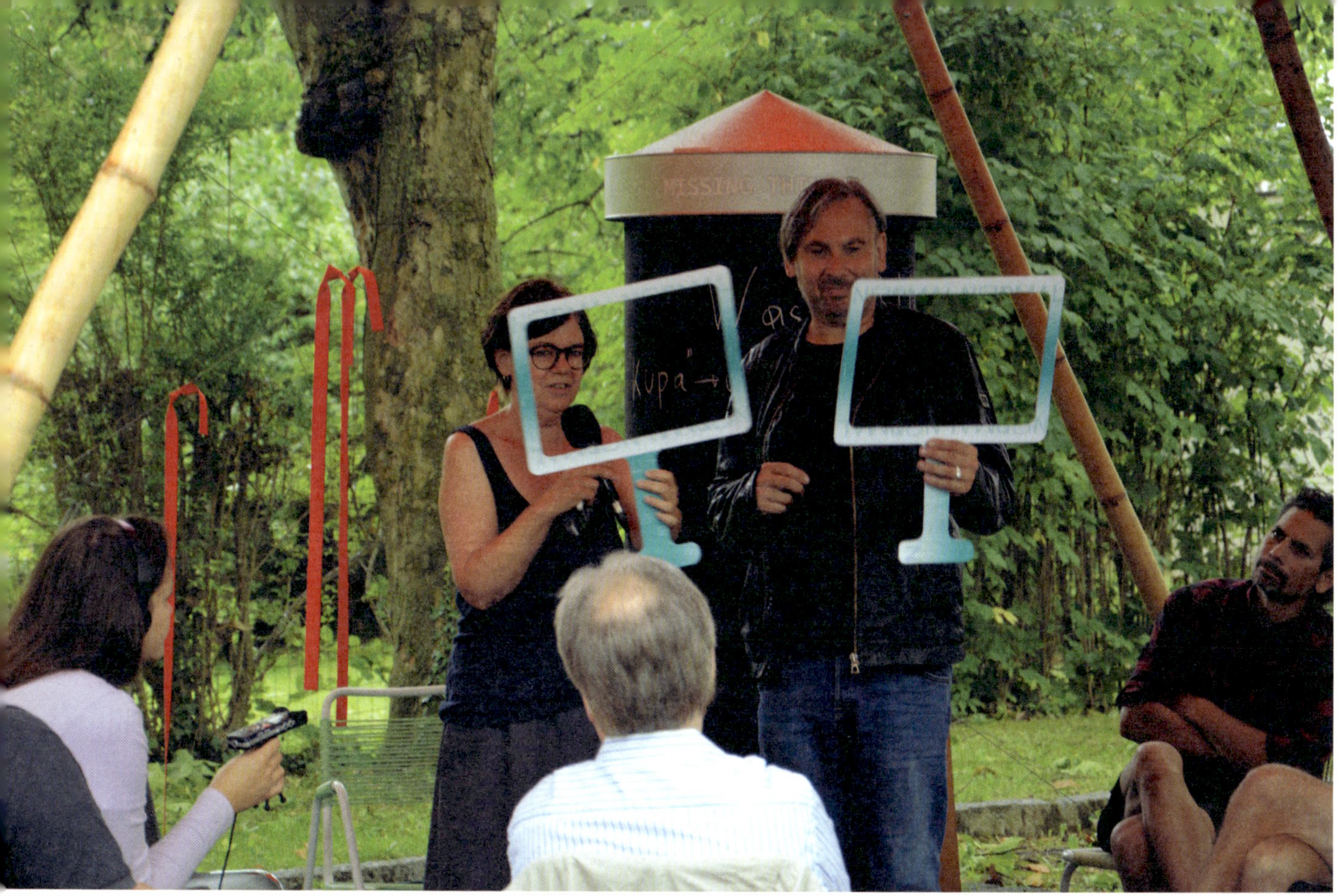

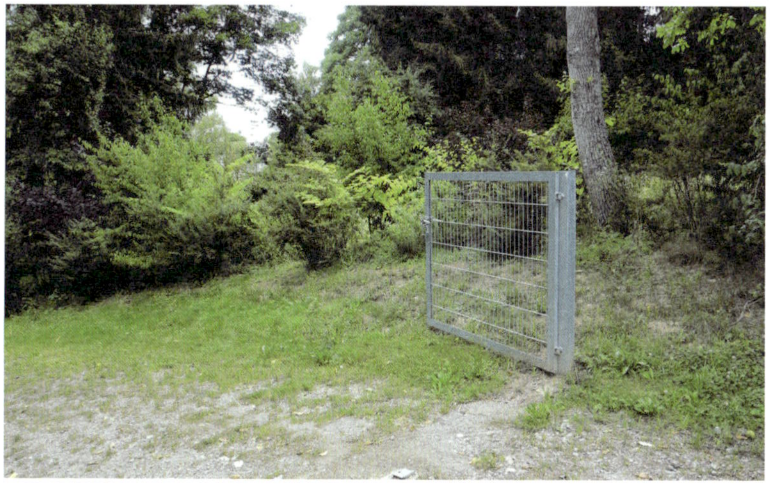

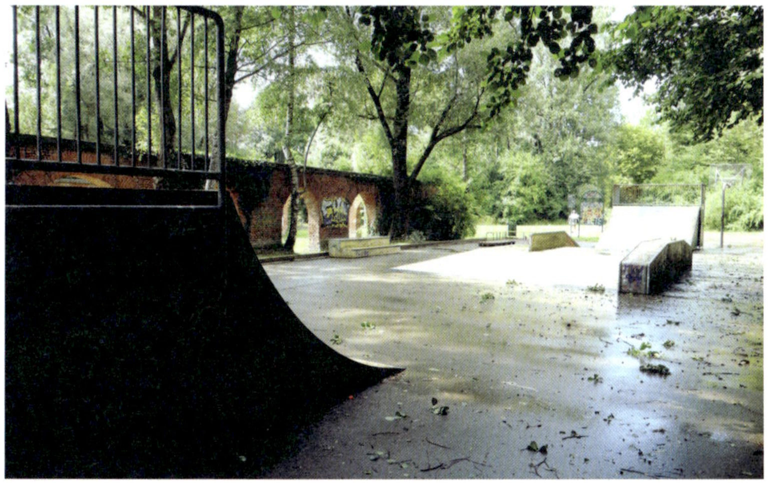

"Moment catchers" invited to "dérives" to discover hidden poetic or even whimsical moments.

Die „Momentefänger" luden zu „dérives" ein, um verborgene poetische oder auch skurrile Momente zu entdecken.

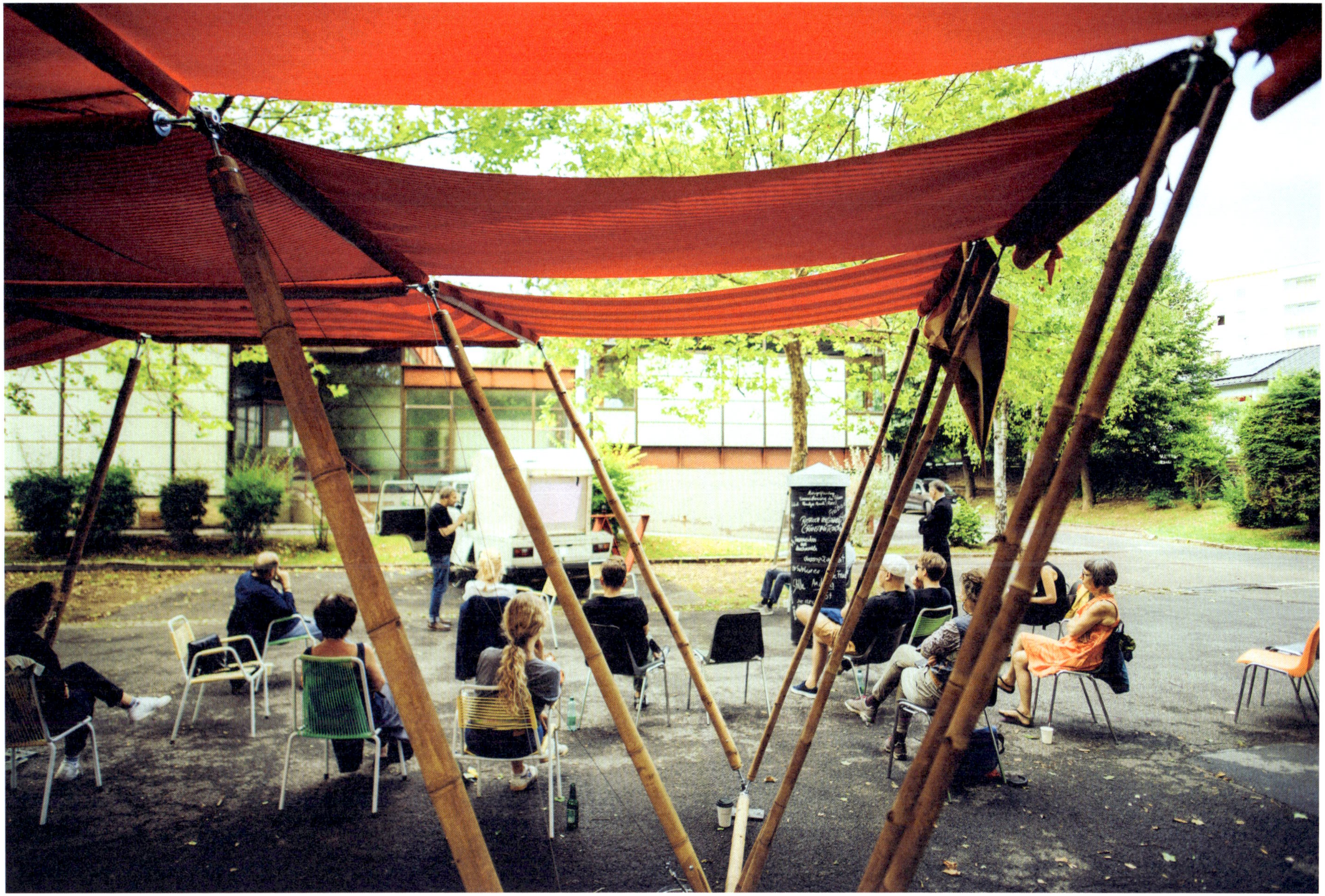

CHARTER OF THE MISSING THINGS

#1 etwas mehr Miteinander
#2 ein (Bezirks)Zentrum für Waltendorf *(vielfach geäußert)*
#3 mehr Rücksicht aufeinander
#4 Geschwindigkeitsbeschränkende Vorkehrungen
#5 Durchgänge für Fußgänger
#6 Grüne Zone ausweiten
#7 Tafeln aufstellen: Hier wohnen Menschen
#8 geschützte und betreute Zone ohne Konsumzwang für Jugendliche im Berliner Ring: eine Utopie?
a) Die Stadt Graz mietet/kauft eine Parterrewohnung und baut sie mit einer Terrasse zum Hof aus
b) Die Stadt Graz pachtet den Keller vom Haus der Begegnung der Pfarre Ragnitz
#9 mehr Wiesen und Bäume im öffentlichen Raum von St. Leonhard und allen anderen Bezirken
#10 neue Formen der „Gemütlichkeit“ - trotz Corona
#11 neue Gruß-, Kommunikations- und Konsumformen
#12 spatial distancing - ja! social distancing - nein!
#13 Durchwegungen für Fußgänger beachten; verordnete Durchwegungen (Bebauungsplan Kaiserwaldweg zur Oberen Teichstraße) durchführen; langjährig bestehende Durchwegungen (Odiliengründe) wieder herstellen. Wäre auch ganz normal!!
#14 Gehsteige in jeder Straße mit Durchzugsverkehr
#15 Professionelle Führung des Mehrgenerationenhauses und Halbtagsplanstelle
#16 mehr Gäste aus der Eisteichsiedlung im Café
#17 ein Tunnel von Süd nach Nord (für den Pendlerverkehr)
#18 rund um das Mehrgenerationenhaus eine gepflegte Grünfläche (ist vorhanden und öffentlicher Grund!!) mit Trinkbrunnen, auf der es sich gerne verweilen lässt. Könnte ein kleiner Dorfbrunnen sein. Das Haus ist denkmalgeschützt und gehört dringend renoviert (Fassade). Wäre alles ganz normal!!
#19 Gestaltung und Aufweitung des alten Dorfzentrums
#20 eine gefrorene Pfütze, in die man hinein springt, sodass es schön kracht und spritzt
#21 Schmetterlingsfänger, die sich aus Leidenschaft im Dickicht unentdeckter Spezies verirren
#22 ein Spielplatz für Erwachsene
#23 Umwertung des Begriffs „Sandler“: der Sandler streute die Formen zum Ziegelbrennen mit Sand aus (hier in der Eisteichsiedlung)
#24 eine zwecklose Nutzlosigkeit oder Müßiggang, bis Poesie geschaffen wird
#25 zwischen schreien und flüstern: die Land schaft hören
#26 so viele Dinge, die fehlen *(mehrfach geäußert)*
#27 Sonnenuntergang am Meer
#28 Wasser in Badequalität in meiner Stadt

The 3rd World Congress of the Missing Things - Graz-Waltendorf

CHARTER OF THE MISSING THINGS

#29 wildes Kombinieren
#30 Institutionen des Wissens hinterfragen
#31 weniger Parkplätze auf öffentlichem Grund
#32 besseres Radwegsystem
#33 neue Kulturen des Lernens
#34 Stille
#35 wenn auch naiv: Weltfrieden
#36 bedingungsloses Grundeinkommen
#37 bessere Bildung - auf allen Ebenen
#38 ein großzügiger Hundeauslauf
#39 prekäre Arbeitsverhältnisse von KünstlerInnen/WissenschafterInnen/ArchitektInnen nicht beschönigen oder gar als „role model“ verherrlichen
#40 mehr Mut sich zu engagieren, auch wenn man scheinbar nicht viel bewirken kann
#41 Strand in Waltendorf
#42 pure Freude
#43 Grosszügigkeit
#44 das halbierte Tor
#45 „Kupa“ (jüdisch) > „verkuppeln“
#46 ein Urwald ohne Sicherheitsbeschränkungen
#47 Messe im Freien
#48 natürliche Sukzession
#49 mehr grüne und unverbaute Flächen
#50 ein Stuhl für den Bettler vor der Kirche
#51 Himalaya Musk (spezielle Rose)
#52 Freibad in St.Peter: Pammerbad mit Hilfe der Stadt
#53 statt zugepflastertem „Zentrum“: Atrium in einem neuen Zentrum
#54 keine geschnittenen Sträucher
#55 Lösungen und Konzept
#56 Freude an kleinen Dingen
#57 Straßenfest
#58 keine Zäune
#59 Kennzeichnung der (seltenen) Bäume
#60 zum Tischtennis durchs Unterholz
#61 Wurzel-Baum
#62 Waltendorf hören
#63 Böschungen Terrassenhaussiedlung
#64 Alu-Hut
#65 Nutzlosigkeit
#66 Rostloch im (grünen) Grünschnittcontainer
#67 die elegant rankende Erbsenblüte vor der Polizeischule
#68 mehr Baumpflege
#69 Selbstlosigkeit
#70 die steile Straße
#71 Glockenkubus
#72 Autos haben mehr Platz als Füße > Umwertung
#73 Hängematte
#74 Gemüsegarten zum gemeinsam Pflanzen
#74 „Maß-Mensch“
#75 freie Sicht aufs Mittelmeer (man muss nur tief genug graben)

The 3rd World Congress of the Missing Things - Graz-Waltendorf

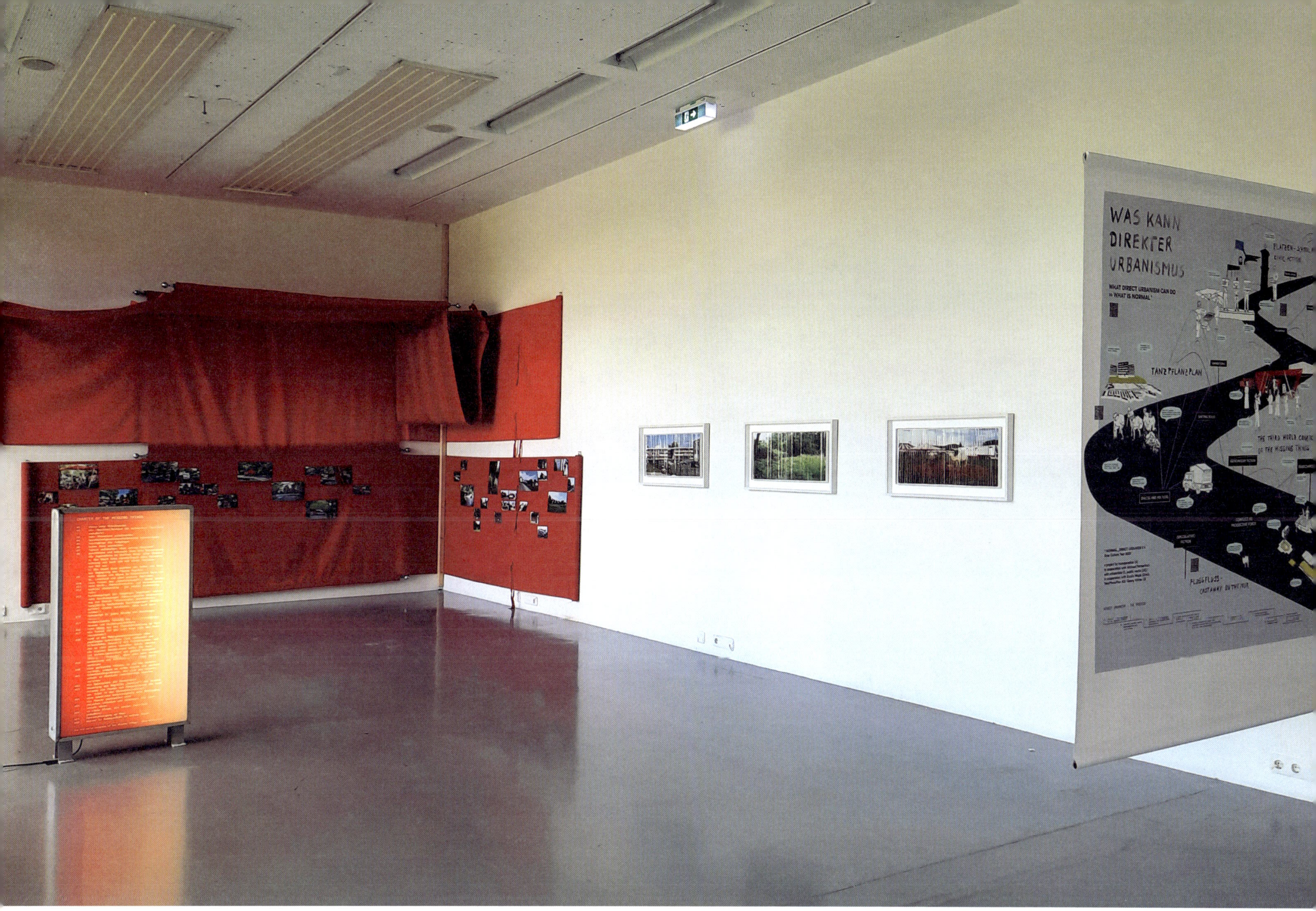

NORMAL, exhibition view, Forum Stadtpark, Graz, 2021

NORMAL, Ausstellungsansicht, Forum Stadtpark, Graz, 2021

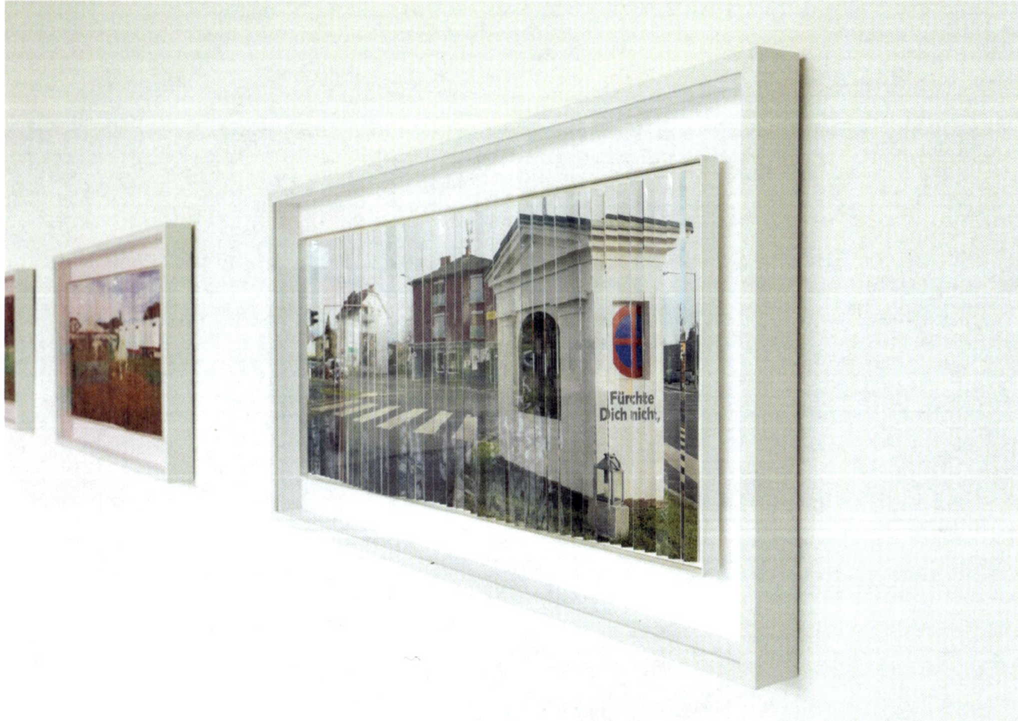

TURNER OF PERSPECTIVES,
2020

PERSPEKTIVENWENDER,
2020

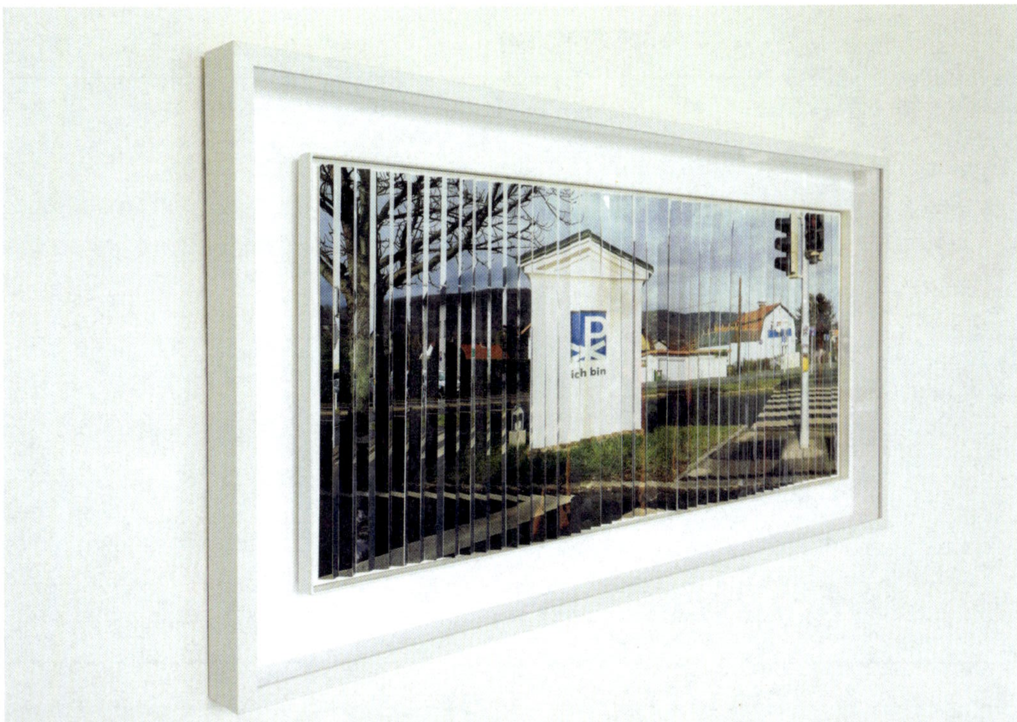

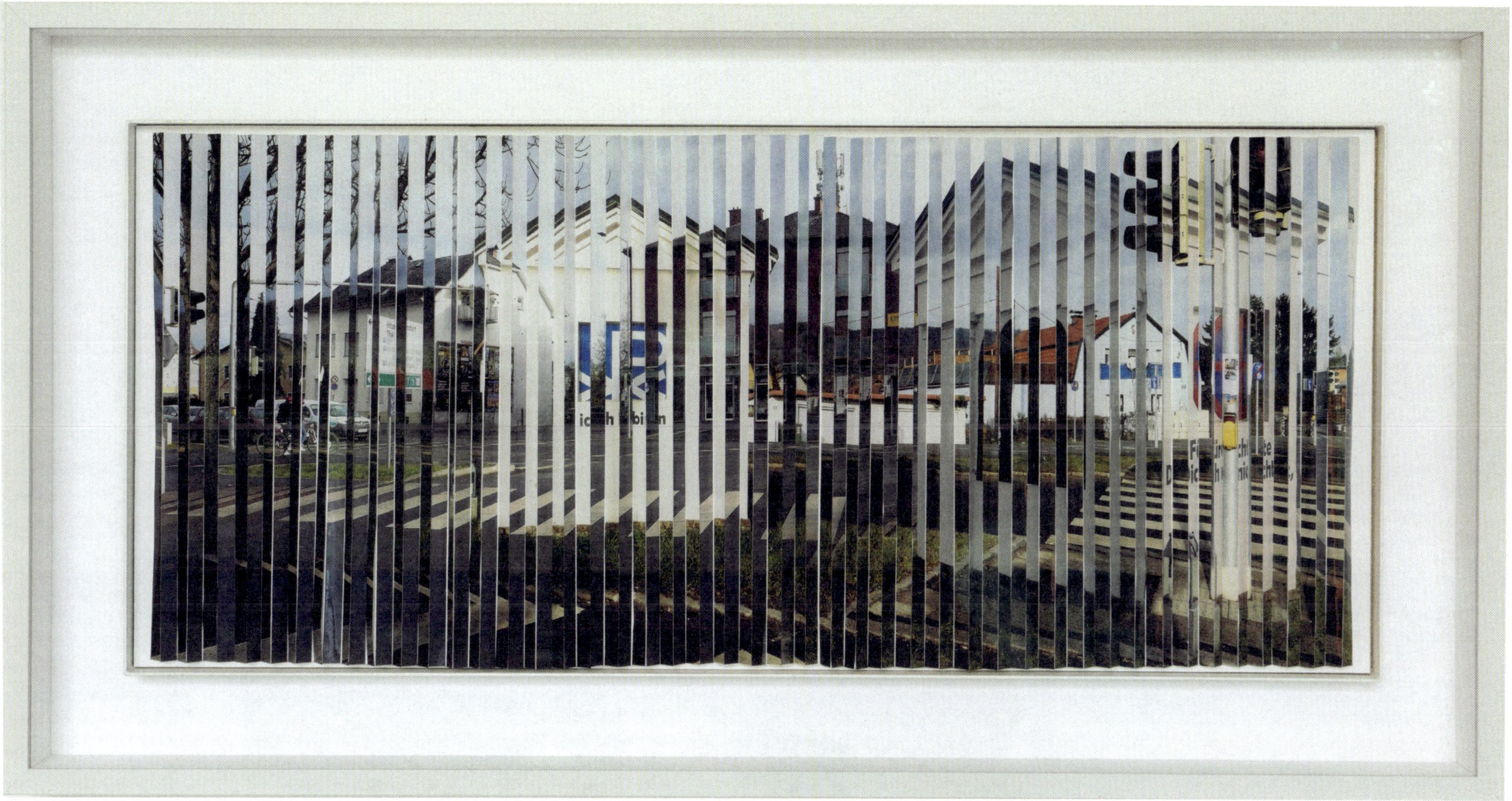

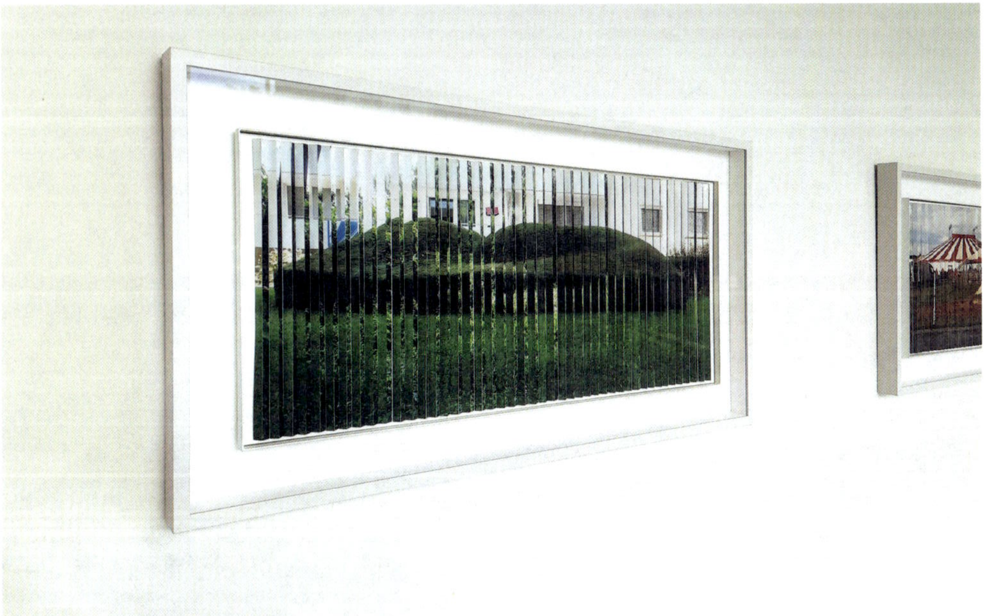

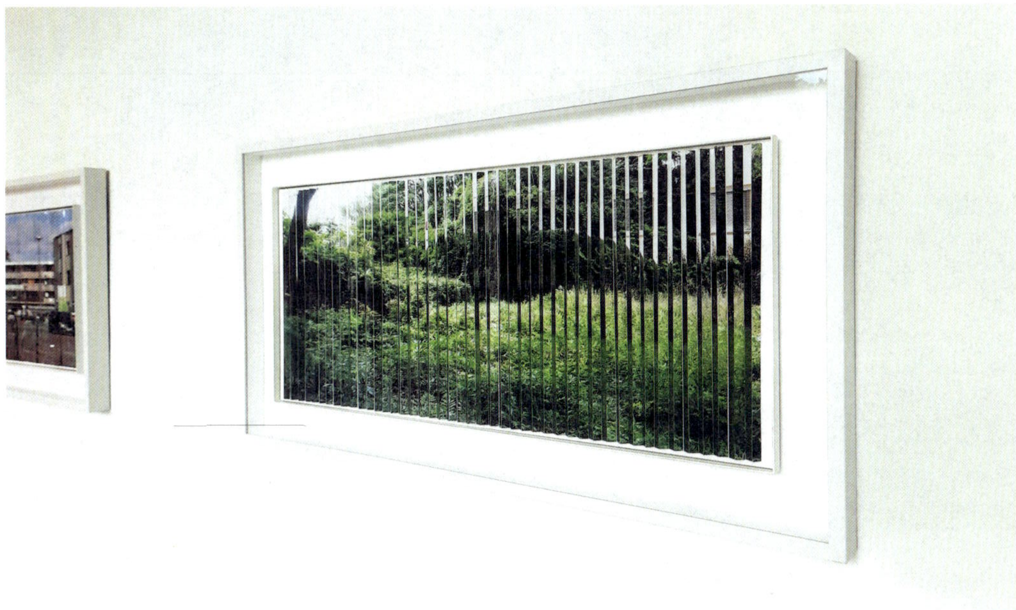

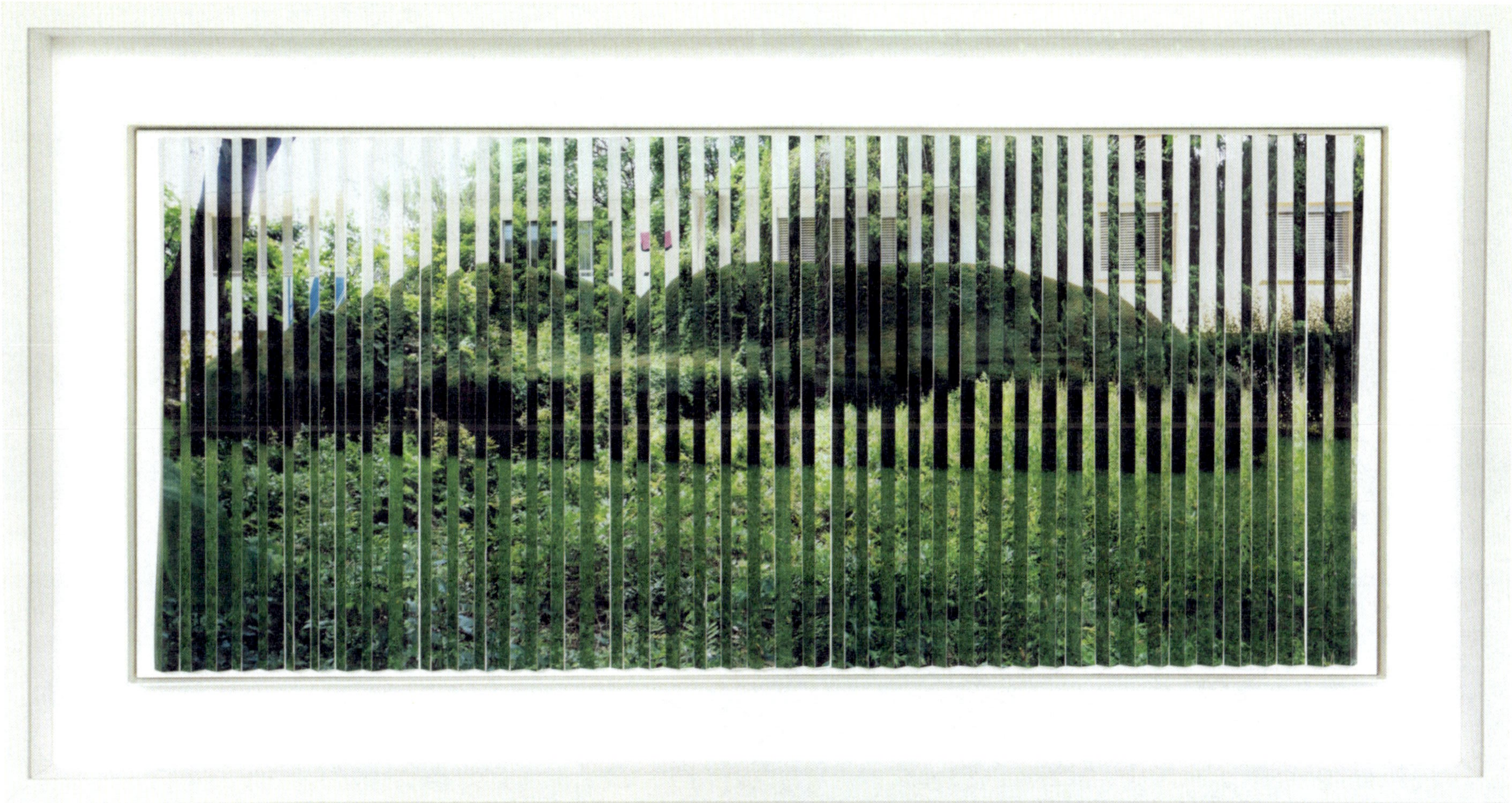

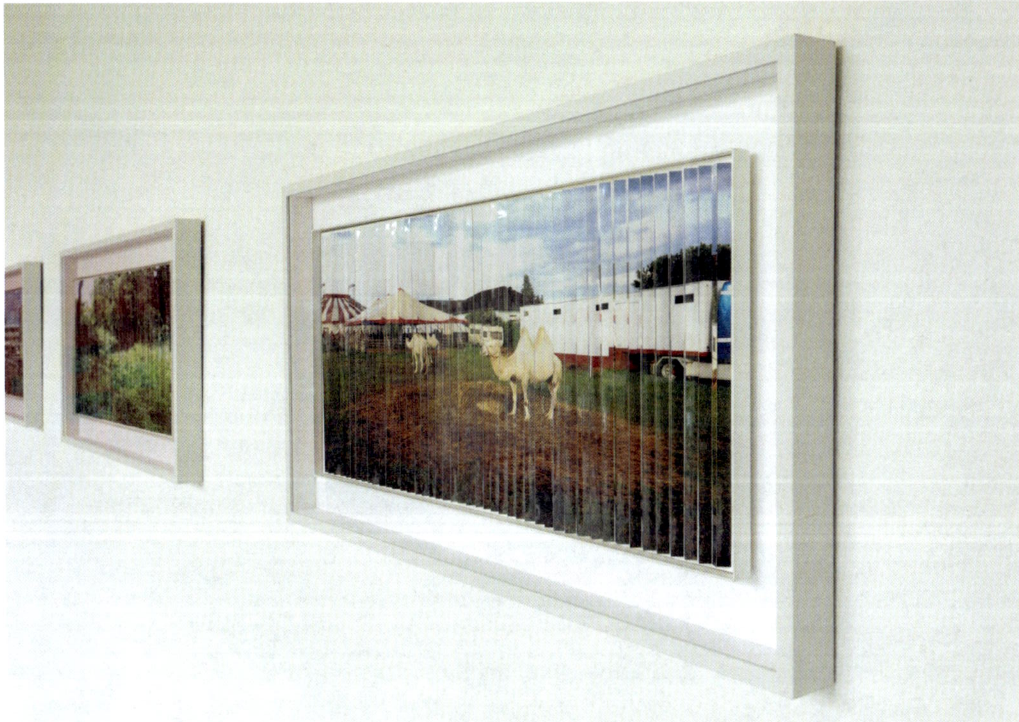

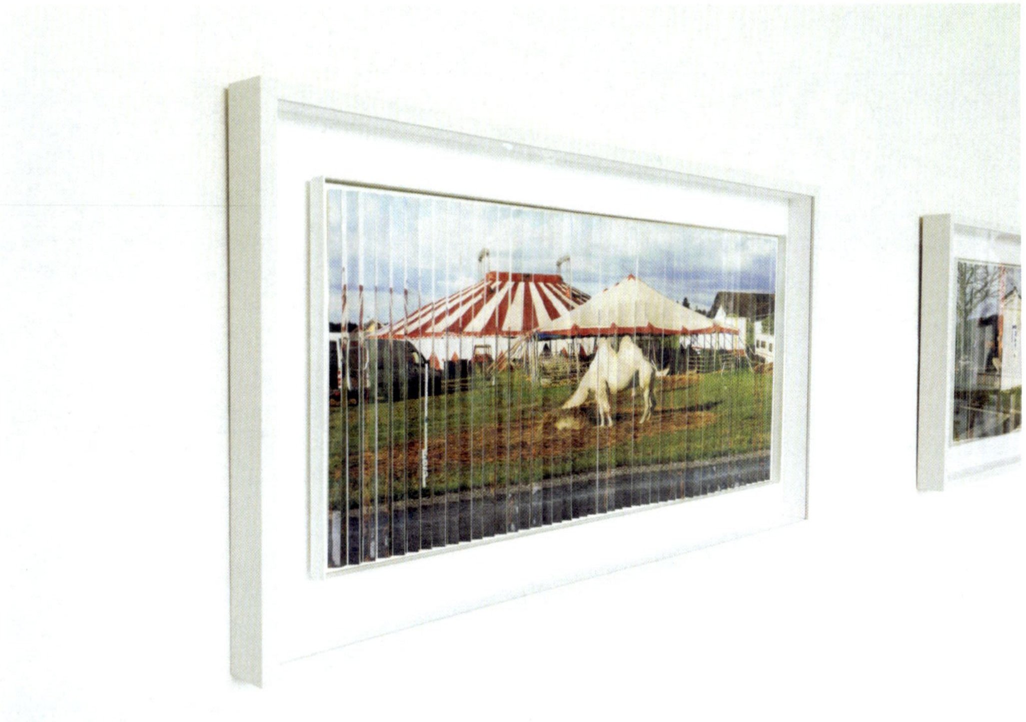

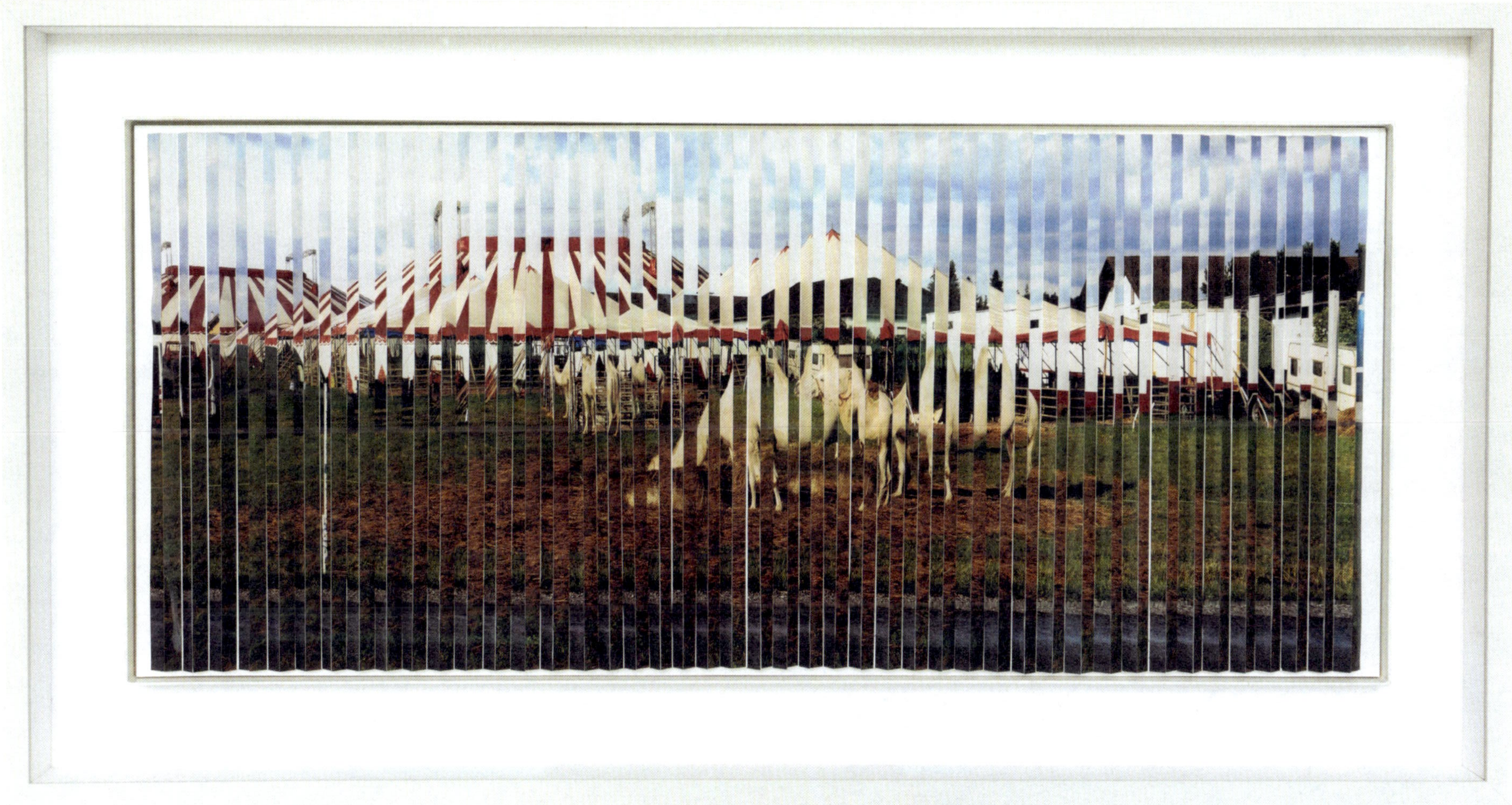

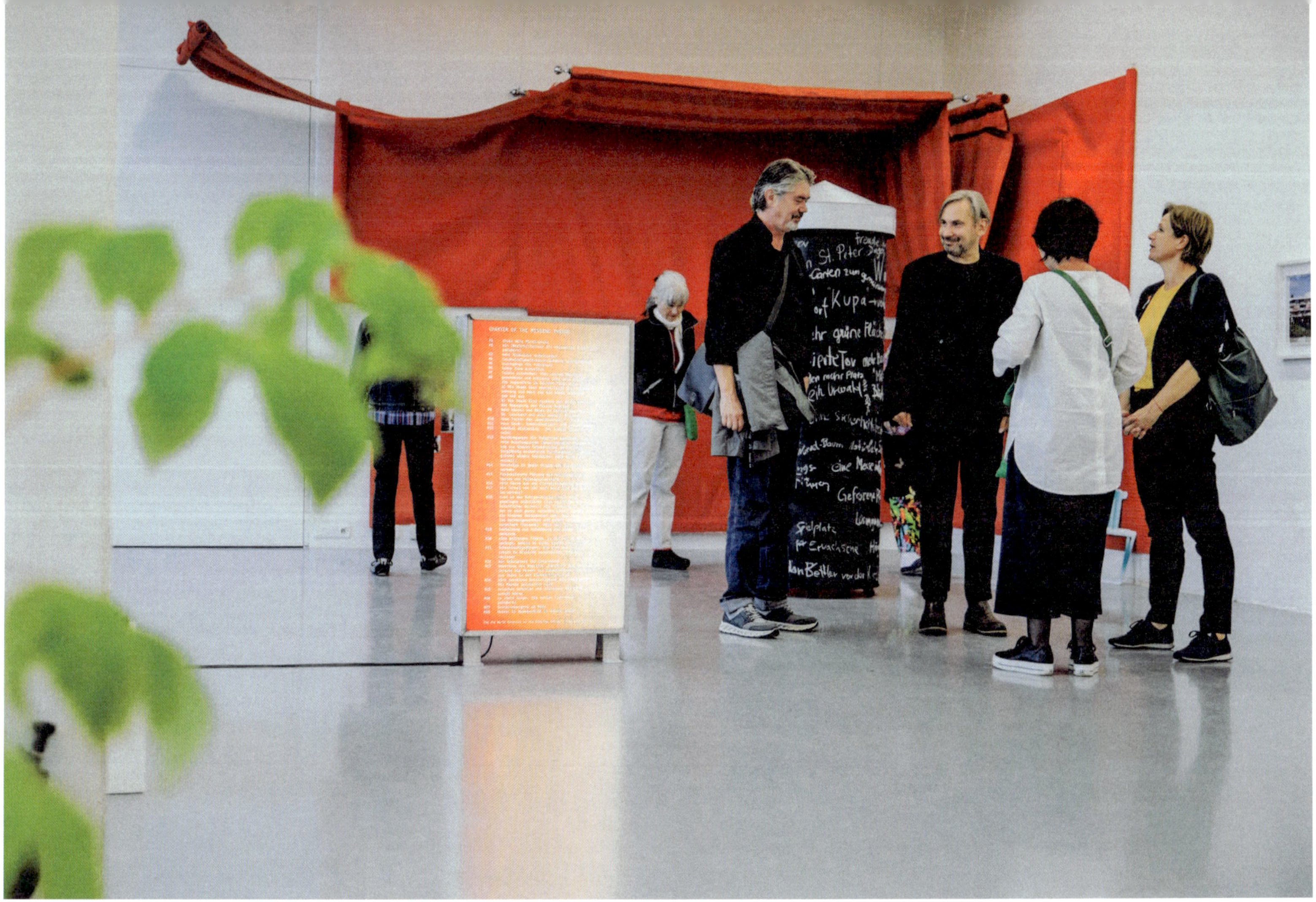
CHARTER OF THE MISSING THINGS

A Sign or Measure of Something: Silent Activism

by Jane Rendell

Index the fore-finger: so called because used in pointing; a piece of wood, metal, or the like, which serves as a pointer; esp. in scientific instruments, a pointer which moves along a graduated scale (or which is itself fixed while a graduated scale moves across its extremity) so as to indicate movements or measurements; the arm of a surveying instrument; an alidade; the hand of a clock or watch; also, the style or gnomon of a sun-dial; that which serves to direct or point to a particular fact or conclusion; a guiding principle; a sign, token, or indication of something; a table of contents prefixed to a book, a brief list or summary of the matters treated in it, an argument; also, a preface, prologue; an alphabetical list, placed (usually) at the end of a book, of the names, subjects, etc. occurring in it, with indication of the places in which they occur.[1]
1. (in a book or set of books) an alphabetical list of names, subjects, etc. with reference to the pages on which they are mentioned.
2. a sign or measure of something.[2]

absence PP. 21–2 then silence turns into a form of non-existence, into the experience of understanding one's own presence as synonymous with.

accumulation P. 24 this, and clustering, are most evident in Holub's non-hierarchical public WORLD CONGRESSES OF THE MISSING THINGS (2014 and 2021).

across PP. 63, 50 the channel between the city of Valletta and Manoel Island in Valletta, Malta, where, for TIMES OF DILEMMA (2018), *għannejja* performed scripted texts about their concerns with urban development and other pressing social matters in Maltese society, these two locations prompting the memory of a time when leprosy patients were quarantined on the island and a priest would hold his prayers for the hospital from across the channel; the borders of public and private properties, connecting citizens of diverse social backgrounds, which, in WE PARAPOM!, the parade of apple trees crosses.

act, the emancipatory PP. 20, 113 consists of hearing silence, the not-being-heard, the experience of being left alone with a problem or having been forgotten; in the urban contexts to which she is invited, Holub identifies thorny or uncomfortable issues and proposes, in discussion and collaboration with the people concerned, to give them an aesthetic form (in the broadest possible sense).

action PP. 112, 228 the concept of direct; extending the invitation for direct with a future imaginary.

activism PP. 220, 113 the four well-trodden tenets—advocacy, subversion, facilitation and healing—are constantly embroiled in a convoluted tension between the artist's desire for poetic forms of social resistance and the need for more direct approaches to imminent structural change; more focused on the search for an agreed and shared experience in a certain time and place than on the production of a particular object or the achievement of a specific goal.

activism, silent PP. 164, 166, 113, 21 is neither silent nor merely activist; as a method of creating platforms for art to channel social change while keeping artistic independence and integrity; a vision that might even manage to resist the ideals of stupidity and futility which signify the time we live in; is deployed to broaden the spectrum of the possible, or simply revive confidence in the ability to transform reality; would lead to a slow but irrepressible spread of awareness of the values of solidarity, sharing, egalitarianism and respect for the environment (in the broadest sense, i.e. respect for living things); is not about being silent or secretive, but rather a mode of articulation—an expression of the encounter with discriminatory structures that do not provide a right to, nor a place for, rebuttal and reply unless adhering to the difference of Us and You, One and the Other, not equating a notion of the public arena and democracy with the notion of the majority.

activistically P. 19 in hearing the concerns of others, the artistic approach starts off from the reception and subsequently transforms this itself into an act of participation, of sharing and attempting to proactively communicate this sharing to others.

advocacy P. 220 with subversion, facilitation and healing, the four well-trodden tenets of activism.

"amateur" PP. 222, 220 Holub situates herself often as a dedicated; as non-expert, as an important intellectual figure of our times, someone who doesn't know yet; following Edward Said:

> what today the intellectual ought to be, someone who considers that to be a thinking and concerned member of a society one is entitled to raise moral issues at the heart of even the most technical and professionalised activity as it involves one's country, its power, its mode of interacting with its citizens as well as other societies. In addition, the intellectual's spirit as an amateur can enter and transform the merely professional routine most of us go through into something much more lively and radical; instead of doing what one is supposed to do one can ask why one does it, who benefits from it, how can it reconnect with a personal project and original thought.[3]

apple P. 50 trees, a European parade of, for WE PARAPOM! (2021–2025, European Capital of Culture Chemnitz 2025).

approaches P. 282 direct, to imminent structural change.

architecture P. 82 before the arrival of, a wild area next to the future Lake-City Aspern – the habitat of THE BLUE FROG SOCIETY.

art PP. 20, 23, 224 the, begins with hearing and the awareness of the need to be heard; in public space, does not mean confronting a public with or familiarizing it with outside of an institutional framework, rather regarding itself as a public agenda; the work of, configured as a cluster of interventions and interactions over time to result in more dispersed forms of distribution.

artist-curator P. 222 as intellectual amateur in the context of predetermined, inflexible or over-professionalized processes, aiming to create a non-hierarchical setting for different kinds of questions to be asked of urban space, its residents and its future social use.

authorities P. 112 public, although transparadiso's projects are usually realized with the support of an art center, they aim to highlight what the public authorities neglect, conceal or cannot manage.

BambooKazas PP. 226, 266 fold-out awnings, held together with bamboo supports—specially designed for THE THIRD WORLD CONGRESS OF THE MISSING THINGS, Eisteichsiedlung, Graz (2021), and donated to the district afterwards, for future events based on topics of conflict.

BAKCHICH, DU, POUR LAMPEDUSA P. 40 a garbage container transformed into an oversized savings box placed as a monumental sculpture placed right in front of the Big Mosque in the Medina in Sousse, in which residents of Sousse were called to donate 10% of their irregular income from the last three years—an equivalent percentage was spent on bribery.

bet PP. 69, 76 the winning—"Revaluation contributes to the prosperity of this quarter"—an urban intervention gilding a gully cover on the corner of Treskower Allee and Am Carlsgarten as part of ON THE SLIM PROBABILITY (2014).

bets P. 76 these free, that symbolically revived the potential of these informal spaces for community for ON THE SLIM PROBABILITY (2014).

between PP. 20, 206, 40, 230 artist and audience, Holub works on an art without spectators—not to keep her art hidden nor to keep it secret, but to reject the "uncanny" division of roles between the artist and audience; the city of Valletta and Manoel Island in Malta in TIMES OF DILEMMA (2018); the Hellbrunner Park and the Monats-schlössl (Folklore Museum) in JE SUIS ARABE—THE RIGHT TO POETRY (2015); Vienna and Istanbul in WHAT I AM PROUD OF; art and architecture, public and privat, and theory and practice the triple cross-roads of "critical spatial practices" as described by Jane Rendell.[4]

bonnets P. 40 golden, of gilded satellite dishes connected by CB radio and worn by Holub and Akram al Halabi for JE SUIS ARABE—A RIGHT TO POETRY (2015); traditionally an item of head-dress dating back to the 13th century that remains a part of women's traditional costume in Salzburg and Upper Austria today; since 1975, a word for the Austrian air defense system.

BORDER, CALL AGAINST THE PP. 20, 206 for which people could shout out their concerns or demands across a river to the other bank using a giant megaphone.

borders PP. 163, 206 contravening between so-called "high" and "folk" culture for TIMES OF DILEMMA (2018).

breathing P. 220 of, of porosity.

"catchers, moment" P. 266 previously overlooked qualities of public space, reversing the dictum of efficiency that typifies urban planning by alerting us to the redundancy of things that were once functional, discovered by two dérives through the Eisteichsiedlung, a neighborhood with social housing from the 1960s, for THE THIRD WORLD CONGRESS OF THE MISSING THINGS (2021).

"Charter of Missing Things, The" P. 250 a list handed to the Mayor of Baltimore on the evening of 8 June and read out publicly during THE FIRST WORLD CONGRESS OF THE MISSING THINGS (2014).

collective P. 223 form of public exhibition—bringing amateurs and professionals together in the hope of creating new forms of as-yet unknown knowledge, and questioning the parameters of the authorship of public space through co-operative and post-autonomous modes of production.

commonality P. 24 as a horizon of.

commonplace P. 165 her understanding of, Holub's supplement, as something far from mediocre.

community P. 22 a silenced – a community that pretends to be the public in order to conceal the diversity and contradictions inherent in the concept.

CONFIDENTIALLY, HANDLED P. 178 in which Holub invited employees of the office furniture company Bene to stage a series of images of "under-the-table-activities."

control P. 220 and non-control, a fine balancing act.

conversation P. 220 sometimes in, mostly not, standing or sitting.

conversations P. 221 help structure temporary architecture or built spaces act as physical and conceptual frameworks towards what can be done.

conviviality P. 220 some kind of relationality, intersectionality.

co-operation P. 223 projects involve varying degrees of, with many different artists, architects, urbanists, curators and critics, where these multiple levels of social participation allow for divergent intellectual positions to co-exist, often in contradiction to one another.

co-production P. 223 as part of a growing list—"conversational art" (Homi Bhabha), "dialogical art" (Grant Kester), "new genre public art" (Suzanne Lacy), "new situationism" (Claire Doherty), "connective aesthetics" (Suzi Gablik), "critical spatial practice" (Jane Rendell), "participatory art" (Claire Bishop), "social practice art" (Gregory Sholette), "community-based practice" (Nato Thompson), "Arte Útil" (Tania Bruguera), "durational-specific" (Paul O'Neill/Dave Beech), "curatorial activism" (Maura Reilly), or "activist art"—that frames an illustrative history of the expansion and diversification of the range of co-productive practices in which multiple participants are involved.

co-productivity P. 223 this approach has the aspiration of overcoming, transgressing, evading, renegotiating or bypassing the dominant status in many small gestural ways as part of an accumulation of positions, reactions and propositions.

corruption [P. 44] the silence around the issue, which results in Tunisians' loss of economic means for providing a solid social substance and perspective, challenged by DU BAKCHICH POUR LAMPEDUSA (2014).

critique, instituent Gerald Raunig's writing on "instituent critique" is situated in the terrain of the complex, rather than the neutral, the place of double strategies, social and institutional criticism on the one hand, political and personal parrhesia on the other.

> What is needed here and now is parrhesia as a double strategy: as an attempt of involvement and engagement in a process of hazardous refutation, and as self-questioning. What is needed, therefore, are practices that conduct radical social criticism, yet which do not fancy themselves in an imagined distance to institutions; at the same time practices that are self-critical and yet do not cling to their own involvement, their complicity, their imprisoned existence in the art field, their fixation on institutions, and the institution, their own-being institution.[5]

curatorial [P. 223] proposition, the function of the, is to create situations of potential agency for the co-productive processes initiated by the artist, or curator, as post-autonomous producer of informal knowledge gatherings; proposition, an understanding of, is put forward as an accumulation of interactions, and information.

DILEMMA, TIMES OF [P. 206] in which transparadiso invited għana singers (*għannejja*) and renowned Maltese authors to produce a contemporary għana dialog, transforming the spontaneously improvised traditional Maltese singing of għana into a scripted dialog that discusses the rapid transformation of Malta and the contradictory interests between economic prosperity and regaining communal values.

doings [PP. 161–2] daily, where in HANDLED CONFIDENTIALLY (1997–1999), Holub managed to expose internal power structures, sexism, fantasies, and projections within the daily doings in the office, perhaps revealing what is considered to be okay, to be normal, in the daily doings of that site.

donations [P. 44] those collected as part of DU BAKCHICH POUR LAMPEDUSA (2014), in an official closing ceremony, were handed over to the humanitarian aid organization African Intelligence, founded and directed by Father Jonathan in Sfax, who has been taking care of refugees sent back from Lampedusa.

drawings, color-book [P. 230] part of her series of unplanned or surprising appropriations of the urban public space, see for example WHAT I AM PROUD OF, in which Holub makes a connection between Vienna and Istanbul.

durational [P. 226] process, a starting point for, considering the project as a small gesture to further develop programs and propositions for the future (social) infrastructure for the mix of people who inhabit the space; what transparadiso had serendipitously set out to do.

emancipation [P. 14] social has become self.

emancipatory act [P. 20] the, consists of hearing silence, the not-being-heard, the experience of being left alone with a problem or having been forgotten—while seeing possibilities in sharing and communicating this experience.

emergence [P. 223] like a model of, the staging of publicness engenders new practices, new meanings, values and social relations between things, and in the generative sense of being the possible site of dialectical opposition to the dominant.

emergency [P. 223] often posed in the present tense, flanked by past and future normals, both of which are ideally envisioned as the same. In the moment of rupture created by "the emergency," no normal is present, and this allows us to see the qualities of the normal more clearly, to define what constitutes the normal and the range of nuances of normalcies, and to distinguish between normalcy and emergency more carefully.[6]

facilitation [P. 220] with advocacy, subversion and healing, the four well-trodden tenets of activism.

form, aesthetic [P. 113] which means a sensitive, non-discursive and non-authoritarian expression of the issue: participatory workshops, collective performances, secular processions.

FROG, THE BLUE, SOCIETY [P. 82]—a species that had survived by counteracting the unlimited growth of urban development, detected by Holub in 2010, as part of her project ON THE URBAN PERIPHERY (2010).

function, the [P. 223] of the curatorial proposition is to create situations of potential agency for the co-productive processes initiated by the artist, or curator, as post-autonomous producer of informal knowledge gatherings.

future [P. 229] imaginary, a means for bringing the social into the present with a form of pragmatic realness.

games [P. 163] Holub's, by no means extravagant. On the contrary, this work is, in all its playfulness, quite mundane. Perhaps even sober.

gathered [P. 220] people are mostly, or huddled together, attending to one another and their surroundings, they are mainly in smaller groups.

gathering [P. 220] some form of; some kind of conviviality, relationality, intersectionality.

gesture [P. 44] a modest, which, in the form of DU BAKCHICH POUR LAMPEDUSA (2014), challenged the silence surrounding the issue of corruption in Tunisia.

għana [P. 206] by using the tradition of, in TIMES OF DILEMMA (2018) encouraged Maltese residents to address current social and urban conflicts in a public performance.

għannejja [PP. 163, 206] groups of għana singers.

happening [P. 220] something seems to be, but there is not a lot to see. Instead, there is a sense of lightness, of breathing, of porosity.

healing [P. 220] with advocacy, subversion and facilitation, the four well-trodden tenets of activism.

heard [P. 21] the awareness of the need to be; only what belongs is, and what is not supposed to belong remains unheard.

hearing [P. 20] the art begins with.

heterotopic [P. 224] appropriation, a permitted space of, for those who were already living there precariously.

hierarchy, (deconstructing) an approach emblematic of critical spatial practice, and relating to Michel de Certeau's notion of tactics, as a kind of spatial practice that is opposed to the strategic—and aims "to make the weaker position seem the stronger... turning the tables on the powerful by the way in which they made use of the opportunities offered by the particular situation"[7]—evident in the work of Holub and transparadiso.

hope P. 113 of generating a poetic moment felt by all the participants.

hypernormalization P. 165 the microhistories provided in many of Holub's works also have the capacity to operate as a form of resistance to both grand narratives and mechanisms of.

"improvisation, spontaneous" P. 206 or "spirtu pront" as performed by għanneijja, challenged with the task of committing to a new format, the scripted text, in TIMES OF DILEMMA (2018).

in-between P. 82 space, drawings aimed at fathoming the potential of this "before the arrival of architecture," to allow for unplanned and unplannable wishes, as part of ON THE URBAN PERIPHERY (2010).

in-betweener P. 221 the, working on location as the "artist-in-residence."

infrastructure P. 27 and maintenance, a lack of, causes a (social) decline, in, for example, INITIATIVE ISLAND (2008–2018).

"interdisciplinarity a site where expressions of resistance are latent"[8]; "where individuals move between and across disciplines and in so doing question the ways in which they work."[9]

interlocutor P. 221 Holub as the skilled.

intersectionality P. 220 some kind of conviviality, relationality.

information P. 220 there is always a lot of.

interventions P. 22 in "public" space imply a political agenda—a critique of emptied concepts of the public arena promoting an opening of public space.

labor P. 182 the outsourcing of, for THE SYSTEM: PRÊT-À-PORTER (2006).

LAND, ANYONE'S P. 94 a project by transparadiso whose title is a play on "no-man's land," a familiar military term converted into an invitation to anyone to cross the border between Nova Gorica, Slovenia, and nearby Gorizia, Italy.

language P. 28 the flipside of, contrasted against eloquence.

laughing P. 18 or stuttering, when at a loss for words, even out of despair, unable to continue speaking anymore because words are insufficient or the language is no longer understood by anybody because it is dying out.

lightness P. 220 a sense of.

limbo-zone [P. 94] a space suggesting both a practical space for migrants and a discursive context, explored as part of ANYONE'S LAND (2011) by transparadiso.

listening [P. 18] over the decades her work has pursued a listening to, and hearing of, the concerns and demands of those "quiet voices" who were not born mute, while they have been silenced—for fear of persecution, for fear of being marginalized even further, or for the experience of merely becoming acquainted with hopelessness.

"map, galactic" [P. 27] conceived of by Holub showing the current state of social housing projects in Birmingham for INITIATIVE ISLAND (2008–2018).

mediating [P. 221] openings through the research, finding the gaps and what is missing for people within a specific situation.

megaphones [P. 163] two large, located on either side of the sea between the city of Valletta and Manoel Island in Valletta, Malta, used by two groups of għana singers (known as għannejja) to communicate with each other.

method [PP. 266, 164, 164] transparadiso's signature, asking the public what they feel is missing from urban experience, as, for example, deployed by transparadiso for THE THIRD WORLD CONGRESS OF THE MISSING THINGS (2021); developed further by Holub in her articulation of "silent activism"; of creating platforms for art to channel social change while keeping artistic independence and integrity; of raising the question which and whose knowledge is considered relevant.

middle, silent [P. 228] Chemnitz (formerly Karl-Marx-Stadt in the GDR), is notorious for right-wing movements, and WE PARAPOM! (2021–2025) thus addresses also the.

modest [P. 229] symbolic gesture, what begins as a, offers huge potential for extensive layers of social and civic action, culminating in non-functioning poetics alongside actualized propositions whilst contributing to change for a more just society.

moment [P. 113] a poetic, that could open up unknown horizons.

neutrality perhaps actively choosing to be neutral was what the art critic Jan Verwoert was getting at when he suggested that we need to enact refusal, not as a negation, but in order to open up the space for other options, this is an approach we see often in the work of Holub and transparadiso. Verwoert writes:

> Maybe the secret of autonomous agency and the good life lies precisely in opening up the space of those other options through a categorical refusal to accept the forceful imposition of any terms, leaving us no choice but to choose between either yes or no?[10]

neutralizing [P. 20] instead of representing others, a moment of solidarity is expressed, without necessarily negating or neutralizing the inequality and difference between the positions from which somebody is speaking or remaining silent.

NON-CONGRESS, THE SECOND WORLD, OF THE MISSING THINGS [P. 225] described as such by Holub to reflect the fact it was a more incognito, clandestine and unpredictable gathering—to refocus on vital issues of urban development in this Viennese district on the outskirts, the largest new urban residential extension of the city.

non-control P. 222 each project, a fine balancing act between control and, setting the structure or framework of invitation and response that is both focused enough while remaining flexible at the same time.

non-hierarchical P. 222 a setting for different kinds of questions to be asked of urban space, its residents and its future social use.

NORMAL P. 226 project by transparadiso, an introductory gallery exhibition at the Haus der Architektur in Graz, presenting research and a series of four interrelated public art interventions framed around the single question—"What is normal?"

normal, the new On 20 May 2020, during the UK's Covid-19 first "lockdown," *W1A*, the BBC political comedy show, aired their special zoom "Initial Lockdown Meeting," and as this quote makes clear, by then, the manipulation of normals, old and new, had already become a full-fledged aspect of managing the crisis and communicating the government message:

> Welcome to the first ever lockdown meeting of the BBC COVID19 "Bounce Back Group." I know we've all got used to thinking of ourselves as the "Way Ahead Group," but in the current circumstances it didn't seem to ring true with the realities of the new normal, whereas the Bounce Back Group seems positive, clear, and very much does what it says on the tin... but really the remit couldn't be more exciting, to try to imagine what the new normal will look like, and to begin to plot a path towards it, from wherever it is that we are now... What we know of course is that it won't look anything like the old normal, or as I think we can safely call it now, the past, which really frees us up to think creatively.[11]

Working through public performance to expose the constructions of "normal"—and new—is a frequent hallmark of the practice of Holub and transparadiso.

normal P. 158 isn't that new, that we're entering, or desiring, now precisely such a retrotopia rather than utopia?

normalcy PP. 62, 162, 166 the question of, can also be seen as a red thread that runs throughout Holub's practice; investigations of, the norms that govern understandings of; not returning-to, but enduring, obfuscating and altering the concept of.

"normalcy, return to" P. 158 was United States presidential candidate Warren G. Harding's campaign slogan for the election of 1920. It evoked a return to the way of life before World War I, the First Red Scare, and the Spanish flu pandemic. One hundred years later this notion of an ill-defined cliché return to some non-existent golden past seems to be exactly what the world wants to hear from its politicians.

opening P. 23 and restoration of the public arena; when Holub shows solidarity with various excluded or marginalized groups in her projects, when the artistic act essentially expresses an interrogation and solidarity, then it is in the sense of this.

OPPORTUNITIES, MORE P. 112 in which Holub staged a demonstration with white, message-less placards, in reference to the dockers' strikes of the 1960s, which occurred after almost three centuries of good relations between the naval port—for a long time the city's main employer—and the citizens, a cohabitation which was considered beneficial to both parties.

"other, the concrete" For psychoanalyst Jean Laplanche, it is the embedding of the alterity of the mother in the child, which places an "other" in the subject, as this message is also other to the mother, it is an enigma both to the receiver, but also to the sender of the message: the "messages are enigmatic," he writes, "because... [they] are strange to themselves."[12] Such strangeness, as a quality of the other (including the mother, in Laplanche, as "concrete other"), is to be found in the work of Holub, and it is this opacity which renders her work distinct from much other contemporary participatory practice. In never quite revealing their workings, in delinking signifying chains, participants and audience are kept guessing, and so engage in self-transformatory processes.[13]

"parade, European, of apple trees," P. 228 the quite radical gesture of.

PARAPOM!, WE P. 50 (parade, apple = pomme Fr.), conceived of for the program of the European Capital of Culture Chemnitz 2025, involving planting as many as 2000 trees of different European apple varieties along an axis that runs right through the city, across districts and property boundaries.

patient P. 113 and unspectacular, silent activism inserts itself into the shadowy areas of pretentious urban policies and aims, above all, to raise awareness of the mechanisms that underpin them and the subjugations they induce.

"performance, laughter" P. 35 members of the refugee choir Hor. 29 Novembar, who at a given signal (bird noise), laughed sarcastically while five people read to each other using scripts based on texts by Herbert Marcuse, Joseph Beuys, Henri Bergson and others, to a small crowd gathered by the path in Sigmund Freud Park, Vienna, for THE LAUGHTER THAT GETS CAUGHT IN YOUR THROAT (2015) Sigmund Freud Park, Vienna.

"perruque, la" visible in the work of Holub, and according to Michel de Certeau, "a diversionary practice":

> With these examples of terrains on which one can locate the specific modalities of "enunciative" practices (manipulations of imposed spaces, tactics relative to particular situations), the possibility is opened up of analyzing the immense field of an "art of practice" differing from the models that (in theory) reign from top to bottom in a culture certified by education (from the universities to the elementary schools)...[14]

place, taking where much listening and speaking seems to be, but without many spectators; and the name of a feminist architectural collective; and a mode of feminist critical spatial practice put forward by Teresa Hoskyns.[15]

play P. 163 taken seriously, could mean that we can use it to transform our actions with exciting, uncertain outcomes.

poetic P. 258 the content more, than pragmatic, perhaps inspired by the eerie spectacle of a brand new but almost entirely uninhabited settlement, evokes the interests of immigrant populations brought together for THE SECOND WORLD *NON*-CONGRESS OF THE MISSING THINGS (2014).

poetics PP. 229, 266, 206 a non-functioning; transparadiso's ongoing assertion of, over pragmatic aspects of urban space, consolidated for THE THIRD WORLD CONGRESS OF THE MISSING THINGS (2021); highlighted as the potential for "silent activism," via the repositioning of the (today underrecognized) tradition of folk singing in "high culture" in għana as an artistic method for addressing conflicts in an open process in TIMES OF DILEMMA (2018).

possibility P. 108 the, of other worlds.

possibilities P. 20 seeing, and communicating this experience.

practice Holub's, has its own rules and objectives, which are unfixed and open; critical spatial, a term that defines self-reflective artistic and architectural modes of practice which seek to question and to transform the social conditions of the sites into which they intervene, and as such describes the work of transparadiso.[16]

problematization with respect to Michel Foucault's processes of problematization, in Clive Barnett's view, "Problematization is an object of study," where the "process by which modes of living or modes of self-care become problems." Problematization is located in the mode of interpretation itself, "in which the task of analysis is primarily to call into question taken-for-granted assumptions and identities and settlements,"[17] and it is this quality of self and social questioning the many taken-for-granted of lived space that we find in the work of Holub.

protest P. 35 commemorative, a kind of, composed of laughter, choreographed by composer Tamara Friebel, for THE LAUGHTER THAT GETS CAUGHT IN YOUR THROAT, 2015 Sigmund Freud Park, Vienna.

public PP. 223, 23 exhibition, a focus on, as a collective form of co-productivity; space, questioning the parameters of the authorship through co-operative and post-autonomous modes of production; spaces, Holub locates most of her projects in; arena, opening and restoration of the.

radical P. 223 gesture, a, "European parade of apple trees."

recite P. 40 alternately in German and Arabic by Barbara Holub and Akram al Halabi, "La volonté de vivre" ("The Will to Live," 1933) a poem by the Tunisian poet Aboul-Qacem Echebbi, now the "Hymn of the Arab Spring," for JE SUIS ARABE—THE RIGHT TO POETRY (2015), outside and inside the Schwarzenberg Barracks, and between the Hellbrunner Park and the Monatsschlössl (Folklore Museum), two locations that, in different ways, are equally committed to the concept of homeland.

refugee P. 19 politics.

relational it is only by paying attention to the more relational, psychic and thus emotional aspects of inter and transdisciplinary practices that we can understand their transitional status and transformational potential, and so better position ourselves to act differently[18]—this is something developed over the past 20 years through the projects of transparadiso and Holub.

relationality P. 220 some kind of conviviality, intersectionality.

responses P. 222 lead to discussions by participant-observers and bring them into the fold of urban planning and decision-making within the architectural or artistic commissioning context.

retrotopia P. 158 the pertinent concept of, explored in Zygmunt Bauman's posthumous book from 2017, where with an ideologically critical gaze Bauman argues that the past has taken over the role of the future as desirable, and that "retrotopia" has replaced utopia.

routine, undermining P. 161 (in corporate companies) as we see in projects like Holub's HANDLED CONFIDENTIALLY (1997–1999).

"ruin, future" P. 258 paraphrasing Robert Smithson, the collection of missing things that shows that settlements are never truly "finished," but always in flux—THE SECOND WORLD *NON*-CONGRESS OF THE MISSING THINGS (2014).

say P. 20 what the work cannot; aimed at, in Macharey's words, "the task of measuring silence, whether acknowledged or unacknowledged":

> what work cannot say is important, because there the elaboration of the utterance is acted out in a sort of journey to silence.[19]

scenarios P. 220 within these spatial, there is an unfolding of the social—some form of gathering.

SECRETS, CARRIERS OF P. 159 Holub's 1996 installation for Neue Galerie in Graz comprised seven large jigsaw fragments upholstered with padded vinyl, in which each button was a peep-hole through which a number that referred to images in the accompanying brochure of the foyers of iconic institutional buildings in Chicago: the City of Chicago Police Department, the Richard J. Daley Centre, the Everett Mc. Kinley Dirksen Building, could be seen; in which Holub explored questions of surveillance, state secrets, cartels, cold war games, in a claustrophobic environment.

setting 45, 55, 78 the structure or framework of invitation and response; the psychoanalytic, as a space of transition, activated through the psychic processes of transference and counter-transference.[20]

shared P. 20 concern, a, to join others in engaging with.

sharing P. 20 while seeing possibilities in, and communicating this experience.

silence PP. 220, 18 instead of, there is an undercurrent of mumbling voices, a rumbling swell of noisy resistance, where the resultant works can also be bold, unequivocally loud, even full of ranting and raving; a representational, manifested in silenced speech, a loud, even shrill silence that can only be heard with the eyes; an unheard, that interrupts the supposed "order of things," which alludes to something more than just pausing for reflection—it is a means of expression for those who are not heard when they raise their voices, the people nobody listens to when they try to articulate their wishes or suggestions.

silent P. 18 the last possibility being to remain, the last way to say something.

site responsive; -specific, in the 1990s, the term site became charged with a critical valency in art theory, as artists, working outside the gallery and often in urban conditions, embraced the term site-specific to describe their particular form of practice. In 2002, in *One Place after Another*, Miwon Kwon outlined a history of the development of a number of approaches to site in contemporary art practice, from phenomenological and experiential to critical and discursive.[21] In distinguishing between different approaches to "site-specific" practice and in arguing that some site-specific works did not adequately engage with their relations to site, Kwon positioned site specificity as a particular strand, if not genre, of art practice. Her critical intervention in the discourse around public art, community practice, and context-based work raised the stakes of the debate and encouraged critics to define key spatial terms and address the specific qualities, conditions, and impacts of site-specific artistic practice.

situated knowledge, in her 1988 essay "Situated Knowledges," Donna Haraway argued that "feminist objectivity means quite simply *situated knowledges*"[22]; practice, Nick Kaye, a critic from theater and performance has drawn attention to the temporal aspects of site-specific practice through his focus on performance, while I have linked the concepts of situation, situating, and situatedness in site-specific practice;[23] aspects of all three can be found in the work of Holub and transparadiso.

situation created by transparadiso in TIMES OF DILEMMA (2018) for the Maltese to take action concerning the contradictory interests between economic prosperity and the need to regain communal values; the specific; each, and each community calling for a different solution; a, Lauren Berlant's elaboration of a situation as "something which will perhaps matter," in her essay "Thinking about Feeling Historical," where she writes about two men "in the now":

> A situation has forced them to think. A situation has changed the ordinary into something they can no longer presume… A situation is a state of things in which something that will perhaps matter is unfolding amidst the usual activity of life.[24]

situations P. 164 and spaces, Holub's trick seems to be to prepare them to be open enough to support and take this into account—open yet regulated—to allow site-sensitivity, coherent narratives, coherences, and contradictions (dialog rather than dialectics); set up through curating, Claire Doherty, for example, has drawn attention to the temporarality of site-based sculpture, through the Bristol-based curatorial commissioning project Situations, which she set up, and *One Day Sculpture,* the program of artworks using time as material, which she curated in collaboration with Australian artist David Cross and with curators, galleries, and museums across New Zealand;[25] constructing, as defined in the rallying manifesto of the Situationist International (SI) from 1957. Guy Debord writes:

> Our central idea is the construction of situations, that is to say, the concrete construction of momentary ambiences of life and their transformation into a superior passional quality. We must develop a systematic intervention based on the complex factors of two components in perpetual interaction: the material environment of life and the behaviors which that environment gives rise to and which radically transform it.[26]

SLIM PROBABILITY, ON THE P. 76 a project developed by transparadiso that searches for possible connotations and correlations between the action of betting and the notion of "fortune," which first took place in Berlin-Karlshorst, and then at the horse racetrack Krieau, Vienna.

social P. 228 is often suggested through a simple evocative image, a symbol, a trope, a gesture, akin to the poetic image, or the quite radical gesture of a "European parade of apple trees"; can be said to often take as its territory, as metaphor and as evocation in Holub's works.

solidarity PP. 22–3 with them as part of the (democratic) public, this means showing, hearing their silence as a mode of speaking, and confronting the emptied concept of the "public"; to demonstrate does not mean becoming part of a community, but to stand up for concerns and demands beyond the boundaries of the respective communities that are denied the claim to public relevance; can only be shown with a community to which one does not belong, still supporting it within the horizon of a notion of the public sphere in order to defend the significance of the public arena itself.

"space, potential" the ability to keep inner and outer realities separate yet inter-related results in an intermediate area of experience, the "potential space," which D. W. Winnicott claimed is located between "the individual and the environment (originally the object)," retained, and later in life contributes to the intensity of cultural experiences around art and religion.[27] This potential space is the pivot point for many of the projects devised by Holub, a place in which a tension is produced between loosing and gaining control, located:

> at the interplay between there being nothing but me and there being objects and phenomena outside omnipotent control.[28]

"Speak, can the Subaltern?" P. 18 is a question that asks whether, how, and under what conditions, people can speak who are excluded from hegemonic cultures or pushed to the various margins of society. This not only provides the title for Gayatri Spivak's essay, but is also the point of departure for Holub's art projects.[29]

speaking P. 20 in a language that does not have to be either translated into the "governing" hegemonic jargon, nor to assimilate itself in order to be heard.

"spectator, the emancipated" P. 19 by refusing to orientate her artistic practice toward an audience that is solely assigned the passive role of reception, for years Holub has been pursuing a path that Jacques Rancière outlined:

> "What is required is a theatre without spectators, where those in attendance learn from as opposed to being seduced by images; where they become active participants as opposed to passive voyeurs."[30]

spectators P. 220 often, you will see people standing among other people and things, lots of groups, where much listening and talking seems to be taking place but without many.

speechlessness P. 18 a display of, screaming soundlessly when all demands and arguments remain unheard.

structures, power [PP. 182, 116, 82] are challenged through the tactics of critical spatial practice across the oeuvre of Holub's work, but especially in works which address the corporate infrastructures and processes governing fashion, labor and urban regneration, in projects like THE SYSTEM*:*
PRÊT-À-PORTER (2006); MORE OPPORTUNITIES (2007); and
ON THE URBAN PERIPHERY (2010).

stuttering [P. 18] or laughing, when at a loss for words.

style [P. 183] how it migrates from one cultural context to another, highlighting the potential difference between what is desirable in Europe and what is desirable in Africa, raised as a crucial part of THE SYSTEM: PRÊT-À-PORTER (2006). During the exhibition, Humana staff members are invited to model Humana clothing at a photoshoot.

subversion [P. 220] with advocacy, facilitation and healing, the four well-trodden tenets of activism.

SYSTEM, THE: PRÊT-À-PORTER [P. 182] analyses the economy of the second-hand clothing industry by looking at a range of models: clothing exchanges, yard sales, and charity donations.

tables [PP. 224, 162] a rhizomatic set of, designed to enable seating arrangements in non-hierarchical manners, turning the underused public space at the entrance of Lexington Market Subway Station into a permitted space of heterotopic appropriation for those who were already living there precariously. for FIRST WORLD CONGRESS OF THE MISSING THINGS (2014); under the, as in HANDLED CONFIDENTIALLY (1997–1999).

temporary [P. 220] architecture settings; architecture or built spaces act as physical and conceptual frameworks and help structure conversations towards what can be done.

"theatre of cruelty" [P. 23] when Antonin Artaud speaks of a,[31] this could also be applied to the concept of being public: the public arena as a theater of cruelty. The theater of the public is the material from which Holub develops her works, and at the same time their location and their destination; of solidarity that can only articulate itself in public.

"things: missing" [P. 250] the public invited to submit whatever they felt was missing from Baltimore life for THE FIRST WORLD CONGRESS OF THE MISSING THINGS (2014).

THINGS, THE FIRST WORLD CONGRESS OF THE MISSING [PP. 250, 258, 266] a two-day event curated by Holub in the Lexington Market area of Baltimore, in which a rhizomatic structure of tables assembled in front of the subway station provided a discursive platform to disenfranchized citizens (the homeless, drug addicts, ex-convicts), inviting them to set the agenda by submitting "missing things"; THINGS, THE SECOND WORLD *NON*-CONGRESS OF THE MISSING (2014), which, in contrast to its predecessor in Baltimore four months earlier, took place in a community at its earliest stage of development, Lake-City Aspern, Vienna; and THINGS, THE THIRD WORLD CONGRESS OF THE MISSING (2021), where, in the parking lot of the parish St. Paul in the Eisteich housing estate in Waltendorf, Graz, for NORMAL (2020–2021), transparadiso asked the public what they felt was missing from urban experience, compiling the responses into a charter submitted to the local authorities.

threshold P. 196 of such divisions, where we are placed by CARRIERS OF SECRETS (1996), which makes us feel that we are on the cusp of gathering knowledge without ever quite achieving enlightenment—reminding us of one of art's signature characteristics—its ability to its tendency to prolong rather than resolve experience.

THROAT, LAUGHTER GETS CAUGHT IN YOUR P. 35 Sigmund Freud Park, Vienna, a moment of protest, in response to the policy of Austria's Minister of Interior Affairs, who sent many asylum seekers back to their home countries, including Syrians displaced by war.

"tongue, mother" P. 244 a reference to the English expressions often used in Austria but sometimes with a different meaning, such as "name dropping," "happy hour," "sex appeal," or "handy," overlaid on the large photographic portraits of people Holub encountered in her home city of Vienna, and inserted into corresponding locations in New York, for IMAGE TRANSFER (1996), Austrian Cultural Forum, New York/ Vienna made in response to the Austrian Cultural Forum's temporary homelessness while its new building in New York was being constructed.

"transcription, loud" P. 18 an unheard that addresses the eyes as it falls upon deaf ears, a silence that bears witness to speechlessness and wants to be witnessed—nobody wants to listen, while everybody sees the speechlessness.

transfer P. 244 made, as part of IMAGE TRANSFER (1996), Austrian Cultural Forum, New York/ Vienna, in which photographic portraits of workers from Vienna, overlaid with English expressions, were hung on the empty storefront of the former Austrian Cultural Forum, alongside a sound piece by the rapper Mr. Complex, drawing a subtle equivalence between the global ubiquity of America's biggest cultural export—rap/hip-hop—and English as an international lingua franca, the mother-tongue of all those phrases that have worked their way into Austrian speech.

transformations P. 230 premeditated urban, and the areas developed without regulations and order, the areas between these opposite poles are explored in WHAT I AM PROUD OF (2011).

"transitional object" D. W. Winnicott's concept of the transitional object is related to, but distinct from, both the external object, the mother's breast, and the internal object, the introjected breast. For Winnicott, this transitional object or original "not-me" possession "stands for" the breast or first object, suggesting the child's use of symbolism and ability to make a distinction between fantasy and fact, between internal and external objects,[32] and become aware of the relation between "primary unawareness of indebtedness and the acknowledgement of indebtedness,"[33]—it is here that the art practices of both transparadiso and Holub hover.

transparadiso P. 13 Barbara Holub's collaborative practice with the architect/urbanist Paul Rajakovics since 1999.

traversing P. 228 social boundaries, crossing property lines laying the ground for artistic interventions, for questioning standards and deconstructing the figure of a "parade" as a manifestation of power in WE PARAPOM! (2021–2025) for the European Capital of Culture Chemnitz 2025.

UNINTENTIONALITY, DEVOTION TO P. 162 in which Holub was invited to the headquarters of Porsche, Porschehof, in Salzburg, where she asked white-collar employees of Porsche to play with Carrera racetracks in the lobby of their offices, outside of office hours and without salary.

urbanism P. 113 in which the resulting, tramples mercilessly under the cover of misleading and perversely indoctrinating communication.

"urbanism, direct" PP. 13, 73, 112 a term often used to describe the approach of transparadiso; the concept that transparadiso developed for their practice, in reference to the concept of "direct action" theorized at the beginning of the twentieth century to define interventions in the economic or political context of a city without the intermediary of institutional representatives.

utopia, concrete P. 113 the concept proposed by Bert Theis[34], an artist whose work is complementary to Holub's, undertaken without the arrogance of turn-key solutions imposed by those who claim to know what is good for others; macro-, Holub's practice has its own rules and objectives, which are unfixed and open, enhancing a concrete utopia.

"vivre: La volonté de" P. 40 ("The Will to Live," 1933) a poem by the Tunisian poet Aboul-Qacem Echebbi, now the "Hymn of the Arab Spring," alternately recited in German and Arabic by Barbara Holub and Akram al Halabi, for JE SUIS ARABE—THE RIGHT TO POETRY (2015).

VOICE, LISTEN TO THE QUIET P. 113 presents itself not only as an imperative, and the title of one of Holub's works, in which she highlights the social weight of fashion on Muslim women in Austria, but as the paradigm behind her entire practice.

voice P. 20 their own concerns, FAVORIT (2021), a wooden pavilion with an integrated stage was installed on a public square in Vienna, primarily to provide a tool to empower an audience to now step onto the stage, to participate proactively.

voices P. 18 other, with this listening to—however quiet, wounded or silenced they may be—as the basis of her approach, Holub has turned away from a concept of art that seeks to associate or identify the "artwork" with the person of the artist.

voices, quiet P. 18 over the decades, Holub's work has pursued listening, a listening to, and hearing of, the concerns and demands of those who were not born mute.

"what I miss, I am afraid of losing, I find problematic, I treasure, I am proud of, I want to change" PP. 230, 206—a list of simple topics framing a discussion of conflicting and sometimes contradictory interests between economic wealth and communal values, as part of a singing performance by Maltese għana singers for TIMES OF DILEMMA (2018, and based on WHAT I AM PROUD OF (2011)

witnessed P. 18 a silence, that bears witness to speechlessness and wants to be.

who PP. 189, 225 decides?

you P. 220 will see.

1 www.oed.com [accessed 14 October 2022].

2 www.lexico.com/definition/index [accessed 14 October 2022].

3 Edward W. Said, Representations of the Intellectual, (New York: Pantheon Books, 1994). Unpaginated.

4 Jane Rendell, Art and Architecture: A Place Between, (London: IB Tauris, 2006). See also criticalspatialpractice.co.uk/ [accessed 21 June 2022].

5 Gerald Raunig, "Instituent Practices: Fleeing, Instituting, Transforming," trans. Aileen Derieg, Gerald Raunig and Gene Ray (eds), Art and Contemporary Critical Practice: Reinventing Institutional Critique, (London: MayFlyBooks, 2009), pp. 3–13, pp. 10–11. Available at http://eipcp.net/transversal/0106/raunig/en [accessed 21 June 2022].

6 Jane Rendell, "After the Emergency," Sevcan Ercan and Eray Çaylı (eds.), Architectures of Emergency in Turkey: Heritage, Displacement and Catastrophe, (London: Bloomsbury, 2021).

7 Michel de Certeau, The Practice of Everyday Life, (Berkeley: University of California Press, 1988), p. xx.

8 Julia Kristeva, "Institutional Interdisciplinarity in Theory and Practice: an Interview," Alex Coles and Alexia Defert (eds.), The Anxiety of Interdisciplinarity, De-, Dis-, Ex-, v. 2, (London: Black Dog Publishing, 1998), pp. 5–6.

9 Rendell, Art and Architecture, p. 11.

10 Jan Verwoert, "Exhaustion and Exuberance: Ways to Defy the Pressure to Perform," What's Love (or Care, Intimacy, Warmth, Affection) Got to Do with It? (e-flux, Inc., Sternberg Press, 2017), pp. 205–246, p. 208.

11 British Comedy Guide, "W1A: Lockdown Special, www.comedy.co.uk/tv/w1a/episodes/2020/1/. [accessed 21 June 2022].

12 Cathy Caruth, "An Interview with Jean Laplanche," © 2001 Cathy Caruth. See http://www3.iath.virginia.edu/pmc/text-only/issue.101/11.2caruth.txt [accessed 14 October 2022]. Laplanche notes that Freud uses the terms der Andere and das Andere to distinguish the other person from the other thing. See Jean Laplanche, "The Kent Seminar, 1 May 1990," John Fletcher and Martin Stanton (eds.), Jean Laplanche: Seduction, Translation and the Drives, (London: Institute of Contemporary Arts, 1992), pp. 21–40, p. 25.

13 Jean Laplanche, "Transference: Its Provocation by the Analyst," (1992), trans. Luke Thurston, John Fletcher (ed.), Essays on Otherness, (London: Routledge, 1999), pp. 214–33, p. 222.

14 de Certeau, The Practice of Everyday Life, p. 25.

15 See for example, Doina Petrescu and Teresa Hoskyns, "Taking Place and Altering It," Doina Petrescu (ed.), Altering Practices: Feminist Politics and Poetics of Space, (London: Routledge, 2007), and Katie Lloyd Thomas, Helen Stratford and Teresa Hoskyns "Taking Place," Scroope, Vol. 14, (2001).

16 Rendell, Art and Architecture.

17 Clive Barnett, "On Problematization: Elaborations on a Theme in 'Late Foucault,'" nonsite.org, No. 16, (22 June 2015), nonsite.org/article/on-problematization/ [accessed 14 October 2022].

18 Jane Rendell, "The Transitional Space of Interdisciplinarity," in Daniel Hinchcliffe, Jane Calow and Laura Mansfield (eds.), Speculative Strategies in Interdisciplinary Arts Practice, (Underwing Press, 2013).

19 Pierre Macherey, A Theory of Literary Production, trans. Geoffrey Wall (London/New York: Routledge, 1978), p. 97.

20 See a discussion of the psychoanalytic setting as transitional space in Jane Rendell, The Architecture of Psychoanalysis: Transitional Spaces (London: IB Tauris, 2017).

21 Miwon Kwon, One Place after Another: Site-Specific Art and Locational Identity, (Cambridge: MIT Press, 2002).

22 Donna Haraway, "Situated Knowledges: The Science Question in Feminism and the Privilege of Partial Knowledge," Feminist Studies, Vol. 14, No. 3, (Fall 1988), pp. 575–99, p. 581.

23 Nick Kaye, Site-Specific Art: Performance, Place and Documentation, (London: Routledge, 2000), and Rendell, Art and Architecture.

24 Lauren Berlant, "Thinking about Feeling Historical," Emotion, Space and Society, Vol. 1, No. 1, (October 2008), pp. 4–9

25 Claire Doherty and David Cross, (eds.), One Day Sculpture, (Bielefeld, Germany: Kerber Verlag, 2009).

26 Guy Debord, "Report on the Construction of Situations and on the International Situationist Tendency's Conditions of Organization and Action, Revolution and Counterrevolution in Modern Culture," (1957). See 391.org/manifestos/1957-report-on-the-construction-of-situations-guy-debord/ [accessed 14 October 2022].

27 D. W. Winnicott, "The Location of Cultural Experience," The International Journal of Psycho-Analysis, Vol. 48, (1967), pp. 368–372, p. 371. See also D. W. Winnicott, Playing and Reality, (London: Routledge, 1991).

28 Winnicott, "The Location of Cultural Experience," pp. 371–2.

29 Gayatri Chakravorty Spivak, Can the Subaltern Speak? Reflections on the History of an Idea, (Columbia University Press, 2010).

30 Jacques Rancière, The Emancipated Spectator, (London/New York: Verso, 2009), p. 4.

31 Antonin Artaud, "The Theater of Cruelty," The Theater and its Double, trans. Mary Caroline Richards, (New York: Grove Press, 1958), 84ff.

32 D. W. Winnicott, "Transitional Objects and Transitional Phenomena – A Study of the First Not-Me Possession," International Journal of Psycho-Analysis, Vol. 34 (1953) pp. 89–97, see in particular pp. 89 and 94. See also D. W. Winnicott, "The Use of an Object," The International Journal of Psycho-Analysis, Vol. 50 (1969) pp. 711–6.

33 Winnicott, "Transitional Objects and Transitional Phenomena," p. 89.

34 See berttheis.com [accessed October 14, 2022].

LIST OF WORKS

LEISURE ENERGY
Installation, 2006
Wallpaper with drawing, 86 × 293 cm; used SUV car window, varnish

SILENT ACTIVISM AND POLITICAL ENGAGEMENT

FAVORIT (transparadiso)
Installation at Sonnwendplatz, 1100 Vienna, 2021
Installation at Zukunftshof, 1100 Vienna, 2022–2023
Pavilion, larch wood, 408 × 637 × 381–231 cm

AT THE URBAN PERIPHERY–2nd WALK AT THE URBAN PERIPHERY
Lake City Aspern, Vienna, June 20, 2010: with "Voices From a Future International City" (soccer talk); Lambda print on Fujicolor, 46 × 80 cm, 2010/2012

AT THE URBAN PERIPHERY–2nd WALK AT THE URBAN PERIPHERY,
Lake-City Aspern, Vienna, June 20, 2010: with "Voices From a Future International City" (asphalt talk); Lambda print on Fujicolor, 46 × 80 cm, 2010/2012

ISH BIN EIN... (transparadiso)
Lambda print on Fujicolor, 100 × 140 cm, 2007

INITIATIVE ISLAND
Installation, 2008–2018
Curtain, black molleton, embroidery by Enkhjargal Bajinnyam (Mongolia), Otgon Tulga (Mongolia), Svetlana Tsal-Tsalko (Ukraine), Ketino Merebaschwili (Georgia), Sabine Ott and Cornelia Silli (Austria), 1060 × 530 cm
Billboard (façade), 250 × 500 cm, 2008
Billboard (inside), 250 × 500 cm, 2008

THE LAUGHTER THAT GETS CAUGHT IN YOUR THROAT(transparadiso)
Performance, 2015; Performers: Christiane Beinl, Xenia Gala, Akram al Halabi, Nancy Mensah-Offei, and Johanna Orsini-Rosenberg; composition: Tamara Friebel; performed together with the Vienna refugee choir "Hor 29. Novembar"; in cooperation with SOS Mitmensch, Integrationshaus, and Vinzi-Rast, Vienna

THE LAUGHTER THAT GETS CAUGHT IN YOUR THROAT
Video, color, sound, 4' 48", 2015
Videography: Reinhard Mayr, Matthias Jahn, and Ewa Stern; sound technician: Felix Zwerger; editing: Marie-Christin Rissinger; photos: Violetta Rajakovics

JE SUIS ARABE—A RIGHT TO POETRY (transparadiso)
Performance, 2015
Performers: Akram al Halabi, Barbara Holub
2 gilded satellite dish objects; 2 walkie-talkies

JE SUIS ARABE—A RIGHT TO POETRY
Video, color, sound, 12' 41", German/Arabic, 2015
Performers: Akram al Halabi, Barbara Holub; videography: Matthias Jahn, Marie-Christin Rissinger; editing: Tatia Skhirtladze

DU BAKCHICH POUR LAMPEDUSA (transparadiso)
Performative installation, 2014
Room dividers, repurposed garbage container, carpet
Color pencil drawing, 70 × 100 cm, 2014
Notebook with color photos, 2016

DU BAKCHICH POUR LAMPEDUSA
Video, b&w, sound, 4' 56", 2016
In: *This Human World*, International Human Rights Film Festival, Vienna, 2016

WE PARAPOM!
Performance, 2021
Text: Barbara Holub; performers: Egmond Elschner, Muriel Wenger, Beate Düber, Stefan Schmidtke; director: René Schmidt

PARTICIPATORY STRATEGIES, VISIONS AND SPECULATIVE FICTION

MASSAGE À LA MEXICANA
Varnish on used car windows, about 140 × 160 cm, 2006

ON THE SLIM PROBABILITY (transparadiso)
Urban intervention, trotting track Karlshorst/Berlin, trotting track Krieau/Vienna, 2014
Object "Bauchladen" (design: Sabine Ott), betting tickets, vintage car hubcaps, gilded gully, golf clubs

AT THE URBAN PERIPHERY
Performance, installation, 2010
4 walks at the urban periphery, Lake City Aspern, Vienna
3 billboards, Erwin-Schrödinger-Platz, 1220 Vienna, 238 × 336 cm
3 billboards, Lake City Aspern, 1220 Vienna, 238 × 336 cm

WERKLISTE

LEISURE ENERGY
Installation, 2006
Wandzeichnung/Tapete, 86 × 293 cm; Autoscheibe eines SUV, Lack

STILLER AKTIVISMUS UND POLITISCHES ENGAGEMENT

FAVORIT (transparadiso)
Installation am Sonnwendplatz, 1100 Wien, 2021
Installation im Zukunftshof, 1100 Wien, 2022–2023
Pavillon, Lärchenholz, 408 × 637 × 381–231 cm

AM STADTRAND – 2. STADTRANDSPAZIERGANG
Wien-Aspern, 20. Juni 2010: Stimmen aus einer internationalen Stadt der Zukunft (Fussballfeldrede); Lambda-Print auf Fujicolor, 46 × 80 cm, 2010/2012

AM STADTRAND – 2. STADTRANDSPAZIERGANG
Wien-Aspern, 20. Juni 2010: Stimmen aus einer internationalen Stadt der Zukunft (Asphaltrede); Lambda-Print auf Fujicolor, 46 × 80 cm, 2010/2012

ISH BIN EIN ... (transparadiso)
Lambda-Print auf Fujicolor, 100 × 140 cm, 2007

INITIATIVE ISLAND
Installation, 2008–2018
Vorhang, schwarzer Bühnenmolton, Stickerei von Enkhjargal Bajinnyam (Mongolei), Otgon Tulga (Mongolei), Svetlana Tsal-Tsalko (Ukraine), Ketino Merebaschwili (Georgien), Sabine Ott und Cornelia Silli (Österreich), 1060 × 530 cm
Plakat (Fassade), 250 × 500 cm, 2008
Plakat (Innenraum), 250 × 500 cm, 2008

DAS LACHEN, DAS EINEM IM HALSE STECKEN BLEIBT (transparadiso)
Performance, 2015; PerformerInnen: Christiane Beinl, Xenia Gala, Akram al Halabi, Nancy Mensah-Offei, Johanna Orsini-Rosenberg; Komposition: Tamara Friebel; Aufführung unter Mitwirkung von: MigrantInnenchor Hor 29. Novembar; in Kooperation mit: SOS Mitmensch, Integrationshaus und Vinzi-Rast, Wien

DAS LACHEN, DAS EINEM IM HALSE STECKEN BLEIBT
Video, Farbe, Ton, 4' 48", 2015
Videografie: Reinhard Mayr, Matthias Jahn, Ewa Stern; Tontechnik: Felix Zwerger; Schnitt: Marie-Christin Rissinger; Fotos: Violetta Rajakovics

JE SUIS ARABE – EIN RECHT AUF POESIE (transparadiso)
Performance, 2015
PerformerInnen: Akram al Halabi, Barbara Holub; Text „Der Wille zum Leben" (Kazem El-Chebbi), Deutsch/Arabisch; 2 vergoldete Satellitenschüssel-Objekte; 2 Walkie-Talkies

JE SUIS ARABE – EIN RECHT AUF POESIE
Video, Farbe, Ton, 12' 41", Deutsch/Arabisch, 2015
PerformerInnen: Akram al Halabi, Barbara Holub; Videografie: Matthias Jahn, Marie-Christin Rissinger; Schnitt: Tatia Skhirtladze

DU BAKCHICH POUR LAMPEDUSA (transparadiso)
Performative Installation, 2014
Paravents, umfunktionierte Mülltonne, Teppich
Buntstiftzeichnung auf Papier, 70 × 100 cm, 2014
Notizbuch mit Fotos, 2016

DU BAKCHICH POUR LAMPEDUSA
Video, s/w, Ton, 4' 56", 2016
In: *This Human World*, Filmfestival, Wien, 2016

WE PARAPOM!
Performance, 2021
Text: Barbara Holub; PerformerInnen: Egmond Elschner, Muriel Wenger, Beate Düber, Stefan Schmidtke; Regisseur: René Schmidt

PARTIZIPATIVE STRATEGIEN, VISIONEN UND SPEKULATIVE FIKTION

MASSAGE À LA MEXICANA
Lack auf gebrauchten Glasscheiben, ca. 140 × 160 cm, 2006

AUF DIE GERINGE WAHRSCHEINLICHKEIT (transparadiso)
Urbane Interventionen, Trabrennbahn Karlshorst/Berlin, Trabrennbahn Krieau/Wien, 2014
Objekt „Bauchladen" (Design: Sabine Ott), Wettlose, Oldtimer-Radkappen, Gullydeckel vergoldet, Golfschläger

AM STADTRAND
Performance, Installation, 2010
4 Stadtrandspaziergänge, Aspern-Seestadt, Wien
3 Billboards, Erwin-Schrödinger-Platz, 1220 Wien, 238 × 336 cm
3 Billboards, Aspern-Seestadt, 1220 Wien, 238 × 336 cm

THE BLUE FROG SOCIETY WALKS TO THE MOON
[audio piece], Barbara Holub, Bruno Pisek, (Ö1 Kunstradio, November 14, 2010), 37′ 28″; speakers: Anne Bennent and Dirk Nocker; sound: Martin Leitner

AT THE URBAN PERIPHERY–3rd WALK AT THE URBAN PERIPHERY,
Lake City Aspern, Vienna, September 19, 2010: "Walk to the Moon"
Lambda print on Fujicolor, 110 × 75 cm, 2010/2012

AT THE URBAN PERIPHERY—GATX [without image]
Ink on paper, 108 × 158 cm, 2010

AT THE URBAN PERIPHERY—TELEPHONE LANE [without image]
Ink on paper, 140 × 100 cm, 2010

AT THE URBAN PERIPHERY—BILLBOARD 1 [without image]
Lake City Aspern, ink on paper, 100 × 140 cm, 2010
Salzburg Regional Collections

AT THE URBAN PERIPHERY—2nd WALK AT THE URBAN PERIPHERY
Vienna-Aspern, ink on paper, 100 × 130 cm, 2010
Salzburg Regional Collections

ANYONE'S LAND (transparadiso)
Installation at a deserted border control building, Gorizia/Nova Gorica, 2011
Video, color, sound, 20′, 1998 (Paul Rajakovics, transbanana), 2011

HARBOUR FOR CULTURES (transparadiso, Trieste Contemporanea, Betta Porro)
Workshops and participatory events, 2017–2020

SHARED VALUES, AMBULANT GARDENS, AND OTHER SPACES (transparadiso)
Urban intervention, 2017; Used carpets from different cultures, hand embroidery, various formats, map for the production of desires for HARBOUR FOR CULTURES, with copy paper, 41.8 × 59.5 cm, 2017

A PROMISE FOR HARBOUR FOR CULTURES (transparadiso)
Gilded bollard, Porto Vecchio/Trieste, 2018

100 DESIRES FOR HARBOUR FOR CULTURES (transparadiso)
Video, color, sound, 12′ 04″, 2018

SILENT ACTIVISM, DIALOG AND POETIC MOMENTS

CALL AGAINST THE BORDER (transparadiso)
Performance, St. Nikola (Upper Austria)—Neustadtl (Lower Austria), Grein (Upper Austria)—Wiesen/Neustadtl (Lower Austria), Festival of Regions (curated by Airan Berg), 2019; Text dialog, 2 megaphone sculptures, steel, aluminum, megaphone with Ø 20–46 cm, length 200 cm, height of tripod 160 cm; mixer, technical equipment; Performers: Anna Maria Brandstätter, kohelet3 (Bohdan and Ewa Hanushevsky), Pelin Ovat, Christine Scholl, Andrea Taspinarli, and the St. Nikola brass band

UNTITLED
(hard work—asphalting the studio), C-type print, 100 × 140 cm, 2000/2003

BEAUTIFUL RADIANT THINGS
Hectography, 29.7 × 21 cm, 2013
Artists' Edition, Secession Vienna, 2013

MORE OPPORTUNITIES
Video, color, sound, 4′ 50″, 2007

TAKING THE FUTURE INTO OUR HANDS
3D/double-sided silkscreen print, 100 × 52 cm, 2007

WELCOME TO THE NAVY BASE VISITOR'S CENTRE
Curtain, inkjet print on fabric, 235 × 310 cm, 2007

WHO SAYS WE ARE NOT...
7 placards, white, reflecting paint on hardboard,
various dimensions from 40 × 30 cm to 70 × 50 cm, 2007

CRYSTAL TURN
Rotary airer, Swarovski pearls, approx. 140 × 140 × 100 cm, 2007

PREY GRAB
Video, color, sound, 4′ 18″, 2007

BURNING SKY [without image]
Acrylic paint on canvas, 120 × 180 cm, 2007

FROM THE DISTANCE OF OUR REALITY WE BECOME TOURISTS IN OUR OWN CITY
Double slide projection, Kodak Carousel, color, 4′, 2007

FORGET THE TECHNICALITIES [without image]
Acrylic glass, wood, PVC sheet, 100 × 200 × 12 cm, 2007

MAKE NEWS INSTEAD OF [without image]
Double video projection, color, sound, 22′ 53″, 2008
Speakers: Céline Condorelli; sound and editing: Maria Garfield/Gunfield Studios, London, Ursula Blickle Video Archive/Belvedere, Medien Kunst Archiv Vienna

DIE BLUE FROG SOCIETY SPAZIERT AUF DEN MOND
[Hörstück], Barbara Holub, Bruno Pisek (Ö1 Kunstradio, 14. November 2010), 37′ 28″; SprecherInnen: Anne Bennent und Dirk Nocker; Ton: Martin Leitner

AM STADTRAND – 3. STADTRANDSPAZIERGANG
Wien-Aspern, 19. September 2010: Spaziergang auf dem Mond
Lambda-Print auf Fujicolor, 75 × 110 cm, 2010/2012

AM STADTRAND – GATX [ohne Abb.]
Tusche auf Papier, 108 × 158 cm, 2010

AM STADTRAND – TELEFONWEG [ohne Abb.]
Tusche auf Papier, 100 × 140 cm, 2010

AM STADTRAND – BILLBOARD 1 [ohne Abb.]
Wien-Aspern, Tusche auf Papier, 100 × 140 cm, 2010
Sammlung Land Salzburg

AM STADTRAND – 2. STADTRANDSPAZIERGANG
Wien-Aspern, Tusche auf Papier, 100 × 130 cm, 2010
Sammlung Land Salzburg

JEMANDSLAND (transparadiso)
Installation in ehemaliger Grenzstation, Gorizia/Nova Gorica, 2011
Video, Farbe, Ton, 20′, 1998 (Paul Rajakovics, transbanana)/2011

HARBOUR FOR CULTURES (transparadiso, Trieste Contemporanea, Betta Porro)
Workshops und partizipative Events, 2017–2020

SHARED VALUES, AMBULANT GARDENS, AND OTHER SPACES (transparadiso)
Urbane Intervention, 2017; Gebrauchte Teppiche aus verschiedenen Kulturen, handbestickt, verschiedene Formate; Plan für die Wunschproduktion für HARBOUR FOR CULTURES, mit Durchschlagpapier, 41,8 × 59,5 cm, 2017

A PROMISE FOR HARBOUR FOR CULTURES (transparadiso)
Vergoldeter Poller, Porto Vecchio/Triest, 2018

100 WÜNSCHE FÜR HARBOUR FOR CULTURES (transparadiso)
Video, Farbe, Ton, 12′ 04″, 2018

STILLER AKTIVISMUS, DIALOG UND POETISCHE MOMENTE

RUF GEGEN DIE GRENZE (transparadiso)
Performance, St. Nikola (Oberösterreich) – Neustadtl (Niederösterreich), Grein (Oberösterreich) – Wiesen/Neustadtl (Niederösterreich), Festival der Regionen (kuratiert von Airan Berg), 2019; Textual-Dialog; 2 Megaphon-Skulpturen, Stahl, Aluminium, Megaphone mit Ø 20–46 cm, Länge 200 cm, Stativhöhe 160 cm; Mischpult, technisches Equipment; performerInnen: Anna Maria Brandstätter, kohelet3 (Bohdan und Ewa Hanushevsky), Pelin Ovat, Christine Scholl, Andrea Taspinarli, Blasmusikkapelle St. Nikola

O. T.
(Harte Arbeit – Atelier asphaltieren), C-Print, 100 × 140 cm, 2000/2003

BEAUTIFUL RADIANT THINGS
Hektografie, 29,7 × 21 cm, 2013
KünstlerInnen-Edition, Secession Wien, 2013

MORE OPPORTUNITIES
Video, Farbe, Ton, 4′ 50″, 2007

TAKING THE FUTURE INTO OUR HANDS
3-D-/doppelseitiger Siebdruck auf Glas, 100 × 52 cm, 2007

WELCOME TO THE NAVY BASE VISITOR'S CENTRE
Vorhang, Inkjet-Print auf Stoff, 235 × 310 cm, 2007

WHO SAYS WE ARE NOT ...
7 Demonstrationstafeln, weiße, reflektierende Farbe auf Hartfaserplatten
Verschiedene Größen, von 40 × 30 cm bis 70 × 50 cm, 2007

CRYSTAL TURN
Wäschespinne, Swarovski-Perlen, ca. 140 × 140 × 100 cm, 2007

BEUTEGRIFF
Video, Farbe, Ton, 4′ 18″, 2007

BURNING SKY [ohne Abb.]
Acryl auf Leinwand, 180 × 120 cm, 2007

FROM THE DISTANCE OF OUR REALITY WE BECOME TOURISTS IN OUR OWN CITY
Doppel-Diainstallation, Kodak-Karussell, Farbe, 4′, 2007

FORGET THE TECHNICALITIES [ohne Abb.]
Acrylglas, Holz, PVC-Folie, 200 × 100 × 12 cm, 2007

MAKE NEWS INSTEAD OF [ohne Abb.]
Doppel-Videoprojektion, Farbe, Ton, 22′ 53″, 2008
Sprecherin: Céline Condorelli; Ton und Schnitt: Maria Garfield/Gunfield Studios, London; Ursula Blickle Video Archiv/Belvedere, Medien Kunst Archiv Wien

WE SHALL OVERCOME
4 digital prints on Kodak Endura Metallic, mounted on aluminum, ca. 30 × 45 cm, 2007/2014

WELCOME TO THE NAVY BASE VISITOR'S CENTRE
Lambda print, 50 × 70 cm, 2007/2014

LOST PERSPECTIVES
Lambda print, 50 × 70 cm, 2007/2014

UNFULFILLED VISIONS
Lambda print, 70 × 50 cm, 2007/2022

LISTEN TO THE QUIET VOICE
4 headscarves of worn nylons, 4 poster stands of wood
with 2 posters each, each 84.1 × 59.4 cm, 2008

THE BLUE FROG SOCIETY | A HABITAT WITHOUT TERRITORY
10 plackards, mirror glass, permanent marker, wood,
100 × 70 cm, 80 × 60 cm, 70 × 50 cm, 2010

MAP OF THE TERRITORY WITHOUT HABITAT—THE BLUE FROG SOCIETY
Inkjet print on satin, hand embroidery, 180 × 250 cm, 2011
filled-in post cards, 2011–2019

MAKE TRUTH OUT OF THE WORLD
4 inkjet prints on PVC sheet, 220 × 86 cm, 213 × 86 cm, 213 × 210 cm, 213 × 193 cm, 2011

A STATE VISIT TO THE BLUE FROG SOCIETY
Performative installation
Untitled, (minority languages in Europe №1), silkscreen on fabric, 120 × 180 cm, 2018
4 videos of speeches held on the occasion of a state visit to THE BLUE FROG SOCIETY, 2018: Nancy Black "The Speech of the Great Dictator" (Romanes, Vienna), color, sound, 7' 19"; Selma Selman (Romanes, Syracuse, New York), color, sound, 1' 53"
Costanza Travaglini (Friulan, Udine), color, sound, 6' 42"
Gabriele Zanello (Friulan, Udine), color, sound, 9' 14"
lectern, 2018

BETWEEN ROLES
Installation of a garden with lawn and fence at Barbara Holub's studio, 2nd district, Vienna, 2000; Performers: Mark Gilbert, Veronika Hofer, Teresa Hohenlohe, Sabine Pollak, Wolfgang Reuscher, Andrea van der Straeten, Heinz Trnka et. al.

BETWEEN ROLES
Video, color, sound, English subtitles, 31' 43", 2000
Ursula Blickle Video Archive/Belvedere, Media Art Archive Vienna

BETWEEN ROLES
Installation of a garden with lawn, fence, porch swing, mole sculpture, cherry tree, projection of the video SWINGING, video studio for live editing, "casting car", 2002
Performers: Josef Adam, Ari Griffner, Anne Grünhagen, Reni Hofmüller, Herbert Lachmayr, Hansjörg Luser, Jeanette Pacher, Charlotte Pöchacker, Julius Salamon, Jan Tabor, Mechthild Widrich, Wolfgang Zinggl and many others

SWINGING
Video, color, sound, 5' 10", 2002; vocals: Nita Tandon
Ursula Blickle Video Archive/Belvedere, Media Art Archive Vienna

SYSTEMS, SECRETS, VOICES

DRIVEN
Performative urban intervention, pickup-truck gallery 7562LR, Chicago, 1998
Performance with stripper, Art Chicago, 1998

SILVER ARMPIT STIMULATOR [without image]
PVC, inflatable object, ca. 30 × 30 × 10 cm, 1998

VELVET BREAST FLATTERY [without image]
PVC, inflatable object, ca. 20 × 20 × 10 cm, 1998

DRIVEN
Video, color, sound, 35' 56", 1998
Published in: VIDEO EDITION AUSTRIA release 01 DVD 3. Reflections, Medienwerkstatt Wien

SPIELEN, BEGEHREN, BRAUCHEN
(Admiral betting shop, Prater), color photo on acrylic glass, varnish, 50 × 75 cm, 1998

SPIELEN, BEGEHREN, BRAUCHEN
(Mudokwan martial arts centre), color photo on acrylic glass, varnish, 50 × 75 cm, 1998

SPIELEN, BEGEHREN, BRAUCHEN
(Horse racetrack in Freudenau), color photo on acrylic glass, varnish, 50 × 75 cm, 1998

SPIELEN, BEGEHREN, BRAUCHEN
(Betting cash desk in, Freudenau), color photo on acrylic glass, varnish, 50 × 75 cm, 1998

WE SHALL OVERCOME
4 Digital-Prints auf Kodak Endura Metallic, auf Aluminium kaschiert, je 45 × 30 cm, 2007/2014

WELCOME TO THE NAVY BASE VISITOR'S CENTRE
Lambda-Print, 70 × 50 cm, 2007/2014

VERLORENE PESPEKTIVEN
Lambda-Print, 70 × 50 cm, 2007/2014

UNERFÜLLTE VISIONEN
Lambda-Print, 70 × 50 cm, 2007/2022

LISTEN TO THE QUIET VOICE
4 Kopftücher aus getragenen Nylonstrümpfen; 4 Plakatständer aus Holz
mit jeweils 2 Plakaten, je 84,1 × 59,4 cm, 2008

THE BLUE FROG SOCIETY | A HABITAT WITHOUT TERRITORY
10 Demonstrationstafeln, Spiegelglas, Lackstift, Holz,
100 × 70 cm, 80 × 60 cm, 70 × 50 cm, 2010

MAP OF THE TERRITORY WITHOUT HABITAT – THE BLUE FROG SOCIETY
Inkjet-Print auf Satin, handbestickt, 180 × 250 cm, 2011
Postkarten, ausgefüllt, 2011–2019

MAKE TRUTH OUT OF THE WORLD
4 Inkjet-Prints auf PVC-Folie, 220 × 86 cm, 213 × 86 cm, 213 × 210 cm, 213 × 193 cm, 2011

A STATE VISIT TO THE BLUE FROG SOCIETY
Performative Installation
O. T., (Minderheitensprachen in Europa №1), Siebdruck auf Stoff, 120 × 180 cm, 2018
4 Videos von Ansprachen anlässlich des Staatsbesuchs bei THE BLUE FROG SOCIETY, 2018: Nancy Black, „The Speech of the Great Dictator" (Romanes, Wien), Farbe, Ton, 7' 19"
Selma Selman (Romanes, Syracuse/New York), Farbe, Ton, 1' 53"
Costanza Travaglini (Friulanisch, Udine), Farbe, Ton, 6' 42"
Gabriele Zanello (Friulanisch, Udine), Farbe, Ton, 9' 14"
Rednerpult, 2018

ZWISCHENROLLEN
Installation eines Gartens mit Rasen und Zaun im Atelier Barbara Holub, 2. Bezirk/Wien, 2000; PerformerInnen: Mark Gilbert, Veronika Hofer, Teresa Hohenlohe, Sabine Pollak, Wolfgang Reuscher, Andrea van der Straeten, Heinz Trnka u. a.

ZWISCHENROLLEN
Video, Farbe, Ton, engl. Untertitel, 31' 43", 2000
Ursula Blickle Video Archiv/Belvedere, Medien Kunst Archiv Wien

ZWISCHENROLLEN
Installation eines Gartens mit Rasen und Zaun, Hollywoodschaukel, Maulwurfskulptur, Kirschbaum, Video-Projektion SWINGING, Video-Studio für Live-Editing, Casting-Auto, 2002
PerformerInnen: Josef Adam, Ari Griffner, Anne Grünhagen, Reni Hofmüller, Herbert Lachmayr, Hansjörg Luser, Jeanette Pacher, Charlotte Pöchacker, Julius Salamon, Jan Tabor, Mechthild Widrich, Wolfgang Zinggl u. v. a.

SWINGING
Video, Farbe, Ton, 5' 10", 2002, Gesang: Nita Tandon
Ursula Blickle Video Archiv/Belvedere, Medien Kunst Archiv Wien

SYSTEME, GEHEIMNIS, STIMMEN

DRIVEN
Performative urbane Intervention, Pickup-Truck-Galerie 7562LR, Chicago, 1998
Performance mit Stripper, Art Chicago, 1998

SILVER ARMPIT STIMULATOR [ohne Abb.]
PVC, aufblasbares Objekt, ca. 30 × 30 × 10 cm, 1998

VELVET BREAST FLATTERY [ohne Abb.]
PVC, aufblasbares Objekt, ca. 20 × 20 × 10 cm, 1998

DRIVEN
Video, Farbe, Ton, 35' 56", 1998
Erschienen in VIDEO EDITION AUSTRIA release 01 DVD 3. Reflections, Medienwerkstatt Wien

SPIELEN, BEGEHREN, BRAUCHEN
(Admiral Wettbüro/Prater), C-Print, Acrylglas, Lack, 75 × 50 cm, 1998

SPIELEN, BEGEHREN, BRAUCHEN
(Mudokwan Centre für asiatischen Kampfsport), C-Print, Acrylglas, Lack, 75 × 50 cm, 1998

SPIELEN, BEGEHREN, BRAUCHEN
(Galopprennbahn Freudenau), C-Print, Acrylglas, Lack, 75 × 50 cm, 1998

SPIELEN, BEGEHREN, BRAUCHEN
(Wettkassa Freudenau), C-Print, Acrylglas, Lack, 75 × 50 cm, 1998

UNREQUESTED VOLUNTARY INTERLINGUISTICALITY (transparadiso)
Design of the new village square, Pottenhofen, 2016
Bilingual (German–Czech) Scrabble game, computer keyboard letters, board game on paper,seating-table sculpture, steel tube lacquered, with fiber concrete disc, text printed in white, Ø 241 cm; Gingko biloba; Czech street lamp

SUBMISSION TO UNINTENTIONALITY
2 inkjet prints on PVC sheet, 265 × 540 cm, 265 × 298 cm, 1999

WITH VEILING HANDS
Installation with double video projection, 1999
2 videos, b&w, sound, 45' each, looped; airport seats

WARUMEN/WHYING
Installation, 1999
Audio play, 22'; inflatable cushions/PU sheet, oil pastel on terrazzo floor

UNTITLED (Watching from the model space of desires)
curtain, inkjet print on satin, 245 × 380 cm, 1999

HANDLED CONFIDENTIALLY
Permanent photo installation on the façade of the Bene showroom, Renngasse/Vienna, 1997–2010
4 lightboxes, Duratrans, 135 × 300 cm each

HANDLED CONFIDENTIALLY
Video, color, sound, 13', 1999
Ursula Blickle Video Archive/Belvedere, Media Art Archive Vienna

PLAYING ALONG...?
Installation at the Bene showroom, Renngasse/Vienna, 1999–2001
Wall text; 2 Calsi prints on PVC sheet, 180 × 240 cm, 125 × 280 cm

THE SYSTEM: PRÊT-À-PORTER
Installation at Künstlerhaus/Künstlerhauspassage, Vienna, 2006
Billboard on scaffolding, inkjet print on PVC sheet, 204 × 515 cm; cutout letters on glass façade; fashion show with secondhand clothes, photo shoot, in cooperation with Humana, Vienna

YARDSALE
Video, color, without sound, 2' 32", 2004
Ursula Blickle Video Archive/Belvedere, Media Art Archive Vienna

THE SYSTEM: PRÊT-À-PORTER
Performative installation in *Slow*, Plymouth Arts Centre, Plymouth, 2007
Room deviders, inkjet prints on fabric, metall construction; fashion show with secondhand clothes, in cooperation with Oxfam, Plymouth

PERSONAL INVESTIGATION [without image]
Sandblasted glass, 10 × 90 cm, 1994

VOID
Calsi print on PVC sheet, sandblasted glass, metal frame, metal shoes, 100 × 300 cm, 1994

NEUTRAL
Calsi print on PVC sheet, sandblasted glass, metal frame, 100 × 300 cm, 1994

VALID
Calsi print on PVC sheet, sandblasted glass, metal frame, 100 × 300 cm, 1994

CONCERNS
Used typewriter tapes on acrylic glass, sandblasted glass, metal frame, 100 × 200 cm, 1994

PRIVATE
Used typewriter tapes on acrylic glass, sandblasted glass, metal frame, 100 × 200 cm, 1994

CONCERNS
Lino printing ink on acrylic glass, sandblasted glass, metal frame, 100 × 200 cm, 1994

PRIVATE
Lino printing ink on acrylic glass, sandblasted glass, metal frame, 100 × 200 cm, 1994

WHAT CONCERNS [without image]
Emergency lighting, acrylic paint on acrylic glass, 5.5 × 30 × 9 cm, 1994

CARRIERS OF SECRETS
8 padded jigsaw objects, faux leather, foam material, about 160 × 125 cm each, 1996
Leaflet with photos of important government and commerce buildings in reference to the jigsaw objects: Everett Mc. Kinley Dirksen Building (Courthouse, 219 S. Dearborn); City of Chicago Police Department (113 W. Chicago); Richard J. Daley Centre (Chicago Civic Centre, 50 W. Washington); John C. Kluczynski Building (Federal Building, 230 S. Dearborn); Immigration and Naturalization Service (10 E. Jackson); Cook County Building (118 N. Clark); Chicago Board of Trade (400 S. LaSalle)

UNAUFGEFORDERTE FREIWILLIGE INTERSPRACHLICHKEIT (transparadiso)
Platzgestaltung, Pottenhofen, 2016
Zweisprachiges Scrabble-Spiel, Deutsch/Tschechisch, Computertastaturbuchstaben, Spielfeld auf Papier; Sitz-Tisch-Skulptur, Stahlrohr lackiert, mit Eternitscheibe, weiß bedruckt, Ø 241 cm; Gingko biloba; tschechische Straßenleuchte

HINGABE AN DIE ABSICHTSLOSIGKEIT
2 Inkjet-Prints auf PVC, 265 × 540 cm, 265 × 298 cm, 1999

MIT VORGEHALTENER HAND
Installation mit Doppel-Videoprojektion, 1999
2 Videos, s/w, Ton, je 45', geloopt; Flughafenbestuhlung

WARUMEN
Installation, 1999
Hörspiel, 22'; aufblasbare Polster/PU-Folie; Ölkreide auf Terrazzoboden

O. T. (Zuschauen aus dem Modellraum von Sehnsüchten)
Vorhang, Inkjet-Print auf Satin, 380 × 245 cm, 1999

VERTRAULICH BEHANDELT
Permanente Installation an der Fassade des Bene-Schauraums, 1. Bezirk/Wien, 1997–2010
4 Leuchtkästen, Duratrans, je 300 × 135 cm

VERTRAULICH BEHANDELT
Video, Farbe, Ton, 13', 1999
Ursula Blickle Video Archiv/Belvedere, Medien Kunst Archiv Wien

MITSPIELEN ...?
Installation im Bene–Schauraum, 1. Bezirk/Wien, 1999–2001
Wandtext; 2 Calsi-Prints auf PVC-Folie, 180 × 240 cm, 125 × 280 cm

THE SYSTEM: PRÊT-À-PORTER
Installation Künstlerhaus/Künstlerhauspassage, Wien, 2006
Billboard auf Baugerüst, Inkjet-Print auf PVC-Folie, 204 × 515 cm; Klebebuchstaben auf Glasfassade; Modenschau mit Secondhandkleidung, Fotoshooting, in Kooperation mit Humana, Wien

YARDSALE
Video, Farbe, ohne Ton, 2' 32", 2004
Ursula Blickle Video Archiv/Belvedere, Medien Kunst Archiv Wien

THE SYSTEM: PRÊT-À-PORTER
Performative Installation in der Ausstellung *Slow*, Plymouth Arts Centre, Plymouth, 2007; Paravents, Inkjet-Prints auf Stoff, Metallkonstruktion; Modenschau mit Secondhandkleidung, Fotoshooting, in Kooperation mit Oxfam, Plymouth

PERSONAL INVESTIGATION [ohne Abb.]
Sandgestrahltes Glas, 10 × 90 cm, 1994

VOID
Calsi-Print auf PVC-Folie, sandgestrahltes Glas, Metallrahmen, Metallfüße, 100 × 300 cm, 1994

NEUTRAL
Calsi-Print auf PVC-Folie, sandgestrahltes Glas, Metallrahmen,100 × 300 cm, 1994

VALID
Calsi-Print auf PVC-Folie, sandgestrahltes Glas, Metallrahmen, 100 × 300 cm, 1994

BETRIFFT
Schreibmaschinenbänder auf Acrylglas, sandgestrahltes Glas, Metallrahmen, 100 × 200 cm, 1994

PRIVAT
Schreibmaschinenbänder auf Acrylglas, sandgestrahltes Glas, Metallrahmen, 100 × 200 cm, 1994

BETRIFFT
Linoldruckfarbe auf Acrylglas, sandgestrahltes Glas, Metallrahmen, 100 × 200 cm, 1994

PRIVAT
Linoldruckfarbe auf Acrylglas, sandgestrahltes Glas, Metallrahmen, 100 × 200 cm, 1994

WAS BETRIFFT [ohne Abb.]
Notbeleuchtung, Acrylfarbe auf Acrylglas, 5,5 × 30 × 9 cm, 1994

GEHEIMNISTRÄGER
8 gepolsterte Puzzle-Objekte, Kunstleder, Schaumstoff, je ca. 160 × 125 cm, 1996
Folder mit Fotos von Gebäuden wesentlicher politischer und wirtschaftlicher Institutionen in Chicago – in Referenz auf die Puzzle-Objekte, 1996: Everett Mc. Kinley Dirksen Building (Courthouse, 219 S. Dearborn); City of Chicago Police Department (113 W. Chicago); Richard J. Daley Centre (Chicago Civic Centre, 50 W. Washington); John C. Kluczynski Building (Federal Building, 230 S. Dearborn); Immigration and Naturalization Service (10 E. Jackson); Cook County Building (118 N. Clark); Chicago Board of Trade (400 S. LaSalle)

TIMES OF DILEMMA (transparadiso)
Performance, Manoel Island/St. Roche Chapel, Malta, 2018
Għana dialogs/texts: Jean Paul Borg, Jo Burden, Immanuel Mifsud; Għanneijja: Il-Bukku Vince, Angelo Theuma, Mikkelina, Josmick Agius as well as Maria Agius/Oħt iż -Żebbuġin'; guitarists: John Saliba, Victor Grech, Frans Casha, Ruben Schembri; coordination of the performances of the Għana dialogs: Rachelle Deguara in cooperation with Il-Bukku Vince, Angelo Theuma, Mikkelina, Josmick Agius; 2 megaphone sculptures, steel, aluminium; megaphones: Ø 20–46 cm, length 200 cm, height of tripod 160 cm; mixer, technical equipment

MISSING THINGS—NOISY ACTIVISM

PLATFORM FOR ARGUMENTS (Barbara Holub/Christine Hohenbüchler with students of the Institute of Art and Design, Vienna University of Technology)
Performative installation, 2018; wooden sculpture, paint, Ø approx. 400 cm, height 20–150 cm; Performances and speeches by: Die BrutpflegerInnen, Dokumentations- und Beratungsstelle für Islamfeindlichkeit/Elif Adam, Katharina Ernst, Janea Hansen, Anna Mendelssohn, Susi Rogenhofer, Raimar Stange, Marlene Streeruwitz, Yasmo, Yosi Wanunu, among others

NEUWERTIG
Keyboard letters, car window (Citroën DS), solid-colored HDF board, 31 × 107 × 138 cm, 2016

WHAT I AM PROUD OF
Ink on Fabriano, 115 × 180 cm, 2011
Zorlu Collection, Istanbul

WHAT I WOULD LIKE TO HANDLE DISCRETELY
Ink on Fabriano, 198 × 151 cm, 2017

WHAT I LET GO
Ink on Fabriano, 53.5 × 68.5 cm, 2019

WHAT I FIGHT FOR
Ink on Fabriano, 53.5 × 68.5 cm, 2013

WHAT I AM AFRAID OF
Ink on Fabriano, 53.5 × 68.5 cm, 2013

WHAT I SUPPORT [without image]
Ink on Fabriano, 53.5 × 68.5 cm, 2013

WHAT I PRACTICE [without image]
Ink on Fabriano, 53.5 × 68.5 cm, 2013

WHAT I NEED TO REMEMBER [without image]
Ink on Fabriano, 53.5 × 68.5 cm, 2013

EXCHANGE OF FAVORITE PASTIMES AND NECESSITIES
Room devider, 210 × 130 cm, inkjet print on Bertex, 200 × 260 cm, rotatable, white steel construction, 2003

WHEN OTHERS DO THEIR WORK
10 vintage car windows, varnish, about 135 × 178 cm, 2003, Lentos Collection, Linz

FENSTERLN
Hanging lamp, Ø 50 cm, ink on cardboard, 2003

PATTING HANDS
Carpet (logo mat), velours on rubber, 115 × 170 cm, 2003

SHAKING SHOULDERS
Carpet (logo mat), velours on rubber, 115 × 170 cm, 2003

BANDEROLA
Sofa, jersey fabric, various color combinations, 80 × 182 cm
2 inflatable cushions, about 80 × 80 × 40 cm each, 2003

CULTIVATING IDLENESS [without image]
Drawing on vintage car window, 58.5 × 120–145 cm
foam pedestal, covered with jersey fabric, 62.5 × 45 × 12 cm, 2003

UNTITLED
(Run), C-type print, 68 × 86 cm, 2003

AWAY FROM THE LIVING ROOM
Lambda print, 56 × 78 cm, 2003

AWAY FROM THE LIVING ROOM [without image]
Lambda print, 56 × 78 cm, 2003

UNTITLED
(Panorama picture, Umag, Croatia), Lambda print, 56 × 167 cm, 2003

THE MAKING OF BEAUTY [without image]
Video, VHS, 3 parts, 48'–60' each, 2003

IMAGE TRANSFER
(Hairdresser "Haarsalat"), Calsi print on PVC sheet, 127 × 112 cm, 1996

TIMES OF DILEMMA (transparadiso)
Performance, Manoel Island/St. Roche Chapel, Malta, 2018
Għana-Dialoge/Texte: Jean Paul Borg, Jo Burden, Immanuel Mifsud; Għanneijja: Il-Bukku Vince, Angelo Theuma, Mikkelina, Josmick Agius sowie Maria Agius/Oħt iż -Żebbuġin'; Gitarristen: John Saliba, Victor Grech, Frans Casha, Ruben Schembri; Koordination der Aufführung der Għana-Dialoge: Rachelle Deguara in Zusammenarbeit mit Il-Bukku Vince, Angelo Theuma, Mikkelina, Josmick Agius; 2 Megaphon-Skulpturen: Stahl Aluminium, Megaphone mit Ø 20–46 cm, Länge 200 cm, Stativhöhe 160 cm; Mischpult, technisches Equipment

DINGE, DIE FEHLEN – GERÄUSCHVOLLER AKTIVISMUS

PLATTFORM FÜR STREITREDEN (Barbara Holub/Christine Hohenbüchler mit StudentInnen des Instituts für Kunst und Gestaltung, TU Wien)
Performative Installation, 2018; Holzskulptur, Farbe, Ø ca. 400 cm, Höhe 20–150 cm
Performances und Reden von: Die BrutpflegerInnen, Dokumentations- und Beratungsstelle für Islamfeindlichkeit/Elif Adam, Katharina Ernst, Janea Hansen, Anna Mendelssohn, Susi Rogenhofer, Raimar Stange, Marlene Streeruwitz, Yasmo, Yosi Wanunu u. a.

NEUWERTIG
Computertastaturbuchstaben, Windschutzscheibe (Citroën DS), durchgefärbte MDF-Platten, 31 × 107 × 138 cm, 2016

WHAT I AM PROUD OF
Tusche auf Fabriano 180 × 115 cm, 2011
Sammlung Zorlu, Istanbul

WHAT I WOULD LIKE TO HANDLE DISCRETELY
Tusche auf Fabriano, 198 × 151 cm, 2017

WHAT I LET GO
Tusche auf Fabriano, 53,5 × 68,5 cm, 2019

WHAT I FIGHT FOR
Tusche auf Fabriano, 53,5 × 68,5 cm, 2013

WHAT I AM AFRAID OF
Tusche auf Fabriano, 53,5 × 68,5 cm, 2013

WHAT I SUPPORT [ohne Abb.]
Tusche auf Fabriano, 53,5 × 68,5 cm, 2013

WHAT I PRACTICE [ohne Abb.]
Tusche auf Fabriano, 53,5 × 68,5 cm, 2013

WHAT I NEED TO REMEMBER [ohne Abb.]
Tusche auf Fabriano, 53,5 × 68,5 cm, 2013

TAUSCH VON LIEBLINGSBESCHÄFTIGUNGEN UND NOTWENDIGKEITEN
Paravent, 210 × 130 cm, Inkjet-Print auf Bertex, 200 × 260 cm, verdrehbar, weiße Stahlkonstruktion, 2003

WENN ANDERE IHRE ARBEIT TUN
10 Oldtimer-Autofensterscheiben, Lack, ca. 135 × 178 cm, 2003, Sammlung Lentos, Linz

FENSTERLN
Hängelampe, Ø 50 cm, Tusche auf Karton, 2003

HÄNDE KLOPFEN
Teppich (Logomatte), Velours auf Gummi, 170 × 115 cm, 2003

SCHULTER SCHÜTTELN
Teppich (Logomatte), Velours auf Gummi, 170 × 115 cm, 2003

BANDEROLA
Sofa, Jersey, div. Farbkombinationen, 80 × 182 cm
2 Polster, aufblasbar, je ca. 80 × 80 × 40 cm, 2003

DEN MÜSSIGGANG PFLEGEN [ohne Abb.]
Lack-Zeichnung auf Windschutzscheibe, 58,5 × 120–145 cm
Schaumstoffsockel mit Jersey überzogen, 62,5 × 45 × 12 cm, 2003

O. T.
(Laufmasche), C-Print, 86 × 68 cm, 2003

DEM WOHNZIMMER ENTRÜCKT
Lambda-Print, 78 × 56 cm, 2003

DEM WOHNZIMMER ENTRÜCKT [ohne Abb.]
Lambda-Print, 78 × 56 cm, 2003

O. T.
(Panoramabild, Umag, Kroatien), Lambda-Print, 167 × 56 cm, 2003

THE MAKING OF BEAUTY [ohne Abb.]
VHS-Video, 3-teilig, je ca. 48–60', 2003

IMAGE TRANSFER
(Friseur „Haarsalat"), Calsi-Print auf PVC-Folie, 127 × 112 cm, 1996

IMAGE TRANSFER
(Photo lab technician "Fotokarussell"), Calsi print on PVC sheet, 80 × 120 cm, 1996

IMAGE TRANSFER
(Drycleaner, "Putzerei Maunz"), Calsi print on PVC sheet, 80 × 110 cm, 1996

IMAGE TRANSFER
(Bank employee, Erste Bank), Calsi print on PVC sheet, 264 × 165 cm, 1996

IMAGE TRANSFER
Audio installation and CD, 8' 40", 1996

THE FIRST WOLRD CONGRESS OF THE MISSING THINGS
Performances, urban interventions for collecting "Missing Things", May–June 2014; Congress, June 7–8, 2014; Installation of a congress office at the artist-run Current Space; installation of the Congress with re-purposed tables (transparadiso) at the entrance of Lexington Market Subway Station.
Team: Marie-Christin Rissinger, Elisabeth Stephan, Julian Verocai; further contributions by: Simone Klien, Nika Kupyrova, Marit Wolters; Design/CI: Lucia Hofer; cooperation partners: University of Applied Arts Vienna/Social Design—Arts as Urban Innovation; Austrian Cultural Forum Washington, Washington D. C.; Bromo Tower Arts & Entertainment Inc.; in the frame of EUNIC (European Network of Institutes of Culture).

THE SECOND WORLD *NON*-CONGRESS OF THE MISSING THINGS
Collection of the "Missing Things", September–October 2014
Non-Congress with performances, urban interventions, November 23, 2014
The Non-Congress was held at the canteen of the construction site at Lake City Aspern. Projects by: Oldooz Ahmadzadeh, Cornelia Bast, Antonia Eggeling, Dilruba Erkan, Roland Hampl, Katharina Heinrich, Wookseob Jeong, Lydia Kaminski, Sally Kotter, Hana Krizanova, Jan Phillip Ley, Alejandra Loreto, Anna Ilona Misovicz, Bo Mu, Vera Nikolaeva Naydenova, Peter Oroszlany, Madeleine Salinger, Christoph Steininger, Cosima Terrasse, Ana-Marija Vasicek, Klelija Zhivkovikj; special guest: Shaheen Merali; cooperation partner: University of Applied Arts Vienna/Social Design—Arts as Urban Innovation

WORKERS IN THE DUNES AFTER KOBO ABE
Lampda print on Fujicolor, 46 × 80 cm, 2014/2017

THE THIRD WORLD CONGRESS OF THE MISSING THINGS (transparadiso)
Congress, performances, urban interventions, July 31–August 1 2021
Installation of the congress at the parking lot of the Parish St. Paul, Eisteichsiedlung housing estate/Waltendorf, Graz; performance by the chapel choir (text: Barbara Holub; directed by: Edith Draxl); dérives at Eisteichsiedlung housing estate and on Ruckerlberg, Graz; Cooperation partner: Michael Petrowitsch; partnering institutions: HDA/Haus der Architektur, Graz, and Forum Stadtpark, Graz; media partner: dérive—magazine for urban research, Vienna

BAMBOOKAZA (transparadiso)
Bamboo, Mero knots, awning fabric, 404 × 673 × 237 cm, 2021
Realization: Stefan Lozar; civil engineering: HELT, Vienna

MOMENT CATCHER (transparadiso)
Cardboard, 42 × 30 cm, 2021

UNTITLED (transparadiso)
Advertising column, painted with blackboard paint, white chalk, height 200 cm, 2021

CHARTA OF THE MISSING THINGS (transparadiso)
Light box, 115 × 64 cm, 2021

PERSPECTIVE CHANGER #1
(Don't be afraid), 2 C-type prints , cardboard, 44.7 × 86.5 cm, 2021

PERSPECTIVE CHANGER #2
(Domesticated nature or wilderness), 2 C-type prints, cardboard, 44.7 × 86.5 cm, 2021

PERSPECTIVE CHANGER #3
(Before extinction/circus), 2 C-prints, cardboard, 44.7 × 86.5 cm, 2021

PERSPECTIVE CHANGER #4 [without image]
(Living at the periphery—between parking lot and minimum green spaces), 2 C-type prints, cardboard, 44.7 × 86.5 cm, 2021

SEEDS OF POETRY UNDISCOVERED
Text of the speech performance for THE THIRD WORLD CONGRESS OF THE MISSING THINGS, video, b&w, without sound, 3' 40", 2021

IMAGE TRANSFER
(Fotolabor „Fotokarussell"), Calsi-Print auf PVC-Folie, 80 × 120 cm, 1996

IMAGE TRANSFER
(Chemische Reinigung, „Putzerei Maunz"), Calsi-Print auf PVC-Folie, 80 × 110 cm, 1996

IMAGE TRANSFER
(Bankangestellte, Erste Bank), Calsi-Print auf PVC-Folie, 264 × 165 cm, 1996

IMAGE TRANSFER
Audio-Installation und CD, 8' 40", 1996

THE FIRST WOLRD CONGRESS OF THE MISSING THINGS
Performances, urbane Interventionen zur Sammlung der „Missing Things", Mai–Juni 2014; Kongress, 7.–8. Juni 2014; Etablierung eines Kongresslokals im Kunstraum Current Space; Installation des Kongresses mit umfunktionierten Tapeziertischen (transparadiso) vor dem Eingang der U-Bahn-Station Lexington Market;
Team: Marie-Christin Rissinger, Elisabeth Stephan, Julian Verocai; weitere Beiträge von: Simone Klien, Nika Kupyrova, Marit Wolters; Design/CI: Lucia Hofer; KooperationspartnerInnen: Universität für angewandte Kunst Wien/Social Design – Arts as Urban Innovation; Österreichisches Kulturforum Washington, Washington D. C.; Bromo Tower Arts & Entertainment Inc.; im Rahmen von: EUNIC (European Network of Institutes of Culture)

THE SECOND WORLD *NON*-CONGRESS OF THE MISSING THINGS
Sammlung der „Missing Things", September–Oktober 2014
Non-Kongress mit Performances, urbanen Interventionen, 23. November 2014
Installation des Non-Kongresses im Kiosk-Lokal der Baustelle Seestadt Aspern
Projekte von: Oldooz Ahmadzadeh, Cornelia Bast, Antonia Eggeling, Dilruba Erkan, Roland Hampl, Katharina Heinrich, Wookseob Jeong, Lydia Kaminski, Sally Kotter, Hana Krizanova, Jan Phillip Ley, Alejandra Loreto, Anna Ilona Misovicz, Bo Mu, Vera Nikolaeva Naydenova, Peter Oroszlany, Madeleine Salinger, Christoph Steininger, Cosima Terrasse, Ana-Marija Vasicek, Klelija Zhivkovikj; Special Guest: Shaheen Merali; Kooperationspartnerin: Universität für angewandte Kunst Wien/Social Design – Arts as Urban Innovation

DIE ARBEITER IN DEN DÜNEN NACH KOBO ABE
Lambda-Print auf Fujicolor, 46 × 80 cm, 2014/2017

THE THIRD WORLD CONGRESS OF THE MISSING THINGS (transparadiso)
Kongress, Performances, urbane Interventionen, 31. Juli–1. August 2021
Installation des Kongresses auf dem Parkplatz der Pfarre St. Paul, Eisteichsiedlung/Waltendorf, Graz; Sprechperformance der Kapellknaben und -mädchen (Text: Barbara Holub; geleitet von: Edith Draxl); dérives in der Eisteichsiedlung und am Ruckerlberg, Graz; Kooperationspartner: Michael Petrowitsch; Partnerinstitutionen: HDA/Haus der Architektur, Graz, und Forum Stadtpark, Graz; Medienpartnerin: dérive – Zeitschrift für Stadtforschung, Wien

BAMBOOKAZA (transparadiso)
Bambus, Mero-Knoten, Markisenstoff, 404 × 673 × 237 cm, 2021
Realisierung: Stefan Lozar; Statik: HELT, Wien

MOMENTEFÄNGER (transparadiso)
Karton, 42 × 30 cm, 2021

O.T. (transparadiso)
Litfaßsäule, bemalt mit schwarzer Tafelfarbe, weiße Tafelkreide, Höhe 200 cm, 2021

CHARTA OF THE MISSING THINGS (transparadiso)
Leuchtbox, 115 × 64 cm, 2021

PERSPEKTIVENWENDER #1
(Fürchte dich nicht), Fotografie, Karton, 44,7 × 86,5 cm, 2021

PERSPEKTIVENWENDER #2
(Domestizierte Natur oder Wildnis), Fotografie, Karton, 44,7 × 86,5 cm, 2021

PERSPEKTIVENWENDER #3
(Vor dem Aussterben/Zirkus), Fotografie, Karton, 44,7 × 86,5 cm, 2021

PERSPEKTIVENWENDER #4 [ohne Abb.]
(Wohnen an der Peripherie – Zwischen Parkplatz und Abstandsgrün), Fotografie, Karton, 44,7 × 86,5 cm, 2021

SAMEN DER POESIE UNENTDECKT
Text der Sprechperformance für THE THIRD WORLD CONGRESS OF THE MISSING THINGS, Video, s/w, ohne Ton, 3' 40", 2021

Sean Ashton

From 2007 to 2011, Sean Ashton was associate editor of *MAP Magazine*, and from 2012 to 2017 he wrote for *Art Review*. His book *Sunsets and Dogshits* (Alma Books, 2008) is a collection of reviews of imaginary artworks and books. *Living in a Land* (Ma Bibliothèque, 2017) is the memoir of a hypothetical citizen, written in sentences constructed in the negative. Asthon has also contributed poems, essays, and stories to many other publications, including *Oxford Poetry, Poetry London, Poetry Ireland Review, Magma, Poetry Salzburg Review, Artenol,* the philosophy journal *Collapse,* and the book *Walking Cities.* His poetry collection *Sampler* (Valley Press, 2020) is a selection of pieces from an imaginary encyclopedia written entirely by poets. In 2020, a vinyl LP of excerpts from *Living in a Land* was issued with the journal *Inscription* (Issue 1: *Beginnings, Information as Material,* 2020). *Living in a Land* was also used as a libretto by the artist Lina Lapelyte in *The Mutes*, a choral work for untrained singers (Paris: Lafayette Anticipations, 2022). In 2017, Sean Ashton was awarded second prize in the International Award for Art Criticism. He teaches fine arts at Leeds Beckett University and the Royal College of Art.

Von 2007 bis 2011 war Sean Ashton Mitherausgeber des *MAP Magazine* und von 2012 bis 2017 schrieb er für *Art Review.* Sein Buch *Sunsets and Dogshits* (Alma Books, 2008) ist eine Sammlung von Rezensionen zu imaginären Kunstwerken und Büchern. Mit *Living in a Land* (Ma Bibliothèque, 2017) veröffentlichte er ein vorwiegend in negativen Sätzen verfasstes Memoire eines hypothetischen Bürgers. Darüber hinaus trug er Gedichte, Essays und Geschichten in vielen anderen Publikationen bei, etwa in *Oxford Poetry, Poetry London, Poetry Ireland Review, Magma, Poetry Salzburg Review, Artenol,* der Philosophiezeitschrift *Collapse* und dem Buch *Walking Cities*. Seine Gedichtsammlung *Sampler* (Valley Press, 2020) beinhaltet ausgewählte Texte einer imaginären Enzyklopädie, die ausnahmslos von DichterInnen geschrieben wurde. Im Jahr 2020 wurde eine Vinyl-LP mit Auszügen aus *Living in a Land* in der Zeitschrift *Inscription* herausgegeben (Ausgabe 1: *Beginnings, Information as Material,* 2020). *Living in a Land* wurde außerdem von der Künstlerin Lina Lapelyte als Libretto für *The Mutes*, einem Chorstück für ungeübte SängerInnen, verwendet (Paris: Lafayette Anticipations, 2022). 2017 wurde Sean Ashton beim International Award for Art Criticism mit dem zweiten Preis ausgezeichnet. Er lehrt bildende Kunst an der Leeds Beckett University und dem Royal College of Art.

Jonatan Habib Engqvist

Jonatan Habib Engqvist is an author, curator and occasional teacher with a background in philosophy and aesthetic theory. He is the co-editor of the quarterly journal *Ord&Bild* and editor-in-mischief of *tsnoK.se.* He has curated several experimental projects and over fifty exhibitions on four continents including international biennials and festivals such as: the 5th Project Biennial of Contemporary Art D-0 ARK Underground (2019), the VR Pavilion at the 58th Venice Biennale (2019), or the Cycle Music and Art Festival Berlin/Reykjavík/Koparvogur (2018). He founded and directed the curatorial residency CRIS, in Stockholm (2015–2020) and was the first artistic director of Nya Småland on commission by four regional art museums and a university including the first edition of their triennial (2016–2020). He is also the former project manager for visual art at IASPIS (2009–2014) and was a curator at Moderna Museet (2008–2009) and employed at The Royal Institute of Art in Stockholm (2005–2007). His writing has been published widely in various languages in books and catalogs around the world including: *Letters Sent from Heaven—Frozen and Vaporized Water: Ukichiro Nakaya and Fujiko Nakaya's Science and Art* (OK BOOK, 2022), *Big Dig—Om passivitet och samtidskonst* (CLP Works, 2018), *Studio Talks: Thinking Through Painting* (Arvinius+Orfeus Publishing, 2014), or *In Dependence—Collaboration and Artists' Initiatives* (Torpedo Press, 2013).

Jonatan Habib Engqvist ist Autor, Kurator und gelegentlich Lehrender mit einem Hintergrund in Philosophie und ästhetischer Theorie. Er ist Mitherausgeber der vierteljährlich erscheinenden Zeitschrift *Ord&Bild* und Chefredakteur *von tsnoK.se.* Engqvist kuratierte mehrere experimentelle Projekte und über fünfzig Ausstellungen auf vier Kontinenten, darunter internationale Biennalen und Festivals wie die 5. Projekt-Biennale für zeitgenössische Kunst D-0 ARK Underground (2019), den VR-Pavillon auf der 58. Biennale in Venedig (2019) und das CYCLE Music and Art Festival Berlin/Reykjavík/Kópavogur (2018). Er gründete und leitete die kuratorische Residenz CRIS in Stockholm (2015–2020) und war der erste künstlerische Leiter von Nya Småland im Auftrag von vier regionalen Kunstmuseen und einer Universität, einschließlich der ersten Ausgabe ihrer Triennale (2016–2020). Engqvist war außerdem Projektmanager für bildende Kunst bei IASPIS (2009–2014), Kurator am Moderna Museet (2008–2009) und war am Kungliga Konsthögskolan KKH in Stockholm (2005–2007) beschäftigt. Seine Texte wurden in verschiedenen Sprachen in Büchern und Katalogen auf der ganzen Welt veröffentlicht, darunter: *Letters Sent from Heaven – Frozen and Vaporized Water: Ukichiro Nakaya and Fujiko Nakaya's Science and Art* (OK BOOK, 2022), *Big Dig – Om passivitet och samtidskonst* (CLP Works, 2018), *Studio Talks: Thinking Through Painting* (Arvinius+Orfeus Publishing, 2014) und *In Dependence – Collaboration and Artists' Initiatives* (Torpedo Press, 2013).

Enrico Lunghi

Enrico Lunghi was born in Luxembourg in 1962. He studied history and art history at the University of Human Sciences in Strasbourg. He was a scientific assistant at the National Museum of History and Art of Luxembourg from 1991 to 1995, then Artistic Director of Casino Luxembourg—Forum of Contemporary Art, which he founded with Jo Kox, from 1996 to 2008. He was also General Director of Mudam—The Contemporary Art Museum of Luxembourg from 2009 to 2016. He was the curator for Luxembourg at the Venice Biennale in 1995 (Bert Theis, *Potemkin Lock*), in 1999

Enrico Lunghi wurde 1962 in Luxemburg geboren. Er studierte Geschichte und Kunstgeschichte an der Universität Straßburg. Von 1991 bis 1995 war er wissenschaftlicher Assistent am Nationalmuseum für Geschichte und Kunst Luxemburg, anschließend von 1996 bis 2008 künstlerischer Leiter des Casino Luxembourg – Forum d'art contemporain, das er zusammen mit Jo Kox gründete. Von 2009 bis 2016 war er außerdem Generaldirektor des Mudam – Musée d'Art Moderne Grand-Duc Jean in Luxembourg. Lunghi war Kurator für Luxemburg bei der Biennale in Venedig 1995 (Bert Theis,

(Simone Decker, *Chewing and Folding Projects*) and in 2007 (Jill Mercedes, *Endless Lust*). In 2009, he was the curator in Venice for the French Community of Wallonia-Brussels with Jacques Charlier's *100 Sexes d'artistes*. From 2005 to 2011, he was president of the IKT (International Association of Curators of Contemporary Art). As curator of multiple exhibitions, he has also published numerous texts on art and contemporary artists. Since 2017, he has been in charge of studies for the Ministry of Education (SCRIPT) and at the University of the Grand Duchy of Luxembourg (IRMA). He has recently curated the Bert Theis retrospective *Building Philosophy—Curating Utopi* at Mudam Luxembourg, *Un monde, un seul, pour demeure—Œuvres des collections des Frac Nouvelle Aquitaine* at the Château de Biron (Dordogne), and Filip Markiewicz's *Celebration Factory* at Kunsthalle Osnabrück.

Potemkin Lock), 1999 (Simone Decker, *Chewing and Folding Projects*) und 2007 (Jill Mercedes, *Endlose Lust*). 2009 kuratierte er in Venedig für die Französische Gemeinschaft Wallonie-Brüssel mit Jacques Charliers *100 Sexes d'artistes*. Von 2005 bis 2011 war Lunghi Präsident der IKT (International Association of Curators of Contemporary Art). Als Kurator mehrerer Ausstellungen veröffentlichte er zudem zahlreiche Texte zu Kunst und zeitgenössischen KünstlerInnen. Seit 2017 ist er Studienleiter beim Bildungsministerium (SCRIPT) und an der Universität Luxemburg (IRMA). Kürzlich kuratierte er die Bert-Theis-Retrospektive *Building Philosophy – Curating Utopi* im Mudam Luxembourg, *Un monde, un seul, pour demeure – Œuvres des collections des Frac Nouvelle Aquitaine* im Château de Biron (Dordogne) und Filip Markiewiczs *Celebration Factory* in der Kunsthalle Osnabrück.

Paul O'Neill

Dr. Paul O'Neill is an Irish curator, artist, writer and educator. Since 2007 he has been the Artistic Director of PUBLICS, a curatorial agency and event space with a dedicated library, and reading room in Helsinki. From 2013 to 2017, he was Director of the Graduate Program at the Centre for Curatorial Studies (CCS), Bard College, New York. O'Neill has held numerous curatorial and research positions over the last twenty years and he has taught on many curatorial and visual arts programs in Europe, the USA, Asia, and the UK. He has curated over seventy exhibitions across the globe and his writing has been published in many books, catalogs, journals, and magazines. O'Neill is author of the critically acclaimed book The *Culture of Curating and the Curating of Culture(s)* (Cambridge: The MIT Press, 2012), which has been translated into many languages. He is responsible for the agenda-setting series of three recent curatorial anthologies, *The Curatorial Conundrum, How Institutions Think,* and *Curating After the Global: Roadmaps to the Present,* co-edited with Lucy Steeds, Mick Wilson et al. and published with the MIT Press, CCS Bard College and Luma Foundation, in 2016, 2017 and 2019, respectively. More recently, he completed an artist's book with Maryam Jafri and is working on books with artists Kathrin Bohm and Dave McKenzie, as well as a new collection of curatorial texts called *CURED*.

Dr. Paul O'Neill ist ein irischer Kurator, Künstler, Autor und Pädagoge. Seit 2007 ist er künstlerischer Leiter von PUBLICS, einer kuratorischen Agentur mit Veranstaltungsort, eigener Bibliothek und Lesesaal in Helsinki. Von 2013 bis 2017 war O'Neill Direktor des Graduiertenprogramms am Centre for Curatorial Studies (CCS), Bard College, New York. Er hatte in den letzten zwanzig Jahren zahlreiche kuratorische und wissenschaftliche Positionen inne und lehrte Curatorial Studies und bildende Kunst an zahlreichen Hochschulen in Europa, den USA, Asien und Großbritannien. Er hat über siebzig Ausstellungen weltweit kuratiert, seine Texte wurden in zahlreichen Büchern, Katalogen, Zeitschriften und Magazinen veröffentlicht. O'Neill ist Autor des von KritikerInnen gefeierten Buches *The Culture of Curating and the Curating of Culture(s)* (Cambridge: The MIT Press, 2012), das in viele Sprachen übersetzt wurde. Er ist verantwortlich für die wegbereitende Reihe von drei kürzlich erschienenen kuratorischen Anthologien, *The Curatorial Conundrum, How Institutions Think* und *Curating After the Global: Roadmaps to the Present,* die zusammen mit Lucy Steeds, Mick Wilson et al. herausgegeben und durch MIT Press, CCS Bard College und Luma Foundation in den Jahren 2016, 2017 bzw. 2019 veröffentlicht wurden. Zuletzt stellte O'Neill mit Maryam Jafri ein KünstlerInnenbuch fertig; aktuell arbeitet er an Büchern mit den KünstlerInnen Kathrin Bohm und Dave McKenzie und an einer neuen Sammlung kuratorischer Texte mit dem Titel *CURED*.

Jane Rendell

Jane Rendell (BSc, DipArch, MSc, PhD) is Professor of Critical Spatial Practice at the Bartlett School of Architecture, UCL, where she co-initiated the master's program Situated Practice and supervises MA and PhD projects. Her research, writing, and pedagogic practice crosses architecture, art, feminism, history, and psychoanalysis. She has introduced concepts of "critical spatial practice" and "site-writing" through her books: *The Architecture of Psychoanalysis* (2017), *Silver* (2016), *Site-Writing* (2010), *Art and Architecture* (2006), and *The Pursuit of Pleasure* (2002). Her co-edited collections include Reactivating the *Social Condenser* (2017), *Critical Architecture* (2007), *Spatial Imagination* (2005), *The Unknown City* (2001), *Intersections* (2000), *Gender, Space, Architecture* (1999), and *Strangely Familiar* (1995). Working With Dr. David Roberts, she led the Bartlett's Ethics Commission and, with Dr. Yael Padan, The Ethics of Research Practice for KNOW (the ESRC-funded project, Knowledge in Action for Urban Equality: PI Prof. Caren Levy). In 2018, she received the RIBA Research Award for History and Theory for her research on housing and psychoanalysis, *May Mo(u)rn*, and a UCL Provost's Education Award for her work on ethics. In 2019, she launched *Site-Reading Writing Quarterly*, which releases dialogic situated reviews each quarter. In 2021, she received, with others, an RIBA Research Award for Education.

Jane Rendell (BSc, DipArch, MSc, PhD) ist Professorin für Critical Spatial Practice an der Bartlett School of Architecture, UCL, wo sie das Masterprogramm Situated Practice mitinitiierte und Master- und Doktorats-Projekte betreut. Ihre Forschungs-, Schreib- und Lehrpraxis verbindet Architektur, Kunst, Feminismus, Geschichte und Psychoanalyse. Mit ihren Büchern T*he Architecture of Psychoanalysis* (2017), *Silver* (2016), *Site-Writing* (2010), *Art and Architecture* (2006) und *The Pursuit of Pleasure* (2002) führte sie Konzepte der „kritischen räumlichen Praxis" und des „Site-Writing" ein. Sie ist Mitherausgeberin der Sammlungen *Reactivating the Social Condenser* (2017), *Critical Architecture* (2007), *Spatial Imagination* (2005), *The Unknown City* (2001), *Intersections* (2000), *Gender, Space, Architecture* (1999) und *Strangely Familiar* (1995). In Zusammenarbeit mit Dr. David Roberts leitete sie die Bartlett's Ethics Commission und mit Dr. Yael Padan The Ethics of Research Practice für KNOW (das ESRC-finanzierte Projekt Knowledge in Action for Urban Equality: PI Prof. Caren Levy). 2018 erhielt sie den RIBA Research Award for History and Theory für *May Mo(u)rn*, ihre Forschungsarbeit zu Wohnen und Psychoanalyse, sowie den UCL Provost's Education Award für ihre Arbeit zur Ethik. Im Jahr 2019 gründete sie *Site-Reading Writing Quarterly*, wo sie jedes Quartal dialogisch situierte Rezensionen veröffentlicht. 2021 erhielt sie, gemeinsam mit anderen, einen RIBA Research Award for Education.

Birgit Rinagl

Birgit Rinagl works as an author, curator, artistic photographer, and secretary, based in Vienna. She studied comparative literature at the University of Vienna and Université Jean Monnet in St. Etienne. She was a lecturer at the University of Art and Design Linz (*Digital Storytelling*) and has given guest lectures at the University of Vienna ("Digital Literature and Media Art"), MUSA Museum Startgalerie Artothek Vienna ("Von öffentlichen Handlungen und ästhetischen Reisen. Fotografie und Netz"), Adalbert-Stifter-Institut des Landes OÖ, Linz ("Digital Literature"), and Museum of Modern and Contemporary Art, Rijeka ("CUREDITING—Contextualising [New] Media Art"). Her publications (ed.) and texts (author) include: *Origo (At Point Zero of the Point of View)* (Revolver, 2013), *Content I Form I Im-material* (Verlag für moderne Kunst Nürnberg, 2011), *ÜBERSETZUNG IST EINE FORM I TRANSLATION IS A MODE* (Kunstraum Niederösterreich, 2010), "Club 27" (David Eisl, 2019, exhibition text), "Between Abstraction and Narration, or: the Brush Stroke as 'Bar-Code'" in Astrid Esslinger. *Paintings/Cut Outs* (Ambra /V, 2014), or "Coincidence of Image Rhetoric and the Visual Appearance of Language" (Michael Endlicher, 2017, endlicher.at). She curated several exhibitions in collaboration with Franz Thalmair/CONT3XT.NET in Vienna, Berlin, and Ljubljana.

Birgit Rinagl lebt in Wien und arbeitet als Autorin, Kuratorin, künstlerische Fotografin und Sekretärin. Sie studierte Vergleichende Literaturwissenschaft an der Universität Wien und der Université Jean Monnet, Saint-Etienne. Sie lehrte an der Kunstuniversität Linz (*Digital Storytelling*) und hielt Gastvorträge an der Universität Wien („Digitale Literatur und Medienkunst"), dem MUSA Museum Startgalerie Artothek Wien („Von öffentlichen Handlungen und ästhetischen Reisen. Fotografie und Netz"), dem Adalbert-Stifter-Institut des Landes OÖ in Linz („Digitale Literatur") und dem Muzej moderne i suvremene umjetnosti in Rijeka („CUREDITING – Contextualising [New] Media Art"). Als Herausgeberin und Autorin publizierte sie unter anderem: *Origo (Am Nullpunkt des Standpunkts)* (Revolver: Berlin 2013), *Content I Form I Im-material* (Verlag für moderne Kunst Nürnberg 2011), *ÜBERSETZUNG IST EINE FORM I TRANSLATION IS A MODE* (Kunstraum Niederösterreich 2010), „Club 27" (David Eisl, 2019, Ausstellungstext), „Zwischen Abstraktion und Narration oder: Der Pinselstrich als ‚Strichcode'" (in: Astrid Esslinger. *Paintings/Cut Outs*, 2014) und „Koinzidenz von Bildrhetorik und Optik der Sprache" (Michael Endlicher, 2017, endlicher.at). Sie hat zahlreiche Ausstellungen in Zusammenarbeit mit Franz Thalmair/CONT3XT.NET in Wien, Berlin und Ljubljana kuratiert.

Başak Şenova

Başak Şenova is a curator and designer; she earned her MFA in Graphic Design and PhD in Art, Design, and Architecture at Bilkent University, and received her associate professorship in Turkey. Currently, she holds a senior postdoctoral researcher position at the University of Applied Arts Vienna with her PEEK project, awarded by FWF. Şenova is one of the founding members of *Nomad*, initiator of the "ctrl_alt_del" and "Upgrade!Istanbul." She is the Turkish correspondent of Flash Art International, a member of the editorial board of PASS, International Biennial Association's journal, and a corresponding member of the Secession. Acted as an advisory board member of the Turkish Pavilion in Venice Biennale, the Istanbul Biennial, and the D-0 ARK Underground in B&H. She was the curator of the Pavilion of Turkey at the 53rd Venice Biennale. Co-curated the *Uncovered* project in Cyprus (2011–2013); and the 2nd and 5th Biennials of Contemporary Art, *D-O Ark Underground* (2013/2019). She acted as the Art Gallery Chair of (ACM) *Siggraph* 2014 (Vancouver), curator of the Helsinki Photography Biennial 2014, and the *Jerusalem Show VII: Fractures* (2014); curated the Pavilion of North Macedonia at the 56th Venice Biennale (2015); the inaugural exhibition of B7L9, *Climbing Through the Tide* (2019) in Tunis. She developed and curated the *CrossSections* project (2017–2019). From 2020 to 2022, as a visiting professor, she led the Octopus Program at the University of Applied Arts Vienna.

Başak Şenova ist Kuratorin und Designerin, Sie studierte Literatur und Grafikdesign (MFA in Grafikdesign und PhD. in Kunst, Design und Architektur an der Bilkent-Universität) und erhielt ein Extraordinariat in der Türkei. Derzeit ist sie Senior-Postdoc-Forscherin an der Universität für angewandte Kunst Wien, mit einem PEEK-Projekt, ausgezeichnet vom FWF. Şenova ist eines der Gründungsmitglieder von *Nomad*, Organisatorin von „ctrl_alt_del" und „Upgrade!Istanbul". Sie ist türkische Korrespondentin von Flash Art International, Mitglied des Editorial Boards von PASS, der Zeitschrift der International Biennial Association und korrespondierendes Mitglied der Wiener Secession. Sie fungierte als Beiratsmitglied für den türkischen Pavillon auf der Biennale in Venedig, für die Biennale in Istanbul sowie für D-0 ARK Underground in B&H. Şenova kuratierte den türkischen Pavillon auf der 53. Biennale in Venedig. Sie war Co-Kuratorin von *Uncovered* in Zypern (2011–2013) sowie für die zweite und fünfte Projekt-Biennale für zeitgenössische Kunst *D-O Ark Underground* (2013/2019). Sie fungierte als Art Gallery Chair für (ACM) *Siggraph* 2014 (Vancouver) und war Kuratorin der Fotografie-Biennale in Helsinki 2014 sowie der *Jerusalem Show VII: Fractures* (2014). Sie kuratierte den nordmazedonischen Pavillon auf der 56. Biennale in Venedig (2015) und die Eröffnungsausstellung von B7L9, *Climbing Through the Tide,* (2019) in Tunis. Sie initiierte und kuratierte *CrossSections* (2017–2019). Von 2020 bis 2022 leitete sie, als Gastprofessorin, das Octopus-Programm an der Universität für angewandte Kunst Wien.

Andreas Spiegl

Andreas Spiegl studied art history at the University of Vienna and is teaching and researching as Senior Scientist at the Academy of Fine Arts Vienna at the Institute for Art Theory and Cultural Studies, which he has been head of since 2015. He held the position as Vice Rector for Academic Affairs and Research from 2003 to 2011 and has been Chair of the Senate since 2022. He has published numerous publications on contemporary art and cultural studies and media theory.

Andreas Spiegl studierte Kunstgeschichte an der Universität Wien und lehrt und forscht als Senior Scientist an der Akademie der bildenden Künste Wien am Institut für Kunst- und Kulturwissenschaften, das er seit 2015 leitet. Von 2003 bis 2011 hatte er die Funktion als Vizerektor für Lehre und Forschung inne und seit 2022 ist er Vorsitzender des Senats. Er publizierte zahlreiche Texte zur zeitgenössischen Kunst, Kulturwissenschaft und Medientheorie.

Barbara Holub lives and works in Vienna. After studying architecture at Stuttgart University of Technology she developed a socially and politically engaged artistic practice that questions the role of art in society, be it in the context of art itself, in public space or in relation to companies. In order to propagate dialogic action aimed at appropriating spaces, she creates performative situations for the specific cultural context so as to view conflicts as a productive force, to question systems and norms and to encourage participants to transcend boundaries. She has coined the term "silent activism" to describe this practice.

In 1999 Barbara Holub and Paul Rajakovics co-founded the transparadiso collective that operates at the intersection of art, architecture and urban intervention and developed the method of direct urbanism. Holub is curating the flagship project WE PARAPOM! for Chemnitz European Capital of Culture 2025.

Barbara Holub was President of the Vienna Secession from 2006 until 2007. She has been a member of the Advisory Board of *Art & the Public Sphere Journal* since 2010, of the World Council of Peoples for the United Nations, New York, since 2013 and a member of the jury of the Innovation Fund for Culture in Public Space, Stuttgart, since 2018. She was external examiner for Situated Practice at the Bartlett School of Architecture/UCL, London (2018–2022), and led the artistic research project "Planning Unplanned" at Vienna University of Technology (2010–2013). She is a member of the editorial board of the urban research journal *dérive*, Vienna (since 2002), and partner of the EU project SPACEX—Spatial Practices in Art and Architecture for Empathetic Exchange (2022–2025).

Since 1997 Barbara Holub has been teaching at various universities including the UIC/School of Art and Design, Chicago; Vienna University of Technology/Institute of Art and Design; f+f School of Art and Media Design, Zurich; and the Universidad Católica, Valparaíso, Chile. She was a visiting professor at the University of Applied Arts Vienna, where she is currently a senior lecturer.

Barbara Holub was awarded the research prize of the Austrian Chamber of Architects in 2022. Other awards include the Austrian National Art Award (2018), the Otto Wagner Prize for Urban Design (2007), the Schindler Scholarship of the MAK Centre for Art and Architecture, Los Angeles (2004), and the Outstanding Artist Award for Artistic Photography of the Austrian Federal Chancellery (1999)

Barbara Holub lebt und arbeitet in Wien. Nach ihrem Architekturstudium an der Technischen Universität Stuttgart entwickelte sie eine sozial und politisch engagierte Kunstpraxis, die die Rolle von Kunst in der Gesellschaft – ob im Kunstkontext, im öffentlichen Raum oder in Bezug auf Unternehmen – befragt. Um dialogisches Handeln für die Aneignung von Räumen zu propagieren, schafft sie für den spezifischen kulturellen Kontext performative Situationen, die Konflikte als Produktivkraft betrachten, Systeme und Normen hinterfragen und die TeilnehmerInnen anregen, Grenzen zu überschreiten. Dafür prägte sie den Begriff „stiller Aktivismus".

1999 gründete Barbara Holub gemeinsam mit Paul Rajakovics das Kollektiv transparadiso, das an der Schnittstelle von Kunst, Architektur und urbaner Intervention agiert und die Methode des direkten Urbanismus entwickelte. Holub kuratiert für die Europäische Kulturhauptstadt Chemnitz 2025 das Flagship-Projekt WE PARAPOM!.

Barbara Holub war von 2006 bis 2007 Präsidentin der Wiener Secession. Seit 2010 ist sie Beiratsmitglied des *Art & Public Sphere Journal*, seit 2013 des World Council of Peoples for the United Nations, New York, und seit 2018 ist sie Jurymitglied des Innovationsfonds für Kultur im öffentlichen Raum, Stuttgart. An der Bartlett School of Architecture/UCL, London, war sie externe Prüferin für Situated Practice (2018–2022) und an der Technischen Universität Wien leitete sie das künstlerische Forschungsprojekt „Planning Unplanned" (2010–2013). Sie ist Redaktionsmitglied von *dérive – Magazin für Stadtforschung*, Wien (seit 2002), und Partnerin des EU-Projekts SPACEX – Spatial Practices in Art and Architecture for Empathetic Exchange (2022–2025).

Seit 1997 lehrt Barbara Holub an folgenden Hochschulen und Universitäten: UIC/School of Art and Design, Chicago; Technischen Universität Wien/Institut für Kunst und Gestaltung; f+f Schule für Design und Mediendesign, Zürich; Universidad Católica, Valparaíso/Chile. Sie war Gastprofessorin an der Universität für angewandte Kunst Wien, wo sie derzeit als Senior Lecturer tätig ist

2022 wurde Barbara Holub mit dem Forschungspreis der Bundeskammer der ZiviltechnikerInnen Österreichs ausgezeichnet. Weitere Auszeichnungen sind der Österreichische Kunstpreis (2018), der Otto-Wagner-Städtebaupreis (2007), das Schindler-Stipendium des MAK Centre for Art and Architecture, Los Angeles (2004), und der Outstanding Artist Award for Artistic Photography des österreichischen Bundeskanzleramtes (1999).

BIBLIOGRAPHY

NORMAL #1 /NORMAL #2
Barbara Holub/Paul Rajakovics, 108 p./132 p., German/English,
Salon für Kunstbuch, Vienna, 2020 /2021

CALL AGAINST THE BORDER
Barbara Holub/Paul Rajakovics, 40 p., German/English,
Kunst im öffentlichen Raum Niederösterreich, St.Pölten, 2020

DAS BIENVENUE: EIN RECHT AUF RAUM FÜR ALLE
(Social Design Reader), Barbara Holub (ed.), 116 p., German, 2017

PLANNING UNPLANNED. DARF KUNST EINE FUNKTION HABEN?
TOWARDS A NEW FUNCTION OF ART IN SOCIETY
Barbara Holub/Christine Hohenbüchler (eds.), 256 p., German/English,
Verlag für moderne Kunst, 2015

DIRECT URBANISM
Barbara Holub/Paul Rajakovics, 216 p., German/English,
Verlag für moderne Kunst Nürnberg, 2013

FOUND, SET, APPROPRIATED,
Barbara Holub, 176 p., German/English, Verlag für moderne Kunst Nürnberg, 2010;
CD supplement: DIE BLUE FROG SOCIETY SPAZIERT AUF DEN MOND

INITIATIVE ISLAND
Barbara Holub, 32 p., English, Eastside Projects, Birmingham, 2009

BARBARA HOLUBS MUSTERBUCH: IDEAL LIVING
Barbara Holub, 176 p., German/English, Triton Verlag, Vienna, 2003

ONE HUNDRED DESIRES FOR HARBOUR FOR CULTURES
Barbara Holub/Paul Rajakovics, in: H/C. The Harbour for Cultures' Logbook,
Giuliana Carbi (ed.), pp. 113–135, English/Italian, Juliet Editrice, Trieste, 2022

WHAT IS NORMAL
Barbara Holub, in: The Art and Public Sphere Journal, Volume 9, Issue 1–2, Mel Jordan
(ed.), pp. 15–27, English, Intellect, Bristol, Dec. 2020

HARBOUR FOR CULTURES
Barbara Holub/Paul Rajakovics, Giuliana Carbi, Elisabetta Porro, in: Centrepoint
Now, World Council of Peoples for the United Nations (ed.), pp. 128–129, English,
New York, 2020

DIREKTER URBANISMUS. EINE NEUE METHODE FÜR URBANES HANDELN
Barbara Holub und Paul Rajakovics, in: Andere Urbanitäten. Zur Pluralität des Städtischen, Brigitta Schmidt-Lauber (ed.), pp. 135–150, German, Böhlau, Vienna, 2018

PLANNING UNPLANNED. ОТХОД ОТ ПЛАНИРОВАНИЯ —К НОВОМУ ПОЗИЦИОНИРОВА-НИЮ ИСКУССТВА В КОНТЕКСТЕ ГРАДОСТРОИТЕЛЬСТВА
Barbara Holub,in the publication of the Intellectual Forum of the 4th Ural
Industrial Biennial Ekaterinburg, Dmitrii Bezouglov (ed.), pp. 167–230, Russian,
Ekaterinburg, 2018

STRATEGIES IN THE URGENCY OF RADICAL SOCIETAL CHANGES
Barbara Holub, in: Bodied Spaces. Discursos cruzados entre corpo e espaço, Gabriela
Vaz-Pinheiro (ed.), pp. 26–55, English/Portuguese, Cadernos do Rivoli 06, Porto, 2018

WHY IS TAKING ACTION BEAUTIFUL? EXPLORATIONS IN ACTOLOGY
Barbara Holub, in: New Stakeholders of Urban Change: A Question of Culture and
Attitude?, Perspectives in Metropolitan Research 4; Hilke Marit Berger/Gesa Ziemer
(ed.), pp. 80–93, English, Jovis, Berlin, 2017

BIENVENUE – NEUE FORMEN DES ZUSAMMENLEBENS
Barbara Holub, in: Räume des Ankommens – Topographische Perspektiven auf Migration und Flucht, Amalia Barboza, Stefanie Eberding, Ulrich Pantle, Georg Winter (ed.),
pp. 181–196, German, transcript, Bielefeld, 2016

COLLABORATIVE SETTINGS: FROM THE BLUE FROG SOCIETY TO DIRECT
URBANISM, Barbara Holub, in: THIS Troublesome Uncomfortable and Questionable
RELEVANCE of Art in Public Space, Laznia Centre for Contemporary Art, pp. 109–122,
English/Polish, Gdánsk, 2013

BIBLIOGRAFIE

NORMAL #1 /NORMAL #2
Barbara Holub/Paul Rajakovics, 108 S./132 S., Dt/Engl.,
Salon für Kunstbuch, Wien, 2020 /2021

RUF GEGEN DIE GRENZE
Barbara Holub/Paul Rajakovics, 40 S., Dt/Engl., Kunst im öffentlichen Raum
Niederösterreich, St. Pölten, 2020

DAS BIENVENUE: EIN RECHT AUF RAUM FÜR ALLE
(Social Design Reader), Barbara Holub /Social Design (Hg.), 116 S., dt., Wien, 2017

PLANNING UNPLANNED. DARF KUNST EINE FUNKTION HABEN?
TOWARDS A NEW FUNCTION OF ART IN SOCIETY
Barbara Holub und Christine Hohenbüchler (Hg.), 256 S., Dt/Engl.,
Verlag für moderne Kunst, 2015

DIREKTER URBANISMUS
Barbara Holub/Paul Rajakovics, 216 S., Dt/Engl.,
Verlag für moderne Kunst Nürnberg, 2013

FOUND, SET, APPROPRIATED,
Barbara Holub, 176 S., Dt/Engl., Verlag für moderne Kunst Nürnberg, 2010,
Beilage CD: DIE BLUE FROG SOCIETY SPAZIERT AUF DEN MOND

INITIATIVE ISLAND
Barbara Holub, 32 S., Engl., Eastside Projects, Birmingham, 2009.

BARBARA HOLUBS MUSTERBUCH: IDEAL LIVING
Barbara Holub, 176 S., Dt/Engl., Triton Verlag, Wien, 2003

ONE HUNDRED DESIRES FOR HARBOUR FOR CULTURES
Barbara Holub/Paul Rajakovics, in: H/C. The Harbour for Cultures' Logbook,
Giuliana Carbi (Hg.), S. 113–135, Juliet Editrice, Triest, 2022

WHAT IS NORMAL
Barbara Holub, in: The Art and Public Sphere Journal, Volume 9, Issue 1–2,
Mel Jordan (Hg.), S. 15–27, Engl., Intellect, Bristol, Dez. 2020

HARBOUR FOR CULTURES
Barbara Holub/Paul Rajakovics, Giuliana Carbi, Elisabetta Porro, in: Centrepoint
Now, World Council of Peoples for the United Nations (Hg.), S. 128–129, Engl.,
New York, 2020

DIREKTER URBANISMUS. EINE NEUE METHODE FÜR URBANES HANDELN
Barbara Holub und Paul Rajakovics, in: Andere Urbanitäten. Zur Pluralität des Städtischen, Brigitta Schmidt-Lauber (Hg.), S. 135–150, dt., Böhlau, Wien, 2018

PLANNING UNPLANNED. ОТХОД ОТ ПЛАНИРОВАНИЯ — К НОВОМУ
ПОЗИЦИОНИРОВА-НИЮ ИСКУССТВА В КОНТЕКСТЕ ГРАДОСТРОИТЕЛЬСТВА
Barbara Holub, in der Publikation des Intellectual Forum of the 4th Ural
Industrial Biennial Ekaterinburg, Dmitrii Bezouglov (Hg.), S. 167–230, Russisch,
Jekaterinburg, 2018

STRATEGIES IN THE URGENCY OF RADICAL SOCIETAL CHANGES
Barbara Holub, in: Bodied Spaces. Discursos cruzados entre corpo e espaço,
Gabriela Vaz-Pinheiro (Hg.), S. 26–55, Engl./Port., Cadernos do Rivoli 06, Porto, 2018

WHY IS TAKING ACTION BEAUTIFUL? EXPLORATIONS IN ACTOLOGY
Barbara Holub, in: New Stakeholders of Urban Change: A Question of Culture and Attitude?, Perspectives in Metropolitan Research 4; Hilke Marit Berger/Gesa Ziemer (Hg.),
S. 80–93, engl., Jovis, Berlin, 2017

BIENVENUE – NEUE FORMEN DES ZUSAMMENLEBENS
Barbara Holub, in: Räume des Ankommens – Topographische Perspektiven auf Migration und Flucht, Amalia Barboza, Stefanie Eberding, Ulrich Pantle, Georg Winter (Hg.),
S. 181–196, Dt., transcript, Bielefeld, 2016

COLLABORATIVE SETTINGS: FROM THE BLUE FROG SOCIETY TO DIRECT
URBANISM, Barbara Holub, in: THIS Troublesome Uncomfortable and Questionable
RELEVANCE of Art in Public Space, Laznia Centre for Contemporary Art, S. 109–122,
Engl./Polnisch, Gdánsk, 2013

Picture Credits

All images by Barbara Holub, except: p. 9 transparadiso; p. 28, p. 29 (bottom), p. 30, p. 32, p. 33 Gavin Wade; p. 34, p. 36, p. 39, p. 41, p. 42, p. 43, p. 45, p. 47, p. 48 transparadiso; p. 51, p. 52 Ernesto Uhlmann; p. 54 Folke Köbberling; p. 56, p. 58 (top left) Ernesto Uhlmann; p. 66 Christian Leitner; p. 71 Darius Bork; p. 77 (bottom) Michael Hauffen; p. 81 Violetta Rajakovics; p. 85, p. 90 transparadiso; p. 96 transbanana; p. 99, p. 100 Christine Hohenbüchler; p. 109 unknown; p. 110 Gertraud Sonntag; p. 141 Otto Wieser; p. 144 transparadiso; p. 147 Mathias Bildstein; p. 164 Wolfgang Woessner; p. 166 transparadiso; p. 169, p. 171 Rainer Iglar; p. 174, p. 176 Christian Wachter; p. 177 (left) Matthias Herrmann; (right) Christian Wachter; p. 181 (bottom) Rembert Rayon; p. 185 Pilo Pichler; p. 188, pp. 190–195 Pilo Pichler; p. 204 Neue Galerie Graz; pp. 207–213 transparadiso; p. 218 Natascha Sturny; p. 221 Christine Hohenbüchler; p. 226 Matthias Bildstein; p. 235 Paul Vincenth Schütz; p. 252, p. 253 (left), p. 256 (bottom right) Elisabeth Stephan, p. 255; p. 268 transparadiso; p. 269 Lex Karelly; p. 270 transparadiso; p. 271 Lex Karelly; p. 273 transparadiso; pp. 274–279 Alexandra Gschiel; p. 280 Johanna Lamprecht

Acknowledgments

Barbara Holub would like to thank:
Gerald Bast, Katharina Blaas, Giuliana Carbi, Maia Damianovic, Laura Carlini Fanfogna, Kaye Geipel, Shamina de Gonzaga, Teresa Hohenlohe, Andrea Holzmann, Grita Insam, Mel Jordan, Jakob Lena Knebl, Karo a Kraus, Bettina Leidl, Christian Mayer, Michael Mayr, Christof Nardin, Işın Önol, Michael Petrowitsch, Katrina Petter, Barbara Putz-Plecko, Jane Rendell, Maren Richter, Désirée Schellerer, Anja Seipenbusch-Hufschmied, Başak Şenova, Nita Tandon, Eliette Thurn-Valsassina-Zeiler, Martin Walde, Kathrin Wildner, Georg Winter, Olga Wukounig, as well as the curators and authors of this publication

Special thanks to Paul Rajakovics and Violetta Rajakovics.

COLOPHON

Editor: Başak Şenova
University of Applied Arts Vienna
FWF Peek Program—Senior Postdoctoral Researcher

Artist: Barbara Holub
www.barbaraholub.com

With contributions by Jonatan Habib Engqvist, Enrico Lunghi, Paul O'Neill, Jane Rendell, Başak Şenova, and Andreas Spiegl

Project texts: Sean Ashton (SA), Birgit Rinagl (BR), and Başak Şenova (BS)

Project Management "Edition Angewandte" on behalf of the University of Applied Arts Vienna: Olga Wukounig, Vienna, Austria

Content and Production Editor on behalf of the Publisher: Katharina Holas, Vienna, Austria

Managing editor: Birgit Rinagl

Proofreading/Copyediting: Birgit Rinagl (German), Vienna, Austria; Scott Clifford Evans (English), Vienna, Austria; scriptophil/Miha Tavčar (German/English), Hinterbrühl, Austria

Translation from German into English: Jonathan Quinn, Vienna, Austria; Richard Watts, Vienna, Austria

Translation from English into German: Andrea and Matei Bellu, Berlin, Germany; Wilfried Prantner, Berlin, Germany

Translation from French into English: Ken Peat, Limoges, France

Graphic design: Bueronardin, Vienna, Austria

Image editing: Mario Rott, Vienna, Austria

Cover image: transparadiso, Vienna, Austria

Paper: Munken Print White 15 90 g/m^2, Amber Graphic 70 g/m^2, Gerinica weiß 120 g/m^2

Typeface: Recta™ by Canada Type
Happy Times at the IKOB by Lucas Le Bihan, Velvetyne Type Foundry

Printing: Holzhausen, die Buchmarke der Gerin Druck GmbH, Wolkersdorf, Austria

Library of Congress Control Number: 2022935565

Bibliographic information published by the German National Library. The German National Library lists this publication in the Deutsche Nationalbibliografie; detailed bibliographic data are available on the Internet at http://dnb.dnb.de.

ISSN 1866-248X
ISBN 978-3-11-079081-8
e-ISBN (PDF) 978-3-11-079082-5

www.degruyter.com

The publication was realized with the financial support from

Federal Ministry
Republic of Austria
Arts, Culture,
Civil Service and Sport

Stadt Wien

LAND SALZBURG

Das Land Steiermark
→ Kultur, Europa, Sport

STADT : SALZBURG

GRAZ

MIX
Papier aus verantwortungsvollen Quellen
FSC® C108696